A Century of
CRICKET TESTS

First published in 2013 by
New Holland Publishers
London • Sydney • Cape Town • Auckland
www.newhollandpublishers.com

Garfield House 86–88 Edgware Road London W2 2EA United Kingdom
1/66 Gibbes Street Chatswood NSW 2067 Australia
Wembley Square First Floor Solan Road Gardens Cape Town 8001 South Africa
218 Lake Road Northcote Auckland New Zealand

A catalogue record of this book is available at the British Library and at the National Library of Australia

ISBN: 9781742572840

Managing director: Fiona Scultz
Publisher: Alan Whiticker
Project editor: Kate Sherington
Proofreader: Kersi Meher-Homji
Designer: Kimberley Pearce
Production director: Olga Dementiev
Printer: Toppan Leefung Printing Limited

10 9 8 7 6 5 4 3 2 1

Follow New Holland Publishers on
Facebook: www.facebook.com/NewHollandPublishers

A Century of
CRICKET TESTS

100 of the greatest Tests ever played

LIAM HAUSER

NEW
HOLLAND

Contents

From left to right: Victor Trumper, Jack Hobbs, Don Bradman, Harbhajan Singh and Sachin Tendulkar.

Introduction

The Test match remains the pinnacle of cricket, in spite of the burgeoning popularity of 50-overs per side and the Twenty20 format. Despite the passion and thrills that often go with limited overs cricket – particularly under floodlights – Test matches remain the ultimate challenge, with many rivalries long established, none more so than Australia versus England.

When asked to put together a compilation of 100 classic Tests, there were certain criteria I had to use. The ancient Test-playing nations – England and Australia – were to be strongly featured, but other nations would also be included. Another key aspect was that no more than one Test in one series could be covered. This has ensured that some worthy Tests have been omitted due to another classic Test in the same series being featured. Whilst many individual cricket achievements and feats stick in people's minds, whether it be the heroics of cricketing icons such as Don Bradman, Jim Laker, Shane Warne, Richard Hadlee or Brian Lara, this book focuses on great matches. All 100 in this list were hard-fought, and many were decided by a very small margin. Others were a lot closer than the margin might suggest.

Test matches have been known as five-day games, although in the era featuring a lot of limited overs cricket, it has not been at all unusual for Tests to be decided in four days. Nonetheless it is worth noting that historically some Tests were allowed to run for six days, or in some cases an unlimited number of days. One of the most remarkable Tests was a 1938–39 contest involving South Africa and England, with no result after 10 days of cricket.

Falling apart and then recovering can happen to any team, particularly in one-day cricket, as things can change quickly due to the limited number of overs available. Being able to win a Test match, however, requires much more patience, skill, strategy, tactics, stamina and fitness, due to the two teams having the chance to bat twice. There are second chances in a Test, unlike in one-day cricket.

Being able to lift when the chips are down is one big challenge in Test cricket, as is the ability to stay in control after gaining control in the first place. A number of Test matches appear to have been dominated by one side, but such is the unpredictable nature of cricket that one bad session can cost a team dearly. A team can be on top for four days and then lose the match on the last day. While limited overs cricket has often been a contest favouring batsmen, due to the intention of scoring quickly, Test cricket represents just what the word "test" implies in the sport: an even contest between batsmen and bowlers.

This book explores a selection of 100 Tests in depth, so readers can relive the contests, each of which had its own unique ebb and flow, and illuminates the vital incidents that shaped the outcome of each match. Because there are usually well over 1,000 or even 2,500 deliveries bowled in Test matches, every one of them counts, whether they involve wickets, runs or no runs. The unpredictability of the sequence and pattern of events that transpires in each Test makes for interesting and compelling investigation.

Many classic Tests are decided on the last day, with a result that was far from predictable early on. Test cricket is truly a survival of the fittest, and requires patience, will, want and determination. Sometimes mind games such as sledging and unsporting behaviour can arise and potentially affect a player's mindset. If a Test goes down to the wire, coping and dealing with pressure can be more fascinating than in limited overs cricket, given the lengthy lead-up. Yet rather than becoming too caught up in the climax of a Test, it is worth noting the events that led to the climax from the very start, as those instances were every bit as decisive. Many Test matches have numerous turning points over a period of a few days, ensuring that the conclusion is far from the most telling part of the game.

In this book, the ups and downs of each Test are explored, and some background information given, while match statistics are included to satisfy avid cricket fans.

Note that the following abbreviations are used in match scorecards: * denotes captain and † denotes wicketkeeper; in sundries, b is byes, lb is leg byes, nb is no-balls, w is wides. For batting dismissals, c is caught, b is bowled, lbw is leg before wicket, st is stumped.

Liam Hauser

Chapter 1:
The Early Years

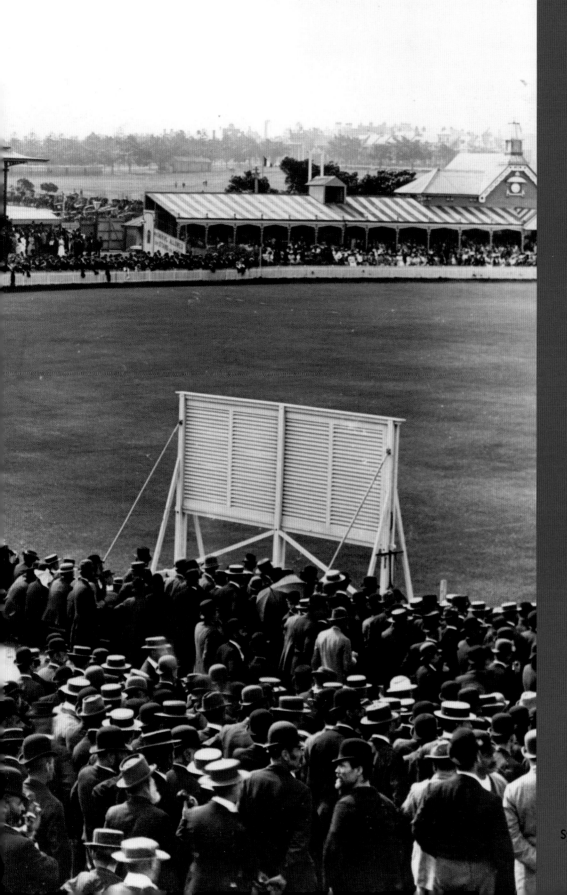

Sydney Cricket Ground, Australia (1895).

Australia v England
First Test at the Melbourne Cricket Ground

1876-77
March 15, 16, 17, 19 (1877)

England's 1876–77 touring squad in Australia. Back row: H. Jupp, T. Emmett, R. Humphrey, A. Hill, T. Armitage, G. Ulyett. Middle row: E. Pooley, J. Southerton, James Lillywhite (captain), A. Greenwood, A. Shaw. Front: H. R. Charlwood, J. Selby.

The first official Test match took place at the Melbourne Cricket Ground in March 1877 following four major tours by England squads to Australia. The English tour in 1876–77 was a business venture, and little did anyone know that a cricket phenomenon was about to start, featuring England and Australia.

Play started in sunny conditions at 1pm. Alfred Shaw bowled Test cricket's first delivery to Charles Bannerman after Australian captain Dave Gregory won the toss and chose to bat. Interestingly, it was a case of one England-born player bowling to an opponent who was also born in England. Just two runs were on the board when Allen Hill took the first wicket, bowling Nat Thomson in the fourth over (as overs consisted of four deliveries). Hill also took Test cricket's first catch as Tom Horan was dismissed for 12, before Dave Gregory was run out one run later and Australia struggled to 41-3.

Bannerman, however, strengthened Australia's position after gaining an early reprieve when Tom Armitage muffed a straightforward chance to catch him. Bannerman dominated the scoring as Bransby Cooper scored just 15 in a partnership of 77, before Billy Midwinter and Edward 'Ned' Gregory were dismissed cheaply. Amazingly, Bannerman was on 126 as day one ended, after three-and-a-half hours of play, while the total was a modest 166-6.

John 'Jack' Blackham made 17 before becoming 49-year-old slow bowler James Southerton's third victim, and Bannerman reached 165 before retiring hurt after a George Ulyett delivery split his finger as Australia was 240-7. Shaw polished off the tail and Australia tallied 245, with Tom Garrett the second-best scorer with 18 not out. Controversy erupted early in England's innings, when Harry Jupp trod on the stumps as he played a leg glance. The umpires seemingly didn't notice it, and the crowd jeered the decision of not out.

John Hodges became Australia's first Test wicket-taker when he had John Selby caught by Cooper with the total on 23. Jupp and Harry Charlwood took the total to 79 before the latter became the first Test batsman to be caught behind. Ulyett became Test cricket's first leg before wicket (lbw) victim, and England was 109-4 at stumps after the dismissal of Andrew Greenwood. Jupp was unbeaten on 54.

Midwinter accounted for Armitage and Shaw before Garrett took the prized scalp of Jupp. Midwinter promptly claimed a five-wicket haul as England sank to 145-8, before number nine Hill batted to good effect. He made 35 not out, and brief resistance from captain James Lillywhite and Southerton helped lower Australia's lead to just 49 runs.

The injured Bannerman was given a warm ovation and was promptly dropped before he scored, but the crowd was silenced when Ulyett bowled him after his sole scoring stroke was a boundary. The hosts reached 27-1 before Shaw had Thomson and Garrett caught by Tom Emmett, and then Hill had Horan caught behind after Horan scored 20 in Australia's wobbling 31-4. Cooper's dismissal made the score 35-5, then Midwinter and Ned Gregory put on 23 runs, before Ulyett and Shaw caused another collapse. Shaw bowled unchanged from one end in Australia's second innings and became the first English player to claim five wickets. Australia finished the day on 83-9 before a rest day took place. Kendall and Hodges added another 21 precious runs before Lillywhite struck with the last ball of his only over, leaving England with a target of 154.

England's run chase began disastrously after Hill and Greenwood opened instead of Jupp and Selby. Hill swung at the second ball of the innings and was caught at mid on. Kendall struck again when Greenwood was caught with the total on seven. Jupp made just four before Midwinter had him lbw, and Charlwood made 13 before Kendall bowled him, rendering England in trouble at 22-4. Selby and Ulyett consolidated, and the total crept to 62 to raise England's hopes, before slow bowler Kendall struck again, bowling Ulyett. The tourists sank to 68-6 when Kendall lured Shaw out of the crease and had him stumped. Kendall rose to the challenge as he bowled for the duration of England's second innings without being replaced.

With England needing a further 86 runs, the determined Selby appeared to be England's last hope, and he badly needed support. Armitage hung around while 24 runs were added before Selby succumbed to the temptation of attacking 21-year-old Hodges. On 38, Selby sought a big hit off Hodges but was caught by Horan, and Armitage was caught behind off Kendall moments later, seeing England plunge to 93-8. The 100 was raised before Hodges bowled Lillywhite, leaving Emmett and Southerton with the task of putting together a last wicket partnership of 54 runs for an England victory. Eight runs were added in 12 minutes before Emmett attempted a pull shot and played the ball onto his stumps, producing Kendall's seventh wicket of the innings. It was an intriguing coincidence that Kendall, Bannerman, Midwinter and Hodges were all born in England, yet all made decisive contributions in Australia beating England by 45 runs in this first ever Test match. Horan was born in Ireland and Cooper in India.

England levelled the two-match series with a four-wicket win in the second Test, also at Melbourne, after Australia scored 122 batting first, before eventually setting the tourists a target of 121. Australia subsequently won a one-off Test against England by 10 wickets at Melbourne in 1878–79, before England won the next one-off Test by five wickets on its home turf at the Oval in 1880. The England versus Australia rivalry was well and truly underway.

AUSTRALIA 1ST INNINGS

C Bannerman	retired hurt	165
NFD Thomson	b Hill	1
TP Horan	c Hill b Shaw	12
DW Gregory*	run out	1
BB Cooper	b Southerton	15
WE Midwinter	c Ulyett b Southerton	5
EJ Gregory	c Greenwood b Lillywhite	0
JM Blackham†	b Southerton	17
TW Garrett	not out	18
TK Kendall	c Southerton b Shaw	3
JR Hodges	b Shaw	0
Extras	(b 4, lb 2, w 2)	8
Total		245

Fall of wickets 2, 40, 41, 118, 142, 143, 197, 243, 245

	O	M	R	W
A Shaw	55.3	34	51	3
A Hill	23	10	42	1
G Ulyett	25	12	36	0
J Southerton	37	17	61	3
T Armitage	3	0	15	0
James Lillywhite jnr	14	5	19	1
T Emmett	12	7	13	0

AUSTRALIA 2ND INNINGS

C Bannerman	b Ulyett	4
NFD Thomson	c Emmett b Shaw	7
TP Horan	c Selby b Hill	20
TW Garrett	c Emmett b Shaw	0
BB Cooper	b Shaw	3
WE Midwinter	c Southerton b Ulyett	17
EJ Gregory	c Emmett b Ulyett	11
JM Blackham†	lbw b Shaw	6
DW Gregory*	b Shaw	3
TK Kendall	not out	17
JR Hodges	b Lillywhite	8
Extras	(b 5, lb 3)	8
Total		104

Fall of wickets 7, 27, 31, 31, 35, 58, 71, 75, 75, 104

	O	M	R	W
A Shaw	34	16	38	5
G Ulyett	19	7	39	3
A Hill	14	6	18	1
James Lillywhite jnr	1	0	1	1

ENGLAND 1ST INNINGS

H Jupp	lbw b Garrett	63
J Selby†	c Cooper b Hodges	7
HRJ Charlwood	c Blackham b Midwinter	36
G Ulyett	lbw b Thomson	10
A Greenwood	c EJ Gregory b Midwinter	1
T Armitage	c Blackham b Midwinter	9
A Shaw	b Midwinter	10
T Emmett	b Midwinter	8
A Hill	not out	35
James Lillywhite jnr*	c & b Kendall	10
J Southerton	c Cooper b Garrett	6
Extras	(lb 1)	1
Total		196

Fall of wickets 23, 79, 98, 109, 121, 135, 145, 145, 168, 196

	O	M	R	W
JR Hodges	9	0	27	1
TW Garrett	18.1	10	22	2
TK Kendall	38	16	54	1
WE Midwinter	54	23	78	5
NFD Thomson	17	10	14	1

ENGLAND 2ND INNINGS

A Hill	c Thomson b Kendall	0
A Greenwood	c Midwinter b Kendall	5
H Jupp	lbw b Midwinter	4
HRJ Charlwood	b Kendall	13
J Selby†	c Horan b Hodges	38
G Ulyett	b Kendall	24
A Shaw	st Blackham b Kendall	2
T Armitage	c Blackham b Kendall	3
T Emmett	b Kendall	9
James Lillywhite jnr*	b Hodges	4
J Southerton	not out	1
Extras	(b 4, lb 1)	5
Total		108

Fall of wickets 0, 7, 20, 22, 62, 68, 92, 93, 100, 108

	O	M	R	W
TK Kendall	33.1	12	55	7
WE Midwinter	19	7	23	1
DW Gregory	5	1	9	0
TW Garrett	2	0	9	0
JR Hodges	7	5	7	2

Toss: Australia   Umpires: CA Reid and RB Terry   Australia won by 45 runs

England v Australia
One-off Test at the Oval, London

1882
August 28, 29 (1882)

A rare photo of an Australian lineup from the 1882 cricket tour of England. Back row: J. Blackham, T. Horan, L. Greenwood (umpire), Midwinter (unknown), P. McDonnell, T. Garrett. Sitting: G. Giffen, H. Boyle , W. Murdoch (captain), G. Bonnor, G. Palmer. Front: A. Bannerman, F. Spofforth.

Following a four-match England versus Australia series in Australia in early 1882, a one-off Test was held in London later in the year. Australia had won the 1881–82 series 2-0 before this Test in London, which was the most tense and famous of the first nine Tests involving the archrivals.

Australian skipper Billy Murdoch won the toss and chose to bat despite two days of rain, which made the pitch very difficult to bat on. George Ulyett gave England an early breakthrough when he bowled Hugh Massie with a yorker as the total was six. More than half of the four-ball overs were maidens throughout the innings and runs were at a premium, with England relying heavily on Ted Peate's left-arm orthodox spin and Dick Barlow's left-arm medium-pace. Murdoch and opener Alec Bannerman slowly took the total to 21 before the tourists collapsed, with Murdoch playing a Peate delivery onto the stumps before Barlow removed George Bonnor's middle-stump. Legendary England all-rounder William 'WG' Grace took a great left-handed catch at point to remove Bannerman,

Australian wicketkeeper John 'Jack' Blackham.

who scored nine runs in 70 minutes.

Tom Horan and George Giffen were bowled and Australia crumbled to 30-6, before Jack Blackham and Tom Garrett reached double figures. Garrett was caught in the deep for 10, then Barlow struck the top of Harry Boyle's stumps. Blackham skied a catch before Sammy Jones was caught at third man, and Barlow finished with 5-19 as Australia tallied just 63 from 80 overs. Australia's bowlers were determined to keep the team in the match, despite the non-selection of the injured George Palmer.

England had 13 runs on the board when Spofforth claimed the key scalp of Grace with a yorker, and Barlow was caught five runs later. Ulyett and Alfred 'Bunny' Lucas took England to within seven runs of a first innings lead before the hosts surrendered their strong position with a collapse of 6-4. Ulyett perhaps looked the most confident of the batsmen, scoring 26 in nearly an hour, before charging at Spofforth and being stumped. Lucas was caught behind off Boyle, Studd was bowled by Spofforth for a third-ball duck, and Alfred Lyttelton was caught behind off Spofforth. Billy Barnes hit a single and a boundary before being bowled, then Maurice Read and Allan Steel put on 26 runs, the second-highest partnership of the innings, before Garrett accounted for Steel. England's lead reached 38 before Spofforth took the last two wickets, just prior to the scheduled close of day one.

The playing arena became wet after further rain, and Massie decided that attack was the best method of defence. He raced to 38 before Lucas dropped him in the deep from Barnes' first delivery. This looked costly as Massie raced to 55 in 57 minutes with nine fours, before Steel bowled him. The total, however, was only 66, and just four more runs were scored before the next two wickets were down. Bonnor again lost his middle peg, with Ulyett the bowler this time, then Bannerman was caught off Barnes after scoring a circumspect 13 in 70 minutes. After Horan and Giffen were caught by Grace off Peate in quick succession, Australia was five wickets down and just 41 runs in front.

Murdoch and Blackham quickly put on 20 runs before rain halted play. Blackham was caught behind before a run was added, and then the determined Murdoch found support from Jones. Jones scored six in 30 minutes but controversy erupted after he left his crease to repair a divot. After completing a run, Jones believed the ball was dead, but Grace thought otherwise, breaking the wicket and successfully appealing for a run out. The Australians were incensed, but had little choice other than try to dismiss England a second time. The chance came quickly as Australia's lower order crashed, with four wickets falling for just eight runs. Spofforth was bowled without scoring as Peate

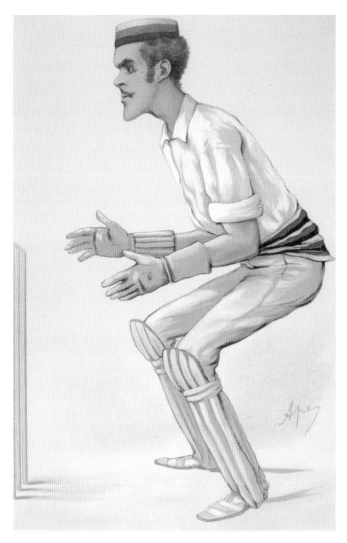

A stylish painted cartoon of the period, depicting England wicketkeeper Alfred Lyttelton.

England's W. G. Grace, perhaps the most famous cricketer before the 20th century.

claimed his eighth wicket of the match, before the last two wickets fell at 122. Murdoch's brave and patient innings ended on 29 as he was run out by some good fielding, then Boyle was bowled second ball. England's target was a small 85, but the tourists were not about to surrender.

England had 15 runs on the board when Spofforth bowled England captain Albert 'Monkey' Hornby and Barlow with consecutive deliveries. Grace and Ulyett subsequently took the score to 51-2 with some confident batting to put the hosts in the box seat, before England slipped to 53-4. Ulyett was caught by the wicketkeeper off Spofforth, and Grace departed for 32 as he miscued his stroke and was caught at mid off.

The run flow stalled with Lyttelton and Lucas bogged down, and 12 consecutive maidens were delivered as Spofforth and Boyle bowled in tandem. Spofforth, a fast bowler known as 'The Demon', decided he wanted to bowl to Lyttelton, so Murdoch allowed a misfield to concede a crucial single. A few more maidens followed before Spofforth had his reward,

bowling Lyttelton, and England required 19 runs with five wickets remaining. The nervous crowd cheered as Lucas hit a precious boundary, before Steel pushed at a slower Spofforth delivery and gave a simple return catch. Spofforth bowled Read second ball as England fell to 70-7, and Blackham conceded three vital byes, which took the total to 75.

Lucas's 65-minute resistance ended as he played a Spofforth ball onto the stumps, giving 'The Demon' his second seven-wicket haul of the match. Boyle had Barnes caught off his glove, and England still needed 10 runs with only one wicket standing. Peate scored a two but then had his stumps rattled as he chanced his arm, and Australia had won a brilliant Test by seven runs.

The tension in the closing stages was such that one spectator reportedly dropped dead with heart failure, while another chewed through his umbrella handle. *The Sporting Times* subsequently published a mock obituary of English cricket.

AUSTRALIA 1ST INNINGS

AC Bannerman	c Grace b Peate	9
HH Massie	b Ulyett	1
WL Murdoch*	b Peate	13
GJ Bonnor	b Barlow	1
TP Horan	b Barlow	3
G Giffen	b Peate	2
JM Blackham†	c Grace b Barlow	17
TW Garrett	c Read b Peate	10
HF Boyle	b Barlow	2
SP Jones	c Barnes b Barlow	0
FR Spofforth	not out	4
Extras	(b 1)	1
Total		63

Fall of wickets 6, 21, 22, 26, 30, 30, 48, 53, 59, 63

	O	M	R	W
E Peate	38	24	31	4
G Ulyett	9	5	11	1
RG Barlow	31	22	19	5
AG Steel	2	1	1	0

ENGLAND 1ST INNINGS

RG Barlow	c Bannerman b Spofforth	11
WG Grace	b Spofforth	4
G Ulyett	st Blackham b Spofforth	26
AP Lucas	c Blackham b Boyle	9
Hon. A Lyttelton†	c Blackham b Spofforth	2
CT Studd	b Spofforth	0
JM Read	not out	19
W Barnes	b Boyle	5
AG Steel	b Garrett	14
AN Hornby*	b Spofforth	2
E Peate	c Boyle b Spofforth	0
Extras	(b 6, lb 2, nb 1)	9
Total		101

Fall of wickets 13, 18, 57, 59, 60, 63, 70, 96, 101, 101

	O	M	R	W
FR Spofforth	36.3	18	46	7
TW Garrett	16	7	22	1
HF Boyle	19	7	24	2

AUSTRALIA 2ND INNINGS

AC Bannerman	c Studd b Barnes	13
HH Massie	b Steel	55
GJ Bonnor	b Ulyett	2
WL Murdoch*	run out	29
TP Horan	c Grace b Peate	2
G Giffen	c Grace b Peate	0
JM Blackham†	c Lyttelton b Peate	7
SP Jones	run out	6
FR Spofforth	b Peate	0
TW Garrett	not out	2
HF Boyle	b Steel	0
Extras	(b 6)	6
Total		122

Fall of wickets 66, 70, 70, 79, 79, 99, 114, 117, 122, 122

	O	M	R	W
E Peate	21	9	40	4
G Ulyett	6	2	10	1
RG Barlow	13	5	27	0
AG Steel	7	0	15	2
W Barnes	12	5	15	1
CT Studd	4	1	9	0

ENGLAND 2ND INNINGS

WG Grace	c Bannerman b Boyle	32
AN Hornby*	b Spofforth	9
RG Barlow	b Spofforth	0
G Ulyett	c Blackham b Spofforth	11
AP Lucas	b Spofforth	5
Hon. A Lyttelton†	b Spofforth	12
AG Steel	c & b Spofforth	0
JM Read	b Spofforth	0
W Barnes	c Murdoch b Boyle	2
CT Studd	not out	0
E Peate	b Boyle	2
Extras	(b 3, nb 1)	4
Total		77

Fall of wickets 15, 15, 51, 53, 66, 70, 70, 75, 75, 77

	O	M	R	W
FR Spofforth	28	15	44	7
TW Garrett	7	2	10	0
HF Boyle	20	11	19	3

Toss: Australia   Umpires: L Greenwood and RA Thoms   Australia won by 7 runs

Australia v England
Third Test at the Sydney Cricket Ground

1882-83
January 26, 27, 29, 30 (1883)

Spectatators on the SCG hill watch the action.

The third Test of the 1882–83 Australia versus England series was marked afterwards by some Australian ladies burning a bail, sealing the ashes in an urn and presenting it to the triumphant English captain. The urn became the most famous prize in cricket, although replicas of the trophy were subsequently created, as the frail original came to be housed at Lord's in England.

The third Test of the 1882–83 series was a decider after the teams won one Test each in Melbourne. As England won the toss in the third Test and elected to bat, Charles Studd edged a George Giffen delivery to fine leg for four. Studd and Dick Barlow established a good start before wicketkeeper Jack Blackham took a great catch to dismiss Studd. A fast yorker from Fred Spofforth dismissed Charles Leslie for nought and England slipped from 41-0 to 44-2. Australia struck another blow just before lunch when Barlow fell to a one-handed catch by Murdoch, making the score 67-3. The departures of Allan Steel and Billy Barnes after the break left England 75-5.

Australia, however, had to wait a while for its next success, as Walter Read and Edmund Tylecote established a century partnership that featured a great contest between bat and ball. The batting duo resisted the best that Spofforth, Joey Palmer, Tom Garrett and a somewhat wayward Giffen could offer. Tylecote, who hit two successive fours off Garrett to raise England's 100, repeatedly played the cut shot well. Tylecote gave a chance to Palmer at mid off, before running himself out for 66, producing the breakthrough Australia desperately wanted. A splendid straight drive from Read raised England's score to 200, but then he played an uncharacteristically poor shot and was caught, to make the score 223-7. The next wicket fell one run later before the tail boosted the total to 247, and then Australia batted on a fresh pitch.

A shower of rain fell before the start of day two, a weather-affected day that saw England drop five regulation catches. Conditions were windy in the morning and England's bowlers failed to make an impact, with Giffen and Alec Bannerman taking the total to 72-0 at lunch. Another shower after lunch rendered the turf pitch very wet and the bowlers struggled to control the ball, but wind dried things up somewhat and left the pitch soft underneath to assist the bowlers. Giffen was dropped at mid off, but then was stumped soon afterwards with the total on 76. Leslie dropped a sitter at mid on to reprieve Billy Murdoch before another spell of rain halted proceedings. Forty-five minutes of play followed the interruption, and Barnes dropped Bannerman as Australia progressed from 100-1 to 133-1.

Day three followed a rest day, and the players discovered

The obituary notice that first appeared in *The Sporting Times* newspaper in August 1882 which prompted the creation of 'the Ashes' trophy, which England 'regained and returned home' at the end of the 1882–83 series in Australia.

a sticky pitch that cut up easily. This ensured that Australia's batsmen would find it hard to maintain the team's good position. Accurate bowling from Steel accounted for Murdoch and McDonnell on 140, and Bannerman was lucky not to be run out 20 runs later. Bannerman was just six runs shy of a century when Australia lost 2-3, tumbling to 178-6. Bannerman and Massie were caught at point before George Bonnor skied a ball where a running George Studd took a good catch.

Another 18 runs were added before left-arm fast bowler Fred Morley struck two quick blows, followed by Blackham raising Australia's 200 with a four. Australia lost its last two wickets on 218 to give England a 29-run lead, although the lead would surely have been far greater had England's fielding been better on day two.

England batted on the same pitch as in its first innings. A dropped catch from Blackham reprieved Studd before Leslie was first out with the total on 13. Charles Studd looked in form before falling for 25, and Spofforth's third wicket made the score 55-3. Read looked to make another strong contribution before being bowled by a ball that kept low as soon as Horan was brought into the attack. Horan bowled superbly and finished with three scalps, with Garrett and Palmer proving ineffective. Barlow's resistance ended as he was caught off Horan, before Spofforth had Barnes lbw. Tylecote and Bates were caught as England slipped to 98-8, with Horan having exceptional figures of 3-2 from 10 overs before George Studd cut him for four. Ivo Bligh made some handy runs before Spofforth claimed the last

Left: Australia captain W. L. Murdoch.
Above: Sketches of the 1882–83 MCC Team in Australia.

two wickets to finish with 11 for the match. Australia needed 153 runs to win the series, and the openers failed to score in the seven overs before stumps.

The pitch was dead on the last day and very difficult to bat on, after rain earlier in the match was followed by sunny conditions. The first four overs of the day were maidens until Bannerman clubbed a long-hop for four to open the scoring. From then on, Australia was never in the hunt. Barlow bowled an immaculate line and length, an impeccable delivery bowling Giffen before Bannerman was caught at point. Morley broke through twice with the score on 18, as Murdoch came forward to a bumpy delivery and was caught in close, and McDonnell was caught at point.

Australia progressed to 30 before Horan was run out, followed by Massie caught at third man from an attacking shot. Blackham handled the conditions better than his team-mates,

his 26 being 15 more than the next top score. Bonnor's stumps were scattered from a ball that kept low, and Spofforth batted recklessly in his innings of seven. Blackham played a ball onto the stumps before Barlow made a mess of Garrett's stumps to claim his seventh wicket of the innings and seal a 69-run win for England.

England had won the series but a fourth Test was played, and Australia won following another intriguing contest at the SCG. The match was well balanced before Australia reached its target of 199 for the loss of six wickets.

ENGLAND 1ST INNINGS

RG Barlow	c Murdoch b Spofforth	28
CT Studd	c Blackham b Garrett	21
CFH Leslie	b Spofforth	0
AG Steel	b Garrett	17
WW Read	c Massie b Bannerman	66
W Barnes	c Blackham b Spofforth	2
EFS Tylecote†	run out	66
W Bates	c McDonnell b Spofforth	17
GB Studd	b Palmer	3
Hon. IFW Bligh*	b Palmer	13
F Morley	not out	2
Extras	(b 8, lb 3, nb 1)	12
Total		247

Fall of wickets 41, 44, 67, 69, 75, 191, 223, 224, 244, 247

	O	M	R	W
G Giffen	12	3	37	0
GE Palmer	38	21	38	2
FR Spofforth	51	19	73	4
TW Garrett	27	8	54	2
AC Bannerman	11	2	17	1
PS McDonnell	4	0	16	0

ENGLAND 2ND INNINGS

CFH Leslie	b Spofforth	8
CT Studd	b Spofforth	25
RG Barlow	c Palmer b Horan	24
AG Steel	lbw b Spofforth	6
WW Read	b Horan	21
W Barnes	lbw b Spofforth	3
EFS Tylecote†	c Bonnor b Spofforth	0
W Bates	c Murdoch b Horan	4
Hon.IFW Bligh*	not out	17
GB Studd	c Garrett b Spofforth	8
F Morley	b Spofforth	0
Extras	(b 5, lb 2)	7
Total		123

Fall of wickets 13, 45, 55, 87, 92, 94, 97, 98, 115, 123

	O	M	R	W
FR Spofforth	41.1	23	44	7
TW Garrett	13	3	31	0
GE Palmer	9	3	19	0
TP Horan	17	10	22	3

AUSTRALIA 1ST INNINGS

G Giffen	st Tylecote b Bates	41
AC Bannerman	c Bates b Morley	94
WL Murdoch*	lbw b Steel	19
PS McDonnell	b Steel	0
TP Horan	c Steel b Morley	19
HH Massie	c Bligh b Steel	1
GJ Bonnor	c GB Studd b Morley	0
JM Blackham†	b Barlow	27
TW Garrett	c Barlow b Morley	0
GE Palmer	c GB Studd b Barnes	7
FR Spofforth	not out	0
Extras	(b 6, lb 2, w 1, nb 1)	10
Total		218

Fall of wickets 76, 140, 140, 176, 177, 178, 196, 196, 218, 218

	O	M	R	W
F Morley	34	16	47	4
RG Barlow	47.1	31	52	1
W Bates	45	20	55	1
W Barnes	13	6	22	1
CT Studd	14	11	5	0
AG Steel	26	14	27	3

AUSTRALIA 2ND INNINGS

G Giffen	b Barlow	7
AC Bannerman	c Bligh b Barlow	5
WL Murdoch*	c GB Studd b Morley	0
TP Horan	run out	8
PS McDonnell	c Bligh b Morley	0
HH Massie	c CT Studd b Barlow	11
GJ Bonnor	b Barlow	8
JM Blackham†	b Barlow	26
FR Spofforth	c Steel b Barlow	7
GE Palmer	not out	2
TW Garrett	b Barlow	0
Extras	(b 6, lb 2, w 1)	9
Total		83

Fall of wickets 11, 12, 18, 18, 30, 33, 56, 72, 80, 83

	O	M	R	W
F Morley	35	19	34	2
RG Barlow	34.2	20	40	7

Toss: England   Umpires: EH Elliott and JS Swift   England won by 69 runs

Australia v England
First Test at the Sydney Cricket Ground

1886-87
January 28, 29, 31 (1887)

One could be forgiven for thinking a Test series might become lopsided when a team is dismissed for fewer than 50 runs in the first innings of the opening Test. This start to the 1886–87 two-Test series, however, was the beginning of a contest full of many twists and turns.

Australia's Percy McDonnell won the toss in his first Test as captain and created a first in Test history by electing to bowl. Debutants Charlie Turner and John James 'JJ' Ferris opened the bowling, with Charles Bannerman umpiring his first Test while younger brother Alec still played. Billy Bates began well for England, hitting two fours before he attempted a third and was caught, giving left-armer Ferris his first wicket. England was 11-2 when a great left-handed catch by Fred Spofforth at point gave Turner his first wicket, Billy Barnes being dismissed without scoring.

Arthur Shrewsbury was next to go as George McShane, chosen to replace an unwell George Palmer, jumped and took a great catch at the second attempt. England crashed to 13-5 as Turner bowled both Dick Barlow and debutant Billy Gunn, who was unlucky when the ball hit him on the thigh and rolled onto the stumps. William Scotton was caught at mid off, and Maurice Read was superbly caught by a diving Spofforth from a cut shot to make the score 21-7. It became 29-8 as Briggs was caught at mid on, and several maidens were delivered before Wilfred Flowers was bowled by a yorker. George Lohmann top scored with 17 before he was caught near the boundary, and Australia must have already been sniffing victory, with England dismissed for just 45. Turner (with 6-15) and the 19-year-old Ferris (4-27) must have found it hard to believe their luck as they bowled unchanged, thoroughly routing England within 36 four-ball overs. England's score in this innings remains, to this day, its lowest in Test cricket.

Australia's Charlie Turner took match figures of 8-68 on debut, but England still won the Test, despite being dismissed for just 45 in its first innings.

Jack Blackham hit a four through square leg before edging to give wicketkeeper Mordecai Sherwin his first Test catch and leaving Australia 8-1. It was 18-2 when McDonnell fell, and could have been 32-3 had Read not misjudged a high hit from Sammy Jones. Australia gained a first innings lead before debutant Harry Moses drove a handsome four to raise the 50. Jones struck the ball hard as he played several drives, before hitting a catch to point with the total on 64. Turner's first Test innings ended three runs later and Australia went to stumps at 76-4.

The home side lost a further three wickets before the total reached 100, ensuring that Australia's lead would not be ample despite stonewalling tactics from Alec Bannerman, who made a slow 15 not out. Moses matched Jones' score of 31 before Barlow struck, followed by Briggs accounting for McShane. Shrewsbury took a superb left-handed catch to dismiss Billy Midwinter, and another 20 runs were scored before the last three wickets fell cheaply. Lohmann landed the ball on the right spot to bowl Garrett before Spofforth was similarly dismissed, and Barnes accounted for Ferris. Australia had gained a lead of 74.

With England battling to remain in contention, Bates scored 24 in an opening partnership of 31 before he went forward and then back to a delivery. He paid the price for changing his mind as he was bowled. Shrewsbury and Barnes found some form and erased England's deficit, although seven successive maidens were bowled at one stage. After Shrewsbury was clean bowled to make the score 80-2, there was some brief resistance, but then England crashed from 92-2 to 103-7 at stumps. Barlow fell to an overhead catch by Jones on the off side before Read was bowled first ball, and Barnes was fifth out when he was caught in close. Gunn was bowled attempting a big hit before Lohmann was lbw, and England led by just 29 runs with three wickets remaining.

Following a rest day, Blackham crucially dropped Scotton off Ferris' bowling with the first ball of day three. England's tail contributed invaluably as Scotton, Briggs, Flowers and Sherwin made the Australians work hard. An eighth wicket partnership of 25 ended when Scotton was caught off a short ball, and another 25 runs were added before Spofforth decisively beat Briggs, just after Spofforth returned to the attack. Another crucial catch was missed in the next over when McDonnell dropped Sherwin in the slips. Sherwin played some good strokes and gained another reprieve when Jones threw the ball to the wrong end when a run out beckoned. A crucial last wicket partnership of 31 ensured Australia needed 111 for victory.

Barnes raised England's hopes as he removed Australia's openers with only five runs on the board. Jones and a patient Moses halted the collapse, and an over from Barlow cost 10 runs, with a boundary from Jones soon followed by Gunn almost taking a catch. But the total was still only 29 when Read ran in from long off to take a great catch and dismiss Jones, the fielder hurting his hand in the process. Turner skied a catch to Barnes nine runs later.

Amidst very slow scoring, Barnes bowled nine straight maidens, and Alec Bannerman lasted about an hour without scoring before he was out for four. McShane was bowled trying to cut as Australia sank to 61-6, but Midwinter luckily hit a four past Sherwin before some byes were conceded. The total crept to 80 when Moses' painstaking innings ended as he edged a prod to slip. Midwinter's dismissal left Australia needing 28 runs with two wickets left, and 12 were scored before Garrett paid for unwisely hitting the ball in the air, enabling Gunn to take a well-judged catch. Spofforth scored a two off Lohmann before Spofforth hit out in Lohmann's next over and was bowled, sealing an amazing 13-run win for England. The tourists subsequently clinched the series with a 71-run win in the second Test, again leaving the Australians wondering what might have been.

Fred Spofforth (aka 'The Demon') took 94 wickets in his 18 Tests for Australia.

ENGLAND 1ST INNINGS		
W Bates	c Midwinter b Ferris	8
A Shrewsbury snr*	c McShane b Ferris	2
W Barnes	c Spofforth b Turner	0
RG Barlow	b Turner	2
JM Read	c Spofforth b Ferris	5
W Gunn	b Turner	0
WH Scotton	c Jones b Turner	1
J Briggs	c Midwinter b Turner	5
GA Lohmann	c Garrett b Ferris	17
W Flowers	b Turner	2
M Sherwin†	not out	0
Extras	(b 2, lb 1)	3
Total		45

Fall of wickets 11, 11, 13, 13, 13, 17, 21, 29, 41, 45

	O	M	R	W
CTB Turner	18	11	15	6
JJ Ferris	17.3	7	27	4

AUSTRALIA 1ST INNINGS		
JM Blackham†	c Sherwin b Lohmann	4
PS McDonnell*	b Barnes	14
H Moses	b Barlow	31
SP Jones	c Shrewsbury b Bates	31
CTB Turner	b Barlow	3
AC Bannerman	not out	15
PG McShane	lbw b Briggs	5
WE Midwinter	c Shrewsbury b Barlow	0
TW Garrett	b Lohmann	12
FR Spofforth	b Lohmann	2
JJ Ferris	c Barlow b Barnes	1
Extras	(b 1)	1
Total		119

Fall of wickets 8, 18, 64, 67, 86, 95, 96, 116, 118, 119

	O	M	R	W
W Barnes	22.1	16	19	2
GA Lohmann	21	12	30	3
J Briggs	14	5	25	1
RG Barlow	35	23	25	3
W Bates	21	9	19	1

ENGLAND 2ND INNINGS		
W Bates	b Ferris	24
A Shrewsbury snr*	b Ferris	29
W Barnes	c Moses b Garrett	32
RG Barlow	c Jones b Ferris	4
JM Read	b Ferris	0
W Gunn	b Turner	4
GA Lohmann	lbw b Ferris	3
J Briggs	b Spofforth	33
WH Scotton	c Spofforth b Garrett	6
W Flowers	c McDonnell b Turner	14
M Sherwin†	not out	21
Extras	(b 9, lb 5)	14
Total		184

Fall of wickets 31, 80, 92, 92, 98, 99, 103, 128, 153, 184

	O	M	R	W
CTB Turner	44.2	22	53	2
JJ Ferris	61	30	76	5
FR Spofforth	12	3	17	1
WE Midwinter	4	1	10	0
TW Garrett	12	7	8	2
PG McShane	3	0	6	0

AUSTRALIA 2ND INNINGS		
JM Blackham†	b Barnes	5
PS McDonnell*	lbw b Barnes	0
H Moses	c Shrewsbury b Barnes	24
SP Jones	c Read b Barnes	18
CTB Turner	c & b Barnes	7
AC Bannerman	b Lohmann	4
PG McShane	b Briggs	0
WE Midwinter	lbw b Barnes	10
TW Garrett	c Gunn b Lohmann	10
FR Spofforth	b Lohmann	5
JJ Ferris	not out	0
Extras	(b 12, lb 2)	14
Total		97

Fall of wickets 4, 5, 29, 38, 58, 61, 80, 83, 95, 97

	O	M	R	W
W Barnes	46	29	28	6
GA Lohmann	24	11	20	3
J Briggs	7	5	7	1
RG Barlow	13	6	20	0
W Bates	17	11	8	0

Toss: Australia   Umpires: C Bannerman and H Rawlinson   England won by 13 runs

England v Australia
Second Test at the Oval, London

1890
August 11, 12 (1890)

Australia, 1890. Standing: J. E. Barrett, B. P. Jones, H. F. Boyle (Manager), H. Trott, E. J. K. Burn, H. Trumble, J. Blackham. Sitting: J. J. Lyons, C. T. B. Turner, W. L. Murdoch (captain), F. H. Walters, J. J. Ferris. Front: P. C. Charlton, S. E. Gregory.

The second Ashes Test of 1890 featured a memorable debut for England left-arm seam bowler Fred Martin, who intriguingly would not have played had England not had an issue with selection. After winning the first at Lord's by seven wickets, the hosts were depleted for the second Test, in which they sought another win to seal the three-match series. County took priority over country for professionals Bobby Peel and George Ulyett, with Yorkshire refusing to release them for England because Yorkshire had a county contest on with Middlesex. Another England player, Andrew Stoddart, was allowed to choose to play for his country or his county, as he was an amateur, and opted for his county, Middlesex. If that was not enough challenge for

England, injuries ruled out William Attewell and Johnny Briggs. England subsequently had three Test debutants: Martin, James Cranston and John Sharpe.

Martin bowled first after Australia won the toss and chose to bat following rain in the lead-up. John Lyons scored 13 runs in an opening partnership of 16 before becoming Martin's first victim. Charlie Turner and Jack Barrett were caught with the total on 27, and England's bowlers subsequently maintained the upper hand. Billy Murdoch was bowled by Martin for two, Kenny Burn caught behind off George Lohmann for seven, and Jack Blackham bowled by Martin for one, and the tourists tumbled to 46-6. Harry Trott resisted and JJ Ferris hung around while 24 runs were added, before he became Sharpe's first Test scalp.

Trott scored a brave 39 in 80 minutes, but his effort was almost single-handed as Australia tallied just 92 runs in less than 66 overs, which contained five deliveries. Trott was bizarrely dismissed when he played the ball onto his pad, before the ball ran up his arm and was caught down the leg-side by wicketkeeper, Gregor MacGregor. Lohmann bowled unchanged and had fine figures of 3-34 from 32.2 overs, but the star was Martin with 6-50 from 27 overs.

England began dreadfully, with Arthur Shrewsbury facing a maiden first up, before WG Grace was caught at slip from Ferris' first delivery. Shrewsbury departed for four when Trott took a good catch at point off Turner, who subsequently bowled Walter Read to have England 16-3. The score could have been 19-4, but Trumble missed a chance to catch Billy Gunn at slip. Cranston scored 16 in a fourth wicket partnership of 39, then ran himself out needlessly, risking a single.

Gunn sought to capitalise on his reprieve, and Maurice Read also reached double digits. Gunn scored 32 in 105 minutes, then Ferris dismissed him as England trailed by 13 runs. The deficit shrank to two runs before the hosts flopped from 90-5 to be all out in 55 overs, with a lead of just eight runs. Maurice Read and Barnes were caught by Murdoch off Percie Charlton, then McGregor and Lohmann were caught off Ferris. A last wicket partnership of six took the score to 100 before Charlton had his third wicket. Ferris was the pick of the bowlers with 4-25 from 25 overs, before Australia's batting slumped again. Barrett was bowled by Martin before Lohmann bowled the promoted Ferris, and the visitors were 5-2 at stumps. Twenty two wickets fell for just 197 runs in the day, not to mention several near misses when the ball beat the bat.

Lyons batted aggressively as he and Burn took Australia to a 28-run lead before Lyons departed. Australia fell to 54-7 as Murdoch, Burn, Turner and Blackham were bowled, with Martin and Lohmann sharing the wickets. Trott and Charlton

provided respite and put on a precious 36-run stand in difficult conditions, and Trott became the only Australian victim in the second innings not to be bowled. Following Charlton's demise, Hugh Trumble and Gregory took Australia from 92-9 to 102-9, and Trumble's dismissal left England with a not-so-easy target of 95. Martin was again England's best bowler, with 6-52 as he bowled unchanged from one end throughout Australia's innings, comprising 60.2 overs.

Grace should have made another first-ball duck, but Trott dropped a cut shot at point. Grace scored 16 in an opening stand of 24 before Trumble caught him off Ferris. The successful bowler soon had Shrewsbury lbw and Gunn stumped, before Turner bowled Walter Read to have England in strife at 32-4. Maurice Read and Cranston, however, swung the pendulum, with the latter showing good composure for a debutant. Maurice Read was on 17 and England 63-4 when he offered a priceless chance to Murdoch at mid on, but the catch was spilled. The error looked certain to quash Australia's victory hopes, with Read adding 18 more runs to take England to 83-4. The hosts needed just 12 runs to win with six wickets remaining, but little did anyone know what was coming.

Turner took two wickets with consecutive deliveries, as Maurice Read unnecessarily chanced his arm and was caught at long on, then Cranston was caught by Trumble. Another three runs were added before Ferris had Lohmann caught at the wicket. With England suddenly under pressure, Barnes scored five precious runs and MacGregor two, ensuring the hosts needed only two more with three wickets standing. Ferris subsequently trapped Barnes lbw, and the tension hit fever pitch in the next five overs. Sharpe played and missed every ball in a Ferris over, but then managed a single to tie the scores. An England victory was far from certain as three maiden overs followed, before Sharpe and MacGregor got into a terrible mix-up after Sharpe played the ball in front of point. The batsmen were stranded in mid-pitch and a run out beckoned, but Barrett crumbled under pressure; his throw went awry and enabled the batsmen to complete the winning run.

In this Test, Martin became the first bowler to take 12 wickets on debut. His record remained until 1972, when Australia's Bob Massie took 16-137 in his first Test (v. England, at Lord's, London).

The third Test was washed out and, curiously, the heroic Martin played only one more Test. It was in South Africa in 1892, with England winning by an innings. Martin bowled in South Africa's second innings and took 2-39. Interestingly, his new-ball partner was JJ Ferris, who took 13 wickets in the match.

AUSTRALIA 1ST INNINGS		
JJ Lyons	c WW Read b Martin	13
CTB Turner	c Sharpe b Lohmann	12
WL Murdoch*	b Martin	2
JE Barrett	c Lohmann b Martin	0
GHS Trott	c MacGregor b Martin	39
EJK Burn	c MacGregor b Lohmann	7
JM Blackham†	b Martin	1
JJ Ferris	c Lohmann b Sharpe	6
PC Charlton	b Martin	10
SE Gregory	b Lohmann	2
H Trumble	not out	0
Extras		0
Total		92

Fall of wickets 16, 27, 27, 32, 39, 46, 70, 85, 92, 92

	O	M	R	W
F Martin	27	9	50	6
GA Lohmann	32.2	19	34	3
JW Sharpe	6	3	8	1

ENGLAND 1ST INNINGS		
A Shrewsbury snr	c Trott b Turner	4
WG Grace*	c Trumble b Ferris	0
W Gunn	b Ferris	32
WW Read	b Turner	1
J Cranston	run out	16
JM Read	c Murdoch b Charlton	19
W Barnes	c Murdoch b Charlton	5
GA Lohmann	c Gregory b Ferris	3
G MacGregor†	c Turner b Ferris	1
JW Sharpe	not out	5
F Martin	c Turner b Charlton	1
Extras	(b 9, lb 3, nb 1)	13
Total		100

Fall of wickets 0, 10, 16, 55, 79, 90, 91, 93, 94, 100

	O	M	R	W
CTB Turner	22	12	37	2
JJ Ferris	25	14	25	4
H Trumble	2	0	7	0
PC Charlton	6	0	18	3

AUSTRALIA 2ND INNINGS		
JE Barrett	b Martin	4
EJK Burn	b Martin	15
JJ Ferris	b Lohmann	1
JJ Lyons	b Martin	21
WL Murdoch*	b Lohmann	6
GHS Trott	c Cranston b Martin	25
CTB Turner	b Martin	0
JM Blackham†	b Lohmann	1
PC Charlton	b Sharpe	11
H Trumble	b Martin	6
SE Gregory	not out	4
Extras	(b 7, lb 1)	8
Total		102

Fall of wickets 4, 5, 36, 43, 49, 53, 54, 90, 92, 102

	O	M	R	W
F Martin	30.2	12	52	6
GA Lohmann	21	8	32	3
JW Sharpe	9	5	10	1

ENGLAND 2ND INNINGS		
A Shrewsbury snr	lbw b Ferris	9
WG Grace*	c Trumble b Ferris	16
W Gunn	st Blackham b Ferris	1
WW Read	b Turner	6
JM Read	c Barrett b Turner	35
J Cranston	c Trumble b Turner	15
GA Lohmann	c Blackham b Ferris	2
W Barnes	lbw b Ferris	5
G MacGregor†	not out	2
JW Sharpe	not out	2
Extras	(lb 1, nb 1)	2
Total	(8 wickets)	95

Did not bat: F Martin

Fall of wickets 24, 25, 28, 32, 83, 83, 86, 93

	O	M	R	W
CTB Turner	25	9	38	3
JJ Ferris	23	8	49	5
PC Charlton	3	1	6	0

Toss: Australia   Umpires: CK Pullin and J Street   England won by 2 wickets

Australia v England

First Test at the Sydney Cricket Ground

1894-95

December 14, 15, 17, 18, 19, 20 (1894)

The first Test of the 1894–95 Ashes series was as unpredictable as the first Test of 1886–87, once again after the home side was in a seemingly impregnable position.

Australia's decision to bat first appeared to backfire as the score slumped to 21-3 within 35 minutes. Tom Richardson bowled John Lyons, Harry Trott and Test debutant Joe Darling, with the latter two out in successive deliveries – Trott lost his off peg, then Darling lost middle and off. England subsequently missed two vital chances before Australia reached 78-3 at lunch. Test debutant Frank Iredale avoided being run out, and wicketkeeper Leslie Gay missed a catch after a delivery hit the handle of George Giffen's bat.

Iredale batted confidently and hit two successive fours off Johnny Briggs after play resumed. Giffen, meanwhile, defended and drove well, and England was disrupted when an ill Bill Lockwood departed. Gay gave Giffen another reprieve, this time while the batsman was on 90. The partnership reached 171 just before tea, and change bowler Francis Ford took a wicket in his first Test as Iredale presented a catch to mid on. Giffen reached his century with a leg-side boundary off Richardson soon after the break, and the scoring increased rapidly while Syd Gregory hit the ball around. Giffen was finally out for 161 when he edged to slip, before Australia closed day one on 346-5, with Gregory on 85.

England's fortunes worsened as day two began, with John Reedman dropped off Richardson's bowling. Gay claimed his first catch to make Australia 409-8 with the dismissal of Charlie Turner, but the wicketkeeper could ill afford to reprieve Gregory on 131. Jack Blackham batted vigorously as he and Gregory put on 154 runs in just 75 minutes before Gregory fell, having scored 201 in just 244 minutes. Blackham's dismissal for 74 left Australia just 14 runs shy of 600.

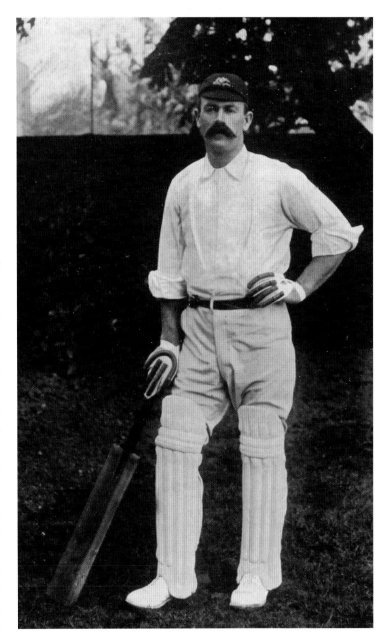

Australian batsman Joe Darling.

Archie MacLaren scored four in his first Test innings before being caught at cover point, and Giffen's dismissal of Andrew Stoddart made the score 43-2. Jack Brown hit two successive fours through the off side from Trott's bowling before being run out while attempting a suicidal single. England finished day two on 130-3, with Albert Ward on 67, and rain interrupted the first session of day three following a rest day. The ball was greasy before the sun came out and dried the grass after the lunch break. Iredale took an important running catch to dismiss Ward, then Bobby Peel failed to profit from a reprieve and England slipped to 155-5.

Ford played some good drives and added 56 runs with Bill Brockwell, until they succumbed to Blackham's glovework in quick succession. Another 41 runs were added before Lockwood gave Giffen an easy catch, then Gay was dropped before going on to make 33 in an audacious 73-run partnership that ended when Briggs was confused by Giffen's slower ball. Australia's fielding was sub-par, and McLeod deputised as wicketkeeper after Blackham suffered a thumb injury late in the day. Australia nonetheless was in a commanding position as England trailed by 261 runs and had to follow on, according to the rules.

England began its second innings on day four in cool and overcast weather, and scored slowly. MacLaren was out for 20, then Ward gained a crucial reprieve on 28 as McLeod fumbled behind the stumps. The *Sydney Morning Herald* reported: "If the Englishmen suffered from the absence of their bowler Lockwood, the Australians certainly lost a great deal by Blackham not being able to take his usual place." After lunch, Ernie Jones paid for bowling too short, and Stoddart hit two fours in a Giffen over. A cut shot by Stoddart gave Giffen an easy catch with the score on 115, and a succession of bowling changes proved fruitless as England reached 183-2 at tea with Ward in form. Reedman took over the wicketkeeping as McLeod had a bowl. Giffen bowled Ward for 117, and Brown fell for 53, England finishing the day with a seven-run lead and six wickets remaining.

England's lead was just 35 runs when Brockwell and Peel were dismissed, then McLeod missed stumping Ford, who was on five. It was decisive, as Ford and Briggs went on to score 40s before McLeod succeeded as a bowler. Lockwood, however, hit McLeod for two fours in an over and shared in vital partnerships of 22 and 17 for the last two wickets, leaving Australia a target of 177. Lyons gave Australia a flying start with 25 runs in 17 minutes but fell to a reckless swish. After Trott's downfall left Australia 45-2, Darling and a more cautious Giffen profited from some wayward bowling and lacklustre fielding to take Australia to stumps.

Only another 64 runs were needed, with eight wickets in hand, but overnight rain changed things dramatically. The *Sydney Morning Herald* reported that the pitch "had been laid with stiff black soil" on the final day. Darling hit Peel out of the ground, before Giffen edged Richardson just past leg-stump for a boundary. Sawdust was brought on to each end to help the bowlers, and Darling skied a catch to long on, Australia 130-3.

Luck still seemed on Australia's side as Giffen survived an lbw appeal before Brown dropped him. But replacing Richardson with Briggs immediately paid off, with Giffen lbw and Australia still needing 42 runs. Another 12 were added before Iredale skied a catch, but there was no sign of trouble as Australia reached 158-5, until four wickets fell for just four runs. Peel took the first three, with Gregory caught behind before Reedman advanced and was freakishly stumped as the ball ricocheted from Gay's chest into the stumps. Turner was caught at cover point, then Jones was caught behind off Briggs. The injured Blackham scored two, and Australia required another 11 runs, but he played the ball back to Peel for a caught-and-bowled. England had snatched an incredible 10-run win, and went on to win the series 3-2.

George Giffen's match tally of 202 runs and eight wickets weren't enough to prevent England recording a remarkable victory after following on.

AUSTRALIA 1ST INNINGS

JJ Lyons	b Richardson	1
GHS Trott	b Richardson	12
G Giffen	c Ford b Brockwell	161
J Darling	b Richardson	0
FA Iredale	c Stoddart b Ford	81
SE Gregory	c Peel b Stoddart	201
JC Reedman	c Ford b Peel	17
CE McLeod	b Richardson	15
CTB Turner	c Gay b Peel	1
JM Blackham*†	b Richardson	74
E Jones	not out	11
Extras	(b 8, lb 3, w 1)	12
Total		586

Fall of wickets 10, 21, 21, 192, 331, 379, 400, 409, 563, 586

	O	M	R	W
T Richardson	55.3	13	181	5
R Peel	53	14	140	2
J Briggs	25	4	96	0
W Brockwell	22	7	78	1
FGJ Ford	11	2	47	1
AE Stoddart	3	0	31	1
WH Lockwood	3	2	1	0

ENGLAND 1ST INNINGS

AC MacLaren	c Reedman b Turner	4
A Ward	c Iredale b Turner	75
AE Stoddart*	c Jones b Giffen	12
JT Brown	run out	22
W Brockwell	c Blackham b Jones	49
R Peel	c Gregory b Giffen	4
FGJ Ford	st Blackham b Giffen	30
J Briggs	b Giffen	57
WH Lockwood	c Giffen b Trott	18
LH Gay†	c Gregory b Reedman	33
T Richardson	not out	0
Extras	(b 17, lb 3, w 1)	21
Total		325

Fall of wickets 14, 43, 78, 149, 155, 211, 211, 252, 325, 325

	O	M	R	W
E Jones	19	7	44	1
CTB Turner	44	16	89	2
G Giffen	43	17	75	4
GHS Trott	15	4	59	1
CE McLeod	14	2	25	0
JC Reedman	3.3	1	12	1
JJ Lyons	2	2	0	0

ENGLAND 2ND INNINGS

AC MacLaren	b Giffen	20
A Ward	b Giffen	117
AE Stoddart*	c Giffen b Turner	36
JT Brown	c Jones b Giffen	53
W Brockwell	b Jones	37
R Peel	b Giffen	17
FGJ Ford	c & b McLeod	48
J Briggs	b McLeod	42
WH Lockwood	b Trott	29
LH Gay†	b Trott	4
T Richardson	not out	12
Extras	(b 14, lb 8)	22
Total		437

Fall of wickets 44, 115, 217, 245, 290, 296, 385, 398, 420, 437

	O	M	R	W
E Jones	19	0	57	1
CTB Turner	35	14	78	1
G Giffen	75	25	164	4
GHS Trott	12.4	2	22	2
CE McLeod	30	6	67	2
JC Reedman	6	1	12	0
JJ Lyons	2	0	12	0
FA Iredale	2	1	3	0

AUSTRALIA 2ND INNINGS

JJ Lyons	b Richardson	25
GHS Trott	c Gay b Peel	8
G Giffen	lbw b Briggs	41
J Darling	c Brockwell b Peel	53
SE Gregory	c Gay b Peel	16
FA Iredale	c & b Briggs	5
JC Reedman	st Gay b Peel	4
CE McLeod	not out	2
CTB Turner	c Briggs b Peel	2
E Jones	c MacLaren b Briggs	1
JM Blackham*	c & b Peel	2
Extras	(b 2, lb 1, nb 4)	7
Total		166

Fall of wickets 26, 45, 130, 135, 147, 158, 159, 161, 162, 166

	O	M	R	W
T Richardson	11	3	27	1
R Peel	30	9	67	6
WH Lockwood	16	3	40	0
J Briggs	11	2	25	3

Toss: Australia   Umpires: C Bannerman and J Phillips
England won by 10 runs

Australia v England
Third Test at the Adelaide Oval

1901-02
January 17, 18, 20, 21, 22, 23 (1902)

The 1901–02 Ashes series seemed unpredictable after England's innings and 124-run victory in the first Test was followed by a 229-run win to Australia in the second Test. The third Test was much closer, and the series swung in the process.

After England skipper Archie MacLaren won his third successive toss and chose to bat on a cool day, openers MacLaren and Tom Hayward put on 88 runs before lunch. Not long after play resumed, James Kelly missed a difficult leg-side stumping to reprieve Hayward. MacLaren also had a slice of luck when he swished and was bowled by a Warwick Armstrong no-ball. A hesitation in running between the wickets ultimately produced the first wicket, as MacLaren departed for 67.

John Tyldesley settled in but didn't score when he skied a return catch to Hugh Trumble, and England's strong position weakened, the score slipping to 171-4. Ten runs shy of a century, Hayward advanced Monty Noble and touched the ball before it ricocheted from Kelly onto the stumps. Gilbert Jessop was caught from an attempted big hit, and then Noble caused some trouble for the batsmen after tea. Trumble, however, missed a catch, before he trapped Arthur 'Dick' Lilley lbw. Slow scoring duo Len Braund and Willie Quaife halted the mid-innings slump as England reached 266-5 at stumps.

The total neared 300 on a sultry day two, before Quaife was caught behind. Arthur Jones hit a four but he was run out when Braund took off for a third run as soon as Jones stopped running. England recovered from 302-7, with John Gunn playing some neat cut shots, and Braund played a lovely straight drive for four. Braund survived a chance to Trumble after lunch, and Braun compounded this by driving Trumble for four. Braund hit further boundaries, playing more forcefully than he had earlier, and Gunn became more defensive until he was bowled by Noble, who also took the last two wickets. Sydney Barnes was caught at

Australian left-hander Clem Hill was perhaps best known for scoring 99, 98 and 97 in consecutive Test innings.

short leg by Clem Hill, who subsequently caught Colin 'Charlie' Blythe superbly, running from square leg to pursue a skier.

Braund remained undefeated on 103, and England's 388 looked very good when Blythe's first ball accounted for Joe Darling, before Victor Trumper and Hill scored briskly, unleashing cuts and drives. Australia's 50 came up in 31 minutes and the 100 was up in 78 minutes, with England meanwhile suffering a cruel blow as Barnes exited the series with a knee injury. Trumper was on 65 when a suicidal single cost him his wicket, before Hill and Reg Duff took Australia to 172-2 at stumps, with Hill on 83.

Following the rest day, Hill gave a chance in the slips on 92. Hill's 11th four took him to 98, but he was denied a century, as a high hit was intercepted by Tyldesley on the bike track. Duff survived a chance at slip before Braund had him lbw for 43, which included eight fours. Syd Gregory also scored most of his runs from boundaries, and Gunn was finally rewarded when Armstrong offered a soft return catch. After Gregory gave a catch to mid on, Trumble was bowled one run later, Australia still 99 runs behind. The 300 was passed before Gunn took the last three wickets and England claimed a 67-run lead.

MacLaren and Hayward again began well for England, putting on 80 before MacLaren was clean bowled, the previous ball rearing and hitting his arm. Hayward again survived a stumping chance, and at one stage some impatient spectators yelled, with the intention of distracting the batsman on strike. Noble sportingly declined to bowl the ball.

Some overnight rain fell before England began day three on 98-1, with the pitch still in a reasonable state. Trumble's first over cost 11 runs, then Hill grassed a sharp chance at short mid on to reprieve Tyldesley. A good ball from Trumble bowled Hayward, before Tyldesley was run out following some athletic fielding from Trumper. Quaife was again slow, while Jessop struck the ball hard several times until Trumble bowled him. Braund survived a run out chance, and the sun came out with a strong wind. After lunch, however, a dust storm ended the day's play early, with England 204-5, Braun and Lilley having scored runs to assist the dogged Quaife.

Day four featured a clear sky with lovely sunshine and breeze. Lilley was bowled by Charlie McLeod without a run added, and Jones scored 11 before Trumble struck twice in the space of six runs, despite Gunn being dropped. With Barnes injured, the ninth wicket was the last, Quaife dubiously adjudged lbw after a partnership of 23. Further controversy arose as the Englishmen were deprived of the chance to bowl seven minutes before lunch. It was reported that one of the umpires misjudged the time because his watch had stopped.

With Australia needing 315 runs, Duff glanced a leg-side four before he was unusually dismissed, having stepped too far back and onto the stumps. Trumper and Hill again batted confidently before Gunn beat Trumper to make the score 50-2. Gregory looked in form and was caught with the score on 98, then Darling was in good touch. Hill reached 97 when he survived an lbw appeal off Jessop, but a faulty stroke off Jessop's bowling caused his downfall, giving him an unfortunate sequence of 99, 98 and 97 in successive Test innings. Australia needed 114 runs and England six wickets as day six began.

England sorely missed Barnes as Darling and Trumble pushed on, Darling eventually caught for 69. Noble was involved in a 32-run partnership before he was run out, and the remaining 28 runs were scored as Trumble moved to 62 while Armstrong scored nine. England's bowling shortcomings were exposed as just four main bowlers were used, and Australia went on to win the series 4-1.

Above: Syd Gregory played 58 Tests for Australia from 1890 to 1912. Following page: Victor Trumper made 65 and 25 in Australia's win in the third Ashes Test of 1901–02.

ENGLAND 1ST INNINGS		
AC MacLaren*	run out	67
TW Hayward	run out	90
JT Tyldesley	c & b Trumble	0
GL Jessop	c Trumper b Trumble	1
AFA Lilley†	lbw b Trumble	10
WG Quaife	c Kelly b Howell	68
LC Braund	not out	103
AO Jones	run out	5
JR Gunn	b Noble	24
SF Barnes	c Hill b Noble	5
C Blythe	c Hill b Noble	2
Extras	(b 9, w 1, nb 3)	13
Total		388

Fall of wickets 149, 160, 164, 171, 186, 294, 302, 371, 384, 388

	O	M	R	W
H Trumble	65	23	124	3
MA Noble	26	10	58	3
WP Howell	36	10	82	1
WW Armstrong	18	5	45	0
VT Trumper	6	3	17	0
CE McLeod	19	5	49	0

AUSTRALIA 1ST INNINGS		
J Darling*	c MacLaren b Blythe	1
VT Trumper	run out	65
C Hill	c Tyldesley b Braund	98
RA Duff	lbw b Braund	43
SE Gregory	c Blythe b Braund	55
WW Armstrong	c & b Gunn	9
H Trumble	b Gunn	13
WP Howell	c Braund b Gunn	3
MA Noble	b Gunn	14
JJ Kelly†	not out	5
CE McLeod	b Gunn	7
Extras	(b 2, lb 6)	8
Total		321

Fall of wickets 1, 138, 197, 229, 260, 288, 289, 302, 309, 321

	O	M	R	W
LC Braund	46	9	143	3
C Blythe	11	3	54	1
SF Barnes	7	0	21	0
JR Gunn	42	14	76	5
GL Jessop	7	0	19	0

ENGLAND 2ND INNINGS		
AC MacLaren*	b Trumble	44
TW Hayward	b Trumble	47
JT Tyldesley	run out	25
WG Quaife	lbw b Trumble	44
GL Jessop	b Trumble	16
LC Braund	b Howell	17
AFA Lilley†	b McLeod	21
AO Jones	c & b Trumble	11
JR Gunn	lbw b Trumble	5
C Blythe	not out	10
SF Barnes	absent hurt	-
Extras	(b 6, w 1)	7
Total		247

Fall of wickets 80, 113, 126, 144, 165, 204, 218, 224, 247

	O	M	R	W
H Trumble	44	18	74	6
MA Noble	21	7	72	0
WP Howell	27	9	54	1
WW Armstrong	5	0	9	0
CE McLeod	14	3	31	1

AUSTRALIA 2ND INNINGS		
RA Duff	hit wicket b Gunn	4
VT Trumper	b Gunn	25
C Hill	b Jessop	97
SE Gregory	c Braund b Gunn	23
J Darling*	c Hayward b Jessop	69
H Trumble	not out	62
MA Noble	run out	13
WW Armstrong	not out	9
Extras	(b 9, lb 3, nb 1)	13
Total	(6 wickets)	315

Did not bat WP Howell, JJ Kelly†, CE McLeod

Fall of wickets 5, 50, 98, 194, 255, 287

	O	M	R	W
LC Braund	25	5	79	0
C Blythe	41	16	66	0
JR Gunn	38	14	88	3
GL Jessop	23	9	41	2
TW Hayward	7	0	28	0

Toss: England   Umpires: P Argall and RM Crockett   Australia won by 4 wickets

England v Australia
Fourth Test at Old Trafford, Manchester

1902
July 24, 25, 26 (1902)

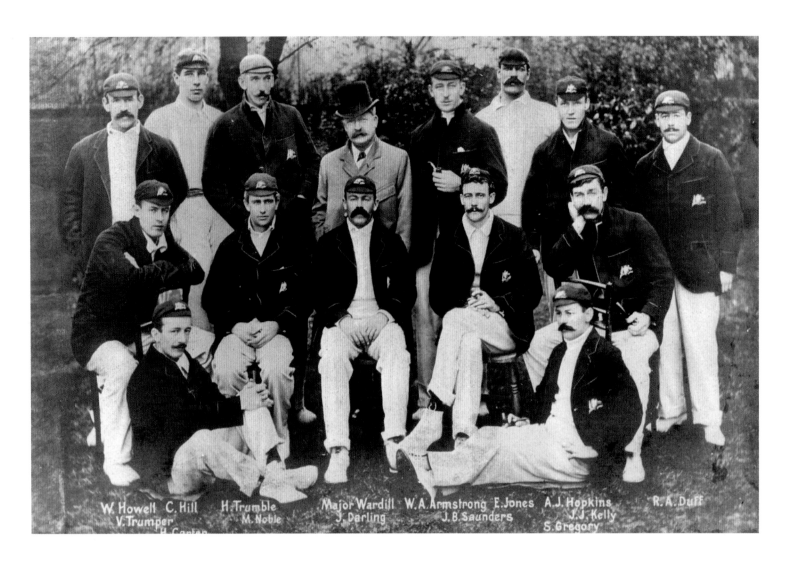

Australia's touring party to England in 1902. Standing: W. Howell, C. Hill, H. Trumble, Major Wardill (Manager), W. W. Armstrong, E. Jones, A. J. Y. Hopkins, R. A. Duff. Sitting: V. T. Trumper, M. A. Noble, J. Darling, J. V. Saunders, J. J. Kelly. Front: H. Carter, S. E. Gregory.

The fourth Ashes Test of 1902 was described by David Frith as one of the most famous cricket matches of all time. The match was certainly enthralling in many ways, with Australia leading the series 1-0 after three of the five Tests.

Australia won the toss and chose to bat, as the Old Trafford venue was soft following rain. England's bowlers unwisely bowled short on many occasions in the first session. Bill Lockwood wasn't used at first because of the slippery run-up. Victor Trumper, meanwhile, was in superb form and hit the ball all around the park. Reg Duff supported him and Australia's 100 was raised in a mere 57 minutes. The total amounted to 135 in the next 20 minutes, until Lockwood snared Duff to a catch behind for 54. After striking two leg-side fours off Lockwood, Trumper became the first batsman to score a century before lunch on the opening day of a Test. He was on 103 with Australia on 173-1.

Trumper added only a single before edging a cut off Wilfred Rhodes to wicketkeeper Dick Lilley. The momentum changed when Rhodes dismissed Monty Noble and Syd Gregory cheaply to have Australia 183-4. The pendulum shifted again as Clem Hill and Joe Darling put on 73 runs, before Lockwood dismissed Hill and Bert Hopkins on the same total. Darling was in an aggressive mood and smashed two huge sixes off Rhodes, however Lockwood bowled brilliantly as the pitch dried out. Darling helped the total race to 288-6, but Lockwood claimed three wickets and Rhodes one to dismiss Australia for 299.

England was in trouble as openers Bobby Abel and debutant Lionel Palairet were caught off John 'Jack' Saunders for six each. Accurate bowling from Hugh Trumble accounted for Archie MacLaren and KS Ranjitsinhji, leaving the hosts 30-4. Johnny Tyldesley scored 22 before becoming Saunders' third scalp, and England was 44-5 until Stanley Jackson and Len Braund took the total to 70-5 at stumps.

Jackson and Braund played some good cricket, with Saunders missing a hard return catch to reprieve Jackson on 41. The sixth wicket partnership reached 141 when Braund succumbed, pulling at a Noble outswinger. England's last four batsmen tallied just 24 runs, but Jackson held firm and registered an impressive century. Jackson gave an easy chance to Gregory on 123 and was last out for 128, caught in the deep. The visitors led by 37 runs, Jackson having struck 16 boundaries and lasted 255 minutes.

England quickly gained the initiative as Trumper steered a ball from Lockwood into the slips cordon, where Braund held a catch on the second attempt. A fired-up Lockwood accounted for Hill and Duff, with the former playing onto his stumps before the latter's off-stump was dislodged, to have

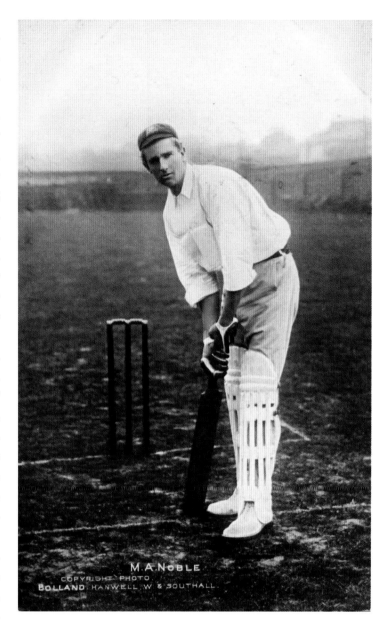

Australia's middle-order batsman Monty Noble.

Australia 10-3. But another turning point came with the total on 16 – Fred Tate, an off spinner who turned 35 the previous day in his Test debut, dropped Darling at deep square leg off Braund's bowling. Darling and Gregory led a recovery before Tate claimed his first wicket with Gregory lbw. Australia sank from 74-4 to 79-8 after Rhodes' dismissal of Darling to a catch at long on was followed by another two wickets to Lockwood and one to Rhodes, who bowled Warwick Armstrong for three.

Australia was 85-8 when several hours of rain caused a late start to day three. Tate and Rhodes claimed a wicket each, with only one run added to the Australian total, leaving England a target of 124 to square the series. MacLaren opened with Palairet, and both had a near miss as they put on 36 runs in 50 minutes before lunch. England seemed on course despite the pitch being less than ideal for batting, and another eight runs were added before Saunders bowled Palairet. MacLaren and Tyldesley quickly took the score to 68-1 and all but ensured an England victory, until both batsmen departed in the space of four runs to show that the match was far from over – Tyldesley was caught by Armstrong at slip off Saunders, then MacLaren lashed out at Trumble and was caught in the outfield as dark clouds hovered.

Abel survived a crucial chance to Saunders at mid on before rain halted play for 15 minutes. Abel subsequently played some attacking shots while Ranjitsinhji looked out of form, but England was on course at 92-4, when Ranjitsinhji was lbw to Trumble. Australia suddenly lifted, with Trumble and Saunders bowling well and the fielding standards picking up sharply.

Abel drove at Trumble and was bowled, but the addition of 10 runs ensured England needed just 17 more with five wickets remaining. Saunders overpitched, but Jackson struck a catch to Gregory at mid off, before Braund was stumped after momentarily lifting his back foot. Lockwood didn't deserve to be on the losing team, having taken match figures of 11-76, but he missed a big hit and was bowled for zero. England looked vulnerable at 109-8. With Lilley and Rhodes batting, three scoring strokes produced seven runs before the next twist came. Lilley pulled hard, only for Hill to run at full speed and snare a spectacular one-handed catch at deep square leg. Tate walked towards the pitch, but the incredible climax was delayed when rain returned and forced a 45-minute stoppage.

The tension was immense as Tate jabbed his first ball for four, making the score 120-9. Two dot balls followed, and then Saunders delivered a quicker full-pitched ball that Tate was unable to keep out. His stumps were wrecked and Australia was home by three runs to seal the series. Unfortunately for Tate, it was his only Test, following his crucial dropped catch in Australia's second innings.

The final Ashes Test of 1902 was another classic, with England winning by one wicket after looking lost at 48-5 while chasing 263. Gilbert Jessop was the star with 104 runs in 77 minutes.

BOBBY ABEL, TO W. G.:—"LOOK HERE, WE PLAYERS INTEND TO BE SUFFICIENTLY PAID, AS WELL AS THE SO-CALLED GENTLEMEN!"

Top: Victor Trumper, who scored a century before lunch on the first day of the 1902 Ashes Test at Manchester.
Bottom: A cartoon of W. G. Grace (left) and Bobby Abel … a case of the 'old' meeting the 'new' at the turn of the last century.

AUSTRALIA 1ST INNINGS		
VT Trumper	c Lilley b Rhodes	104
RA Duff	c Lilley b Lockwood	54
C Hill	c Rhodes b Lockwood	65
MA Noble	c & b Rhodes	2
SE Gregory	c Lilley b Rhodes	3
J Darling*	c MacLaren b Rhodes	51
AJY Hopkins	c Palairet b Lockwood	0
WW Armstrong	b Lockwood	5
JJ Kelly†	not out	4
H Trumble	c Tate b Lockwood	0
JV Saunders	b Lockwood	3
Extras	(b 5, lb 2, w 1)	8
Total		299

Fall of wickets 135, 175, 179, 183, 256, 256, 288, 292, 292, 299

	O	M	R	W
W Rhodes	25	3	104	4
Hon. FS Jackson	11	0	58	0
FW Tate	11	1	44	0
LC Braund	9	0	37	0
WH Lockwood	20.1	5	48	6

ENGLAND 1ST INNINGS		
LCH Palairet	c Noble b Saunders	6
R Abel	c Armstrong b Saunders	6
JT Tyldesley	c Hopkins b Saunders	22
AC MacLaren*	b Trumble	1
KS Ranjitsinhji	lbw b Trumble	2
Hon. FS Jackson	c Duff b Trumble	128
LC Braund	b Noble	65
AFA Lilley†	b Noble	7
WH Lockwood	run out	7
W Rhodes	c & b Trumble	5
FW Tate	not out	5
Extras	(b 6, lb 2)	8
Total		262

Fall of wickets 12, 13, 14, 30, 44, 185, 203, 214, 235, 262

	O	M	R	W
H Trumble	43	16	75	4
JV Saunders	34	5	104	3
MA Noble	24	8	47	2
VT Trumper	6	4	6	0
WW Armstrong	5	2	19	0
AJY Hopkins	2	0	3	0

AUSTRALIA 2ND INNINGS		
VT Trumper	c Braund b Lockwood	4
RA Duff	b Lockwood	3
C Hill	b Lockwood	0
J Darling*	c Palairet b Rhodes	37
SE Gregory	lbw b Tate	24
MA Noble	c Lilley b Lockwood	4
AJY Hopkins	c Tate b Lockwood	2
WW Armstrong	b Rhodes	3
JJ Kelly†	not out	2
H Trumble	lbw b Tate	4
JV Saunders	c Tyldesley b Rhodes	0
Extras	(b 1, lb 1, nb 1)	3
Total		86

Fall of wickets 7, 9, 10, 64, 74, 76, 77, 79, 85, 86

	O	M	R	W
W Rhodes	14.4	5	26	3
FW Tate	5	3	7	2
LC Braund	11	3	22	0
WH Lockwood	17	5	28	5

ENGLAND 2ND INNINGS		
LCH Palairet	b Saunders	17
AC MacLaren*	c Duff b Trumble	35
JT Tyldesley	c Armstrong b Saunders	16
KS Ranjitsinhji	lbw b Trumble	4
R Abel	b Trumble	21
Hon. FS Jackson	c Gregory b Saunders	7
LC Braund	st Kelly b Trumble	3
AFA Lilley†	c Hill b Trumble	4
WH Lockwood	b Trumble	0
W Rhodes	not out	4
FW Tate	b Saunders	4
Extras	(b 5)	5
Total		120

Fall of wickets 44, 68, 72, 92, 97, 107, 109, 109, 116, 120

	O	M	R	W
H Trumble	25	9	53	6
JV Saunders	19.4	4	52	4
MA Noble	5	3	10	0

Toss: Australia   Umpires: J Moss and T Mycroft   Australia won by 3 runs

South Africa v England
First Test at Old Wanderers, Johannesburg

1905-06
January 2, 3, 4 (1906)

England had won its first four series against South Africa before the turning of the tide began in exciting fashion in the opening Test of the 1905–06 series in South Africa. The hosts introduced Aubrey Faulkner, Reggie Schwarz, Percy Sherwell, Sibley 'Tip' Snooke, Bert Vogler and Gordon White to Test cricket. England meanwhile had four debutants: Jack Crawford, Frederick Fane, Ernie Hayes and Walter Lees.

England's decision to bat first seemed to backfire as the top three batsmen were caught for a total of only seven runs. Schwarz had a brilliant start to his Test career, dismissing Pelham Warner and David 'Lucky' Denton before taking a catch off Faulkner to dismiss Fane, after Faulkner had caught Denton. Hayes and Teddy Wynyard added 38 runs, then Volger took a return catch to dismiss Hayes, and Wynyard went on to score 29, but was stumped off Schwarz to leave the tourists 76-5.

Crawford batted in fine style, while White chipped in with his first wicket when he bowled Albert Relf for eight. Schofield Haigh gave Crawford good support, and their 48-run partnership was the highest of the innings when Haigh was bowled by Faulkner. Just two more runs were added before Crawford was caught off Jimmy Sinclair, and Lees scored 11 before becoming White's second scalp. A crucial last wicket partnership of 25 unfolded, with Charlie Blythe hitting three fours in his 17 until Sinclair bowled him. The total of 184 was far from embarrassing in light of the top order slump.

South Africa's top order also flopped. Lees had Louis Tancred caught behind for three, before Blythe accounted for William Shalders. South Africa was reeling at 13-3 when Maitland Hathorn was bowled by Lees, and then a 22-run partnership was followed by a collapse of 9-4. Lees accounted for White and Sinclair, before Blythe dismissed Snooke and

Faulkner. Vogler hit a four and a six, then the introduction of Crawford paid off, as the only change bowler accounted for Vogler. South Africa was 71-8 at the end of day one, meaning 18 wickets had fallen for 255 runs in the day.

Arthur 'Dave' Nourse remained undefeated on 18 the next morning after Crawford claimed his second wicket and Lees his fifth of the innings. England led by 93 runs, and soon lost Fane for three when he became Snooke's first Test victim. Warner and Denton, however, looked intent on building a sizable lead, and Denton struck six fours as he moved to 34, while Warner also scored the majority of his runs in boundaries. England was 55-1 but then lost 1-2, with Denton bowled by Faulkner, and Wynyard bowled by Vogler without scoring.

Hayes was caught off Snooke for three, but then Crawford again looked good. Warner reached 51 before falling to Vogler, then Relf combined with Crawford for a crucial 53-run partnership, Crawford again departing in the 40s. From 166-6, England fell away as the lower order struggled. Nourse and Faulkner claimed an lbw each, and the last two wickets fell on 190, Faulkner claiming them to finish with 4-26 from 12.5 overs. South Africa thus needed 284 runs to win.

Tancred scored 10 of the first 11 runs but was caught off Blythe, and South Africa was teetering at 22-2 when Hathorn again fell cheaply to Lees. Shalders and White took the hosts to 68-2 at stumps, before England maintained the initiative the next morning, with Shalders run out before a run was added. It was a crucial blow, Shalders having hit six fours in his 38. Snooke and Sinclair hit a four each before falling to Lees for single figure scores, and Faulkner also hit a four in a single figure score before he was another run out victim. South Africa had crashed to 105-6, and White seemed to be the team's last hope.

White found the left-handed Nourse a willing ally, and they chiselled away at the deficit. White resisted superbly on debut, and this seventh wicket partnership took South Africa to within sight of victory at 226-6. But Relf made a breakthrough when he bowled White, who had lasted four hours and struck 11 fours in his 81. Nourse was now the senior player, and he was well settled, having registered a half-century. The end for the hosts seemed nigh, however, as Vogler and Schwarz scored just two each, with Hayes bowling Vogler before Schwarz was caught-and-bowled by Relf.

Nourse was joined by last man Sherwell, who was not only a Test debutant but also South Africa's wicketkeeper and captain. Sherwell had crucially conceded 23 byes in England's second innings while there were no wides or no-balls, and he had his chance to compensate, as his team needed a last wicket

partnership of 45 for victory. Sherwell was up to the task as he hit four fours in an unbeaten 22, while Nourse moved to 93 not out, having batted for three hours and 40 minutes and accumulated 11 fours. The scores were tied, and then a boundary in Relf's 22nd over sealed a thrilling one-wicket win to the hosts.

Snatching victory from the jaws of defeat may have given the hosts a psychological edge, as they subsequently crushed the visitors by nine wickets in the second Test and 243 runs in the third Test. England scraped home by four wickets in the fourth Test before South Africa regained the ascendancy with a mighty innings and 16-run defeat in the final Test, for a 4-1 series win.

Pelham 'Plum' Warner, England captain in 1905 (opposite) and later as manager (above) of the MCC team in the infamous 'Bodyline' tour of 1932–33.

ENGLAND 1ST INNINGS		
PF Warner*	c Snooke b Schwarz	6
FL Fane	c Schwarz b Faulkner	1
D Denton	c Faulkner b Schwarz	0
EG Wynyard	st Sherwell b Schwarz	29
EG Hayes	c & b Vogler	20
JN Crawford	c Nourse b Sinclair	44
AE Relf	b White	8
S Haigh	b Faulkner	23
JH Board†	not out	9
WS Lees	st Sherwell b White	11
C Blythe	b Sinclair	17
Extras	(b 6, lb 9, nb 1)	16
Total		184

Fall of wickets 6, 6, 15, 53, 76, 97, 145, 147, 159, 184

	O	M	R	W
RO Schwarz	21	5	72	3
GA Faulkner	22	7	35	2
JH Sinclair	11	1	36	2
AEE Vogler	3	0	10	1
GC White	5	1	13	2
AW Nourse	1	0	2	0

SOUTH AFRICA 1ST INNINGS		
LJ Tancred	c Board b Lees	3
WA Shalders	c Haigh b Blythe	4
CMH Hathorn	b Lees	5
GC White	c Blythe b Lees	8
SJ Snooke	c Board b Blythe	19
JH Sinclair	c & b Lees	0
GA Faulkner	b Blythe	4
AW Nourse	not out	18
AEE Vogler	b Crawford	14
RO Schwarz	c Relf b Crawford	5
PW Sherwell*†	lbw b Lees	1
Extras	(b 9, lb 1)	10
Total		91

Fall of wickets 5, 11, 13, 35, 39, 43, 44, 62, 82, 91

	O	M	R	W
WS Lees	23.1	10	34	5
C Blythe	16	5	33	3
JN Crawford	7	1	14	2

ENGLAND 2ND INNINGS		
PF Warner*	b Vogler	51
FL Fane	b Snooke	3
D Denton	b Faulkner	34
EG Wynyard	b Vogler	0
EG Hayes	c Schwarz b Snooke	3
JN Crawford	b Nourse	43
AE Relf	c Sherwell b Faulkner	17
S Haigh	lbw b Nourse	0
JH Board†	lbw b Faulkner	7
WS Lees	not out	1
C Blythe	b Faulkner	0
Extras	(b 23, lb 8)	31
Total		190

Fall of wickets 3, 55, 56, 73, 113, 166, 174, 185, 190, 190

	O	M	R	W
RO Schwarz	8	1	24	0
GA Faulkner	12.5	5	26	4
JH Sinclair	5	1	25	0
AEE Vogler	11	3	24	2
GC White	4	0	15	0
AW Nourse	6	4	7	2
SJ Snooke	12	4	38	2

SOUTH AFRICA 2ND INNINGS		
LJ Tancred	c Warner b Blythe	10
WA Shalders	run out	38
CMH Hathorn	c Crawford b Lees	4
GC White	b Relf	81
SJ Snooke	lbw b Lees	9
JH Sinclair	c Fane b Lees	5
GA Faulkner	run out	6
AW Nourse	not out	93
AEE Vogler	b Hayes	2
RO Schwarz	c & b Relf	2
PW Sherwell*	not out	22
Extras	(b 6, lb 2, nb 7)	15
Total	(9 wickets)	287

Fall of wickets 11, 22, 68, 81, 89, 105, 226, 230, 239

	O	M	R	W
WS Lees	33	10	74	3
C Blythe	28	12	50	1
JN Crawford	17	4	49	0
S Haigh	1	0	9	0
AE Relf	21.5	7	47	2
EG Wynyard	3	0	15	0
EG Hayes	9	1	28	1

Toss: England   Umpires: J Phillips and FE Smith   South Africa won by 1 wicket

Australia v England
First Test at the Sydney Cricket Ground

1907-08
December 13, 14, 16, 17, 18, 19 (1907)

A number of players had a memorable Test debut in the first Ashes Test of 1907–08, and the result remained in doubt until the very end.

England's wicketkeeper Dick Young began nervously as an opening batsman, snicking a four, and England slipped to 18-2 after Frederick Fane and Young edged catches. A dropped slips catch reprieved debutant Kenneth Hutchings, who unleashed five boundaries before falling for 42, while George Gunn also batted confidently on debut. His driving was attractive, and his first 78 runs included 11 fours, before he reached a century after six successive scoring strokes were fours.

Gunn and Len Braund, who survived a stumping chance on nine, added 117 runs until Gunn was superbly caught by Australian Test debutant Gerry Hazlitt. Joe Hardstaff's first Test innings contained 12 runs before he was bowled, then Wilfred Rhodes was run out following a dropped catch. Albert 'Tibby' Cotter ended Braund's resistance and demolished Sydney Barnes' off-stump, and then Crawford hit three fours in a Warwick Armstrong over before being bowled off his pads. The erratic Cotter claimed his sixth scalp as England was dismissed for 273, before Australia lost Peter McAlister cheaply as he edged to slip.

Victor Trumper and Clem Hill took Australia to 50-1 at stumps, but Arthur Fielder struck the next morning with the dismissal of Trumper for 43. Hill and Monty Noble subsequently ran well between the wickets in a productive and relatively risk-free partnership. Hill, however, had a lucky escape when he played a ball that touched the stumps without dislodging the bails. Reminiscent of England's innings, a great catch ended a lengthy partnership – Braund took a splendid one-hander to snare Noble, before Fielder had Armstrong caught at first slip and Hill caught at third man from a flashy

Australian bowler Albert 'Tibby' Cotter had bowling figures of 6-101 and 2-101 in the Test against England at the SCG.

drive, as Australia's solid position collapsed.

From 184-5, Australia recovered somewhat via debutants Vernon Ransford and Charles Macartney, who was cautious at first but soon played more freely. Ransford fell to a juggling catch by Braund for 24, before another debutant, Hanson 'Sammy' Carter, was also productive. Macartney made 35 and Carter 25, and Australia gained a first innings lead. Hazlitt generated plenty of applause when he raised Australia's 300, before the last wicket featured Fielder's sixth wicket and Braund's fourth catch.

Rhodes opened England's second innings, instead of Young, and had a first-ball let-off when Carter spilled a catch. England began day three with an eight-run deficit, and Armstrong's bowling was tight while Cotter was wayward again. Macartney came on and had Rhodes caught at first slip, before Gunn again hit his stride with off side drives. A great one-handed catch by Noble dismissed Fane at 82-2, but Gunn was harder to dislodge, combining defence and attack.

Following Hutchings' dismissal, Hardstaff started defensively before going for his strokes. Gunn took 12 runs off one over and survived a tough chance to McAlister off the expensive Hazlitt, who was hit for three straight fours by Hardstaff. Gunn struck 11 fours and Hardstaff 10 fours, but the conclusion of their 113-run stand sparked a collapse of 9-3. England recovered as Braund found form, while Barnes and Blythe made some handy runs, despite gloomy weather and rain returning. England was 293-9 at stumps, and finished with 300 to set Australia a target of 274.

Rain interrupted day four and Australia was in early trouble. Trumper was bowled by an off break that hit his thigh, before a pacy delivery, which kept low, sent Hill's off-stump flying. A subdued Macartney survived an lbw appeal, and Noble opened his account with a boundary before edging another four over slips. Macartney struck a four but was caught next ball and Australia sank to 27-3. Australia reached 63-3 when play finished early, Armstrong having survived a chance to second slip.

Rain abandoned day five and then Australia struggled on a slow pitch. Armstrong hit two fours past mid off in quick succession, before Noble offered no stroke to a ball that clipped his off-stump. Ransford presented a soft caught-and-bowled to make the score 95-5, but then the pitch became easier to bat on. A full-toss from Blythe hit McAlister on the jaw, but a bigger blow occurred when Armstrong was bowled and Australia was left 124-6. All was not lost, however, as Carter arrived. At the same venue, just over a week earlier, Carter batted at number nine for New South Wales in a Sheffield Shield match, his team 356-7 and chasing 593 against South Australia. Carter had blazed 125 runs in 128 minutes as NSW almost stole a miraculous victory.

Now under pressure for his country, Carter cut two fours in a Crawford over and was off and running. Young, meanwhile, continued to disappoint as he dropped McAlister at 156-6 after lunch. Carter hit the ball all around the field and generated plenty of excitement, but Australia was set back when McAlister was bowled with the score at 185. Barnes repeatedly sent the ball past Carter's bat in one over, but Carter passed 50 with a four from a full-toss, and soon reached 61, before Young finally held a crucial catch. Australia needed 55 more runs with only two wickets remaining.

Hazlitt luckily edged a four and went on to reduce the margin further, and a lofted hit from Cotter fell safely. Cotter otherwise defended more, while the 19-year-old Hazlitt, who failed to take a wicket, showed batting skills as he played confident strokes. A boundary to square leg by Hazlitt reduced the deficit to 30, and Hardstaff missed a difficult catch to reprieve Hazlitt, before Australia needed just 14 runs after tea. A few more runs were scored, and then overthrows turned one run into three. Cotter straight drove Fielder for three, and spectators jumped around excitedly when only two more runs were needed. Australia triumphed when Hazlitt hit Fielder to the leg-side boundary. The *Sydney Morning Herald* described jubilant scenes in the aftermath: "…members in the pavilion held up the two not-out men in front of the pavilion, and gave them an ovation."

Hanson 'Sammy' Carter, who top-scored in Australia's second innings, later captained his country in 1909.

ENGLAND 1ST INNINGS		
FL Fane*	c Trumper b Cotter	2
RA Young†	c Carter b Cotter	13
G Gunn	c Hazlitt b Cotter	119
KL Hutchings	c & b Armstrong	42
LC Braund	b Cotter	30
J Hardstaff snr	b Armstrong	12
W Rhodes	run out	1
JN Crawford	b Armstrong	31
SF Barnes	b Cotter	1
C Blythe	b Cotter	5
A Fielder	not out	1
Extras	(b 7, lb 6, w 1, nb 2)	16
Total		273

Fall of wickets 11, 18, 91, 208, 221, 223, 246, 253, 271, 273

	O	M	R	W
A Cotter	21.5	0	101	6
JV Saunders	11	0	42	0
GR Hazlitt	9	2	32	0
WW Armstrong	26	10	63	3
CG Macartney	3	0	5	0
MA Noble	6	1	14	0

ENGLAND 2ND INNINGS		
W Rhodes	c McAlister b Macartney	29
FL Fane*	c Noble b Saunders	33
G Gunn	c Noble b Cotter	74
KL Hutchings	c Armstrong b Saunders	17
J Hardstaff snr	b Noble	63
LC Braund	not out	32
RA Young†	b Noble	3
JN Crawford	c Hazlitt b Cotter	5
SF Barnes	b Saunders	11
C Blythe	c Noble b Saunders	15
A Fielder	lbw b Armstrong	6
Extras	(b 2, w 3, nb 7)	12
Total		300

Fall of wickets 56, 82, 105, 218, 223, 227, 241, 262, 293, 300

	O	M	R	W
A Cotter	26	1	101	2
JV Saunders	23	6	68	4
GR Hazlitt	4	2	24	0
WW Armstrong	27	14	33	1
CG Macartney	14	2	39	1
MA Noble	15	5	23	2

AUSTRALIA 1ST INNINGS		
VT Trumper	b Fielder	43
PA McAlister	c Hutchings b Barnes	3
C Hill	c Gunn b Fielder	87
MA Noble*	c Braund b Fielder	37
WW Armstrong	c Braund b Fielder	7
VS Ransford	c Braund b Rhodes	24
CG Macartney	c Young b Fielder	35
H Carter†	b Braund	25
GR Hazlitt	not out	18
A Cotter	b Braund	2
JV Saunders	c Braund b Fielder	9
Extras	(b 4, lb 2, w 2, nb 2)	10
Total		300

Fall of wickets 4, 72, 164, 177, 184, 222, 253, 277, 281, 300

	O	M	R	W
A Fielder	30.2	4	82	6
SF Barnes	22	3	74	1
C Blythe	12	1	33	0
LC Braund	17	2	74	2
JN Crawford	5	1	14	0
W Rhodes	5	2	13	1

AUSTRALIA 2ND INNINGS		
VT Trumper	b Barnes	3
CG Macartney	c Crawford b Fielder	9
C Hill	b Fielder	1
MA Noble*	b Barnes	27
WW Armstrong	b Crawford	44
VS Ransford	c & b Blythe	13
PA McAlister	b Crawford	41
H Carter†	c Young b Fielder	61
A Cotter	not out	33
GR Hazlitt	not out	34
Extras	(b 6, nb 3)	9
Total	(8 wickets)	275

Did not bat JV Saunders

Fall of wickets 7, 12, 27, 75, 95, 124, 185, 219

	O	M	R	W
A Fielder	27.3	4	88	3
SF Barnes	30	7	63	2
C Blythe	19	5	55	1
LC Braund	7	2	14	0
JN Crawford	8	2	33	2
W Rhodes	7	3	13	0

Toss: England   Umpires: RM Crockett and W Hannah   Australia won by 2 wickets

Australia v England
Third Test at the Adelaide Oval

1920–21
January 14, 15, 17, 18, 19, 20 (1921)

Australia, 1921. Standing: Sydney Smith (Manager), J. S. Ryder, J. M. Gregory, E. L. Hendry, E. A. Macdonald, A. A. Mailey. Sitting: W. Bardsley, C. C. Macartney, W. W. Armstrong, H. L. Collins, H. Carter. Front: J. M. Taylor, T. J. Andrews.

In his book, *Australia versus England*, David Frith reported that the third Test of the 1920–21 Ashes series was "a classic batsman's match, and England were well in it for three days." Australia had dominated the first two Tests, with a 377-run win in Sydney and an innings win in Melbourne, before heading to Adelaide seeking a series-clinching win.

Australia batted first for the third successive time, reaching 32-0 before Warren Bardsley was stumped. Charles Kelleway was superbly caught by Test debutant Percy Fender at slip, then Johnny Taylor was needlessly run out, making Australia 55-3. Warwick Armstrong's dismissal to a catch behind left Australia 96-4. Providing stability at the top of the innings, Herb Collins presented a catch to square leg, but Wilfred Rhodes dropped it off paceman Harry Howell. On 60, Collins was again reprieved off the luckless Howell. Clarence 'Nip' Pellew scored 35 in an 80-run stand before being run out just after tea. Jack Gregory scored a quick 10 before becoming Fender's maiden Test victim when Bert Strudwick took a catch behind.

Jack Ryder gave Collins good support. The opener hit 20 fours and scored 162 in 258 minutes until Rhodes belatedly caught him, with off spinner Cecil Parkin the successful bowler. Ryder and Bert Oldfield took Australia to 313-7 at stumps, and 347-7 the next morning, but Parkin quickly claimed the last three wickets to have Australia out for 354. Oldfield posted a half-century before he was last out.

England openers Jack Hobbs and Rhodes began confidently, but Rhodes was run out at 25. Hobbs was caught-and-bowled by Arthur Mailey 24 runs later. Elias 'Patsy' Hendren also perished after a good start, bowled by Gregory after scoring 36 in an hour. A 50-run partnership unfolded for the fourth wicket, and Joseph 'Harry' Makepeace progressed to a promising 60 in his second Test, then was caught off Armstrong. Frank Woolley batted in attractive fashion, moving to 73 at stumps, while Charles 'Jack' Russell was on 21, and England a promising 233-4.

Woolley joined the list of Englishmen who would squander a chance for a big score, adding just six more runs before he was caught at slip off Gregory, after hitting 10 fours and a six in his two-hour knock. England established a lead as Russell and captain Johnny Douglas found form. Douglas scored 60 within two hours before Mailey had him lbw as England led by 20 runs. Fender's first Test knock was short-lived when he was bowled by Australia's debutant paceman Ted McDonald. England's tail-enders offered brief resistance and scored some handy runs. Russell finished unconquered on 135, scored in 250 minutes and including 10 fours and a six, leaving Australia with a deficit of 93.

England captain Johnny Douglas.

Thirty-four runs were wiped off the deficit when Howell bowled Bardsley, and England faltered at a crucial time again, Fender dropping Kelleway at slip before the batsman had scored, Howell again the unfortunate bowler. England was well in the series with Australia 71-3 at stumps, after the dismissals of Collins and Ryder, who edged the last ball of day three to slip. Kelleway's let-off, however, proved as vital as Collins' first innings reprieves. Kelleway batted throughout the fourth day in dogged fashion, taking his score from 19 to 115, after scoring just 24 runs in the second session. Armstrong meanwhile scored a fluent 121 in a 194-run partnership in 206 minutes and Australia regained the initiative, before Armstrong was bowled by the deserving Howell. Taylor hit six fours as he scored 38 in nearly an hour, and Pellew helped Kelleway take Australia to 364-5 at stumps.

Pellew struck the ball superbly and picked the gaps on day five, dominating a 126-run partnership with Kelleway, who finished with 147 in 417 minutes when Howell belatedly

dismissed him. Pellew soon registered a century with 16 runs in a Howell over, before he was caught behind off Parkin after scoring 104 in just 128 minutes. From 477-7, Australia was far from done and Gregory kept the scoring rate moving, making 78 not out as the last three wickets added 105 runs. The tourists only had themselves to blame for allowing the target to be as high as 490, although they had all the time in the world while the pitch was still playing well.

McDonald trapped Rhodes for just four, then Hobbs raced to 50 as England reached 66-1 at stumps. Another 59 runs were added before Makepeace was out to a bad shot, and Hobbs showed his class, determined to keep England in the hunt. He scored 123 of England's first 183 runs in just 151 minutes until Gregory bowled him and Woolley in quick succession, as England slid from 183-2 to 185-4. Hendren reached a half-century but didn't build on it, and England was still just short of the halfway mark when Mailey bowled him.

England wasn't prepared to surrender despite the task appearing impossible, and several batsmen showed good form. Russell scored a half-century before Mailey bowled him, and Douglas hit six fours in his 32, but he and Strudwick fell to

make the score 321-8. In a vain attempt to keep the contest alive, Parkin struck two fours and a six, but was stumped for 17. Fender showed some ability with the bat after having copped a mauling in Australia's second innings, and scored 42 before becoming Mailey's fifth victim. Australia sealed the series with a 119-run win.

The tourists were left to rue reprieving Collins and Kelleway at crucial times, and several England batsmen not converting good starts into big scores. The unfortunate Howell, who ironically claimed his best Test figures in Australia's second innings, played only three more Tests and went wicketless. Bad luck was obvious – he finished his five-match Test career with just seven wickets at an average of 79.85.

Top left: The towering figure of Australian captain Warwick Armstrong. Above: Australian pair Charles Kellaway (left) and Herb 'Lucky' Collins (right).

AUSTRALIA 1ST INNINGS

HL Collins	c Rhodes b Parkin	162
W Bardsley	st Strudwick b Douglas	14
C Kelleway	c Fender b Parkin	4
JM Taylor	run out	5
WW Armstrong*	c Strudwick b Douglas	11
CE Pellew	run out	35
JM Gregory	c Strudwick b Fender	10
J Ryder	c Douglas b Parkin	44
WAS Oldfield†	lbw b Parkin	50
EA McDonald	b Parkin	2
AA Mailey	not out	3
Extras	(b 6, lb 8)	14
Total		354

Fall of wickets 32, 45, 55, 96, 176, 209, 285, 347, 349, 354

	O	M	R	W
H Howell	26	1	89	0
JWHT Douglas	24	6	69	2
CH Parkin	20	2	60	5
FE Woolley	21	6	47	0
PGH Fender	12	0	52	1
W Rhodes	5	1	23	0

ENGLAND 1ST INNINGS

JB Hobbs	c & b Mailey	18
W Rhodes	run out	16
JWH Makepeace	c Gregory b Armstrong	60
EH Hendren	b Gregory	36
FE Woolley	c Kelleway b Gregory	79
CAG Russell	not out	135
JWHT Douglas*	lbw b Mailey	60
PGH Fender	b McDonald	2
CH Parkin	st Oldfield b Mailey	12
H Strudwick†	c Pellew b Mailey	9
H Howell	c Gregory b Mailey	2
Extras	(b 8, lb 5, nb 5)	18
Total		447

Fall of wickets 25, 49, 111, 161, 250, 374, 391, 416, 437, 447

	O	M	R	W
EA McDonald	24	1	78	1
JM Gregory	36	5	108	2
C Kelleway	11	4	25	0
AA Mailey	32.1	3	160	5
WW Armstrong	23	10	29	1
J Ryder	6	0	29	0

AUSTRALIA 2ND INNINGS

HL Collins	c Hendren b Parkin	24
W Bardsley	b Howell	16
C Kelleway	b Howell	147
J Ryder	c Woolley b Howell	3
WW Armstrong*	b Howell	121
JM Taylor	c Strudwick b Fender	38
CE Pellew	c Strudwick b Parkin	104
JM Gregory	not out	78
WAS Oldfield†	b Rhodes	10
AA Mailey	b Rhodes	13
EA McDonald	b Rhodes	4
Extras	(b 5, lb 10, w 4, nb 5)	24
Total		582

Fall of wickets 34, 63, 71, 265, 328, 454, 477, 511, 570, 582

	O	M	R	W
H Howell	34	6	115	4
JWHT Douglas	19	2	61	0
CH Parkin	40	8	109	2
FE Woolley	38	4	91	0
PGH Fender	22	0	105	1
W Rhodes	25.5	8	61	3
JB Hobbs	7	2	16	0

ENGLAND 2ND INNINGS

JB Hobbs	b Gregory	123
W Rhodes	lbw b McDonald	4
JWH Makepeace	c & b McDonald	30
EH Hendren	b Mailey	51
FE Woolley	b Gregory	0
CAG Russell	b Mailey	59
JWHT Douglas*	c Armstrong b Gregory	32
PGH Fender	c Ryder b Mailey	42
H Strudwick†	c Armstrong b Mailey	1
CH Parkin	st Oldfield b Mailey	17
H Howell	not out	4
Extras	(lb 3, nb 4)	7
Total		370

Fall of wickets 20, 125, 183, 185, 243, 292, 308, 321, 341, 370

	O	M	R	W
EA McDonald	24	0	95	2
JM Gregory	20	2	50	3
C Kelleway	8	2	16	0
AA Mailey	29.2	3	142	5
WW Armstrong	16	1	41	0
J Ryder	9	2	19	0

Toss: Australia   Umpires: RM Crockett and DA Elder   Australia won by 119 runs

South Africa v England
Second Test at Newlands, Cape Town

1922-23
January 1, 2, 3, 4 (1923)

The conclusion to the second Test of the 1922–23 South Africa versus England series proved as thrilling as the ending of the first Test that had involved the countries in the 1905–06 series. Interestingly, Dave Nourse, having played in 1905–06, was still playing in 1922–23. Meanwhile the two debutants in the second Test of the 1922–23 series had a huge influence in a brilliant contest: Alfred Hall for South Africa and George Macaulay for England.

South Africa had won the first Test by 168 runs, and Macaulay had a dream start to the second Test. He bowled the second over and struck with his first delivery, having George Hearne caught by Percy Fender without a run on the board. Fender came on as first change bowler, and had Bob Catterall caught behind before bowling South African skipper Herbie Taylor, to make the score 31-3. The total nearly doubled before Fender struck again when he had Nourse lbw.

South Africa's innings disintegrated further, and Alex Kennedy's dismissal of William Brann was followed by William Ling becoming Fender's fourth scalp, as 67-4 became 67-6. Cyril Francois provided some lower order resistance, but his effort was virtually single-handed. Jimmy Blanckenberg hung around long enough for 29 runs to be added, before he and Tommy Ward fell to Vallance Jupp's off-spin. Eiulf 'Buster' Nupen became Macaulay's second victim before Francois was run out for a gallant 28. The miserable total of 113 from 56 overs would have been even less had there not been 14 byes.

England's first innings began well, with Andy Sandham scoring just 19 in an opening stand of 59 before he was caught by Francois off Blanckenberg. Francois soon took another catch, this time off Hall, to dismiss Frank Woolley without him scoring, then Charles 'Jack' Russell was caught by Catterall to become Hall's second victim. The visitors looked like they might surrender their advantage as they flopped to 60-3, but Phil Mead and Arthur Carr took England to the lead with seven wickets still remaining. Carr scored 42 runs to Mead's 17 before Carr was caught behind off Hall just before stumps, as England led by 15 runs.

The significance of Carr's dismissal was illuminated the next morning when England collapsed again. Blanckenberg bowled superbly, and had Mead caught by Francois before Hall took his fourth wicket when he accounted for Fender. Blanckenberg followed up with the wickets of Mann and Kennedy, then Nupen struck as Hearne matched Francois with three catches. England was 155-9 before George Brown and Macaulay put on a vital last wicket stand of 28, with last man Macaulay scoring 19 before his dismissal gave Blanckenberg a five-wicket haul.

South Africa again began disastrously, with Hearne bagging a pair when he played a Kennedy delivery onto the stumps. Catterall and Taylor, however, were in superb form, the former moving to 74 and the latter to 48 before stumps, and the hosts finished the day 64 runs in front.

Taylor looked the better of the duo the following morning, while Catterall added just two runs before falling to Macaulay. Taylor was caught by Jupp just one run later, and 158-3 looked a lot different from 157-1. Amidst an excellent spell, Macaulay went on to dismiss Ling and Brann cheaply, before a 30-run stand between Nourse and Francois took the total to 200. Nourse and Francois scored 19 each, with Nourse bowled by Fender before the next two wickets fell on 212. Macaulay claimed a caught-and-bowled to make Francois his fifth victim in the innings. Kennedy hit the stumps for the last three wickets, although handy partnerships of 12 and 18 for the last two wickets helped South Africa set England 173 runs for victory.

South Africa made early inroads as Russell was lbw to Blanckenberg for eight and Woolley bowled by Hall for five. Sandham and Mead hinted at a recovery, but Hall wreaked havoc yet again; the left-arm paceman had Sandham lbw, Carr caught by Brann and Fender caught by Nourse, seeing England tumble to 59-5. Mead looked the most comfortable against Hall before the left-armer struck a crucial blow just before stumps, trapping Mead for 31. The balance was with South Africa, as England needed 87 runs on the final day with only four wickets remaining.

Mann found form after starting the day on 12, and Jupp helped the score move along steadily as England seemingly gained the ascendancy. The South Africans could have remained in control but faltered under pressure, missing vital chances to dismiss both batsmen. Jupp fell to Hall just before lunch for an invaluable 38, and England needed just 19 more runs.

Mann and Kennedy inched their way towards the target before the unpredictable nature of the game became evident. Blanckenberg took a great slips catch off Hall, dismissing Mann while England still needed six runs. A single was scored before a great throw from deep point ran out Brown, and suddenly the match was on a knife's edge, Kennedy and Macaulay needing to put on five runs for an England triumph. Hall had had an heroic debut thus far, but it remained to be seen if he or England's debutant, Macaulay, would taste victory.

A leg-side delivery proved costly when Kennedy hit it for four to tie the scores, before Macaulay took strike as Hall began his 38th over. Macaulay managed a single from the third ball to clinch a one-wicket win for England, and finish a memorable debut, his match figures of 7-83 coupled with 20 runs at number 11, including the match-winning single. Hall, having taken 11-112 from 62.3 overs and come achingly close to winning the match for the hosts, was carried off the field shoulder high.

The remainder of the series was not nearly as thrilling. Two draws were followed by England winning the final Test at Durban by 109 runs to win the series 2-1.

Frank Woolley, regarded as one of the finest all-rounders England has produced, though he had little success with the bat or the ball in England's narrow win against South Africa in January 1923.

SOUTH AFRICA 1ST INNINGS

RH Catterall	c Brown b Fender	10
GAL Hearne	c Fender b Macaulay	0
HW Taylor*	b Fender	9
AW Nourse	lbw b Fender	16
WVS Ling	c Mann b Fender	13
WH Brann	b Kennedy	0
JM Blanckenberg	c Carr b Jupp	9
CM Francois	run out	28
TA Ward†	b Jupp	4
EP Nupen	c & b Macaulay	2
AE Hall	not out	0
Extras	(b 14, lb 6, nb 2)	22
Total		113

Fall of wickets 0, 22, 31, 60, 67, 67, 96, 108, 111, 113

	O	M	R	W
AS Kennedy	18	10	24	1
GG Macaulay	13	5	19	2
PGH Fender	14	4	29	4
FE Woolley	2	1	1	0
VWC Jupp	9	3	18	2

ENGLAND 1ST INNINGS

CAG Russell	c Catterall b Hall	39
A Sandham	c Francois b Blanckenberg	19
FE Woolley	c Francois b Hall	0
CP Mead	c Francois b Blanckenberg	21
AW Carr	c Ward b Hall	42
FT Mann*	lbw b Blanckenberg	4
PGH Fender	c Hearne b Hall	3
VWC Jupp	c Hearne b Nupen	12
AS Kennedy	c Hearne b Blanckenberg	2
G Brown†	not out	10
GG Macaulay	b Blanckenberg	19
Extras	(b 5, lb 4, w 1, nb 2)	12
Total		183

Fall of wickets 59, 59, 60, 128, 134, 137, 147, 149, 155, 183

	O	M	R	W
EP Nupen	15	2	48	1
AE Hall	25	8	49	4
JM Blanckenberg	24.1	5	61	5
CM Francois	4	1	13	0

SOUTH AFRICA 2ND INNINGS

RH Catterall	b Macaulay	76
GAL Hearne	b Kennedy	0
HW Taylor*	c Jupp b Macaulay	68
AW Nourse	b Fender	19
WVS Ling	c Fender b Macaulay	2
WH Brann	lbw b Macaulay	4
CM Francois	c & b Macaulay	19
JM Blanckenberg	b Kennedy	5
TA Ward†	not out	15
EP Nupen	b Kennedy	6
AE Hall	b Kennedy	5
Extras	(b 15, lb 6, nb 2)	23
Total		242

Fall of wickets 2, 157, 158, 162, 170, 200, 212, 212, 224, 242

	O	M	R	W
AS Kennedy	35.2	13	58	4
GG Macaulay	37	11	64	5
PGH Fender	20	3	52	1
FE Woolley	11	3	22	0
VWC Jupp	11	3	23	0

ENGLAND 2ND INNINGS

CAG Russell	lbw b Blanckenberg	8
A Sandham	lbw b Hall	17
FE Woolley	b Hall	5
CP Mead	lbw b Hall	31
AW Carr	c Brann b Hall	6
PGH Fender	c Nourse b Hall	2
FT Mann*	c Blanckenberg b Hall	45
VWC Jupp	st Ward b Hall	38
AS Kennedy	not out	11
G Brown†	run out	0
GG Macaulay	not out	1
Extras	(b 4, lb 5)	9
Total	(9 wickets)	173

Fall of wickets 20, 29, 49, 56, 59, 86, 154, 167, 168

	O	M	R	W
EP Nupen	24	8	41	0
AE Hall	37.3	12	63	7
JM Blanckenberg	24	7	56	1
CM Francois	3	0	4	0

Toss: South Africa   Umpires: AG Laver and GJ Thompson   England won by 1 wicket

Australia v England
Third Test at the Adelaide Oval

1924-25
January 16, 17, 19, 20, 21, 22, 23 (1925)

England's Ashes squad for 1924–25.

Injuries rocked England in the third Test of the 1924–25 Ashes series, yet a close and classic meeting unfolded.

After losing the first two Tests decisively, England was in trouble. John Hearne was missing, while captain Arthur Gilligan carried an injury into the game. When Gilligan lost the toss, he bowled into the wind, while Maurice Tate had the wind at his back. Tate rattled the off-stump after just 10 minutes, Herb Collins having offered no stroke, before Jack Gregory played an Alfred 'Tich' Freeman delivery onto the stumps. Australia sank to 22-3 when Johnny Taylor was lbw, before Arthur Richardson and Bill Ponsford consolidated. Richardson looked ominous, pulling four boundaries off Freeman in quick succession. A 92-run partnership, however, was followed by England regaining the initiative, Gilligan's dismissal of Ponsford to a catch behind followed by Roy Kilner dismissing Arthur and Victor Richardson, to make the score 119-6.

But England was rocked when Tate succumbed to a toe injury and Gilligan to a strained thigh, and left-armers Kilner and Frank Woolley were grossly overbowled as a consequence. Jack Ryder and Tommy Andrews turned the game Australia's way after both were recalled to the team. Ryder drove well,

while Andrews played good onside strokes, especially hooks. Half of Andrews' 72 runs came in fours, and Ryder was on 72 when Australia reached 275-7 at stumps.

A crucial chance to run out Ryder was missed before Charles Kelleway was eighth out at 308, but Australia was in control as Ryder registered a century and combined with Bert Oldfield for a ninth wicket stand of 108. England suffered another blow when a thumping hit from Ryder injured Freeman's wrist. As Arthur Mailey approached the wicket following Oldfield's dismissal for 47, laughter erupted from the crowd, because a cat had appeared on the field near the players' gate.

After scoring 21 and 46 not out in the first Test, Mailey cover drove a four and scored 27, again looking like a batsman. Ryder meanwhile recorded his highest Test score of 201 not out and Australia tallied 489. England bafflingly opened with Tate and 37-year-old debutant Bill Whysall, who hit two fours before Gregory bowled him for nine. In another surprise, Bert Strudwick batted at three and was soon caught at slip. Tate and Percy Chapman, who was also promoted, took England to 36-2 at stumps before both were dismissed in the 20s, and England slipped to 69-4 following the rest day.

Jack Hobbs and Herb Sutcliffe restored order, having put on opening partnerships of 157, 110, 283 and 36 in the first two Tests. Scoring was slow at times, despite Mailey bowling some full-tosses, and Gregory reprieved Hobbs in the slips. Hobbs batted more freely after lunch while Sutcliffe was painstaking, scoring 33 from about 180 balls, before touching a rising Ryder delivery to the wicketkeeper. Woolley was well caught at cover, then Hobbs found support from 'Patsy' Hendren. Hobbs, who treated Mailey with respect, reached 99 just before stumps thanks to a misfield, but was off strike until the following morning. Hendren was on 47 as England was 270-6.

Hobbs reached 119 before being superbly caught by Gregory at slip from a rising Mailey delivery. Hendren pushed on but didn't get much support from Kilner and Gilligan, both of whom fell to Arthur Richardson. Freeman eked out six runs in 44 minutes, and Hendren forged to 92 before his dismissal left Australia with a 124-run lead.

Australia's lead had extended to 160 when Arthur Richardson was caught at silly mid off, and Collins looked solid until his defensive shot bounced onto the stumps in Freeman's first over after tea. Ryder was promoted to first drop and continued his brilliant match with quick scoring against England's depleted attack. Taylor likewise scored briskly before he was bowled for 34, and Ponsford also scored freely. Ryder was on 86 and Ponsford 40 as Australia led by 335 runs at the end of day four.

Rain, however, changed things dramatically in the lead-up to day five. The pitch resembled a gluepot and Australia's batsmen played indiscreet shots in the unpleasant conditions, enabling Woolley and Kilner to take regular wickets. Kelleway played a lone hand of 22 not out in 56 minutes, as Australia flopped from 215-3 to 250 all out. England consequently needed 375 runs to keep the series alive.

Hobbs and Sutcliffe resumed their opening combination, which produced a steady 63 runs before Hobbs was inexplicably caught off a long-hop. Woolley also made a solid start until Kelleway bowled him and then trapped Hendren lbw to have England tottering at 96-3. Sutcliffe passed 50, he and Whysall helping England to 133-3 at the close of play. Australia missed a few chances but the balance was still with the hosts.

Rain interrupted the sixth day, and Whysall survived a caught behind appeal early on. Sutcliffe hardly progressed before a skied drive ended his innings, and then Chapman teed off and was chancy. A miscued square drive went for four, a stinging hit hurt Collins' hand, and Ponsford just missed a chance in the deep. Chapman struck seven fours and two sixes before a cut was caught by Ryder to end an 89-run partnership. Whysall was composed, eventually caught-and-bowled by Gregory for 75, making the score 254-6 as England again faltered at a crucial time. The injured Tate blasted a quick 21 before Mailey bowled him, and England's hopes seemingly faded. Kilner and Gilligan were patient, however, and the score reached 312 before Kilner was caught. Freeman scored 17, then rain ended the day's play, with England needing 27 runs and Australia two wickets.

About 25,000 spectators came for day seven, as the gates were open. Nine runs were scored before Gilligan was caught off a slower ball, and another six runs were added in nine minutes. Then Freeman edged a Mailey delivery to Oldfield to seal an 11-run margin, and Australia had won the Ashes for the third straight time.

Opposite: England's 'Patsy' Hendren.
Below: England's formidable batting combination of Jack Hobbs (left) and Herb Sutcliffe.
Following page: Arthur Gilligan played only 11 Tests, but captained England in the 1924–25 Ashes.

Arthur E.R. Gilligan

AUSTRALIA 1ST INNINGS

HL Collins*	b Tate	3
AJ Richardson	b Kilner	69
JM Gregory	b Freeman	6
JM Taylor	lbw b Tate	0
WH Ponsford	c Strudwick b Gilligan	31
VY Richardson	c Whysall b Kilner	4
J Ryder	not out	201
TJE Andrews	b Kilner	72
C Kelleway	c Strudwick b Woolley	16
WAS Oldfield†	lbw b Kilner	47
AA Mailey	st Strudwick b Hendren	27
Extras	(lb 9, nb 4)	13
Total		489

Fall of wickets 10, 19, 22, 114, 118, 119, 253, 308, 416, 489

	O	M	R	W
MW Tate	18	1	43	2
AER Gilligan	7.7	1	17	1
AP Freeman	18	0	107	1
FE Woolley	43	5	135	1
R Kilner	56	7	127	4
JB Hobbs	3	0	11	0
EH Hendren	5.1	0	27	1
WW Whysall	2	0	9	0

AUSTRALIA 2ND INNINGS

HL Collins*	b Freeman	26
AJ Richardson	c Kilner b Woolley	14
J Ryder	c & b Woolley	88
JM Taylor	b Freeman	34
WH Ponsford	c Hendren b Kilner	43
TJE Andrews	c Whysall b Kilner	1
VY Richardson	c Tate b Woolley	0
C Kelleway	not out	22
JM Gregory	c Hendren b Woolley	2
WAS Oldfield†	b Kilner	4
AA Mailey	c Sutcliffe b Kilner	5
Extras	(b 4, lb 4, nb 3)	11
Total		250

Fall of wickets 36, 63, 126, 215, 216, 217, 217, 220, 242, 250

	O	M	R	W
MW Tate	10	4	17	0
AP Freeman	17	1	94	2
FE Woolley	19	1	77	4
R Kilner	22.1	7	51	4

ENGLAND 1ST INNINGS

WW Whysall	b Gregory	9
MW Tate	c Andrews b Mailey	27
H Strudwick†	c Gregory b Kelleway	1
APF Chapman	b Gregory	26
JB Hobbs	c Gregory b Mailey	119
H Sutcliffe	c Oldfield b Ryder	33
FE Woolley	c Andrews b Mailey	16
EH Hendren	c Taylor b Gregory	92
R Kilner	lbw b AJ Richardson	6
AER Gilligan*	c Collins b AJ Richardson	9
AP Freeman	not out	6
Extras	(b 8, lb 10, nb 3)	21
Total		365

Fall of wickets 15, 18, 67, 69, 159, 180, 297, 316, 326, 365

	O	M	R	W
JM Gregory	26.2	0	111	3
C Kelleway	15	6	24	1
AA Mailey	44	5	133	3
AJ Richardson	21	7	42	2
J Ryder	6	2	15	1
HL Collins	5	1	19	0

ENGLAND 2ND INNINGS

JB Hobbs	c Collins b AJ Richardson	27
H Sutcliffe	c Ponsford b Mailey	59
FE Woolley	b Kelleway	21
EH Hendren	lbw b Kelleway	4
WW Whysall	c & b Gregory	75
APF Chapman	c Ryder b Kelleway	58
R Kilner	c VY Richardson b AJ Richardson	24
MW Tate	b Mailey	21
AER Gilligan*	c VY Richardson b Gregory	31
AP Freeman	c Oldfield b Mailey	24
H Strudwick†	not out	2
Extras	(b 5, lb 5, w 1, nb 6)	17
Total		363

Fall of wickets 63, 92, 96, 155, 244, 254, 279, 312, 357, 363

	O	M	R	W
JM Gregory	23	6	71	2
C Kelleway	22	4	57	3
AA Mailey	30.2	4	126	3
AJ Richardson	25	5	62	2
J Ryder	2	0	11	0
HL Collins	9	4	19	0

Toss: Australia   Umpires: RM Crockett and DA Elder

Australia won by 11 runs

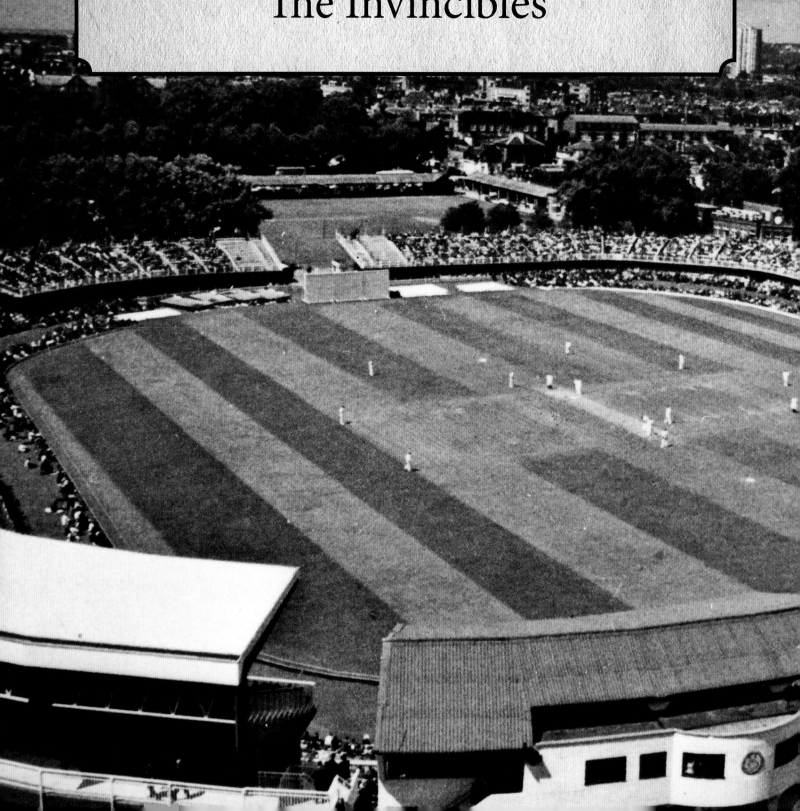

Chapter 2:
Bodyline, Bradman and "The Invincibles"

1930 — 1959

Lord's Cricket Ground, London.

South Africa v England

First Test at Old Wanderers, Johannesburg

1930-31

December 24, 26, 27 (1930)

South Africa pair Bruce Mitchell (left) and Bob Catterall, pictured in 1929. Catterall captained South Africa against England the following year.

The last innings of this intriguing Test in December 1930 took place on a matting wicket, which arguably proved decisive. South Africa and England had four more Tests to play after the series opener at Johannesburg, but the first Test ultimately decided the series.

The hosts were sent into bat on Christmas Eve after losing the toss, and debutant opener Syd Curnow hit two fours as South Africa moved to 19 without loss, before Maurice Tate trapped Curnow lbw. Bill Voce put England in control, dismissing Bruce Mitchell, Jack Siedle and Bob Catterall to make the score 42-4. Ian Peebles chipped in with the wicket of debutant Ken Viljoen to a catch behind, then bowled Jock Cameron for a duck, and South Africa crashed to 53-6 on a pitch that had some life for the bowlers.

Xen Balaskas showed some resistance in his first Test innings, but scored only seven before Peebles caught him in front of his stumps. South African skipper 'Buster' Nupen was bowled immediately as his team plunged to 78-8, and then Voce matched Peebles with four wickets, seeing Cyril Vincent depart for two. The hosts, however, were far from finished. Quintin McMillan showed some confidence and received solid support from number 11 Bob Newson, who was one of four Test debutants in the team. A 45-run partnership for the last wicket took the score to 126 until Tate bowled Newson for 10, leaving McMillan unconquered on 45, which included seven boundaries.

With Maurice Leyland looking more assured than fellow opener Bob Wyatt, England moved to 33 without loss, but then crumbled to 51-3. Nupen had Wyatt lbw and Leyland caught behind, and Patsy Hendren hit a four before falling cheaply, caught behind off McMillan. Wally Hammond looked in striking form, while Maurice Turnbull hit three fours and a six before he was stumped off Vincent for 28, ending a 52-run partnership. England was still four wickets down when a first innings lead was established. Percy Chapman hit four fours but also perished for 28 against Vincent's spin bowling. Hammond was on 45 at stumps as the tourists led by 41 runs, and England's hopes of obtaining a formidable lead lay heavily on Hammond.

After the teams had a rest day for Christmas, Nupen ensured England would not gain a sizable advantage. Hammond was one run shy of 50 when he was lbw, White was caught three runs later, and Peebles was bowled for a duck (this was some sort of revenge, after Peebles had earlier bowled Nupen without scoring). Voce hit a four before the last two wickets fell on 193, Vincent claiming his third scalp before Voce was run out.

Siedle hit a series of boundaries as South Africa began

England batsman Wally Hammond top-scored in both innings in the Test against South Africa in Johannesburg in 1930.

its second innings, while Curnow was still in single figures when he was run out. Voce made a huge breakthrough when he won an lbw appeal against Siedle, who looked threatening before his dismissal left the score 50-2. Mitchell and Catterall subsequently repaired the damage, putting their heads down and playing intelligently. Peebles was wayward this time and didn't bowl again after delivering seven expensive overs, while White was also ineffective. Mitchell and Catterall played some confident strokes, and the latter hit a six as he scored 54 in a 122-run partnership, eventually falling to a smart slips catch by Hendren off Hammond. Mitchell's 72 ended just two runs later, when Hammond had him caught behind, and the game had changed again to see South Africa four-down and 107 runs in front after the hard work of Mitchell and Catterall.

The hosts were effectively 115-5 when Balaskas was lbw to Tate, before South Africa's prospects lifted again with Viljoen and Cameron batting soundly. Cameron scored a brisk 51 in a partnership of 81 until Voce had him caught behind. McMillan hit a six before Voce bowled him for 14, and Viljoen moved to 43 as South Africa finished the day leading by 236, with three wickets remaining. Only three runs were added the following morning before it was England's turn to bat again. Hammond bowled Nupen and Viljoen before Voce bowled Vincent, and then South Africa sprang a surprise, as Catterall – who rarely bowled, and didn't in the first innings – opened the bowling with Newson.

The risk paid off handsomely, Catterall dismissing openers Wyatt and Leyland to have England 22-2. The score was 30-3 when Hendren was caught at slip off Nupen, but Hammond and Turnbull turned the tide again. Turnbull looked in control, scoring freely, with six fours and a six. He reached 61 in just 75 minutes, and the partnership reaped 101 runs before Nupen again came to the rescue for his side as he bowled Turnbull.

Chapman helped the score pass 150 when Nupen had him caught at slip. Nupen soon trapped White lbw, and England needed a further 86 runs with only four wickets remaining. Hammond was restrained as Nupen and Vincent bowled well, and the champion English all-rounder needed support. Hammond registered only four boundaries and reached 63 in 140 minutes before he was superbly stumped, and England looked lost at 164-7, and then 169-8, when Voce was caught.

Tate had a couple of near misses against Vincent, but produced some attacking strokes to keep the contest alive. Nupen, however, came back to haunt the tourists again when Tate became the third batsman caught at slip by Mitchell, leaving George Duckworth and Peebles with the requirement of a 45-run last wicket partnership for an England victory. Tate stayed on as a runner for the injured Peebles, who hit a couple of precious boundaries, but Nupen sealed a 28-run win for his team when he had Duckworth lbw. Nupen had impressive match figures of 11-150.

The remaining four Tests in the series were drawn, leaving South Africa with a 1-0 series win.

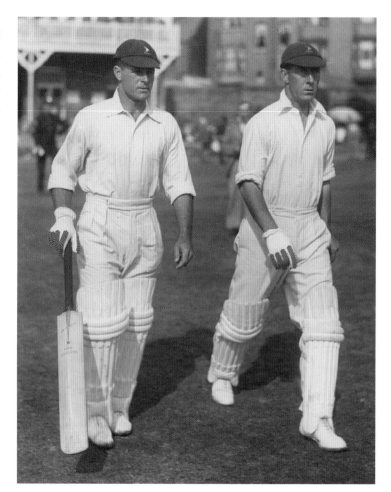

Top: South Africa wicketkeeper Jock Cameron (right), pictured with future captain Dudley Nourse in the 1930s.
Bottom: England bowler Maurice Tate, who played an important cameo role as his team tried to win the Test against South Africa.

SOUTH AFRICA 1ST INNINGS

IJ Siedle	b Voce	13
SH Curnow	lbw b Tate	13
B Mitchell	c Hammond b Voce	6
RH Catterall	b Voce	5
KG Viljoen	c Duckworth b Peebles	7
XC Balaskas	lbw b Peebles	7
HB Cameron†	b Peebles	0
Q McMillan	not out	45
EP Nupen*	b Peebles	0
CL Vincent	c Hammond b Voce	2
ES Newson	b Tate	10
Extras	(b 12, lb 5, nb 1)	18
Total		126

Fall of wickets 19, 28, 37, 42, 51, 53, 78, 78, 81, 126

	O	M	R	W
MW Tate	12.2	4	20	2
W Voce	26	11	45	4
IAR Peebles	14	2	43	4

ENGLAND 1ST INNINGS

RES Wyatt	lbw b Nupen	8
M Leyland	c Cameron b Nupen	29
WR Hammond	lbw b Nupen	49
EH Hendren	c Cameron b McMillan	8
MJL Turnbull	st Cameron b Vincent	28
APF Chapman*	c Newson b Vincent	28
JC White	c Curnow b Nupen	14
MW Tate	c Mitchell b Vincent	8
IAR Peebles	b Nupen	0
W Voce	run out	8
G Duckworth†	not out	0
Extras	(b 9, lb 3, w 1)	13
Total		193

Fall of wickets 33, 42, 51, 103, 149, 176, 179, 185, 193, 193

	O	M	R	W
ES Newson	8	2	11	0
KG Viljoen	4	1	10	0
Q McMillan	9	0	47	1
EP Nupen	26.1	1	63	5
CL Vincent	21	8	49	3

SOUTH AFRICA 2ND INNINGS

IJ Siedle	lbw b Voce	35
SH Curnow	run out	8
B Mitchell	c Duckworth b Hammond	72
RH Catterall	c Hendren b Hammond	54
XC Balaskas	lbw b Tate	3
KG Viljoen	b Hammond	44
HB Cameron†	c Duckworth b Voce	51
Q McMillan	b Voce	14
EP Nupen*	b Hammond	1
CL Vincent	b Voce	1
ES Newson	not out	0
Extras	(b 16, lb 7)	23
Total		306

Fall of wickets 34, 50, 172, 174, 182, 263, 291, 305, 306, 306

	O	M	R	W
MW Tate	18	2	47	1
W Voce	27.2	8	59	4
IAR Peebles	7	0	41	0
WR Hammond	25	5	63	4
JC White	16	3	53	0
RES Wyatt	2	0	20	0

ENGLAND 2ND INNINGS

RES Wyatt	c McMillan b Catterall	5
M Leyland	c & b Catterall	15
WR Hammond	st Cameron b Vincent	63
EH Hendren	c Mitchell b Nupen	3
MJL Turnbull	b Nupen	61
APF Chapman*	c Mitchell b Nupen	11
JC White	lbw b Nupen	2
MW Tate	c Mitchell b Nupen	28
W Voce	c Nupen b Vincent	0
G Duckworth†	lbw b Nupen	4
IAR Peebles	not out	13
Extras	(lb 6)	6
Total		211

Fall of wickets 13, 22, 30, 131, 152, 154, 164, 169, 195, 211

	O	M	R	W
ES Newson	14	2	30	0
Q McMillan	4	0	25	0
EP Nupen	25.3	3	87	6
CL Vincent	17	1	44	2
RH Catterall	5	0	12	2
XC Balaskas	2	0	7	0

Toss: England   Umpires: WB Ryan and GB Treadwell   South Africa won by 28 runs

Australia v England
Third Test at the Adelaide Oval

1932–33
January 13, 14, 16, 17, 18, 19 (1933)

The England cricket team at the Adelaide Test on the controversial Bodyline tour of Australia in 1932–33. Back row: G. Duckworth, R. Mitchell, Nawab of Pataudi, M. Leyland, H. Larwood, E. Paynter, Ferguson (scorer). Middle row: P. Warner (co-manager), L. Ames, H. Verity, W. Voce, W. Bowes, F. Brown, M. Tate, R. Palairet (co-manager). Front row: H. Sutcliffe, R. Wyatt, D. Jardine, G. Allen, W. Hammond.

The infamous Bodyline series in 1932–33 reached its boiling point at Adelaide in the third Test, one of the most hostile and controversial in history. The teams entered the match with the series level at 1-all, England captain Douglas Jardine's leadership and the vicious short-pitched bowling of Harold Larwood and Bill Voce having gained notoriety.

The third Test started in fine weather following rain the previous day, and the hosts began well after losing the toss and fielding first. A full-pitched ball from Tim Wall bowled Jardine, then Wally Hammond and Herb Sutcliffe departed as the score was 16. Sutcliffe fell to a superb catch by Wall at short leg, before England fell to 30-4, a fast ball from slow medium-pacer Bert Ironmonger beating Les Ames. Maurice Leyland and Bob Wyatt led an impressive recovery following lunch as the pitched dried out, the ball having kicked in the first session. Leyland hooked and drove well, scoring 83 in three hours, and registered 13 fours before playing a Bill O'Reilly delivery onto his wicket. England slipped to 196-6 when Wyatt was caught, having hit three fours and three sixes in his 78. A quick ball from Clarrie Grimmett had Gubby Allen lbw, and England was 236-7 at stumps.

Eddie Paynter survived a crucial run out chance, and subsequently played some exquisite cover drives, pulls and cuts. He used his feet well to the spinners in a controlled innings. Hedley Verity, meanwhile, gave a chance to slip on 16. Paynter was on 77 when he perished to a hook, and Wall finished with five scalps. Verity was last out for a stubborn 45 as England tallied 341.

Allen had Jack Fingleton caught behind without scoring in the second over of Australia's reply. In the next over, a rearing Larwood delivery struck Australian captain Bill Woodfull over the heart. The batsman reeled away in agony but opted to keep batting, and the crowd jeered Larwood. Australia was in strife at 18-2, Don Bradman succumbing to the leg trap off Larwood's bowling, and a hook caused Stan McCabe's downfall 16 runs later. Woodfull, after facing more hostile bowling, succumbed to a low ball from Allen and Australia became 51-4. Bill Ponsford's unbeaten 45 helped Australia reach 109-4 at stumps, an ankle injury keeping Voce out of the attack. The aftermath of the day's play was unpleasant, Woodfull telling MCC manager Pelham Warner that only one side was playing cricket.

Following the rest day, 22 runs were added before Victor Richardson played a ball onto his stumps. Ponsford played some fine cuts shots while also combating the leg theory. Oldfield was resistant, and Ponsford was on 85 as Australia neared 200 when Voce bowled him round his legs. Grimmett

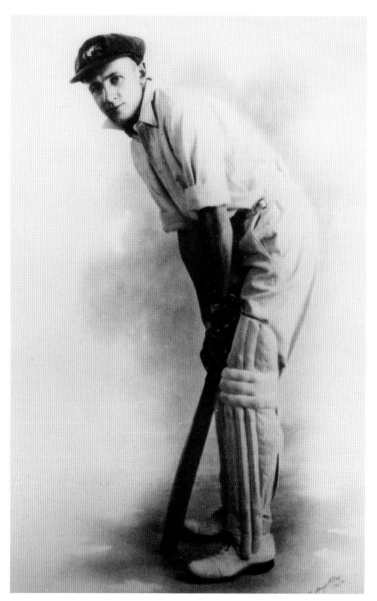

Not even legendary Australian batsman Don Bradman could conquer England's tactics in the 1932–33 Ashes series.

fell for 10, Voce taking an excellent slips catch, and the score was 218-7 when Oldfield hooked at Larwood and edged the ball into his head. The injured Oldfield, who didn't blame Larwood for the injury, was helped off the field, and police surrounded the boundary as the crowd became infuriated. Only four more runs were added before Wall and O'Reilly were bowled, and Australia was all out, Oldfield unable to resume. Richardson kept wicket as England began its second innings.

Sutcliffe had seven runs on the board before a faulty hook shot was superbly caught by substitute fielder Leo O'Brien. O'Reilly spilled a difficult slips catch when Wyatt was on nine, and Wyatt added 40 more runs before departing early on day four to a great catch by Wall at short leg. The promoted Allen was again lbw to Grimmett for 15, and Jardine scored a painstaking 56 in 254 minutes before he was lbw to Ironmonger.

Douglas Jardine, the England captain who gained few friends in Australia during the 1932–33 'Bodyline' series.

Australian wicketkeeper Bert Oldfield suffered an injury as a result of England's bowling tactics.

Hammond knuckled down and showed his class, and Leyland scored 42 in a 91-run partnership until he was caught by Wall, as Fingleton nearly hindered Wall. Hammond was on 85 just before stumps when he surprisingly missed a full-toss, giving Bradman a rare wicket. England was 415 runs in front, only 211 having been scored in the day.

Overnight rain did not help the bowlers. Ames and Verity extended England's lead to 513 until O'Reilly dismissed them in quick succession; both played many fine strokes. England finished with 412 when Paynter came in at number 10 due to an ankle injury. With a massive 532-run target, Australia had just 10 batsmen, the injured Oldfield being absent.

The hosts began woefully. Fingleton fell for another duck, bowled by a great Larwood delivery, and Ponsford made three until a cut was caught behind point. But Bradman was in command, racing to 60 with 10 fours. He then struck a six off Verity, but a hard-hit next ball was caught by the bowler. McCabe hooked a catch to deep square leg, and Australia's cause was lost at 120-4 when bad light ended day five.

Day six began in intense heat, and Woodfull and Richardson showed some resistance. The score reached 171 before Richardson was struck on the thumb trying to hook

Larwood, and Allen took a catch. Grimmett lasted 10 minutes before he was bowled by Allen, and it barely took another 10 minutes for the last three wickets to fall, seeing England record a 338-run victory – Wall was bowled fourth ball, and O'Reilly hit a boundary before Larwood bowled him. Ironmonger was bowled first ball by Allen, leaving the gallant Woodfull unconquered on 73 from 235 minutes. It was a courageous if somewhat unnoticeable achievement from the Australian skipper in this spiteful contest.

On the fifth day, the Australian Board of Control protested against Bodyline tactics and labelled it 'unsportsmanlike' in a message delivered via cable to the MCC. In reply, the MCC said an amendment to the laws would be considered if proposed, and that the MCC would reluctantly agree to abandon the tour if that's what Australia wanted. Instead, the tour continued, and England won the infamous series 4-1.

Right: England duo Bill Voce (left) and Harold Larwood, England's dangerous pace duo in the 1932–33 Ashes series.
Inset: Australian batsman Bill Ponsford.

ENGLAND 1ST INNINGS

H Sutcliffe	c Wall b O'Reilly	9
DR Jardine*	b Wall	3
WR Hammond	c Oldfield b Wall	2
LEG Ames†	b Ironmonger	3
M Leyland	b O'Reilly	83
RES Wyatt	c Richardson b Grimmett	78
E Paynter	c Fingleton b Wall	77
GOB Allen	lbw b Grimmett	15
H Verity	c Richardson b Wall	45
W Voce	b Wall	8
H Larwood	not out	3
Extras	(b 1, lb 7, nb 7)	15
Total		341

Fall of wickets 4, 16, 16, 30, 186, 196, 228, 324, 336, 341

	O	M	R	W
TW Wall	34.1	10	72	5
WJ O'Reilly	50	19	82	2
H Ironmonger	20	6	50	1
CV Grimmett	28	6	94	2
SJ McCabe	14	3	28	0

AUSTRALIA 1ST INNINGS

JHW Fingleton	c Ames b Allen	0
WM Woodfull*	b Allen	22
DG Bradman	c Allen b Larwood	8
SJ McCabe	c Jardine b Larwood	8
WH Ponsford	b Voce	85
VY Richardson	b Allen	28
WAS Oldfield†	retired hurt	41
CV Grimmett	c Voce b Allen	10
TW Wall	b Hammond	6
WJ O'Reilly	b Larwood	0
H Ironmonger	not out	0
Extras	(b 2, lb 11, nb 1)	14
Total		222

Fall of wickets 1, 18, 34, 51, 131, 194, 212, 222, 222

	O	M	R	W
H Larwood	25	6	55	3
GOB Allen	23	4	71	4
WR Hammond	17.4	4	30	1
W Voce	14	5	21	1
H Verity	16	7	31	0

ENGLAND 2ND INNINGS

H Sutcliffe	c sub (LPJ O'Brien) b Wall	7
DR Jardine*	lbw b Ironmonger	56
RES Wyatt	c Wall b O'Reilly	49
GOB Allen	lbw b Grimmett	15
WR Hammond	b Bradman	85
M Leyland	c Wall b Ironmonger	42
LEG Ames†	b O'Reilly	69
H Verity	lbw b O'Reilly	40
H Larwood	c Bradman b Ironmonger	8
E Paynter	not out	1
W Voce	b O'Reilly	8
Extras	(b 17, lb 11, nb 4)	32
Total		412

Fall of wickets 7, 91, 123, 154, 245, 296, 394, 395, 403, 412

	O	M	R	W
TW Wall	29	6	75	1
WJ O'Reilly	50.3	21	79	4
H Ironmonger	57	21	87	3
CV Grimmett	35	9	74	1
SJ McCabe	16	0	42	0
DG Bradman	4	0	23	1

AUSTRALIA 2ND INNINGS

JHW Fingleton	b Larwood	0
WM Woodfull*	not out	73
WH Ponsford	c Jardine b Larwood	3
DG Bradman	c & b Verity	66
SJ McCabe	c Leyland b Allen	7
VY Richardson	c Allen b Larwood	21
CV Grimmett	b Allen	6
TW Wall	b Allen	0
WJ O'Reilly	b Larwood	5
H Ironmonger	b Allen	0
WAS Oldfield†	absent hurt	-
Extras	(b 4, lb 2, w 1, nb 5)	12
Total		193

Fall of wickets 3, 12, 100, 116, 171, 183, 183, 192, 193

	O	M	R	W
H Larwood	19	3	71	4
GOB Allen	17.2	5	50	4
WR Hammond	9	3	27	0
W Voce	4	1	7	0
H Verity	20	12	26	1

Toss: England   Umpires: GE Borwick and GA Hele

England won by 338 runs

West Indies v England

First Test at Kensington Oval, Bridgetown, Barbados

1934-35

January 8, 9, 10 (1935)

A completed Test match featuring just 309 runs, yet involving two declarations, is hard to imagine. But this was the case in the first Test of the West Indies versus England series in 1934–35.

England had contested the West Indies in three previous series, England winning 3-0 in 1928 and 2-0 in 1933, both on home soil, while the 1929–30 series was drawn 1-all in the Caribbean. The opening match of the 1934–35 series was interrupted by rain, but this led to a fascinating sequence of events. It was certainly a memorable introduction to Test cricket for five English players and four West Indian players. Cedric 'Jim' Smith, Jack Iddon, Errol Holmes, George Paine and Eric Hollies were England's debutants, while Leslie Hylton, Rolph Grant, Cyril Christiani and George Carew debuted for the West Indies.

England captain Bob Wyatt sent the hosts into bat on a sticky wicket after he won the toss, and paceman Ken Farnes made the ball lift uncomfortably. Carew began his Test career with a duck, caught by an opposing debutant, Holmes. Paine also took his first catch off Farnes' bowling, Clifford Roach being the batsman, with the total on 11. Farnes followed up by dismissing Charles Jones and Derek Sealy with the score on 20, before slow bowling proved effective. West Indies captain George 'Jackie' Grant and Rolph Grant were Hollies's first Test victims, while George Headley showed resistance. He led some sort of comeback, although he was reprieved twice.

Hylton scored 15 as the total moved from 49-6 to 81-6, and became Paine's first Test scalp, Les Ames producing a stumping. Headley lasted two hours and scored 44 of the batting team's 86 runs when he was run out after Christiani turned down a run. Ellis 'Puss' Achong became another stumping victim, then Christiani and Manny Martindale put on a 14-run last

West Indies batsman George Headley opens his shoulders during the 1934–35 Test series.

wicket stand to take the total to 102 before Paine claimed his third scalp. The hosts lasted 47 overs on the diabolical pitch, and then it was England's turn.

Openers Wyatt and Maurice Leyland put on 12 runs, but Martindale dismissed both in the space of two runs. Wally Hammond proved as vital to England's innings as Headley had been in the West Indies innings. Hammond was solid, while the batting at the other end was fragile. 'Patsy' Hendren became the second batsman to be caught by Rolph Grant off Martindale, then a 24-run partnership took the total to 52. Grant took his first wicket when he had Ames lbw. Hylton soon had his first wicket when another debutant, Smith, was caught by Jones without scoring. England moved from 54-5 to 81-5 at stumps, Hammond progressing to 43 while Iddon reached 14.

Overnight rain made the pitch even worse, and it wasn't until after tea on day two that play resumed. Hammond and Holmes were caught off Hylton without the addition of a run, and Wyatt declared, as he wanted the opposition to bat on the even more diabolical pitch. The West Indies subsequently reshuffled the batting line-up in the hope that the pitch might improve, but their makeshift top order flopped. Smith dismissed Rolph Grant, Martindale and Achong without scoring and the hosts fell to 4-3, but Hylton and Christiani survived and carefully took the score to 33-3 at stumps.

Further rain soaked the pitch and delayed the start of play until 3.30pm on day three. Sunshine and breeze didn't make the pitch any easier to bat on, and the overnight batsmen made little progress before falling to Smith. With Roach on 10, Headley was caught off Farnes for a duck to leave the hosts 51-6. Jackie Grant declared on this total, obviously confident that his bowlers could prevent England scoring 73 runs for victory as more than a day remained.

Smith and Farnes opened the batting as the visitors also rearranged their order. Martindale bowled very fast, he and Hylton making the ball bounce awkwardly, and the duo bowled unchanged throughout the innings. Martindale had Smith caught behind for zero and Hylton accounted for Farnes to have England 7-2. Hendren scored some vital runs, but England struggled, Holmes and Leyland caught off Martindale to make the score 29-4. Hendren and Hammond added 14 runs before the former was bowled for 20, and Martindale claimed his fifth wicket in the innings when Paine was caught for two. A winner was impossible to pick with England at 48-6 and Wyatt joining Hammond at the crease.

Wyatt watched the ball carefully and defended resolutely, while Hammond played some strokes without looking too risky. The deficit shrank quickly, and England triumphed by four wickets halfway through the 17th over, when a huge drive by Hammond off Martindale went for six. Martindale was the standout bowler in the match with figures of 8-61, while Hammond's scores of 43 and 29 not out were majestic under the circumstances. According to *The Illustrated History of the Test Match*, he described the two innings in this Test as the hardest he'd ever played.

Above: England captain Bob Wyatt.

Below: West Indies batsman George Headley

Right: Wally Hammond top-scored in both innings for England in the Test win over the West Indies, but with modest scores of 43 and 29. Right inset: Hammond in his prime as a player.

WEST INDIES 1ST INNINGS

CA Roach	c Paine b Farnes	9
GM Carew	c Holmes b Farnes	0
GA Headley	run out	44
CEL Jones	c Leyland b Farnes	3
JED Sealy	c Paine b Farnes	0
GC Grant*	c Hendren b Hollies	4
RS Grant	c Hammond b Hollies	5
LG Hylton	st Ames b Paine	15
CM Christiani†	not out	9
EE Achong	st Ames b Paine	0
EA Martindale	c Leyland b Paine	9
Extras	(lb 2, nb 2)	4
Total		102

Fall of wickets 1, 11, 20, 20, 31, 49, 81, 86, 88, 102

	O	M	R	W
K Farnes	15	4	40	4
CIJ Smith	7	3	8	0
WE Hollies	16	4	36	2
GAE Paine	9	3	14	3

ENGLAND 1ST INNINGS

RES Wyatt*	c RS Grant b Martindale	8
M Leyland	c & b Martindale	3
WR Hammond	c RS Grant b Hylton	43
EH Hendren	c RS Grant b Martindale	3
LEG Ames†	lbw b RS Grant	8
CIJ Smith	c Jones b Hylton	0
J Iddon	not out	14
ERT Holmes	c Achong b Hylton	0
Extras	(b 1, nb 1)	2
Total	(7 wickets dec)	81

Did not bat K Farnes, GAE Paine, WE Hollies
Fall of wickets 12, 14, 28, 52, 54, 81, 81

	O	M	R	W
EA Martindale	9	0	39	3
LG Hylton	7.3	3	8	3
EE Achong	6	1	14	0
RS Grant	7	0	18	1

WEST INDIES 2ND INNINGS

LG Hylton	lbw b Smith	19
RS Grant	c Paine b Smith	0
EA Martindale	lbw b Smith	0
EE Achong	b Smith	0
CM Christiani†	b Smith	11
CA Roach	not out	10
GA Headley	c Paine b Farnes	0
GC Grant*	not out	0
Extras	(b 4, lb 4, nb 3)	11
Total	(6 wickets dec)	51

Did not bat GM Carew, CEL Jones, JED Sealy
Fall of wickets 4, 4, 4, 40, 47, 51

	O	M	R	W
K Farnes	9	2	23	1
CIJ Smith	8	4	16	5
GAE Paine	1	1	0	0
WR Hammond	1	0	1	0

ENGLAND 2ND INNINGS

K Farnes	c GC Grant b Hylton	5
CIJ Smith	c Christiani b Martindale	0
ERT Holmes	c GC Grant b Martindale	6
EH Hendren	b Martindale	20
M Leyland	c RS Grant b Martindale	2
WR Hammond	not out	29
GAE Paine	c RS Grant b Martindale	2
RES Wyatt*	not out	6
Extras	(b 2, nb 3)	5
Total	(6 wickets)	75

Did not bat LEG Ames†, J Iddon, WE Hollies
Fall of wickets 3, 7, 25, 29, 43, 48

	O	M	R	W
EA Martindale	8.3	1	22	5
LG Hylton	8	0	48	1

Toss: England   Umpires: CW Reece and EL Ward   England won by 4 wickets

Australia v England
Fourth Test at the Adelaide Oval

1936-37
January 29, 30, February 1, 2, 3, 4 (1937)

The England team that travelled to Australia for the 1936–37 Ashes.

The 1936–37 Ashes series did not have the unpleasantness of the corresponding series in Australia four years earlier, but England, after having lost the Ashes on home soil in 1934, this time appeared dominant. England decisively won the first two Tests of the 1936–37 series before Australia won the third Test to keep the series alive. The fourth Test proved crucial, with the tourists only one win away from regaining the prized urn.

Batting first on a good wicket, Australia was 26-1 when Jack Fingleton was disastrously run out. Bill Brown and Keith Rigg put on 46 runs, but the lunch break might have disturbed their concentration, as Ken Farnes dismissed both in quick succession just after the interval. Brown dangled his bat and was caught in close, before Rigg edged behind. Don Bradman was not at his best but he and Stan McCabe put on 63 runs, before Bradman was bowled trying to hook Gubby Allen.

McCabe was in sublime form and went on a scoring spree after tea, but the pendulum swung again as McCabe hooked a Walter Robins half-tracker and was splendidly caught by Allen for 88. Twenty-year-old Test debutant Ross Gregory scored a careful 23 before he was lbw to Wally Hammond, who had been given the new ball. Australia was 249-7 when Bert Oldfield became another run out casualty. Arthur Chipperfield progressed to 45 at stumps, with Australia an unexceptional 267-7. Chipperfield added only 12 more runs before being stranded, Australia dismissed for a disappointing 288 when the conditions suggested a 400-plus total might have beckoned.

Charlie Barnett looked more convincing than Hedley Verity as England made a slow but steady start. Ernie McCormick generated a fair bit of pace, and delivered Barnett a bouncer immediately after Barnett hit a lovely boundary. Shortly after tea, McCormick muffed a return catch following a pulled four from Barnett. Left-arm wrist-spinner Leslie 'Chuck' Fleetwood-Smith threatened at times, although a full-toss was dispatched by Barnett for six. Verity scored just 19 in 101 minutes before lashing out and being caught in the deep off Bill O'Reilly. Hammond had a couple of near misses, then fell for 20 when he glanced a leg-side catch off O'Reilly. England nonetheless was well placed at stumps, with the score at 174-2, Barnett on 92 and Maurice Leyland 35, before a rest day.

Leyland added 10 runs before edging Fleetwood-Smith to slip, and England was 195-4 when Bob Wyatt was caught at forward short leg. Barnett was slow but posted his first Test century, and hit four fours in a McCormick over until a Fleetwood-Smith yorker had him lbw for 129 just after lunch. Ames assumed responsibility, and a vital half-century took England to an 11-run lead before he swished at McCormick and was bowled. McCormick caught-and-bowled Joe Hardstaff, then a wicket each to Fleetwood-Smith and O'Reilly made England 322-9. Bill Voce hit two of his first three deliveries for four before holing out from his fourth delivery, and England's lead was restricted to 42. Australia had halved its deficit when Fingleton was lbw to Hammond, before Brown and Bradman took the hosts to a 21-run lead at stumps.

Australia was 88-2 when wicketkeeper Ames snared a

England captain 'Gubby' Allen with Australian counterpart Don Bradman at the coin toss before the Fourth Test at the Adelaide Oval.

magnificent leg-side catch to send Brown on his way. Australia, however, slowly gained control, and a leg injury restricted Allen's bowling. Bradman was not in his most masterful form but he nonetheless seemed impossible to dislodge. McCabe again showed good touch, hitting seven fours and scoring 55 in a 109-run partnership, before Rigg scored just seven in a 40-run partnership. Bradman, who raised his century with two successive fours off Robins, was on 174 at stumps while Gregory was on 36 and Australia 299 runs in front with six wickets remaining.

Gregory reached 50 with a two but was run out chasing a third. Chipperfield made 31, and Bradman finally succumbed as Hammond took a return catch. Bradman's 212 included 14 fours and 99 singles in 437 minutes. Australia slid from 422-5 to 433 all out thanks largely to Hammond, who finished with five wickets and three catches in the innings. The tourists nonetheless had a big target of 392, although the weather remained fine and the pitch was still playing well.

England had some luck as Fingleton dropped Barnett, who hit the next ball for four. But Fleetwood-Smith bowled Verity shortly after, and England was a shaky 50-2 when the same bowler had Barnett caught at slip. The promoted Hardstaff combined with Hammond to put on 70 runs, before Hardstaff was bowled by a turning O'Reilly delivery for 43. On 39 at stumps, Hammond was virtually England's best hope, as the score was 148-3.

Hammond's score hadn't changed when a Fleetwood-Smith delivery spun from outside off-stump and bowled him. With their team looking sure to lose, Leyland and Wyatt added 41 runs, but Leyland was caught at slip and then Ames lbw first ball as Fleetwood-Smith gained something from the pitch.

Wyatt was not prepared to surrender, and Allen hung around while 35 runs were added, before England's skipper was caught off McCormick. Wyatt reached 50 before he was caught at the wicket off McCabe, who had earlier opened the bowling but delivered just five overs in the innings. With England 231-8, it was only a matter of time until Australia levelled the series. Fleetwood-Smith claimed his 10th wicket in the match before McCormick bowled Robins. All of the Australians had contributed in their 148-run victory, although Australia would surely have lost without Bradman's double century and Fleetwood-Smith's haul of wickets.

Australia completed the rare feat of winning the Ashes after trailing 2-0 in the series, as the hosts won the fifth and deciding Test in Melbourne by an innings and 200 runs. Bradman, Clayvel 'Jack' Badcock and McCabe set up the victory with centuries, as Australia racked up 604 runs batting first.

Top: Champion Australian bowler Bill O'Reilly.
Above: A commemorative MCC cup to mark the 150th anniversary of the club in 1937.

AUSTRALIA 1ST INNINGS

JHW Fingleton	run out	10
WA Brown	c Allen b Farnes	42
KE Rigg	c Ames b Farnes	20
DG Bradman*	b Allen	26
SJ McCabe	c Allen b Robins	88
RG Gregory	lbw b Hammond	23
AG Chipperfield	not out	57
WAS Oldfield†	run out	5
WJ O'Reilly	c Leyland b Allen	7
EL McCormick	c Ames b Hammond	4
LO Fleetwood-Smith	b Farnes	1
Extras	(lb 2, nb 3)	5
Total		288

Fall of wickets 26, 72, 73, 136, 206, 226, 249, 271, 283, 288

	O	M	R	W
W Voce	12	0	49	0
GOB Allen	16	0	60	2
K Farnes	20.6	1	71	3
WR Hammond	6	0	30	2
H Verity	16	4	47	0
RWV Robins	7	1	26	1

AUSTRALIA 2ND INNINGS

JHW Fingleton	lbw b Hammond	12
WA Brown	c Ames b Voce	32
DG Bradman*	c & b Hammond	212
SJ McCabe	c Wyatt b Robins	55
KE Rigg	c Hammond b Farnes	7
RG Gregory	run out	50
AG Chipperfield	c Ames b Hammond	31
WAS Oldfield†	c Ames b Hammond	1
WJ O'Reilly	c Hammond b Farnes	1
EL McCormick	b Hammond	1
LO Fleetwood-Smith	not out	4
Extras	(b 10, lb 15, w 1, nb 1)	27
Total		433

Fall of wickets 21, 88, 197, 237, 372, 422, 426, 427, 429, 433

	O	M	R	W
W Voce	20	2	86	1
GOB Allen	14	1	61	0
K Farnes	24	2	89	2
WR Hammond	15.2	1	57	5
H Verity	37	17	54	0
RWV Robins	6	0	38	1
CJ Barnett	5	1	15	0
M Leyland	2	0	6	0

ENGLAND 1ST INNINGS

H Verity	c Bradman b O'Reilly	19
CJ Barnett	lbw b Fleetwood-Smith	129
WR Hammond	c McCormick b O'Reilly	20
M Leyland	c Chipperfield b Fleetwood-Smith	45
RES Wyatt	c Fingleton b O'Reilly	3
LEG Ames†	b McCormick	52
J Hardstaff jnr	c & b McCormick	20
GOB Allen*	lbw b Fleetwood-Smith	11
RWV Robins	c Oldfield b O'Reilly	10
W Voce	c Rigg b Fleetwood-Smith	8
K Farnes	not out	0
Extras	(b 6, lb 2, w 1, nb 4)	13
Total		330

Fall of wickets 53, 108, 190, 195, 259, 299, 304, 318, 322, 330

	O	M	R	W
EL McCormick	21	2	81	2
SJ McCabe	9	2	18	0
LO Fleetwood-Smith	41.4	10	129	4
WJ O'Reilly	30	12	51	4
AG Chipperfield	9	1	24	0
RG Gregory	3	0	14	0

ENGLAND 2ND INNINGS

H Verity	b Fleetwood-Smith	17
CJ Barnett	c Chipperfield b Fleetwood-Smith	21
J Hardstaff jnr	b O'Reilly	43
WR Hammond	b Fleetwood-Smith	39
M Leyland	c Chipperfield b Fleetwood-Smith	32
RES Wyatt	c Oldfield b McCabe	50
LEG Ames†	lbw b Fleetwood-Smith	0
GOB Allen*	c Gregory b McCormick	9
RWV Robins	b McCormick	4
W Voce	b Fleetwood-Smith	1
K Farnes	not out	7
Extras	(b 12, lb 2, nb 6)	20
Total		243

Fall of wickets 45, 50, 120, 149, 190, 190, 225, 231, 235, 243

	O	M	R	W
EL McCormick	13	1	43	2
SJ McCabe	5	0	15	1
LO Fleetwood-Smith	30	1	110	6
WJ O'Reilly	26	8	55	1

Toss: Australia   Umpires: GE Borwick and JD Scott
Australia won by 148 runs

South Africa v England
Fifth Test at Kingsmead, Durban

1938-39
March 3, 4, 6, 7, 8, 9, 10, 11, 13, 14 (1939)

Timeless Tests came to an end after the final Test of the 1938–39 South Africa versus England series, which was scheduled to be played to a finish. A fascinating battle and extraordinary conclusion showed just how strange a game cricket could be.

England led the series 1-0 after four Tests, and the finale at Durban was a survival of the fittest contest from the outset. After South Africa won the toss, its openers Alan Melville and Pieter van der Bijl braved some testing fast bowling. Van der Bijl didn't score for 45 minutes, and only 49 runs were on the board by lunchtime. More than two hours passed before Melville hit the first boundary, and he scored 78, before playing back and stepping on his wicket. Eric Rowan scored 33, then became debutant Reg Perks' first Test victim, and South Africa was 229-2 at stumps with van der Bijl on 105. He survived a chance on 71, and was dogged, briefly accelerating with 22 runs in a Doug Wright over before pulling a six.

Bruce Mitchell departed early on day two but van der Bijl soldiered on, despite being struck on the body repeatedly in another slow session. The opener scored 125 in just over seven hours, eventually being bowled after lunch, and Ken Viljoen soon edged behind. Batting resistance resumed, with Dudley Nourse crawling to 50 in three-and-a-half hours, while Eric Dalton was livelier before departing for 57. Nourse and Ronnie Grieveson took the home side to 423-6 at stumps, and rain fell on the first rest day.

The pitch remained batsman-friendly, Nourse passing 100 before Perks yorked him. Grieveson posted South Africa's 500 with a four off Hedley Verity, until Perks bowled him for 75. Chud Langton clubbed a six in his 27 and was last out, caught in the deep. South Africa tallied 530 from nearly 203 eight-ball overs, and England began uncertainly with only 10 runs in 45

Dudley Nourse, the son of South Africa batsman Dave Nourse, scored a century in the first innings against England in 1939 but the match finished in a prolonged draw.

South Africa's Dudley Nourse batting against Australia in the 1930s. Nourse was named after Earl Dudley, the Governor General of Australia, because his father Dave Nourse was touring Australia in 1910 when his son was born.

minutes, during which time Paul Gibb fell to an inswinger. The total reached 35-1 before rain ended the day's play, and the next day was overcast.

Len Hutton made a gritty 38 before being run out, and captain Wally Hammond was not at his best, stumped for 24. Eddie Paynter looked out of form and had some narrow escapes, struggling to 62 in 260 minutes until Langton had him lbw and Bill Edrich caught in close, seeing England fall to 171-5. Les Ames and Bryan Valentine added 58 before Valentine was stumped off Dalton, who subsequently bowled Verity for three. Ames cut and drove well, and was on 82 as

England finished the day on 268-7. Ames scored only two more runs before Dalton took a good running catch. Wright and Ken Farnes scored 20s and England was dismissed for 316, although South Africa did not enforce the follow-on.

With Melville injured, Mitchell and van der Bijl put on 191 runs, but then South Africa lost 0-3 shortly before stumps. In an unusual similarity to the first wicket of the match, Mitchell was out hit wicket, Rowan was superbly caught by Edrich, and van der Bijl caught at short leg, but Nourse survived a hard chance to Hammond. Following overnight rain, Nourse moved to 25 before perishing to a miscued hook. Melville and

Viljoen plugged away to put on 104 runs before Viljoen fell for 74, and then Dalton scored an aggressive 21 when Wright took an impressive caught-and-bowled. Melville braved injury and scored an attractive century before being bowled. Grieveson took 40 minutes to score before making 39, and South Africa finished with 481. Only one ball was bowled in England's second innings before bad light ended day six, with England's target a phenomenal 696.

Hutton scored 55 in an error-free opening stand of 78 until Hutton uncharacteristically played the ball onto his stumps. The out-of-form Edrich was promoted, and responded confidently as he drove and used his feet well. Edrich registered 12 fours on his way to a maiden Test century. Gibb stonewalled at the other end and battled at times as drizzle affected his spectacles. Bad light caused stumps to be drawn 10 minutes early, with Edrich on 107 and Gibb 78, and England 253-1. There was no play for the next two days, as a washed out day was followed by the second rest day.

After the pitch rolled out well, England's second wicket partnership reached 280 until Gibb was bowled, having hit just two fours in his nine-hour knock of 120. Edrich reached 219 before Langton had him caught, and Hammond established himself after another scratchy start, advancing England to 496-3 when bad light halted play. Day 10 was sure to be the last, as England's touring party had arranged commitments to return home.

Good bowling and fielding restricted England to 39 runs in the first hour as rain clouds threatened. Hammond and Paynter subsequently forced the pace, with Hammond in masterful form, the total reaching 611 before Paynter was well caught by wicketkeeper Grieveson for 75. The new ball was taken, and rain caused two stoppages before Hammond was stumped for 140. Valentine survived a stumping chance, and England was 42 runs away from a historic victory with five wickets remaining at the tea adjournment. A downpour, however, prevented any more play, and the two captains consulted. The match was declared a draw, as the touring party had to board a train in Durban that night so they could catch their boat in Cape Town on time.

There was little point speculating what the result might have been, even though England finished well on course for victory. England won the series 1-0 in any case. Ultimately, in a match featuring numerous records, it was incredible to think that there was no result after more than 43 hours of play in 10 days, comprising 5463 deliveries bowled and 1981 runs scored. Such is the unpredictable nature of cricket.

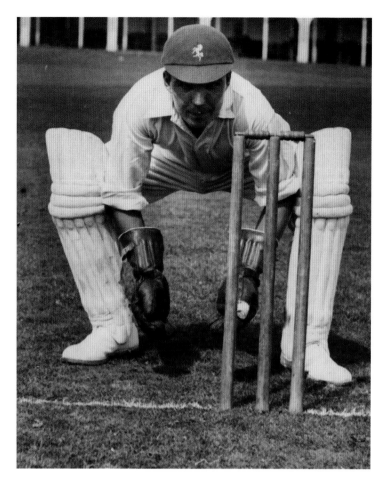

Top: England wicketkeeper Les Ames.

Above: England batsman Len Hutton.

SOUTH AFRICA 1ST INNINGS

A Melville*	hit wicket b Wright	78
PGV van der Bijl	b Perks	125
EAB Rowan	lbw b Perks	33
B Mitchell	b Wright	11
AD Nourse	b Perks	103
KG Viljoen	c Ames b Perks	0
EL Dalton	c Ames b Farnes	57
RE Grieveson†	b Perks	75
ACB Langton	c Paynter b Verity	27
ES Newson	c & b Verity	1
N Gordon	not out	0
Extras	(b 2, lb 12, nb 6)	20
Total		530

Fall of wickets 131, 219, 236, 274, 278, 368, 475, 522, 523, 530

	O	M	R	W
K Farnes	46	9	108	1
RTD Perks	41	5	100	5
DVP Wright	37	6	142	2
H Verity	55.6	14	97	2
WR Hammond	14	4	34	0
WJ Edrich	9	2	29	0

ENGLAND 1ST INNINGS

L Hutton	run out	38
PA Gibb	c Grieveson b Newson	4
E Paynter	lbw b Langton	62
WR Hammond*	st Grieveson b Dalton	24
LEG Ames†	c Dalton b Langton	84
WJ Edrich	c Rowan b Langton	1
BH Valentine	st Grieveson b Dalton	26
H Verity	b Dalton	3
DVP Wright	c Langton b Dalton	26
K Farnes	b Newson	20
RTD Perks	not out	2
Extras	(b 7, lb 17, w 1, nb 1)	26
Total		316

Fall of wickets 9, 64, 125, 169, 171, 229, 245, 276, 305, 316

	O	M	R	W
ES Newson	25.6	5	58	2
ACB Langton	35	12	71	3
N Gordon	37	7	82	0
B Mitchell	7	0	20	0
EL Dalton	13	1	59	4

SOUTH AFRICA 2ND INNINGS

B Mitchell	hit wicket b Verity	89
PGV van der Bijl	c Paynter b Wright	97
EAB Rowan	c Edrich b Verity	0
AD Nourse	c Hutton b Farnes	25
KG Viljoen	b Perks	74
A Melville*	b Farnes	103
EL Dalton	c & b Wright	21
RE Grieveson†	b Farnes	39
ACB Langton	c Hammond b Farnes	6
ES Newson	b Wright	3
N Gordon	not out	7
Extras	(b 5, lb 8, nb 4)	17
Total		481

Fall of wickets 191, 191, 191, 242, 346, 382, 434, 450, 462, 481

	O	M	R	W
K Farnes	22.1	2	74	4
RTD Perks	32	6	99	1
DVP Wright	32	7	146	3
H Verity	40	9	87	2
WR Hammond	9	1	30	0
WJ Edrich	6	1	18	0
L Hutton	1	0	10	0

ENGLAND 2ND INNINGS

L Hutton	b Mitchell	55
PA Gibb	b Dalton	120
WJ Edrich	c Gordon b Langton	219
WR Hammond*	st Grieveson b Dalton	140
E Paynter	c Grieveson b Gordon	75
LEG Ames†	not out	17
BH Valentine	not out	4
Extras	(b 8, lb 12, w 1, nb 3)	24
Total	(5 wickets)	654

Did not bat H Verity, DVP Wright, K Farnes, RTD Perks

Fall of wickets 78, 358, 447, 611, 650

	O	M	R	W
ES Newson	43	4	91	0
ACB Langton	56	12	132	1
N Gordon	55.2	10	174	1
B Mitchell	37	4	133	1
EL Dalton	27	3	100	2

Toss: South Africa   Umpires: RGA Ashman and GL Sickler   Match drawn

England v Australia
Fourth Test at Headingley, Leeds

1948
July 22, 23, 24, 26, 27 (1948)

The 1948 Australian team in England, 'The Invincibles': Back row: N. Harvey, S. Barnes, R. Lindwall, R. Saggers, D. Ring, W. Johnston, E. Toshack, K. Miller, D. Tallon, S. Loxton. In front: G. Johnson (manager), R. Hamence, I. Johnson, L. Hassett (vice-captain), D. Bradman (captain), W. Brown, A. Morris, C. McCool, W. Ferguson (manager).

Much has been said and written about the 1948 Ashes series in England, the 'Invincibles' tag prominent, after Australia won the five-match series 4-0. A memorable aspect was Don Bradman's second-ball duck in his final Test innings, but another part of the series that deserves to be well remembered is the fourth Test.

England had a great start when captain Norman Yardley won the toss and chose to bat on an ideal pitch for batsmen. Len Hutton and Cyril Washbrook put on an opening stand of 168 in just over three hours before Ray Lindwall bowled Hutton for 81. Washbrook went on to score 143, including 22 fours, but was caught by Lindwall off Bill Johnston in the last over of the day. The hosts were a commanding 268-2 before usual tail-ender Alec Bedser did a sterling job on day two, having survived the last four balls of day one. England was well and truly back in the series after heavy defeats in the first two

Neil Harvey receives congratulations from Sam Loxton upon scoring a century on debut in the first innings of the fourth Test at Leeds.

Tests were followed by a rain-interrupted drawn third Test.

Bedser hit eight fours and two sixes as he scored a Test-best 79 in nearly three hours, then fell to Ian Johnson, after Bedser and Bill Edrich added 155 runs. The number three batsman departed shortly afterwards for 111, having lasted 314 minutes and struck 13 fours and a six. Jack Crapp made just five before Ernie Toshack bowled him, and Denis Compton reached 23 when Lindwall had him caught behind by Ron Saggers, who made his Test debut in place of an injured Don Tallon.

England's last four wickets fell for just 10 runs after three successive wickets to Sam Loxton were followed by Keith Miller bowling Yardley for 25. The total of 496 was big but disappointing given the hosts had been unassailably placed at 423-2. Australia was on the back foot when Arthur Morris was caught off Bedser for six, before Lindsay Hassett and Bradman took the total to 63-1 at stumps.

Dick Pollard put England in the box seat in his first over on day three, with Hassett caught and Bradman bowled. Australia was 68-3. The complexion changed, however, as 19-year-old Neil Harvey made a strong impression in his first Ashes Test.

Harvey and Miller played many aggressive strokes, adding 121 runs in a mere 95 minutes. Yardley broke through when he had Miller caught for 58, then Loxton unleashed some powerful strokes, particularly drives.

Harvey hit 17 fours and reached 112 in just over three hours, while the fifth wicket partnership reaped 105 in 95 minutes before Harvey departed. Loxton continued his hard hitting, registering eight fours and five sixes, until Yardley bowled him just seven runs shy of a century. Loxton's departure left Australia 344-7, Johnson having been dismissed 15 runs earlier.

Saggers's maiden Test innings yielded just five runs before he was stumped, leaving Australia 355-8. Lindwall subsequently found form and gained control, while Johnston hung around until the total reached 403. An injured Toshack needed a runner but he resisted well, and scored 12 not out. Lindwall meanwhile moved to 77 before he was dismissed early on day four, following a rest day, having put on 55 runs with Toshack for the last wicket to prune England's lead to just 38.

The hosts regained the ascendancy, with Hutton and Washbrook scoring half-centuries before the duo were caught off Johnson with the total on 129. Edrich and Compton subsequently added 103 runs quickly before Lindwall had Edrich lbw. Crapp scored 18 before he too fell to Lindwall, and Yardley made little impact before he and Ken Cranston fell to Johnston in quick succession. England had stuttered to 278-6, and the innings threatened to collapse when Compton departed with the total on 293.

Godfrey Evans, however, led a counterattack, and he received support from Bedser who made 17. Laker scored an unbeaten 15, and Evans was on 47 when Yardley oddly declared, after three runs were scored in two overs on the final morning. Yardley hoped the roller would break up the pitch, and Australia's task was a daunting 404 in 344 minutes, as the surface was conducive to spin. No team in history had ever successfully chased such a target in Test cricket.

Morris and Hassett put on 57 for the first wicket when Hassett was caught-and-bowled by Compton. Left-arm Compton should have dismissed Morris for 32, but Evans missed a regulation stumping chance. It proved costly, as did a dropped catch by Crapp at slip that reprieved Bradman, who edged a Compton googly. Morris and Bradman put on 64 runs in just 30 minutes before lunch, and subsequently kept the runs flowing as loose deliveries were punished. Laker failed to land the ball on a good length, and Bradman was in the 50s when he gained another reprieve off Compton.

The unfortunate Compton was punished after he should have broken through, and Yardley accepted the new ball even though the pitch benefited spin. Morris and Bradman posted centuries, and Evans missed another stumping chance, this time to reprieve the lucky Bradman on 108. Morris was on 126 when Laker dropped him at square leg. It was easy to say with hindsight that England should have picked a second recognised spinner, rather than utilise part-timers Compton and Hutton to support Laker. On the other hand, the second-string spin attack could have worked well had chances been taken.

The second wicket partnership was worth 301 runs in just 217 minutes, when Morris was caught by Pollard off Yardley, Morris having scored 182 in 291 minutes. Miller scored 12 before he was lbw to Cranston, with victory just eight runs away. Harvey sealed Australia's famous win with 13 minutes left when he struck Cranston to the mid-wicket boundary. Bradman batted for 255 minutes and was unbeaten on 173, having hit 29 fours, while Morris had hit 33, Miller two, and Hassett and Harvey one each.

Right: Don Bradman and Arthur Morris put on a match-winning 301-run partnership in the second innings of the Fourth Test.
Bottom: Australia captain Don Bradman shakes hands with King George VI before presenting his team on the 1948 Invincibles tour.

ENGLAND 1ST INNINGS

L Hutton	b Lindwall	81
C Washbrook	c Lindwall b Johnston	143
WJ Edrich	c Morris b Johnson	111
AV Bedser	c & b Johnson	79
DCS Compton	c Saggers b Lindwall	23
JF Crapp	b Toshack	5
NWD Yardley*	b Miller	25
K Cranston	b Loxton	10
TG Evans†	c Hassett b Loxton	3
JC Laker	c Saggers b Loxton	4
R Pollard	not out	0
Extras	(b 2, lb 8, w 1, nb 1)	12
Total		496

Fall of wickets 168, 268, 423, 426, 447, 473, 486, 490, 496, 496

	O	M	R	W
RR Lindwall	38	10	79	2
KR Miller	17.1	2	43	1
WA Johnston	38	12	86	1
ERH Toshack	35	6	112	1
SJE Loxton	26	4	55	3
IWG Johnson	33	9	89	2
AR Morris	5	0	20	0

AUSTRALIA 1ST INNINGS

AR Morris	c Cranston b Bedser	6
AL Hassett	c Crapp b Pollard	13
DG Bradman*	b Pollard	33
KR Miller	c Edrich b Yardley	58
RN Harvey	b Laker	112
SJE Loxton	b Yardley	93
IWG Johnson	c Cranston b Laker	10
RR Lindwal	c Crapp b Bedser	77
RA Saggers†	st Evans b Laker	5
WA Johnston	c Edrich b Bedser	13
ERH Toshack	not out	12
Extras	(b 9, lb 14, nb 3)	26
Total		458

Fall of wickets 13, 65, 68, 189, 294, 329, 344, 355, 403, 458

	O	M	R	W
AV Bedser	31.2	4	92	3
R Pollard	38	6	104	2
K Cranston	14	1	51	0
WJ Edrich	3	0	19	0
JC Laker	30	8	113	3
NWD Yardley	17	6	38	2
DCS Compton	3	0	15	0

ENGLAND 2ND INNINGS

L Hutton	c Bradman b Johnson	57
C Washbrook	c Harvey b Johnston	65
WJ Edrich	lbw b Lindwall	54
DCS Compton	c Miller b Johnston	66
JF Crapp	b Lindwall	18
NWD Yardley*	c Harvey b Johnston	7
K Cranston	c Saggers b Johnston	0
TG Evans†	not out	47
AV Bedser	c Hassett b Miller	17
JC Laker	not out	15
Extras	(b 4, lb 12, nb 3)	19
Total	(8 wickets dec)	365

Did not bat R Pollard

Fall of wickets 129, 129, 232, 260, 277, 278, 293, 330

	O	M	R	W
RR Lindwall	26	6	84	2
KR Miller	21	5	53	1
WA Johnston	29	5	95	4
SJE Loxton	10	2	29	0
IWG Johnson	21	2	85	1

Toss: England   Umpires: HG Baldwin and F Chester
Australia won by 7 wickets

AUSTRALIA 2ND INNINGS

AR Morris	c Pollard b Yardley	182
AL Hassett	c & b Compton	17
DG Bradman*	not out	173
KR Miller	lbw b Cranston	12
RN Harvey	not out	4
Extras	(b 6, lb 9, nb 1)	16
Total	(3 wickets)	404

Did not bat SJE Loxton, IWG Johnson, RR Lindwall, RA Saggers†, WA Johnston, ERH Toshack

Fall of wickets 57, 358, 396

	O	M	R	W
AV Bedser	21	2	56	0
R Pollard	22	6	55	0
K Cranston	7.1	0	28	1
JC Laker	32	11	93	0
NWD Yardley	13	1	44	1
DCS Compton	15	3	82	1
L Hutton	4	1	30	0

South Africa v England
First Test at Kingsmead, Durban

1948-49
December 16, 17, 18, 20 (1948)

A four-day Test in which the result could go any of four ways with three scheduled balls remaining is truly worthy of the 'classic' label. This was the case in the first Test of the 1948–49 series involving South Africa and England. Having been trounced by Australia's 1948 'Invincibles', England made some changes, George Mann, Roly Jenkins and Reg Simpson being newcomers. In an unusual move, Mann also took on the captaincy. Denis Begbie, Cuan McCarthy and Owen Wynne, meanwhile, were debutants for the hosts.

Humid conditions on day one suited swing bowling, but the forecast of thunderstorms on day two was another telling factor as the captains had the pre-match toss. South African captain Dudley Nourse won and chose to bat, and his side slipped to 18-2, after Wynne was caught at backward short leg and Eric Rowan caught behind. A 51-run stand between Bruce Mitchell and Nourse increased South Africa's prospects, until Allan Watkins lunged to his right at short leg and took a splendid one-handed catch near the ground to dismiss Nourse.

South Africa was 80-4 when Mitchell was caught behind, and 99-5 when a superb throw from Cyril Washbrook ran out Billy Wade. Begbie and Ossie Dawson provided some respite with a 49-run partnership before a collapse of 13-5 saw South Africa dismissed for just 161. Begbie fell to the same bowler-fielder combination that Wynne did, before Cliff Gladwin went to work, bowling Dawson and trapping Lindsay Tuckett lbw, then having Norman 'Tufty' Mann caught behind. Bedser finished with 4-39 when he bowled McCarthy, and bad light and rain brought about an early finish to day one.

Bad light and rainstorms interrupted day two, which featured less than three hours of play. England openers Len Hutton and Washbrook, however, seemed unfazed. They put on 50 runs in as many minutes, and Dawson and Tuckett were

England's opening batsmen Len Hutton (left) and Cyril Washbrook

a bit wayward before spinners Athol Rowan and Tufty Mann slowed things down. Mann had Washbrook caught behind with the total on 84, before having Simpson caught by Begbie for five. Mann conceded only 15 runs in 13 overs, but Hutton moved to 81 and Denis Compton to 17 as England trailed by

England's Len Hutton skies a ball from South Africa bowler Athol Rowan in a 1949 Test match.

South African trio (from left) Eric Rowan, Athol Rowan and Dudley Nourse on tour in the late 1940s – with suitable springbok mascot.

just 17 runs with eight wickets remaining at stumps.

The pitch crumbled on day three, and the hosts relied on their spinners to get their team back into the match. Hutton added just two runs before he was caught by McCarthy, and the spinners kept extracting lift and turn. Compton was gutsy and determined, and Watkins resisted for 39 minutes before falling to Athol Rowan. England advanced to 212-4 when the rot set in, as Rowan accounted for George Mann and Evans with consecutive deliveries. Jenkins fell to 'Tufty' Mann, and Compton kept plugging away, while Bedser chipped in with 11. Mann, however, claimed three wickets in the space of six runs, and finished with six scalps to Athol Rowan's four, England's lead confined to 92.

South Africa lost both openers with the total on 22 before Mitchell and Nourse again provided resistance, but once more they only started a recovery, poor weather repeatedly interrupting the play. Nourse again fell in the 30s, caught-and-bowled by Bedser, before Mitchell was bowled by Doug

Wright for a slow 19. Bad light stopped play entirely for the day, as South Africa remained two runs in arrears with six wickets remaining.

Wade and Begbie breathed life back into the contest on the final day with energetic batting. The partnership reached 85, with Begbie on 48 when he was caught off Bedser. Dawson didn't last long, but Wade took the total past 200 before his three-hour knock ended on 63. Athol Rowan added a slow 15, and Tuckett scored three not out in 55 minutes at number nine before South Africa folded for 219. Following a 12-minute rain delay, England had 28 eight-ball overs in which to score 128 runs on a difficult pitch in drizzling rain.

Washbrook gained a vital early reprieve, dropped in the deep, and the score reached 25 before Hutton was caught off Tuckett. George Mann came in at first drop, and he too was reprieved on the boundary, the ball proving hard to field cleanly in the conditions. The total quickly moved to 49 when 'Tufty' Mann had Washbrook lbw, although the spinners were

deliveries rose sharply while others skidded. Compton and Jenkins, however, coped with McCarthy's and Tuckett's pace, and lifted England back into a winning position. Just 13 runs were needed when a shooter from McCarthy rattled Compton's stumps, and Jenkins was caught behind one run later. England needed 12 runs in 10 minutes in the dark, and an unfortunate fielder missed a chance to catch Gladwin first ball. Gladwin soon registered a boundary that illuminated the significance of his reprieve.

With Tuckett bowling the final over, Bedser managed a single to level the scores from the third-last ball. Gladwin swung at the penultimate ball but missed, and the England players in the pavilion could not bear to watch the final delivery. The ball struck Gladwin's thigh as he missed another swing, and 'Tufty' Mann swooped at short leg, but Bedser ran for his life and scurried home for the winning single. Excited spectators invaded the field and chaired off numerous players in the darkness, to cap off a spectacular Test match.

hardly used due to the wet ball. Nineteen-year-old paceman McCarthy soon claimed his maiden scalp when Mitchell took a great slips catch to account for the England skipper. This seemed to inject a spark into McCarthy, who controlled the wet ball and bowled with hostility. He bowled Watkins and had Simpson caught from successive balls, then bowled Evans in his next over, and England crashed to 70-6 with an hour remaining.

The captains agreed to continue playing in the drizzle as the pitch became greasier and the skies grew darker. Some

Above: England's Denis Compton receiving an award from the Minister for Sport as British Sportsman of the Year in 1949.
Inset: England bowler Alec Bedser tamed South Africa in 1948.

SOUTH AFRICA 1ST INNINGS

EAB Rowan	c Evans b Jenkins	7
OE Wynne	c Compton b Bedser	5
B Mitchell	c Evans b Bedser	27
AD Nourse*	c Watkins b Wright	37
WW Wade†	run out	8
DW Begbie	c Compton b Bedser	37
OC Dawson	b Gladwin	24
AMB Rowan	not out	5
L Tuckett	lbw b Gladwin	1
NBF Mann	c Evans b Gladwin	4
CN McCarthy	b Bedser	0
Extras	(b 3, lb 2, nb 1)	6
Total		161

Fall of wickets 9, 18, 69, 80, 99, 148, 150, 152, 160, 161

	O	M	R	W
AV Bedser	13.5	2	39	4
C Gladwin	12	3	21	3
RO Jenkins	14	3	50	1
DVP Wright	9	3	29	1
DCS Compton	2	0	5	0
AJ Watkins	3	0	11	0

SOUTH AFRICA 2ND INNINGS

EAB Rowan	c Compton b Jenkins	16
OE Wynne	c Watkins b Wright	4
B Mitchell	b Wright	19
AD Nourse*	c & b Bedser	32
WW Wade†	b Jenkins	63
DW Begbie	c Mann b Bedser	48
OC Dawson	c Compton b Wright	3
AMB Rowan	b Wright	15
L Tuckett	not out	3
NBF Mann	c Mann b Compton	10
CN McCarthy	b Jenkins	0
Extras	(b 1, lb 5)	6
Total		219

Fall of wickets 22, 22, 67, 89, 174, 179, 208, 208, 219, 219

	O	M	R	W
AV Bedser	18	5	51	2
C Gladwin	7	3	15	0
RO Jenkins	22.3	6	64	3
DVP Wright	26	3	72	4
DCS Compton	16	11	11	1

ENGLAND 1ST INNINGS

L Hutton	c McCarthy b AMB Rowan	83
C Washbrook	c Wade b Mann	35
RT Simpson	c Begbie b Mann	5
DCS Compton	c Wade b Mann	72
AJ Watkins	c Nourse b AMB Rowan	9
FG Mann*	c EAB Rowan b AMB Rowan	19
TG Evans†	c Wynne b AMB Rowan	0
RO Jenkins	c Mitchell b Mann	5
AV Bedser	c Tuckett b Mann	11
C Gladwin	not out	0
DVP Wright	c Tuckett b Mann	0
Extras	(b 2, lb 12)	14
Total		253

Fall of wickets 84, 104, 146, 172, 212, 212, 221, 247, 253, 253

	O	M	R	W
CN McCarthy	9	2	20	0
OC Dawson	3	0	16	0
L Tuckett	6	0	36	0
AMB Rowan	44	8	108	4
NBF Mann	37.4	14	59	6

ENGLAND 2ND INNINGS

L Hutton	c Dawson b Tuckett	5
C Washbrook	lbw b Mann	25
FG Mann*	c Mitchell b McCarthy	13
DCS Compton	b McCarthy	28
AJ Watkins	b McCarthy	4
RT Simpson	c EAB Rowan b McCarthy	0
TG Evans†	b McCarthy	4
RO Jenkins	c Wade b McCarthy	22
AV Bedser	not out	1
C Gladwin	not out	7
Extras	(b 9, lb 10)	19
Total	(8 wickets)	128

Did not bat DVP Wright

Fall of wickets 25, 49, 52, 64, 64, 70, 115, 116

	O	M	R	W
CN McCarthy	12	2	43	6
L Tuckett	10	0	38	1
AMB Rowan	4	0	15	0
NBF Mann	2	0	13	1

Toss: South Africa   Umpires: RGA Ashman and GL Sickler   England won by 2 wickets

Australia v West Indies
Fourth Test at the Melbourne Cricket Ground

1951-52
December 31 (1951), January 1, 2, 3 (1952)

Australian captain Lindsay Hassett struggles to make his ground in the Test series against the West Indies in January 1952.

A classic fourth Test unfolded in the Australia versus West Indies series on Australian soil in 1951–52, after the hosts led the five-match series 2-1. The series held sufficient interest, 21 years after the first series involving Australia and the West Indies. Many of Australia's 1948 'Invincibles' remained, and the West Indies had beaten England 3-1 in 1950.

Batting first seemed the wrong option for the tourists, as Keith Miller dismissed the openers before left-armer Bill Johnston's dismissal of Everton Weekes made the score 30-3. Frank Worrell suffered a painful blow on the right hand from a Miller delivery, but Worrell and Gerry Gomez led a recovery. Worrell overcame a scratchy start, playing some attractive drives and cuts despite a sore hand. Gomez was on 30 when he appeared lucky not to be adjudged hit wicket, having kicked off his bails as the bat flew out of his hands during a hook shot. Gomez added seven more runs before becoming Miller's third victim.

Worrell copped further blows and was dropped several times, and Ian Johnson missed a chance to catch Robert Christiani. The tourists lost their fifth wicket at 194, when good fielding from Neil Harvey accounted for Christiani. Worrell effectively batted one-handed as he reached a chancy but gutsy century. When Ray Lindwall bowled him for 108, he had hit just seven fours. With the tourists 242-8, Australia's bowlers were booed, as they seemed intent on slowing down so that they wouldn't have to bat before stumps. Johnston delivered a number of wide balls, and Sonny Ramadhin touched one down leg-side to the wicketkeeper. There was no appeal, but then as Johnston was about to run in for the next ball, captain Lindsay Hassett stopped him and appealed. Umpire Ronald Wright gave Ramadhin out, and the crowd booed. Alf Valentine and Sammy Guillen put on a crucial last wicket stand of 24 to take the score to 272, then Miller's fifth wicket ended the innings just before stumps.

Worrell didn't field on day two due to injury, while Australian opener Arthur Morris had a leg injury and used a runner. Morris didn't look comfortable, playing a ball onto his stumps after scoring six. Jack Moroney and Hassett took the score to 48 before Australia fell to 49-3. Hassett was run out by a fast throw from Gomez to wicketkeeper Guillen, before Moroney was bowled with the first ball he faced from spinner Ramadhin, Moroney having timed the ball well against the quicks.

Australia recovered as Harvey played a fine innings while Miller was steady. The batting duo was settled against spin, and the West Indies surprisingly didn't take the new ball as the score was 138-3 at the 50-over mark. The total reached 173, with Harvey on 83 including 15 fours when he was too early on a drive and hit a return catch to Ramadhin. Valentine soon

Bowler Keith Miller took seven wickets in the match against the West Indies to set up Australia's one-wicket victory in Melbourne.

bowled Graeme Hole, and the new ball was taken at 187-5. The 36-year-old John Trim went to work with 4-11 in six overs, dismissing Miller, Lindwall, Johnson and Ring, before Gomez dismissed Johnston as Australia fell from 208-5 to 216 all out.

Strangely, Guillen opened the West Indies' second innings when 25 minutes remained before stumps. Lindwall dismissed Guillen third ball and the promoted Goddard second ball without a run scored, before the tourists finished the day 20-2 and 76 runs in front. English Test star Alec Bedser commented in the press that two tactical errors could cost the West Indies dearly: not taking the new ball when it was due, and then reshuffling the batting order.

The tourists wobbled to 60-4 as Johnston had Kenneth Rickards and Weekes lbw. Jeff Stollmeyer batted gracefully for 54, but the total was only 97 when he was lbw. Christiani looked settled before falling for 33, and the injured Worrell was effective after being reprieved on five. Gomez defended well, and the score reached 190 when Johnston bowled Worrell. Trim and Ramadhin were run out for ducks, and Gomez's departure for 52 ended the innings, leaving Australia with a target of 260.

Moroney retired hurt on 13-0 after a Trim delivery struck him on the elbow. Valentine had Morris lbw for 12, and Hassett and Harvey took Australia to 93-1 the following morning, before Valentine bowled Harvey with a great delivery. Moroney's return was brief as Ramadhin had him lbw, and Australia collapsed to 109-4 when Miller was hit wicket from a late cut. Hassett nonetheless showed magnificent concentration, as he was solid yet ready to smack stray deliveries. On 59 he was crucially reprieved when Guillen missed a catch and stumping. Australia nonetheless looked shaky at 147-5 as Hole departed.

Hassett took 75 minutes to go from 70 to 80, and Lindwall was slow before he took 14 runs from a Valentine over. Australia seemed on course when Lindwall edged a cut behind to make the score 192-6. Johnson stuck around as Hassett reached a splendid century, then Johnson was caught behind off Ramadhin with the score on 218. The game swung the tourists' way with Hassett lbw to Valentine, also on 218, before Langley was similarly dismissed four runs later. Hassett's 323-minute innings was heroic, but Australia's cause appeared lost, as Ring and Johnston needed a last wicket partnership of 38 for an Australian victory.

The tension was immense. Johnston was passive while Ring took some risks, playing some airy shots that fell safely, as the fielders were not placed for lofted hits into the deep. There were some near misses as the batsmen prodded at the spinners. The crowd, according to the *Argus* newspaper, "yelled louder than a bigger crowd did at the Collingwood-Essendon football final last year." The scores were tied before Johnston turned a Worrell delivery to the leg-side for the winning run. Johnston had scored just seven as the required 38 runs were polished off in 35 minutes to seal the series.

Top: Australia batsman Lindsay Hassett practising in the nets.
Bottom: Lindsay Hassett scored a fine 102 in his team's one-wicket defeat of the West Indies at Melbourne.

WEST INDIES 1ST INNINGS		
KR Rickards	b Miller	15
JB Stollmeyer	c Langley b Miller	7
FMM Worrell	b Lindwall	108
ED Weekes	c Johnson b Johnston	1
GE Gomez	c Langley b Miller	37
RJ Christiani	run out	37
JDC Goddard*	b Miller	21
SC Guillen†	not out	22
J Trim	run out	0
S Ramadhin	c Langley b Johnston	1
AL Valentine	c Lindwall b Miller	14
Extras	(b 2, lb 6, w 1)	9
Total		272

Fall of wickets 16, 29, 30, 102, 194, 221, 237, 242, 248, 272

	O	M	R	W
RR Lindwall	18	2	72	1
KR Miller	19.3	1	60	5
WA Johnston	20	1	59	2
DT Ring	9	0	43	0
IWG Johnson	7	0	23	0
GB Hole	2	0	6	0

WEST INDIES 2ND INNINGS		
SC Guillen†	c Johnston b Lindwall	0
JB Stollmeyer	lbw b Miller	54
JDC Goddard*	lbw b Lindwall	0
KR Rickards	lbw b Johnston	22
ED Weekes	lbw b Johnson	2
RJ Christiani	b Miller	33
GE Gomez	b Johnston	52
FMM Worrell	b Johnston	30
J Trim	run out	0
S Ramadhin	run out	0
AL Valentine	not out	1
Extras	(b 4, lb 5)	9
Total		203

Fall of wickets 0, 0, 53, 60, 97, 128, 190, 194, 194, 203

	O	M	R	W
RR Lindwall	17	2	59	2
KR Miller	16	1	49	2
WA Johnston	14.3	2	51	3
DT Ring	7	1	17	0
IWG Johnson	5	0	18	1

AUSTRALIA 1ST INNINGS		
J Moroney	lbw b Ramadhin	26
AR Morris	b Trim	6
AL Hassett*	run out	15
RN Harvey	c & b Ramadhin	83
KR Miller	b Trim	47
GB Hole	b Valentine	2
RR Lindwall	lbw b Trim	13
IWG Johnson	c Guillen b Trim	1
DT Ring	b Trim	6
GRA Langley†	not out	0
WA Johnston	b Gomez	1
Extras	(b 12, lb 4)	16
Total		216

Fall of wickets 17, 48, 49, 173, 176, 208, 209, 210, 215, 216

	O	M	R	W
J Trim	12	2	34	5
GE Gomez	13.3	7	25	1
AL Valentine	23	8	50	1
S Ramadhin	17	4	63	2
JDC Goddard	8	0	28	0

AUSTRALIA 2ND INNINGS		
J Moroney	lbw b Ramadhin	5
AR Morris	lbw b Valentine	12
AL Hassett*	lbw b Valentine	102
RN Harvey	b Valentine	33
KR Miller	hit wicket b Valentine	2
GB Hole	c Gomez b Worrell	13
RR Lindwall	c Guillen b Ramadhin	29
IWG Johnson	c Guillen b Ramadhin	6
DT Ring	not out	32
GRA Langley†	lbw b Valentine	1
WA Johnston	not out	7
Extras	(b 14, lb 4)	18
Total	(9 wickets)	260

Fall of wickets 27, 93, 106, 109, 147, 192, 218, 218, 222

	O	M	R	W
J Trim	10	3	25	0
GE Gomez	9	1	18	0
AL Valentine	30	9	88	5
S Ramadhin	39	15	93	3
FMM Worrell	9	1	18	1

Toss: West Indies   Umpires: MJ McInnes and RJJ Wright   Australia won by 1 wicket

Australia v South Africa
Fifth Test at the Melbourne Cricket Ground

1952–53
February 6, 7, 9, 10, 11, 12 (1953)

The South African touring party to Australia in 1952–53.

The fifth and final Test of the 1952–53 series in Australia was memorable as South Africa sought to draw the series 2-all after Australia had won all seven series involving the two nations since 1902–03. The 1952–53 series was level at 1-all before an Australian win was followed by a draw. The hosts therefore couldn't lose the series, but they were handicapped for the final Test as Ray Lindwall and Keith Miller were absent with injuries.

The start of the final Test was delayed until just before lunch, but Australia looked at ease batting on the damp pitch. Arthur Morris batted fluently and was well supported by Colin McDonald, who scored 41 in a 122-run opening stand. Morris was unfortunately run out just one run shy of a century, while Neil Harvey was in sublime form. He finished the day on 71 while captain Lindsay Hassett was on 30 and his team 243-2. Hassett became another run out casualty after adding 10 runs to his overnight score, before 17-year-old Ian Craig played many superb strokes in his Test debut. Craig and Harvey were a joy to watch as they put on 148 runs in 107 minutes before Craig, on 53, was caught by South Africa's Test debutant, Headley Keith.

Harvey went on to score his first Test double century, and he lasted 295 minutes before being caught for 205, which included 19 fours. Ron Archer scored 18 in his maiden Test innings before being caught behind, and Richie Benaud and Doug Ring also made starts before Australia lost 5-3 as a 500-run total neared. Bill Johnston and Geff Noblet added 25 runs for the last wicket before off spinner Hugh Tayfield took his third scalp after paceman Eddie Fuller had earlier taken three wickets. Amazingly, three leg byes were the only sundries in the huge total of 520. At stumps on day two, South Africa had 48 runs on the board for the loss of Russell Endean, who was caught at the wicket off Johnston.

Like the hosts, the visitors found the pitch good for batting as day three followed a rest day. Also like Australia, South Africa lost its second wicket to a run out, with John Waite gone for 64. John Watkins looked set for a century, but 189-2 became 189-4. Ken Funston was lbw to Johnston, and Archer took his first Test wicket when he bowled Watkins for 92. Roy McLean attacked the Australian bowlers while Keith's first Test knock yielded 10 runs in an hour before Johnston bowled him. McLean struck 10 fours and a six before Noblet had him lbw for 81, scored in just 93 minutes.

South Africa finished day three 195 runs behind, and a seventh wicket partnership of 111 involving skipper Jack Cheetham and Percy Mansell took the total to 401 on day four before the duo departed in quick succession. Anton Murray and Tayfield scored 17 each before both were dismissed on 435, leaving Australia with an 85-run lead. The hosts carefully

Australian batsman Arthur Morris was run out on 99 in the first innings against South Africa in Melbourne in 1953.

reached 36-0 before Fuller put South Africa right back in the match as he had McDonald caught for 11 and Harvey bowled for seven. Morris scored a solid 44 in two hours before Tayfield trapped him lbw, and Australia led by 174 runs with two days left in this six-day match.

Australia was slower and less comfortable than in the first innings despite Craig again showing impressive composure. Hassett took two hours to score 30, although the Australians nonetheless looked on course to set a big target as they reached 128-3. Hassett's dismissal, however, was soon followed by Archer departing without scoring as Australia slipped to 129-5. Craig was three runs shy of another half-century before falling to Tayfield with the score on 152. Mansell struck with the dismissal of Ring as Australia faltered to 152-7, before Benaud and Gil Langley pushed the lead beyond 250. A last wicket partnership of 16 enabled Australia to set South Africa 295 runs to square the series. Fuller claimed the last three Australian wickets to finish with fine figures of 5-66 and complement spinners Tayfield and Mansell.

Endean and Waite put on 42 runs before Waite succumbed to Archer's first Test catch. Endean went on to reach 57 by stumps while Watkins supported him, and the tourists needed 201 runs on the last day with nine wickets in hand. Cracks were evident in the pitch as the final day began, but the batsmen looked settled.

Arthur Morris, Ian Craig, Ron Archer (Australia) and H. J. Keith (South Africa) exchange pleasantries during the 1952–53 Test series.

South Africa appeared well placed, but some minor hurdles unfolded.

Endean added 13 runs to his overnight score before Johnston bowled him, and Watkins worked his way to 50 before he was bowled by Ring just after a 50-run partnership was raised for the third wicket. Funston reached 35 before Benaud bowled him, and the match was in the balance as South Africa needed 104 runs with six wickets remaining. A tight contest looked likely. Just 80 minutes later, the match was over.

Following Funston's departure, Keith was under some pressure in his first Test while McLean had a bruised eye. McLean, however, took up where he left off in the first innings as he again struck the ball all over the place. There was little point wondering what Lindwall or Miller could have done as McLean clubbed 14 fours and scored an unbeaten 76, enabling South Africa to finish level with Australia in a Test series for the first time. Whilst McLean's innings was memorable, Keith deserved credit for his 40 not out in 118 minutes. Hassett had a bowl with the score reading 285-4, and he delivered just five balls out of a possible eight as 12 runs were scored to take South Africa to a memorable six-wicket win. The result seemed hard to believe after Australia was 417-3 in its first innings, South Africa 189-4 in its first innings in response to 520, and Australia 213 runs in front with seven wickets remaining in its second innings.

AUSTRALIA 1ST INNINGS

CC McDonald	c McLean b Mansell	41
AR Morris	run out	99
RN Harvey	c Cheetham b Fuller	205
AL Hassett*	run out	40
ID Craig	c Keith b Fuller	53
RG Archer	c Waite b Fuller	18
R Benaud	c & b Tayfield	20
DT Ring	b Tayfield	14
GRA Langley†	b Murray	2
WA Johnston	c Endean b Tayfield	12
G Noblet	not out	13
Extras	(lb 3)	3
Total		520

Fall of wickets 122, 166, 269, 417, 450, 459, 490, 493, 495, 520

	O	M	R	W
ERH Fuller	19	4	74	3
JC Watkins	23	3	72	0
HJ Tayfield	35.4	4	129	3
ARA Murray	25	3	84	1
PNF Mansell	22	0	114	1
HJ Keith	9	0	44	0

SOUTH AFRICA 1ST INNINGS

WR Endean	c Langley b Johnston	16
JHB Waite†	run out	64
JC Watkins	b Archer	92
KJ Funston	lbw b Johnston	16
HJ Keith	b Johnston	10
RA McLean	lbw b Noblet	81
JE Cheetham*	c McDonald b Johnston	66
PNF Mansell	lbw b Johnston	52
ARA Murray	c & b Johnston	17
HJ Tayfield	c Benaud b Ring	17
ERH Fuller	not out	0
Extras	(b 1, lb 3)	4
Total		435

Fall of wickets 31, 129, 189, 189, 239, 290, 401, 402, 435, 435

	O	M	R	W
G Noblet	30	6	65	1
RG Archer	33	4	97	1
WA Johnston	46	8	152	6
DT Ring	19.1	1	62	1
R Benaud	15	3	55	0

AUSTRALIA 2ND INNINGS

CC McDonald	c Watkins b Fuller	11
AR Morris	lbw b Tayfield	44
RN Harvey	b Fuller	7
AL Hassett*	c Endean b Mansell	30
ID Craig	c Endean b Tayfield	47
RG Archer	c Watkins b Tayfield	0
R Benaud	c Watkins b Fuller	30
DT Ring	c Endean b Mansell	0
GRA Langley†	not out	26
WA Johnston	c Cheetham b Fuller	5
G Noblet	b Fuller	1
Extras	(b 7, lb 1)	8
Total		209

Fall of wickets 36, 44, 70, 128, 129, 152, 152, 187, 193, 209

	O	M	R	W
ERH Fuller	30.2	4	66	5
JC Watkins	14	4	33	0
HJ Tayfield	32	8	73	3
PNF Mansell	8	3	29	2

SOUTH AFRICA 2ND INNINGS

WR Endean	b Johnston	70
JHB Waite†	c Archer b Noblet	18
JC Watkins	b Ring	50
KJ Funston	b Benaud	35
HJ Keith	not out	40
RA McLean	not out	76
Extras	(b 2, lb 6)	8
Total	(4 wickets)	297

Did not bat JE Cheetham*, PNF Mansell, ARA Murray, HJ Tayfield, ERH Fuller

Fall of wickets 42, 124, 174, 191

	O	M	R	W
G Noblet	24	9	44	1
RG Archer	5	0	23	0
WA Johnston	38	7	114	1
DT Ring	13	2	55	1
R Benaud	15	4	41	1
AL Hassett	0.5	0	12	0

Toss: Australia   Umpires: MJ McInnes and RJJ Wright   South Africa won by 6 wickets

England v Australia
Second Test at Lord's, London

1953
June 25, 26, 27, 29, 30 (1953)

Australia 1953. Standing: Keith Miller, Doug Ring, Richie Benaud, Bill Johnston, Alan Davidson, Ray Lindwall. Sitting: Gil Langley, Neil Harvey, Lindsay Hassett (captain), Arthur Morris, Graeme Hole.

The 1953 Ashes series was decided only in the fifth and final Test after the first four Tests were drawn, but the second Test at Lord's was perhaps the most memorable of the series.

A packed crowd led to the gates being closed after Australian captain Lindsay Hassett won the toss and opened the batting with Arthur Morris. Hassett was scratchy as his strained arm was strapped, but he settled in, while Morris scored 30 until quick glovework from Godfrey Evans had him stumped, 20 minutes before lunch. Hassett and Neil Harvey batted into the final session of the day, after Hassett gave a chance at slip when 55. The batting was steady but not very attractive, and Harvey was lbw after scoring 59 in nearly three hours. Australia 190-2.

Hassett completed his second century in as many Tests before retiring on 101 due to cramps. Keith Miller struck a six to reach 25 but was bowled next ball by Johnny Wardle, who ripped through the middle order to provide some joy for the locals during an otherwise sedate day. Richie Benaud was lbw for zero, and Hole caught by Denis Compton for 13 as Australia fell to 240-5, before finishing the day at 263-5.

Hassett returned at the fall of the sixth wicket and added just three runs before he was caught off Alec Bedser. Alan Davidson cut and drove with authority as he scored the majority of his runs in boundaries, but there was little substance from the rest of the lower order. Davidson went from 17 to 76 on day two while the team scored only 24 runs. Bedser finished with five wickets and Wardle four but Australia's total could have been far less than 346 had there not been dropped catches, with Len Hutton the main culprit.

England was set back as Don Kenyon was caught at short leg from the last ball of the third over, before the hosts gained control. Hutton and Tom Graveney survived everything the Australians threw at them, and the batting duo produced some fine strokeplay as the score moved to 177-1 at stumps.

A Lindwall yorker rattled Graveney's stumps without a run added on day three, before Hutton and Compton were resistant as Lindwall and Miller couldn't strike with the new ball. Hutton reached 145 with a hit to deep square leg for his 16th four, before his elegant innings ended as he was caught off Bill Johnston. England 279-3.

The visitors made further inroads after lunch, with Willie Watson's only scoring stroke being a four before he was unluckily stumped off wicketkeeper Gil Langley's pads. England was 301-5 when Compton departed as he misread a Benaud delivery, and 328-7 after Lindwall struck with successive balls. The recalled 42-year-old Freddie Brown hit four fours in his 22 before he was caught behind, and then Evans was bowled first ball. Trevor Bailey fell to Miller for two, and England was still five runs behind when Bedser was ninth out and Lindwall's fifth victim. Wardle and Statham added 31 runs for the last wicket, and then Statham had Hassett caught behind for three.

Australia recovered to 96-1 at stumps before Morris and Miller pressed on following the rest day. After they were cautious on day three, they showed more urgency on day four. Morris was on 89 and the total on 168 when he departed as Statham ran backwards and tumbled to take a superb catch. The score moved to 227-2 after lunch before Australia lost 21-3, with Harvey and Miller bowled before Benaud was caught. Miller batted for nearly five hours, and hit 14 fours and a six in his 109. Hole helped push the total towards 300, before Australia slipped to 308-8 after Brown took three wickets without assistance from teammates. Lindwall counterattacked with some breathtaking hitting, as he raced to 50 with eight fours and two sixes. The ninth wicket stand featured 54 runs in a mere 25 minutes as Langley scored just nine. After Lindwall was last out, England needed 343 runs for victory with an hour of day four and all of day five remaining.

Lindwall made two huge breakthroughs as Kenyon was caught at mid on and Hutton caught at slip. A brilliant diving catch by Langley off Johnston snared Graveney to have England reeling at 12-3, before a chance at short leg was missed to reprieve Watson in the last over of the day. Little did anyone know how crucial this would be, even though England was in big trouble at 20-3 with a day left.

Lord's Cricket Ground in the heart of London, 'the home of cricket'.

Watson and Compton added 53 runs in 95 minutes on day five, with Compton hitting three powerful fours in a Benaud over. A low ball from Johnston had Compton lbw, before Bailey and Watson showed remarkable concentration and patience as they played straight and resisted Australia's pace and spin. The hosts were 116-4 at lunch, with a draw their best option. Lindwall and Miller took the new ball midway through the afternoon, and Bailey suffered two fierce blows on the hands as just nine runs came in 10 overs. Importantly for England, no wickets fell.

England still had six wickets left when tea was taken, before Watson posted a century when he swung a Ring delivery for four. Watson was on 109 when he finally departed as Ring had him caught off bat and pad. Just 40 minutes remained, after Watson batted for 346 minutes and hit 16 fours. Five minutes later, Bailey uncharacteristically played a needless attacking shot and was caught at cover.

Brown played a couple of risky shots but he and Evans survived against some testing spin bowling. Australia needed three wickets in four balls after Benaud had Brown caught at slip. Wardle survived, and a fascinating draw had resulted, with England 61 runs and Australia three wickets shy of victory.

England went on to win the Ashes for the first time since 1932–33 courtesy of an eight-wicket victory in the last Test.

Above left: Century-maker Willie Watson.

Above right: Bowler Brian Statham.

Right: England wicketkeeper Godfrey Evans.

AUSTRALIA 1ST INNINGS

AL Hassett*	c Bailey b Bedser	104
AR Morris	st Evans b Bedser	30
RN Harvey	lbw b Bedser	59
KR Miller	b Wardle	25
GB Hole	c Compton b Wardle	13
R Benaud	lbw b Wardle	0
AK Davidson	c Statham b Bedser	76
DT Ring	lbw b Wardle	18
RR Lindwall	b Statham	9
GRA Langley†	c Watson b Bedser	1
WA Johnston	not out	3
Extras	(b 4, lb 4)	8
Total		346

Fall of wickets 65, 190, 225, 229, 240, 280, 291, 330, 331, 346

	O	M	R	W
AV Bedser	42.4	8	105	5
JB Statham	28	7	48	1
FR Brown	25	7	53	0
TE Bailey	16	2	55	0
JH Wardle	29	8	77	4

ENGLAND 1ST INNINGS

L Hutton*	c Hole b Johnston	145
D Kenyon	c Davidson b Lindwall	3
TW Graveney	b Lindwall	78
DCS Compton	c Hole b Benaud	57
W Watson	st Langley b Johnston	4
TE Bailey	c & b Miller	2
FR Brown	c Langley b Lindwall	22
TG Evans†	b Lindwall	0
JH Wardle	b Davidson	23
AV Bedser	b Lindwall	1
JB Statham	not out	17
Extras	(b 11, lb 1, w 1, nb 7)	20
Total		372

Fall of wickets 9, 177, 279, 291, 301, 328, 328, 332, 341, 372

	O	M	R	W
RR Lindwall	23	4	66	5
KR Miller	25	6	57	1
WA Johnston	35	11	91	2
DT Ring	14	2	43	0
R Benaud	19	4	70	1
AK Davidson	10.5	2	25	1

AUSTRALIA 2ND INNINGS

AL Hassett*	c Evans b Statham	3
AR Morris	c Statham b Compton	89
KR Miller	b Wardle	109
RN Harvey	b Bedser	21
GB Hole	lbw b Brown	47
R Benaud	c Graveney b Bedser	5
AK Davidson	c & b Brown	15
DT Ring	lbw b Brown	7
RR Lindwall	b Bedser	50
GRA Langley†	b Brown	9
WA Johnston	not out	0
Extras	(b 8, lb 5)	13
Total		368

Fall of wickets 3, 168, 227, 235, 248, 296, 305, 308, 362, 368

	O	M	R	W
AV Bedser	31.5	8	77	3
JB Statham	15	3	40	1
FR Brown	27	4	82	4
TE Bailey	10	4	24	0
JH Wardle	46	18	111	1
DCS Compton	3	0	21	1

ENGLAND 2ND INNINGS

L Hutton*	c Hole b Lindwall	5
D Kenyon	c Hassett b Lindwall	2
TW Graveney	c Langley b Johnston	2
DCS Compton	lbw b Johnston	33
W Watson	c Hole b Ring	109
TE Bailey	c Benaud b Ring	71
FR Brown	c Hole b Benaud	28
TG Evans†	not out	11
JH Wardle	not out	0
Extras	(b 7, lb 6, w 2, nb 6)	21
Total	(7 wickets)	282

Did not bat AV Bedser, JB Statham

Fall of wickets 6, 10, 12, 73, 236, 246, 282

	O	M	R	W
RR Lindwall	19	3	26	2
KR Miller	17	8	17	0
WA Johnston	29	10	70	2
DT Ring	29	5	84	2
R Benaud	17	6	51	1
AK Davidson	14	5	13	0
GB Hole	1	1	0	0

Toss: Australia   Umpires: HG Baldwin and FS Lee   Match drawn

England v Pakistan

Fourth Test at the Oval, London

1954

August 12, 13, 14, 16, 17 (1954)

The Pakistan touring party to England in 1954.

Pakistan's 1954 tour of England had an unexpected final twist after the series didn't appear attractive. A rain-reduced first Test was drawn before an innings win to England in the second Test was followed by rain preventing a certain England win in the third Test. The fourth and final Test, however, was one to savour, despite rain interruptions.

England's selectors were perhaps a little complacent as they excluded Alec Bedser and Trevor Bailey in favour of debutants Frank Tyson and Peter Loader as the Australian tour was approaching. Pakistan elected to bat first despite rain delaying the start until 2.30pm, and Brian Statham promptly trapped Hanif Mohammad lbw from the sixth ball without a run scored. Tyson's first over was wayward, but in his third over he bowled Alimuddin and Maqsood Ahmed with successive balls after Alimuddin had hit two fours and scored the first 10 runs. Loader came on at first change and claimed his maiden scalp as he bowled Waqar Hasan with the score on 26. Imtiaz Ahmed hit four fours before Pakistan collapsed from 51-4 to 51-7. Imtiaz was caught behind off a bouncer, Wazir Mohammad was run out and Fazal Mahmood caught behind off a good length ball.

Captain Abdul Kardar reached 36 before wicketkeeper Godfrey Evans accepted his third catch as Pakistan became 77-8. Shujauddin, however, showed strong tail-end resistance, while Zulfiqar Ahmed hit three fours before becoming Loader's third victim. Mahmood Hussain struck four fours in an invaluable 23 before becoming Tyson's fourth scalp as Pakistan totalled 133. Shujauddin remained unbeaten on 16 from 113 minutes.

England scored one run in two overs before stumps, and there was no chance of play the next day after heavy rain saturated the field. Day three began 45 minutes late, and balls regularly rose sharply off a good length in sunny weather. Reg Simpson departed early when he edged to slip, and Len Hutton fell 20 runs later to a catch behind. Runs weren't easy to score, as shown by Fazal delivering 11 maidens in 15 overs at one stage. England remained two wickets down at lunch, before Peter May's dismissal to a catch at slip was followed by Tom Graveney and Evans departing cheaply as England slipped to 69-5.

Denis Compton, however, was dropped a few times, and he subsequently showed determination and aggression. Johnny Wardle and Tyson departed similarly, and Compton passed 50 before becoming Fazal's fourth caught behind victim. Statham soon fell to Hussain as England still trailed by 17 runs, before Jim McConnon and Loader narrowed the deficit. Catches accounted for all 10 dismissals after Fazal took the final catch to go with his six wickets. The Pakistani fans in the crowd were

England's Frank Tyson took 4-35 in his Test debut as Pakistan was dismissed for 133, before Pakistan recovered to win the Test.

happy with their team's three-run lead as the country marked its seventh Independence Day.

The pitch became conducive to spin as the conditions dried out, and Shujauddin opened after his stonewalling first innings. Hanif scored the first 19 runs, including 16 from boundaries before he was caught at slip off Wardle. Shujauddin was solid for nearly an hour before he too fell to Wardle, who subsequently caught Maqsood off McConnon. Waqar was run out, and Pakistan struggled to 63-4 at stumps before collapsing further as Wardle starred on day four.

Imtiaz was caught by Wardle off Tyson before a run was added, and then Kardar and Alimuddin resisted briefly before Wardle dismissed both, with Alimuddin lbw for a 28-minute duck. Wardle also dismissed Fazal as Pakistan flopped to 82-8, but once again the tail made precious runs. Wazir and Zulfiqar were stoic and had some luck, and Zulfiqar scored 34 in a 58-run stand in 117 minutes. The last wicket partnership produced 24 runs as Wazir moved to an unbeaten 42 in 160 minutes. Wardle finished with seven wickets and three catches, including one off his bowling. Although Pakistan's last two partnerships doubled

England's Peter May (left) and Peter Loader (right) in action during the 1950s.

the total, England's target of 168 did not seem daunting.

Hutton edged an outswinger behind with the score on 15 before Simpson and May added 51 runs in 40 minutes. May played splendidly while Simpson looked comfortable until he was caught-and-bowled by Zulfiqar. Compton established himself while May elegantly progressed to 53. Kardar sought to take Fazal out of the attack but the bowler snatched the ball and was able to overrule his captain. Fazal incredibly broke through immediately as May was caught by none other than Kardar. With England only 59 runs shy of victory, Evans was sent in, perhaps in an attempt to win the game in the remaining 30 minutes that day. Fazal, however, bowled Evans behind his legs for three, and the match suddenly swung Pakistan's way. Shujauddin trapped Graveney lbw for a duck before Compton edged a Fazal leg cutter to the wicketkeeper in the second-last over before stumps. England needed 43 runs with four wickets remaining on day five, and McConnon was nursing a finger injury.

Wardle gained a reprieve when he was dropped at slip, before Tyson became the third batsman to be caught behind off Fazal for the second time. A fielding change paid off as Wardle directed a catch to backward short leg, before Loader

was caught off Hussain as the total was still 138. England needed a 30-run last wicket partnership for victory, and scored five before McConnon pushed the ball to cover and called for a risky single. Hanif had just one stump to aim at but he struck it with perhaps the most crucial throw of his career to seal a remarkable win for Pakistan. Amidst several Pakistanis who contributed well, the star was Fazal with match figures of 12-99 from 60 overs.

Amazingly, Pakistan had drawn the series after being outplayed in the first three Tests and in parts of the fourth Test. Just as incredible was Pakistan becoming the first country to win a Test in its maiden series in England. Pakistan's only previous Test series was in 1952–53, when India won 2-1 at home.

PAKISTAN 1ST INNINGS		
Hanif Mohammad	lbw b Statham	0
Alimuddin	b Tyson	10
Waqar Hasan	b Loader	7
Maqsood Ahmed	b Tyson	0
Imtiaz Ahmed†	c Evans b Tyson	23
AH Kardar*	c Evans b Statham	36
Wazir Mohammad	run out	0
Fazal Mahmood	c Evans b Loader	0
Shujauddin	not out	16
Zulfiqar Ahmed	c Compton b Loader	16
Mahmood Hussain	b Tyson	23
Extras	(nb 2)	2
Total		133

Fall of wickets 0, 10, 10, 26, 51, 51, 51, 77, 106, 133

	O	M	R	W
JB Statham	11	5	26	2
FH Tyson	13.4	3	35	4
PJ Loader	18	5	35	3
JE McConnon	9	2	35	0

ENGLAND 1ST INNINGS		
L Hutton*	c Imtiaz Ahmed b Fazal Mahmood	14
RT Simpson	c Kardar b Mahmood Hussain	2
PBH May	c Kardar b Fazal Mahmood	26
DCS Compton	c Imtiaz Ahmed b Fazal Mahmood	53
TW Graveney	c Hanif Mohammad b Fazal Mahmood	1
TG Evans†	c Maqsood Ahmed b Mahmood Hussain	0
JH Wardle	c Imtiaz Ahmed b Fazal Mahmood	8
FH Tyson	c Imtiaz Ahmed b Fazal Mahmood	3
JE McConnon	c Fazal Mahmood b Mahmood Hussain	11
JB Statham	c Shujauddin b Mahmood Hussain	1
PJ Loader	not out	8
Extras	(lb 1, w 1, nb 1)	3
Total		130

Fall of wickets 6, 26, 56, 63, 69, 92, 106, 115, 116, 130

	O	M	R	W
Fazal Mahmood	30	16	53	6
Mahmood Hussain	21.3	6	58	4
Zulfiqar Ahmed	5	2	8	0
Shujauddin	3	0	8	0

PAKISTAN 2ND INNINGS		
Hanif Mohammad	c Graveney b Wardle	19
Shujauddin	c May b Wardle	12
Waqar Hasan	run out	9
Maqsood Ahmed	c Wardle b McConnon	4
Imtiaz Ahmed†	c Wardle b Tyson	12
AH Kardar*	c & b Wardle	17
Alimuddin	lbw b Wardle	0
Wazir Mohammad	not out	42
Fazal Mahmood	b Wardle	6
Zulfiqar Ahmed	c May b Wardle	34
Mahmood Hussain	c Statham b Wardle	6
Extras	(b 3)	3
Total		164

Fall of wickets 19, 38, 43, 54, 63, 73, 76, 82, 140, 164

	O	M	R	W
JB Statham	18	7	37	0
FH Tyson	9	2	22	1
PJ Loader	16	6	26	0
JE McConnon	14	5	20	1
JH Wardle	35	16	56	7

Toss: Pakistan   Umpires: D Davies and FS Lee

ENGLAND 2ND INNINGS		
L Hutton*	c Imtiaz Ahmed b Fazal Mahmood	5
RT Simpson	c & b Zulfiqar Ahmed	27
PBH May	c Kardar b Fazal Mahmood	53
DCS Compton	c Imtiaz Ahmed b Fazal Mahmood	29
TG Evans†	b Fazal Mahmood	3
TW Graveney	lbw b Shujauddin	0
JH Wardle	c Shujauddin b Fazal Mahmood	9
FH Tyson	c Imtiaz Ahmed b Fazal Mahmood	3
PJ Loader	c Waqar Hasan b Mahmood Hussain	5
JE McConnon	run out	2
JB Statham	not out	2
Extras	(lb 2, nb 3)	5
Total		143

Fall of wickets 15, 66, 109, 115, 116, 121, 131, 138, 138, 143

	O	M	R	W
Fazal Mahmood	30	11	46	6
Mahmood Hussain	14	4	32	1
Zulfiqar Ahmed	14	2	35	1
Shujauddin	10	1	25	1

Pakistan won by 24 runs

Australia v England
Second Test at the Sydney Cricket Ground

1954–55
December 17, 18, 20, 21, 22 (1954)

It takes a lot of character for a team to bounce back after losing the opening Test of a series by an innings and 154 runs. Yet the second Test of the 1954–55 Ashes proved nothing like the first Test which Australia won so comprehensively.

England entered the second Test with a somewhat different look as Godfrey Evans, Tom Graveney, Johnny Wardle and Bob Appleyard were chosen in place of Keith Andrew, Denis Compton, Reg Simpson and Alec Bedser. Australia meanwhile included Jim Burke and Alan Davidson in place of injured duo Ian Johnson and Keith Miller. After England opted to field first and conceded 601 runs in the first Test at Brisbane, Australia opted to field first in the second Test at Sydney following an overnight thunderstorm. Australia's decision appeared worthwhile.

Trevor Bailey hadn't scored in 37 minutes when Ray Lindwall uprooted his middle-stump, and England was 19-2 when Peter May drove at a Ron Archer inswinger and was caught at short square leg. Len Hutton was intent on survival, scoring 30 in 132 minutes before Davidson snared a great one-handed catch at short leg. Bill Johnston struck again when Tom Graveney edged a push and was caught at slip. Colin Cowdrey provided resistance but the visitors were still on the slide. John Edrich was easily caught at gully off Archer, Frank Tyson bowled by Lindwall, and Evans caught behind off Archer as the tourists collapsed to 88-7.

Davidson had Cowdrey caught behind and Appleyard brilliantly caught by Graeme Hole at slip as England plunged to 111-9. Left-handers Wardle and Brian Statham exceeded expectations as they hit out and put on the highest stand of the innings, 43. Wardle struck 17 runs in a Johnston over, and top-scored with 35 before being caught at long on.

England's Peter May (left) and Australia's Ian Johnson (right) signing autographs during the 1954–55 Ashes series.

Bailey struck a vital blow with the final ball before stumps when he had Arthur Morris glove a catch to leg slip. Australia 18-1. Les Favell and Burke added 47 in 40 minutes the next morning before Bailey struck after changing ends, with Favell caught at second slip. Australia reached 100-2 before Bailey and Tyson bowled superbly to curtail Australia's progress after lunch. Australia slipped to 104-4

following the departures of Burke and Neil Harvey. Hole and Richie Benaud looked unconvincing although they made starts, but were dismissed before the hosts established a lead. Archer had a few narrow escapes as he and Davidson pushed the score along, and Australia led by 39 runs when Statham bowled Davidson. Another 20 runs were added before Archer, who had pulled Appleyard for the only six of the match, was caught at third slip for 49. Tyson and Bailey finished with four wickets each as Australia's lead was restricted to 74 with three days remaining.

Bailey avoided a pair but he failed again when Archer had him caught behind. Hutton again departed after making a start, before Graveney edged behind three balls later as England fell to 55-3. After lunch, May and Cowdrey overcame adversity and toughed it out, defending repeatedly while ready to pounce on loose deliveries. May pulled well while Cowdrey's driving was impressive. The duo added 116 runs in 193 minutes before Cowdrey surprisingly lost his cool and was caught trying to clout a Benaud delivery.

England was 204-4 at stumps with May on 98, before

Australia delayed taking the new ball as the outfield was wet. May quickly reached 100 but scored only three runs in the next 50 minutes. After the new ball was taken, May was bowled as he came forward to a late inswinger from Lindwall, before Tyson ducked into a short Lindwall delivery and was struck on the back of the head.

With Tyson retired hurt, Hole dropped Evans before Edrich was bowled by Archer, leaving England 232-6. Tyson returned and was again bowled by Lindwall, Archer's third wicket being followed by Lindwall's third wicket. England was 250-9 before another vital last wicket partnership unfolded. Statham hit three fours and scored 25 as 46 runs were added before Johnston also claimed a third scalp.

Australia's target of 223 looked tough as Statham bowled with hostility. Edrich spilled a sharp chance to reprieve Favell in Statham's first over, before Statham beat Morris four times and then trapped him lbw just before tea. Australia 27-1. Tyson also bowled with venom despite his head knock, and his sixth delivery after tea dismissed Favell as Edrich made no mistake this time. Harvey began

scratchily but settled in, and Burke didn't score for nearly an hour before Australia began the final day on 72-2 following overnight rain. With the pitch having been covered, the surface became less lively but was not slow.

Tyson's first over on day five was crucial as yorkers wrecked Burke's and Hole's stumps. Hutton surprisingly brought on Bailey and Appleyard, and the batsmen may have felt relief. But this proved false as Benaud skied a hook in Appleyard's second over and was caught by Tyson. Harvey reached a defiant half-century and was Australia's best hope as the lunch score was 118-5, before another collapse followed. Tyson bowled Archer before Statham had Davidson brilliantly caught behind. Tyson gained some payback as he bowled Lindwall with another splendid yorker, before Statham cracked Langley's off-stump. England's last wicket partnerships, having tallied 89 runs, were telling as the hosts needed a final wicket partnership of 78.

A miracle was possible as Harvey sought as much of the strike as he could. Johnston managed two boundaries, and

scored 11 from 15 balls as 39 runs were added in 79 balls before Tyson had him caught behind. Harvey was stranded on 92 and must have lamented a lack of support. After adopting a shorter run-up following unflattering figures of 1-160 in the first Test, Tyson had match figures of 10-130, while Bailey's bowling in Australia's first innings and Statham's contribution in Australia's second innings could not be underestimated. The complexion of the series had turned, and England's eventual 3-1 series win would have seemed incomprehensible after the first Test.

Opposite: The England touring party to Australia in 1954–55.
Above left: Australia spin bowler Richie Benaud.
Above right: England fast bowler Frank 'Typhoon' Tyson.

ENGLAND 1ST INNINGS		
L Hutton*	c Davidson b Johnston	30
TE Bailey	b Lindwall	0
PBH May	c Johnston b Archer	5
TW Graveney	c Favell b Johnston	21
MC Cowdrey	c Langley b Davidson	23
WJ Edrich	c Benaud b Archer	10
FH Tyson	b Lindwall	0
TG Evans†	c Langley b Archer	3
JH Wardle	c Burke b Johnston	35
R Appleyard	c Hole b Davidson	8
JB Statham	not out	14
Extras	(lb 5)	5
Total		154

Fall of wickets 14, 19, 58, 63, 84, 85, 88, 99, 111, 154

	O	M	R	W
RR Lindwall	17	3	47	2
RG Archer	12	7	12	3
AK Davidson	12	3	34	2
WA Johnston	13.3	1	56	3

AUSTRALIA 1ST INNINGS		
LE Favell	c Graveney b Bailey	26
AR Morris*	c Hutton b Bailey	12
JW Burke	c Graveney b Bailey	44
RN Harvey	c Cowdrey b Tyson	12
GB Hole	b Tyson	12
R Benaud	lbw b Statham	20
RG Archer	c Hutton b Tyson	49
AK Davidson	b Statham	20
RR Lindwall	c Evans b Tyson	19
GRA Langley†	b Bailey	5
WA Johnston	not out	0
Extras	(b 5, lb 2, nb 2)	9
Total		228

Fall of wickets 18, 65, 100, 104, 122, 141, 193, 213, 224, 228

	O	M	R	W
JB Statham	18	1	83	2
TE Bailey	17.4	3	59	4
FH Tyson	13	2	45	4
R Appleyard	7	1	32	0

ENGLAND 2ND INNINGS		
L Hutton*	c Benaud b Johnston	28
TE Bailey	c Langley b Archer	6
PBH May	b Lindwall	104
TW Graveney	c Langley b Johnston	0
MC Cowdrey	c Archer b Benaud	54
WJ Edrich	b Archer	29
FH Tyson	b Lindwall	9
TG Evans†	c Lindwall b Archer	4
JH Wardle	lbw b Lindwall	8
R Appleyard	not out	19
JB Statham	c Langley b Johnston	25
Extras	(lb 6, nb 4)	10
Total		296

Fall of wickets 18, 55, 55, 171, 222, 232, 239, 249, 250, 296

	O	M	R	W
RR Lindwall	31	10	69	3
RG Archer	22	9	53	3
AK Davidson	13	2	52	0
WA Johnston	19.3	2	70	3
R Benaud	19	3	42	1

AUSTRALIA 2ND INNINGS		
LE Favell	c Edrich b Tyson	16
AR Morris*	lbw b Statham	10
JW Burke	b Tyson	14
RN Harvey	not out	92
GB Hole	b Tyson	0
R Benaud	c Tyson b Appleyard	12
RG Archer	b Tyson	6
AK Davidson	c Evans b Statham	5
RR Lindwall	b Tyson	8
GRA Langley†	b Statham	0
WA Johnston	c Evans b Tyson	11
Extras	(lb 7, nb 3)	10
Total		184

Fall of wickets 27, 34, 77, 77, 102, 122, 127, 136, 145, 184

	O	M	R	W
JB Statham	19	6	45	3
TE Bailey	6	0	21	0
FH Tyson	18.4	1	85	6
R Appleyard	6	1	12	1
JH Wardle	4	2	11	0

Toss: Australia   Umpires: MJ McInnes and RJJ Wright   England won by 38 runs

Pakistan v Australia
One-off Test at National Stadium, Karachi

1956-57
October 11, 12, 13, 15, 17 (1956)

As Peter Arnold wrote in *The Illustrated Encyclopedia of World Cricket*, "the first Test match ever played between Australia and Pakistan was historic in various ways." The contest was a one-off and occurred after Australia's 2-1 Ashes series loss in England, remembered for England spinner Jim Laker's 19 wickets in the fourth Test at Old Trafford. Pakistan was still finding its way in Test cricket after the country's memorable drawn series in England in 1954. A decisive factor in the inaugural Pakistan versus Australia Test was the use of a matting pitch. Pakistan's biggest hero in the country's 1954 win over England, Fazal Mahmood, was known to be good at swinging and cutting the ball on these pitches.

Australia faced the music after winning the toss, and the batsmen struggled to adjust to the matting after being familiar with turf pitches. Australia reached 19-0 before losing 5-3 as Fazal dismissed Jim Burke, Neil Harvey and Colin McDonald. Keith Miller top scored but in one over had no answer to Fazal, who dismissed Ian Craig for a duck and accounted for Miller next as the tourists scored very slowly and struggled to 48-5. Richie Benaud became Fazal's sixth scalp before the accurate and persistent Khan Mohammad took the last four wickets as Australia was dismissed after tea for just 80 in 53.1 overs. Fazal and Khan bowled unchanged and were rewarded with great figures as nine victims were caught, including three by wicketkeeper Imtiaz Ahmed.

Miller struck early for Australia as he had Hanif Mohammad caught behind without scoring. Ron Archer had Alimuddin caught just before stumps, and the hosts finished the day uncertainly placed at 15-2. It was incredible to think that only 95 runs were scored in a day's play.

Alan Davidson struck first on day two before Waqar Hasan became the second batsman caught behind off Miller. From

Neil Harvey in classic attacking pose. Harvey had no answer to Pakistan's Fazal Mahmood as Pakistan routed the Australians on a matting pitch when the teams first met in Test cricket.

35-4, Pakistan doubled its total as the ball turned sharply, before Imtiaz edged a drive to slip off Benaud. The match was interestingly placed but the pendulum gradually swung Pakistan's way as captain Abdul Kardar was a bit bolder than the batsmen who preceded him. Wazir Mohammad was effective as well, although the scoring rate was slow throughout. Kardar scored 69 in a sixth wicket partnership of 104 before Ian Johnson trapped Kardar lbw and then bowled Wallis Mathias as the total was still 174. Wazir went on to score 67 before he too fell to Johnson, who finished with four wickets as Pakistan was all out for 199 just before stumps.

Fazal set the Australians back on their heels as he bowled McDonald and Harvey with just 10 runs on the board. Burke and Craig reached double figures before they too fell to Fazal, and then Khan bowled Miller who had also registered double figures without reaching 20. As the scoring remained slow, the strongest resistance from the Australians followed with the sixth wicket partnership. Archer scored 27 before he was caught by Fazal off Khan, and another 27 runs were added before stumps to take Australia to a 19-run lead as Benaud registered a gallant half-century. A rest day followed, and then Benaud added just three runs to his overnight score before Fazal bowled him.

Further accuracy from Fazal saw Lindwall and Johnson dismissed for ducks, and Australia led by just 24 runs. Gil Langley, however, combined with Davidson for a gritty last wicket stand as they sought to make Pakistan earn the last wicket. Davidson reached 37 before he was caught behind off Khan, leaving Langley unbeaten on 13. Khan finished with seven wickets for the Test while Fazal had magical figures of 13-114, and Pakistan had 160 minutes of play on day four as well as all of day five to score the necessary 69 runs to win.

Hanif was caught off Davidson with the total on seven, and then Alimuddin and Gul Mahomed were extremely careful as the Australians persisted without necessarily looking threatening. The scoring dawdled as many overs conceded one or no runs, and this earned the ire of the spectators who yelled and booed at the batsmen. "It got so bad at one stage that Alimuddin, who was at the crease, offered his bat to the crowd in disgust," Imtiaz commented in an article published in *Wisden Asia Cricket* magazine.

Pakistan amazingly finished day four still six runs shy of victory. The next day was a rest day due to a public holiday to mark the anniversary of the death of Pakistan's first Prime Minister, Liaquat Ali Khan. The cricketers subsequently returned to the action after the public holiday, and Pakistan polished off the required runs without loss to ensure the country had now beaten the two ancient Test-playing cricket nations.

Australia's Ray Lindwall (top) and Alan Davidson (below).

AUSTRALIA 1ST INNINGS		
CC McDonald	c Imtiaz Ahmed b Fazal Mahmood	17
JW Burke	c Mathias b Fazal Mahmood	4
RN Harvey	lbw b Fazal Mahmood	2
ID Craig	c Imtiaz Ahmed b Fazal Mahmood	0
KR Miller	c Wazir Mohammad b Fazal Mahmood	21
RG Archer	c Imtiaz Ahmed b Khan Mohammad	10
R Benaud	c Waqar Hasan b Fazal Mahmood	4
AK Davidson	c Kardar b Khan Mohammad	3
RR Lindwall	c Mathias b Khan Mohammad	2
IWG Johnson*	not out	13
GRA Langley†	c Waqar Hasan b Khan Mohammad	1
Extras	(lb 2, nb 1)	3
Total		80

Fall of wickets 19, 23, 24, 43, 48, 52, 56, 65, 76, 80

	O	M	R	W
Fazal Mahmood	27	11	34	6
Khan Mohammad	26.1	9	43	4

PAKISTAN 1ST INNINGS		
Hanif Mohammad	c Langley b Miller	0
Alimuddin	c Lindwall b Archer	10
Gul Mahomed	b Davidson	12
Imtiaz Ahmed†	c McDonald b Benaud	15
Waqar Hasan	c Langley b Miller	6
Wazir Mohammad	c & b Johnson	67
AH Kardar*	lbw b Johnson	69
W Mathias	b Johnson	0
Fazal Mahmood	not out	10
Zulfiqar Ahmed	c Langley b Lindwall	0
Khan Mohammad	b Johnson	3
Extras	(b 5, lb 2)	7
Total		199

Fall of wickets 3, 15, 25, 35, 70, 174, 174, 189, 190, 199

	O	M	R	W
RR Lindwall	27	8	42	1
KR Miller	17	5	40	2
RG Archer	4	0	18	1
AK Davidson	6	4	6	1
R Benaud	17	5	36	1
IWG Johnson	20.3	3	50	4

AUSTRALIA 2ND INNINGS		
CC McDonald	b Fazal Mahmood	3
JW Burke	c Mathias b Fazal Mahmood	10
RN Harvey	b Fazal Mahmood	4
ID Craig	lbw b Fazal Mahmood	18
KR Miller	b Khan Mohammad	11
RG Archer	c Fazal Mahmood b Khan Mohammad	27
R Benaud	b Fazal Mahmood	56
AK Davidson	c Imtiaz Ahmed b Khan Mohammad	37
RR Lindwall	lbw b Fazal Mahmood	0
IWG Johnson*	b Fazal Mahmood	0
GRA Langley†	not out	13
Extras	(lb 2, nb 6)	8
Total		187

Fall of wickets 6, 10, 23, 46, 47, 111, 141, 141, 143, 187

	O	M	R	W
Fazal Mahmood	48	17	80	7
Khan Mohammad	40.5	13	69	3
Zulfiqar Ahmed	9	1	18	0
AH Kardar	12	5	12	0

PAKISTAN 2ND INNINGS		
Hanif Mohammad	c Harvey b Davidson	5
Alimuddin	not out	34
Gul Mahomed	not out	27
Extras	(lb 1, nb 2)	3
Total	(1 wicket)	69

Did not bat Imtiaz Ahmed†, Waqar Hasan, Wazir Mohammad, AH Kardar*, W Mathias, Fazal Mahmood, Zulfiqar Ahmed, Khan Mohammad

Fall of wickets 7

	O	M	R	W
RR Lindwall	16	8	22	0
KR Miller	12	4	18	0
RG Archer	3.5	3	1	0
AK Davidson	9	5	9	1
IWG Johnson	7.5	2	16	0

Toss: Australia   Umpires: Daud Khan and Idrees Baig   Pakistan won by 9 wickets

South Africa v England
Fourth Test at New Wanderers Stadium, Johannesburg

1956-57
February 15, 16, 18, 19, 20 (1957)

South Africa had never beaten England on a turf pitch in South Africa, until a memorable Test took place at Johannesburg in February 1957. England looked set for a series win after victories by 131 and 312 runs in the first two Tests, before a drawn third Test meant South Africa remained a chance of drawing the series.

The hosts won the toss and made use of a surface that looked batsman-friendly. Tony Pithey scored just 10, before Trevor Goddard and John Waite provided a platform for a strong total. A couple of edges fell safely, but the duo showed good skill. When Brian Statham had Waite caught behind, Waite had scored 61 in a 112-run partnership in 190 minutes. When Goddard was bowled by Trevor Bailey for 67, South Africa was more modestly placed at 151-3. A turning point, however, came as Doug Insole spilled a slips catch to reprieve Roy McLean on three.

Bailey, however, accounted for Ken Funston to have South Africa 172-4 and bring debutant Chris Duckworth to the crease while McLean was scratchy. Duckworth was tied down but McLean warmed to the task and posted a half-century, before Duckworth was out early on day two as he remained on 13, which included two boundaries in 87 minutes. McLean failed to score for the next 17 minutes as Russell Endean sped to 13 before Statham bowled him, leaving the score 251-6.

Clive van Ryneveld was steady while McLean eyed his second century in consecutive Tests, before he was run out for 93 after hitting 13 fours and a six in his 274-minute innings. South Africa's captain, van Ryneveld, scored 36 in more than two hours before Johnny Wardle and Jim Laker combined to take 3-12 and have South Africa dismissed for 340.

England openers Peter Richardson and Bailey were so slow and unconvincing that the score was 40-2 after 102 minutes

when they were removed. Insole and Peter May added 47 runs before stumps, and continued in a similar vein on day three. The third wicket fell in bizarre circumstances with the total on 131 after Insole survived an lbw appeal against off spinner Hugh Tayfield. Goddard fielded the ball at slip but Insole started running as he thought the ball went through the cordon, and he was run out. The needless dismissal was compounded just four runs later and in the last over before lunch when May played a Neil Adcock delivery onto the stumps, after hitting seven fours and a six in his 61 from 189 minutes.

Denis Compton scored only 13 runs in the next session as Tayfield bowled impeccably, and had Colin Cowdrey and Godfrey Evans caught. Wardle clubbed two sixes and a four in a quick 16 before he too was caught off Tayfield, making England a precarious 176-7. The lower order, however, provided resistance. Laker added 37 runs with Compton, whose innings comprised of 42 runs in 205 minutes before he was ninth out when he was caught off Peter Heine. A last wicket partnership of 24 reduced England's deficit to 89 before Goddard took a well-deserved wicket, having conceded just 22 runs in 25.2 overs.

Pithey and Goddard survived the one over before stumps, and were painfully slow the next day against admittedly very accurate bowling. Just 62 runs were eked out in an opening stand that lasted 145 minutes before Pithey was bowled by Laker for just 18. Funston hit a six before South Africa crashed from 91-1 to 104-6 to put England right back in the match. Goddard was caught behind off Bailey for 49, McLean caught off Statham for a duck, Funston run out for 23, Endean caught off Bailey for two and Duckworth bowled by Wardle for three. Another 25 runs were added before South Africa lost 2-3, with Statham dismissing van Ryneveld and Waite before Wardle dismissed Heine for a duck. Tayfield helped put on 11 runs for the last wicket before Adcock was run out, leaving England a target of 232 to seal the series.

Tayfield came on early and had Bailey caught for one. England was 19-1 at stumps after 45 minutes of batting. Tayfield subsequently bowled unchanged from one end on the last day and again was accurate as he spun the ball. Richardson progressed to 39 before Tayfield bowled him, and then Cowdrey knuckled down while Insole was already entrenched. Their battle with Tayfield and Goddard was absorbing, and England slowly gained the upper hand as the score reached 147-2, 25 minutes after lunch.

The match suddenly changed as Insole was caught by Tayfield off Goddard, ending an 82-run stand from 100 minutes. May was caught by Endean without scoring, and Compton caught

by Goddard for one as England fell to 156-5. Wardle, however, hit the ball confidently while Cowdrey was tied down, and 30 runs were added before Tayfield claimed his fifth wicket of the innings as Wardle was caught behind. England needed 46 runs in the last session as four wickets remained, and Evans hit a vital boundary before Tayfield bowled him for eight.

England was in trouble at 199-8 when Tayfield took a caught-and-bowled to dismiss Cowdrey, England's best hope, after he lasted 200 minutes for his 55. Another nine runs were added before Duckworth held a catch to account for Laker. Six runs were added in the next nine minutes, meaning England needed 19 more when Loader chanced his arm and lofted Tayfield to long-on. Stationed there was Tayfield's brother Arthur, substituting for an injured Funston. Arthur Tayfield took the catch to seal South Africa's win and give his brother his ninth wicket of the innings and 13th of the match. Hugh Tayfield was chaired off the field as South Africa's win was its first against England on South African soil for 26 years. The hosts went on to win the last Test by 58 runs to draw the series, an impressive feat after starting the series with heavy losses.

Opposite: England bowler Jim Laker.
Above: South Africa's Neil Adcock.
Below: Trevor Goddard.

SOUTH AFRICA 1ST INNINGS

AJ Pithey	c Wardle b Bailey	10
TL Goddard	b Bailey	67
JHB Waite†	c Evans b Statham	61
KJ Funston	c Evans b Bailey	20
RA McLean	run out	93
CAR Duckworth	c Wardle b Loader	13
WR Endean	b Statham	13
CB van Ryneveld*	c Cowdrey b Laker	36
HJ Tayfield	c Bailey b Wardle	10
PS Heine	not out	1
NAT Adcock	lbw b Wardle	6
Extras	(lb 8, w 1, nb 1)	10
Total		340

Fall of wickets 22, 134, 151, 172, 238, 251, 309, 328, 333, 340

	O	M	R	W
JB Statham	23	5	81	2
PJ Loader	23	3	78	1
TE Bailey	21	3	54	3
JH Wardle	19.6	4	68	2
JC Laker	15	3	49	1

ENGLAND 1ST INNINGS

PE Richardson	c Tayfield b Heine	11
TE Bailey	c Waite b Adcock	13
DJ Insole	run out	47
PBH May*	b Adcock	61
DCS Compton	c Pithey b Heine	42
MC Cowdrey	c Goddard b Tayfield	8
TG Evans†	c Endean b Tayfield	7
JH Wardle	c Goddard b Tayfield	16
JC Laker	lbw b Tayfield	17
PJ Loader	c Endean b Goddard	13
JB Statham	not out	12
Extras	(lb 1, nb 3)	4
Total		251

Fall of wickets 25, 40, 131, 135, 152, 160, 176, 213, 227, 251

	O	M	R	W
NAT Adcock	21	5	52	2
PS Heine	23	6	54	2
TL Goddard	25.2	15	22	1
HJ Tayfield	37	15	79	4
CB van Ryneveld	8	0	40	0

SOUTH AFRICA 2ND INNINGS

AJ Pithey	b Laker	18
TL Goddard	c Evans b Bailey	49
KJ Funston	run out	23
RA McLean	c Cowdrey b Statham	0
WR Endean	c Insole b Bailey	2
CAR Duckworth	b Wardle	3
JHB Waite†	c Cowdrey b Statham	17
CB van Ryneveld*	c & b Statham	12
HJ Tayfield	not out	12
PS Heine	c Insole b Wardle	0
NAT Adcock	run out	1
Extras	(b 4, lb 1)	5
Total		142

Fall of wickets 62, 91, 94, 95, 97, 104, 129, 130, 131, 142

	O	M	R	W
JB Statham	13	1	37	3
PJ Loader	13	3	33	0
TE Bailey	13	4	12	2
JH Wardle	14	4	29	2
JC Laker	7	1	26	1

ENGLAND 2ND INNINGS

PE Richardson	b Tayfield	39
TE Bailey	c Endean b Tayfield	1
DJ Insole	c Tayfield b Goddard	68
MC Cowdrey	c & b Tayfield	55
PBH May*	c Endean b Tayfield	0
DCS Compton	c Goddard b Tayfield	1
JH Wardle	c Waite b Tayfield	22
TG Evans†	b Tayfield	8
JC Laker	c Duckworth b Tayfield	5
PJ Loader	c sub (A Tayfield) b Tayfield	7
JB Statham	not out	4
Extras	(b 1, lb 3)	4
Total		214

Fall of wickets 10, 65, 147, 148, 156, 186, 196, 199, 208, 214

	O	M	R	W
NAT Adcock	8	1	22	0
PS Heine	8	1	21	0
TL Goddard	25	5	54	1
HJ Tayfield	37	11	113	9

Toss: South Africa   Umpires: JH McMenamin and BV Malan   South Africa won by 17 runs

England v West Indies
First Test at Edgbaston, Birmingham

1957
May 30, 31, June 1, 3, 4 (1957)

England touring team to the West Indies in 1957.

Test cricket's return to Edgbaston after a 28-year absence "generated a Test match that had more twists and turns than an Alfred Hitchcock thriller, and it produced cricket of outstanding quality". This was Norman Giller's description in his book *The World's Greatest Cricket Matches*, with regard to the first Test of the 1957 series involving England and the West Indies.

Roy Gilchrist bowled with hostility in his Test debut after England won the toss and chose to bat. Gilchrist and fellow debutant Rohan Kanhai combined for the first dismissal when Brian Close was caught behind for 15. However it was soon evident that Sonny Ramadhin was the danger. England's batsmen were confused and may have become mentally disturbed as they found it hard to tell if Ramadhin would bowl off-breaks or leg-breaks. Interestingly, his stock delivery seemed to be the straight ones. Ramadhin bowled Doug Insole with the total on 61 before captain Peter May looked solid, as did opener Peter Richardson. They added 43 runs before Richardson was caught off Ramadhin, who caused a collapse after the score reached 115-3.

May was caught by Weekes before Trevor Bailey and Tony Lock were bowled cheaply. Colin Cowdrey was caught by Gilchrist as England crashed to 121-7, and then 130-8 when Jim Laker became Ramadhin's seventh scalp. The total was 150 when Gilchrist bowled Godfrey Evans, before 36 runs were added for the last wicket. Brian Statham scored 13 when Denis Atkinson bowled him, leaving Fred Trueman unconquered on 29, which included three fours and a six. Trueman struck early in the West Indies reply when he yorked Bruce Pairaudeau, but it was England's only joy of the day as Kanhai and Clyde Walcott took the visitors to 83-1 at stumps.

Statham had Kanhai lbw with the first ball of day two, before Walcott pulled a leg muscle as he ran a single. He collapsed and soon had Pairaudeau run for him. Walcott batted well but Everton Weekes scratched around for nine, before Garry Sobers showed confidence. Walcott reached 90 after more than four hours before being caught behind off Laker as the West Indians were just four runs shy of a first innings lead. Sobers was on 53 while the tourists led by 11 runs when he cut venomously, only to see Bailey take a splendid diving catch. Trueman and Statham used the new ball, but England's recovery was dented despite O'Neill 'Collie' Smith and Frank Worrell playing and missing at times. Smith forged to 70 and Worrell to 48 as the visitors finished the day on 316-5. Worrell was hampered by a knee injury, and Pairaudeau was again used as a runner.

The sixth wicket partnership extended to 190 before Statham bowled Worrell with the last ball before lunch on day

three. All up, Pairaudeau was a runner for nearly nine hours after being dismissed for one. In his first appearance against England, Smith scored 161 before the last four wickets fell quickly, with three scalps to Laker before Gilchrist was run out. The West Indies led by 288 runs but took to the field without injured duo Worrell and Walcott, before suffering another setback as Gilchrist limped off after opening the bowling with Ramadhin. Richardson scored 34 in an opening stand of 63 when caught by a substitute fielder off Ramadhin, who soon bowled Insole for a duck. After entering the rest day on 102-2, England was in strife when a revitalised Gilchrist struck just 20 minutes into day four with the dismissal of Close.

May and Cowdrey subsequently knuckled down, and nullified Ramadhin by coming well forward to him and often using their pads. The batting duo showed marvellous concentration, and by the end of the day the game had changed dramatically as England was 378-3, with May on 193 and Cowdrey 78. Ramadhin bowled 48 wicketless overs during the day and conceded just 74 runs. The batsmen didn't take risks, and May's cover driving was a sight to behold.

After defending resolutely until he reached his century, Cowdrey unleashed an array of drives and cuts. When he was caught at long on for 154, he and May had put on 411 runs in 500 minutes. Evans hit five fours as he and May put on 59 runs in a mere 30 minutes before England declared on 583-4. May finished with 285 not out, which included 25 fours and two sixes in nearly 10 hours. Only two balls were used in England's second innings, and the second ball was used for 162 overs. Ramadhin had incredibly bowled 588 deliveries in the innings, and 774 in the match. It was equally amazing that no wides or no-balls were delivered in the entire contest.

A draw appeared inevitable as the tourists needed 296 runs in 140 minutes for victory. Trueman had other ideas as he had Kanhai caught by Close for one before bowling Pairaudeau for seven. Statham and Trueman tallied only seven overs before spinners Laker and Lock bowled in tandem while there were several fielders in close. Sobers hit three fours before being caught by Cowdrey off Lock, and Sobers' departure spelt doom for the tourists. The injured Worrell was caught by May off Lock for nought, and the wounded Walcott was caught by Lock off Laker

for one to reignite England's victory hopes as the score was 43-5.

Weekes and Smith, however, were stubborn, and Weekes scored half of the team's 66 runs before Trueman caught him off Lock with 41 minutes left. Smith and captain John Goddard defended grimly, with Goddard mostly using his pads as time ticked away. Smith lasted 64 minutes before Laker had him lbw with seven minutes left, and time ran out on England. Goddard remained scoreless while Atkinson struck a boundary before surviving until the finish with the West Indies 72-7 from 60 overs. Having almost snatched an unbelievable come-from-behind victory at Edgbaston, England went on to record three innings victories to win the series 3-0.

Opposite: Everton Weekes, who, with fellow Barbados cricketers Clyde Walcott (below left) and Frank Worrell (inset), formed the 'Three Ws' in the great West Indies teams of the 1940s and 1950s. Following page: A young Garry Sobers in action for the West Indies against England in 1957.

ENGLAND 1ST INNINGS

PE Richardson	c Walcott b Ramadhin	47
DB Close	c Kanhai b Gilchrist	15
DJ Insole	b Ramadhin	20
PBH May*	c Weekes b Ramadhin	30
MC Cowdrey	c Gilchrist b Ramadhin	4
TE Bailey	b Ramadhin	1
GAR Lock	b Ramadhin	0
TG Evans†	b Gilchrist	14
JC Laker	b Ramadhin	7
FS Trueman	not out	29
JB Statham	b Atkinson	13
Extras	(b 3, lb 3)	6
Total		186

Fall of wickets 32, 61, 104, 115, 116, 118, 121, 130, 150, 186

	O	M	R	W
FMM Worrell	9	1	27	0
R Gilchrist	27	4	74	2
S Ramadhin	31	16	49	7
DS Atkinson	12.4	3	30	1

WEST INDIES 1ST INNINGS

BH Pairaudeau	b Trueman	1
RB Kanhai†	lbw b Statham	42
CL Walcott	c Evans b Laker	90
ED Weekes	b Trueman	9
GS Sobers	c Bailey b Statham	53
OG Smith	lbw b Laker	161
FMM Worrell	b Statham	81
JDC Goddard*	c Lock b Laker	24
DS Atkinson	c Statham b Laker	1
S Ramadhin	not out	5
R Gilchrist	run out	0
Extras	(b 1, lb 6)	7
Total		474

Fall of wickets 4, 83, 120, 183, 197, 387, 466, 469, 474, 474

	O	M	R	W
JB Statham	39	4	114	3
FS Trueman	30	4	99	2
TE Bailey	34	11	80	0
JC Laker	54	17	119	4
GAR Lock	34.4	15	55	0

ENGLAND 2ND INNINGS

PE Richardson	c sub b Ramadhin	34
DB Close	c Weekes b Gilchrist	42
DJ Insole	b Ramadhin	0
PBH May*	not out	285
MC Cowdrey	c sub b Smith	154
TG Evans†	not out	29
Extras	(b 23, lb 16)	39
Total	(4 wickets dec)	583

Did not bat TE Bailey, GAR Lock, JC Laker, FS Trueman, JB Statham
Fall of wickets 63, 65, 113, 524

	O	M	R	W
R Gilchrist	26	2	67	1
S Ramadhin	98	35	179	2
DS Atkinson	72	29	137	0
GS Sobers	30	4	77	0
OG Smith	26	4	72	1
JDC Goddard	6	2	12	0

WEST INDIES 2ND INNINGS

BH Pairaudeau	b Trueman	7
RB Kanhai†	c Close b Trueman	1
GS Sobers	c Cowdrey b Lock	14
ED Weekes	c Trueman b Lock	33
FMM Worrell	c May b Lock	0
CL Walcott	c Lock b Laker	1
OG Smith	lbw b Laker	5
JDC Goddard*	not out	0
DS Atkinson	not out	4
Extras	(b 7)	7
Total	(7 wickets)	72

Did not bat S Ramadhin, R Gilchrist
Fall of wickets 1, 9, 25, 27, 43, 66, 68

	O	M	R	W
JB Statham	2	0	6	0
FS Trueman	5	3	7	2
JC Laker	24	20	13	2
GAR Lock	27	19	31	3
DB Close	2	1	8	0

Toss: England   Umpires: DE Davies and CS Elliott   Match drawn

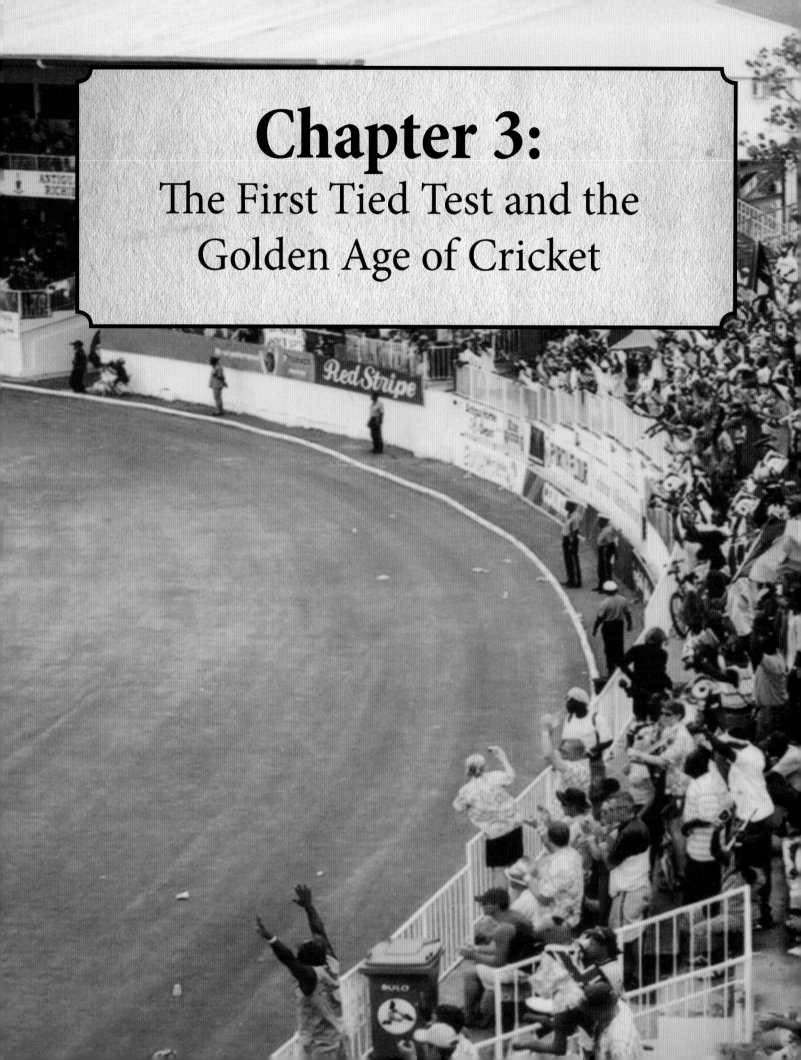

Chapter 3:
The First Tied Test and the Golden Age of Cricket

1960 – 1977

Antigua Recreation Ground.

Australia v West Indies

First Test at the Brisbane Cricket Ground (Woolloongabba)

1960-61

December 9, 10, 12, 13, 14 (1960)

A rare photo showing the extraordinary moment the West Indies players celebrated the final wicket of first Test of the 1960–61 series against Australia, which resulted in an historic tie.

Classic cricket matches cannot be discussed without mention of the first tied Test, which featured Australia and the West Indies at the Brisbane Cricket Ground in December 1960.

This historic Test fluctuated many times, as each team took it in turns to dominate while the contest was even at other times. Bowling first, Australia had the upper hand as three wickets to left-arm paceman Alan Davidson left the visitors 65-3. But the Australians hadn't made significant inroads, as legendary all-rounder Garry Sobers showed. He and captain Frank Worrell tilted the balance back the visitors' way with a 174-run partnership. Sobers played sumptuous strokes all around the wicket and accumulated 21 fours in his 174-minute innings. He reached 50 in 57 minutes and 100 in 125 minutes. Benaud generously applauded one thunderous straight drive off his bowling. Ian Meckiff was punished before he dismissed Sobers for 132, and Worrell scored a quieter 65 before the dismissals of the duo reduced the tourists from 239-3 to 243-5.

There was no sign of a collapse as the West Indies reached 359-7 at stumps. Joe Solomon matched Worrell's score, before the tail pushed on during the second morning. The eighth wicket fell at 366, before wicketkeeper Gerry Alexander and Wes Hall showed the class of top order batsmen. The tourists had compiled 453 by the time Lindsay Kline dismissed Alexander for 60 and Hall for 50.

Bob Simpson anchored Australia's first innings while fellow opener Colin McDonald scored more freely. McDonald contributed 57 of the first 84 runs before Sobers dismissed him. Neil Harvey made 15, and Simpson was eight runs shy of a century when Sonny Ramadhin bowled him. It was a crucial blow not long before stumps, which arrived with Australia trailing by 257 runs.

Norm O'Neill took centre stage on day three as he scored 181 in a marathon six-and-a-half hour performance. The game's complexion however could have been much different had O'Neill not had three escapes around the time he reached 50. O'Neill was not quite as sparkling as Sobers but was still very watchable as he hit 22 fours. Les Favell scored 45 before he was run out, and then left-handers Ken Mackay and Davidson also made vital runs without going on to a big score. Australia still had five wickets in hand when a first innings lead was established, but the lower order was far less effective than the West Indies' had been. There were two lbws to Hall and the second run out of the innings as a collapse of 36-5 confined the home side's lead to 52.

Davidson again dismissed Cammie Smith cheaply, this time as Smith incredibly drove a half-volley straight to the only outfielder. Davidson was again dangerous at times, although

Above: Bowler Sonny Ramadhin jokes with his West Indies teammates before the first Test in Brisbane in 1960.
Right: Wes Hall scored 50 in the first innings and took 9 wickets in the tied Test against Australia.

Conrad Hunte and Rohan Kanhai put on a second wicket partnership of 75 before a mini collapse of 39-3 somewhat changed the momentum. Mackay dismissed Hunte while Davidson took the key wickets of Kanhai and Sobers, who was bowled for 14. Worrell and Solomon however stonewalled the hosts once more; Worrell again making 65. The West Indians advanced from 127-4 before 210-4 was quickly reduced to 210-6. Another 31 runs were added before three wickets fell for 12 runs, and then the West Indies finished day four on 259-9. Hall and Valentine added 25 crucial runs on the final morning before Davidson claimed his 11th wicket of the match, and Australia had a shade over five hours in which to reach a target of 233.

Australia crashed to 7-2 after Hall dismissed Simpson and Harvey. Sobers dislocated his finger as he caught Harvey from a full length dive, before Alexander yanked the finger into place. Hall was still menacing after lunch, and he dismissed O'Neill and Favell while Worrell chipped in with the wicket of McDonald as a collapse of 8-3 reduced Australia to 57-5. Mackay grafted his way to 28 before Ramadhin bowled him, and an Australian victory looked fanciful with the score 92-6.

Davidson and Benaud however seemed unfazed. They launched a great counterattack which included speedy running between the wickets as they scored at the required run rate after Australia needed 123 runs and the West Indies four wickets in the last session. Benaud and Davidson withstood Hall's ferocity, and Hall took the new ball with 40 deliveries remaining. In the subsequent over there were four singles, a no-ball and a hooked boundary from Davidson. Davidson just avoided being run out off another delivery. Benaud drove Sobers for four in the next over, which cost nine runs to reduce Australia's task to just 10 runs in three overs. Only one run was scored in the third-last over, but Australia needed just seven runs when a splendid throw from Solomon ran out Davidson in the second-last over as a quick single was sought. Little did anyone know how crucial this would be.

Australia needed six runs from the last over with three wickets standing, and a leg bye from the first ball was followed by Benaud hooking at a risky bouncer from Hall and gloving a catch behind. Meckiff faced a dot ball before the batsmen stole a bye after the ball went down the leg-side to Alexander, and an alert Valentine prevented overthrows after Hall threw at the non-striker's stumps. Wally Grout spooned to mid wicket from the fifth ball, and fortuitously gained a single after Hall beat Kanhai to the ball and muffed the catch. Meckiff swung the next ball into the deep at square leg and sought a match-winning three. Hunte however chased and threw superbly, and Alexander

broke the stumps with Grout just short. With the scores tied, the left-handed Kline steered the second-last ball to square leg and took off. Solomon had one stump at which to aim at the striker's end, and his accuracy was again faultless as Meckiff was short of his ground when the bails flew. It took some conferring amongst players and umpires before the historic tied result was determined.

Top: Alf Valentine, the veteran 'calypso' bowler.
Bottom: Australia's Norm O'Neill, who scored 181 in the first innings of the tied Test in Brisbane.

WEST INDIES 1ST INNINGS

CC Hunte	c Benaud b Davidson	24
CW Smith	c Grout b Davidson	7
RB Kanhai	c Grout b Davidson	15
GS Sobers	c Kline b Meckiff	132
FMM Worrell*	c Grout b Davidson	65
JS Solomon	hit wicket b Simpson	65
PD Lashley	c Grout b Kline	19
FCM Alexander†	c Davidson b Kline	60
S Ramadhin	c Harvey b Davidson	12
WW Hall	st Grout b Kline	50
AL Valentine	not out	0
Extras	(lb 3, w 1)	4
Total		453

Fall of wickets 23, 42, 65, 239, 243, 283, 347, 366, 452, 453

	O	M	R	W
AK Davidson	30	2	135	5
I Meckiff	18	0	129	1
KD Mackay	3	0	15	0
R Benaud	24	3	93	0
RB Simpson	8	0	25	1
LF Kline	17.6	6	52	3

AUSTRALIA 1ST INNINGS

CC McDonald	c Hunte b Sobers	57
RB Simpson	b Ramadhin	92
RN Harvey	b Valentine	15
NC O'Neill	c Valentine b Hall	181
LE Favell	run out	45
KD Mackay	b Sobers	35
AK Davidson	c Alexander b Hall	44
R Benaud*	lbw b Hall	10
ATW Grout†	lbw b Hall	4
I Meckiff	run out	4
LF Kline	not out	3
Extras	(b 2, lb 8, w 1, nb 4)	15
Total		505

Fall of wickets 84, 138, 194, 278, 381, 469, 484, 489, 496, 505

	O	M	R	W
WW Hall	29.3	1	140	4
FMM Worrell	30	0	93	0
GS Sobers	32	0	115	2
AL Valentine	24	6	82	1
S Ramadhin	15	1	60	1

WEST INDIES 2ND INNINGS

CC Hunte	c Simpson b Mackay	39
CW Smith	c O'Neill b Davidson	6
RB Kanhai	c Grout b Davidson	54
GS Sobers	b Davidson	14
FMM Worrell*	c Grout b Davidson	65
JS Solomon	lbw b Simpson	47
PD Lashley	b Davidson	0
FCM Alexander†	b Benaud	5
S Ramadhin	c Harvey b Simpson	6
WW Hall	b Davidson	18
AL Valentine	not out	7
Extras	(b 14, lb 7, w 2)	23
Total		284

Fall of wickets 13, 88, 114, 127, 210, 210, 241, 250, 253, 284

	O	M	R	W
AK Davidson	24.6	4	87	6
I Meckiff	4	1	19	0
KD Mackay	21	7	52	1
R Benaud	31	6	69	1
RB Simpson	7	2	18	2
LF Kline	4	0	14	0
NC O'Neill	1	0	2	0

AUSTRALIA 2ND INNINGS

CC McDonald	b Worrell	16
RB Simpson	c sub (LR Gibbs) b Hall	0
RN Harvey	c Sobers b Hall	5
NC O'Neill	c Alexander b Hall	26
LE Favell	c Solomon b Hall	7
KD Mackay	b Ramadhin	28
AK Davidson	run out	80
R Benaud*	c Alexander b Hall	52
ATW Grout†	run out	2
I Meckiff	run out	2
LF Kline	not out	0
Extras	(b 2, lb 9, nb 3)	14
Total		232

Fall of wickets 1, 7, 49, 49, 57, 92, 226, 228, 232, 232

	O	M	R	W
WW Hall	17.7	3	63	5
FMM Worrell	16	3	41	1
GS Sobers	8	0	30	0
AL Valentine	10	4	27	0
S Ramadhin	17	3	57	1

Toss: West Indies   Umpires: CJ Egar and C Hoy   Match tied

England v Australia
Fourth Test at Old Trafford, Manchester

1961
July 27, 28, 29, 31, August 1 (1961)

Bill Lawry is applauded by the England players on making his century in the second innings of the 1961 Ashes Test at Old Trafford.

With regard to the fourth Test of the 1961 Ashes series, Peter Arnold wrote in his book *The Illustrated Encyclopedia of World Cricket* that "the scene was set for one of the greatest of all Test matches." The match ultimately decided the series after it was level at 1-all after three Tests, with Australia needing only one more win to regain the urn.

England missed Colin Cowdrey for the all-important fourth Test, and more changes were made. Thirty-two-year-old fast bowler Jack Flavell made his Test debut, while Australia introduced Brian Booth in place of the injured Colin McDonald. Australian skipper Richie Benaud chose to bat despite a greenish pitch, and Bob Simpson was an early casualty as he was caught behind off Brian Statham. Statham had changed ends when he dismissed Neil Harvey to make the score 51-2.

Norm O'Neill looked out of sorts and was hit on the body many times, particularly by Flavell. O'Neill departed when he fell onto his stumps as he tried to hook Fred Trueman, before Flavell gained his first wicket after lunch when he bowled Peter Burge. More than three hours of play were lost due to rain, and Australia was 124-4 at stumps with opener Bill Lawry on 64.

Lawry added another 10 runs when Statham had him lbw. Statham and Ted Dexter swung the ball on a lively pitch, and kept England on top despite Booth making a gallant 46. After dismissing Ken Mackay at 174, Statham claimed a five-wicket haul when he accounted for Booth to trigger a collapse which saw Australia slide from 185-6 to 190 all out. Dexter took the final three wickets, before Alan Davidson was involved in the dismissals of Raman Subba Row and Dexter as England wobbled to 43-2.

Davidson was also involved in the third wicket as he bowled Geoff Pullar, but not before Pullar and Peter May added 111 runs. May was on 90 at stumps as his team was 187-3, before reaching 212-3 and then slipping to 212-5. May fell unfortunately for 95 when Simpson caught him at slip after wicketkeeper Wally Grout dived and scooped up the ball. Graham McKenzie took his second wicket when he had Brian Close lbw, although England regained the ascendancy as Ken Barrington and John Murray put on 60 runs before Mackay dismissed Murray.

England furthered its lead, with Barrington hitting 10 fours in his 78 while Allen hit seven fours in his 42. Simpson unexpectedly took the last four wickets as England lost 9-4, but its lead of 177 was strong. Subba Row however let Australia off the hook when he dropped a slips catch to give Lawry a life on 25. Australia was 63-0 at stumps and, following the rest

Australia, led by Neil Harvey, takes to the field during the 1961 Ashes tour.

day, added another 50 runs before Flavell had Simpson caught behind. Harvey survived slips chances on two and 26 before wicketkeeper Murray caught him for 35, and Australia soon erased the deficit. Lawry played some good hooks and drives, and he reached 102 before falling to a great catch by Trueman at backward short leg.

O'Neill was struck on the thigh but he showed much greater resolve than in the first innings. Burge failed to impress before falling to Dexter, and O'Neill's 67 ended when Murray took his seventh catch of the match. Booth's departure left Australia 296-6, and then Mackay and Davidson added 35 runs at the close of play. Allen suddenly thwarted Australia's progress on the final morning when his off-spin dismissed Mackay, Benaud and Grout to have Australia nine-down and just 157 runs in front. Davidson however was far from finished, and McKenzie showed he was no mug with the bat. Davidson hit two towering sixes in an Allen over that cost 20 runs, and Allen was promptly replaced. The partnership reached a staggering 98 in 102 minutes before McKenzie was bowled by Flavell for 32. Davidson was unbeaten on 77, having hit 10 fours and two sixes in 174 minutes. England needed 256 runs in 230 minutes, an attainable task, but the situation would have been far easier were it not for dropped catches and the last wicket stand.

Left-handers Pullar and Subba Row put on 40 runs in as many minutes before Pullar hooked a catch off Davidson. With Subba Row batting solidly, Dexter produced a splendid array of drives and cross-batted strokes as he accumulated 14 fours and a six and

raced to 76 in 84 minutes. Twenty minutes before tea, England was 150-1. Benaud then made an important breakthrough as he came around the wicket and had Dexter caught behind from an attempted cut. Benaud kept coming around the wicket and landing the ball in the rough, courtesy of Trueman's footholds. May swept at his second delivery and was bowled round his legs, and Close swept a catch soon after driving a big six. Subba Row was bowled by a Benaud yorker, leaving England 163-5 at the break and needing 93 in 85 minutes. "Benaud could not wait to get back into action after a tea interval that left the England batsmen with indigestion," Norman Giller commented in *The World's Greatest Cricket Matches*.

Benaud showed no ill-effects of a shoulder injury as he continued to use the rough to his advantage. Benaud had five wickets in 25 balls when Murray edged to Simpson at slip, before Mackay trapped Barrington lbw while the total was still 171. A few boundaries helped the total to 189-7 before Simpson dived and snared a superb slips catch off Benaud – who was now bowling over the wicket – to dismiss Allen. With Simpson bowling, Benaud took a catch at short leg to account for Trueman, and Australia had 32 minutes in which to claim the last wicket. Davidson returned to the attack and settled the matter with 20 minutes remaining as he comprehensively beat Statham. Benaud was understandably considered Australia's hero after taking 6-70 in the second innings, although a look at the scoreboard suggests virtually all of the Australians made worthwhile contributions during the match.

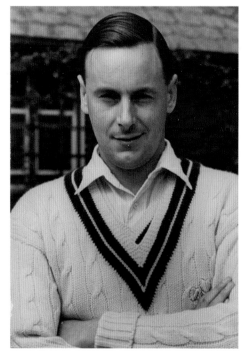

From left: Peter May (England), Bill Lawry (Australia) and Fred Trueman (England).

AUSTRALIA 1ST INNINGS		
WM Lawry	lbw b Statham	74
RB Simpson	c Murray b Statham	4
RN Harvey	c Subba Row b Statham	19
NC O'Neill	hit wicket b Trueman	11
PJP Burge	b Flavell	15
BC Booth	c Close b Statham	46
KD Mackay	c Murray b Statham	11
AK Davidson	c Barrington b Dexter	0
R Benaud*	b Dexter	2
ATW Grout†	c Murray b Dexter	2
GD McKenzie	not out	1
Extras	(b 4, lb 1)	5
Total		190

Fall of wickets 8, 51, 89, 106, 150, 174, 185, 185, 189, 190

	O	M	R	W
FS Trueman	14	1	55	1
JB Statham	21	3	53	5
JA Flavell	22	8	61	1
ER Dexter	6.4	2	16	3

ENGLAND 1ST INNINGS		
G Pullar	b Davidson	63
R Subba Row	c Simpson b Davidson	2
ER Dexter	c Davidson b McKenzie	16
PBH May*	c Simpson b Davidson	95
DB Close	lbw b McKenzie	33
KF Barrington	c O'Neill b Simpson	78
JT Murray†	c Grout b Mackay	24
DA Allen	c Booth b Simpson	42
FS Trueman	c Harvey b Simpson	3
JB Statham	c Mackay b Simpson	4
JA Flavell	not out	0
Extras	(b 2, lb 4, w 1)	7
Total		367

Fall of wickets 3, 43, 154, 212, 212, 272, 358, 362, 367, 367

	O	M	R	W
AK Davidson	39	11	70	3
GD McKenzie	38	11	106	2
KD Mackay	40	9	81	1
R Benaud	35	15	80	0
RB Simpson	11.4	4	23	4

AUSTRALIA 2ND INNINGS		
WM Lawry	c Trueman b Allen	102
RB Simpson	c Murray b Flavell	51
RN Harvey	c Murray b Dexter	35
NC O'Neill	c Murray b Statham	67
PJP Burge	c Murray b Dexter	23
BC Booth	lbw b Dexter	9
KD Mackay	c Close b Allen	18
AK Davidson	not out	77
R Benaud*	lbw b Allen	1
ATW Grout†	c Statham b Allen	0
GD McKenzie	b Flavell	32
Extras	(b 6, lb 9, w 2)	17
Total		432

Fall of wickets 113, 175, 210, 274, 290, 296, 332, 334, 334, 432

	O	M	R	W
FS Trueman	32	6	92	0
JB Statham	44	9	106	1
JA Flavell	29.4	4	65	2
ER Dexter	20	4	61	3
DA Allen	38	25	58	4
DB Close	8	1	33	0

ENGLAND 2ND INNINGS		
G Pullar	c O'Neill b Davidson	26
R Subba Row	b Benaud	49
ER Dexter	c Grout b Benaud	76
PBH May*	b Benaud	0
DB Close	c O'Neill b Benaud	8
KF Barrington	lbw b Mackay	5
JT Murray†	c Simpson b Benaud	4
DA Allen	c Simpson b Benaud	10
FS Trueman	c Benaud b Simpson	8
JB Statham	b Davidson	8
JA Flavell	not out	0
Extras	(b 5, w 2)	7
Total		201

Fall of wickets 40, 150, 150, 158, 163, 171, 171, 189, 193, 201

	O	M	R	W
AK Davidson	14.4	1	50	2
GD McKenzie	4	1	20	0
KD Mackay	13	7	33	1
R Benaud	32	11	70	6
RB Simpson	8	4	21	1

Toss: Australia   Umpires: JG Langridge and WE Phillipson   Australia won by 54 runs

Pakistan v England

First Test at Lahore Stadium

1961-62

October 21, 22, 24, 25, 26 (1961)

More than six years had passed between Pakistan's historic 1954 win over England and the next England versus Pakistan series. This time a three-Test series was held in Pakistan, and Hanif Mohammad, Imtiaz Ahmed and Mahmood Hussain were the only Pakistan players from the 1954 victory to line up in the first Test of the 1961–62 series. Afaq Hussain was a Test debutant, as were English trio Eric Russell, David 'Butch' White and Alan Brown, while Tony Lock was absent with a thigh injury.

White and Brown were effectively thrown in at the deep end as they opened the bowling after Imtiaz won the toss and opened the batting. Hanif gave a very brief exhibition of scoring, and White struck in his second over when Imtiaz was caught behind. White landed a bigger blow in his next over when he bowled Hanif, who had scored 19 before his dismissal rendered Pakistan 24-2.

Saeed Ahmed and Javed Burki however seemed like a brick wall for the tourists, as a 138-run partnership swung the complexion Pakistan's way. Bob Barber finally made the breakthrough when Saeed was caught behind after hitting 12 fours in his 74. Javed nonetheless kept going, and he reached his maiden Test hundred before stumps while Mushtaq Mohammad moved to 46 as Pakistan finished the day on 254-3. The fourth wicket partnership produced another 61 runs before David Allen had Javed caught behind for 138, which came in 375 minutes and featured 17 fours and one six.

Mushtaq soon progressed to 76 after hitting 11 fours, but the pendulum changed just nine runs after Javed's dismissal. Mushtaq was run out before Wallis Mathias departed on the same score, and the next wicket fell 13 runs later. Intikhab Alam smacked two fours and two sixes before being bowled for 24, and some further runs from the tail took the total to 387

Ken Barrington – his 139 against Pakistan was a highlight among more than 6,000 Test runs.

before Pakistan declared with one wicket remaining. The total was not as big as it could have been, although it looked ample as Mohammad Munaf dismissed England openers Geoff Pullar and Peter Richardson for a total of just four runs. But as was the case in Pakistan's innings, a third wicket partnership built a platform for a decent total. Ken Barrington advanced to 51 and Mike Smith to 45 as the visiting team finished day two on 109-2 before the following day was a rest day.

Barrington and Smith kept working steadily after play resumed, and Barrington passed a century whereas Smith reached 99 before chancing a single cost him as he was run out. The 192-run partnership was followed by a 62-run stand before Afaq claimed his first Test scalp in an unusual way as Ted Dexter was out hit wicket. Barrington passed Javed's score by one run, and the Englishman batted for 55 minutes longer than Javed before being run out. Imtiaz claimed a stumping to remove Barber, although the Pakistani skipper had a poor time behind the stumps as he conceded 21 byes in the innings. England finished day three on 321-6, and added only one more run before Munaf accounted for John Murray. The battle for a first innings lead was on in earnest, and Allen was more than handy at number nine while Russell's maiden Test innings was productive. England was just 26 runs behind when Russell was bowled, and then White's maiden Test innings produced no runs as he too was bowled. Allen went on to score a satisfying 40, and the deficit was seven runs when Allen was lbw to Munaf, who was easily the pick of the bowlers.

Pakistan's second innings began soundly as White was not so effective before Pakistan crashed from 33-0 to 33-3. After going wicketless in Pakistan's first innings, Brown claimed his first two scalps as Hanif and Saeed were caught behind, while Imtiaz was bowled by Dexter. Javed and Mushtaq made some progress but couldn't repeat their first innings heroics. Mushtaq scored 23 and Javed a much slower 15 as Pakistan struggled to 93-5. Allen was a key figure as he accounted for Mushtaq before catching Javed and later trapping Mathias lbw for 32. Twenty-five runs were added before Munaf departed, and Mahmood hit a six before being bowled for seven. Intikhab was soon bowled after he had earlier hit a four and a six, and Pakistan was in trouble at 149-9 at stumps. It was telling that five Pakistanis were dismissed between 10 and 20 while two others scored between 20 and 35.

England had to earn the last wicket as Afaq and Haseeb put a high price on their wickets. After scoring 10 not out in his first innings, Afaq struck five fours in an invaluable 35 not out while Haseeb hit two fours before he was caught off Barber for 14. Pakistan made exactly 200 after a last wicket stand of 52, and England had 250 minutes in which to score 208 runs. Munaf bowled Pullar for a duck before the tourists fell to 17-2 as Mahmood trapped Barrington lbw. Richardson and Smith steered England on course before an erratic Haseeb had Smith caught for 34. The run rate was under control as Richardson

and Dexter took the score to 108, before Intikhab made a double breakthrough with Richardson caught behind for 48 and Russell bowled for zero. The game hung in the balance as England needed 100 runs in two hours, before Dexter and Barber hit their stride. Defence and attack were wisely combined as Dexter cruised to 66 not out with nine fours while Barber hit three fours in his unbeaten 39 as 101 runs were scored in 85 minutes.

The five-wicket margin didn't reflect the closeness of the contest, before England headed to India where the host nation won a five-match series 2-0. Strangely, the England versus Pakistan series resumed afterwards in Pakistan, and England salvaged two draws for a 1-0 series triumph.

England's Mike Smith, run out on 99 in the first innings against Pakistan in 1961.

PAKISTAN 1ST INNINGS		
Hanif Mohammad	b White	19
Imtiaz Ahmed*†	c Murray b White	4
Saeed Ahmed	c Murray b Barber	74
Javed Burki	c Murray b Allen	138
Mushtaq Mohammad	run out	76
W Mathias	c Smith b Barber	3
Intikhab Alam	b Barber	24
Mohammad Munaf	b Allen	7
Mahmood Hussain	b White	14
Afaq Hussain	not out	10
Haseeb Ahsan	not out	7
Extras	(b 4, lb 3, nb 4)	11
Total	(9 wickets dec)	387

Fall of wickets 17, 24, 162, 315, 324, 324, 337, 365, 369

	O	M	R	W
DW White	22	3	65	3
A Brown	15.5	3	44	0
ER Dexter	7	1	26	0
RW Barber	40	4	124	3
DA Allen	33	14	67	2
WE Russell	19	9	25	0
KF Barrington	6	0	25	0

PAKISTAN 2ND INNINGS		
Hanif Mohammad	c Murray b Brown	17
Imtiaz Ahmed*†	b Dexter	12
Saeed Ahmed	c Murray b Brown	0
Javed Burki	c Allen b Barber	15
Mushtaq Mohammad	c Pullar b Allen	23
W Mathias	lbw b Allen	32
Intikhab Alam	b Barber	17
Mohammad Munaf	c Dexter b Brown	12
Mahmood Hussain	b Allen	7
Afaq Hussain	not out	35
Haseeb Ahsan	c Smith b Barber	14
Extras	(b 9, lb 2, nb 5)	16
Total		200

Fall of wickets 33, 33, 33, 69, 93, 113, 138, 146, 148, 200

	O	M	R	W
DW White	12	2	42	0
A Brown	14	4	27	3
ER Dexter	7	2	10	1
DA Allen	22	13	51	3
RW Barber	20.5	6	54	3

ENGLAND 1ST INNINGS		
PE Richardson	c Afaq Hussain b Mohammad Munaf	4
G Pullar	c Mahmood Hussain b Mohammad Munaf	0
KF Barrington	run out	139
MJK Smith	run out	99
ER Dexter*	hit wicket b Afaq Hussain	20
WE Russell	b Intikhab Alam	34
RW Barber	st Imtiaz Ahmed b Haseeb Ahsan	6
JT Murray†	b Mohammad Munaf	4
DA Allen	lbw b Mohammad Munaf	40
DW White	b Saeed Ahmed	0
A Brown	not out	3
Extras	(b 21, lb 1, nb 9)	31
Total		380

Fall of wickets 2, 21, 213, 275, 294, 306, 322, 361, 362, 380

	O	M	R	W
Mahmood Hussain	25	8	35	0
Mohammad Munaf	31.1	15	42	4
Intikhab Alam	48	6	118	1
Afaq Hussain	23	6	40	1
Haseeb Ahsan	36	7	95	1
Saeed Ahmed	11	3	19	1

ENGLAND 2ND INNINGS		
PE Richardson	c Imtiaz Ahmed b Intikhab Alam	48
G Pullar	b Mohammad Munaf	0
KF Barrington	lbw b Mahmood Hussain	6
MJK Smith	c Afaq Hussain b Haseeb Ahsan	34
ER Dexter*	not out	66
WE Russell	b Intikhab Alam	0
RW Barber	not out	39
Extras	(b 10, lb 4, nb 2)	16
Total	(5 wickets)	209

Did not bat JT Murray†, DA Allen, DW White, A Brown

Fall of wickets 1, 17, 86, 108, 108

	O	M	R	W
Mohammad Munaf	15	1	54	1
Mahmood Hussain	12	3	30	1
Haseeb Ahsan	9	0	42	1
Intikhab Alam	16	3	37	2
Afaq Hussain	5	0	21	0
Saeed Ahmed	2	0	9	0

Toss: Pakistan   Umpires: KA Saeed and Shujauddin   England won by 5 wickets

South Africa v New Zealand
Fifth Test at Crusaders Ground, St George's Park, Port Elizabeth

1961-62
February 16, 17, 19, 20 (1962)

South Africa had won its first three series against New Zealand, and the Africans sought four on the trot as they led 2-1 in the 1961–62 series with one Test remaining, which turned out to be a thriller.

The series proved fascinating, as South Africa won the first Test by just 30 runs before a drawn second Test was followed by New Zealand beating South Africa for the first time with a 72-run margin. South Africa bounced back with an innings victory at Johannesburg, ensuring the host nation couldn't lose the series as the teams headed to Port Elizabeth for the final encounter.

The Kiwis chose to bat first after winning the toss on a pitch that looked tailor-made for runs, but the decision looked like backfiring as Neil Adcock and Peter Pollock dismissed the openers cheaply. Captain John Reid showed some initiative as he struck six fours, only to be bowled by Adcock for 26. Paul Barton however built on after a good start as he showed a disciplined and correct style despite battling a shoulder injury. Barton however lost two more partners, with Pollock dismissing Noel McGregor before the amazingly economical Harry Bromfield had Zin Harris caught as New Zealand tumbled to 115-5. Barton however kept going, while Artie Dick provided resistance.

Barton reached his first and only Test century with his 19th four, and found the boundary once more before his 276-minute innings ended as he was caught off Herbert 'Tiger' Lance. Despite Barton's great knock, his team was still perilously placed at 180-6. Gary Bartlett settled in, and Dick went on to score 46 before he was caught behind. Another 17 runs were added before New Zealand closed the day on 242-7.

Bartlett and John 'Jack' Alabaster scored some useful runs the following morning before Bartlett was out hit wicket,

South Africa pair Eddie Barlow (left) going out to bat with team-mate Peter Pollock.

and then Godfrey 'Goofy' Lawrence claimed two scalps as New Zealand quickly folded for 275. Lawrence was sent in as an opening batsman in place of captain Jackie McGlew, who had dislocated his shoulder in a fielding mishap during New Zealand's innings. South Africa lost its first wicket when Dick Motz dismissed Eddie Barlow for 20, and then John Waite fell for a duck as Graham Dowling took his second catch. William 'Buster' Farrer's dismissal to a catch behind left South Africa 65-3, but the makeshift opener provided solidity.

Roy McLean meanwhile struck four fours and a six in a quick 25 before his departure made the score 92-4. Colin Bland made 12 before he was lbw, and a major breakthrough occurred three runs later when Lawrence was caught behind after grafting his way to 43 in 141 minutes with eight fours. From 115-6, South Africa stuttered to 143-9 before number 11 Bromfield resisted while McGlew braved injury. The duo put on 47 runs, easily the highest partnership of the innings as South Africa trimmed its deficit to 85 runs.

The Africans received another boost when Pollock dismissed John Sparling cheaply for the second time in the match, before Dowling and the promoted Harris took the score to 36-1 at stumps. After a rest day, Adcock gave South Africa a strong start to day three with the dismissals of Harris and Barton, reducing the Kiwis to 50-3 before Dowling and Reid changed the course of the match. They were cautious as they built a 125-run partnership in 201 minutes before Reid was caught for 69, which included eight fours and two sixes. The pendulum changed 10 runs later when Lawrence had Dowling lbw for 78, which included eight fours in a 290-minute stay at the crease. Dick was lbw for one, and then McGregor and Bartlett added a few handy runs before the fall of the seventh wicket at 216 was followed by the last three wickets falling on 228 as Lawrence and Pollock cleaned up the tail. Farrer was promoted to open South Africa's second innings with Barlow, who advanced to 25 before stumps as the locals were 38-0 and needing 276 runs on the final day of this four-day Test.

The opening partnership reached 57 before Frank Cameron struck Farrer's pads in front of the stumps. McGlew came in next, and settled in while Barlow passed 50 and helped South Africa to 101-1 before Reid landed a decisive blow as he bowled the opener. The home side could ill afford to lose another wicket at a crucial time, but it happened in the form of a run out as McGlew was gone for 26. Reid and Alabaster were splendidly economical, and they worked their way through the middle order as Waite, McLean and Lance were dismissed and South Africa crumbled to 142-6.

Bland and Lawrence fought for survival, and added 51

runs before Reid trapped Bland in front after the batsman hit four fours and a six in his 32. Alabaster subsequently bowled Lawrence to make South Africa 199-8. New Zealand had about one-and-three-quarter hours in which to take the last two wickets as a Kiwi victory looked a formality. Pollock and Adcock however had other ideas as they resisted the bowling and played some confident strokes. Pollock hit boundaries from time to time, and Adcock registered his highest Test score of 24.

The Kiwis however took the chance to use the new ball against the tail-enders, and Motz bowled Adcock to leave one wicket remaining. Pollock and Bromfield needed to put on a 55-run partnership for victory or survive 57 minutes for a draw, and the latter was the only real option as Bromfield focused on survival. Pollock meanwhile reached 54 not out, which included 10 fours. Bromfield didn't score but time ticked away with the Kiwis desperately seeking one more wicket while Pollock and Bromfield tried to keep their opponents at bay. Twenty-one minutes remained when Cameron had Bromfield caught by McGregor, and the Kiwis had drawn the series 2-all in an eye-catching climax to the series.

New Zealand captain John Reid in the early 1960s.

NEW ZEALAND 1ST INNINGS

GT Dowling	lbw b Adcock	2
JT Sparling	c Lance b Pollock	3
PT Barton	c Bromfield b Lance	109
JR Reid*	b Adcock	26
SN McGregor	b Pollock	10
PGZ Harris	c McGlew b Bromfield	7
AE Dick†	c Waite b Pollock	46
GA Bartlett	hit wicket b Adcock	29
JC Alabaster	lbw b Lawrence	24
RC Motz	c McLean b Lawrence	2
FJ Cameron	not out	1
Extras	(b 1, lb 7, nb 8)	16
Total		275

Fall of wickets 4, 20, 82, 108, 115, 180, 225, 269, 272, 275

	O	M	R	W
NAT Adcock	27	11	60	3
PM Pollock	28	9	63	3
GB Lawrence	26.2	7	71	2
HR Lance	14	4	50	1
HD Bromfield	16	7	15	1

SOUTH AFRICA 1ST INNINGS

EJ Barlow	c Dowling b Motz	20
GB Lawrence	c Dick b Alabaster	43
JHB Waite†	c Dowling b Cameron	0
WS Farrer	c Dick b Motz	7
RA McLean	c McGregor b Bartlett	25
KC Bland	lbw b Bartlett	12
HR Lance	st Dick b Reid	9
DJ McGlew*	not out	28
PM Pollock	lbw b Motz	8
NAT Adcock	c Dowling b Reid	5
HD Bromfield	c Dick b Alabaster	21
Extras	(lb 6, nb 6)	12
Total		190

Fall of wickets 34, 39, 65, 92, 112, 115, 125, 137, 143, 190

	O	M	R	W
FJ Cameron	11	2	46	1
GA Bartlett	8	4	10	2
RC Motz	14	7	33	3
JC Alabaster	25.4	7	63	2
JR Reid	14	6	26	2

NEW ZEALAND 2ND INNINGS

GT Dowling	lbw b Lawrence	78
JT Sparling	c Bromfield b Pollock	4
PGZ Harris	c Bland b Adcock	13
PT Barton	lbw b Pollock	2
JR Reid*	c Bromfield b Lance	69
SN McGregor	b Lawrence	24
AE Dick†	lbw b Lance	1
GA Bartlett	c Barlow b Lawrence	18
JC Alabaster	c Adcock b Lawrence	7
RC Motz	c Waite b Pollock	0
FJ Cameron	not out	0
Extras	(b 4, lb 6, nb 2)	12
Total		228

Fall of wickets 4, 37, 50, 175, 185, 192, 216, 228, 228, 228

	O	M	R	W
NAT Adcock	21	11	25	1
PM Pollock	24.1	5	70	3
GB Lawrence	28	5	85	4
HR Lance	8	0	36	2
HD Bromfield	2	2	0	0

SOUTH AFRICA 2ND INNINGS

EJ Barlow	b Reid	59
WS Farrer	lbw b Cameron	10
DJ McGlew*	run out	26
JHB Waite†	c Dowling b Reid	7
RA McLean	b Alabaster	10
KC Bland	lbw b Reid	32
HR Lance	c Dick b Reid	9
GB Lawrence	b Alabaster	17
PM Pollock	not out	54
NAT Adcock	b Motz	24
HD Bromfield	c McGregor b Cameron	0
Extras	(b 6, lb 3, w 2, nb 14)	25
Total		273

Fall of wickets 57, 101, 117, 125, 133, 142, 193, 199, 259, 273

	O	M	R	W
FJ Cameron	18	6	48	2
GA Bartlett	9	3	26	0
RC Motz	20	11	34	1
JC Alabaster	52	23	96	2
JR Reid	45	27	44	4

Toss: New Zealand   Umpires: GD Gibbon and G Parry   New Zealand won by 40 runs

England v West Indies
Second Test at Lord's, London

1963
June 20, 21, 22, 24, 25 (1963)

West Indies captain Frank Worrell (right) is greeted in England by team manager Mr Gaskin in April 1963 as wicketkeeper David Allen (centre) looks on.

England captain Ted Dexter commented in *Wisden Asia Cricket* magazine that the second England versus West Indies Test from 1963 "was possibly the greatest Test played at Lord's".

After rain delayed the start by 23 minutes, Conrad Hunte struck the first three balls for four after West Indian skipper Frank Worrell won the toss and chose to bat. Intriguingly, only 35 more runs were scored before lunch. Derek Shackleton had Hunte in some trouble after Shackleton was recalled for his first Test in 11 years. Hunte survived two sharp chances off Shackleton, and Dexter felt England should have taken three or four wickets before lunch. He considered this was decisive in the outcome despite the many twists and turns that ensued until the very end.

Fred Trueman dismissed openers Easton McMorris and Hunte as the tourists went from 51-0 to 64-2. Garry Sobers and Rohan Kanhai put on 63 runs in quick time before Sobers was caught off spinner David Allen: a crucial blow. Following Basil Butcher's demise for 14, Kanhai and Joe Solomon steered the visitors into a potentially strong position. But it quickly came undone as two wickets fell on 219, with Trueman dismissing Kanhai for 73 and Worrell for zero. Solomon and Deryck Murray added 26 runs before stumps and a further 18 the next day before Murray became Trueman's sixth victim. Solomon posted a half-century while Wes Hall also made runs as the tourists reached 297-7 before Shackleton dismissed Solomon,

Charlie Griffith and Lance Gibbs in the space of four balls across his 50th and 51st overs.

The fiery Griffith dismissed England openers Micky Stewart and John Edrich as the hosts struggled to 20-2 at lunch. Dexter counterattacked with an array of attacking strokes, and he copped a couple of painful blows to the left knee from Griffith thunderbolts. Dexter struck 10 fours and scored 70 at nearly a run per ball before Sobers trapped him lbw. Gibbs dismissed Colin Cowdrey cheaply, but Ken Barrington took control after being outshone by Dexter. Brian Close scored just nine in a 36-run partnership, before Jim Parks helped England pass 200. Barrington scored 80 in 190 minutes before driving Worrell for a catch at cover, and Worrell later bowled Parks for 35 before England ended the day on 244-7.

Fred Titmus pushed the score along while Trueman supported him until the total reached 271. Allen departed cheaply before Shackleton hung around long enough for Titmus to post a half-century. The last wicket stand of 23 bridged the visiting team's lead to just four runs, and the West Indies' response began disastrously despite Hunte hitting a six and Morris two fours. Both were caught by Cowdrey at slip with the total on 15, and Kanhai departed in similar fashion after scoring 21. Sobers hit two fours but scored no further runs before he was caught behind, and Solomon failed as the West Indies sank to 104-5.

Perhaps unfazed by the collapse or desperate to hit the West

Indies out of it, Butcher launched an astonishing assault on the bowling. He raced past 100 before stumps, while Worrell reached 33 and the score 214-5. Following the rest day, the complexion swung dramatically. Trueman racked up 11 wickets for the match after he dismissed Worrell, Murray and Hall. Butcher added just four runs before he was lbw to Shackleton for 133, which included 17 fours and two sixes. The tourists lost 15-5 as Shackleton finished the innings with his seventh wicket of the match, leaving England with a victory target of 234.

England fell to 27-2 as Hall dismissed the openers, and the hosts were in bigger trouble four runs later when Dexter was bowled by Gibbs. Barrington however proved an obstacle for the West Indians again, and Cowdrey scored 19 in a partnership of 41 before a ferocious Hall delivery broke Cowdrey's left wrist and made him retire hurt. Barrington hammered Gibbs over the mid-wicket boundary twice in one over, before progressing to 55 as England reached 116-3 until bad light caused an early finish to the day.

Rain and poor light unfortunately delayed the start of day five until 2.20pm, and Hall was promptly fired up to bowl unchanged for the remaining three-and-a-third hours. The first hour yielded only 18 runs for the loss of Barrington who was caught behind off Griffith. On an uneasy pitch, Close and Parks added 28 runs before Griffith had Parks lbw. England required 63 runs in the last 85 minutes, and weren't helped by a slow over rate. Close was the key for England, and he seemed to tolerate pain as a lot of fearsome deliveries hit his body. He also struck some cross-batted boundaries, and ran singles.

The score reached 203 before Titmus was caught by McMorris, and then Trueman was caught behind first ball. Close changed his approach as he advanced from his crease to distract bowlers Hall and Griffith. Close reached 70 before he edged a swing to Murray, and England needed 15 runs in 19 minutes with two wickets in hand. Hall bowled the last over, and any result was possible as England needed eight runs from six balls. Shackleton missed a swing from ball one before two successive singles were pushed. After Shackleton missed the fourth delivery, Murray's throw missed the stumps but Worrell fielded the ball and beat fellow 38-year-old Shackleton to the bowler's end for a run out.

With England needing six runs from two balls, Cowdrey heroically strode to the non-striker's end with his left arm in plaster below the elbow. Rather than risk death or glory shots, Allen blocked the last two balls to salvage a thrilling draw. England thus remained 1-0 down in the series, before winning the third Test. The West Indies however won the series 3-1 after big wins in the last two Tests.

Top: Lance Gibbs took 309 wickets in his 79 Tests as an off-spinner for the West Indies.
Bottom: England bowler Derek Shackleton took seven wickets in the Test against the West Indies in 1963, second only to Fred Trueman's 11 scalps.

WEST INDIES 1ST INNINGS

CC Hunte	c Close b Trueman	44
EDAS McMorris	lbw b Trueman	16
GS Sobers	c Cowdrey b Allen	42
RB Kanhai	c Edrich b Trueman	73
BF Butcher	c Barrington b Trueman	14
JS Solomon	lbw b Shackleton	56
FMM Worrell*	b Trueman	0
DL Murray†	c Cowdrey b Trueman	20
WW Hall	not out	25
CC Griffith	c Cowdrey b Shackleton	0
LR Gibbs	c Stewart b Shackleton	0
Extras	(b 10, lb 1)	11
Total		301

Fall of wickets 51, 64, 127, 145, 219, 219, 263, 297, 297, 301

	O	M	R	W
FS Trueman	44	16	100	6
D Shackleton	50.2	22	93	3
ER Dexter	20	6	41	0
DB Close	9	3	21	0
DA Allen	10	3	35	1

ENGLAND 1ST INNINGS

MJ Stewart	c Kanhai b Griffith	2
JH Edrich	c Murray b Griffith	0
ER Dexter*	lbw b Sobers	70
KF Barrington	c Sobers b Worrell	80
MC Cowdrey	b Gibbs	4
DB Close	c Murray b Griffith	9
JM Parks†	b Worrell	35
FJ Titmus	not out	52
FS Trueman	b Hall	10
DA Allen	lbw b Griffith	2
D Shackleton	b Griffith	8
Extras	(b 8, lb 8, nb 9)	25
Total		297

Fall of wickets 2, 20, 102, 115, 151, 206, 235, 271, 274, 297

	O	M	R	W
WW Hall	18	2	65	1
CC Griffith	26	6	91	5
GS Sobers	18	4	45	1
LR Gibbs	27	9	59	1
FMM Worrell	13	6	12	2

WEST INDIES 2ND INNINGS

CC Hunte	c Cowdrey b Shackleton	7
EDAS McMorris	c Cowdrey b Trueman	8
RB Kanhai	c Cowdrey b Shackleton	21
BF Butcher	lbw b Shackleton	133
GS Sobers	c Parks b Trueman	8
JS Solomon	c Stewart b Allen	5
FMM Worrell*	c Stewart b Trueman	33
DL Murray†	c Parks b Trueman	2
WW Hall	c Parks b Trueman	2
CC Griffith	b Shackleton	1
LR Gibbs	not out	1
Extras	(b 5, lb 2, nb 1)	8
Total		229

Fall of wickets 15, 15, 64, 84, 104, 214, 224, 226, 228, 229

	O	M	R	W
FS Trueman	26	9	52	5
D Shackleton	34	14	72	4
DA Allen	21	7	50	1
FJ Titmus	17	3	47	0

ENGLAND 2ND INNINGS

MJ Stewart	c Solomon b Hall	17
JH Edrich	c Murray b Hall	8
ER Dexter*	b Gibbs	2
KF Barrington	c Murray b Griffith	60
MC Cowdrey	not out	19
DB Close	c Murray b Griffith	70
JM Parks†	lbw b Griffith	17
FJ Titmus	c McMorris b Hall	11
FS Trueman	c Murray b Hall	0
DA Allen	not out	4
D Shackleton	run out	4
Extras	(b 5, lb 8, nb 3)	16
Total	(9 wickets)	228

Fall of wickets 15, 27, 31, 130, 158, 203, 203, 219, 228

	O	M	R	W
WW Hall	40	9	93	4
CC Griffith	30	7	59	3
GS Sobers	4	1	4	0
LR Gibbs	17	7	56	1

Toss: West Indies   Umpires: JS Buller and WE Phillipson   Match drawn

England v South Africa

First Test at Lord's, London

1965

July 22, 23, 24, 26, 27 (1965)

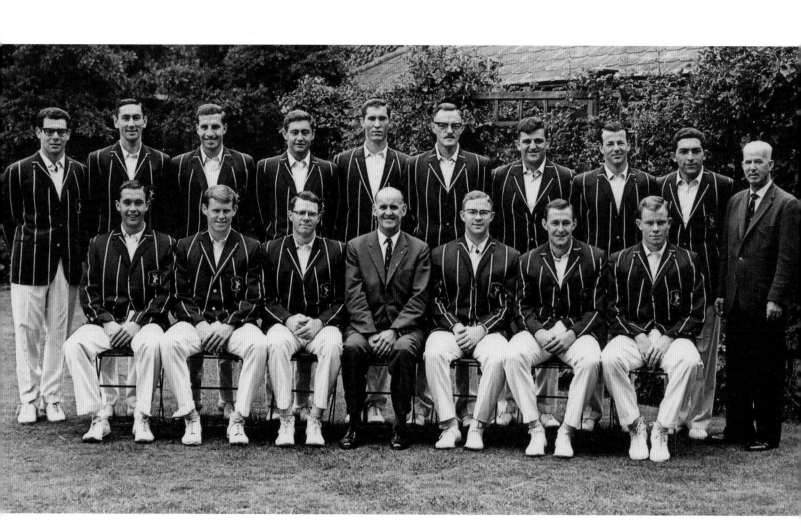

The South Africa team in England, 1963.

Three great Tests unfolded in the last series involving England and South Africa before the intrusion of apartheid in South Africa. The first Test at Lord's was arguably the most fascinating of the three, as it went down to the wire. It was the 100th Test featuring England against South Africa.

Batting first, the visitors were 1-1 when Bob Barber took a good catch at short fine leg off Fred Rumsey's bowling to account for Eddie Barlow. Herbert 'Tiger' Lance and Denis Lindsay appeared to be putting South Africa in a sound position before Test debutant and first change bowler David Brown struck. He impressively took his maiden Test wicket and catch with an ankle high caught-and-bowled to dismiss Lance for 28. Lindsay reached 40 but the tourists were tottering at 75-3 when another good piece of fielding took place. Fred Titmus dived full length at gully to catch Lindsay off Rumsey.

Two successive South African batsmen known by their middle names, Robert Graeme Pollock and Kenneth Colin Bland, added 80 runs. But another wicket fell when South Africa could ill afford it, with Pollock caught off Titmus for 56 as a lengthy partnership threatened. Brown made another key breakthrough when he bowled Bland, and then Ali Bacher's debut Test innings ended on four when Titmus had him lbw. Richard Dumbrill's maiden Test innings yielded three runs before he fell to Barber's part-time bowling, and the tourists were in strife at 178-7. Skipper Peter van der Merwe and another Test rookie, James 'Jackie' Botten, put on 34 runs before the captain became Rumsey's third victim.

South Africa resumed day two on 227-8 but rain washed out the first session before Brown bowled Botten with the total on 241. Peter Pollock frustrated England's bowlers and scored 34 while Harry Bromfield made an unbeaten nine as the last wicket pair took the total to 280. A little more than two hours of play was possible on the day, which finished with England on 26 without loss.

Barber scored a half-century as he and Geoff Boycott put on an 82-run opening stand before the game changed unexpectedly in a short space of time. Botten made the breakthrough with his first wicket as Boycott was caught by Barlow, before two wickets fell on 88. Barber was bowled by Bromfield, and John Edrich lbw to Peter Pollock for nought as the hosts suddenly looked vulnerable.

Colin Cowdrey made 29 before becoming medium-pacer Dumbrill's first Test victim. Ken Barrington however gave England's innings the strength it needed as he found form. Barrington dominated the scoring while captain Mike Smith played a minor role. Barrington struck 11 fours and a six as he reached 91 in three hours, and the hosts looked like assuming

control before sensational fielding from Bland turned the tide. He ran from mid wicket towards mid on and produced a direct hit to run out Barrington. With the total still on 240, Smith was caught behind.

Parks and Titmus took England to a seven-run lead at stumps before a rest day followed. Only seven runs were added on day four when Bland produced another accurate throw to run out Parks. Titmus went on to score 59, although the last three batsmen tallied just four runs as England claimed a 58-run lead.

David Larter copped some punishment as Barlow gave South Africa's second innings a strong start. Lance meanwhile scored just nine in a 55-run opening partnership before he was caught by Titmus off Brown. The same bowler soon had Barlow caught behind for 52, before bowling Graeme Pollock for five as South Africa crumbled to 68-3.

Bland looked capable of a big innings, but the visitors were still struggling when Larter had Lindsay caught behind. Four for 120. Bacher supported Bland who reached 70 before Barber took his wicket. South Africa had a mere 128-run lead with five wickets in hand when the last day began. Brown and Titmus deserved much credit for very tight bowling.

Bacher and van der Merwe stretched South Africa's lead to 158 before Titmus bowled Bacher for 37. Another 14 runs

South Africa captain Peter van der Merwe (left) and 'Ali' Bacher.

Above: South Africa's Eddie Barlow practises his catching before a Test match in England.
Opposite: The South Africa team arrive in England by Boeing 707 in 1963.

were added when Rumsey chimed in with successive wickets, and then Peter Pollock scored some vital runs before Rumsey's third wicket and a run out saw South Africa dismissed for 248. England had nearly four hours in which to reach its target of 191.

Peter Pollock had Barber caught behind with the total on 23, and the same bowler caused another big blow when one of his deliveries struck Edrich in the side of the head. Edrich retired hurt to leave England effectively 37-2, and the home side's cause was not helped as the tourists bowled their overs slowly. Boycott and Barrington took the total to 70 before Dumbrill dismissed the duo in the space of 10 runs. Cowdrey was steady, but England's winning chances dwindled as the scoring rate never gained momentum. Dumbrill gave South Africa hope as he dismissed Smith and Parks to have the score 121-5 while Edrich was injured. Dumbrill had a memorable debut with match figures of 7-61 from 42 overs, including 19 maidens.

Cowdrey scored 37 before Peter Pollock trapped him lbw,

and Graeme Pollock bowled four maiden overs for the wicket of Brown, who was caught by Barlow. However the South Africans were unable to take wickets often enough to threaten a victory, and the innings lasted 68 overs. Titmus and Rumsey saw the hosts to safety, and an intriguing Test finished with England 46 runs and South Africa three wickets away from victory. It was a matter of conjecture as to what would have resulted had rain not shortened day two.

The Pollocks starred in the second Test at Trent Bridge, with Graeme scoring 125 and 59 while Peter took 5-53 and 5-34 in South Africa's 94-run victory. The weather unfortunately prevented a thrilling conclusion to the series, as England was 308-4 chasing 399 when a thunderstorm cancelled the last scheduled 70 minutes.

SOUTH AFRICA 1ST INNINGS

EJ Barlow	c Barber b Rumsey	1
HR Lance	c & b Brown	28
DT Lindsay†	c Titmus b Rumsey	40
RG Pollock	c Barrington b Titmus	56
KC Bland	b Brown	39
A Bacher	lbw b Titmus	4
PL van der Merwe*	c Barrington b Rumsey	17
R Dumbrill	b Barber	3
JT Botten	b Brown	33
PM Pollock	st Parks b Barber	34
HD Bromfield	not out	9
Extras	(lb 14, nb 2)	16
Total		280

Fall of wickets 1, 60, 75, 155, 170, 170, 178, 212, 241, 280

	O	M	R	W
JDF Larter	26	10	47	0
FE Rumsey	30	9	84	3
DJ Brown	24	9	44	3
FJ Titmus	29	10	59	2
RW Barber	10.3	3	30	2

SOUTH AFRICA 2ND INNINGS

EJ Barlow	c Parks b Brown	52
HR Lance	c Titmus b Brown	9
DT Lindsay†	c Parks b Larter	22
RG Pollock	b Brown	5
KC Bland	c Edrich b Barber	70
A Bacher	b Titmus	37
PL van der Merwe*	c Barrington b Rumsey	31
R Dumbrill	c Cowdrey b Rumsey	2
JT Botten	b Rumsey	0
PM Pollock	not out	14
HD Bromfield	run out	0
Extras	(b 4, lb 2)	6
Total		248

Fall of wickets 55, 62, 68, 120, 170, 216, 230, 230, 247, 248

	O	M	R	W
JDF Larter	17	2	67	1
FE Rumsey	21	8	49	3
DJ Brown	21	11	30	3
FJ Titmus	26	13	36	1
RW Barber	25	5	60	1

ENGLAND 1ST INNINGS

G Boycott	c Barlow b Botten	31
RW Barber	b Bromfield	56
JH Edrich	lbw b PM Pollock	0
KF Barrington	run out	91
MC Cowdrey	b Dumbrill	29
MJK Smith*	c Lindsay b Botten	26
JM Parks†	run out	32
FJ Titmus	c PM Pollock b Bromfield	59
DJ Brown	c Bromfield b Dumbrill	1
FE Rumsey	b Dumbrill	3
JDF Larter	not out	0
Extras	(b 1, lb 4, w 1, nb 4)	10
Total		338

Fall of wickets 82, 88, 88, 144, 240, 240, 294, 314, 338, 338

	O	M	R	W
PM Pollock	39	12	91	1
JT Botten	33	11	65	2
EJ Barlow	19	6	31	0
HD Bromfield	25.2	5	71	2
R Dumbrill	24	11	31	3
HR Lance	5	0	18	0
RG Pollock	5	1	21	0

ENGLAND 2ND INNINGS

G Boycott	c & b Dumbrill	28
RW Barber	c Lindsay b PM Pollock	12
JH Edrich	retired hurt	7
KF Barrington	lbw b Dumbrill	18
MC Cowdrey	lbw b PM Pollock	37
MJK Smith*	c Lindsay b Dumbrill	13
JM Parks†	c van der Merwe b Dumbrill	7
FJ Titmus	not out	9
DJ Brown	c Barlow b RG Pollock	5
FE Rumsey	not out	0
Extras	(lb 7, w 1, nb 1)	9
Total	(7 wickets)	145

Did not bat JDF Larter

Fall of wickets 23, 70, 79, 113, 121, 135, 140

	O	M	R	W
PM Pollock	20	6	52	2
JT Botten	12	6	25	0
EJ Barlow	9	1	25	0
HD Bromfield	5	4	4	0
R Dumbrill	18	8	30	4
RG Pollock	4	4	0	1

Toss: South Africa   Umpires: JS Buller and AEG Rhodes   Match drawn

New Zealand v England
First Test at Lancaster Park, Christchurch

1965-66
February 25, 26, 28, March 1 (1966)

'Tanned by the Antipodean sun' noted one press report of the time, as members of the MCC party arrived at London Airport from the Australasian tour of 1965–66. From left: Colin Cowdrey, Billy Griffiths (tour manager), Mike Smith, Ken Higgs, David Brown and Geoff Boycott.

New Zealand's quest for its first ever Test series win against England received a blow with the retirement of influential Kiwi captain John Reid. England had won the past six series against the Kiwis, yet the 1965–66 series had a different complexion after an interesting first Test.

New Zealand's new captain Murray Chapple lost the toss, and England skipper Mike Smith somewhat surprisingly opted to bat first after several days of rain produced a soft pitch. England lost its first wicket at 19 as Dick Motz had Geoff Boycott caught behind, and the bowlers subsequently dominated for a while despite a solid effort from opener Eric Russell. Motz dismissed John Edrich for two, before Colin Cowdrey departed for a duck after spending half an hour at the crease. Before a run was added, Russell was bowled by Motz for 30 as England was a worrying 47-4.

Smith and Peter Parfitt improved England's position as they batted into the second session. Coincidentally, both scored 54 including three boundaries before falling with the total on 160 as New Zealand regained the ascendancy. Change bowler Vic Pollard was expensive but he broke the partnership as Indian-born Narotam 'Tom' Puna made his mark in his Test debut with a superb catch to dismiss Smith. Gary Bartlett took the next wicket when Parfitt was caught by Bev Congdon.

David Allen acquitted himself well, while Jim Parks struck three fours and a six before falling to a catch behind for 30. With the pitch improving for batting, David Brown and Allen put on 33 runs and England finished the day on 242-7. Brown and Allen continued in the same vein the next day as they added a further 74 runs before Allen was caught after striking eight fours in his 88, which spanned 222 minutes. Brown progressed

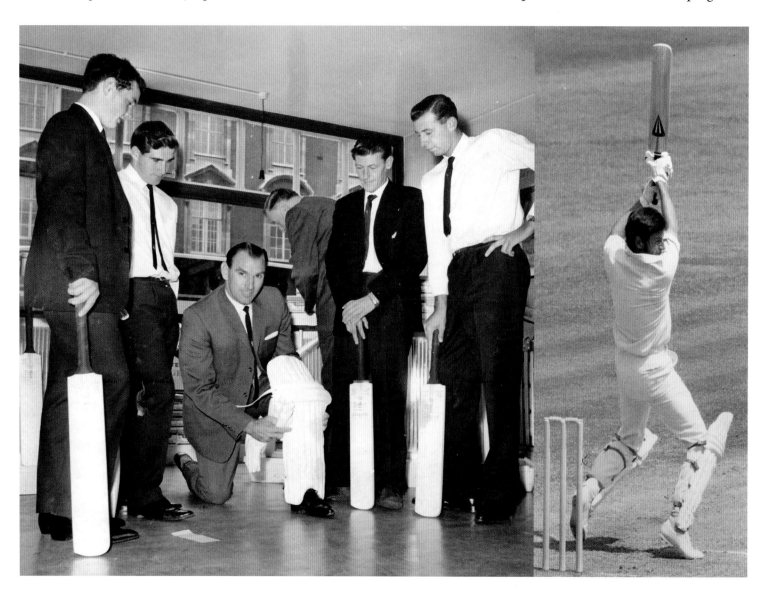

New Zealand players, with captain John Reid in the centre trying on pads, on the Kiwis' 1965 tour of England.
Right: New Zealand batsman Bevan Congdon scored a first-innings century against England in Christchurch in 1966.

to 44 before he and Jeff Jones were bowled with the score on 342, a total that England should have been pleased with after being 47-4.

Grahame Bilby dominated the scoring in New Zealand's first wicket partnership as he was in his first Test, before the Kiwis fell from 39-0 to 41-2. Mike Shrimpton and Bilby were caught behind, before Congdon and Barry Sinclair batted doggedly. Sinclair scored 23 in two hours before being caught-and-bowled by Ken Higgs, while Congdon moved to 78 to guide the home side to 174-3 at stumps. Pollard hit a six but slowly reached 21.

Following the rest day, Pollard added only two runs before becoming Higgs's third scalp. Chapple helped the Kiwis past 200 before his dismissal to a simple catch at slip was followed by Bartlett departing just one run later. Congdon posted a century before falling not long afterwards as New Zealand trailed by 105 runs with only three wickets remaining. But just as Allen and Brown had frustrated the Kiwis, now Petrie and Motz did likewise to the Englishmen. Motz showed some aggression as he struck six fours and two sixes in an innings of 58 in a partnership of 89 in 105 minutes. After a five-year absence from Test cricket, Petrie scored 55 in three hours before becoming the fifth Kiwi caught behind by Parks. Petrie's 18-run partnership with Bob Cunis took New Zealand to a two-run lead, before Jones took the last wicket to restrict the lead to five runs.

Russell again dominated the scoring without being brisk, while Boycott was run out for four. It was the second time in the Test that Boycott departed after opening his account with a boundary and not adding to his score. Cunis struck a big blow when he trapped Edrich lbw, and England was 32-2 at stumps with one day remaining in this four-day Test.

Russell added only five runs to his overnight score before Bartlett bowled him, and another 20 runs were added before Cowdrey exited as England struggled at 68-4. Smith and Parfitt however proved hard to dislodge yet again, and their 113-run partnership in the first innings was bettered by 12 runs. Off spinner Puna copped some stick but he had the satisfaction of making the breakthrough with his first Test wicket when Smith was caught by New Zealand's other debutant, Bilby, who had caught Cowdrey on day one. Puna's wicket was soon followed by a declaration that left New Zealand a target of 197 runs in two hours and 20 minutes.

Brown struck early when he had Bilby caught behind, before Higgs sparked a remarkable collapse to put England on the verge of victory. Congdon's sole scoring stroke was a four before he was caught by Cowdrey off Higgs to make the

Basil D'Oliveira (left), the former South African player who became a British citizen in 1964, and England team-mate Tom Graveney.

score 19-2. Incredibly, two wickets fell on 21 before the next three fell on 22. Higgs had Sinclair caught at the wicket before Allen accounted for Shrimpton, who scored 13 of the first 21 runs. Higgs struck twice and Parfitt once when the score was 22, and Higgs had phenomenal figures of 4-5 from nine overs. New Zealand meanwhile was in danger of recording a new lowest score in Test cricket after being dismissed for 26 in Len Hutton's final Test, which took place in Auckland just over a decade earlier.

The total reached 32 before Motz was caught off Parfitt, and England needed just two more wickets in the last 32 minutes. The visitors were denied, as Cunis scored 16 not out while the stonewalling Pollard, who was at the non-striker's end as five wickets fell, finished with six not out in 92 minutes. The Kiwis remarkably scored at a mere one run per over as they finished on 48-8 to escape with a draw. The second and third Tests were also drawn, and it was the first time since 1949 that New Zealand did not lose a Test series to England.

ENGLAND 1ST INNINGS		
G Boycott	c Petrie b Motz	4
WE Russell	b Motz	30
JH Edrich	c Bartlett b Motz	2
MC Cowdrey	c Bilby b Cunis	0
MJK Smith*	c Puna b Pollard	54
PH Parfitt	c Congdon b Bartlett	54
JM Parks†	c Petrie b Chapple	30
DA Allen	c Chapple b Bartlett	88
DJ Brown	b Cunis	44
K Higgs	not out	8
IJ Jones	b Bartlett	0
Extras	(b 6, lb 6, nb 16)	28
Total		342

Fall of wickets 19, 28, 47, 47, 160, 160, 209, 316, 342, 342

	O	M	R	W
RC Motz	31	9	83	3
GA Bartlett	33.2	6	63	3
RS Cunis	31	9	63	2
N Puna	18	6	54	0
ME Chapple	9	3	24	1
V Pollard	5	1	27	1

ENGLAND 2ND INNINGS		
G Boycott	run out	4
WE Russell	b Bartlett	25
JH Edrich	lbw b Cunis	2
MC Cowdrey	c Pollard b Motz	21
MJK Smith*	c Bilby b Puna	87
PH Parfitt	not out	46
JM Parks†	not out	4
Extras	(b 4, lb 1, nb 7)	12
Total	(5 wickets dec)	201

Did not bat DA Allen, DJ Brown, K Higgs, IJ Jones

Fall of wickets 18, 32, 48, 68, 193

	O	M	R	W
RC Motz	20	6	38	1
GA Bartlett	14	2	44	1
RS Cunis	19	3	58	1
N Puna	14	6	49	1

NEW ZEALAND 1ST INNINGS		
GP Bilby	c Parks b Higgs	28
MJF Shrimpton	c Parks b Brown	11
BE Congdon	c Smith b Jones	104
BW Sinclair	c & b Higgs	23
V Pollard	lbw b Higgs	23
ME Chapple*	c Cowdrey b Jones	15
GA Bartlett	c Parks b Brown	0
EC Petrie†	c Parks b Brown	55
RC Motz	c Parks b Jones	58
RS Cunis	not out	8
N Puna	c Smith b Jones	1
Extras	(b 7, lb 13, nb 1)	21
Total		347

Fall of wickets 39, 41, 112, 181, 202, 203, 237, 326, 344, 347

	O	M	R	W
DJ Brown	30	3	80	3
IJ Jones	28.4	9	71	4
K Higgs	30	6	51	3
DA Allen	40	14	80	0
G Boycott	12	6	30	0
PH Parfitt	3	0	14	0

NEW ZEALAND 2ND INNINGS		
GP Bilby	c Parks b Brown	3
MJF Shrimpton	c Smith b Allen	13
BE Congdon	c Cowdrey b Higgs	4
BW Sinclair	c Parks b Higgs	0
V Pollard	not out	6
EC Petrie†	lbw b Higgs	1
ME Chapple*	c Parks b Higgs	0
GA Bartlett	c Brown b Parfitt	0
RC Motz	c Russell b Parfitt	2
RS Cunis	not out	16
Extras	(b 2, lb 1)	3
Total	(8 wickets)	48

Did not bat N Puna

Fall of wickets 5, 19, 21, 21, 22, 22, 22, 32

	O	M	R	W
DJ Brown	4	2	6	1
IJ Jones	7	3	13	0
K Higgs	9	7	5	4
DA Allen	19	15	8	1
PH Parfitt	6	3	5	2
JM Parks	3	1	8	0

Toss: England   Umpires: FR Goodall and WT Martin

Match drawn

South Africa v Australia
First Test at New Wanderers Stadium, Johannesburg

1966-67
December 23, 24, 26, 27, 28 (1966)

South Africa had not beaten Australia on South African soil in 21 attempts from 1902–03 to 1957–58, yet there was hope for the Africans that the drought could break in 1966–67 after Transvaal defeated the Australians in a tour match. A classic first Test captured the attention of the faithful and ensured an eye-catching series ahead.

South Africa batted first after winning the toss despite plenty of rain in the lead-up. Fourteen runs were on the board when debutant Australian wicketkeeper Brian Taber took his first catch. Trevor Goddard was the batsman and Neil Hawke the bowler, before Taber was involved in the second dismissal as well with Eddie Barlow the batsman and Graham McKenzie the bowler. In a great spell, McKenzie had Ali Bacher caught by Bob Cowper before having Colin Bland lbw. McKenzie subsequently took a catch to produce debutant bowler David Renneberg's first Test scalp, a key one in the form of Graeme Pollock. South Africa was on the skids at 41-5 after just 90 minutes, before 'Tiger' Lance and wicketkeeper Denis Lindsay provided the home side with fresh hope.

Lindsay scored at a speedy rate while Lance was more defensive. Lindsay scored most of his 69 runs in the 110-run partnership before he fell to the combination of Australia's debutants. Just five more runs were added before Lance departed, and then a 24-run partnership ensued before the last three wickets fell for nine runs. Bob Simpson claimed two wickets before the innings finished with McKenzie's fifth wicket and Taber's fifth catch. The tourists held all the aces at stumps as they were 99-0, with Simpson on 52 and Bill Lawry 41.

Simpson scored 13 of the first 19 runs on day two before Peter Pollock dismissed him. Australia remained in control as Lawry and Ian Redpath took Australia to the lead with nine wickets remaining, before the tourists declined from 204-

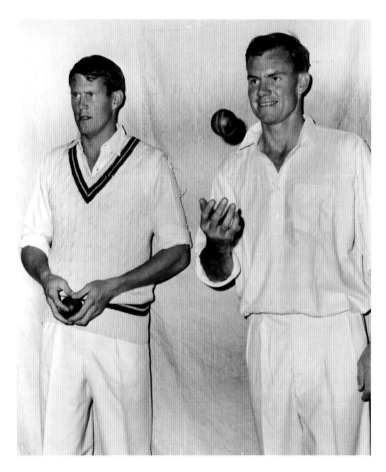

Brothers Graeme and Peter Pollock were an enormously vital part of South African teams in the 1960s.

1 to 207-4. Lawry was just two runs shy of a century when Goddard had him caught behind, before Barlow had Redpath caught behind for 41. Cowper and Keith Stackpole fell likewise without scoring as Australia became 218-5, before Ian Chappell and Tom Veivers provided resistance. Chappell made 37 and Veivers 18 before both fell on 267. Taber scored 13 before

his counterpart exceeded him with six catches. Australia's tail provided some resistance, and there was a last wicket stand of 26, but the eventual 126-run lead was measly considering how strong Australia's position was at 204-1. South Africa's openers had four runs on the board before play resumed after the teams spent Christmas Day away from cricket.

The first South African wicket was again that of Goddard to Hawke's bowling, before Barlow and Bacher steadied the ship. Barlow's solid 50 included seven fours before Renneberg had him caught behind, and then Graeme Pollock showed his talent with great timing and placement as well as aggressive strokes as South Africa built a lead. Australia was not helped as a groin injury prevented Hawke completing his 15th over. South Africa however was not helped as a run out accounted for Bacher after he scored 63 and helped Pollock take the score from 87-2 to 178-2.

Bland made a start before falling for 32, and Pollock went on to hammer 90 in just 114 minutes, including 15 fours and two sixes. The match was interestingly poised when Cowper bowled Pollock, as South Africa was effectively 142-5.

Lance took on a forceful role, and Lindsay had a crucial reprieve on 10 when he was dropped. Lance and Lindsay extended South Africa's lead to 210 at stumps, and Lance added just four runs before falling to McKenzie. Lance's 70 included 10 fours and a six. Another crucial catch was spilled as South African captain Peter van der Merwe was on two, and the two batsmen at the crease made the most of their second chances.

A breathtaking 221-run partnership unfolded, with Lindsay's first Test century containing 25 fours and five sixes as he scored 182 from just 227 balls in 273 minutes. Van der Merwe scored 76 and Richard Dumbrill 29 as South Africa raced past 600. The last two wickets fell on 620 as Taber took a catch and a stumping to complete eight dismissals. The Australians however had their backs to the wall as they needed 495 runs in eight hours. Lawry lasted 90 minutes before Atholl McKinnon bowled him, and Australia finished the day on 97-1 with Simpson on 48 and Redpath 17.

The tourists were in trouble from the second ball of the final day as Simpson unwisely risked a single and was run out. Goddard had Cowper caught behind just one run later, and not even 30 minutes of the day's play had passed when Redpath and Stackpole were back in the pavilion. Australia was 112-5, but Chappell and Veivers were not about to surrender. They showed determination as survival was Australia's only hope, but they did not last. Veivers made 55 and Chappell 34, and McKenzie struck five fours and two sixes in his 34 as Australia was doomed to defeat.

Above: Australia's Bob Simpson, who formed a steady opening batting combination with Bill Lawry.

Opposite: South African wicketkeeper Denis Lindsay.

The 35-year-old Goddard took his best Test figures, 6-53, including the final wickets of Hawke and McKenzie to catches by 20-year-old substitute fielder Mike Procter, who made his Test debut later in the series. Both wicketkeepers finished with eight dismissals after Lindsay caught Chappell in Australia's second innings, completing a phenomenal match for Lindsay. His 251 runs was easily the most decisive figure as the hosts won by 233 runs, an unthinkable result after Australia led on the first innings with nine wickets remaining. South Africa's first win against Australia on South African soil was memorable in numerous ways.

Australian team manager Bill Jacobs denied allegations that Australia's defeat followed a wild champagne Christmas party. The tourists levelled the series with a six-wicket win in the second Test before the hosts went on to win the five-match series 3-1. Lindsay was continually prominent, scoring 606 runs and taking 24 catches in the series.

SOUTH AFRICA 1ST INNINGS

TL Goddard	c Taber b Hawke	5
EJ Barlow	c Taber b McKenzie	13
A Bacher	c Cowper b McKenzie	5
RG Pollock	c McKenzie b Renneberg	5
KC Bland	lbw b McKenzie	0
HR Lance	hit wicket b McKenzie	44
DT Lindsay†	c Taber b Renneberg	69
PL van der Merwe*	c Taber b Simpson	19
R Dumbrill	c Chappell b Simpson	19
PM Pollock	c Taber b McKenzie	6
AH McKinnon	not out	0
Extras	(b 11, w 3)	14
Total		199

Fall of wickets 14, 31, 31, 35, 41, 151, 156, 190, 199, 199

	O	M	R	W
GD McKenzie	21.5	6	46	5
NJN Hawke	8	1	25	1
DA Renneberg	16	3	54	2
IM Chappell	2	0	16	0
TR Veivers	9	1	13	0
RM Cowper	6	0	21	0
RB Simpson	4	1	10	2

SOUTH AFRICA 2ND INNINGS

TL Goddard	c Simpson b Hawke	13
EJ Barlow	c Taber b Renneberg	50
A Bacher	run out	63
RG Pollock	b Cowper	90
KC Bland	c Simpson b Chappell	32
HR Lance	c Simpson b McKenzie	70
DT Lindsay†	c Chappell b Stackpole	182
PL van der Merwe*	c Chappell b Simpson	76
R Dumbrill	c Taber b Chappell	29
PM Pollock	st Taber b Simpson	2
AH McKinnon	not out	0
Extras	(b 7, lb 5, w 1)	13
Total		620

Fall of wickets 29, 87, 178, 228, 268, 349, 570, 614, 620, 620

	O	M	R	W
GD McKenzie	39	4	118	1
NJN Hawke	14.2	1	46	1
DA Renneberg	32	8	96	1
IM Chappell	21	3	91	2
TR Veivers	18	3	59	0
RM Cowper	16	2	56	1
RB Simpson	16.1	3	66	2
KR Stackpole	21	6	75	1

AUSTRALIA 1ST INNINGS

RB Simpson*	c Goddard b PM Pollock	65
WM Lawry	c Lindsay b Goddard	98
IR Redpath	c Lindsay b Barlow	41
RM Cowper	c Lindsay b Barlow	0
KR Stackpole	c Lindsay b Barlow	0
IM Chappell	c Lindsay b Goddard	37
TR Veivers	b Lance	18
HB Taber†	c Lindsay b McKinnon	13
GD McKenzie	run out	16
NJN Hawke	not out	18
DA Renneberg	c Goddard b McKinnon	9
Extras	(lb 5, w 2, nb 3)	10
Total		325

Fall of wickets 118, 204, 207, 207, 218, 267, 267, 294, 299, 325

	O	M	R	W
PM Pollock	25	6	74	1
R Dumbrill	18	3	55	0
TL Goddard	26	11	39	2
HR Lance	17	6	35	1
AH McKinnon	27.2	9	73	2
EJ Barlow	17	3	39	3

AUSTRALIA 2ND INNINGS

RB Simpson*	run out	48
WM Lawry	b McKinnon	27
IR Redpath	c van der Merwe b Barlow	21
RM Cowper	c Lindsay b Goddard	1
KR Stackpole	b Goddard	9
IM Chappell	c Lindsay b Dumbrill	34
TR Veivers	b Goddard	55
HB Taber†	b Goddard	7
GD McKenzie	c sub (MJ Procter) b Goddard	34
NJN Hawke	c sub (MJ Procter) b Goddard	13
DA Renneberg	not out	2
Extras	(lb 6, w 2, nb 2)	10
Total		261

Fall of wickets 62, 97, 98, 110, 112, 183, 210, 212, 248, 261

	O	M	R	W
PM Pollock	18	3	33	0
R Dumbrill	16	6	43	1
TL Goddard	32.5	14	53	6
HR Lance	3	0	6	0
AH McKinnon	30	14	64	1
EJ Barlow	15	1	47	1
RG Pollock	3	1	5	0

Toss: South Africa   Umpires: LM Baxter and HC Kidson
South Africa won by 233 runs

Australia v West Indies
Fourth Test at the Adelaide Oval

1968-69
January 24, 25, 27, 28, 29 (1969)

Sir Don Bradman raising the Australian flag in the traditional Australia Day weekend Test at the Adelaide Oval in 1968. Rival captains Garry Sobers (left) and Bill Lawry (right) stand at attention.

Garry Sobers rated the fourth Test of the 1968–69 series involving the West Indies and Australia at Adelaide as the most exciting Test he played in other than the 1960 tied Test. Eight years passed between West Indian tours to Australia, although the West Indians defeated Australia 2-1 in the Caribbean in 1964–65 after Australia won by the same margin in 1960–61.

Australia led the 1968–69 series 2-1 after losing the first Test, so there was much interest in the fourth Test. Batting first after winning the toss, the tourists began soundly before Alan Connolly trapped Roy Fredericks for 17. Rohan Kanhai was dismissed in the same fashion for 11, before Michael 'Joey' Carew and Basil Butcher were separated after putting on a 50-partnership. Carew lasted two hours before he was caught by Ian Chappell off John Gleeson for 36, and the West Indies struggled to 107-4 when Graham McKenzie accounted for Seymour Nurse. Indiscreet strokes were responsible for the wickets that fell, although Sobers played another splendid innings to give the total some respectability.

Butcher scored a solid 52 before he suffered the same fate as Carew, and Clive Lloyd hit a six before departing for 10 as the tourists became 215-6. After David Holford departed, Sobers went on to score 110 before Eric Freeman bowled him, after hitting 15 fours and two sixes in a sublime 132-minute stay. Freeman finished with four wickets as the tourists tallied a modest 276, before Australia was 37-0 at stumps with Keith Stackpole on 30.

Stackpole and fellow opener Bill Lawry scored 62 each, and then the two Ians, Chappell and Redpath, kept the score moving before falling in quick succession as 248-2 became 254-4. Australia's momentum was not lost as two players known by their middle name, Kevin Douglas Walters and Andrew Paul Sheahan, joined the run flow. Sheahan scored 51, and Australia led by 71 runs when he became the second of off spinner Lance Gibbs' victims. Freeman wielded the bat to good effect as he hit five fours and a six in his 33, before he was lbw to Charlie Griffith as Australia finished the day in the box seat at 424-6.

Following the rest day, Barry Jarman fell cheaply before Walters went on to match Sobers' score. Walters struck 13 fours and batted 62 more minutes than Sobers did, and Australia's innings was far from finished after Walters' demise. McKenzie hit five fours and a six in his 59, one of only two half-centuries in his 60 Tests from 1961 to 1971. Gleeson scored a handy 17 as Australia gained a commanding 257-run lead.

Fredericks departed after making another start, this time 23 runs in 48 minutes. The following batsmen however knuckled

Australian Cricketer of the Year for 1967–68, 27-year-old Graham McKenzie became the youngest player to capture 200 Test wickets the following season (a record since beaten).

down and found form on the pitch which remained favourable for batting. Carew and Kanhai added 132 runs in 140 minutes for the second wicket, with Kanhai registering 10 fours and a six before Connolly bowled him for 80. Carew gave Gleeson some harsh treatment, and Butcher batted much more freely than in the first innings. Carew scored 90 in nearly four hours before Chappell again caught him, and then nightwatchman Griffith combined with Butcher to take the tourists to a four-run lead at the close of play.

Griffith was run out soon after the 300 was raised, before an aggressive Nurse scored at nearly a run per minute for his 40. Nurse was Gleeson's only victim in the West Indian second innings, in which Gleeson bowled 35 overs and conceded 176 runs. Butcher went on to score 118 in 191 minutes with 18 fours before McKenzie had him caught, and the tourists were effectively 147-6 as it appeared many batsmen would rue squandering chances to build big scores. Left-handers Sobers and Lloyd also made good starts before Connolly dismissed them both to claim five wickets in the innings, and the tourists led by 235 runs with two wickets in hand.

Holford subsequently played a fine innings while Jackie Hendriks proved a stumbling block to ensure a challenging target would be set. The partnership produced 122 runs before Holford departed at the end of the day after scoring 80 in nearly three hours. Just two runs were added the following morning before Gibbs was dismissed, leaving Hendriks stranded on 37 from 147 minutes and Australia needing 360 runs in five hours and 45 minutes.

Stackpole gave the hosts a flying start with a half-century. The opening partnership produced 86 runs in as many minutes before Gibbs had Stackpole caught behind. Lawry and Chappell kept the scoring rate going at about a run per minute as 99 runs were added before Lawry was caught off Sobers for 89. There was some unpleasantness when the third wicket fell at 215, as Griffith ran out Redpath in the 'Mankad' fashion without a warning after Redpath backed up too far as Griffith came in to bowl.

Walters however helped Chappell take the hosts to the brink of success, and only 62 runs were needed from the final 15 eight-ball overs with seven wickets standing. Chappell was just four runs shy of 100 when Griffith had him lbw, before the game changed drastically in 15 minutes as Australia went from the brink of victory to the brink of defeat. Walters was run out soon after he reached 50, and Sheahan shouldered much of the blame as Freeman and Jarman were run out cheaply as Australia wastefully flopped to 322-7.

Sheahan and McKenzie put on 11 runs before McKenzie skied a sweep to square leg. When Griffith trapped Gleeson, Sheahan and Connolly had to survive 26 balls for a draw or score 27 runs for victory. This bore some resemblance to the Adelaide Test in 1960–61, when Ken Mackay and Lindsay Kline survived 100 minutes to secure a draw. Eight years on, Sheahan and Connolly survived 10 deliveries with the old ball before the new ball was taken. Sobers sent the new ball swinging down leg, and Australia hung on for a thrilling draw while 21 runs shy of victory.

Above: Garry Sobers.

Right: A young Doug Walters, who scored a century and a half-century against the West Indies in Adelaide.

WEST INDIES 1ST INNINGS

RC Fredericks	lbw b Connolly	17
MC Carew	c Chappell b Gleeson	36
RB Kanhai	lbw b Connolly	11
BF Butcher	c Chappell b Gleeson	52
SM Nurse	c & b McKenzie	5
GS Sobers*	b Freeman	110
CH Lloyd	c Lawry b Gleeson	10
DAJ Holford	c McKenzie b Freeman	6
CC Griffith	b Freeman	7
JL Hendriks†	not out	10
LR Gibbs	c Connolly b Freeman	4
Extras	(b 5, lb 2, nb 1)	8
Total		276

Fall of wickets 21, 39, 89, 107, 199, 215, 228, 261, 264, 276

	O	M	R	W
GD McKenzie	14	1	51	1
AN Connolly	13	3	61	2
EW Freeman	10.3	0	52	4
JW Gleeson	25	5	91	3
KR Stackpole	3	1	13	0

WEST INDIES 2ND INNINGS

RC Fredericks	c Chappell b Connolly	23
MC Carew	c Chappell b Connolly	90
RB Kanhai	b Connolly	80
BF Butcher	c Sheahan b McKenzie	118
CC Griffith	run out	24
SM Nurse	lbw b Gleeson	40
GS Sobers*	c Walters b Connolly	52
CH Lloyd	c Redpath b Connolly	42
DAJ Holford	c Stackpole b McKenzie	80
JL Hendriks†	not out	37
LR Gibbs	b McKenzie	1
Extras	(b 5, lb 12, nb 12)	29
Total		616

Fall of wickets 35, 167, 240, 304, 376, 404, 476, 492, 614, 616

	O	M	R	W
GD McKenzie	22.2	4	90	3
AN Connolly	34	7	122	5
EW Freeman	18	3	96	0
JW Gleeson	35	2	176	1
KR Stackpole	12	3	44	0
IM Chappell	14	0	50	0
KD Walters	1	0	6	0
IR Redpath	1	0	3	0

AUSTRALIA 1ST INNINGS

WM Lawry*	c Butcher b Sobers	62
KR Stackpole	c Hendriks b Holford	62
IM Chappell	c Sobers b Gibbs	76
IR Redpath	lbw b Carew	45
KD Walters	c & b Griffith	110
AP Sheahan	b Gibbs	51
EW Freeman	lbw b Griffith	33
BN Jarman†	c Hendriks b Gibbs	3
GD McKenzie	c Nurse b Holford	59
JW Gleeson	b Gibbs	17
AN Connolly	not out	1
Extras	(b 3, lb 6, nb 5)	14
Total		533

Fall of wickets 89, 170, 248, 254, 347, 424, 429, 465, 529, 533

	O	M	R	W
GS Sobers	28	4	106	1
CC Griffith	22	4	94	2
DAJ Holford	18.5	0	118	2
LR Gibbs	43	8	145	4
MC Carew	9	3	30	1
CH Lloyd	6	0	26	0

AUSTRALIA 2ND INNINGS

WM Lawry*	c sub b Sobers	89
KR Stackpole	c Hendriks b Gibbs	50
IM Chappell	lbw b Griffith	96
IR Redpath	run out	9
KD Walters	run out	50
AP Sheahan	not out	11
EW Freeman	run out	1
BN Jarman†	run out	4
GD McKenzie	c sub b Gibbs	4
JW Gleeson	lbw b Griffith	0
AN Connolly	not out	6
Extras	(b 8, lb 10, nb 1)	19
Total	(9 wickets)	339

Fall of wickets 86, 185, 215, 304, 315, 318, 322, 333, 333

	O	M	R	W
GS Sobers	22	1	107	1
CC Griffith	19	2	73	2
DAJ Holford	15	1	53	0
LR Gibbs	26	7	79	2
MC Carew	2	0	8	0

Toss: West Indies   Umpires: CJ Egar and LP Rowan

Match drawn

England v West Indies
Third Test at Headingley, Leeds

1969
July 10, 11, 12, 14, 15 (1969)

The West Indies touring team to England, captained by legendary all-rounder Garry Sobers (seated third from left).

England was in sight of successive series wins over the West Indies, with England having won the 1967–68 five-match series 1-0 before leading the three-match series 1-0 in 1969 with one Test remaining. Headingley was the venue for the final Test, which was one to remember.

England chose to bat after winning the toss, although rain caused play to begin 80 minutes late. Garry Sobers struck a big blow for the visitors when he trapped Geoff Boycott lbw for 12. John Edrich produced decent form, but the batting at the other end seemed vulnerable. Vanburn Holder had Phil Sharpe and John Hampshire caught behind as England stumbled to 64-3. Edrich and Basil D'Oliveira worked hard in damp and cloudy conditions, and put on 76 runs before Edrich was lbw to John Shepherd, having registered just six fours on a slow outfield in his 190-minute knock of 79.

D'Oliveira hit three fours and a six before he was caught by Sobers off Shepherd for 48, sparking a collapse. Ray Illingworth was bowled by Shepherd for one, and Barry Knight caught off Lance Gibbs for seven. England was 194-7 at stumps, and 199-8 the next day when Derek Underwood departed. Alan Knott made a solid 44 before becoming the fourth batsman caught by wicketkeeper Mike Findlay. Holder finished the innings with the wicket of David Brown, before the West Indies began uncertainly in response to England's 223.

Steve Camacho scratched around for 40 minutes before he was caught behind off Knight, who followed up with the wickets of Charlie Davis and Roy Fredericks as the visitors sank to 46-3. Basil Butcher looked confident but the batting side remained in trouble, as Knight had Sobers caught at slip for 13 before Butcher departed for 35 when John Snow bowled him. When D'Oliveira had Findlay lbw for one, the West Indies were 91-6 and had only three wickets left as a back injury prevented Shepherd batting.

Clive Lloyd and Holder hinted at a recovery, with Lloyd hitting a six before he was caught off Brown as the total was 151. Holder and Grayson Shillingford soon followed, and the hosts led by 62 runs. The momentum quickly changed again as Sobers had Boycott caught behind for a second-ball duck, before England finished day two on 13-1.

The weather was fine on day three but batting didn't seem to become easier, as the scoring rate was very slow while Sobers bowled superbly. Edrich and Sharpe were both lbw to Sobers for 15, with Edrich's innings lasting 71 minutes and Sharpe's 117 minutes. Hampshire scored a slightly quicker 22 before he too was lbw, albeit to Shillingford. Sobers took a staggering 2-18 from 18 overs before lunch, as Shepherd was unable to bowl.

Garry Sobers failed with the bat as his beloved West Indies team went down by 30 runs to concede the Wisden Trophy to England.

D'Oliveira scored a little quicker than in the first innings, while Knott played a stonewalling role. England was 102-5 when D'Oliveira was caught off Davis, before Illingworth gave Knott solid support. Sobers however came back for another spell, and again proved hard to get away as he took 2-14 in 10 overs. Knott took just over two hours to score 31, before he was again caught behind off Sobers. Illingworth was caught off Holder with the total still on 147, and then Underwood scored a handy 16 before Sobers bowled him, as England led by 233 runs.

Knight and Brown added 32 runs for the ninth wicket, before the last wicket partnership frustrated the tourists further. Thirty-seven runs were added in 57 minutes, including 26 runs on day four which followed a rest day. Snow remained undefeated on 15, while Brown was bowled by Shillingford after scoring 34 in 115 minutes, and facing 126 balls. The West Indies could not have been satisfied with England's total of 240 after the score had been 58-4 and later 147-7. Nonetheless, the tourists had a little less than two days in which to score 303 runs to square the series.

The pitch had become less moist, but it didn't help Fredericks who failed again as he edged Snow to Sharpe at slip with the total on just eight. Camacho and Davis added 61 runs before the latter was caught-and-bowled by Underwood, and then the West Indies gained control. Camacho and Butcher set up a platform for victory, as Camacho played the anchor role while Butcher went for his strokes and hit regular boundaries. Camacho scored more than half of his 71 runs in boundaries before he was caught off Underwood, having batted for 231 minutes and added 108 runs with Butcher.

Lloyd settled in while Butcher kept the runs flowing, and the West Indies were in sight of victory at 219-3 when the next twist came. On 91 after striking 16 fours, Butcher was controversially adjudged caught behind off Underwood. The game was still there for the visiting team's taking, but the complexion swung England's way as Sobers played a Knight delivery onto the stumps before Sobers had scored. Illingworth had Lloyd caught behind, and the tourists had lost 9-3 in 16 minutes. The collapse worsened to 9-4 as the injured Shepherd was caught behind off Underwood, who had the knack of striking just when England needed it. Findlay and Holder survived the rest of the day, before the West Indies needed 63 runs on the last day.

Illingworth took the new ball at the start of the final day, and the tension mounted as 11 runs were added in 30 minutes before Brown had Holder caught at slip. Gibbs scored four before departing as Knott claimed his fourth catch of the innings and sixth in the Test. This left Findlay, who had also taken six catches, with the responsibility of putting together a last wicket stand of 48 with Shillingford.

A West Indian victory remained a possibility as 17 runs were added in 30 minutes. Knight however had the final say as he won an lbw appeal against Findlay, who scored 16 in 103 minutes. England retained the Wisden Trophy with its 30-run win.

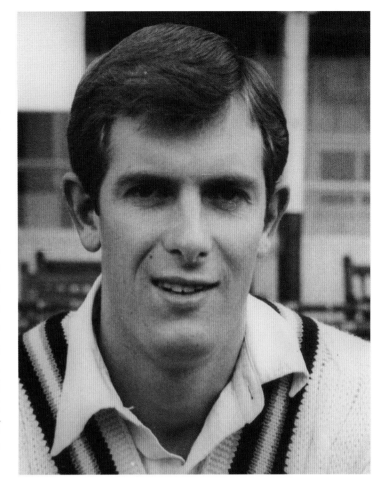

Top: England paceman David Brown took 79 wickets in 26 Tests in the 1960s, for an average of 28.31.
Bottom: England's stoic opening batsman Geoff Boycott, who averaged 47.72 in his 108 Tests from 1964 to 1982.

ENGLAND 1ST INNINGS		
G Boycott	lbw b Sobers	12
JH Edrich	lbw b Shepherd	79
PJ Sharpe	c Findlay b Holder	6
JH Hampshire	c Findlay b Holder	1
BL D'Oliveira	c Sobers b Shepherd	48
APE Knott†	c Findlay b Sobers	44
R Illingworth*	b Shepherd	1
BR Knight	c Fredericks b Gibbs	7
DL Underwood	c Findlay b Holder	4
DJ Brown	b Holder	12
JA Snow	not out	1
Extras	(b 4, lb 3, nb 1)	8
Total		223

Fall of wickets 30, 52, 64, 140, 165, 167, 182, 199, 217, 223

	O	M	R	W
GS Sobers	21	1	68	2
VA Holder	26	7	48	4
GC Shillingford	7	0	21	0
LR Gibbs	19	6	33	1
JN Shepherd	24	8	43	3
CA Davis	1	0	2	0

WEST INDIES 1ST INNINGS		
RC Fredericks	lbw b Knight	11
GS Camacho	c Knott b Knight	4
CA Davis	c Underwood b Knight	18
BF Butcher	b Snow	35
GS Sobers*	c Sharpe b Knight	13
CH Lloyd	c Snow b Brown	27
TM Findlay†	lbw b D'Oliveira	1
VA Holder	b Snow	35
LR Gibbs	not out	6
GC Shillingford	c Knott b Brown	3
JN Shepherd	absent hurt	-
Extras	(lb 7, nb 1)	8
Total		161

Fall of wickets 17, 37, 46, 80, 88, 91, 151, 153, 161

	O	M	R	W
JA Snow	20	4	50	2
DJ Brown	7.3	2	13	2
BR Knight	22	5	63	4
BL D'Oliveira	15	8	27	1

ENGLAND 2ND INNINGS		
G Boycott	c Findlay b Sobers	0
JH Edrich	lbw b Sobers	15
PJ Sharpe	lbw b Sobers	15
JH Hampshire	lbw b Shillingford	22
BL D'Oliveira	c Sobers b Davis	39
APE Knott†	c Findlay b Sobers	31
R Illingworth*	c Lloyd b Holder	19
BR Knight	c Holder b Gibbs	27
DL Underwood	b Sobers	16
DJ Brown	b Shillingford	34
JA Snow	not out	15
Extras	(lb 5, w 1, nb 1)	7
Total		240

Fall of wickets 0, 23, 42, 58, 102, 147, 147, 171, 203, 240

	O	M	R	W
GS Sobers	40	18	42	5
VA Holder	33	13	66	1
GC Shillingford	20.4	4	56	2
LR Gibbs	21	6	42	1
CA Davis	17	8	27	1

WEST INDIES 2ND INNINGS		
RC Fredericks	c Sharpe b Snow	6
GS Camacho	c Hampshire b Underwood	71
CA Davis	c & b Underwood	29
BF Butcher	c Knott b Underwood	91
CH Lloyd	c Knott b Illingworth	23
GS Sobers*	b Knight	0
TM Findlay†	lbw b Knight	16
JN Shepherd	c Knott b Underwood	0
VA Holder	c Sharpe b Brown	13
LR Gibbs	c Knott b Brown	4
GC Shillingford	not out	5
Extras	(lb 11, nb 3)	14
Total		272

Fall of wickets 8, 69, 177, 219, 224, 228, 228, 251, 255, 272

	O	M	R	W
JA Snow	21	7	43	1
DJ Brown	21	8	53	2
BR Knight	18.2	4	47	2
BL D'Oliveira	10	3	22	0
R Illingworth	14	5	38	1
DL Underwood	22	12	55	4

Toss: England   Umpires: CS Elliott and AE Fagg   England won by 30 runs

Australia v England

Seventh Test at the Sydney Cricket Ground

1970-71

February 12, 13, 14, 16, 17 (1971)

Australian tail-end batsman Terry Jenner is felled by a bouncer from England paceman John Snow.

The 1970–71 Ashes series featured a seventh Test, which proved the most decisive of the series after the third Test was washed out. England led 1-0 with the seventh Test remaining, ensuring ample interest as Australia needed a win to retain the urn it had held since 1958–59.

Both sides lost a dogged opening batsman, as a broken arm sidelined England's Geoff Boycott while Australia's Bill Lawry was dropped following a dispute with the board. Lawry's Victorian team-mate Ken Eastwood subsequently played his only Test while Queensland left-arm paceman Tony Dell played the first of his two Tests. Dell shared the new ball with Dennis Lillee after new Australian skipper Ian Chappell won the toss and sent England in. Brian Luckhurst lasted 37 minutes but hadn't scored when Doug Walters' first over saw him caught at short leg via bat and pad.

John Edrich and Keith Fletcher slowly put on 55 runs before Dell claimed his maiden wicket as Edrich edged to third slip. Kerry O'Keeffe ended Fletcher's resistance before Basil D'Oliveira played a Dell delivery onto the stumps, making England 69-4. John Hampshire drove Lillee for four before edging him behind, and then Alan Knott helped Ray

Illingworth steady the ship. Illingworth dug in well, but England's innings resumed deteriorating when Knott was splendidly caught by Keith Stackpole at short leg for 27.

Terry Jenner bowled John Snow and Illingworth, whose 42 occupied 135 minutes. Peter Lever was caught by Jenner off O'Keeffe without a run added, and then a 19-run partnership occurred for the last wicket before Jenner matched fellow leg spinner O'Keeffe with three wickets. England's 184 did not look substantial, but the hosts fell to 13-2 in six overs before stumps. Eastwood glanced a catch behind off Lever, and a Snow delivery beat Stackpole.

Having been promoted to first drop, Rod Marsh scored a miserly four before falling to a leaping catch from Bob Willis. Ian Chappell looked settled before Willis bowled him for 25, and Australia was 66-4. The innings could have collapsed had Walters not been reprieved three times. When Walters was stumped for 42, Australia trailed by 37. Ian Redpath made a vital 59, but Australia was still 22 runs in arrears when he departed. O'Keeffe also departed before Australia hit the lead.

Australia was 195-7 when Jenner ducked into a short ball from Snow and was hit on the head. Jenner fell in agony before

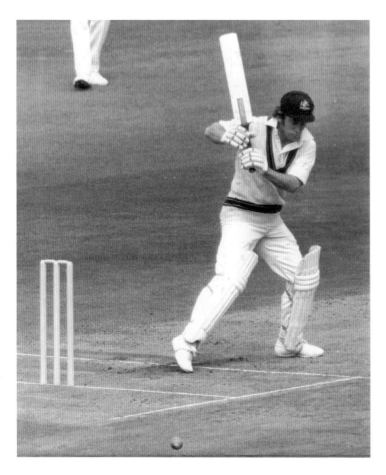

Ian Chappell's first Test as Australian captain was the seventh and final Test of the 1970–71 Ashes series.

Terry Jenner took 24 wickets in his nine Tests for Australia as a leg-spin bowler.

John Snow has his shirt grabbed by an irate spectator after the England fast bowler's bouncer felled Terry Jenner.

retiring hurt, and umpire Lou Rowan warned Snow before Snow fielded on the boundary and had his shirt grabbed by an unruly spectator. More unruly spectators threw cans and bottles onto the field, and the game was halted as Illingworth took his team off the field. The tourists returned after the umpires warned that England would lose on a forfeit if the England players did not return.

Greg Chappell seemed unfazed as he and Lillee helped Australia to 235-7 at stumps, before Willis had Lillee caught behind first thing on day three. Chappell fell just four runs later, but Jenner returned upon Lillee's dismissal and went from eight to 30 before Lever bowled him. Edrich and Luckhurst turned England's 80-run deficit into a 14-run lead before Luckhurst, on 59, lofted O'Keeffe and was well caught by Lillee. England unexpectedly lost its second wicket 36 runs later as Eastwood's rarely used chinaman bowling saw Fletcher hit a full-toss to short mid wicket. England stuttered from 158-2 to 165-4 after Edrich

and Hampshire were caught by Ian Chappell off O'Keeffe. Edrich fell to a googly, before Hampshire miscued a sweep and fell to a great running and diving catch. Illingworth had a couple of near misses early on, and later was painfully struck on the left knee by a Dell delivery. Illingworth and D'Oliveira however survived until stumps as England reached 229-4.

Lillee dismissed D'Oliveira and Illingworth before they made much impact on day four, and England was effectively 171-6. Knott, Snow and Lever made useful contributions before England lost its last three wickets for four runs, Dell finishing with the best figures. The stage was set: would Australia score the required 223 and hold the Ashes for a seventh successive series?

Snow yorked Eastwood from the sixth ball of the chase without a run on the board, leaving the 35-year-old Eastwood with an average of 2.50. England sustained a setback when Snow raced towards a skied hook from Stackpole, and injured

Victorious England skipper Ray Illingworth pours a drink for his bowler, John Snow, after England won the Ashes in the final Test of 1970–71.

a finger on his bowling hand against the fence. Snow was consequently unable to bowl more than two overs, but Lever struck a huge blow when he had Ian Chappell caught behind. Australia 22-2.

Stackpole survived a caught behind appeal on 13, and batted with confidence. Redpath however was much less convincing, scoring a slow 14 before being caught off Illingworth. Walters was caught at third man from an indiscreet stroke, leaving Australia in trouble at 82-4. Stackpole quickly moved to 67, having struck six fours and two sixes, but then Australia fell to 96-5 when Illingworth bowled him. Greg Chappell and Marsh began a potential revival, although Marsh survived a difficult stumping chance at 103-5 before the hosts needed exactly 100 runs on day five.

Only eight runs were added on day five when Underwood bowled Marsh, before Illingworth drifted a ball past Greg Chappell who was stumped to leave Australia needing 81 runs with only three wickets in hand. O'Keeffe and Jenner resisted for a while, but the total was still only 154 when D'Oliveira had O'Keeffe and Lillee caught from successive deliveries. Jenner and Dell needed to accumulate 69 runs to secure Australia a one-wicket win to draw the series. The partnership lasted only 12 minutes, with Jenner caught by Fletcher off Underwood to seal a 62-run win for England and a 2-0 series victory. Illingworth was chaired off the field, having become the first England captain since Douglas Jardine to regain the Ashes in enemy territory. Bizarrely, no Australian batsman was dismissed lbw in the 1970–71 series.

ENGLAND 1ST INNINGS

JH Edrich	c GS Chappell b Dell	30
BW Luckhurst	c Redpath b Walters	0
KWR Fletcher	c Stackpole b O'Keeffe	33
JH Hampshire	c Marsh b Lillee	10
BL D'Oliveira	b Dell	1
R Illingworth*	b Jenner	42
APE Knott†	c Stackpole b O'Keeffe	27
JA Snow	b Jenner	7
P Lever	c Jenner b O'Keeffe	4
DL Underwood	not out	8
RGD Willis	b Jenner	11
Extras	(b 4, lb 4, w 1, nb 2)	11
Total		184

Fall of wickets 5, 60, 68, 69, 98, 145, 156, 165, 165, 184

	O	M	R	W
DK Lillee	13	5	32	1
AR Dell	16	8	32	2
KD Walters	4	0	10	1
GS Chappell	3	0	9	0
TJ Jenner	16	3	42	3
KJ O'Keeffe	24	8	48	3

ENGLAND 2ND INNINGS

JH Edrich	c IM Chappell b O'Keeffe	57
BW Luckhurst	c Lillee b O'Keeffe	59
KWR Fletcher	c Stackpole b Eastwood	20
JH Hampshire	c IM Chappell b O'Keeffe	24
BL D'Oliveira	c IM Chappell b Lillee	47
R Illingworth*	lbw b Lillee	29
APE Knott†	b Dell	15
JA Snow	c Stackpole b Dell	20
P Lever	c Redpath b Jenner	17
DL Underwood	c Marsh b Dell	0
RGD Willis	not out	2
Extras	(b 3, lb 3, nb 6)	12
Total		302

Fall of wickets 94, 130, 158, 165, 234, 251, 276, 298, 299, 302

	O	M	R	W
DK Lillee	14	0	43	2
AR Dell	26.7	3	65	3
KD Walters	5	0	18	0
TJ Jenner	21	5	39	1
KJ O'Keeffe	26	8	96	3
KH Eastwood	5	0	21	1
KR Stackpole	3	1	8	0

Toss: Australia   Umpires: TF Brooks and LP Rowan

AUSTRALIA 1ST INNINGS

KH Eastwood	c Knott b Lever	5
KR Stackpole	b Snow	6
RW Marsh†	c Willis b Lever	4
IM Chappell*	b Willis	25
IR Redpath	c & b Underwood	59
KD Walters	st Knott b Underwood	42
GS Chappell	b Willis	65
KJ O'Keeffe	c Knott b Illingworth	3
TJ Jenner	b Lever	30
DK Lillee	c Knott b Willis	6
AR Dell	not out	3
Extras	(lb 5, w 1, nb 10)	16
Total		264

Fall of wickets 11, 13, 32, 66, 147, 162, 178, 235, 239, 264

	O	M	R	W
JA Snow	18	2	68	1
P Lever	14.6	3	43	3
BL D'Oliveira	12	2	24	0
RGD Willis	12	1	58	3
DL Underwood	16	3	39	2
R Illingworth	11	3	16	1

AUSTRALIA 2ND INNINGS

KH Eastwood	b Snow	0
KR Stackpole	b Illingworth	67
IM Chappell*	c Knott b Lever	6
IR Redpath	c Hampshire b Illingworth	14
KD Walters	c D'Oliveira b Willis	1
GS Chappell	st Knott b Illingworth	30
RW Marsh†	b Underwood	16
KJ O'Keeffe	c sub (K Shuttleworth) b D'Oliveira	12
TJ Jenner	c Fletcher b Underwood	4
DK Lillee	c Hampshire b D'Oliveira	0
AR Dell	not out	3
Extras	(b 2, nb 5)	7
Total		160

Fall of wickets 0, 22, 71, 82, 96, 131, 142, 154, 154, 160

	O	M	R	W
JA Snow	2	1	7	1
P Lever	12	2	23	1
BL D'Oliveira	5	1	15	2
RGD Willis	9	1	32	1
DL Underwood	13.6	5	28	2
R Illingworth	20	7	39	3
KWR Fletcher	1	0	9	0

England won by 62 runs

West Indies v India

Fifth Test at Queen's Park Oval, Port of Spain, Trinidad

1970-71
April 13, 14, 15, 17, 18, 19 (1971)

The 1970–71 West Indies versus India series in the Caribbean was intriguing as the West Indian pace attack looked less than lethal following the retirements of Wes Hall and Charlie Griffith. With a gifted 21-year-old batsman named Sunil Gavaskar on the rise, India led the five-match series 1-0 before the final Test was extended to six days.

Indian skipper Ajit Wadekar chose to bat, and the score was 26-1 when he arrived at the crease following the wicket of Syed Abid Ali. Wadekar scored 28 before he was caught off John Shepherd, while Gavaskar was established. India was 68-2 and should have been three-down soon after, but Dilip Sardesai had a let-off as a slips catch was fumbled.

Sardesai was scratchy but he registered a crisp half-century, and then improved while the gritty Gavaskar seemed unshiftable. The partnership reaped 122 runs in 130 minutes before David Holford had Sardesai caught by wicketkeeper Desmond Lewis for 75. Gundappa Viswanath and Gavaskar took India to 238-3 before the score became 239-5 after Viswanath and Motganhalli Jaisimha were removed. Gavaskar was on 102 at stumps while India was 247-5, before Uton Dowe had Eknath Solkar caught without a run added the next day.

Srinivas Venkataraghavan subsequently showed how effective he could be with the bat. The total neared 300 before Gavaskar was finally out, caught behind off Holford for 124 after stroking 11 fours in his 392-minute innings. The tail wagged as Venkataraghavan made 51, Pochiah Krishnamurthy 20 and Erapalli Prasanna 16, while Holford and Shepherd finished with three wickets each. The total of 360 however was by no means daunting in a six-day Test.

The Indians bowled accurately, and relied heavily on spinners Bishan Bedi, Prasanna and Venkataraghavan, although the medium-fast Abid Ali bowled a fair bit as well.

Above: Clive Lloyd's 64 in the second innings helped the West Indies salvage a draw.
Right: Garry Sobers scored a century in the first innings and a duck in the second innings.

Joey Carew scored 28 in an opening stand of 52 before he was caught off Prasanna. Rohan Kanhai was inexcusably run out for 13, but an unbeaten 59 from Lewis and a start from Charlie Davis took the hosts to 117-2 at stumps.

Lewis reached 72 before Bedi had him caught behind, and the West Indies were in a spot of bother at 153-4 when Clive Lloyd was caught by Venkataraghavan off Prasanna. India however missed a golden chance to dismiss Davis for 29, and the hosts regained the ascendancy as Davis and Garry Sobers knuckled down. The tourists believed Bedi had caught-and-bowled Sobers for 34, but Sobers survived the appeal and added 177 runs with Davis. It was by no means easygoing as the batsmen had to earn their runs against an honest and gallant attack. Bedi delivered 42 overs in the day.

Davis'ss innings comprised of 105 runs in five-and-a-half hours before he was caught off Venkataraghavan. India's spinners seemed to suffer fatigue late in the day, and Maurice Foster briskly moved to 26 before stumps while Sobers registered a century and finished the day on 114 as the hosts took a 17-run lead into the rest day.

Foster maintained the momentum on day four, and was particularly strong with strokes off the back foot. Sobers reached 132 before Prasanna bowled him, and Holford kept the runs flowing, scoring 44. Foster was unfortunately bowled for 99, before Venkataraghavan polished off the tail. Venkataraghavan's figures of 100-4 were respectable but not enough to prevent the hosts leading by 166 runs. The West Indies' hopes of squaring the series were boosted when Sobers dismissed Abid Ali for three. India however wiped 94 runs off its deficit in the two hours before stumps, with Gavaskar on 57 and Wadekar 29.

Gavaskar was rock solid again despite battling a painful toothache, while the batting at the other end was steady as the bowling was tidy but not penetrative. Only three wickets fell on day five: Wadekar for 54, Sardesai 21 and Viswanath 38. Gavaskar toiled away to 180 as India led by 158 runs with a day left. The West Indies missed three vital chances to dismiss Jaisimha in session one of day six, and the Indians added 50 runs to their overnight score before Jaisimha departed. Gavaskar was bowled by Shepherd soon afterwards for a monumental 220, scored in 529 minutes and including 22 fours.

Solkar, Venkataraghavan and Prasanna made some handy runs as Jack Noreiga worked his way through the tail to claim the last four wickets. An untimely shower extended the lunch break by 20 minutes, and left the West Indies two hours and 35 minutes to score 262 runs to level the series.

The target seemed a long way off as Carew was run out and Shepherd caught-and-bowled by Abid Ali to leave the hosts 16-2. Lloyd came in at first drop and hit the ball hard, while Kanhai made a start before Abid Ali bowled him for 21. The home side's hopes effectively died with the ensuing delivery which was a shooter that bowled Sobers, making the score 50-4.

Lloyd and Foster put on 51 runs before Foster was run out, and the dismissal of Holford left the hosts needing 148 runs from a little under 20 overs with only four wickets in hand. There was no urgency as salvaging a draw and a 1-0 series loss was all the hosts could realistically achieve. India's spinners were finally brought on with 12 overs remaining, and a draw beckoned as the overs dwindled away.

India's remote chance of a remarkable victory, however, remained alive, as Lloyd and Davis were caught in consecutive Venkataraghavan overs. Just nine deliveries remained as India sought two wickets, and Noreiga must have been nervous as he padded up. But Lewis and Dowe survived under pressure to secure a draw. The match had many characteristics of a Test to remember, despite no result in six days as the West Indies finished 97 runs shy of victory with only two wickets in hand. There was no way of knowing how different the outcome would have been had there been fewer dropped catches.

Gravaskar became the second batsman after Australia's Doug Walters to score a century and a double century in the same Test.

Bishan Bedi, one of India's spinners, who could always be relied upon to bowl long spells.

INDIA 1ST INNINGS		
S Abid Ali	c Davis b Sobers	10
SM Gavaskar	c Lewis b Holford	124
AL Wadekar*	c Sobers b Shepherd	28
DN Sardesai	c Lewis b Holford	75
GR Viswanath	c Lewis b Shepherd	22
ML Jaisimha	c Carew b Dowe	0
ED Solkar	c sub b Dowe	3
S Venkataraghavan	c Carew b Shepherd	51
P Krishnamurthy†	c Lewis b Noreiga	20
EAS Prasanna	c Lloyd b Holford	16
BS Bedi	not out	1
Extras	(lb 1, nb 9)	10
Total		360

Fall of wickets 26, 68, 190, 238, 239, 247, 296, 335, 354, 360

	O	M	R	W
GS Sobers	13	3	30	1
UG Dowe	29	1	99	2
JN Shepherd	35	7	78	3
CA Davis	10	0	28	0
JM Noreiga	16	3	43	1
DAJ Holford	28.3	5	68	3
MLC Foster	2	0	4	0

INDIA 2ND INNINGS		
S Abid Ali	lbw b Sobers	3
SM Gavaskar	b Shepherd	220
AL Wadekar*	c Shepherd b Noreiga	54
DN Sardesai	c & b Foster	21
GR Viswanath	b Sobers	38
ML Jaisimha	lbw b Shepherd	23
ED Solkar	c Sobers b Noreiga	14
S Venkataraghavan	b Noreiga	21
P Krishnamurthy†	c sub b Noreiga	2
EAS Prasanna	not out	10
BS Bedi	c Sobers b Noreiga	5
Extras	(b 6, lb 8, nb 2)	16
Total		427

Fall of wickets 11, 159, 194, 293, 374, 377, 409, 412, 413, 427

	O	M	R	W
GS Sobers	42	14	82	2
UG Dowe	22	2	55	0
JN Shepherd	24	8	45	2
CA Davis	10	2	12	0
JM Noreiga	53.4	8	129	5
DAJ Holford	27	3	63	0
MLC Foster	12	4	10	1
MC Carew	7	2	15	0

WEST INDIES 1ST INNINGS		
MC Carew	c Wadekar b Prasanna	28
DM Lewis†	c Krishnamurthy b Bedi	72
RB Kanhai	run out	13
CA Davis	c Solkar b Venkataraghavan	105
CH Lloyd	c Venkataraghavan b Prasanna	6
GS Sobers*	b Prasanna	132
MLC Foster	b Abid Ali	99
DAJ Holford	st Krishnamurthy b Venkataraghavan	44
JN Shepherd	c Abid Ali b Venkataraghavan	0
UG Dowe	lbw b Venkataraghavan	3
JM Noreiga	not out	0
Extras	(b 14, lb 8, nb 2)	24
Total		526

Fall of wickets 52, 94, 142, 153, 330, 424, 517, 522, 523, 526

	O	M	R	W
S Abid Ali	31	7	58	1
ED Solkar	11	1	35	0
BS Bedi	71	19	163	1
EAS Prasanna	65	15	146	3
S Venkataraghavan	37.3	6	100	4
ML Jaisimha	1	1	0	0

WEST INDIES 2ND INNINGS		
MC Carew	run out	4
JN Shepherd	c & b Abid Ali	9
CH Lloyd	c Wadekar b Venkataraghavan	64
RB Kanhai	b Abid Ali	21
GS Sobers*	b Abid Ali	0
MLC Foster	run out	18
DAJ Holford	c Bedi b Solkar	9
CA Davis	c Viswanath b Venkataraghavan	19
DM Lewis†	not out	4
UG Dowe	not out	0
Extras	(b 9, lb 8)	17
Total	(8 wickets)	165

Did not bat JM Noreiga

Fall of wickets 10, 16, 50, 50, 101, 114, 152, 161

	O	M	R	W
S Abid Ali	15	1	73	3
ED Solkar	13	1	40	1
BS Bedi	2	1	1	0
EAS Prasanna	5	0	23	0
S Venkataraghavan	5	1	11	2

Toss: India   Umpires: RG Gosein and D Sang Hue
Match drawn

England v Pakistan

Third Test at Headingley, Leeds

1971

July 8, 9, 10, 12, 13 (1971)

Pakistan captain Intikhab Alam introduces the Queen to the Pakistan players during the team's 1971 tour of England.

Zaheer Abbas made 72 in the first innings of the deciding Test, but was out for a duck in the second innings as Pakistan fell short in a run chase.

A classic third and deciding Test involving England and Pakistan in 1971 followed several successive drawn Tests featuring the two countries. Political riots spoilt the 1968–69 series in Pakistan before rain spoilt the first two Tests of the 1971 series in England.

The tourists lost the toss in the deciding Test but made an ideal start. Brian Luckhurst edged Salim Altaf behind in the second over before John Edrich edged Asif Masood in the subsequent over as England tumbled to 10-2. An in-form Geoff Boycott however made use of the good batting surface, and scored somewhat quicker than his usual standard. Pervez Sajjad broke a third wicket partnership of 64 when Dennis Amiss became another caught behind victim.

Basil D'Oliveira and Boycott steered England on track as they knuckled down, struck wayward deliveries to the boundary and scored at better than a run per minute. D'Oliveira registered 12 fours in a 124-minute innings of 74 before Intikhab Alam bowled him with the total on 209. Boycott passed 100, but England faltered as Alan Knott was bowled by Masood for 10 before Intikhab had Boycott caught behind without the addition of a run.

Ray Illingworth and Richard Hutton led a revival, with Hutton hitting six fours before Asif Iqbal dismissed the duo and Robin Hobbs. England reached 309-9 at stumps, and Peter Lever's useful 19 helped the home side to 316. Pakistan openers Aftab Gul and Sadiq Mohammad put on a 54-run stand before Norm Gifford dismissed both to have Pakistan 69-2. Zaheer Abbas and Mushtaq Mohammad however were a formidable presence after Zaheer scored 274 and Mushtaq 100 in the first Test. They looked capable of repeating those performances as they plugged away against some tidy if not so penetrative bowling. The duo added 129 runs before the pendulum suddenly changed after the new ball was taken. Zaheer was caught by Edrich off Lever, and Mushtaq caught behind off Hutton as 198-2 became 198-4. The match was interestingly poised at stumps, with Pakistan 208-4.

England's position improved as D'Oliveira accounted for Iqbal and Intikhab after they appeared to have settled in. D'Oliveira also ended Saeed Ahmed's painstaking two-hour knock of 22 as Pakistan limped to 256-7, before Wasim Bari and Altaf were amazingly dogged. It really was a game of patience for both sides as scoring was painfully slow, although England had only itself to blame for dropped catches. Just 57 runs were added in 144 minutes, and Pakistan trailed by three runs when Altaf was caught behind for 22 from 161 balls. Masood was caught-and-bowled next ball, before Pervez hung on while Bari pushed ahead. Thirty-seven vital runs in 72 minutes gave

the visitors a 34-run lead before Bari was caught for 63, having faced 238 balls in 247 minutes. After succumbing for a golden duck, Masood's disappointment turned to joy when he had Luckhurst edging the first ball of England's second innings to Bari. Luckhurst completed a pair, and only 159 runs were scored during the day after England reached 17-1 at stumps.

Only four runs were added on day four when Masood struck gold again, removing Boycott. Edrich was defensive while Amiss was lively, hitting 10 fours and scoring half of England's 112 runs until Saeed dismissed him. Edrich's resistance ended when Mushtaq took his second catch, and England was effectively 108-5 when Knott departed.

A turning point soon occurred as a catch was missed at gully to reprieve Illingworth. The complexion changed as Illingworth provided the perfect foil for the in-form D'Oliveira. Steady batting produced a 106-run partnership before England plunged from 248-5 to 264 all out in 50 minutes after Altaf was devastating with the new ball. D'Oliveira and Illingworth were caught behind off Altaf, who then bowled Hobbs third ball before Intikhab had Hutton caught. Altaf had magical figures

Above left: England's Geoff Boycott. Right: The Pakistan players arrive at their hotel on the tour of England in 1971.

of 4-11 from 14.3 overs when he bowled Lever, and Aftab subsequently helped wipe 25 runs off Pakistan's 231-run target before stumps.

England quickly stole the initiative as Aftab softly hit a catch to mid wicket from Illingworth's third ball of day five before Zaheer was caught at short leg next ball. The left-handed Sadiq knuckled down but Mushtaq and Saeed scratched around nervously before Pakistan struggled to 65-4. Iqbal however provided Sadiq with necessary support. Illingworth relied a lot on his off-spin and Gifford's left-arm orthodox spin, and the spinners utilised the rough. Sadiq's defence however was rock solid, and he was harsh on loose deliveries. Sadiq's boundaries were convincing, while Iqbal's supporting role was immaculate as Pakistan seemingly gained the ascendancy. Iqbal reached 33 in 102 minutes, and Pakistan was 71 runs shy of victory when a crucial moment occurred. Record-breaking wicketkeeper Knott, who took four catches in the first innings but went a bit off the boil as he conceded 17 byes in the second innings, made no mistake with a stumping chance to dismiss Iqbal.

Illingworth's captaincy was tested as Sadiq hit his 16th four and looked capable of guiding Pakistan home, until D'Oliveira's medium-pacers – which reaped three first innings scalps – proved a trump card. D'Oliveira had Intikhab caught by Hutton on 184, and three runs later D'Oliveira caught-and-bowled Sadiq for a glorious but not necessarily match-winning 91. Bari and Altaf were under intense pressure to produce another partnership, and Bari's eight catches and first innings 63 suggested that he – as well as Sadiq – deserved to be on the winning side. But Bari suddenly had more responsibility. The match was tantalisingly placed as the score reached 203-7, and then suddenly it was over in the space of five deliveries with the new ball.

The scarcely used Lever instantly had Bari caught behind before Masood followed suit two runs later. Pervez was lbw first ball, and England's 25-run win snared a 1-0 series triumph while Pakistan was left to rue what might have been. Rain had prevented a certain Pakistan win in the first Test before the tourists crumbled at vital stages in the decider.

ENGLAND 1ST INNINGS		
G Boycott	c Wasim Bari b Intikhab Alam	112
BW Luckhurst	c Wasim Bari b Salim Altaf	0
JH Edrich	c Wasim Bari b Asif Masood	2
DL Amiss	c Wasim Bari b Pervez Sajjad	23
BL D'Oliveira	b Intikhab Alam	74
APE Knott†	b Asif Masood	10
R Illingworth*	b Asif Iqbal	20
RA Hutton	c Sadiq Mohammad b Asif Iqbal	28
RNS Hobbs	c Wasim Bari b Asif Iqbal	6
P Lever	c Salim Altaf b Intikhab Alam	19
N Gifford	not out	3
Extras	(b 5, lb 5, nb 9)	19
Total		316

Fall of wickets 4, 10, 74, 209, 234, 234, 283, 286, 294, 316

	O	M	R	W
Asif Masood	18	2	75	2
Salim Altaf	20.1	4	46	1
Asif Iqbal	13	2	37	3
Pervez Sajjad	20	2	65	1
Intikhab Alam	27.1	12	51	3
Saeed Ahmed	4	0	13	0
Mushtaq Mohammad	3	1	10	0

ENGLAND 2ND INNINGS		
BW Luckhurst	c Wasim Bari b Asif Masood	0
G Boycott	c Mushtaq Mohammad b Asif Masood	13
JH Edrich	c Mushtaq Mohammad b Intikhab Alam	33
DL Amiss	c & b Saeed Ahmed	56
BL D'Oliveira	c Wasim Bari b Salim Altaf	72
APE Knott†	c Zaheer Abbas b Intikhab Alam	7
R Illingworth*	c Wasim Bari b Salim Altaf	45
RA Hutton	c Zaheer Abbas b Intikhab Alam	4
RNS Hobbs	b Salim Altaf	0
P Lever	b Salim Altaf	8
N Gifford	not out	2
Extras	(b 6, lb 11, w 2, nb 5)	24
Total		264

Fall of wickets 0, 21, 112, 120, 142, 248, 252, 252, 262, 264

	O	M	R	W
Asif Masood	20	7	46	2
Salim Altaf	14.3	9	11	4
Pervez Sajjad	16	3	46	0
Intikhab Alam	36	10	91	3
Saeed Ahmed	15	4	30	1
Mushtaq Mohammad	6	1	16	0

PAKISTAN 1ST INNINGS		
Aftab Gul	b Gifford	27
Sadiq Mohammad	c Knott b Gifford	28
Zaheer Abbas	c Edrich b Lever	72
Mushtaq Mohammad	c Knott b Hutton	57
Saeed Ahmed	c Knott b D'Oliveira	22
Asif Iqbal	c Hutton b D'Oliveira	14
Intikhab Alam*	c Hobbs b D'Oliveira	17
Wasim Bari†	c Edrich b Gifford	63
Salim Altaf	c Knott b Hutton	22
Asif Masood	c & b Hutton	0
Pervez Sajjad	not out	9
Extras	(b 6, lb 11, w 1, nb 1)	19
Total		350

Fall of wickets 54, 69, 198, 198, 223, 249, 256, 313, 313, 350

	O	M	R	W
P Lever	31	9	65	1
RA Hutton	41	8	72	3
N Gifford	53.4	26	69	3
R Illingworth	28	14	31	0
RNS Hobbs	20	5	48	0
BL D'Oliveira	36	18	46	3

PAKISTAN 2ND INNINGS		
Aftab Gul	c Hobbs b Illingworth	18
Sadiq Mohammad	c & b D'Oliveira	91
Zaheer Abbas	c Luckhurst b Illingworth	0
Mushtaq Mohammad	c Edrich b Illingworth	5
Saeed Ahmed	c D'Oliveira b Gifford	5
Asif Iqbal	st Knott b Gifford	33
Intikhab Alam*	c Hutton b D'Oliveira	4
Wasim Bari†	c Knott b Lever	10
Salim Altaf	not out	8
Asif Masood	c Knott b Lever	1
Pervez Sajjad	lbw b Lever	0
Extras	(b 17, lb 9, w 1, nb 3)	30
Total		205

Fall of wickets 25, 25, 54, 65, 160, 184, 187, 203, 205, 205

	O	M	R	W
P Lever	3.3	1	10	3
RA Hutton	6	0	18	0
N Gifford	34	14	51	2
R Illingworth	26	11	58	3
RNS Hobbs	4	0	22	0
BL D'Oliveira	15	7	16	2

Toss: England   Umpires: DJ Constant and AE Fagg

England won by 25 runs

India v England
Second Test at Eden Gardens, Calcutta

1972–73
December 30, 31 (1972), January 1, 3, 4 (1973)

England's tour to India in 1972–73 was the first of its type since a five-Test series was drawn 0-all nine years earlier, although India had since toured England for a couple of three-match series. England won 3-0 in 1967 before India won 1-0 in 1971, and England began the 1972–73 series with a six-wicket win before a classic second Test unfolded at Calcutta.

The hosts won the toss but found batting hard going as England's bowlers were very accurate while the fielding was top-notch. Chris Old made a good impression on debut as illness sidelined seam bowler Geoff Arnold. India's total was just 29 after 89 minutes when a Derek Underwood delivery exploded from a good length and had Sunil Gavaskar superbly caught by Old at short leg. The score slowly reached 68-1 before Old had Ramnath Parkar caught behind, and Gundappa Viswanath fell 10 runs later when Barry Wood took a brilliant catch at gully from Bob Cottam's bowling.

Indian skipper Ajit Wadekar looked the most confident of the top-order batsmen despite copping a painful blow in the ribs from an Old delivery. Wadekar struck 16 runs in an Underwood over before he was run out for 44, and then a Tony Greig inswinger bowled Salim Durani to leave India in trouble at 100-5. Only 53, 47 and 48 runs were scored in each session after Eknath Solkar and Farokh Engineer guided India safely to stumps.

Engineer scored 49 runs the next morning but there were only 10 other runs off the bat and three sundries before India succumbed for 210 before lunch. Solkar hadn't added to his overnight score when Old bowled him, and then Cottam claimed the next two wickets. Bishan Bedi was run out without facing a ball, before Bhagwath Chandrasekhar scored one not out in a last wicket stand of 18. Engineer was last out, bowled by Underwood after scoring 75 in 215 minutes and hitting 10 fours.

England's top order also struggled, and India introduced spin in the first 10 overs. Eighteen runs were scored in 50 minutes before Bedi bowled Wood. Dennis Amiss gained a reprieve before Chandrasekhar had him caught on the leg-side. Keith Fletcher attacked a full-toss but hit a catch straight to Gavaskar off Erapalli Prasanna, who was picked in place of Srinivas Venkataraghavan. England crumbled to 56-4 when Tony Lewis played no stroke and was lbw to Bedi. Mike Denness and Greig looked like building a good partnership until Solkar took a splendid catch off Chandrasekhar to send Denness packing. England 84-5. Greig and Alan Knott added another 33 runs before Greig was caught off a miscued stroke, and then Old showed his worth as a lower order batsman.

Knott was stumped for 35 the next morning, before the dismissals of Pat Pocock and Underwood left England 154-9. Cottam hung around before becoming Chandrasekhar's fifth wicket, while Old was unconquered on 33 after helping trim India's lead to 36. Old quickly had the hosts reeling as he trapped Gavaskar lbw from the fourth ball of the innings as the total was two. Thirty-one runs were added before Old had Parkar caught by Fletcher, while Durani had a thigh injury and used Gavaskar as a runner. Durani was resistant at first before going for his strokes, while Viswanath was slow while hitting the occasional boundary. The total passed 100 before Fletcher took another two catches to dismiss the well-set batsmen. Old accounted for Viswanath before Greig dismissed Durani, as Fletcher reached to his left to take a great catch low down.

India led by 157 runs with six wickets left as day four began, and extended the lead to 169 before losing 2-4 as Greig mixed cutting deliveries with straight balls. Underwood had Engineer caught behind before Solkar was caught behind off Greig. Wadekar was lbw and Prasanna bowled with successive Greig deliveries, before 20 runs were added for the last two wickets. Greig finished with

5-24 and Old 4-43, and the visitors required 192 runs for victory.

Bedi was introduced to the Indian attack in just the fourth over, and he quickly had England in trouble. Wood was bowled by Abid Ali, before Bedi had Fletcher lbw, Amiss caught behind and Lewis caught by Solkar to leave England in tatters at 17-4. Greig however came to the rescue as he progressed to 60 at stumps while Denness very slowly reached 28. England seemed on target at 105-4 with a day remaining.

The next twist came with the total on 114 when a Chandrasekhar top-spinner hit Greig on the pads and he was adjudged lbw. Knott scored just two when he pulled a catch to mid wicket. Denness needed support but England's chances soon faded further when Chandrasekhar had him lbw for 32, scored off 186 balls in 234 minutes. Chandrasekhar had 3-5 in his fifth over as England still required 69 runs with only three wickets in hand.

Old held firm, while Pocock and Underwood hit a boundary each before falling to Bedi. Cottam joined Old with 54 runs wanted for the last wicket, and Cottam offered Bedi a straightforward return catch but the bowler bungled it after taking a caught-and-bowled to dismiss Pocock. Cottam had another life, this time off Chandrasekhar, and England's hopes remained alive as Cottam and Old put on 22 runs before lunch was taken. Three more runs were scored upon the resumption before Chandrasekhar won an lbw appeal against Cottom, producing Chandrasekhar's ninth wicket of the match while Bedi had seven wickets. Although England lost by 28 runs, Old had reason to be satisfied with his Test debut as he scored 50 runs without being dismissed in addition to match figures of 6-115 from 47 overs.

Crowd attendances tallied about 70,000 each day for this memorable Test that featured only 702 runs across four completed innings. England could easily have led the series 2-0, but instead the tourists ended up losing the series 2-1 after an Indian win by four wickets in the third Test was followed by two draws.

Above: E.A.S. Prasanna, the off-spinner who took an India cricket record of 100 wickets in just 20 Tests during the 1960s and 1970s. Insert: All-rounder Tony Greig put in a fine performance in England's 28-run loss to India in the second Test of the 1972–73 series.

INDIA 1ST INNINGS

SM Gavaskar	c Old b Underwood	18
RD Parkar	c Knott b Old	26
AL Wadekar*	run out	44
GR Viswanath	c Wood b Cottam	3
SA Durani	b Greig	4
ED Solkar	b Old	19
FM Engineer†	b Underwood	75
S Abid Ali	b Cottam	3
EAS Prasanna	lbw b Cottam	6
BS Bedi	run out	0
BS Chandrasekhar	not out	1
Extras	(lb 3, nb 8)	11
Total		210

Fall of wickets 29, 68, 78, 99, 100, 163, 176, 192, 192, 210

	O	M	R	W
CM Old	26	7	72	2
RMH Cottam	23	6	45	3
DL Underwood	20.4	11	43	2
PI Pocock	19	10	26	0
AW Greig	9	1	13	1

ENGLAND 1ST INNINGS

B Wood	b Bedi	11
DL Amiss	c Solkar b Chandrasekhar	11
KWR Fletcher	c Gavaskar b Prasanna	16
MH Denness	c Solkar b Chandrasekhar	21
AR Lewis*	lbw b Bedi	4
AW Greig	c sub b Prasanna	29
APE Knott†	st Engineer b Chandrasekhar	35
CM Old	not out	33
PI Pocock	b Prasanna	3
DL Underwood	c Solkar b Chandrasekhar	0
RMH Cottam	lbw b Chandrasekhar	3
Extras	(lb 4, nb 4)	8
Total		174

Fall of wickets 18, 37, 47, 56, 84, 117, 144, 153, 154, 174

	O	M	R	W
S Abid Ali	4	1	4	0
ED Solkar	3	1	5	0
BS Bedi	26	7	59	2
BS Chandrasekhar	26.2	5	65	5
EAS Prasanna	16	4	33	3

INDIA 2ND INNINGS

SM Gavaskar	lbw b Old	2
RD Parkar	c Fletcher b Old	15
SA Durani	c Fletcher b Greig	53
GR Viswanath	c Fletcher b Old	34
FM Engineer†	c Knott b Underwood	17
ED Solkar	c Knott b Greig	6
AL Wadekar*	lbw b Greig	0
S Abid Ali	c Amiss b Old	3
EAS Prasanna	b Greig	0
BS Bedi	not out	9
BS Chandrasekhar	b Greig	1
Extras	(b 8, lb 2, nb 5)	15
Total		155

Fall of wickets 2, 33, 104, 112, 133, 133, 135, 135, 147, 155

	O	M	R	W
CM Old	21	6	43	4
RMH Cottam	5	0	18	0
DL Underwood	14	4	36	1
PI Pocock	8	1	19	0
AW Greig	19.5	9	24	5

ENGLAND 2ND INNINGS

B Wood	b Abid Ali	1
DL Amiss	c Engineer b Bedi	1
KWR Fletcher	lbw b Bedi	5
MH Denness	lbw b Chandrasekhar	32
AR Lewis*	c Solkar b Bedi	3
AW Greig	lbw b Chandrasekhar	67
APE Knott†	c Durani b Chandrasekhar	2
CM Old	not out	17
PI Pocock	c & b Bedi	5
DL Underwood	c Wadekar b Bedi	4
RMH Cottam	lbw b Chandrasekhar	13
Extras	(b 6, lb 5, nb 2)	13
Total		163

Fall of wickets 3, 8, 11, 17, 114, 119, 123, 130, 138, 163

	O	M	R	W
S Abid Ali	8	2	12	1
ED Solkar	1	1	0	0
BS Bedi	40	12	63	5
BS Chandrasekhar	29	14	42	4
EAS Prasanna	9	0	19	0
SA Durani	4	1	14	0

Toss: India   Umpires: AM Mamsa and J Reuben   India won by 28 runs

West Indies v England

Fifth Test at Queen's Park Oval, Port of Spain, Trinidad

1973-74

March 30, 31, April 2, 3, 4, 5 (1974)

The great Garry Sobers' final Test was fascinating. Ironically, in his autobiography it was included in a chapter titled "Boring England". The match took place at Trinidad in early 1974, after the West Indies led England 1-0 following four Tests in the five-match series. The last Test was extended to six days considering it could affect the series outcome.

England skipper Mike Denness chose to bat on a pitch that had turn from one end but was considerably flatter at the other end. Geoff Boycott and Dennis Amiss were very slow in their opening partnership, and a poor throw from Rohan Kanhai wasted a golden chance to run out Boycott for nine. Amiss scored 44 in 171 minutes before Sobers dismissed him, and then Denness and Keith Fletcher failed as England faltered to 133-3. Boycott meanwhile played a typically defensive game, and at one stage he didn't score for 50 minutes. Tony Greig got his eye in until he became Lance Gibbs' second scalp, before Boycott and an equally stubborn Frank Hayes saw England to 198-4 at stumps, with Boycott on 97. Despite his snail-like scoring rate, Boycott hit 13 fours.

The West Indies gained the upper hand the next morning as Hayes fell at 204-5 before Boycott departed unluckily for 99. Wicketkeeper Deryck Murray dived down the leg-side to snare a one-handed catch off Bernard Julien. Alan Knott made 33 not out in 113 minutes but the tail contributed little, and the tourists were dismissed for 267 as Gibbs and Inshan Ali had three wickets each.

Although the hosts would surely have been better placed had Boycott not been reprieved, the West Indies attained control as Roy Fredericks and Lawrence Rowe put on a confident opening stand of 110. Fredericks scored 67 before he was caught off Pat Pocock, who subsequently took a return catch to dismiss Alvin Kallicharran without scoring. Rowe and Clive Lloyd took the

Above: Rohan Kanhai, a mainstay of the West Indies team since 1957, near the end of his career.

Opposite: Garry Sobers didn't achieve the farewell victory he craved, with the West Indies going down to England by 26 runs as England squared the series.

total to 174-2 at stumps, and a commanding 224-2 following the rest day. The complexion however changed suddenly as the score plunged to 232-6. From the end that helped spin bowling, Greig gained spin and bounce with his two-metre frame, and was supported with good catching. Lloyd was caught behind and then Sobers caught by Jack Birkenshaw for a third-ball duck, with Greig bowling a good line from around the wicket to the left-handers. Two right-handers subsequently departed, with Kanhai caught-and-bowled, and Murray caught by Pocock.

Rowe however remained steadfast and scored a century, while Julien and Keith Boyce made useful contributions to take the hosts to 300-8. But then when Rowe departed without a run added, the hosts' chance of a decent lead virtually disappeared. Rowe, who scored 123 runs in 437 minutes and hit 10 fours and a six, struck a full-toss for a catch to Boycott. The West Indies had a mere 38-run advantage when Inshan Ali was lbw, giving Greig his eighth wicket. Greig finished with 8-86 after starting the day with 0-53, and England pruned the deficit to 15 runs without loss before day three concluded.

Lloyd broke through when he bowled Amiss, before Denness was run out to leave England floundering at 44-2. Boycott however was stonewalling again, while Fletcher proved a worthy ally. Two-hundred minutes yielded 101 runs before Julien bowled Fletcher for 45. Despite painfully slow scoring and some rain interruptions during the match, a hard fought battle was on. Only 135 runs were scored on day four, including 70 to Boycott.

England flopped from 169-3 to 176-6 after Boyce's dismissal of Pocock and Julien's dismissals of Greig and Hayes. Knott was resistant again, while Boycott bettered his first innings score by 13 runs before he was controversially dismissed after lasting nearly seven hours. A bail was dislodged after he defended at a turning Gibbs delivery, and the umpires conferred before adjudging Boycott out. England was 213-7 before Knott went on to score 44. Birkenshaw scored seven and Geoff Arnold 13, including three priceless boundaries. The West Indies needed 226 runs to win, and were 30-0 when day six began.

The hosts looked comfortable before Birkenshaw had Rowe lbw, and then Kallicharran bagged a pair when he edged onto his pad and was caught at slip off Greig. Another turning point occurred moments later as Fredericks chanced a risky second run. Lloyd waited until Fredericks was in the middle of the pitch, and then ran past him to result in Fredericks being run out by metres. The hosts went from 63-0 to 65-3 within 10 minutes, and tension was evident.

Like Kallicharran, Kanhai was caught Fletcher, bowled Greig. Lloyd was soon caught-and-bowled by Greig to leave the hosts tottering at 85-5. Sobers however felt in good form, while Murray also showed a cool head under pressure. Fifty runs were added before Sobers tried to clip a full-toss from Derek Underwood through mid wicket, but missed and was bowled. A triumphant farewell for Sobers appeared dashed, particularly when Julien was caught off Pocock eight minutes later to leave the score 138-7.

Murray and Boyce slowly added 28 runs before Murray drove at Greig and gave Fletcher another catch. The visitors felt the match was theirs, but the tail-enders showed it wouldn't be easy. Boyce displayed a rearguard action, and Inshan Ali also showed calmness as he scored 15 in nearly an hour. A West Indian victory was 29 tantalising runs away when he played one shot too many and was caught by Underwood off Greig. Denness had taken the new ball, and the match ended as Arnold delivered only his 14th over of the match. Gibbs couldn't keep out a yorker, and England squared the series with a 26-run triumph.

Sobers felt it was a disappointing way to finish his Test career, but that it was fitting his last game was against England after the country dominated his cricket career home and away. Greig meanwhile deserved credit for his match figures of 13-156, and Boycott for 211 runs in 799 minutes.

ENGLAND 1ST INNINGS		
G Boycott	c Murray b Julien	99
DL Amiss	c Kanhai b Sobers	44
MH Denness*	c Fredericks b Ali	13
KWR Fletcher	c Kanhai b Gibbs	6
AW Greig	lbw b Gibbs	19
FC Hayes	c Rowe b Ali	24
APE Knott†	not out	33
J Birkenshaw	c Lloyd b Julien	8
GG Arnold	run out	6
PI Pocock	c Lloyd b Ali	0
DL Underwood	b Gibbs	4
Extras	(b 2, lb 3, nb 6)	11
Total		267

Fall of wickets 83, 114, 133, 165, 204, 212, 244, 257, 260, 267

	O	M	R	W
KD Boyce	10	3	14	0
BD Julien	21	8	35	2
GS Sobers	31	16	44	1
Inshan Ali	35	12	86	3
LR Gibbs	34.3	10	70	3
CH Lloyd	4	2	7	0

WEST INDIES 1ST INNINGS		
RC Fredericks	c Fletcher b Pocock	67
LG Rowe	c Boycott b Greig	123
AI Kallicharran	c & b Pocock	0
CH Lloyd	c Knott b Greig	52
GS Sobers	c Birkenshaw b Greig	0
RB Kanhai*	c & b Greig	2
DL Murray†	c Pocock b Greig	2
BD Julien	c Birkenshaw b Greig	17
KD Boyce	c Pocock b Greig	19
Inshan Ali	lbw b Greig	5
LR Gibbs	not out	0
Extras	(b 11, lb 4, nb 3)	18
Total		305

Fall of wickets 110, 122, 224, 224, 226, 232, 270, 300, 300, 305

	O	M	R	W
GG Arnold	8	0	27	0
AW Greig	36.1	10	86	8
PI Pocock	31	7	86	2
DL Underwood	34	12	57	0
J Birkenshaw	8	1	31	0

ENGLAND 2ND INNINGS		
G Boycott	b Gibbs	112
DL Amiss	b Lloyd	16
MH Denness*	run out	4
KWR Fletcher	b Julien	45
PI Pocock	c Kallicharran b Boyce	5
AW Greig	c Fredericks b Julien	1
FC Hayes	lbw b Julien	0
APE Knott†	lbw b Sobers	44
J Birkenshaw	c Gibbs b Ali	7
GG Arnold	b Sobers	13
DL Underwood	not out	1
Extras	(lb 4, nb 11)	15
Total		263

Fall of wickets 39, 44, 145, 169, 174, 176, 213, 226, 258, 263

	O	M	R	W
KD Boyce	12	3	40	1
BD Julien	22	7	31	3
GS Sobers	24.2	9	36	2
Inshan Ali	34	12	51	1
LR Gibbs	50	15	85	1
CH Lloyd	7	4	5	1

WEST INDIES 2ND INNINGS		
RC Fredericks	run out	36
LG Rowe	lbw b Birkenshaw	25
AI Kallicharran	c Fletcher b Greig	0
CH Lloyd	c & b Greig	13
RB Kanhai*	c Fletcher b Greig	7
GS Sobers	b Underwood	20
DL Murray†	c Fletcher b Greig	33
BD Julien	c Denness b Pocock	2
KD Boyce	not out	34
Inshan Ali	c Underwood b Greig	15
LR Gibbs	b Arnold	1
Extras	(b 9, lb 2, nb 2)	13
Total		199

Fall of wickets 63, 64, 65, 84, 85, 135, 138, 166, 197, 199

	O	M	R	W
GG Arnold	5.3	1	13	1
AW Greig	33	7	70	5
PI Pocock	25	7	60	1
DL Underwood	15	7	19	1
J Birkenshaw	10	1	24	1

England won by 26 runs

Australia v England
Third Test at the Melbourne Cricket Ground

1974–75
December 26, 27, 28, 30, 31 (1974)

Greg Chappell was the leading scorer in the 1974–75 Ashes, with 608 runs at an average of 55.27.

The 1974–75 Ashes series became well-known for Dennis Lillee's and Jeff Thomson's fiery bowling, as Australia romped to a 4-1 series victory. The third Test, however, was tense, and the only match in the series not to be lopsided.

England welcomed Dennis Amiss and John Edrich back from injury, while Mike Hendrick and Derek Underwood also returned, and Brian Luckhurst, Keith Fletcher, Geoff Arnold and Chris Old were dropped. After the tourists had been thrashed in the first two Tests, England was sent in for the second successive Test as the Melbourne pitch was moist and contained green tinges. The tourists were 4-1 when Amiss edged to a diving Doug Walters in the slips, before David Lloyd and veteran Colin Cowdrey were resistant but slow. Lloyd was reprieved as he scored just 14 in 108 minutes, before fending a rearing Thomson thunderbolt for an easy catch to gully.

Cowdrey copped a couple of body blows thanks to Thomson, and Ian Chappell dislocated a finger as he fumbled a chance to catch Edrich. Cowdrey and the more fluent Edrich pushed the tourists into a potentially solid position, but the rebuilding was damaged as England went from 110-2 to 110-4 in consecutive overs before tea. Cowdrey was lbw to Thomson just after a couple of spectators disrupted play, then Edrich was dubiously ruled caught behind down the legside when Rod Marsh appealed for a stumping off Ashley Mallett.

Tony Greig looked good, but England faltered to 176-7 at stumps. Mike Denness was caught behind trying to cut before Greig was run out chancing a third run, although replays suggested he may have made his ground. Fred Titmus was caught as he fended at a rising Lillee delivery from around the wicket, before a confident Alan Knott progressed from 18 to 52 the following day, and England reached 242. Derek Underwood copped a blow on the right hand before Bob Willis was well caught from a skied slog.

England was rocked when a hamstring injury restricted Hendrick to 2.6 overs in the match, and Australia was 63-0 at stumps after unsatisfactory weather interrupted play. Wally Edwards departed to a rash shot early on day three, then Greg Chappell fell cheaply to a rearing Willis delivery. Australia was 68-3 when Ross Edwards edged a prod, and another 53 runs were added before Walters clipped a legside catch. Ian

Colin Cowdrey turned 42 during the 1974–75 Ashes series after he was recalled to the England team.

Australia's unsung hero in the 1974–75 series, off-spinner Ashley Mallett, took 17 wickets at a cost of just 19.94.

Redpath's four-hour knock yielded 55 runs before he edged a cut, leaving Australia 126-5.

Ian Chappell had some close shaves against Underwood before playing some hooks off Willis. After Australia's skipper was lbw for 36, Marsh and Max Walker played attacking strokes in a slow but productive partnership. Australia went from 173-6 to 237-6 before slumping to finish one run behind England. Marsh top-edged a sweep, Walker edged behind, Mallett was run out and Thomson yorked, before England began day four at one without loss.

Lloyd scored a chancy 44 before offering Mallett a return catch, and Amiss was in great touch, but again a solid platform was squandered. Cowdrey, Edrich and Denness tallied just 14 runs and fell to catches behind the wicket, Greg Chappell taking a sharp left-hander to dismiss Cowdrey. Amiss was 10 runs shy of a well-deserved century when he flicked a catch to wide mid on, then Knott was well caught by a diving Marsh and England sank to 165-6. A Thomson delivery struck Titmus painfully on the knee, before Titmus succumbed to Mallett's spin. Underwood promptly hit a four and then edged to first slip.

Greig rescued England from 182-8 with a fine knock, and Willis put up a rearguard action, hitting a streaky four over the slips. Greig once hit Mallett over the extra cover boundary, and scored 60 before a cut was caught behind point. Willis slogged a boundary and went down swinging, leaving Australia a target of 246.

Wally Edwards was lbw in the first over of day five, and Ian Chappell was also lbw without scoring, as Australia slumped to 5-2. Redpath, however, frustrated the tourists yet again, while Greg Chappell batted more fluently. Redpath gave a chance to mid on, then Greg Chappell raised his 50 with a fortuitously edged boundary. But the pendulum swung as Australia lost 15-3 to be 121-5. Greg Chappell was another lbw victim, Redpath was run out chancing a risky second run, and Ross Edwards was brilliantly caught at short leg. With England's bowling stocks limited, Titmus was impressive as he battled a knee injury.

Fifty runs were added when Walters drove a catch to cover, and Australia needed 75 runs in 105 minutes. Marsh and Walker were again a cautious, effective combination. Australia needed 55 runs in the last hour, and the batting duo seemed intent on survival, scoring just seven runs in seven overs off Titmus and Underwood. Denness subsequently took the new ball after it was available at the start of the last hour and, as if a switch had been flicked, Marsh suddenly changed his approach. He blasted a four in an over that cost nine runs, before Greig had him caught behind down the legside in the next over. Australia needed 38 runs.

Walker and Lillee reduced the equation to 21 runs from four eight-ball overs before the fourth-last over yielded five runs. The third-last over yielded just two, however, as the batsmen seemed extra cautious, perhaps not wanting to risk turning a possible win into a loss. Underwood bowled a superb penultimate over while Lillee didn't score, leaving 14 runs needed from eight balls to be bowled by Greig. Only three runs came in four balls, then Lillee skewed a high catch to cover, and this fascinating contest finished 26 minutes behind schedule, Australia merely eight runs and England two wickets shy of victory.

Australia's dominance continued as the hosts moved to a 4-0 series lead, before England won the dead rubber, as Australia's pace attack was depleted.

Doug Walters had a productive series against England in 1974–75, averaging 42.55.

ENGLAND 1ST INNINGS		
DL Amiss	c Walters b Lillee	4
D Lloyd	c Mallett b Thomson	14
MC Cowdrey	lbw b Thomson	35
JH Edrich	c Marsh b Mallett	49
MH Denness*	c Marsh b Mallett	8
AW Greig	run out	28
APE Knott†	b Thomson	52
FJ Titmus	c Mallett b Lillee	10
DL Underwood	c Marsh b Walker	9
RGD Willis	c Walters b Thomson	13
M Hendrick	not out	8
Extras	(lb 2, w 1, nb 9)	12
Total		242

Fall of wickets 4, 34, 110, 110, 141, 157, 176, 213, 232, 242

	O	M	R	W
DK Lillee	20	2	70	2
JR Thomson	22.4	4	72	4
MHN Walker	24	10	36	1
KD Walters	7	2	15	0
AA Mallett	15	3	37	2

AUSTRALIA 1ST INNINGS		
IR Redpath	c Knott b Greig	55
WJ Edwards	c Denness b Willis	29
GS Chappell	c Greig b Willis	2
R Edwards	c Cowdrey b Titmus	1
KD Walters	c Lloyd b Greig	36
IM Chappell*	lbw b Willis	36
RW Marsh†	c Knott b Titmus	44
MHN Walker	c Knott b Willis	30
DK Lillee	not out	2
AA Mallett	run out	0
JR Thomson	b Willis	2
Extras	(b 2, lb 2)	4
Total		241

Fall of wickets 65, 67, 68, 121, 126, 173, 237, 237, 238, 241

	O	M	R	W
RGD Willis	21.7	4	61	5
M Hendrick	2.6	1	8	0
DL Underwood	22	6	62	0
AW Greig	24	2	63	2
FJ Titmus	22	11	43	2

ENGLAND 2ND INNINGS		
DL Amiss	c IM Chappell b Mallett	90
D Lloyd	c & b Mallett	44
MC Cowdrey	c GS Chappell b Lillee	8
JH Edrich	c Marsh b Thomson	4
MH Denness*	c IM Chappell b Thomson	2
AW Greig	c GS Chappell b Lillee	60
APE Knott†	c Marsh b Thomson	4
FJ Titmus	b Mallett	0
DL Underwood	c IM Chappell b Mallett	4
RGD Willis	b Thomson	15
M Hendrick	not out	0
Extras	(b 2, lb 9, w 2)	13
Total		244

Fall of wickets 115, 134, 152, 156, 158, 165, 178, 182, 238, 244

	O	M	R	W
DK Lillee	17	3	55	2
JR Thomson	17	1	71	4
MHN Walker	11	0	45	0
AA Mallett	24	6	60	4

AUSTRALIA 2ND INNINGS		
IR Redpath	run out	39
WJ Edwards	lbw b Greig	0
IM Chappell*	lbw b Willis	0
GS Chappell	lbw b Titmus	61
R Edwards	c Lloyd b Titmus	10
KD Walters	c Denness b Greig	32
RW Marsh†	c Knott b Greig	40
MHN Walker	not out	23
DK Lillee	c Denness b Greig	14
AA Mallett	not out	0
Extras	(b 6, lb 9, nb 4)	19
Total	(8 wickets)	238

Did not bat JR Thomson

Fall of wickets 4, 5, 106, 120, 121, 171, 208, 235

	O	M	R	W
RGD Willis	14	2	56	1
DL Underwood	19	7	43	0
AW Greig	18	2	56	4
FJ Titmus	29	10	64	2

Toss: Australia   Umpires: RC Bailhache and TF Brooks   Match drawn

England v Australia
Third Test at Headingley, Leeds

1975
August 14, 15, 16, 18, 19 (1975)

Australian bowlers Jeff Thomson (left) and Dennis Lillee (right) were the leading wicket-takers in the 1975 Ashes.

The third Ashes Test of 1975 justifiably earned a place in Andrew Ward's book *Cricket's Strangest Matches*. Certainly nobody could have anticipated what would happen on the last day, as the contest was delicately poised.

With Australia leading 1-0 after two Tests, England began the third Test soundly after skipper Tony Greig won the toss and chose to bat. Barry Wood was dismissed for nine, before John Edrich and David Steele laid the foundation for a solid total. They added 112 runs, and Steele scored just 10 in 90 minutes at one stage. Jeff Thomson produced the breakthrough when he had Edrich caught for 62, and John Hampshire and Keith Fletcher never really got going before the hosts faltered to 189-4. After scoring a gritty 73 in 255 minutes, Steele was caught by Doug Walters off Thomson with the total at 213. Greig however struck a number of boundaries, and his unbeaten 46 took his team to 251-5 at stumps. Ian Chappell bowled two overs of spin as the Australians relied almost exclusively on a four-pronged pace attack.

Greig scored five more runs before his side lost 20-5 to be all out for 288, thanks to left-armer Gary Gilmour. From short leg, Gilmour ran out Greig, before Alan Knott became Gilmour's third lbw victim of the innings. Chris Old showed some resistance before Gilmour bowled him, and John Snow and Derek Underwood were caught off Gilmour who finished with his best first-class figures of 6-85.

Rick McCosker failed to score in 22 minutes before falling to a low catch by Hampshire at slip. Then the makeshift opener Rod Marsh combined with Ian Chappell for a steadying partnership. Marsh scored 25 before Snow bowled him, and Australia reached 78-2 with 70 minutes left on day two before the contest swung dramatically. Underwood bowled a series of maidens, but it was the other left-arm slow bowler, Phil Edmonds, who made the most impact. In his Test debut, he scored a solid 13 not out during England's lower order collapse, before turning the ball in his first over. In Edmonds' second over, Ian Chappell missed a pull shot and was bowled. Edwards, who had a runner after injuring his ankle, was out first ball as he offered no stroke to a straight delivery. Edmonds had the unique achievement of taking his first two Test wickets with successive deliveries, before Doug Walters prevented a hat-trick. Australia was 87-5 at tea after Greg Chappell pulled a catch to Underwood.

Rain interrupted the last session as England remained on top. The left-handed Gilmour also pulled a catch off Edmonds, and Walters was reprieved before being lbw trying to hook Edmonds. Walker was caught at slip, and Australia was 107-8 at stumps after Edmonds had remarkable figures of 5-17

England wicketkeeper Alan Knott watches his miscued pull shot.

from 12 overs. Lillee and Thomson staved off Edmonds the next morning, before Snow returned and dismissed Australia's opening bowlers to secure a 153-run lead for the hosts.

Wood and Edrich made a steady but slow start to England's second innings, and again Wood was first to go. He made 25 in a partnership of 55, and Edrich departed 15 runs later as off spinner Ashley Mallett claimed his first wicket in the match. Steele was gutsy again, while Fletcher again made little impression, before Greig helped Steele take England to 184-3 at stumps.

Leading by 337 runs, England showed more initiative with the bat after play resumed, and runs were scored quickly while wickets fell regularly in the process. Mallett got rid of Greig and Old before Thomson dismissed Hampshire for a duck as England wobbled to 210-6. A 62-run partnership followed, and Steele fell just eight runs shy of a century before Knott departed for an aggressive 31. Edmonds and Snow hit a four each before falling to Gilmour, who finished with nine wickets in the match. A 445-run target was massive for the Australians, but the pitch no longer seemed to offer much for the bowlers.

Australia's opening partnership matched England's second

innings opening stand, with Marsh scoring only 12 before Underwood bowled him. Ian Chappell scored 62 in just over two hours, hitting 11 fours and a six before playing across the line and falling lbw to Old. Greg Chappell hit three quick fours but they were his only scoring shots before he edged a catch off Edmonds. The remaining 49 minutes of the day's play yielded 25 runs to Walters, including 20 from fours, as Australia progressed from 174-3 to 220-3. The match was interestingly poised as the tourists were nearly halfway to the target, with Walters looking good while McCosker was unbeaten on 95, which included 12 fours in 260 minutes.

The last day was ruined as the groundsman discovered the pitch had holes dug in it while oil was poured over various patches. Slogans on the venue's perimeter walls proclaimed that the imprisoned George Davis was innocent. Captains Greig and Ian Chappell inspected the damaged pitch, and it was soon apparent that the game would be abandoned. Rain arrived at noon and would have abandoned most of the day's play in any case, but the vandalism to the pitch was always what would be remembered for destroying a fascinating Test. Gilmour's wickets and Edmonds' debut Test heroics were largely forgotten, as was virtually everything else other than the way the contest ended. The next Test was also drawn, ensuring Australia won the four-match series 1-0.

Left: Captains Ian Chappell and Tony Greig inspect the Headingley pitch, after vandals damaged it with knives and oil, causing the abandonment of the third Test of the 1975 Ashes.
Above: Australias 'Big Three' in the 1970s, from left: Rodney Marsh, Dennis Lillee and Greg Chappell.

ENGLAND 1ST INNINGS		
B Wood	lbw b Gilmour	9
JH Edrich	c Mallett b Thomson	62
DS Steele	c Walters b Thomson	73
JH Hampshire	lbw b Gilmour	14
KWR Fletcher	c Mallett b Lillee	8
AW Greig*	run out	51
APE Knott†	lbw b Gilmour	14
PH Edmonds	not out	13
CM Old	b Gilmour	5
JA Snow	c Walters b Gilmour	0
DL Underwood	c GS Chappell b Gilmour	0
Extras	(b 4, lb 15, w 11, nb 9)	39
Total		288

Fall of wickets 25, 137, 159, 189, 213, 268, 269, 284, 284, 288

	O	M	R	W
DK Lillee	28	12	53	1
JR Thomson	22	8	53	2
GJ Gilmour	31.2	10	85	6
MHN Walker	18	4	54	0
IM Chappell	2	0	4	0

AUSTRALIA 1ST INNINGS		
RB McCosker	c Hampshire b Old	0
RW Marsh†	b Snow	25
IM Chappell*	b Edmonds	35
GS Chappell	c Underwood b Edmonds	13
R Edwards	lbw b Edmonds	0
KD Walters	lbw b Edmonds	19
GJ Gilmour	c Greig b Underwood	6
MHN Walker	c Old b Edmonds	0
JR Thomson	c Steele b Snow	16
DK Lillee	b Snow	11
AA Mallett	not out	1
Extras	(lb 5, w 1, nb 3)	9
Total		135

Fall of wickets 8, 53, 78, 78, 81, 96, 104, 107, 128, 135

	O	M	R	W
JA Snow	18.5	7	22	3
CM Old	11	3	30	1
AW Greig	3	0	14	0
B Wood	5	2	10	0
DL Underwood	19	12	22	1
PH Edmonds	20	7	28	5

ENGLAND 2ND INNINGS		
B Wood	lbw b Walker	25
JH Edrich	b Mallett	35
DS Steele	c GS Chappell b Gilmour	92
KWR Fletcher	c GS Chappell b Lillee	14
AW Greig*	c & b Mallett	49
CM Old	st Marsh b Mallett	10
JH Hampshire	c GS Chappell b Thomson	0
APE Knott†	c Thomson b Lillee	31
PH Edmonds	c sub (A Turner) b Gilmour	8
JA Snow	c Marsh b Gilmour	9
DL Underwood	not out	0
Extras	(b 5, lb 2, w 2, nb 9)	18
Total		291

Fall of wickets 55, 70, 103, 197, 209, 210, 272, 276, 285, 291

	O	M	R	W
DK Lillee	20	5	48	2
JR Thomson	20	6	67	1
GJ Gilmour	20	5	72	3
MHN Walker	15	4	36	1
AA Mallett	19	4	50	3

AUSTRALIA 2ND INNINGS		
RB McCosker	not out	95
RW Marsh†	b Underwood	12
IM Chappell*	lbw b Old	62
GS Chappell	c Steele b Edmonds	12
KD Walters	not out	25
Extras	(b 4, lb 8, nb 2)	14
Total	(3 wickets)	220

Did not bat R Edwards, GJ Gilmour, MHN Walker, JR Thomson, DK Lillee, AA Mallett

Fall of wickets 55, 161, 174

	O	M	R	W
JA Snow	15	6	21	0
CM Old	17	5	61	1
AW Greig	9	3	20	0
DL Underwood	15	4	40	1
PH Edmonds	17	4	64	1

Toss: England   Umpires: DJ Constant and AE Fagg   Match drawn

West Indies v India
Third Test at Queen's Park Oval, Port of Spain, Trinidad

1975-76
April 7, 8, 10, 11, 12 (1976)

India replicated what Australia's 1948 Ashes team had done, chasing more than 400 runs to win a Test. Doing so in the Caribbean was no small feat. Unusually, the West Indies relied more on spin than pace in this classic Test.

The West Indies led the 1975–76 series 1-0 heading into the third Test. The drawn second Test was at Trinidad and the third Test at the same venue, the Georgetown venue being unfit for play after rain. Batting first after winning the toss, the hosts were 45-0 until spinner Bhagwath Chandrasekhar reduced them to a troublesome 52-3. Lawrence Rowe and Roy Fredericks were caught, then Alvin Kallicharran was bowled without scoring.

Viv Richards and Clive Lloyd turned the tide as India relied on spinners Chandrasekhar, Bishan Bedi and Srinivas Venkataraghavan. Lloyd played some aggressive strokes before he was caught off Chandrasekhar for 68. Richards was in a typically domineering mood, having already scored two centuries in the series. Indian wicketkeeper Syed Kirmani paid dearly for missing a catch from a sweep when Richards was 72, before the 'Master Blaster' posted another ton.

Deryck Murray scored just 11 in a 51-run partnership, becoming Chandrasekhar's fifth scalp. There were no more breakthroughs on day one. Richards motored to 151 while Bernard Julien's unbeaten 37 helped the hosts to 320-5. Trying to score quickly the next morning, Bedi picking up four wickets and Chandrasekhar one. Julien departed for 47 and Richards for 177, the latter dismissal triggering a collapse of 2-4. The West Indies flopped to 359 all out.

Michael Holding bowled menacingly on the docile pitch and gave the hosts the upper hand. He had Anshuman Gaekwad caught behind for six before trapping the dangerous Sunil Gavaskar for 26. Mohinder Amarnath and Gundappa Viswanath made starts before spinner Albert Padmore took his first wicket in his maiden

The West Indian 'Master Blaster' Viv Richards scored 177, but India recovered to beat the West Indies following a huge run chase.

Test when he had Amarnath stumped. It was a satisfying moment for Padmore after he had earlier been out first ball. The other West Indian spinner in his debut, Imtiaz Ali, ended Viswanath's promising innings at 41; he was bowled trying to cut. India was 112-4, and later 147-5 when Holding bowled Eknath Solkar. The stumps score was 169-5.

India made little progress on day three despite Madan Lal attacking on his way to 42. Holding was dangerous with the new ball, dismissing Brijesh Patel and Madan Lal to have India 203-7. Venkataraghavan and Kirmani showed some resistance before Ali bowled Venkataraghavan. Then Holding quickly mopped up the tail to finish with 6-65. It was telling that eight Indians reached double figures without registering a half-century as the hosts had a decisive 131-run lead.

Fredericks and Rowe again made starts without reaching 30, and the tourists must have been relieved when Richards was caught by Solkar off Venkataraghavan to leave the West Indies 81-3. India's spinners were tidy, although Kallicharran and Lloyd took the score to 132-3 at stumps. Another 30 runs were added before the reintroduction of Chandrasekhar paid off, as Lloyd was superbly caught by Viswanath at slip. There were no easy runs, though Kallicharran steadily progressed and Murray made a handy 25. Julien failed before Holding hammered a quick 17 not out. Kallicharran meanwhile registered a century before Lloyd declared, setting India 403 runs in a minimum 595 minutes. History suggested the hosts were safe, considering the fourth Ashes Test in 1948 was the only time a 400-plus target had been achieved in Test cricket.

India began soundly, Gavaskar and Gaekwad putting on a first wicket partnership of 69, before Gaekwad was caught by Kallicharran off Jumadeen. Gavaskar appeared the biggest threat, progressing to 85 at stump with 12 fours, while Amarnath was on just 14. India needed 269 runs on the last day with nine wickets remaining.

Gavaskar seemed to lose touch as he struggled to 102, and West Indian hopes rose as he advanced Jumadeen and edged to Murray, who removed the bails to ensure Gavaskar was out. India 177-2. Amarnath was tied down but when Ali dropped a return catch with the batsman on 37, it appeared a crucial chance was missed. Despite Amarnath's slow scoring, Viswanath looked good, and India needed 206 in the four hours.

Viswanath produced some attractive strokeplay while Amarnath remained slow, and India reached 292-2 at tea as Viswanath kept the runs flowing. It was easy to say with hindsight that Lloyd should have taken the new ball when it was due, rather than 29 overs later, after the spinners lacked penetration. Pacemen Julien and Holding conceded 37 runs in eight overs with the new

One of the highest-regarded captains in cricket history, Clive Lloyd.

ball before Holding limped off. Considering the pitch contained some turn, the inexperience in the West Indies spin combination was telling, as the trio was considerably less effective than India's spinners. Viswanath nonetheless used his feet well.

Viswanath raised his century, while his partnership with Amarnath was just 147. India was only 67 runs from victory when Viswanath was run out. He had hit 15 fours and scored 112 runs in his 220-minute innings. India needed to score at about three runs per over in the final 20 overs; Patel became the chief scorer while Amarnath remained slow. Having scored a century in the second Test, Patel played some attacking strokes as India closed in on victory. Amarnath's innings ended when an accurate Lloyd throw ran him out for 85, scored painstakingly in a mammoth 440 minutes. India was just 11 runs shy of winning, and Patel sealed the historic triumph when he struck Jumadeen to the boundary with six overs remaining.

The West Indies subsequently won the final Test by 10 wickets to clinch the series, after a bizarre declaration left the hosts a target of 13 as several Indian batsmen were unfit.

WEST INDIES 1ST INNINGS

RC Fredericks	c Amarnath b Chandrasekhar	27
LG Rowe	c Viswanath b Chandrasekhar	18
IVA Richards	c Chandrasekhar b Bedi	177
AI Kallicharran	b Chandrasekhar	0
CH Lloyd*	c Gaekwad b Chandrasekhar	68
DL Murray†	b Chandrasekhar	11
BD Julien	c Viswanath b Bedi	47
MA Holding	lbw b Bedi	1
Imtiaz Ali	not out	1
AL Padmore	c Gavaskar b Bedi	0
RR Jumadeen	lbw b Chandrasekhar	0
Extras	(lb 7, nb 2)	9
Total		359

Fall of wickets 45, 50, 52, 176, 227, 334, 357, 358, 358, 359

	O	M	R	W
S Madan Lal	6	1	22	0
M Amarnath	5	0	26	0
ED Solkar	9	2	40	0
BS Bedi	30	11	73	4
BS Chandrasekhar	32.2	8	120	6
S Venkataraghavan	27	7	69	0

WEST INDIES 2ND INNINGS

RC Fredericks	c Solkar b Chandrasekhar	25
LG Rowe	c Kirmani b Venkataraghavan	27
IVA Richards	c Solkar b Venkataraghavan	23
AI Kallicharran	not out	103
CH Lloyd*	c Viswanath b Chandrasekhar	36
DL Murray†	c Solkar b Bedi	25
BD Julien	c Kirmani b Venkataraghavan	6
MA Holding	not out	17
Extras	(b 1, lb 7, nb 1)	9
Total	(6 wickets dec)	271

Did not bat Imtiaz Ali, AL Padmore, RR Jumadeen

Fall of wickets 41, 78, 81, 162, 214, 230

	O	M	R	W
S Madan Lal	11	2	14	0
M Amarnath	11	3	19	0
BS Bedi	25	3	76	1
BS Chandrasekhar	27	5	88	2
S Venkataraghavan	30.3	5	65	3

INDIA 1ST INNINGS

SM Gavaskar	lbw b Holding	26
AD Gaekwad	c Murray b Julien	6
M Amarnath	st Murray b Padmore	25
GR Viswanath	b Ali	41
ED Solkar	b Holding	13
BP Patel	c Fredericks b Holding	29
S Madan Lal	c Richards b Holding	42
S Venkataraghavan	b Ali	13
SMH Kirmani†	lbw b Holding	12
BS Bedi*	b Holding	0
BS Chandrasekhar	not out	0
Extras	(b 11, lb 6, w 4)	21
Total		228

Fall of wickets 22, 50, 86, 112, 147, 182, 203, 225, 227, 228

	O	M	R	W
BD Julien	13	4	35	1
MA Holding	26.4	3	65	6
CH Lloyd	1	0	1	0
AL Padmore	29	11	36	1
Imtiaz Ali	17	7	37	2
RR Jumadeen	16	7	33	0

INDIA 2ND INNINGS

SM Gavaskar	c Murray b Jumadeen	102
AD Gaekwad	c Kallicharran b Jumadeen	28
M Amarnath	run out	85
GR Viswanath	run out	112
BP Patel	not out	49
S Madan Lal	not out	1
Extras	(b 8, lb 12, w 1, nb 8)	29
Total	(4 wickets)	406

Did not bat ED Solkar, S Venkataraghavan, SMH Kirmani†, BS Bedi*, BS Chandrasekhar

Fall of wickets 69, 177, 336, 392

	O	M	R	W
BD Julien	13	3	52	0
MA Holding	21	1	82	0
CH Lloyd	6	1	22	0
AL Padmore	47	10	98	0
Imtiaz Ali	17	3	52	0
RR Jumadeen	41	13	70	2
RC Fredericks	2	1	1	0

Toss: West Indies   Umpires: RG Gosein and CF Vyfhuis   India won by 6 wickets

West Indies v Pakistan

First Test at Kensington Oval, Bridgetown, Barbados

1976–77

February 18, 19, 20, 22, 23 (1977)

Champion Pakistani all-rounder Imran Khan rated the Bridgetown Test of 1976–77 as one of the finest he had ever played in. "From start to finish it was completely unpredictable," he wrote in his book *All Round View*. Pakistan entered the series after recording its first Test victory in Australia. The West Indies meanwhile introduced fast bowlers Joel Garner and Colin Croft to Test cricket while Michael Holding was absent with injury.

Croft opened the bowling with Andy Roberts after Pakistan won the toss, and Roberts was a little wayward as the tourists began strongly. Majid Khan and Sadiq Mohammad put on 72 runs before Garner took his first Test wicket and Croft his first Test catch to dismiss Sadiq. Haroon Rasheed also began well, before Pakistan fell from 148-1 to 149-3 as Haroon's dismissal was soon followed by that of skipper Mushtaq Mohammad to a catch behind for Croft's maiden wicket. Majid compiled 88 before Garner rattled his leg-stump. Garner struck again when he trapped Javed Miandad for two, and Asif Iqbal became the third batsman dismissed in the 30s when he fell similarly to his captain. Wasim Raja and Imran took the score to 269-6 at stumps, with the game interestingly poised.

Imran departed cheaply on day two when Garner took his first Test catch, before the left-handed Raja showed good form and found support from the tail. Raja showed some aggression, while Salim Altaf scored 19 in a partnership of 64. Sarfraz Nawaz scored 38 in a decisive ninth wicket stand of 73. Raja finished unconquered on 117, which included 12 fours and a six as Pakistan reached 435. Garner and Croft shared seven wickets although the surprise was Maurice Foster with 2-41 from 27 overs.

Roy Fredericks and Gordon Greenidge put on 59 runs before Sarfraz dismissed Fredericks, and Greenidge progressed to 47 before he fell to Imran. The West Indies were 109-2 at stumps, before Sarfraz and Imran reduced the home side to 183-5. Viv

The West Indians run around the oval as part of their fitness routine.

Richards, Alvin Kallicharran and Foster departed after making starts, before Mushtaq made what Imran deemed a crucial mistake in taking the new ball after the old ball was swinging. Clive Lloyd and Deryck Murray found it hard to score as the old ball didn't come onto the bat, whereas the new ball had the opposite effect and didn't swing. Lloyd went for his strokes and gave Imran's and Sarfraz's figures a bit of a battering as the balance of the game shifted. The tourists paid dearly not only for taking the new ball, but for reprieving Lloyd at slip on 42.

Murray posted a half-century before his departure ended a 151-run partnership, and then Garner helped Lloyd sustain the run flow. The 400 was passed before Salim dismissed Lloyd, who struck 21 fours and three sixes in his 157. Garner hit the ball hard as he registered eight fours until Javed's part-time spin ended his maiden Test innings on 43. Garner was ninth and last out as Vanburn Holder was absent hurt, and Pakistan had a mere 14-run lead. Majid and Sadiq survived a testing period before stumps and put on 18 runs before the match swung the home side's way after the rest day.

Majid hit a six but he and Sadiq made little impression before both were caught by Garner off Croft. Pakistan nonetheless was soundly placed at 102-2 before crashing to 113-6 as Roberts and Croft were destructive. Haroon was bowled by Roberts for 39 – a crucial dismissal – before Asif was bowled by Croft without scoring. Mushtaq and Javed also fell cheaply, and Raja again provided resistance but witnessed Garner take two wickets and Roberts his third to reduce Pakistan to 158-9 in mid-afternoon.

The game was there for the home side's taking, but inexplicably sloppy cricket enabled Pakistan to greatly increase its lead with the two Wasims, Raja and Bari, at the crease. Several catches were missed, with Raja the chief beneficiary as he scored 71 in three hours, including five fours and two sixes. Bari meanwhile hit 10 fours in an unbeaten 60 in 110 minutes. Foster finally had Raja caught, but the home team's target was now a stiff 306. It was telling not only that the West Indians dropped catches and conceded a 133-run last wicket partnership, but also conceded a record 68 sundries (29 byes, 28 no-balls and 11 leg byes).

Sarfraz struck with the cheap removal of Greenidge before the West Indies began the final day on 41-1. Fredericks and Richards gained control with a partnership of 130 before both succumbed in session two as they chanced their arm against Sarfraz. Following the dismissal of Richards for 92, the match swung Pakistan's way when Lloyd was caught behind off Imran to make the score 179-4. The Pakistanis bowled their overs slowly, and this may have upset the West Indian batsmen, who struggled. Foster became Sarfraz's fourth victim, before Salim dismissed Kallicharran, Garner and Murray to have the West Indies 217-8 with 20 overs plus 15 minutes remaining.

Roberts and Murray had put on an unbroken last wicket partnership of 64 to give the West Indies an amazing one-wicket win over Pakistan in a World Cup match in England 20 months earlier. With Murray dismissed this time, Roberts focused on survival, as did Holder. Amidst the pressure, Holder lasted 45 minutes until Imran bowled him with eight overs remaining, leaving one wicket standing. Croft completed a thoroughly successful Test debut as he survived, while Roberts finished with nine not out in 95 minutes as the West Indies salvaged a draw while 55 runs shy of victory.

An intriguing series unfolded, with the series level after four Tests until Pakistan crumbled against some hostile bowling in the final Test. The West Indies won the decider in Jamaica by 140 runs to take the series 2-1. Imran later wrote: "Despite the fiasco of the final Test it had been a close and absorbing series."

Colin Croft (top) and Andy Roberts (bottom) took some wickets, but were more valuable as tail-end batsmen in the first Test against Pakistan in 1976–77, as they helped prevent a Pakistan victory. Following page: Spectators watch play underneath the MCG scoreboard in the Centenary Test in 1977 with Australia batting first and 27 for 3.

PAKISTAN 1ST INNINGS

Majid Khan	b Garner	88
Sadiq Mohammad	c Croft b Garner	37
Haroon Rasheed	c Kallicharran b Foster	33
Mushtaq Mohammad*	c Murray b Croft	0
Asif Iqbal	c Murray b Croft	36
Javed Miandad	lbw b Garner	2
Wasim Raja	not out	117
Imran Khan	c Garner b Roberts	20
Salim Altaf	lbw b Garner	19
Sarfraz Nawaz	c Kallicharran b Foster	38
Wasim Bari†	lbw b Croft	10
Extras	(b 5, lb 6, w 1, nb 23)	35
Total		435

Fall of wickets 72, 148, 149, 186, 207, 233, 271, 335, 408, 435

	O	M	R	W
AME Roberts	30	3	124	1
CEH Croft	31.4	6	85	3
VA Holder	4	0	13	0
J Garner	37	7	130	4
MLC Foster	27	13	41	2
IVA Richards	3	1	3	0
RC Fredericks	1	0	4	0

WEST INDIES 1ST INNINGS

RC Fredericks	c & b Sarfraz Nawaz	24
CG Greenidge	c Majid Khan b Imran Khan	47
IVA Richards	c Salim Altaf b Sarfraz Nawaz	32
AI Kallicharran	c Sarfraz Nawaz b Imran Khan	17
CH Lloyd*	c Sadiq Mohammad b Salim Altaf	157
MLC Foster	b Sarfraz Nawaz	15
DL Murray†	c Mushtaq Mohammad b Imran Khan	52
J Garner	b Javed Miandad	43
AME Roberts	c Wasim Bari b Salim Altaf	4
CEH Croft	not out	1
VA Holder	absent hurt	-
Extras	(b 2, lb 6, nb 21)	29
Total		421

Fall of wickets 59, 91, 120, 134, 183, 334, 404, 418, 421

	O	M	R	W
Imran Khan	28	3	147	3
Sarfraz Nawaz	29	3	125	3
Salim Altaf	21	3	70	2
Javed Miandad	10.4	3	22	1
Mushtaq Mohammad	5	0	27	0
Majid Khan	1	0	1	0

PAKISTAN 2ND INNINGS

Majid Khan	c Garner b Croft	28
Sadiq Mohammad	c Garner b Croft	9
Haroon Rasheed	b Roberts	39
Mushtaq Mohammad*	c Murray b Roberts	6
Asif Iqbal	b Croft	0
Javed Miandad	c Greenidge b Croft	1
Wasim Raja	c Garner b Foster	71
Imran Khan	c Fredericks b Garner	1
Salim Altaf	b Garner	2
Sarfraz Nawaz	c Murray b Roberts	6
Wasim Bari†	not out	60
Extras	(b 29, lb 11, nb 28)	68
Total		291

Fall of wickets 29, 68, 102, 103, 108, 113, 126, 146, 158, 291

	O	M	R	W
AME Roberts	25	5	66	3
CEH Croft	15	3	47	4
J Garner	17	4	60	2
MLC Foster	8	2	34	1
IVA Richards	2	0	16	0

Toss: Pakistan Umpires: RG Gosein and D Sang Hue

Match drawn

WEST INDIES 2ND INNINGS

RC Fredericks	b Sarfraz Nawaz	52
CG Greenidge	c Wasim Raja b Sarfraz Nawaz	2
IVA Richards	c Sadiq Mohammad b Sarfraz Nawaz	92
AI Kallicharran	c Wasim Bari b Salim Altaf	9
CH Lloyd*	c Wasim Bari b Imran Khan	11
MLC Foster	b Sarfraz Nawaz	4
DL Murray†	c Wasim Bari b Salim Altaf	20
J Garner	b Salim Altaf	0
AME Roberts	not out	9
VA Holder	b Imran Khan	6
CEH Croft	not out	5
Extras	(b 1, lb 8, w 1, nb 31)	41
Total	(9 wickets)	251

Fall of wickets 12, 142, 166, 179, 185, 206, 210, 217, 237

	O	M	R	W
Imran Khan	32	16	58	2
Sarfraz Nawaz	34	10	79	4
Salim Altaf	21	7	33	3
Javed Miandad	11	4	31	0
Majid Khan	1	0	1	0
Asif Iqbal	1	0	8	0

Australia v England
Centenary Test at the Melbourne Cricket Ground

1976-77
March 12, 13, 14, 16, 17 (1977)

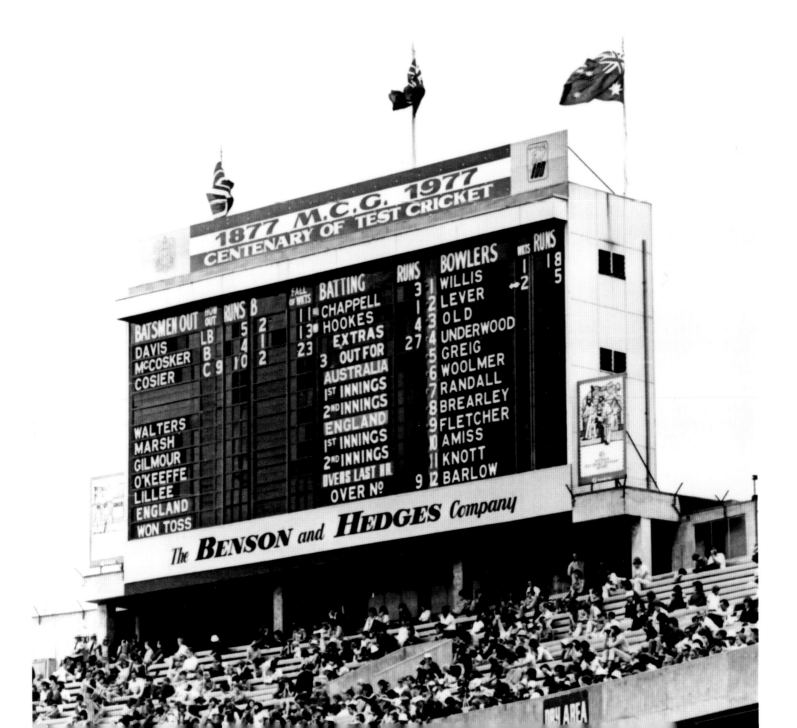

The Centenary Test was played 100 years after the inaugural Test match, involving the same countries, at the same venue. A mighty contest unfolded, ensuring that the one-off match would be one for the ages. A lot of organising and sponsorship went into staging the event, and more than 200 former Test cricketers from both Australia and England were present.

Sent in to bat, the hosts were 13-2 within 35 minutes. John Lever had Ian Davis lbw before Rick McCosker tried to hook a Bob Willis bouncer and was struck on the jaw, the ball ricocheting onto the stumps. McCosker went to hospital and did not field in the match.

Australia's top order faltered through some indiscreet strokeplay. Gary Cosier hooked a catch behind square leg, and Test debutant David Hookes played some fine shots, before fending a rising ball to Tony Greig at second slip for 17. A hook from Doug Walters also went badly wrong, and Australia was 51-5, but Greg Chappell and Rod Marsh led a recovery, doubling the score. England was still in control, though, when Marsh departed, and Gary Gilmour fell to a splendid right-handed catch by Greig. Kerry O'Keeffe went down to a brilliant left-handed catch by Mike Brearley at first slip, before Dennis Lillee held up one end. Chappell didn't register a boundary as he scored 40 in nearly four hours, and he and Max Walker were bowled as they swung at Derek Underwood. Australia tallied a poor 138 in just 43.6 eight-ball overs against a disciplined attack.

Bob Woolmer edged to first slip before England finished day one at 29-1. Lillee and Walker subsequently put Australia on top, ripping through England's middle order. Brearley, nightwatchman Underwood and Dennis Amiss were caught in the cordon, with Brearley an early casualty and Underwood superbly taken at first slip. Derek Randall doffed his cap to Lillee after ducking a bouncer, then edged Lillee behind as England fell to 40-5. Greig made 18 until he was yorked by Walker, who had Keith Fletcher caught right-handed at the wicket as the visitors plunged to 65-7. The score was 78-8 when Chris Old swayed back to a Lillee bouncer and gloved another catch to Marsh. There was no sign of a recovery, and Lillee finished with brilliant figures of 26-6, after having Alan Knott lbw and Lever caught behind. England lasted just 34.3 overs and tallied 43 fewer runs than Australia.

O'Keeffe opened Australia's second innings in the absence of McCosker, and the makeshift opener scored 14 in 50 minutes. Australia fell to 53-3 when Chappell and Cosier succumbed cheaply, the latter after another faulty hook shot. Davis slowly progressed to 45, while Walters reached 32 at

Top: Dennis Lillee after taking a memorable haul of 11-165 in the Centenary Test.

Bottom: Rod Marsh took five catches and scored a century to play his part in Australia's triumph in the Centenary Test.

stumps after having been dropped on 16, and the hosts were reasonably placed with a 147-run lead. Twenty-three wickets having fallen in two days, it was feared that an exhibition match might need to be arranged for the scheduled fifth day, when the Queen was due to visit.

Davis reached a gritty 68 before he was smartly caught right-handed by Knott, and then the chancy Walters' innings ended at 66 to another catch behind. Hookes raced impressively from 36 to 56 with five consecutive fours off Greig, a drive over mid-off followed by a swing down the legside, a cover drive, a clip through mid wicket, and another shot past cover. Still on 56, Hookes was caught one-handed at short leg with the total on 244. Another 33 runs were added before Gilmour departed, and the Englishmen would have hoped to polish off the tail.

Marsh, however, had other ideas, scoring quickly with some punishing strokes, while Lillee again was solid. Lillee scored 25 in a 76-run partnership, and McCosker then returned with his head swathed in bandages. McCosker and Marsh together stretched Australia's lead to 430 at stumps, with Marsh on 95. Following the rest day, Marsh became Australia's first wicketkeeper to score a Test century against England, and he finished with 110 not out. McCosker scored an invaluable 25, and another 12 runs were added prior to Chappell declaring, setting England 463 for victory.

Woolmer departed for 12 when a Walker inswinger trapped him lbw, but Brearley and Randall consolidated. They added 85 runs before Lillee had Brearley lbw, and England reached 191-2 with one day remaining. Randall played many attractive cuts, drives and hooks on his way to 87, and was harsh on Lillee several times. Injury restricted Gilmour to four overs, which were expensive.

Randall passed 100 and had an eventful battle with Lillee, particularly when bouncers were involved. One delivery struck Randall on the head and floored him, and then another sent him tumbling. England was 267-2 with two sessions remaining before Amiss departed for 64, bowled by a Chappell delivery that kept low. When Lillee had Fletcher caught behind for one, the game was back in the balance, with England 290-4.

Randall was given out on 161 after edging Chappell to Marsh, who took the ball low down. Randall started walking but Marsh sportingly disclaimed the catch, and Randall was allowed to continue. Randall reached 174 before edging O'Keeffe to short leg, where Cosier snared a splendid left-handed catch. England progressed from 346-5 to 369-5, and Greig's defiance ended on 41, when he too was caught by Cosier off O'Keeffe.

Knott scored quickly, playing some attacking strokes, but the tail struggled. Old edged a cut shot to slip before Lever was lbw to make the score 385-8. The total passed 400, but the tourists were still 53 runs shy of victory when Underwood chanced his arm and was bowled by Lillee. Willis hit a four, then Lillee trapped Knott lbw to seal the game. Lillee was chaired off in triumph following match figures of 11-165 and, remarkably, the 45-run margin was exactly the same as it had been in the inaugural Test. Nobody could have written a better script for the Centenary Test.

Above: Max Walker took 4-54 to help dismiss England for 95 after Australia batted first and tallied 138.

Following page: England's Derek Randall has a running battle of wits with Dennis Lillee during 1977's Centenary Test in Melbourne. Whatever Lillee is saying to Randall here, who is pictured staring the Australian fast bowler down, Australia captain Greg Chappell (back left) and wicketkeeper Rod Marsh (back right) don't seem to be sharing in the joke.

Inset: The menu for the official Centenary Test dinner.

CENTENARY
TEST MATCH

1877~1977

Dinner

Given by the
MELBOURNE CRICKET CLUB
Melbourne Cricket Ground
16th March 1977

AUSTRALIA 1ST INNINGS

IC Davis	lbw b Lever	5
RB McCosker	b Willis	4
GJ Cosier	c Fletcher b Lever	10
GS Chappell*	b Underwood	40
DW Hookes	c Greig b Old	17
KD Walters	c Greig b Willis	4
RW Marsh†	c Knott b Old	28
GJ Gilmour	c Greig b Old	4
KJ O'Keeffe	c Brearley b Underwood	0
DK Lillee	not out	10
MHN Walker	b Underwood	2
Extras	(b 4, lb 2, nb 8)	14
Total		138

Fall of wickets 11, 13, 23, 45, 51, 102, 114, 117, 136, 138

	O	M	R	W
JK Lever	12	1	36	2
RGD Willis	8	0	33	2
CM Old	12	4	39	3
DL Underwood	11.6	2	16	3

ENGLAND 1ST INNINGS

RA Woolmer	c Chappell b Lillee	9
JM Brearley	c Hookes b Lillee	12
DL Underwood	c Chappell b Walker	7
DW Randall	c Marsh b Lillee	4
DL Amiss	c O'Keeffe b Walker	4
KWR Fletcher	c Marsh b Walker	4
AW Greig*	b Walker	18
APE Knott†	lbw b Lillee	15
CM Old	c Marsh b Lillee	3
JK Lever	c Marsh b Lillee	11
RGD Willis	not out	1
Extras	(b 2, lb 2, w 1, nb 2)	7
Total		95

Fall of wickets 19, 30, 34, 40, 40, 61, 65, 78, 86, 95

	O	M	R	W
DK Lillee	13.3	2	26	6
MHN Walker	15	3	54	4
KJ O'Keeffe	1	0	4	0
GJ Gilmour	5	3	4	0

AUSTRALIA 2ND INNINGS

IC Davis	c Knott b Greig	68
KJ O'Keeffe	c Willis b Old	14
GS Chappell*	b Old	2
GJ Cosier	c Knott b Lever	4
KD Walters	c Knott b Greig	66
DW Hookes	c Fletcher b Underwood	56
RW Marsh†	not out	110
GJ Gilmour	b Lever	16
DK Lillee	c Amiss b Old	25
RB McCosker	c Greig b Old	25
MHN Walker	not out	8
Extras	(lb 10, nb 15)	25
Total	(9 wickets dec)	419

Fall of wickets 33, 40, 53, 132, 187, 244, 277, 353, 407

	O	M	R	W
JK Lever	21	1	95	2
RGD Willis	22	0	91	0
CM Old	27.6	2	104	4
AW Greig	14	3	66	2
DL Underwood	12	2	38	1

ENGLAND 2ND INNINGS

RA Woolmer	lbw b Walker	12
JM Brearley	lbw b Lillee	43
DW Randall	c Cosier b O'Keeffe	174
DL Amiss	b Chappell	64
KWR Fletcher	c Marsh b Lillee	1
AW Greig*	c Cosier b O'Keeffe	41
APE Knott†	lbw b Lillee	42
CM Old	c Chappell b Lillee	2
JK Lever	lbw b O'Keeffe	4
DL Underwood	b Lillee	7
RGD Willis	not out	5
Extras	(b 8, lb 4, w 3, nb 7)	22
Total		417

Fall of wickets 28, 113, 279, 290, 346, 369, 380, 385, 410, 417

	O	M	R	W
DK Lillee	34.4	7	139	5
MHN Walker	22	4	83	1
GJ Gilmour	4	0	29	0
GS Chappell	16	7	29	1
KJ O'Keeffe	33	6	108	3
KD Walters	3	2	7	0

Toss: England   Umpires: TF Brooks and MG O'Connell   Australia won by 45 runs

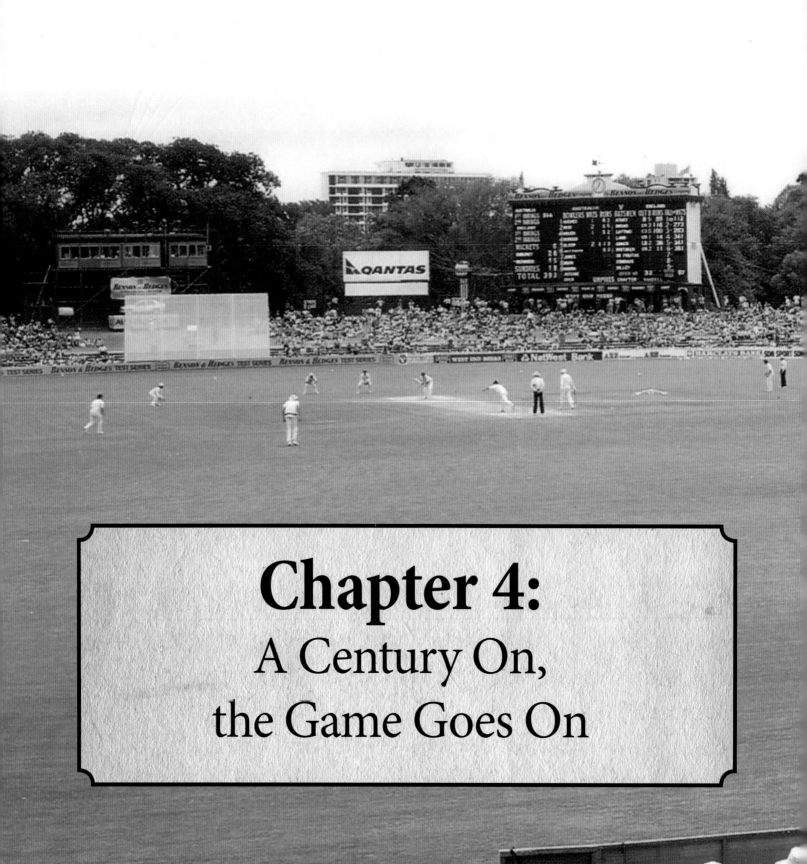

Chapter 4:
A Century On,
the Game Goes On

An Ashes clash at the Adelaide
Oval, Australia, in 1986.

New Zealand v England

First Test at Basin Reserve, Wellington

1977–78

February 10, 11, 12, 14, 15 (1978)

Basin Reserve, Wellington (New Zealand) in the 1970s.

New Zealand entered its series against England in 1977–78 without having beaten England in 48 years and 47 Test matches. The drought had to break sooner or later. Little did anyone know how the first Test of the 1977–78 New Zealand versus England series would pan out after some very tedious batting.

England captain Geoff Boycott won the toss and sent the home side in to bat, and a gale-force wind continually made conditions difficult for the players. In his Test debut, the left-handed John Wright survived an appeal for caught behind off Bob Willis' bowling from the first ball. Wright took 47 minutes to open his account, while opening partner Robert Anderson hit five fours in the first 52 minutes before he was first out. Rain and bad light interruptions somewhat reduced the first day's play, and Boycott must have learned what it was like for others to watch him bat as Wright was agonisingly slow. Wright finished day one on 55 not out as the Kiwis were 152-3, after Geoff Howarth lasted 110 minutes for 13 runs before Mark Burgess scored nine in nearly an hour.

Wright was lbw to Ian Botham before a run was added the next morning, and Wright had faced 244 balls in 348 minutes. Bev Congdon – on his 40th birthday – and John Parker also stonewalled, and put on 39 runs before Parker fell to Willis. New Zealand collapsed as Warren Lees, Congdon and Dayle Hadlee departed quickly thanks to splendid wicketkeeping from Bob Taylor and great bowling from Chris Old into the wind. Richard Hadlee scored an unbeaten 27 in an hour as New Zealand lasted nearly 88 eight-ball overs but was confined to a mediocre 228, thanks largely to Old's 6-54 from 30 overs.

Boycott was his usual slow and stubborn self, while Brian Rose scored 21 in 76 minutes before Richard Collinge had him caught behind. Geoff Miller and Boycott helped the total crawl from 39-1 to 89-1 in 110 minutes before Miller was bowled just before stumps to give left-arm spinner Stephen Boock his maiden wicket in his first Test.

Boycott averaged about 10 runs per hour on day three as New Zealand's bowlers conceded fewer than two runs per over. Congdon bowled seven straight maidens at one stage. Taylor scored just eight runs in 72 minutes before Derek Randall scored four off 45 balls as England limped to 126-4. Wearing contact lenses, Boycott sometimes delayed play as the gale was hell for his eyes. Graham Roope and Boycott saw off the new ball, although Boycott was hit over the right eye on 68 as he attempted a hook shot off Richard Hadlee. Roope made a solid 37 before he was caught behind off Hadlee on 183, and Collinge took the prized scalp of Boycott five runs later. Boycott was caught by Congdon after scoring 77 runs off 302 balls in 442 minutes.

Richard Hadlee bowled New Zealand to a marvellous victory over England, with his 6-26 routing the tourists for just 64 when chasing 137.

The total passed 200 before two wickets to Richard Hadlee and two lbws to Congdon caused England to fall 13 runs shy of New Zealand's score. Two runs to Anderson and 10 sundries stretched the home side's lead to 25 before the rest day was followed by more slow scoring. Anderson again batted solidly before he again fell to Old in the 20s, and then New Zealand slowly moved to 82-1 before Wright was caught after scoring 19 runs from 105 balls in 169 minutes.

New Zealand's steady start and prospects of setting a daunting target fell apart as Willis caused a collapse. He had Howarth and Congdon caught off successive deliveries as the Kiwis fell to 93-4, before Parker and Burgess – who was caught off Botham – followed with the total still in the 90s. England's catching was exemplary, and Richard Hadlee became Willis' fifth victim to make the score 104-7, before Hendrick and Botham cleaned up the tail. The last two wickets fell on 123 as New Zealand had lost 41-9 and left the tourists with a modest target of 137 with two hours of day four and all of day five remaining. The pitch was uneven but the Kiwis didn't have a lot of runs to play with.

Collinge struck gold after only eight minutes as Boycott tried to drive and was bowled off his pads. England became 8-2 when Miller was caught by Anderson, before Rose suffered a bruised right arm and retired hurt. Collinge struck a third time as he trapped Randall lbw, and Richard Hadlee had Roope caught one-handed by Lees to leave England a worrying 18-4.

Botham hit three fours but his impact was brief as he hooked a catch to backward square leg. To make matters worse, Taylor was run out as England plummeted to 38-6. Old hit two fours before Hadlee had him lbw and Hendrick caught at first slip as Hendrick again failed to score. England looked gone at 53-8 as day four ended.

New Zealand's victory bid was delayed as rain caused day five to start 40 minutes late. Edmonds and Willis survived for a while but runs were very hard to score, and Edmonds reached 11 when he emulated Hendrick's dismissal. Rose returned from injury as England needed a last wicket stand of 74 for victory. A single was scored before Willis was caught by a diving Howarth in the gully, giving Hadlee his sixth wicket of the innings and 10th for the match as the Kiwis claimed a memorable 72-run win. The crowd soaked up the occasion, singing and cheering.

England levelled the series in the second Test with a 174-run win, and the three-match series finished at 1-all, but nothing could detract from New Zealand's first Test win over England.

Warren Lees souvenirs the stumps while Geoff Howarth holds the ball aloft after taking the catch for the final wicket to seal New Zealand's memorable Test win over England.

NEW ZEALAND 1ST INNINGS

JG Wright	lbw b Botham	55
RW Anderson	c Taylor b Old	28
GP Howarth	c Botham b Old	13
MG Burgess*	b Willis	9
BE Congdon	c Taylor b Old	44
JM Parker	c Rose b Willis	16
WK Lees†	c Taylor b Old	1
RJ Hadlee	not out	27
DR Hadlee	c Taylor b Old	1
RO Collinge	b Old	1
SL Boock	b Botham	4
Extras	(b 12, lb 3, w 1, nb 13)	29
Total		228

Fall of wickets 42, 96, 114, 152, 191, 193, 194, 196, 208, 228

	O	M	R	W
RGD Willis	25	7	65	2
M Hendrick	17	2	46	0
CM Old	30	11	54	6
PH Edmonds	3	1	7	0
IT Botham	12.6	2	27	2

ENGLAND 1ST INNINGS

BC Rose	c Lees b Collinge	21
G Boycott*	c Congdon b Collinge	77
G Miller	b Boock	24
RW Taylor†	c & b Collinge	8
DW Randall	c Burgess b RJ Hadlee	4
GRJ Roope	c Lees b RJ Hadlee	37
IT Botham	c Burgess b RJ Hadlee	7
CM Old	b RJ Hadlee	10
PH Edmonds	lbw b Congdon	4
M Hendrick	lbw b Congdon	0
RGD Willis	not out	6
Extras	(lb 4, nb 13)	17
Total		215

Fall of wickets 39, 89, 108, 126, 183, 188, 203, 205, 206, 215

	O	M	R	W
RJ Hadlee	28	5	74	4
RO Collinge	18	5	42	3
DR Hadlee	21	5	47	0
SL Boock	10	5	21	1
BE Congdon	17.4	11	14	2

NEW ZEALAND 2ND INNINGS

JG Wright	c Roope b Willis	19
RW Anderson	lbw b Old	26
GP Howarth	c Edmonds b Willis	21
MG Burgess*	c Boycott b Botham	6
BE Congdon	c Roope b Willis	0
JM Parker	c Edmonds b Willis	4
WK Lees†	lbw b Hendrick	11
RJ Hadlee	c Boycott b Willis	2
DR Hadlee	c Roope b Botham	2
RO Collinge	c Edmonds b Hendrick	6
SL Boock	not out	0
Extras	(b 2, lb 9, w 2, nb 13)	26
Total		123

Fall of wickets 54, 82, 93, 93, 98, 99, 104, 116, 123, 123

	O	M	R	W
RGD Willis	15	2	32	5
M Hendrick	10	2	16	2
CM Old	9	2	32	1
PH Edmonds	1	0	4	0
IT Botham	9.3	3	13	2

ENGLAND 2ND INNINGS

BC Rose	not out	5
G Boycott*	b Collinge	1
G Miller	c Anderson b Collinge	4
DW Randall	lbw b Collinge	9
GRJ Roope	c Lees b RJ Hadlee	0
IT Botham	c Boock b RJ Hadlee	19
RW Taylor†	run out (Boock)	0
CM Old	lbw b RJ Hadlee	9
PH Edmonds	c Parker b RJ Hadlee	11
M Hendrick	c Parker b RJ Hadlee	0
RGD Willis	c Howarth b RJ Hadlee	3
Extras	(nb 3)	3
Total		64

Fall of wickets 2, 8, 18, 18, 38, 38, 53, 53, 63, 64

	O	M	R	W
RO Collinge	13	5	35	3
RJ Hadlee	13.3	4	26	6
DR Hadlee	1	1	0	0

Toss: England   Umpires: WRC Gardiner and RL Monteith   New Zealand won by 72 runs

West Indies v Australia

Third Test at Bourda, Georgetown, Guyana

1977-78

March 31, April 1, 2, 4, 5 (1978)

A classic Test involving the West Indies and Australia in early 1978 seemed unlikely after Australia lost the Chappell brothers, Rod Marsh and Dennis Lillee to World Series cricket. It was no surprise that strong West Indian line-ups demolished the second-rate Australians in the first two Tests. The third Test in Guyana however was a different story. The hosts were also depleted as skipper Clive Lloyd and five World Series players withdrew in protest after World Series players Desmond Haynes, Richard Austin and Deryck Murray were dropped. The hosts consequently had six Test debutants: Sylvester Clarke, Alvin Greenidge, David Murray, Norbert Phillip, Sewdatt Shivnarine and Basil Williams. Trevor Laughlin meanwhile made his Test debut for Australia.

Greenidge and Williams opened after stand-in skipper Alvin Kallicharran won the toss. The hosts were 31-0 before crumbling to 48-3. Wayne Clark had Williams lbw and Larry Gomes bowled, before Jeff Thomson bowled Kallicharran without scoring. Greenidge hit 10 fours in his 56, but the hosts were 84-5 when he was lbw to Thomson, after Irvine Shillingford became Laughlin's first Test victim.

Shivnarine registered 10 fours as he scored 53 in two hours to lead a mini fightback. David Murray scored 21 and Phillip 15, before Vanburn Holder fell cheaply to leave the score a disappointing 166-8. Derick Parry and Shivnarine added 27 runs before Shivnarine departed, and Clarke hit a four as the hosts reached 205 before Thomson claimed his fourth wicket. Clark had also picked up four wickets.

Australia slipped from 28-0 to 36-2 as a lively Phillip took his first two Test wickets: Rick Darling and David Ogilvie. With Darling's dismissal, Greenidge took his first Test catch before Phillip took a return catch to dismiss Ogilvie. Graeme Wood and Gary Cosier saw Australia to 68-2 at stumps, before the hosts

Larry Gomes' century in the second innings set up a desperate Australian run chase in Guyana.

regained control. Clarke had Cosier lbw for nine before bowling Craig Serjeant for a duck. Wood reached 50 before falling lbw to Holder, and Australia was in disarray at 90-5.

Captain Bob Simpson found support from Laughlin, who

scored 21 before he was caught off Parry in the lead-up to lunch. Australia was 146-6 at the interval, and then Simpson combined with Rixon to put Australia in the lead as the inexperienced bowling attack was unable to maintain control of the situation. Simpson scored 67 in three hours before he was run out, while his side led by 32 runs. Rixon went on to score 54 in nearly two hours before falling to a superb catch by Holder at second slip. Bruce Yardley hit five fours in a crucial 33, as Australia extended its lead to 81 before Yardley was last out.

Australia's lead was reduced to 45 when Clark bowled Greenidge, and then David Murray played a supporting role to Williams, who went for his shots. He rode his luck at times as he raced to 60 before stumps. Simpson, who took a wicket in the first innings, chipped in again as he had Murray lbw shortly before the end of day two.

The West Indies began day three with a 17-run lead, and seemingly gained control as Williams showed his selection instead of Haynes was worthwhile. Williams had more near misses, and Thomson could have dismissed him any number of times. Williams reached 100 from just 117 balls, having hit 19 fours, before hooking his next delivery for a catch to fine leg. After coming in as nightwatchman late on day two, Parry scored a vital 51 before Clark had him lbw. West Indies 199-4.

Gomes took on the responsibility of building the total, although he was more composed than and not as fast as Williams. Kallicharran and Shillingford departed after making starts, and the hosts were 285-6 as Shivnarine joined Gomes. The left-handed Gomes scored 101 before he too departed from the delivery he faced after he reached three figures. Yardley followed up by dismissing Phillip to make the score 369-8.

The innings however was far from finished, as Shivnarine was in form while Holder struck two fours and two sixes. Sixty-two runs were added for the ninth wicket before Cosier bowled Shivnarine for 63. Clarke hit a four before Holder was out, leaving Australia with a tough target of 359 in two days. The hosts scored enough runs without World Series batsmen Gordon Greenidge and Viv Richards, but the question was whether or not Colin Croft, Joel Garner and Andy Roberts would be missed with the ball.

Clarke had Darling caught by Williams and Ogilvie lbw for ducks, before having Simpson caught behind for four to leave Australia reeling at 22-3 after 40 minutes. Western Australian duo Wood and Serjeant however knuckled down and showed impressive determination, as the West Indian second string attack was again unable to maintain the upper hand.

Wood and Serjeant scored steadily without being too risky. Neither had scored a Test century until this day. Australia went from certain losers to certain winners as the score went from 22-3 to 273-3 in 269 minutes, before Serjeant top-edged a hook and was superbly caught by substitute fielder Faoud Bacchus. Serjeant accumulated 18 fours and a six in his 124, but Australia's chances became shaky again after he departed. Phillip bowled Cosier for zero, and Wood was run out just before stumps, having hit eight fours and a six in his 126, from 335 minutes.

The tourists needed 69 runs while the hosts required four wickets on the last day. The result could have gone either way, but sub-par bowling and a few dropped catches enabled Australia to press towards the target. The visitors were 21 runs shy of their target when Laughlin was caught-and-bowled by Parry. West Indian hopes remained alive but Yardley was unfazed, hitting three fours in a quick 15 not out while Rixon reached an unbeaten 39 as the Australians achieved a memorable three-wicket win. It was their only victory of the series, which the West Indies eventually won 3-1.

Australia's Craig Serjeant replied to his duck in the first innings against the West Indies in 1978 with a century in the second innings.

WEST INDIES 1ST INNINGS

AE Greenidge	lbw b Thomson	56
AB Williams	lbw b Clark	10
HA Gomes	b Clark	4
AI Kallicharran*	b Thomson	0
IT Shillingford	c Clark b Laughlin	3
DA Murray†	c Ogilvie b Clark	21
S Shivnarine	c Rixon b Thomson	53
N Phillip	c Yardley b Simpson	15
VA Holder	c Laughlin b Clark	1
DR Parry	not out	21
ST Clarke	b Thomson	6
Extras	(lb 2, nb 13)	15
Total		205

Fall of wickets 31, 36, 48, 77, 84, 130, 165, 166, 193, 205

	O	M	R	W
JR Thomson	16.2	1	56	4
WM Clark	24	6	65	4
TJ Laughlin	10	4	34	1
GJ Cosier	2	1	1	0
RB Simpson	8	1	34	1

AUSTRALIA 1ST INNINGS

WM Darling	c Greenidge b Phillip	15
GM Wood	lbw b Holder	50
AD Ogilvie	c & b Phillip	4
GJ Cosier	lbw b Clarke	9
CS Serjeant	b Clarke	0
RB Simpson*	run out	67
TJ Laughlin	c Greenidge b Parry	21
SJ Rixon†	c Holder b Phillip	54
B Yardley	b Clarke	33
JR Thomson	c & b Phillip	3
WM Clark	not out	2
Extras	(lb 12, w 1, nb 15)	28
Total		286

Fall of wickets 28, 36, 77, 85, 90, 142, 237, 256, 268, 286

	O	M	R	W
N Phillip	18	0	75	4
VA Holder	17	1	40	1
ST Clarke	22	3	58	3
HA Gomes	3	0	8	0
DR Parry	15	2	39	1
S Shivnarine	8	0	38	0

WEST INDIES 2ND INNINGS

AE Greenidge	b Clark	11
AB Williams	c Serjeant b Clark	100
DA Murray†	lbw b Simpson	16
DR Parry	lbw b Clark	51
HA Gomes	c Simpson b Yardley	101
AI Kallicharran*	b Yardley	22
IT Shillingford	c & b Thomson	16
S Shivnarine	b Cosier	63
N Phillip	st Rixon b Yardley	4
VA Holder	lbw b Clark	31
ST Clarke	not out	5
Extras	(b 4, lb 5, nb 10)	19
Total		439

Fall of wickets 36, 95, 172, 199, 249, 285, 355, 369, 431, 439

	O	M	R	W
JR Thomson	20	2	83	1
WM Clark	34.4	4	124	4
TJ Laughlin	7	1	33	0
GJ Cosier	6	1	14	1
RB Simpson	19	4	70	1
B Yardley	30	6	96	3

AUSTRALIA 2ND INNINGS

WM Darling	c Williams b Clarke	0
GM Wood	run out	126
AD Ogilvie	lbw b Clarke	0
RB Simpson*	c Murray b Clarke	4
CS Serjeant	c sub (SFAF Bacchus) b Phillip	124
GJ Cosier	b Phillip	0
SJ Rixon†	not out	39
TJ Laughlin	c & b Parry	24
B Yardley	not out	15
Extras	(b 8, lb 4, w 2, nb 16)	30
Total	(7 wickets)	362

Did not bat JR Thomson, WM Clark

Fall of wickets 11, 13, 22, 273, 279, 290, 338

	O	M	R	W
N Phillip	19	2	65	2
VA Holder	20	3	55	0
ST Clarke	27	5	83	3
DR Parry	17	1	61	1
S Shivnarine	18	2	68	0

Toss: West Indies   Umpires: RG Gosein and CF Vyfhuis   Australia won by 3 wickets

Australia v England
Fourth Test at the Sydney Cricket Ground

1978-79
January 6, 7, 8, 10, 11 (1979)

Derek Randall's 174 in the Centenary Test will long be remembered, but the innings he rated as his best Down Under was his 150 in the fourth Test of the 1978–79 series. His 150 was pivotal in a memorable Test that was crucial in the destination of the series. Australia was weakened considerably due to the absence of World Series players including the Chappell brothers, Rod Marsh and Dennis Lillee. The second-rate Australians were competitive at times in the first two Tests, but were thrashed by seven wickets at Brisbane and 166 runs at Perth, before winning by 103 runs at Melbourne.

Desperate to level the series in the fourth Test, Australia fielded first after England captain Mike Brearley won the toss. Geoff Boycott and Brearley ground out 18 runs in nearly an hour before first change bowler Alan Hurst made two breakthroughs in three balls, after Rodney Hogg left the steamy arena for supposed health reasons. Boycott edged to slip before Randall couldn't resist a bouncer, hooking it to Graeme Wood. With Hogg back, England remained in trouble as Hogg dislodged Brearley's off-stump. When David Gower edged Hurst behind on the stroke of lunch, England was 51-4.

Hurst, Hogg, Geoff Dymock and Jim Higgs toiled away as the tourists struggled, despite Ian Botham showing some aggression. England slipped to 70-6 before two wickets fell in the 90s. Australian skipper Graham Yallop substituted as wicketkeeper after John Maclean succumbed to illness, and Yallop held a crucial catch as Botham top-edged a hook when on 59. Hurst finished with 5-28 as England was dismissed for just 152, in oppressive conditions that seemed favourable for batsmen.

Wood departed for a duck when he inside-edged a defensive shot onto the stumps, but Australia recovered to 56-1 at stumps. Rick Darling found form the following day and was well supported by Kim Hughes as the Englishmen struggled in

Rodney Hogg was a prolific wicket-taker for Australia in 1978–79, but Australia was still hammered repeatedly.

the heat. Australia was 126-1 at lunch before Hughes perished to a drive from the first ball of the next session. With Bob Willis and Mike Hendrick unwell at various times, Botham and John Emburey were forced to do plenty of bowling.

Darling was on 91 when he leg glanced and was well caught

by Botham, before Peter Toohey edged a rising Botham delivery to Graham Gooch, making it 179-4. Botham later took a superb diving catch at third slip to dismiss Yallop from a late cut after the left-hander scored 44 and was warming to the task. Another left-hander, Allan Border, hit the ball around to good effect in his second Test, but the rest of the Australian batsmen made little impression as England fought back. The underdogs were in a strong position with a 142-run lead when they were all out early on the third day, although Yallop was far from impressed after they had been 178-2.

Australia nonetheless was destined to level the series when Hogg trapped Boycott lbw with the first ball of England's second innings. Dymock however was desperately unlucky not to win an lbw decision against Randall soon afterwards as the batsman was hit in front of middle-stump to a delivery that pitched in line. After lunch, Brearley and Randall accumulated runs as they played a number of fine drives in the hot weather to launch a fightback that mightn't have been. Brearley made 53 before becoming Border's first Test victim, and England finished day three just nine runs behind Australia with eight wickets remaining.

England lost four wickets on day four and led by 162 runs at stumps. The Australians let themselves down with a few dropped catches as the heat remained fierce. Randall hit three fours in four balls from Hogg and raced past 100, before chancing his arm and having a few narrow escapes. Gooch made 22, Gower started well but again fell to a catch behind, before Botham scored an unusually slow six. Randall batted for nearly 10 hours before Hogg had him lbw. England added another 42 runs on day five, and Higgs finished with five scalps after bowling nearly 60 overs in a marathon performance.

Needing 205 to win, Australia was 15-0 at lunch, before a vicious pull from Darling cracked Botham's helmet at short square leg. The opening partnership produced 38 runs before a push from Darling was well caught by Gooch at gully. A turning point came six runs later when Wood was foolishly run out after defending the ball to cover, before an attempted defensive stroke from Yallop resulted in a return catch to Hendrick. With Australia suddenly 45-3 and needing more than a run per minute, a draw seemed Australia's best hope as England's spinners Geoff Miller and Emburey bowled in tandem with the fielders in close. Hughes gave a catch to bat-pad, before Toohey paid the price for leaving his crease and not keeping his head down. Maclean also succumbed to a catch in close, and Australia was six down at tea.

Despite Border driving confidently and punishing the rare loose balls, the Australians were gone for all money. Emburey dismissed Hogg and Dymock without scoring, and then Higgs

lasted 24 minutes before Emburey had him lbw. Emburey wrapped up the match with his fourth wicket when Hurst was bowled, and Australia had lost 73-10 to hand England a 93-run win. In his book *Lambs to the Slaughter*, Yallop suggested that Randall surviving the confident lbw appeal early in his second innings changed the course of the match. Yallop was critical of his players as well, saying he was disgusted when seven of the last eight batsmen tallied just nine runs in the second innings. "The let-down was bad enough. We had this Test in our keeping for four days and then blew it," Yallop wrote.

Australia also had England on the ropes during the fifth Test at Adelaide before England recovered to win by 205 runs. The tourists won the series 5-1 after claiming a nine-wicket victory in the sixth Test at Sydney.

Above: Rodney Hogg and his captain Graham Yallop at the presentations after Australia lost the 1978–79 Ashes series 5-1. The outcome could have been much different had Australia not squandered a winning position in the fourth Test at Sydney.
Opposite: Allan Border's arrival in international cricket ultimately heralded a new era in Australian cricket in the 1980s.

ENGLAND 1ST INNINGS		
G Boycott	c Border b Hurst	8
JM Brearley*	b Hogg	17
DW Randall	c Wood b Hurst	0
GA Gooch	c Toohey b Higgs	18
DI Gower	c Maclean b Hurst	7
IT Botham	c Yallop b Hogg	59
G Miller	c Maclean b Hurst	4
RW Taylor†	c Border b Higgs	10
JE Emburey	c Wood b Higgs	0
RGD Willis	not out	7
M Hendrick	b Hurst	10
Extras	(b 1, lb 1, w 2, nb 8)	12
Total		152

Fall of wickets 18, 18, 35, 51, 66, 70, 94, 98, 141, 152

	O	M	R	W
RM Hogg	11	3	36	2
G Dymock	13	1	34	0
AG Hurst	10.6	2	28	5
JD Higgs	18	4	42	3

AUSTRALIA 1ST INNINGS		
GM Wood	b Willis	0
WM Darling	c Botham b Miller	91
KJ Hughes	c Emburey b Willis	48
GN Yallop*	c Botham b Hendrick	44
PM Toohey	c Gooch b Botham	1
AR Border	not out	60
JA Maclean†	lbw b Emburey	12
RM Hogg	run out	6
G Dymock	b Botham	5
JD Higgs	c Botham b Hendrick	11
AG Hurst	run out	0
Extras	(b 2, lb 3, nb 11)	16
Total		294

Fall of wickets 1, 126, 178, 179, 210, 235, 245, 276, 290, 294

	O	M	R	W
RGD Willis	9	2	33	2
IT Botham	28	3	87	2
M Hendrick	24	4	50	2
G Miller	13	2	37	1
JE Emburey	29	10	57	1
GA Gooch	5	1	14	0

ENGLAND 2ND INNINGS		
G Boycott	lbw b Hogg	0
JM Brearley*	b Border	53
DW Randall	lbw b Hogg	150
GA Gooch	c Wood b Higgs	22
DI Gower	c Maclean b Hogg	34
IT Botham	c Wood b Higgs	6
G Miller	lbw b Hogg	17
RW Taylor†	not out	21
JE Emburey	c Darling b Higgs	14
RGD Willis	c Toohey b Higgs	0
M Hendrick	c Toohey b Higgs	7
Extras	(b 5, lb 3, nb 14)	22
Total		346

Fall of wickets 0, 111, 169, 237, 267, 292, 307, 334, 334, 346

	O	M	R	W
RM Hogg	28	10	67	4
G Dymock	17	4	35	0
AG Hurst	19	3	43	0
JD Higgs	59.6	15	148	5
AR Border	23	11	31	1

AUSTRALIA 2ND INNINGS		
GM Wood	run out	27
WM Darling	c Gooch b Hendrick	13
KJ Hughes	c Emburey b Miller	15
GN Yallop*	c & b Hendrick	1
PM Toohey	b Miller	5
AR Border	not out	45
JA Maclean†	c Botham b Miller	0
G Dymock	b Emburey	0
RM Hogg	c Botham b Emburey	0
JD Higgs	lbw b Emburey	3
AG Hurst	b Emburey	0
Extras	(lb 1, nb 1)	2
Total		111

Fall of wickets 38, 44, 45, 59, 74, 76, 85, 85, 105, 111

	O	M	R	W
RGD Willis	2	0	8	0
M Hendrick	10	3	17	2
JE Emburey	17.2	7	46	4
G Miller	20	7	38	3

Toss: England   Umpires: RC Bailhache and RA French   England won by 93 runs

Australia v Pakistan
First Test at the Melbourne Cricket Ground

1978-79
March 10, 11, 12, 14, 15 (1979)

Pakistan's 100th Test was marked by an astonishing spell of bowling from Sarfraz Nawaz in the opening match of the 1978–79 two-Test series, featuring Pakistan and Australia in Australia. In *The World's Greatest Cricket Matches*, Norman Giller wrote: "Of all the victories recorded in this selection of the world's greatest cricket matches, this was the most improbable of them all."

Graham Yallop's decision to bowl after he won the toss looked good, as Rodney Hogg continued his great season with a spell of 3-5, Pakistan crumbling to 28-3. Majid Khan edged behind, Mohsin Khan was brilliantly caught by Andrew Hilditch at third slip, and Zaheer Abbas was bowled. Wayne Clark struck when Asif Iqbal edged behind with the total on 40, before a stubborn Javed Miandad and captain Mushtaq Mohammad put together a 43-run partnership. Miandad drove a four off Hogg before playing the ball onto the stumps as he attempted another drive.

Mushtaq also proved stubborn, and he scored just 36 in two-and-a-half hours before his demise made the score 122-7, after Wasim Raja was bowled by Alan Hurst just before Pakistan's 100 was raised. Australia's bowlers seemed to tire as they bowled some wayward deliveries, and all-rounder Imran Khan found a willing ally in Sarfraz. They both made 30s before Pakistan was dismissed for 196. Debutant Peter Sleep took a wicket, while Hogg and Hurst were the pick of the bowlers with four and three wickets respectively. Wicketkeeper Kevin Wright also starred, taking five catches.

Australia's innings began poorly as Graeme Wood and Hilditch inattentively ran into each other following a pull shot from Wood. Wood retired hurt with an injured wrist before Hilditch fended at a rearing delivery from Imran and was caught in close. Yallop and Allan Border provided resistance

Graham Yallop was run out in Australia's second innings while the other nine batsmen dismissed were victims of Sarfraz Nawaz.

without looking too comfortable, before Border offered no stroke to an Imran delivery that toppled the off-stump. Yallop was also bowled by Imran as the score became 63-3, before Kim Hughes and debutant Dav Whatmore hinted at a recovery. But Hughes took off for a risky single and was run out after Whatmore sent him back. Imran continued to be economical and destructive, and a great delivery had Sleep caught behind off his glove as the batsman tried to evade it. Imran had four wickets as Australia was perilously placed at 109-5, yet Pakistan's modest score meant the home side was still well in the match.

Whatmore resisted, while Wright and Clark scored nine each before falling to Raja, and the last three wickets fell for one run after Hogg also scored nine. Spite crept into the match after Hogg defended a delivery and left his crease to repair a divot, while Miandad broke the wicket and had a run out appeal upheld. Mushtaq tried to recall Hogg, but umpire Clarence 'Mick' Harvey didn't overturn his decision, and an angry Hogg smacked two stumps out of the ground. Whatmore was last out after top-scoring with 43, Wood's return virtually amounting to nothing.

Pakistan had a 28-run lead on the first innings, and Majid combined with Zaheer for a strong second-wicket partnership on day three. Mohsin fell for 14 when Hogg took a good return catch, before Majid and Zaheer played many aggressive and attractive strokes. They put on 135 runs before Hogg bowled Zaheer. Leg-spinner Sleep learned a harsh lesson as his loose deliveries were punished unmercifully, with Majid whacking eight boundaries in Sleep's first four overs. Majid passed a century, and hit 16 boundaries before he unexpectedly succumbed to a yorker from Border's left-arm spin. Border struck again when Miandad edged behind, and Pakistan was four-down and leading by 237 runs. Asif and Mushtaq put on 52 runs to keep the visiting team on top, with Asif hitting two sixes before finishing the day unbeaten on 41. Pakistan led by 307 runs with five wickets remaining. Mushtaq was fifth out when substitute fielder Jim Higgs took a fine diving catch at deep mid wicket off the erratic Sleep.

Overnight rain delayed the start of day four by 30 minutes, and Asif didn't last long before Hogg had him lbw. Raja and Imran hit out and scored 28 each, and Pakistan declared with one wicket remaining after Hurst took three consecutive scalps. Australia needed 382 runs to win, an apparently impossible task, particularly after Australia had only once topped 300 in 12 team innings in the recent Ashes series.

Whatmore opened with Hilditch as Wood was still hurt, and the opening stand realised 49 runs before Whatmore

played a ball onto his stumps. Hilditch batted positively but gave chances on 26 and 59 before he was bowled as he tried a leg glance, 24 minutes before stumps. Australia needed 265 runs on the last day with eight wickets standing. Yallop was foolishly run out after 11 runs were added to the overnight total, before Border and Hughes batted wonderfully. Elegant strokes, good judgment in their running, and punishing stray deliveries were prominent as the duo put on 177 runs, although there were some missed catches. Border produced his maiden Test century, and Australia needed 77 runs from 4.30pm when a swinging Sarfraz delivery crashed into Border's stumps off a deflection. There was no hint of what was to follow, as Sarfraz went to work.

Wood was out first ball as he edged behind, before Sleep was bowled for nought. On 84 and with the batting around him suddenly crumbling, Hughes lost his cool and played a rare bad shot to produce a catch to mid off. Clark was bowled, Hogg lbw and Hurst caught behind as Sarfraz completed a freakish spell of 7-1 in 33 deliveries to seal a 71-run win to Pakistan. Australia had lost 5-7 in 65 deliveries in 55 minutes, and three of the five runs were leg byes. The Australians were speechless as they couldn't believe what had happened, but they bounced back to square the series in Perth with a seven-wicket win as they chased 236 runs.

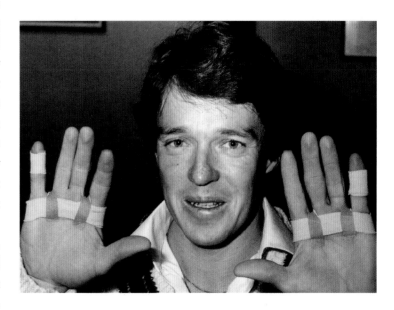

Australia's wicketkeeper Kevin Wright took five first innings catches against Pakistan, and seven overall in the match, in 1979.

PAKISTAN 1ST INNINGS

Majid Khan	c Wright b Hogg	1
Mohsin Khan	c Hilditch b Hogg	14
Zaheer Abbas	b Hogg	11
Javed Miandad	b Hogg	19
Asif Iqbal	c Wright b Clark	9
Mushtaq Mohammad*	c Wright b Hurst	36
Wasim Raja	b Hurst	13
Imran Khan	c Wright b Hurst	33
Sarfraz Nawaz	c Wright b Sleep	35
Wasim Bari†	run out	0
Sikander Bakht	not out	5
Extras	(b 2, lb 7, w 1, nb 10)	20
Total		196

Fall of wickets 2, 22, 28, 40, 83, 99, 122, 173, 177, 196

	O	M	R	W
RM Hogg	17	4	49	4
AG Hurst	20	4	55	3
WM Clark	17	4	56	1
PR Sleep	7.7	2	16	1

AUSTRALIA 1ST INNINGS

GM Wood	not out	5
AMJ Hilditch	c Javed Miandad b Imran Khan	3
AR Border	b Imran Khan	20
GN Yallop*	b Imran Khan	25
KJ Hughes	run out	19
DF Whatmore	lbw b Sarfraz Nawaz	43
PR Sleep	c Wasim Bari b Imran Khan	10
KJ Wright†	c Imran Khan b Wasim Raja	9
WM Clark	c Mushtaq Mohammad b Wasim Raja	9
RM Hogg	run out	9
AG Hurst	c & b Sarfraz Nawaz	0
Extras	(b 1, lb 5, w 2, nb 8)	16
Total		168

Fall of wickets 11, 53, 63, 97, 109, 140, 152, 167, 167, 168

	O	M	R	W
Imran Khan	18	8	26	4
Sarfraz Nawaz	21.6	6	39	2
Sikander Bakht	10	1	29	0
Mushtaq Mohammad	7	0	35	0
Wasim Raja	5	0	23	2

PAKISTAN 2ND INNINGS

Majid Khan	b Border	108
Mohsin Khan	c & b Hogg	14
Zaheer Abbas	b Hogg	59
Javed Miandad	c Wright b Border	16
Asif Iqbal	lbw b Hogg	44
Mushtaq Mohammad*	c sub (JD Higgs) b Sleep	28
Wasim Raja	c Wright b Hurst	28
Imran Khan	c Clark b Hurst	28
Sarfraz Nawaz	lbw b Hurst	1
Wasim Bari†	not out	8
Extras	(b 4, lb 6, nb 9)	19
Total	(9 wickets dec)	353

Did not bat Sikander Bakht

Fall of wickets 30, 165, 204, 209, 261, 299, 330, 332, 353

	O	M	R	W
RM Hogg	19	2	75	3
AG Hurst	19.5	1	115	3
WM Clark	21	6	47	0
PR Sleep	8	0	62	1
AR Border	14	5	35	2

AUSTRALIA 2ND INNINGS

DF Whatmore	b Sarfraz Nawaz	15
AMJ Hilditch	b Sarfraz Nawaz	62
AR Border	b Sarfraz Nawaz	105
GN Yallop*	run out	8
KJ Hughes	c Mohsin Khan b Sarfraz Nawaz	84
GM Wood	c Wasim Bari b Sarfraz Nawaz	0
PR Sleep	b Sarfraz Nawaz	0
KJ Wright†	not out	1
WM Clark	b Sarfraz Nawaz	0
RM Hogg	lbw b Sarfraz Nawaz	0
AG Hurst	c Wasim Bari b Sarfraz Nawaz	0
Extras	(b 13, lb 13, nb 9)	35
Total		310

Fall of wickets 49, 109, 128, 305, 305, 306, 308, 309, 310, 310

	O	M	R	W
Imran Khan	27	9	73	0
Sarfraz Nawaz	35.4	7	86	9
Sikander Bakht	7	0	29	0
Mushtaq Mohammad	11	0	42	0
Wasim Raja	3	0	11	0
Majid Khan	9	1	34	0

Toss: Australia   Umpires: RC Bailhache and CE Harvey   Pakistan won by 71 runs

England v India
Fourth Test at the Oval, London

1979
August 30, 31, September 1, 3, 4 (1979)

The climax to the final Test of the 1979 series involving England and India was sensational as all four results were possible in the final over. This provided an enthralling conclusion to the series, which hosts England led 1-0 after two Tests were rain-reduced. England introduced Alan Butcher and David Bairstow to Test cricket for the decisive match, while Derek Randall and Bob Taylor were omitted. India meanwhile replaced an injured Mohinder Amarnath with Yajurvindra Singh.

Butcher opened with Geoff Boycott after the hosts elected to bat first on a flat pitch. The openers were tied down as pacemen Kapil Dev and Karsan Ghavri bowled accurately, before spinners Bishan Bedi and Srinivas Venkataraghavan caused some problems. Butcher scored just 14 in 117 minutes before presenting a catch to short leg off Venkataraghavan, and Kapil Dev trapped Boycott and David Gower in the space of three balls. England went from 45-0 to 51-3.

Graham Gooch settled in, and the recalled Peter Willey overcame an uncertain start to play some aggressive strokes before departing for 52. Ian Botham also departed after looking dominant, having hit four fours and a six before being stumped for 38. Gooch reached 79 in four hours before departing early on day two with an edge to slip off Ghavri, making the score 245-6. Another 27 runs were added before captain Mike Brearley's two-hour stay ended as Ghavri bowled him for 34. Bairstow's maiden Test knock yielded nine runs in an hour, before Phil Edmonds and Bob Willis managed double figures. England's total of 305 was modest, with the Indian bowlers putting in a good all-round effort.

India was 9-2 following lunch after Willis had Chetan Chauhan and Dilip Vengsarkar caught at second slip. Chauhan steered a short ball, before Vengsarkar was bizarrely dismissed.

Sunil Gavaskar (left) and Chetan Chauhan came close to leading India to a remarkable victory in a big run chase against England at the Oval in 1979.

He edged a leg-cutter, which Bairstow spilled, and the ball speculatively bounced off Brearley's boot and was snaffled one-handed by Botham.

India was 47-3 when Bairstow held his first Test catch, after Sunil Gavaskar edged a splendid Botham outswinger. Yashpal Sharma used his feet well to the spinners, before Willis returned and had Sharma lbw with India's total on 91. Gundappa Viswanath played some delightful drives and cuts on his way to 62 before Botham again made a crucial breakthrough. India was 137-5 when bad light caused stumps to be drawn 40 minutes early.

The tourists reached 161-5 before Mike Hendrick bowled Kapil Dev, and thereafter India was unable to put together a partnership beyond 20 runs as Botham and Hendrick worked their way through the tail. Yajurvindra deserved credit for scoring a gutsy 43 not out in nearly three hours, after coming to the crease at 91-4, but England held the aces with a 103-run lead.

Butcher improved slightly in his second innings, scoring 20 before a miscued stroke produced a catch behind point off Ghavri. Gooch struck a mighty six before Kapil Dev had him lbw for 31, and Gower scored just seven before he was caught behind off Bedi. England scored 52 runs in 75 minutes before stumps, as Boycott and Willey were cautious. Boycott was on 83 and Willey 26 as England entered the rest day with a 280-run lead.

Boycott was hampered by a back injury when play resumed, and Willey added just five runs before England stumbled, with Willey caught behind and Botham run out for a duck. Brearley scored 11 before Bairstow enjoyed some time with the willow in his second Test innings. Boycott scored 125 in seven hours before Ghavri bowled him as England's lead neared 400. Edmonds struck four fours and a six in a quickfire 27 not out, before Bairstow's dismissal for 59 prompted a declaration that left India needing 438 runs to square the series. Gavaskar and Chauhan gave the tourists a sound start with an unbroken 76-run partnership before stumps, meaning India needed about a run per minute on the last day.

Gavaskar and Chauhan were careful as they seemingly became entrenched at the crease, scoring 93 runs in the first two hours of day five. Forty-four runs were added in the next hour before Chauhan was again caught by Botham off Willis, this time after scoring a resolute 80 in 314 minutes. England was set back as a shoulder injury restricted Hendrick to just eight overs, although the hosts kept the run rate under control, particularly when Willey conceded a mere two runs in eight overs at one stage in the afternoon. But an Indian win was not out of the question, as nine wickets remained.

Vengsarkar warmed to the task, while Gavaskar increased

Kapil Dev goes on the attack for India.

his scoring rate. Throughout his innings, Gavaskar flicked a number of deliveries through mid wicket and struck some firm cover drives. India was 304-1 at tea, before the hosts slowed their over rate, as they must have felt their opponents could record the highest successful run chase in Test cricket history. With the mandatory 20 overs left, the visitors required 110 runs with nine wickets still standing.

Gavaskar passed 200, and Botham dropped a vital catch in the deep to reprieve Vengsarkar as India was 365-1, but it mattered little as Botham promptly caught Vengsarkar with the total on 366. The promoted Kapil Dev was soon caught off Willey for zero, but Gavaskar soldiered on. Botham returned for a spell of bowling as India needed an attainable 49 runs from eight overs. Botham struck gold as Gavaskar hit a catch to mid on, having scored 221 in 490 minutes and hit 21 fours.

The scoring climbed as the fielders were spread, and Viswanath picked out Brearley after hitting a quick 15. Botham soon had Yajurvindra lbw before running out Venkataraghavan for six. Botham took a paramount 3-17 from four overs after trapping Sharma lbw, and the field moved in as India needed 15 runs from the last over with two wickets in hand. India managed just six runs from five balls despite a boundary to Bharath Reddy, and a thrilling draw resulted.

ENGLAND 1ST INNINGS

G Boycott	lbw b Kapil Dev	35
AR Butcher	c Yajurvindra Singh b Venkataraghavan	14
GA Gooch	c Viswanath b Ghavri	79
DI Gower	lbw b Kapil Dev	0
P Willey	c Yajurvindra Singh b Bedi	52
IT Botham	st Reddy b Venkataraghavan	38
JM Brearley*	b Ghavri	34
DL Bairstow†	c Reddy b Kapil Dev	9
PH Edmonds	c Kapil Dev b Venkataraghavan	16
RGD Willis	not out	10
M Hendrick	c Gavaskar b Bedi	0
Extras	(lb 9, w 4, nb 5)	18
Total		305

Fall of wickets 45, 51, 51, 148, 203, 245, 272, 275, 304, 305

	O	M	R	W
N Kapil Dev	32	12	83	3
KD Ghavri	26	8	61	2
BS Bedi	29.5	4	69	2
Yajurvindra Singh	8	2	15	0
S Venkataraghavan	29	9	59	3

INDIA 1ST INNINGS

SM Gavaskar	c Bairstow b Botham	13
CPS Chauhan	c Botham b Willis	6
DB Vengsarkar	c Botham b Willis	0
GR Viswanath	c Brearley b Botham	62
Yashpal Sharma	lbw b Willis	27
Yajurvindra Singh	not out	43
N Kapil Dev	b Hendrick	16
KD Ghavri	c Bairstow b Botham	7
B Reddy†	c Bairstow b Botham	12
S Venkataraghavan*	c & b Hendrick	2
BS Bedi	c Brearley b Hendrick	1
Extras	(b 2, lb 3, w 5, nb 3)	13
Total		202

Fall of wickets 9, 9, 47, 91, 130, 161, 172, 192, 200, 202

	O	M	R	W
RGD Willis	18	2	53	3
IT Botham	28	7	65	4
M Hendrick	22.3	7	38	3
P Willey	4	1	10	0
GA Gooch	2	0	6	0
PH Edmonds	5	1	17	0

ENGLAND 2ND INNINGS

G Boycott	b Ghavri	125
AR Butcher	c Venkataraghavan b Ghavri	20
GA Gooch	lbw b Kapil Dev	31
DI Gower	c Reddy b Bedi	7
P Willey	c Reddy b Ghavri	31
IT Botham	run out	0
JM Brearley*	b Venkataraghavan	11
DL Bairstow†	c Gavaskar b Kapil Dev	59
PH Edmonds	not out	27
Extras	(lb 14, w 2, nb 7)	23
Total	(8 wickets dec)	334

Did not bat RGD Willis, M Hendrick

Fall of wickets 43, 107, 125, 192, 194, 215, 291, 334

	O	M	R	W
N Kapil Dev	28.5	4	89	2
KD Ghavri	34	11	76	3
S Venkataraghavan	26	4	75	1
BS Bedi	26	4	67	1
Yajurvindra Singh	2	0	4	0

INDIA 2ND INNINGS

SM Gavaskar	c Gower b Botham	221
CPS Chauhan	c Botham b Willis	80
DB Vengsarkar	c Botham b Edmonds	52
N Kapil Dev	c Gooch b Willey	0
Yashpal Sharma	lbw b Botham	19
GR Viswanath	c Brearley b Willey	15
Yajurvindra Singh	lbw b Botham	1
S Venkataraghavan*	run out	6
KD Ghavri	not out	3
B Reddy†	not out	5
Extras	(b 11, lb 15, w 1)	27
Total	(8 wickets)	429

Did not bat BS Bedi

Fall of wickets 213, 366, 367, 389, 410, 411, 419, 423

	O	M	R	W
RGD Willis	28	4	89	1
IT Botham	29	5	97	3
M Hendrick	8	2	15	0
PH Edmonds	38	11	87	1
P Willey	43.5	15	96	2
GA Gooch	2	0	9	0
AR Butcher	2	0	9	0

Toss: England   Umpires: DJ Constant and KE Palmer   Match drawn

India v Pakistan
Second Test at Feroz Shah Kotla, Delhi

1979-80
December 4, 5, 6, 8, 9 (1979)

Pakistan's 2-0 series win over India in Pakistan in 1978–79 was the first series involving the archenemies since 1960–61, due to the effects of wars involving the two countries. India hosted the subsequent 1979–80 series, and was in a transitional period after the retirements of spinners Bishan Bedi, Bhagwath Chandrasekhar and Erapalli Prasanna, while an out-of-form Srinivas Venkataraghavan was omitted. Pakistan, however, made some puzzling decisions, with key batsman Mushtaq Mohammad and opening bowler Sarfraz Nawaz excluded. Sarfraz was apparently omitted because captain Asif Iqbal found him hard to deal with.

The pick of the Tests was the second at Delhi after a draw in Bangalore featured both teams topping 400 runs before rain intervened. The Delhi surface was conducive to seam bowling, yet Asif chose to bat after he won the toss. In a strong opening spell, Kapil Dev bowled Majid Khan and Zaheer Abbas as Pakistan fell to 13-2. Mudassar Nazar also fell to Kapil Dev, and Javed Miandad worked his way to 34 in nearly two hours before Karsan Ghavri had him lbw. From 90-4, Pakistan rallied to 217-4 at stumps, with Wasim Raja on 94 and Asif 63.

Taking the new ball the next morning, India regained the initiative. Asif added only one run before succumbing to a wild shot, before Raja was lbw after adding just three runs. Imran Khan struck four fours and a six but he had little support, as Kapil Dev's accuracy brought him a five-wicket haul and Ghavri and Roger Binny finished with two scalps each. Pakistan was dismissed for 273 when Iqbal Qasim was run out, before Imran produced a hostile spell of bowling. But he sustained a rib-muscle injury and was unable to complete his eighth over. Sikander Bakht stepped up and produced a devastating spell as he bowled unchanged.

Chetan Chauhan was first out when he was caught behind

Opening batsman Chetan Chauhan scored 2084 runs in 40 Test appearances for India.

off Sikander with the total on 19, before Vengsarkar was caught by Javed for one. Gundappa Viswanath was unluckily run out when Sikander unintentionally deflected a drive from Gavaskar into the stumps at the non-striker's end as Viswanath was out of the crease. Sikander struck another blow several minutes later when Gavaskar, who had hit five fours in his 31, was caught behind to make the score 52-4.

Sikander didn't need any assistance from team-mates for the next four wickets, as Binny was lbw, Syed Kirmani and Kapil Dev bowled, and Ghavri lbw second ball. India crumbled to 87-8. Abdul Qadir caught Shivlal Yadav off Sikander to make the score 94-9, before Yashpal Sharma and Dilip Doshi put on 32 runs until bad light forced stumps to be drawn seven minutes early. The highest partnership of the innings ended without a run added the next morning, when Doshi was caught off Asif. Sikander had taken 8-69, while Sharma was unconquered on 28 from 147 minutes.

Pakistan built on its 147-run lead with an opening stand of 39 before Mudassar was dismissed. Majid made a handy 40, and his departure was quickly followed by the run out of Javed as the visitors went from 68-1 to 68-3. Zaheer reached a half-century before Kirmani gloved his third catch of the innings. Raja and Asif produced another good partnership and expanded the lead to 344 at stumps. But Pakistan collapsed on day four, following the rest day. There were a few reckless strokes as Pakistan slumped from 201-4 to 242 all out. Kapil Dev finished with four wickets while Doshi and Ghavri also chipped in. India had 550 minutes in which to score 390 runs, and Pakistan was set back when Imran aggravated his injury after one over and did not bowl again in the match.

Gavaskar reached 21 before he again fell to a catch behind off Sikander. Chauhan made a gritty 40 before Sikander had him lbw, and India reached 117-2 at stumps with Vengsarkar and Viswanath looking settled. Viswanath confidently reached 34 the following morning before left-arm orthodox spinner Qasim produced a majestic delivery that pitched on leg-stump before hitting the off-stump. Vengsarkar meanwhile scored just 17 runs in the session, while Sikander seemed to lose his sting after peaking at 10 wickets. Vengsarkar remained slow after lunch before Sharma increased the scoring rate. After tea, Vengsarkar belatedly showed more authority, before Sikander took his 11th wicket when he caught-and-bowled Sharma.

India required 114 runs from 20 overs with five wickets left, and Kapil Dev scored a quick 21 before Mudassar had him lbw. Binny was the sixth and last wicket to fall with 23 minutes remaining, and Vengsarkar finished with 146 not out from 370 balls in 522 minutes. After being behind the eight-ball for much of the match, the Indians ended 26 runs shy of victory with four wickets remaining. They could well have won had the scoring been just a little quicker in the first two sessions of day five.

India recorded its first Test win over Pakistan for 27 years with a 131-run triumph in the third Test at Bombay, before a rain-affected fourth Test was drawn. India's 10-wicket win in the fifth Test decided the series, and the last Test was drawn after Pakistan's fielding was particularly poor.

Having lost the series 2-0, the Pakistanis dreaded returning home. Imran, who repeatedly battled injury, wrote in *All*

Round View: "Our failure was attributed to non-stop partying and a thoroughly irresponsible way of life. Apparently we had all indulged in wining, dining and womanising throughout the tour. There was little sympathy for my muscle injury, which I had evidently contracted while performing debauched calisthenics with Indian actresses.

"Realistically, it should have been pointed out that our batting had always tended to collapse under pressure, but in the context of an India-Pakistan series, rational analysis is rare indeed. The press thrives on innuendo, gossip, rumour and outright slander, and still more so at the first sign of defeat."

A rib injury severely hindered champion Pakistan all-rounder Imran Khan in the 1979–80 series against India.

PAKISTAN 1ST INNINGS

Majid Khan	b Kapil Dev	0
Mudassar Nazar	c Chauhan b Kapil Dev	18
Zaheer Abbas	b Kapil Dev	3
Javed Miandad	lbw b Ghavri	34
Wasim Raja	lbw b Kapil Dev	97
Asif Iqbal*	c Vengsarkar b Ghavri	64
Imran Khan	lbw b Binny	30
Wasim Bari†	b Kapil Dev	9
Abdul Qadir	b Binny	9
Iqbal Qasim	run out	2
Sikander Bakht	not out	1
Extras	(lb 2, nb 4)	6
Total		273

Fall of wickets 3, 13, 36, 90, 220, 224, 250, 270, 271, 273

	O	M	R	W
N Kapil Dev	23.5	8	58	5
KD Ghavri	21	4	58	2
RMH Binny	10	3	32	2
DR Doshi	17	3	51	0
NS Yadav	20	2	68	0

PAKISTAN 2ND INNINGS

Majid Khan	c Kirmani b Binny	40
Mudassar Nazar	c Kirmani b Kapil Dev	12
Zaheer Abbas	c Kirmani b Binny	50
Javed Miandad	run out	0
Wasim Raja	c Kapil Dev b Doshi	61
Asif Iqbal*	c Kirmani b Kapil Dev	38
Imran Khan	c Chauhan b Doshi	2
Wasim Bari†	b Ghavri	5
Abdul Qadir	c Vengsarkar b Kapil Dev	11
Iqbal Qasim	not out	5
Sikander Bakht	lbw b Kapil Dev	6
Extras	(b 6, lb 4, nb 2)	12
Total		242

Fall of wickets 39, 68, 68, 143, 201, 209, 210, 230, 232, 242

	O	M	R	W
N Kapil Dev	22.5	6	63	4
KD Ghavri	17	4	59	1
RMH Binny	17	3	56	2
NS Yadav	5	0	21	0
DR Doshi	19	6	31	2

INDIA 1ST INNINGS

SM Gavaskar*	c Wasim Bari b Sikander Bakht	31
CPS Chauhan	c Wasim Bari b Sikander Bakht	11
DB Vengsarkar	c Javed Miandad b Sikander Bakht	1
GR Viswanath	run out	4
Yashpal Sharma	not out	28
RMH Binny	lbw b Sikander Bakht	1
SMH Kirmani†	b Sikander Bakht	5
N Kapil Dev	b Sikander Bakht	15
KD Ghavri	lbw b Sikander Bakht	0
NS Yadav	c Abdul Qadir b Sikander Bakht	4
DR Doshi	c Javed Miandad b Asif Iqbal	10
Extras	(b 2, lb 5, nb 9)	16
Total		126

Fall of wickets 19, 35, 46, 52, 56, 70, 87, 87, 94, 126

	O	M	R	W
Imran Khan	7.3	4	11	0
Sikander Bakht	21	3	69	8
Asif Iqbal	6.2	4	3	1
Majid Khan	1	0	12	0
Iqbal Qasim	3	0	7	0
Mudassar Nazar	3	0	8	0

INDIA 2ND INNINGS

SM Gavaskar*	c Wasim Bari b Sikander Bakht	21
CPS Chauhan	lbw b Sikander Bakht	40
DB Vengsarkar	not out	146
GR Viswanath	b Iqbal Qasim	34
Yashpal Sharma	c & b Sikander Bakht	60
N Kapil Dev	lbw b Mudassar Nazar	21
RMH Binny	c Abdul Qadir b Asif Iqbal	10
SMH Kirmani†	not out	11
Extras	(b 2, lb 5, w 1, nb 13)	21
Total	(6 wickets)	364

Did not bat KD Ghavri, NS Yadav, DR Doshi

Fall of wickets 37, 92, 154, 276, 308, 343

	O	M	R	W
Imran Khan	1	0	2	0
Sikander Bakht	38	7	121	3
Asif Iqbal	20	7	46	1
Iqbal Qasim	30	5	87	1
Mudassar Nazar	25	8	61	1
Abdul Qadir	11	3	16	0
Wasim Raja	2	1	2	0
Majid Khan	4	2	8	0

Toss: Pakistan　Umpires: Mohammad Ghouse and PR Punjabi

Match drawn

New Zealand v West Indies

First Test at Carisbrook, Dunedin

1979–80

February 8, 9, 10, 12, 13 (1980)

Above: West Indies players, with bowlers Colin Croft (left) and Joel Garner (right) centre stage, celebrate a wicket during their turbulent tour of New Zealand in 1979–80.

Opposite: West Indies skipper Clive Lloyd was popular among cricket fans in Australia and New Zealand.

The 1979–80 series involving the Kiwis and West Indians involved plenty of controversy, and the first Test was decided by the smallest possible margin, ensuring its inclusion in this book.

The West Indians were supposedly unbeatable as they arrived in New Zealand, although Viv Richards was absent with a back injury. The tourists, however, seemed not to adjust to the conditions after Clive Lloyd elected to bat. The ball repeatedly kept low while there was some movement. Richard Hadlee took three wickets in his first 13 deliveries, with a miscued hook causing Gordon Greenidge's downfall before Lawrence Rowe and Alvin Kallicharran were adjudged lbw to leave the tourists reeling at 4-3. Desmond Haynes provided resistance as he got on the front foot, while Lloyd lasted nearly two hours in scoring 24, which included a six before he too was lbw. Collis King and Deryck Murray were caught from cross-batted shots off Gary Troup's bowling as the West Indies fell to 105-6. Derick Parry hit a four and a six before he was bowled by left-arm spinner Steve Boock for 17, and Joel Garner was out second ball. Michael Holding hit a boundary before he became Hadlee's fourth lbw victim and fifth scalp of the innings. Haynes was denied the satisfaction of carrying his bat, as he was caught-and-bowled by Lance Cairns after scoring 55 among a dismal total of 140.

New Zealand was 30-0 at stumps, and another 12 runs were added before John Wright was bowled by Holding. The West Indians didn't pitch the ball up as much as the Kiwis did, and the tourists might have had a better reward if they did. The Kiwi batsmen copped some blows but gradually worked their team into a good position. Bruce Edgar and captain Geoff Howarth added 67 runs in 129 minutes before Croft dismissed Howarth and John Parker in one over. Peter Webb's debut Test innings yielded just five runs before Parry had him lbw, and the same fate befell Edgar as New Zealand led by five runs. Edgar lasted five hours for his 65, before Jeremy Coney was bowled by Holding for eight and Warren Lees run out after striking a four and a six.

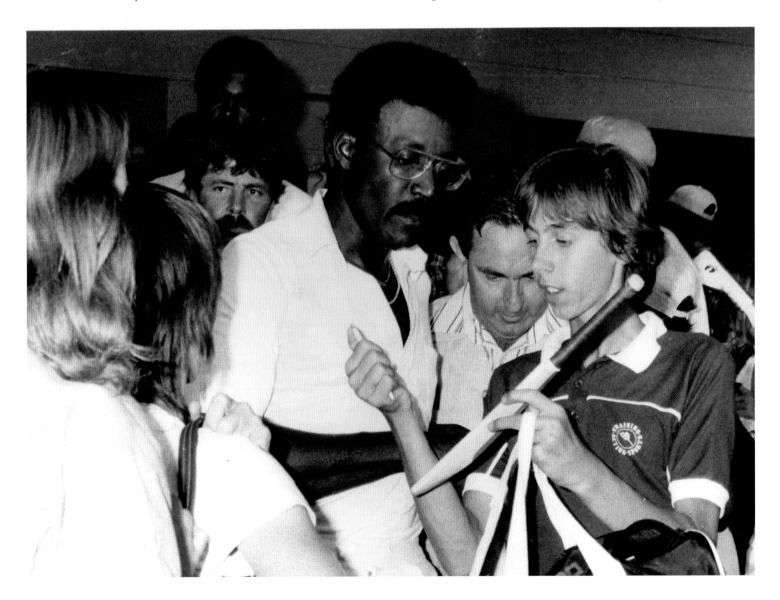

The hosts were 168-7 before the pendulum swung sharply their way. Cairns creamed three sixes in a Parry over, and scored 30 runs off 18 balls. Hadlee struck regular fours before Croft bowled Cairns, and had Troup caught. After New Zealand finished the day on 236-9, Hadlee went from 38 to 51 and had struck nine fours when he was last out. Hadlee subsequently dismissed Greenidge cheaply again. The tourists were left 18-1 at stumps and 91 runs in arrears after rain washed out most of the day's play before a rest day followed.

Rowe failed again before Kallicharran bagged a pair, and Lloyd's dismissal to a catch behind left his team at a worrying 29-4. Haynes, however, was again determined to put up a fight, and King scored 41 before he departed when a big innings looked possible. Murray scored a solid 30, and the West Indies led by 71 runs when Hadlee took a Test-record seventh lbw. Hadlee removed Parry and Garner cheaply to make the score 188-8, before Holding lasted 48 minutes and scored three in a vital 21-run partnership. Haynes reached a well-deserved century before stumps, but again he was last out, this time caught by Webb off Troup early on day five after he added two runs to the overnight total. In the match, Haynes batted for 711 minutes, scored 160 runs and hit only nine fours.

Chasing just 104 runs, New Zealand lost its openers before lunch after Holding produced two breakthroughs to have the hosts 33-2 at the break. The Kiwis could have been three-down but Parker was given not out after gloving a Holding delivery to the wicketkeeper. The tourists, already unhappy at some lbw decisions their batsmen had been dealt, were incensed at Parker's reprieve, and tempers flared as Holding booted the stumps down. After lunch, however, the Kiwis crumbled under pressure.

Howarth was caught off Croft, before New Zealand crashed from 44-3 to 44-6. Coney was lbw to Croft, before Garner had Parker officially caught behind and Lees lbw with successive balls. Another 10 runs were added before Webb was again trapped in front for five. A record 12 lbw decisions had been given in the match.

Having scored crucial runs in New Zealand's first innings, Hadlee and Cairns needed to do so again. Hadlee played some forceful strokes before Garner bowled him for 17, and the Kiwis looked lost at 73-8. But Cairns and Troup showed courage and resilience, and they slowly took the score up to 95-8 at tea. At 96-8, a Holding delivery grazed Cairns' off-stump, but amazingly the bails weren't dislodged.

The contest could hardly have been tenser as the Kiwis needed four runs with one wicket remaining, Holding having Cairns caught behind with the first ball of an over. With a top Test score of just eight, Boock survived the remainder of the

over before Garner bowled to Troup. A bye was run off the first ball, and Boock nearly ran himself out after unsuccessfully seeking a second run. Boock survived an lbw appeal from the second ball before facing two dot balls and then squeezing two runs past point to tie the scores. The last ball of the over ricocheted behind square on the legside from Boock's pad, and a scrambled leg bye sealed a one-wicket win to the hosts as Parry threw errantly to the non-striker's end.

Bill Frindall wrote in the *Wisden Book of Test Cricket* that the result "precipitated much truculent behaviour from the West Indies team and management". In the second Test at Christchurch, the tourists were again upset with the umpires, particularly Fred Goodall. At one point, Croft knocked Goodall sideways as Croft came in to bowl. At the end of the unsavoury three-match series, New Zealand won 1-0.

Gordon Greenidge's failure in both innings precipitated an unlikely Test win for New Zealand in Dunedin.

WEST INDIES 1ST INNINGS		
CG Greenidge	c Cairns b Hadlee	2
DL Haynes	c & b Cairns	55
LG Rowe	lbw b Hadlee	1
AI Kallicharran	lbw b Hadlee	0
CH Lloyd*	lbw b Hadlee	24
CL King	c Coney b Troup	14
DL Murray†	c Edgar b Troup	6
DR Parry	b Boock	17
J Garner	c Howarth b Cairns	0
MA Holding	lbw b Hadlee	4
CEH Croft	not out	0
Extras	(lb 8, nb 9)	17
Total		140

Fall of wickets 3, 4, 4, 72, 91, 105, 124, 125, 136, 140

	O	M	R	W
RJ Hadlee	20	9	34	5
GB Troup	17	6	26	2
BL Cairns	19.5	4	32	2
SL Boock	13	3	31	1

NEW ZEALAND 1ST INNINGS		
JG Wright	b Holding	21
BA Edgar	lbw b Parry	65
GP Howarth*	c Murray b Croft	33
JM Parker	b Croft	0
PN Webb	lbw b Parry	5
JV Coney	b Holding	8
WK Lees†	run out	18
RJ Hadlee	c Lloyd b Garner	51
BL Cairns	b Croft	30
GB Troup	c Greenidge b Croft	0
SL Boock	not out	0
Extras	(b 5, lb 2, nb 11)	18
Total		249

Fall of wickets 42, 109, 110, 133, 145, 159, 168, 232, 236, 249

	O	M	R	W
MA Holding	22	5	50	2
CEH Croft	25	3	64	4
J Garner	25.5	8	51	1
CL King	1	0	3	0
DR Parry	22	6	63	2

WEST INDIES 2ND INNINGS		
CG Greenidge	lbw b Hadlee	3
DL Haynes	c Webb b Troup	105
LG Rowe	lbw b Hadlee	12
AI Kallicharran	c Cairns b Troup	0
CH Lloyd*	c Lees b Hadlee	5
CL King	c Boock b Cairns	41
DL Murray†	lbw b Hadlee	30
DR Parry	c & b Hadlee	1
J Garner	b Hadlee	2
MA Holding	c Cairns b Troup	3
CEH Croft	not out	1
Extras	(lb 4, nb 5)	9
Total		212

Fall of wickets 4, 21, 24, 29, 117, 180, 186, 188, 209, 212

	O	M	R	W
RJ Hadlee	36	13	68	6
GB Troup	36.4	13	57	3
BL Cairns	25	10	63	1
SL Boock	11	4	15	0

NEW ZEALAND 2ND INNINGS		
JG Wright	b Holding	11
BA Edgar	c Greenidge b Holding	6
GP Howarth*	c Greenidge b Croft	11
JM Parker	c Murray b Garner	5
JV Coney	lbw b Croft	2
PN Webb	lbw b Garner	5
WK Lees†	lbw b Garner	0
RJ Hadlee	b Garner	17
BL Cairns	c Murray b Holding	19
GB Troup	not out	7
SL Boock	not out	2
Extras	(b 7, lb 5, nb 7)	19
Total	(9 wickets)	104

Fall of wickets 15, 28, 40, 44, 44, 44, 54, 73, 100

	O	M	R	W
MA Holding	16	7	24	3
CEH Croft	11	2	25	2
J Garner	23	6	36	4

Toss: West Indies   Umpires: FR Goodall and JBR Hastie   New Zealand won by 1 wicket

Australia v India
Third Test at the Melbourne Cricket Ground

1980-81
February 7, 8, 9, 10, 11 (1981)

Rarely does a team threaten to forfeit a Test match, let alone win after threatening to forfeit. But this intriguing set of events took place in the third Test involving Australia and India at the MCG in 1980–81. India had the chance to square the series after drawing the second Test, following Australia's win by an innings in the first Test.

Australian skipper Greg Chappell, who had been vocal in his criticism of the MCG pitches, which contained irregular bounce, chose to bowl after he won the toss. Len Pascoe struck in the second over when he had Chetan Chauhan caught for a duck, before Dennis Lillee accounted for Dilip Vengsarkar in the 11th over. A struggling Sunil Gavaskar scored just 10 in 93 minutes before Pascoe struck again, and India was 43-3.

Gundappa Viswanath proved India's saviour as he consolidated, and Sandeep Patil reached 23 in short order before he and Yashpal Sharma fell to Lillee. Pascoe's dismissal of Kapil Dev made the score 115-6, before Syed Kirmani gave Viswanath solid support. Kirmani scored 25 in a 49-run partnership, before Karsan Ghavri hung around for 25 minutes as Viswanath pushed India's total to 190, until Ghavri was run out for zero. Shivlal Yadav copped several blows on his body thanks to aggressive bowling from Pascoe and the nature of the pitch, but Yadav survived while Viswanath posted a vital century. Viswanath's knock ended on 114 against the spin of Bruce Yardley, who subsequently dismissed Dilip Doshi as India finished with 237. John Dyson and Graeme Wood took Australia to 12-0 at stumps, but both failed the following morning as Australia slipped to 32-2.

Chappell and Kim Hughes added 49 runs before a drive from Hughes was well caught by Chauhan at mid on. The wicket-taker, Yadav, received pain-killing injections after a yorker from Pascoe fractured his toe the previous day.

Australian skipper Greg Chappell was unhappy with the state of the MCG pitch, but offered no excuses for his team surrendering a likely Test victory.

Chappell and Allan Border put on a steady partnership, but had to earn their runs as the pitch became lower and slower. Australia was 48 runs short of India's total when Chappell fell to Ghavri, before Australia gained a 35-run lead by the close of play without further loss. Border, who was on 95 at stumps, had a close shave late in the day when the Indians thought they had him caught behind, but replays supported the decision, as Border's bat hit the ground while the ball deviated from a footmark.

Border reached 124 before Yadav bowled him, and Doug Walters progressed to a workmanlike 78 before being stumped off Doshi. Yardley was lbw five balls later as Australia became 356-7, and then Marsh and Lillee put on a gritty 57-run partnership. The last three wickets fell for six runs but Australia had a formidable 182-run lead.

India fought back as captain Gavaskar scored 59 and Chauhan 41 in a dogged and unbroken 108-run stand before stumps. Gavaskar scored just 11 of the first 57 runs the next day before Lillee struck him on the pads and won an lbw appeal. Gavaskar claimed he edged the ball first, and his frustration boiled over. He felt his team had been handed several tough decisions throughout the series, not to mention his own run drought, so he must have felt ripe for a big score this time. The unhappy Gavaskar stood his ground and then walked off, only to turn back and advise Chauhan to come as well. It was a remarkable scene as a forfeit looked likely, but India's manager Wing Commander Shahid Durrani was at the fence and directed Chauhan and Vengsarkar to the wicket, so proceedings continued. The drama must have unsettled Chauhan, who looked unconvincing as he moved from 77 to 85 before a cut shot produced a catch to cover point.

Vengsarkar and Viswanath put on 67 runs before departing in the space of two runs, as Lillee and Pascoe struck. The deterioration of the pitch was evident as Yashpal was bowled by a shooter, then Patil counterattacked, scoring at better than a run per ball. India reached 296-5 before Yardley dismissed Patil and Kapil Dev with successive balls. Kirmani, Ghavri and Doshi took the score to 324-9, which was the end of the innings as Durrani ordered the injured Yadav not to bat.

As Australia chased 143 runs, India was handicapped without Yadav while Kapil Dev had a thigh injury and Doshi a toe injury. The period of play before stumps proved significant in an unexpected way as Australia went from 11-0 to 11-2 in successive balls. Dyson's dismissal to a catch behind off Ghavri was followed by Chappell being bizarrely bowled behind his legs as he tried to hook a half-tracker that kept low. Wood was stumped, and Australia was in trouble at 24-3 with a day remaining.

Kapil Dev braved his injury to help India's cause on day five, and he bowled in tandem with Doshi as the pitch was fiendish to bat on. Australia reached 40-3 before Doshi bowled Hughes

Above: Len Pascoe achieved outstanding figures of 3-29 from 22 overs in India's first innings.
Following page: Australia wicketkeeper Rod Marsh.

for 16, and Yardley's innings as nightwatchman produced seven runs in 73 minutes when Kapil Dev bowled him with a delivery that skidded and cut in slightly. India's paceman landed the ball on a good length and was assisted by the pitch as the ball often kept low, and the Australians never looked like reaching their modest target despite Walters' determination.

Kapil Dev had Border caught behind down the legside and Marsh bowled behind his legs as he shuffled across the stumps. Lillee was bowled as he drove wildly, before Pascoe was run out and Jim Higgs lbw. Kapil Dev took 5-28 as India drew the series with an unexpected 59-run win after being outplayed in the first two Tests and coming close to forfeiting the third. Peter McFarline described this truly remarkable Test in *Wisden Cricket Monthly* as "the Test that could have died of shame". Chappell meanwhile offered no excuses for Australia's downfall despite his dissatisfaction with the pitch.

INDIA 1ST INNINGS

SM Gavaskar*	c Hughes b Pascoe	10
CPS Chauhan	c Yardley b Pascoe	0
DB Vengsarkar	c Border b Lillee	12
GR Viswanath	c Chappell b Yardley	114
SM Patil	c Hughes b Lillee	23
Yashpal Sharma	c Marsh b Lillee	4
N Kapil Dev	c Hughes b Pascoe	5
SMH Kirmani†	c Marsh b Lillee	25
KD Ghavri	run out	0
NS Yadav	not out	20
DR Doshi	c Walters b Yardley	0
Extras	(b 1, lb 8, w 6, nb 9)	24
Total		237

Fall of wickets 0, 22, 43, 91, 99, 115, 164, 190, 230, 237

	O	M	R	W
DK Lillee	25	6	65	4
LS Pascoe	22	11	29	3
GS Chappell	5	2	9	0
B Yardley	13	3	45	2
JD Higgs	19	2	65	0

AUSTRALIA 1ST INNINGS

J Dyson	c Kirmani b Kapil Dev	16
GM Wood	c Doshi b Ghavri	10
GS Chappell*	c & b Ghavri	76
KJ Hughes	c Chauhan b Yadav	24
AR Border	b Yadav	124
KD Walters	st Kirmani b Doshi	78
RW Marsh†	c sub (KBJ Azad) b Doshi	45
B Yardley	lbw b Doshi	0
DK Lillee	c & b Patil	19
LS Pascoe	lbw b Patil	3
JD Higgs	not out	1
Extras	(b 12, lb 6, nb 5)	23
Total		419

Fall of wickets 30, 32, 81, 189, 320, 356, 356, 413, 413, 419

	O	M	R	W
N Kapil Dev	19	7	41	1
DR Doshi	52	14	109	3
KD Ghavri	39	4	110	2
NS Yadav	32	6	100	2
CPS Chauhan	2	0	8	0
SM Patil	12.3	4	28	2

INDIA 2ND INNINGS

SM Gavaskar*	lbw b Lillee	70
CPS Chauhan	c Yardley b Lillee	85
DB Vengsarkar	c Marsh b Pascoe	41
GR Viswanath	b Lillee	30
SM Patil	c Chappell b Yardley	36
Yashpal Sharma	b Pascoe	9
SMH Kirmani†	run out	9
N Kapil Dev	b Yardley	0
KD Ghavri	not out	11
DR Doshi	b Lillee	7
NS Yadav	absent hurt	-
Extras	(b 11, lb 8, nb 7)	26
Total		324

Fall of wickets 165, 176, 243, 245, 260, 296, 296, 308, 324

	O	M	R	W
DK Lillee	32.1	5	104	4
LS Pascoe	29	4	80	2
JD Higgs	15	3	41	0
B Yardley	31	11	65	2
AR Border	2	0	8	0

AUSTRALIA 2ND INNINGS

J Dyson	c Kirmani b Ghavri	3
GM Wood	st Kirmani b Doshi	10
GS Chappell*	b Ghavri	0
KJ Hughes	b Doshi	16
B Yardley	b Kapil Dev	7
AR Border	c Kirmani b Kapil Dev	9
KD Walters	not out	18
RW Marsh†	b Kapil Dev	3
DK Lillee	b Kapil Dev	4
LS Pascoe	run out	6
JD Higgs	lbw b Kapil Dev	0
Extras	(lb 5, nb 2)	7
Total		83

Fall of wickets 11, 11, 18, 40, 50, 55, 61, 69, 79, 83

	O	M	R	W
KD Ghavri	8	4	10	2
SM Pati	2	0	5	0
DR Doshi	22	9	33	2
N Kapil Dev	16.4	4	28	5

Toss: Australia   Umpires: MW Johnson and RV Whitehead   India won by 59 runs

England v Australia
Third Test at Headingley, Leeds

1981
July 16, 17, 18, 20, 21 (1981)

The 1981 Ashes Test at Headingley will be remembered for what happened after, at one stage during the match, bookmakers rated England a 500-1 chance to win.

With Australia leading 1-0 after two Tests, Mike Brearley regained the England captaincy at Ian Botham's expense following Botham's loss of form. Bob Willis meanwhile was excluded after suffering a chest infection in the drawn second Test at Lord's. Mike Hendrick was named but before the team was publicly announced, selectors called Willis to mention their decision. Willis pleaded for the chance to prove his fitness, and

was named after playing a day for Warwickshire's second team.

Australia clawed its way to 203-3 at stumps on a rain-interrupted first day, after John Dyson worked up to a maiden Test century following the dismissals of Graeme Wood and Trevor Chappell. Wood scored 34, then Botham had him lbw. Chappell was dropped twice when in single figures, before scoring a slow 27 in a partnership of 94. Dyson was third out for 102.

After nightwatchman Ray Bright's dismissal at 220-4, captain Kim Hughes combined with Graham Yallop for a 112-run partnership that featured plenty of defence and attractive strokeplay. Dismissing Hughes for 89, Botham then made further breakthroughs on another rainy day. Hughes declared on 401-9, and England was 7-0 at stumps.

Terry Alderman struck early on day three when he had Graham Gooch lbw, before Geoff Boycott and Mike Brearley batted doggedly. Just 28 runs were scored in 64 minutes before Alderman had Brearley caught behind, and then Geoff Lawson bowled Boycott. David Gower and Mike Gatting also settled in without going on to a decent score, both lasting 58 minutes before England slumped to 87-5.

An aggressive Botham hit eight fours in his speedy half-century before edging Dennis Lillee and enabling Rod Marsh to break Alan Knott's record for most Test catches by a wicketkeeper. England's tail folded quickly, the visitors gaining a 227-run lead and enforcing the follow-on. Just three balls into England's second dig, the home side was reeling further as Lillee had Gooch caught at slip for zero. The hosts were 6-1 as

bad light forced stumps to be drawn early.

Brearley hit three fours but his team's total was still only 18 when he fell in the same manner as Gooch. Alderman accounted for Gower and Gatting cheaply as the score became 41-4, before Boycott and Peter Willey provided resistance. Boycott was his solid self, while Willey hit a series of boundaries before cutting a catch to third man with the total on 105. Boycott's stubborn innings ended when Alderman had him lbw for 46 runs in 215 minutes, and then Alderman had Bob Taylor caught for one. The Australians were poised for an innings win as they led by 92 runs and needed just three more wickets, with the scoreboard showing odds of 500-1 for an England win. The English players were resigned to defeat and subsequently checked out of their hotel rooms.

But they were later forced to rebook. The right-handed Botham and left-handed Graham Dilley decided they had nothing to lose, and so they went for their shots. Runs suddenly flowed, and Botham produced a memorable onslaught as he raced to a century with a series of thumping boundaries. Using Gooch's bat proved worthwhile, as Botham went from 50 to 100 in just 40 minutes, and reached three figures from just 87

Opposite: Headingley, Leeds in the 1980s.
Top left: Dennis Lillee took seven wickets in the Ashes Test at Headingley in 1981, but could not halt a belated England batting onslaught that turned the Test around.
Top right: England players (from left) Ian Botham, Bob Taylor and Graham Gouch dispute a decision.

balls. Dilley was hardly outshone, as he struck nine fours in an innings of 56 in 80 minutes before Alderman bowled him.

England's situation was still bleak, leading by 25 runs with two wickets left. However another left-handed tail-ender in Chris Old kept the runs flowing, while Botham continued blazing away. Botham struck a huge six off Alderman, and Old hit six fours in a crucial 67-run partnership before Lawson bowled him. England was still not done, and Botham farmed the strike as much as he could to take England to 351-9 at stumps. Botham had scored a remarkable 106 runs in the last session, before Willis was last out with five runs added on the final day. Botham's 149 not out came from just 148 balls, and included 27 fours and a six.

Australia's target was still only 130, and Wood struck two fours before edging Botham to Taylor with the score on 13. Chappell was bogged down again but he and Dyson took the score past 50, with Willis having bowled some no-balls. Willis, whose position in the England team was insecure as he hadn't taken a wicket all game, switched to the Kirkstall Lane end with the wind behind him. A rearing delivery had Chappell caught behind, before Hughes edged to third slip. Yallop fended a catch to short leg, and suddenly Willis had three scalps as Australia slipped to 58-4 before lunch.

Old claimed a big wicket after lunch as he bowled Border, before Dyson tried to hook Willis and was caught behind. Marsh middled his hook shot but was caught at deep fine leg, before Willis induced an edge from Lawson to Taylor. England was suddenly poised for a sensational victory as Australia was 75-8, but the pendulum swung again as Lillee and Bright put on 35 runs in just four overs. With Australia requiring 20 more runs, Lillee miscued a hook shot towards mid on. Gatting ran and dived to take a vital low catch, before Old twice dropped Alderman at third slip off Botham. Willis, however, produced a brilliant yorker that flattened Bright's middle-stump and caused the Englishmen to celebrate. Willis had taken 8-43, and a Test team had won after following on, for only the second time ever. What might have happened had Hendrick played instead of Willis?

England won the next Test at Edgbaston, after Australia was again in control, and England later won the series 3-1.

Top: Kim Hughes captained the Australians in their 1981 tour of England, after Greg Chappell made himself unavailable for family reasons.

Bottom: Terry Alderman appeals for an lbw.

AUSTRALIA 1ST INNINGS

J Dyson	b Dilley	102
GM Wood	lbw b Botham	34
TM Chappell	c Taylor b Willey	27
KJ Hughes*	c & b Botham	89
RJ Bright	b Dilley	7
GN Yallop	c Taylor b Botham	58
AR Border	lbw b Botham	8
RW Marsh†	b Botham	28
GF Lawson	c Taylor b Botham	13
DK Lillee	not out	3
TM Alderman	not out	0
Extras	(b 4, lb 13, w 3, nb 12)	32
Total	(9 wickets dec)	401

Fall of wickets 55, 149, 196, 220, 332, 354, 357, 396, 401

	O	M	R	W
RGD Willis	30	8	72	0
CM Old	43	14	91	0
GR Dilley	27	4	78	2
IT Botham	39.2	11	95	6
P Willey	13	2	31	1
G Boycott	3	2	2	0

ENGLAND 1ST INNINGS

GA Gooch	lbw b Alderman	2
G Boycott	b Lawson	12
JM Brearley*	c Marsh b Alderman	10
DI Gower	c Marsh b Lawson	24
MW Gatting	lbw b Lillee	15
P Willey	b Lawson	8
IT Botham	c Marsh b Lillee	50
RW Taylor†	c Marsh b Lillee	5
GR Dilley	c & b Lillee	13
CM Old	c Border b Alderman	0
RGD Willis	not out	1
Extras	(b 6, lb 11, w 6, nb 11)	34
Total		174

Fall of wickets 12, 40, 42, 84, 87, 112, 148, 166, 167, 174

	O	M	R	W
DK Lillee	18.5	7	49	4
TM Alderman	19	4	59	3
GF Lawson	13	3	32	3

ENGLAND 2ND INNINGS

GA Gooch	c Alderman b Lillee	0
G Boycott	lbw b Alderman	46
JM Brearley*	c Alderman b Lillee	14
DI Gower	c Border b Alderman	9
MW Gatting	lbw b Alderman	1
P Willey	c Dyson b Lillee	33
IT Botham	not out	149
RW Taylor†	c Bright b Alderman	1
GR Dilley	b Alderman	56
CM Old	b Lawson	29
RGD Willis	c Border b Alderman	2
Extras	(b 5, lb 3, w 3, nb 5)	16
Total		356

Fall of wickets 0, 18, 37, 41, 105, 133, 135, 252, 319, 356

	O	M	R	W
DK Lillee	25	6	94	3
TM Alderman	35.3	6	135	6
GF Lawson	23	4	96	1
RJ Bright	4	0	15	0

AUSTRALIA 2ND INNINGS

J Dyson	c Taylor b Willis	34
GM Wood	c Taylor b Botham	10
TM Chappell	c Taylor b Willis	8
KJ Hughes*	c Botham b Willis	0
GN Yallop	c Gatting b Willis	0
AR Border	b Old	0
RW Marsh†	c Dilley b Willis	4
RJ Bright	b Willis	19
GF Lawson	c Taylor b Willis	1
DK Lillee	c Gatting b Willis	17
TM Alderman	not out	0
Extras	(lb 3, w 1, nb 14)	18
Total		111

Fall of wickets 13, 56, 58, 58, 65, 68, 74, 75, 110, 111

	O	M	R	W
IT Botham	7	3	14	1
GR Dilley	2	0	11	0
RGD Willis	15.1	3	43	8
CM Old	9	1	21	1
P Willey	3	1	4	0

Toss: Australia   Umpires: DGL Evans and BJ Meyer   England won by 18 runs

England v Pakistan
Third Test at Headingley, Leeds

1982
August 26, 27, 28, 30, 31 (1982)

England and Pakistan produced another third and thrilling deciding Test at Headingley, with Pakistanis Zaheer Abbas and Wasim Bari remaining from the corresponding Test 11 years earlier. England and Pakistan had drawn series in 1972–73, 1974 and 1977–78 nil-all before England won 2-0 in 1978. The 1982 series was intriguing as England won a fluctuating first Test by 113 runs, and Pakistan won the second by 10 wickets.

Pakistan missed the injured duo Sarfraz Nawaz and Tahir Naqqash for the decider, and subsequently brought in Ehteshamuddin from the English league, while Majid Khan and Sikander Bakht returned. England meanwhile introduced left-handed opening batsman Graeme Fowler and off-spinner Vic Marks to Test cricket. Pakistan skipper Imran Khan elected to bat on a sunny morning, but must have been disappointed, when Mohsin Khan departed for 10 and Mansoor Akhtar without scoring in the opening 30 minutes.

Mudassar Nazar and Javed Miandad rallied with a 100-run partnership before Ian Botham bowled Mudassar for 65. Zaheer hit two fours but then edged his fifth ball to wicketkeeper Bob Taylor, and Majid Khan scored 21 of the next 32 runs before Robin Jackman had him lbw. Javed lasted four hours for 54 before his departure left Pakistan a precarious 168-6. Bari scored a rapid 23 before Jackman bowled him, and then the tail supported Imran, who led by example. Abdul Qadir lasted 33 minutes before Imran and Sikander took Pakistan to 255-8 at stumps. Sikander scored seven in a ninth-wicket partnership of 50 before Pakistan was dismissed for 275, with Imran unbeaten on 67 after hitting nine fours and two sixes in a 171-minute stay.

Fowler hit a boundary before Ehteshamuddin bowled him for nine, and then Chris Tavare stonewalled while Mike

Mike Gatting scored 25 in each innings for England in the deciding Test against Pakistan in 1982, falling lbw to Imran Khan both times.

Gatting showed a little more initiative. Imran put in a great spell of bowling and was rewarded with the wickets of Gatting for 25, Allan Lamb for zero and Tavare for 22, as England slumped from 67-1 to 77-4. Leg-spinner Qadir appeared to have David Gower caught behind for seven, but Gower was controversially given not out.

Botham meanwhile entertained the Headingley crowd with another of his blazing exhibitions. He was particularly severe on Qadir, blasting 57 runs in a similar number of minutes and deliveries, before falling to an impressive running catch by substitute fielder Haroon Rasheed. Derek Randall fell cheaply to a run out, and Marks' first Test innings yielded a four before Qadir bowled him for seven. England was 170-7 but the fortunate Gower was the mainstay. He batted sensibly, and shared in partnerships of 39 with Taylor and 46 with Jackman before departing just before stumps. He scored 74 from 233 minutes when Haroon, replacing the injured Ehteshamuddin, took his third catch. Imran claimed a deserved five-wicket haul when he had Jackman caught without a run added on day three.

The Pakistanis led by 19 runs but were instantly in trouble, as Mohsin drove loosely at the first ball of Pakistan's second innings and edged a catch behind. Four balls later, Bob Willis also dismissed Mudassar for a golden duck, with a rising ball edged to third slip. Javed subsequently played an entertaining if risky innings, scoring 52 at nearly a run per ball, before a booming drive produced a catch behind. Zaheer was lbw to Botham just five balls later as Pakistan wobbled to 85-4. Botham's match-turning ability showed again as he dismissed the steady-looking Mansoor and Majid, and the tourists struggled to 115-6.

Imran carefully mixed defence and offence as he sought to lift his team. Bari eked out seven runs in 69 minutes, and then Qadir scored a vital 17 before Jackman bowled him. Imran tried to farm the strike, although Sikander resisted admirably as the total crept from 169-8 to 199-8, before Marks claimed his first Test scalp. Unfortunately the dismissal proved a blight on the game, as replays confirmed the suspicion that the ball touched Sikander's pad only before Gatting took the catch at short leg. Feeling that he had no option but to take risks, Imran was caught without the addition of a run. Botham thus had a five-wicket haul, with the battle of two champion all-rounders shaping up to be as great as the contest itself.

England reached 15 without loss at stumps thanks to nine sundries, and so needed a further 204 runs with two days left after the rest day. Day four featured some brief rain stoppages and England gained control as Tavare was gutsy, while debutant Fowler showed good composure and unleashed some attractive drives. With Ehteshamuddin unable to bowl, Pakistan relied on four bowlers who were economical. England nonetheless had 103 runs on the board when Imran finally made a breakthrough with the dismissal of Tavare.

Gatting was slow but effective, and the light worsened as

England reached a match-winning 168-1. Medium-pacer Mudassar, however, had other ideas after taking 6-32 during the second Test. This time he had Fowler caught behind for a well-made 86, before having Lamb lbw four runs later. The hosts still looked comfortable as they reached 187-3 before Mudassar had Gower caught behind. Imran pinned Gatting and Randall in front of the stumps in the space of three balls as England suddenly became a shaky 189-6. Bad light, however, forced stumps, and crucially robbed Pakistan of its momentum. A thrilling finish was still in store.

England was in a refreshed frame of mind on the morning of day five. Nine runs came from the first 10 balls before Botham was caught by Majid off Mudassar. England needed a further 20 runs, and Marks and Taylor polished them off in 30 minutes, despite Pakistan's best efforts to thwart them. It was easy for Pakistan to single out Gower's first innings reprieve and Sikander's second innings dismissal as turning points. But the tourists faltered at crucial times, and 19 byes were conceded in England's run chase. Regardless, the deciding Test was a classic to cap off a great series.

Wasim Bari, one of Pakistan's most reliable wicketkeepers of all time.

PAKISTAN 1ST INNINGS

Mohsin Khan	c Taylor b Botham	10
Mudassar Nazar	b Botham	65
Mansoor Akhtar	c Gatting b Willis	0
Javed Miandad	c Fowler b Willis	54
Zaheer Abbas	c Taylor b Jackman	8
Majid Khan	lbw b Jackman	21
Imran Khan*	not out	67
Wasim Bari†	b Jackman	23
Abdul Qadir	c Willis b Botham	5
Sikander Bakht	c Tavare b Willis	7
Ehteshamuddin	b Botham	0
Extras	(b 1, lb 7, w 4, nb 3)	15
Total		275

Fall of wickets 16, 19, 119, 128, 160, 168, 207, 224, 274, 275

	O	M	R	W
RGD Willis	26	6	76	3
IT Botham	24.5	9	70	4
RD Jackman	37	14	74	3
VJ Marks	5	0	23	0
MW Gatting	8	2	17	0

ENGLAND 1ST INNINGS

CJ Tavare	c sub (Haroon Rasheed) b Imran Khan	22
G Fowler	b Ehteshamuddin	9
MW Gatting	lbw b Imran Khan	25
AJ Lamb	c Mohsin Khan b Imran Khan	0
DI Gower	c sub (Haroon Rasheed) b Sikander Bakht	74
IT Botham	c sub (Haroon Rasheed) b Sikander Bakht	57
DW Randall	run out	8
VJ Marks	b Abdul Qadir	7
RW Taylor†	c Javed Miandad b Imran Khan	18
RD Jackman	c Mohsin Khan b Imran Khan	11
RGD Willis*	not out	1
Extras	(b 4, lb 10, w 2, nb 8)	24
Total		256

Fall of wickets 15, 67, 69, 77, 146, 159, 170, 209, 255, 256

	O	M	R	W
Imran Khan	25.2	7	49	5
Ehteshamuddin	14	4	46	1
Sikander Bakht	24	5	47	2
Abdul Qadir	22	5	87	1
Mudassar Nazar	4	1	3	0

PAKISTAN 2ND INNINGS

Mohsin Khan	c Taylor b Willis	0
Mudassar Nazar	c Botham b Willis	0
Mansoor Akhtar	c Randall b Botham	39
Javed Miandad	c Taylor b Botham	52
Zaheer Abbas	lbw b Botham	4
Majid Khan	c Gower b Botham	10
Imran Khan*	c Randall b Botham	46
Wasim Bari†	c Taylor b Willis	7
Abdul Qadir	b Jackman	17
Sikander Bakht	c Gatting b Marks	7
Ehteshamuddin	not out	0
Extras	(lb 6, w 4, nb 7)	17
Total		199

Fall of wickets 0, 3, 81, 85, 108, 115, 128, 169, 199, 199

	O	M	R	W
RGD Willis	19	3	55	3
IT Botham	30	8	74	5
RD Jackman	28	11	41	1
VJ Marks	2	1	8	1
MW Gatting	2	1	4	0

ENGLAND 2ND INNINGS

CJ Tavare	c Majid Khan b Imran Khan	33
G Fowler	c Wasim Bari b Mudassar Nazar	86
MW Gatting	lbw b Imran Khan	25
AJ Lamb	lbw b Mudassar Nazar	4
DI Gower	c Wasim Bari b Mudassar Nazar	7
IT Botham	c Majid Khan b Mudassar Nazar	4
DW Randall	lbw b Imran Khan	0
VJ Marks	not out	12
RW Taylor†	not out	6
Extras	(b 19, lb 16, w 1, nb 6)	42
Total	(7 wickets)	219

Did not bat RD Jackman, RGD Willis*

Fall of wickets 103, 168, 172, 187, 189, 189, 199

	O	M	R	W
Sikander Bakht	20	4	40	0
Imran Khan	30.2	8	66	3
Abdul Qadir	8	2	16	0
Mudassar Nazar	22	7	55	4

Toss: Pakistan   Umpires: DJ Constant and BJ Meyer   England won by 3 wickets

Australia v England
Fourth Test at the Melbourne Cricket Ground

1982-83
December 26, 27, 28, 29, 30 (1982)

The 250th Test involving Australia and England was one to behold, as the teams engaged in the closest Ashes battle since 1902.

Leading the series 2-0, Australia chose to bowl first after the MCG turf had been re-laid. England was 11-1 when Graeme Fowler was superbly caught by Greg Chappell off Rodney Hogg. Nearly another hour passed until Chappell caught the other opener, Geoff Cook, off Jeff Thomson. England was 56-3 when David Gower edged Hogg behind, before Chris Tavare and Allan Lamb put on an eye-catching partnership. Tavare batted somewhat more freely than usual as he hit 15 fours in just over four hours. Lamb was more attacking as he struck 13 boundaries in 160 minutes, and the partnership reaped 161 runs in just 32 overs. Tavare was on 89 when he fell to Thomson, before Lamb departed for 83. Ian Botham registered five fours in a quick 27, before Geoff Miller's dismissal made the score 262-7. England was dismissed for 284, and Norman Cowans was last out as Geoff Lawson took a splendid outfield catch, to ensure catches accounted for all 10 wickets.

John Dyson and Kepler Wessels established an opening stand of 55 for Australia on day two before Cowans took two wickets with successive balls. Dyson was lbw before Chappell perished to a hook shot. Wessels scored at a good rate before England captain Bob Willis bowled him, and Allan Border didn't last long before Botham disturbed his stumps. The hosts recovered from 89-4 as Kim Hughes and David Hookes established themselves and made the visitors work hard to gain another breakthrough.

Hookes hit seven boundaries before falling for 53, and fellow left-hander Rod Marsh kept the score moving along, while Hughes played what would have been called a fine captain's knock had he been leading the side. He made 66 in 251 minutes

Greg Chappell returned for the 1982–83 Ashes, and failed in both innings of the Melbourne Test.

before Willis bowled him, then Yardley hit two quick fours before Marsh was also bowled by Willis. Yardley was bowled by Miller without a run added, and Lawson also fell to Miller before Hogg helped Australia earn a three-run lead. Miller's cheap dismissal of Thomson signalled the close of day two.

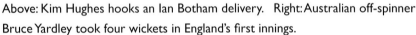

Above: Kim Hughes hooks an Ian Botham delivery.   Right: Australian off-spinner Bruce Yardley took four wickets in England's first innings.

Cook and Fowler put on 40 runs within the first hour of day three before Cook was again caught off Thomson. Hogg bowled Tavare for a duck before Lawson had Gower controversially caught behind to have England 45-3, only for Fowler and Lamb to halt Australia's progress. Fowler suffered a broken bone in his foot following a miscued drive off Thomson, and Gower came on as a runner. It didn't last long, as Fowler's solid knock ended on 65 when Hogg claimed him, and subsequently Lamb, within one run of each other to have England 129-5. Miller made 14, and an attacking Botham scored 46 at a run per ball before he was caught just after the 200 was raised.

The lower order provided resistance, with Derek Pringle steady and Bob Taylor more of a strokemaker as the duo showed determination in a crucial eighth wicket partnership of 61. Another 18 runs were added before the ninth wicket fell, and Cowans struck two fours in a vital 10 before Lawson claimed his fourth scalp. A full day's play consisted of one team's innings for the third straight day, and Australia needed 292 runs on a pitch that involved unpredictable bounce.

Thirty-seven runs were scored before a Cowans delivery ricocheted from Wessels' pads onto the stumps, and Cowans again had Chappell caught cheaply. Dyson looked well set before Botham dismissed him to have Australia 71-3. Hughes and Hookes restored hope although they survived several appeals, and Botham showed frustration at times. A 100-run partnership was raised before Hughes was caught by the wicketkeeper, and Hookes' two-hour knock of 68 ended two runs later when he mistimed a pull off Cowans. Cowans put in a great spell, with Marsh lbw and Yardley bowled on 190.

The total passed 200 before Lawson hooked a Pringle bouncer to Cowans at fine leg, and a boundary was Hogg's only scoring stroke before he became Cowans' sixth victim. Australia needed a last wicket partnership of 74 for victory, seemingly impossible as Thomson was a genuine tail-ender while the senior batsman, Border, had floundered all series. It took him 40 minutes to open his account in this innings. In an attempt to get Thomson on strike, Willis set a defensive field when Border was on strike. The batsmen became settled, sometimes accepting the singles on offer. There was a rain break before the players returned for two overs before stumps, and Thomson was nearly run out on the third-last ball of the day. The batting duo had halved their requirement.

The crowd built up to 18,000 on day five, as admittance was free, and a loud ovation greeted Border and Thomson. They saw off the new ball and the crowd went wild with joy every time Thomson scored, with runs very slowly accumulating. The fielders began to worry as they engaged in plenty of shouting rather than encouragement, while Border and Thomson also abused each other when false strokes were played. Once, two fielders collided as they tried to run out Thomson. The tension was enthralling as replays and

Australia's requirement were flashed on the new electronic scoreboard.

Australia needed just four runs when Botham began the 18th over of the day, after 29 easy singles had been declined during the last wicket partnership. Another telling factor was that Thomson had conceded four runs in overthrows during a run out attempt when England batted. Regardless, the deciding delivery was in a perfect spot to cut: short and wide of off-stump. Thomson, however, poked forward and edged to second slip. Tavare spilled the ball over his shoulder but first slipper Miller bent down to snaffle it, and the Englishmen raced off the field in jubilation. A draw in the fifth and final Test enabled Australia to win back the Ashes.

Top: Jeff Thomson and Allan Border (right) put on a memorable partnership of 70 that nearly pulled off an Australian victory, but England won by three runs.   Inset: Ill-fated Australian batsman David Hookes top-scored in Australia's second innings run chase that fell agonisingly short in the Melbourne Test in 1982. Following page: A poster advertising the 1982–83 Ashes series.

1882~1982
Centenary Ashes Series

AUSTRALIA – 4th and 5th Tests

BACK ROW: Rodney Hogg, Jeff Thomson, David Hookes, Geoff Lawson, Kepler Wessels, John Dyson, Graeme Wood.
FRONT ROW: Bruce Yardley, Kim Hughes (vice-captain), Greg Chappell (captain), Rodney Marsh, Allan Border.

ENGLAND – Touring Side

BACK ROW: Vic Marks, Robin Jackman, Graeme Fowler, Norman Cowans, Derek Pringle, Geoff Cook, Eddie Hemmings, Ian Gould, Allan Lamb.
FRONT ROW: Chris Tavare, Bob Taylor, David Gower (vice-captain), Bob Willis (captain), Ian Botham, Derek Randall, Geoff Miller.

ENGLAND 1ST INNINGS

G Cook	c Chappell b Thomson	10
G Fowler	c Chappell b Hogg	4
CJ Tavare	c Yardley b Thomson	89
DI Gower	c Marsh b Hogg	18
AJ Lamb	c Dyson b Yardley	83
IT Botham	c Wessels b Yardley	27
G Miller	c Border b Yardley	10
DR Pringle	c Wessels b Hogg	9
RW Taylor†	c Marsh b Yardley	1
RGD Willis*	not out	6
NG Cowans	c Lawson b Hogg	3
Extras	(b 3, lb 6, w 3, nb 12)	24
Total		284

Fall of wickets 11, 25, 56, 217, 227, 259, 262, 268, 278, 284

	O	M	R	W
GF Lawson	17	6	48	0
RM Hogg	23.3	6	69	4
B Yardley	27	9	89	4
JR Thomson	13	2	49	2
GS Chappell	1	0	5	0

AUSTRALIA 1ST INNINGS

KC Wessels	b Willis	47
J Dyson	lbw b Cowans	21
GS Chappell*	c Lamb b Cowans	0
KJ Hughes	b Willis	66
AR Border	b Botham	2
DW Hookes	c Taylor b Pringle	53
RW Marsh†	b Willis	53
B Yardley	b Miller	9
GF Lawson	c Fowler b Miller	0
RM Hogg	not out	8
JR Thomson	b Miller	1
Extras	(lb 8, nb 19)	27
Total		287

Fall of wickets 55, 55, 83, 89, 180, 261, 276, 276, 278, 287

	O	M	R	W
RGD Willis	15	2	38	3
IT Botham	18	3	69	1
NG Cowans	16	0	69	2
DR Pringle	15	2	40	1
G Miller	15	5	44	3

ENGLAND 2ND INNINGS

G Cook	c Yardley b Thomson	26
G Fowler	b Hogg	65
CJ Tavare	b Hogg	0
DI Gower	c Marsh b Lawson	3
AJ Lamb	c Marsh b Hogg	26
IT Botham	c Chappell b Thomson	46
G Miller	lbw b Lawson	14
DR Pringle	c Marsh b Lawson	42
RW Taylor†	lbw b Thomson	37
RGD Willis*	not out	8
NG Cowans	b Lawson	10
Extras	(b 2, lb 9, nb 6)	17
Total		294

Fall of wickets 40, 41, 45, 128, 129, 160, 201, 262, 280, 294

	O	M	R	W
GF Lawson	21.4	6	66	4
RM Hogg	22	5	64	3
B Yardley	15	2	67	0
JR Thomson	21	3	74	3
GS Chappell	1	0	6	0

AUSTRALIA 2ND INNINGS

KC Wessels	b Cowans	14
J Dyson	c Tavare b Botham	31
GS Chappell*	c sub (IJ Gould) b Cowans	2
KJ Hughes	c Taylor b Miller	48
DW Hookes	c Willis b Cowans	68
AR Border	not out	62
RW Marsh†	lbw b Cowans	13
B Yardley	b Cowans	0
GF Lawson	c Cowans b Pringle	7
RM Hogg	lbw b Cowans	4
JR Thomson	c Miller b Botham	21
Extras	(b 5, lb 9, w 1, nb 3)	18
Total		288

Fall of wickets 37, 39, 71, 171, 173, 190, 190, 202, 218, 288

	O	M	R	W
RGD Willis	17	0	57	0
IT Botham	25.1	4	80	2
NG Cowans	26	6	77	6
DR Pringle	12	4	26	1
G Miller	16	6	30	1

Toss: Australia   Umpires: AR Crafter and RV Whitehead   England won by 3 runs

Pakistan v England

First Test at National Stadium, Karachi

1983–84

March 2, 3, 4, 6 (1984)

The most significant match in the 1983–84 Pakistan versus England three-Test series was the first at Karachi. It was great to see a competitive Test after the series was threatened by student disruption. Heavy security was necessary, and England batted first after winning the toss. Pakistan had undergone one notable change since previously contesting England, as Imran Khan was out of action with a stress fracture of the leg.

Mike Gatting scored 26 of the first 41 runs before Tauseef Ahmed bowled him, and then David Gower batted steadily while Chris Smith played a Geoff Boycott-like role. The total crawled to 90 late in the second session before Smith was caught off Sarfraz Nawaz for 28 from 177 balls. Allan Lamb departed in Sarfraz's next over after a boundary was Lamb's only scoring shot, and England suddenly looked shaky at 94-3 while Sarfraz was swinging the ball. Derek Randall made just eight before leg-spinner Abdul Qadir found his rhythm and bowled him, while off spinner Tauseef was also hard to get away. Gower looked in control as he carefully built his innings, and Ian Botham displayed only some aggression as he was slower than usual. Gower posted a crucial half-century and England finished day one on 147-4.

Seven runs were added before Pakistani Test debutant Rameez Raja claimed his second catch, an important one off Qadir to dismiss Botham. Rameez held his third catch, and his second off Sarfraz, as Vic Marks' dismissal made the score 159-6. With England in disarray, Qadir took advantage, trapping Bob Taylor and Gower lbw, with the latter not offering a stroke. Nick Cook and captain Bob Willis showed some resistance before Qadir finished with five scalps and Sarfraz four, England's total a disappointing 182.

Mohsin Khan and Qasim Umar put on a steady opening stand of 67 for the home side before left-arm spinner Cook trapped Qasim lbw. Rameez's first Test innings was a disappointment

Pakistan batsman Zaheer Abbas.

as he scored just a single in 29 minutes before falling to Cook. Botham's dismissal of Zaheer Abbas for nought made the score 80-3. Mohsin registered five fours and a six and reached 54 before he too fell to Cook, and Pakistan was vulnerable at 96-4. Only nine more runs were scored before Cook accounted for Wasim Raja, and the home side's batsmen rued some faulty strokeplay, although Cook was impressive. Salim Malik and debutant Anil Dalpat halted the collapse, surviving until stumps and narrowing the deficit to just 51 runs.

Willis broke through early on day three when he had Anil caught behind, before Cook blotted his copybook, missing a return catch with Qadir on one. It proved decisive, as Qadir went on to hit four fours and a six in a decent 40, and Pakistan led by 31 runs when he was belatedly dismissed. Malik went on to score 74 before he was ninth out, with the lead at 58 runs. The next twist came as number 11 Azeem Hafeez batted to good effect while Tauseef survived against the second new ball. Azeem scored 24 in a partnership of 37, and Cook returned to take his sixth wicket when Azeem holed out to deep mid on.

Pakistan maintained the upper hand. Gatting padded up to Sarfraz and was lbw for four, and Smith was also lbw to Sarfraz as the visitors struggled to 21-2. Gower and Lamb added 31 runs before the end of the day's play was followed by a rest day. The total was 63 when wicketkeeper Anil Dalpat claimed his first Test catch, although the dismissal of Lamb was controversial. Gower worked his way to another 50, but Randall again made little impression before Qadir bowled him for the second time with a googly. Botham also failed when he swept at Tauseef and lost his leg-stump, before Qadir bowled Marks through the gate. Before a run was added, Gower departed just after lunch when an edged cut shot was caught at slip, and England was virtually 33-7. Taylor and Cook resisted the bowling, as 29 runs were added before the last three wickets fell for two runs, with Wasim claiming the eighth and tenth scalps.

Willis conceded 13 runs in two overs before Cook came on, with Pakistan 17-0 and needing just 48 more runs. With spinners Cook and Marks bowling in tandem, Pakistan's momentum stalled as Cook removed the openers in quick succession, and then Zaheer hit two fours before Cook bowled him. Pakistan made hard work of the small run chase as Rameez found it virtually impossible to score. Rameez again scored one, and this time faced 45 balls. Malik scored 11 before he was run out, and then Botham showed great reflexes at slip, taking a one-handed catch to snare Rameez. Pakistan was suddenly 38-5. Wasim must have panicked, because he attacked the second ball he faced and was superbly caught by Norman Cowans at long off. England had every chance of an upset, as Pakistan was 40-6.

The 20-year-old Anil, however, showed good composure, and Qadir stuck around as 19 runs were added, but Cook claimed another five-wicket haul as Qadir was bowled. England hung on by a thread as Pakistan reached 62-7 with Anil on 16, and Cowans was back in the attack. Suddenly the match was over with the second ball Sarfraz faced, as he edged a boundary to clinch a tense three-wicket win. Qadir was easily the biggest hero, although Cook deserved praise for his match figures of 11-83.

The second Test took on a different complexion as it was a high scoring draw. The third Test fluctuated, and a draw was good enough for the Pakistanis to win the series after they finished on 217-6 when chasing a target of 243.

Bob Taylor appeals for a wicket during one of his **57** Tests for England.

ENGLAND 1ST INNINGS		
CL Smith	c Wasim Raja b Sarfraz Nawaz	28
MW Gatting	b Tauseef Ahmed	26
DI Gower	lbw b Abdul Qadir	58
AJ Lamb	c Rameez Raja b Sarfraz Nawaz	4
DW Randall	b Abdul Qadir	8
IT Botham	c Rameez Raja b Abdul Qadir	22
VJ Marks	c Rameez Raja b Sarfraz Nawaz	5
RW Taylor†	lbw b Abdul Qadir	4
NGB Cook	c Salim Malik b Abdul Qadir	9
RGD Willis*	c Wasim Raja b Sarfraz Nawaz	6
NG Cowans	not out	1
Extras	(lb 6, nb 5)	11
Total		182

Fall of wickets 41, 90, 94, 108, 154, 159, 164, 165, 180, 182

	O	M	R	W
Azeem Hafeez	11	3	21	0
Sarfraz Nawaz	25.5	8	42	4
Tauseef Ahmed	24	11	33	1
Wasim Raja	3	2	1	0
Abdul Qadir	31	12	74	5

PAKISTAN 1ST INNINGS		
Mohsin Khan	c Botham b Cook	54
Qasim Umar	lbw b Cook	29
Rameez Raja	c Smith b Cook	1
Zaheer Abbas*	c Lamb b Botham	0
Salim Malik	lbw b Willis	74
Wasim Raja	c Cowans b Cook	3
Anil Dalpat†	c Taylor b Willis	12
Abdul Qadir	c Lamb b Botham	40
Sarfraz Nawaz	c Botham b Cook	8
Tauseef Ahmed	not out	17
Azeem Hafeez	c Willis b Cook	24
Extras	(lb 5, nb 10)	15
Total		277

Fall of wickets 67, 79, 80, 96, 105, 138, 213, 229, 240, 277

	O	M	R	W
RGD Willis	17	6	33	2
NG Cowans	12	3	34	0
IT Botham	30	5	90	2
NGB Cook	30	12	65	6
VJ Marks	13	4	40	0

ENGLAND 2ND INNINGS		
CL Smith	lbw b Sarfraz Nawaz	5
MW Gatting	lbw b Sarfraz Nawaz	4
DI Gower	c Mohsin Khan b Tauseef Ahmed	57
AJ Lamb	c Anil Dalpat b Abdul Qadir	20
DW Randall	b Abdul Qadir	16
IT Botham	b Tauseef Ahmed	10
VJ Marks	b Abdul Qadir	1
RW Taylor†	c Mohsin Khan b Tauseef Ahmed	19
NGB Cook	c Mohsin Khan b Wasim Raja	5
RGD Willis*	c Tauseef Ahmed b Wasim Raja	2
NG Cowans	not out	0
Extras	(b 6, lb 6, nb 8)	20
Total		159

Fall of wickets 6, 21, 63, 94, 121, 128, 128, 157, 159, 159

	O	M	R	W
Azeem Hafeez	8	3	14	0
Sarfraz Nawaz	15	1	27	2
Tauseef Ahmed	21	6	37	3
Wasim Raja	3.3	1	2	2
Abdul Qadir	31	4	59	3

PAKISTAN 2ND INNINGS		
Mohsin Khan	b Cook	10
Qasim Umar	c Botham b Cook	7
Rameez Raja	c Botham b Marks	1
Zaheer Abbas*	b Cook	8
Salim Malik	run out	11
Wasim Raja	c Cowans b Cook	0
Anil Dalpat†	not out	16
Abdul Qadir	b Cook	7
Sarfraz Nawaz	not out	4
Extras	(b 1, nb 1)	2
Total	(7 wickets)	66

Did not bat Tauseef Ahmed, Azeem Hafeez

Fall of wickets 17, 18, 26, 38, 38, 40, 59

	O	M	R	W
RGD Willis	2	0	13	0
NG Cowans	2.3	1	10	0
NGB Cook	14	8	18	5
VJ Marks	12	5	23	1

Toss: England   Umpires: Khizer Hayat and Shakoor Rana
Pakistan won by 3 wickets

Sri Lanka v India

Third Test at Asgiriya Stadium, Kandy

1985-86

September 14, 15, 16, 18, 19 (1985)

Sri Lanka was in sight of its first series win when the third Test took place in the Sri Lanka versus India series in 1985–86. Sri Lanka, which had been a Test playing nation for less than five years, had the better of the first Test, which was drawn, before winning the second Test by 149 runs. This was Sri Lanka's maiden Test victory, and all eyes turned from Colombo to Kandy to see if Sri Lanka would seal its first series win.

India captain Kapil Dev had no hesitation in taking first use of a good batting pitch after he won the toss. Ashantha de Mel had Ravi Shastri caught for just six before Kris Srikkanth dominated the scoring. He had 40 runs, the total being 66 when Saliya Ahangama bowled him, and Ahangama made another key breakthrough after India threatened to stabilise its position. Ahangama trapped Mohinder Amarnath in front of his stumps for 30 to make the score 111-3, and the rest of the Indian innings resembled a scorecard from a limited overs match. A wicket fell every time India looked like gaining momentum.

Dilip Vengsarkar scored 62 at number four and helped India to 161-3 before he was run out. Another 19 runs were added before Mohammad Azharuddin was caught behind off Ahangama, who took the prized scalp of Kapil Dev before a run was added, as an lbw appeal was upheld. India struggled at 180-6 but with Sunil Gavaskar now in the middle order, India remained a chance to build a big score. India passed 200 early on day two before Roger Binny became Ahangama's fifth scalp, and another setback came when Chetan Sharma retired hurt as India was 237-7. The score barely passed 240 before Rumesh Ratnayake had Sadanand Viswanath and Gavaskar caught behind, with the latter just one run shy of a half-century. Sharma returned, and was last out as India finished with a disappointing 249.

Sri Lankan openers Sidath Wettimuny and Amal Silva put on 36 runs before Binny dismissed Silva and Ranjan Madugalle to reduce the locals to 44-2. Sri Lanka fell to 80-4 after Roy Dias and Wettimuny went out to catches behind the stumps, before Arjuna Ranatunga and captain Duleep Mendis staged a recovery. Ranatunga hit six fours and a six, but the job had only really started when he was caught off Maninder Singh for 38, shortly before the close of play.

After Sri Lanka began day three on 153-5, Ahangama scored 11 before falling to Maninder, and then Mendis went on to post a half-century. But his dismissal sparked a collapse, with Sri Lanka losing its last four wickets for two runs. Mendis was caught by substitute fielder Laxman Sivaramakrishnan before Test debutant Roshan Jurangpathy was caught behind. Aravinda de Silva was run out, and de Mel's dismissal presented wicketkeeper Viswanath with his fourth catch, and Maninder with his fourth victim, as India gained a 51-run lead.

Srikkanth gave India a flying start, scoring at better than a run per ball as he struck de Mel and Ratnayake around the park. Srikkanth raced to 47 in a partnership of 74 before Ahangama was again the man to produce the goods for Sri Lanka, trapping Srikkanth lbw. With Shastri moving to 68 and Amarnath 28 at stumps, India was in a strong position, with a 200-run lead for the loss of only one wicket, and two days remaining.

Ahangama, however, spoilt India's progress after the rest day, as he had Shastri caught behind for 81 and Vengsarkar lbw for 10. Kapil Dev failed with the bat again when Ranatunga bowled him for two, as India slipped to 211-4, a lead of 262. But Amarnath was solid and Azharuddin batted effectively as India pushed the lead beyond 300. Azharuddin reached 43 before Ratnayake bowled him, and Amarnath went on to 116 not out, while Gavaskar was on 15 when Kapil Dev ordered a declaration. India had eight hours in which to dismiss the home side, which faced a difficult target of 377.

Sharma had Wettimuny caught by Vengsarkar before Kapil Dev had Silva caught behind, as Sri Lanka crashed to 8-2. Madugalle reached double figures before he too edged to Viswanath, and at 34-3 the home side was in strife. Vice-captain Dias and captain Mendis survived until stumps, but the hosts were far from comfortable at 78-3.

Fortunes changed unexpectedly on the final day as Dias and Mendis flayed the bowlers and regularly found the boundary. Playing for a draw didn't appear to be their intention. They looked like surviving until tea as they kept Sri Lanka in with a chance of a spectacular victory. A run out, however, sent Dias packing after he faced 216 balls for his 106 runs, which included 68 in boundaries. The momentum suddenly shifted

India's way as Ranatunga was promptly bowled by Sharma for a duck, and 250-5 was suddenly a lot different from 250-3.

Another 16 runs were added before Mendis was caught off Sharma for 124, which included 11 fours and two sixes from 228 balls and 318 minutes. Jurangpathy was soon left with a batting average of 0.50 after his maiden Test, when Kapil Dev trapped him lbw, and India was suddenly just three wickets shy of victory. Survival seemed Sri Lanka's only hope as the target was 110 runs away. De Silva and de Mel, however, thwarted the Indians as the time remaining shrank, and the Sri Lankan duo had some luck before bad light caused the umpires to close the match with 20 minutes left. Neither side could claim a moral victory, as Sri Lanka finished 70 runs short with three wickets left. A moral victory would have meant nothing in any case, as a draw enabled Sri Lanka to win its first Test series.

The Indian team was not at its best against Sri Lanka in 1985–86 and was unable to win a Test in the series.

INDIA 1ST INNINGS

RJ Shastri	c Madugalle b de Mel	6
K Srikkanth	b Ahangama	40
M Amarnath	lbw b Ahangama	30
DB Vengsarkar	run out	62
M Azharuddin	c Silva b Ahangama	25
SM Gavaskar	c Silva b Ratnayake	49
N Kapil Dev*	lbw b Ahangama	0
RMH Binny	c de Mel b Ahangama	19
C Sharma	c Wettimuny b de Mel	11
S Viswanath†	c Silva b Ratnayake	4
Maninder Singh	not out	0
Extras	(lb 1, w 1, nb 1)	3
Total		249

Fall of wickets 10, 66, 111, 161, 180, 180, 212, 241, 242, 249

	O	M	R	W
ALF de Mel	26.3	5	97	2
RJ Ratnayake	26	5	88	2
FS Ahangama	24	7	52	5
A Ranatunga	8	5	11	0

SRI LANKA 1ST INNINGS

S Wettimuny	c Viswanath b Kapil Dev	34
SAR Silva†	lbw b Binny	19
RS Madugalle	c & b Binny	5
RL Dias	c Viswanath b Sharma	8
LRD Mendis*	c sub (L Sivaramakrishnan) b Maninder Singh	53
A Ranatunga	c Vengsarkar b Maninder Singh	38
FS Ahangama	c Gavaskar b Maninder Singh	11
PA de Silva	run out	8
BR Jurangpathy	c Viswanath b Kapil Dev	1
ALF de Mel	c Viswanath b Maninder Singh	1
RJ Ratnayake	not out	0
Extras	(lb 4, nb 16)	20
Total		198

Fall of wickets 36, 44, 68, 80, 153, 173, 196, 197, 198, 198

	O	M	R	W
N Kapil Dev	19	4	46	2
RMH Binny	12	0	49	2
C Sharma	14	1	40	1
RJ Shastri	6	2	28	0
Maninder Singh	12.3	4	31	4

INDIA 2ND INNINGS

RJ Shastri	c Silva b Ahangama	81
K Srikkanth	lbw b Ahangama	47
M Amarnath	not out	116
DB Vengsarkar	lbw b Ahangama	10
N Kapil Dev*	b Ranatunga	2
M Azharuddin	b Ratnayake	43
SM Gavaskar	not out	15
Extras	(lb 5, w 4, nb 2)	11
Total	(5 wickets dec)	325

Did not bat RMH Binny, C Sharma, S Viswanath†, Maninder Singh

Fall of wickets 74, 178, 206, 211, 289

	O	M	R	W
ALF de Mel	13	2	66	0
RJ Ratnayake	23	2	97	1
FS Ahangama	27	6	72	3
A Ranatunga	16	4	51	1
BR Jurangpathy	4	0	24	0
RS Madugalle	1	0	10	0

SRI LANKA 2ND INNINGS

S Wettimuny	c Vengsarkar b Sharma	5
SAR Silva†	c Viswanath b Kapil Dev	2
RS Madugalle	c Viswanath b Kapil Dev	10
RL Dias	run out	106
LRD Mendis*	c Gavaskar b Sharma	124
A Ranatunga	b Sharma	0
PA de Silva	not out	29
BR Jurangpathy	lbw b Kapil Dev	0
ALF de Mel	not out	9
Extras	(b 8, lb 4, w 4, nb 6)	22
Total	(7 wickets)	307

Did not bat FS Ahangama, RJ Ratnayake

Fall of wickets 5, 8, 34, 250, 250, 266, 267

	O	M	R	W
N Kapil Dev	24	4	74	3
C Sharma	20	4	65	3
Maninder Singh	34	11	99	0
RJ Shastri	24	5	57	0

Toss: India   Umpires: DP Buultjens and MDDN Gooneratne   Match drawn

India v Australia

First Test at MA Chidambaram Stadium, Madras

1986-87

September 18, 19, 20, 21, 22 (1986)

Australia did not win a Test match in 1986, yet the Australians celebrated wildly at the end of the first Test of the series in India. The reason? A tie, albeit after Australia dominated the first four days and could have won convincingly.

After Australia won the toss, an Indian victory looked out of the equation as the Australians batted for just over two days. Following Geoff Marsh's departure for 22, Dean Jones played an unforgettable innings in just his third Test, after more than two years since his previous Test. Jones quickly found his stride, and he and David Boon added 158 runs, with Boon's 122 including 84 in boundaries, before he was caught not long before stumps.

Nightwatchman Ray Bright hit three fours and a six on day two before he became Shivlal Yadav's second victim. After catching Australia's openers, Kapil Dev dropped Australian skipper Allan Border on zero, and it was costly, as Border and Jones put on 178 runs. Jones suffered immensely in the intense heat and was treated for leg cramps and exhaustion. He delayed play as he vomited several times, and when he was well past 100 he felt like giving up. Border famously told the Victorian that a Queenslander, Greg Ritchie, was in next. Perhaps Border was insensitive to Jones' health, but the Victorian summoned up enough strength to bat on and become the first Australian to score a double hundred in India. Jones batted for 503 minutes, hitting 27 fours and two sixes in his mammoth 210 from just 330 balls. Afterwards he was put on a saline drip and spent the night in hospital.

Following Jones' dismissal, Ritchie hit a four and a six before he was run out for 13. Border survived chances on 67 and 98 to score 106 before he was belatedly caught, and fellow left-hander Greg Matthews made 44 before Border declared with Australia on 574-7. Kris Srikkanth gave India a blazing start as he pounced on some wayward bowling from Craig McDermott and Bruce Reid, before Matthews' off-spin changed things.

Sunil Gavaskar contributed just eight runs in an opening stand of 62 before he was caught-and-bowled by Matthews. Three runs later, Mohinder Amarnath was run out before Srikkanth was caught by Ritchie next ball, after striking nine fours and a six in his 53. Mohammad Azharuddin and Ravi Shastri also hit regular boundaries on their way to half-centuries before succumbing to spin bowling. Azharuddin was reprieved three times but didn't fully capitalise, and Chandra Pandit made 35. His departure was followed by Kiran More's dismissal for four. India was 270-7 at stumps and needed another 105 runs to avert the follow-on.

It was time for captain Kapil Dev to come to the rescue, and that he did, with a blazing 119 off only 138 balls after he began day four on 33. Chetan Sharma and Yadav provided resistance, but Australia was still in the box seat with a 177-run lead after India's skipper was last out, becoming Matthews' fifth victim.

The visitors batted for 49 overs before stumps, mainly against spin after Kapil Dev delivered only one over. After Marsh was bowled for 11, Boon scored 49 before the batsmen from three to six made between 24 and 28 each. Australia was 170-5 at stumps, and Border somewhat surprisingly declared, allowing India a full day to score 348 runs. India had a realistic chance of victory as the wicket was still playing well, after Australia had controlled the play so far.

Australia's pacemen were ineffective, and Srikkanth again outscored Gavaskar until Matthews dismissed the former for 39. Gavaskar helped India to a promising 94-1 at lunch, and then 99 runs were scored in the second session for the loss of just one wicket. Gavaskar and Amarnath accumulated runs against the spin duo of Matthews and Bright before Amarnath was caught off Matthews for 51. The Indians needed 155 runs from the last 30 overs, with eight wickets remaining, and Australia relied on Bright and Matthews. The last session was chaotic at times as there was a mixture of good, risky and reckless batting, wayward and accurate spin bowling, and bad sportsmanship. There were plenty of unsavoury and petty quarrels between opponents, and Border had a heated exchange with umpire Dara Dotiwalla.

Eleven runs were added after tea before Gavaskar was caught at cover for 90. Azharuddin pushed on while Pandit scored briskly, and India was on course at 251-3 before losing 2-2 as Azharuddin and Kapil Dev needlessly perished to attacking shots. Shastri hit two big sixes off Matthews, and the total reached 291 when Pandit was bowled by a hysterical Matthews, who was involved in some unsavoury incidents.

India again seemed on track as Sharma scored 23, before he chanced his arm and was caught in the deep. India was 331-7 and then 334-8 as More swung at Bright and was lbw. A result was impossible to pick as India sought 14 runs and Australia two wickets. Yadav lofted a six before an ungainly sweep deflected onto the stumps. Maninder Singh survived the last two balls of Bright's over, and Shastri faced Matthews. India needed four runs and Australia one wicket from the final over.

Shastri advanced the first ball but failed to put it away before he heaved the second ball through the legside for two as Steve Waugh crucially fumbled a wayward bounce. Shastri steered the third ball towards mid wicket for a single to tie the scores, and then Maninder faced a dot ball before stepping across to the penultimate delivery. It struck his pads, and umpire Vikramraju instantly upheld the appeal in his second and last Test. Matthews scurried away in delirium, although the batting duo insisted that Maninder had edged the ball onto his pads. Replays were inconclusive, but a memorable tie resulted regardless.

Opposite: The final ball of a classic Test which ended in a tie.
Top: Mohinder Amarnath's half-century in India's second innings against Australia was vital as the hosts chased a target of 348.
Bottom: Kapil Dev was often a hero amongst Indian fans, including in the tied Test of 1986, when his first innings century rescued his country from a troublesome situation.

AUSTRALIA 1ST INNINGS		
DC Boon	c Kapil Dev b Sharma	122
GR Marsh	c Kapil Dev b Yadav	22
DM Jones	b Yadav	210
RJ Bright	c Shastri b Yadav	30
AR Border*	c Gavaskar b Shastri	106
GM Ritchie	run out	13
GRJ Matthews	c Pandit b Yadav	44
SR Waugh	not out	12
Extras	(b 1, lb 7, w 1, nb 6)	15
Total	(7 wickets dec)	574

Did not bat TJ Zoehrer†, CJ McDermott, BA Reid
Fall of wickets 48, 206, 282, 460, 481, 544, 574

	O	M	R	W
N Kapil Dev	18	5	52	0
C Sharma	16	1	70	1
Maninder Singh	39	8	135	0
NS Yadav	49.5	9	142	4
RJ Shastri	47	8	161	1
K Srikkanth	1	0	6	0

AUSTRALIA 2ND INNINGS		
GR Marsh	b Shastri	11
DC Boon	lbw b Maninder Singh	49
DM Jones	c Azharuddin b Maninder Singh	24
AR Border*	b Maninder Singh	27
GM Ritchie	c Pandit b Shastri	28
GRJ Matthews	not out	27
SR Waugh	not out	2
Extras	(lb 1, nb 1)	2
Total	(5 wickets dec)	170

Did not bat RJ Bright, TJ Zoehrer†, CJ McDermott, BA Reid
Fall of wickets 31, 81, 94, 125, 165

	O	M	R	W
C Sharma	6	0	19	0
N Kapil Dev	1	0	5	0
RJ Shastri	14	2	50	2
Maninder Singh	19	2	60	3
NS Yadav	9	0	35	0

INDIA 1ST INNINGS		
SM Gavaskar	c & b Matthews	8
K Srikkanth	c Ritchie b Matthews	53
M Amarnath	run out	1
M Azharuddin	c & b Bright	50
RJ Shastri	c Zoehrer b Matthews	62
CS Pandit	c Waugh b Matthews	35
N Kapil Dev*	c Border b Matthews	119
KS More†	c Zoehrer b Waugh	4
C Sharma	c Zoehrer b Reid	30
NS Yadav	c Border b Bright	19
Maninder Singh	not out	0
Extras	(b 1, lb 9, nb 6)	16
Total		397

Fall of wickets 62, 65, 65, 142, 206, 220, 245, 330, 387, 397

	O	M	R	W
CJ McDermott	14	2	59	0
BA Reid	18	4	93	1
GRJ Matthews	28.2	3	103	5
RJ Bright	23	3	88	2
SR Waugh	11	2	44	1

INDIA 2ND INNINGS		
SM Gavaskar	c Jones b Bright	90
K Srikkanth	c Waugh b Matthews	39
M Amarnath	c Boon b Matthews	51
M Azharuddin	c Ritchie b Bright	42
CS Pandit	b Matthews	39
N Kapil Dev*	c Bright b Matthews	1
RJ Shastri	not out	48
C Sharma	c McDermott b Bright	23
KS More†	lbw b Bright	0
NS Yadav	b Bright	8
Maninder Singh	lbw b Matthews	0
Extras	(b 1, lb 3, nb 2)	6
Total		347

Fall of wickets 55, 158, 204, 251, 253, 291, 331, 334, 344, 347

	O	M	R	W
CJ McDermott	5	0	27	0
BA Reid	10	2	48	0
GRJ Matthews	39.5	7	146	5
RJ Bright	25	3	94	5
AR Border	3	0	12	0
SR Waugh	4	1	16	0

Toss: Australia   Umpires: DN Dotiwalla and V Vikramraju   Match tied

India v Pakistan
Fifth Test at M Chinnaswamy Stadium, Bangalore

1986-87
March 13, 14, 15, 17 (1987)

India and Pakistan repeatedly had nil-all drawn series until a great fifth and deciding match took place in March 1987. The 1986–87 series in India appeared dull, after four drawn Tests, prior to the thrilling finale in Bangalore.

Indian skipper Kapil Dev may not have been unhappy to lose the toss, as he bowled Rizwan-uz-Zaman for a golden duck in the first over. Roger Binny meanwhile conceded 25 runs in three overs and was replaced, before spin was introduced after only a dozen overs. Kapil Dev meanwhile produced another key breakthrough when he had Rameez Raja caught, after Rameez hit four fours in his 22.

The ball turned square in the first session, and Pakistan reached 60-2 before attempts to unleash forceful strokes caused a batting collapse. Javed Miandad and Manzoor Elahi were caught off Maninder Singh's left-arm spin in one over as Pakistan fell to 60-4, before the same bowler dismissed Salim Malik and Imran Khan on 68. Wasim Akram and Salim Yousuf departed for ducks as the visitors became 74-8, before the last three batsmen showed better survival tactics. Iqbal Qasim scored 19 in 40 minutes before Maninder bowled him, and Maninder claimed his seventh scalp 53 minutes later as Pakistan was routed for 116, while Tauseef Ahmed remained unbeaten on 15 from 72 balls.

Akram bowled just two overs, and Imran took himself off after five expensive overs, thanks largely to Kris Srikkanth scoring quickly. Tauseef broke through when he bowled Srikkanth for 21, and Gavaskar made the same score from 44 extra deliveries before he suffered the same mode of dismissal. Mohinder Amarnath and Dilip Vengsarkar took the home side to 68-2 at stumps, and only three more runs were added when Amarnath became the third successive batsman bowled by Tauseef. Vengsarkar attacked to good effect, but lost

India's Dilip Vengsarkar was one of only two players to score a half-century in the deciding Test against Pakistan in 1986–87.

Mohammad Azharuddin on 102 when Qasim struck. India passed Pakistan's score, and Vengsarkar struck seven fours and a six on his way to 50. The Indians were in the position to build a handy lead but, on the tricky pitch, they virtually replicated the Pakistanis in terms of faulty strokeplay.

Tauseef had Ravi Shastri caught with the total on 126, and Tauseef struck a blow four runs later, when Vengsarkar played an indiscreet stroke and lofted a catch to Manzoor. Qasim took the last four wickets in the space of 10 runs to finish with five scalps, after Tauseef also claimed five. India led by just 29 runs.

Javed Miandad was promoted to open Pakistan's second innings, while Maninder opened the bowling with Kapil Dev. Forty-five runs were scored in an hour before Javed was caught by Srikkanth off Shastri. Rizwan scored his only run of the match before Shastri bowled him, but Pakistan's batsmen showed greater commitment than in the first innings. Maninder wasn't as effective as in the first innings, yet Kapil Dev kept him on. Rameez's solid knock ended on 47 when Shivlal Yadav bowled him, and Qasim came in because Imran felt bringing in a left-hander would be beneficial. Qasim and Malik took the score from 89 to 121 before Kapil Dev bowled Malik, and Qasim scored a vital 26 before Yadav had him caught. Imran and Manzoor were the not out batsmen at stumps as Pakistan led by 126 runs.

Manzoor hit a six but scored just two other runs in his 54-minute stay, and Akram hit a four and a six in his 11. Pakistan was effectively 169-8 when Imran was caught for a gallant 39, before the next partnership assumed huge proportions. Tauseef scored just 10 in 75 minutes, but Yousuf was a little more assertive, and 51 runs were added before the last two wickets fell on 249, leaving Yousuf undefeated on 41.

India was 15-0 chasing 221 until Akram had Srikkanth lbw and Amarnath caught behind with successive balls. Vengsarkar was more defensive than in the first innings, while Gavaskar settled in stubbornly. Forty-nine runs were added before Vengsarkar was bowled by Tauseef, who struck again 30 minutes later when he had Kiran More lbw. Gavaskar meanwhile worked his way to 51 as India reached 99-4 at stumps.

The pitch offered ample spin and bounce following a rest day. Azharuddin scored 19 of the first 24 runs on day four before he was caught-and-bowled by Qasim. Shastri played a passive role in a partnership with Gavaskar, who watched the ball onto the bat and was very judicious in his approach. The total reached 155 before Shastri and then Kapil Dev lost their cool and surrendered their wickets to Qasim, the hosts faltering from 155-5 to 161-7. Gavaskar soldiered on before a Qasim delivery kicked off a good length and had him caught at slip, Rizwan's crucial contribution to the match. Pakistan smelt victory. The score was 180-8, after Gavaskar's 96 was scored from 264 balls in 320 minutes and included eight fours.

Yadav hit a four before Tauseef bowled him, leaving Binny and Maninder to achieve a 36-run partnership for an Indian win. This looked a possibility when they put on 19 runs in 20 minutes, with Binny hitting a six. But Pakistan was not to be denied, and wicketkeeper Yousuf gloved a chance to dismiss Binny. It must have been a relief for Yousuf after he conceded 22 byes in the innings, while Tauseef matched Qasim with nine wickets in the contest.

Pakistan had gained its first series win on Indian soil – a memorable occasion. Imran, who found the match the most difficult he ever had to captain, described it as "a dream Test match". In *All Round View*, he wrote: "The tensions of a great Test are of a different order from those of any other game, or the instant excitement of one-day cricket. It is unique because it is a complex, subtle story that develops over five days and, like great fiction, encompasses many moods and situations." Gavaskar ended his Test career in this match, holding many Test records: most Tests (125), most runs (10,122), most centuries (34), and most century partnerships (58).

India's Ravi Shastri had some success with his left-arm spin in the deciding Test against Pakistan in 1986–87, but he failed with the bat, scoring 7 and 4.

PAKISTAN 1ST INNINGS		
Rameez Raja	c Vengsarkar b Kapil Dev	22
Rizwan-uz-Zaman	b Kapil Dev	0
Salim Malik	b Maninder Singh	33
Javed Miandad	c Shastri b Maninder Singh	7
Manzoor Elahi	c Azharuddin b Maninder Singh	0
Imran Khan*	c Amarnath b Maninder Singh	6
Wasim Akram	b Maninder Singh	0
Salim Yousuf†	c & b Shastri	0
Iqbal Qasim	b Maninder Singh	19
Tauseef Ahmed	not out	15
Salim Jaffer	c Vengsarkar b Maninder Singh	8
Extras	(b 2, lb 1, nb 3)	6
Total		116

Fall of wickets 3, 39, 60, 60, 68, 68, 73, 74, 98, 116

	O	M	R	W
N Kapil Dev	11	2	23	2
RMH Binny	3	0	25	0
M Amarnath	3	1	7	0
Maninder Singh	18.2	8	27	7
RJ Shastri	11	1	19	1
NS Yadav	3	0	12	0

INIDIA 1ST INNINGS		
SM Gavaskar	b Tauseef Ahmed	21
K Srikkanth	b Tauseef Ahmed	21
M Amarnath	b Tauseef Ahmed	13
DB Vengsarkar	c Manzoor Elahi b Tauseef Ahmed	50
M Azharuddin	c Manzoor Elahi b Iqbal Qasim	6
RJ Shastri	c Salim Malik b Tauseef Ahmed	7
N Kapil Dev*	c Salim Malik b Iqbal Qasim	9
RMH Binny	c Tauseef Ahmed b Iqbal Qasim	1
KS More†	not out	9
NS Yadav	b Iqbal Qasim	0
Maninder Singh	c Salim Yousuf b Iqbal Qasim	0
Extras	(b 4, lb 4)	8
Total		145

Fall of wickets 39, 56, 71, 102, 126, 130, 135, 137, 143, 145

	O	M	R	W
Imran Khan	5	0	26	0
Wasim Akram	2	0	9	0
Iqbal Qasim	30	15	48	5
Tauseef Ahmed	27	7	54	5

PAKISTAN 2ND INNINGS		
Rameez Raja	b Yadav	47
Javed Miandad	c Srikkanth b Shastri	17
Rizwan-uz-Zaman	b Shastri	1
Salim Malik	b Kapil Dev	33
Iqbal Qasim	c Srikkanth b Yadav	26
Imran Khan*	c Srikkanth b Shastri	39
Manzoor Elahi	c More b Maninder Singh	8
Wasim Akram	lbw b Maninder Singh	11
Salim Yousuf†	not out	41
Tauseef Ahmed	c Yadav b Shastri	10
Salim Jaffer	c Gavaskar b Maninder Singh	0
Extras	(b 7, lb 8, nb 1)	16
Total		249

Fall of wickets 45, 57, 89, 121, 142, 166, 184, 198, 249, 249

	O	M	R	W
N Kapil Dev	12	2	25	1
Maninder Singh	43.5	8	99	3
RJ Shastri	24	3	69	4
NS Yadav	15	3	41	2

INDIA 2ND INNINGS		
SM Gavaskar	c Rizwan-uz-Zaman b Iqbal Qasim	96
K Srikkanth	lbw b Wasim Akram	6
M Amarnath	c Salim Yousuf b Wasim Akram	0
DB Vengsarkar	b Tauseef Ahmed	19
KS More†	lbw b Tauseef Ahmed	3
M Azharuddin	c & b Iqbal Qasim	26
RJ Shastri	c & b Iqbal Qasim	4
N Kapil Dev*	b Iqbal Qasim	2
RMH Binny	c Salim Yousuf b Tauseef Ahmed	15
NS Yadav	b Tauseef Ahmed	4
Maninder Singh	not out	2
Extras	(b 22, lb 5)	27
Total		204

Fall of wickets 15, 15, 64, 80, 123, 155, 161, 180, 185, 204

	O	M	R	W
Wasim Akram	11	3	19	2
Iqbal Qasim	37	11	73	4
Tauseef Ahmed	45.5	12	85	4

Toss: Pakistan   Umpires: RB Gupta and VK Ramaswamy
Pakistan won by 16 runs

Australia v New Zealand
Third Test at the Melbourne Cricket Ground

1987-88
December 26, 27, 28, 29, 30 (1987)

Australian left-arm paceman Mike Whitney was a genuine number 11 with the bat, but his most memorable moment in his 12 Tests involved the willow. Australia was in sight of winning the Trans Tasman trophy for the first time, after New Zealand won it in 1985–86.

With Australia leading the three-match series 1-0 before the final Test, Whitney and Test debutant Tony Dodemaide replaced injured duo Bruce Reid and Merv Hughes. Whitney opened the bowling with Craig McDermott as the Kiwis batted first, and Phil Horne took 45 minutes to open his account. John Wright meanwhile defended well and attacked loose deliveries. Horne scored just seven runs in 81 minutes before edging behind to give Dodemaide his first Test wicket. Wright and Andrew Jones took New Zealand to 119-1 before Jones was controversially dismissed. Jones leg glanced a delivery, which wicketkeeper Greg Dyer gloved as he rolled over, but replays showed the ball touched the ground as Dyer attempted the catch.

Martin Crowe middled the ball well and picked the gaps while Wright pressed on. Crowe caressed three cover drives to the fence off Steve Waugh at one stage, but Wright fell for 99 when he edged outside off-stump. McDermott took four wickets on day one after accurate deliveries accounted for Jeff Crowe and Dipak Patel in quick succession. Martin Crowe sped to 76 at stumps, as the Kiwis reached 242-5.

Australia claimed the ascendancy with two wickets on 254. McDermott claimed his fifth victim when an attempted on-drive by Martin Crowe to an outswinger found the back of the bat and produced a catch to third slip. Whitney chimed in with the last four wickets to catches, although there was some resistance from the Kiwi tail as the total reached 317. Ian Smith struck seven fours, scoring 44 at a run per ball before he was last out.

A moment of elation for New Zealand's Richard Hadlee as he captures Greg Dyer's wicket at the MCG during the third Test against Australia in December 1987. Hadlee captured 10 wickets, but Australia did just enough to win the series.

The Australians were 24-0 before their nemesis Richard Hadlee reduced them to 31-3. David Boon was lbw in Hadlee's third over, and Hadlee's sixth over was a beauty. Geoff Marsh edged the fourth ball to fourth slip, and then a rearing delivery next ball should have had Allan Border caught at first slip. The next ball, however, cut off the pitch and had Dean Jones snicking to Smith.

Coming off a monumental 205 in the drawn Adelaide Test, Border made 31 before off-spinner John Bracewell had him caught. Australia was 121-5 when Hadlee trapped Mike Veletta in front, and then Steve Waugh reached 55 in a 49-run stand with Peter Sleep. Overnight rain delayed the start of day three by 28 minutes, and then Waugh was caught before a run was added. Sleep, however, was solid, and Dyer scored 21 before he was run out. Dodemaide showed his ability to hang around, as no wickets fell in session two while 69 runs were scored. Sleep posted his highest Test score, 90, in 311 minutes, before Hadlee claimed his third lbw in a five-wicket haul. From 293-8, Australia gained a 40-run lead after McDermott hit the ball around, while Dodemaide plodded along. McDermott scored 33 in 81 minutes while Dodemaide made 50 in just over four hours, before Danny Morrison dismissed the duo shortly prior to stumps.

Wright and Horne put on 73 runs until both were removed shortly before lunch on day four. Andrew Jones and Martin Crowe again occupied the crease for lengthy periods, although Jones scored just 20 in 109 minutes before being run out. Crowe meanwhile scored 79 in 116 minutes and was harsh on Sleep's leg-spin at times. Crowe passed 4000 first class runs in 1987, before Dodemaide's first ball of a new spell produced an edge, which Border snaffled superbly to his left.

Jeff Crowe departed at 220-5 before Hadlee and Patel put on 52 runs. They struck a six each before both departed on 272. Dodemaide continued a fine debut as he dismissed Bracewell and Morrison late in the day, before finishing with 6-58, Smith having been caught behind just three balls into day five. The hosts needed 247 runs for victory, although a draw would have been enough for them to win the series. The Kiwis were set back with the second delivery as Smith suffered a finger injury and was replaced behind the stumps by Horne until lunch. Australia was 52-1 at the break, having lost Marsh.

Martin Crowe took two important catches in session two, removing Dean Jones cheaply and Boon for 54, scored in 184 minutes. Australia, however, was well placed at 137-3 by tea, before Hadlee ended Border's two-hour stay soon afterwards. Waugh fell at 176, and Australia needed 64 from the last 20 overs. They looked capable of doing it with Veletta and Sleep batting together, but the tide turned with the total on 209, as Sleep was again lbw to Hadlee before Veletta was caught off Bracewell. Australia suddenly became intent on survival.

Dyer lasted 31 minutes before he was caught behind, and the stoic Dodemaide scored three in 52 minutes before he became Hadlee's sixth lbw of the match. This left McDermott and Whitney to survive 29 deliveries for a draw, while Hadlee sought his 11th wicket of the match, and 374th Test wicket, to overtake Ian Botham as Test cricket's leading wicket-taker. Morrison rapped McDermott on the pad with the fifth ball of the penultimate over, but umpire Dick French ruled not out. Replays suggested the decision could have gone the other way.

The result came down to the last over as Hadlee bowled to Whitney. The first and third balls passed harmlessly outside off-stump, whereas Whitney played and missed at ball two. The fourth ball was a yorker, which Whitney dug out, before he defended two accurate deliveries up the pitch and subsequently punched the air in triumph. With Australia victorious, Hadlee had to settle for the man of the match and man of the series awards. Moments after Whitney survived the last ball, Hadlee sportingly put his arm around Whitney to congratulate him.

Dean Jones had a disappointing series against New Zealand in 1987–88, with Richard Hadlee getting the better of him.

NEW ZEALAND 1ST INNINGS

PA Horne	c Dyer b Dodemaide	7
JG Wright	c Dyer b McDermott	99
AH Jones	c Dyer b McDermott	40
MD Crowe	c Veletta b McDermott	82
JJ Crowe*	lbw b McDermott	6
DN Patel	b McDermott	0
JG Bracewell	c Dyer b Whitney	9
RJ Hadlee	c Dodemaide b Whitney	11
IDS Smith†	c Jones b Whitney	44
DK Morrison	c Border b Whitney	0
EJ Chatfield	not out	6
Extras	(b 1, lb 4, nb 8)	13
Total		317

Fall of wickets 32, 119, 187, 221, 223, 254, 254, 280, 294, 317

	O	M	R	W
CJ McDermott	35	8	97	5
MR Whitney	33.3	6	92	4
AIC Dodemaide	20	4	48	1
SR Waugh	10	1	44	0
PR Sleep	12	1	31	0

AUSTRALIA 1ST INNINGS

DC Boon	lbw b Hadlee	10
GR Marsh	c sub (KR Rutherford) b Hadlee	13
DM Jones	c Smith b Hadlee	4
AR Border*	c JJ Crowe b Bracewell	31
MRJ Veletta	lbw b Hadlee	31
SR Waugh	c Jones b Bracewell	55
PR Sleep	lbw b Hadlee	90
GC Dyer†	run out (Bracewell/Smith)	21
AIC Dodemaide	c Smith b Morrison	50
CJ McDermott	b Morrison	33
MR Whitney	not out	0
Extras	(lb 8, nb 11)	19
Total		357

Fall of wickets 24, 30, 31, 78, 121, 170, 213, 293, 354, 357

	O	M	R	W
RJ Hadlee	44	11	109	5
DK Morrison	27.4	5	93	2
EJ Chatfield	30	10	55	0
JG Bracewell	32	8	69	2
DN Patel	12	6	23	0

NEW ZEALAND 2ND INNINGS

PA Horne	c Boon b Dodemaide	27
JG Wright	b Sleep	43
AH Jones	run out (Dodemaide/Jones)	20
MD Crowe	c Border b Dodemaide	79
JJ Crowe*	c Boon b Sleep	25
DN Patel	c Dyer b Dodemaide	38
RJ Hadlee	lbw b Sleep	29
JG Bracewell	c Veletta b Dodemaide	1
IDS Smith†	c Dyer b Dodemaide	12
DK Morrison	b Dodemaide	0
EJ Chatfield	not out	1
Extras	(b 2, lb 8, nb 1)	11
Total		286

Fall of wickets 73, 76, 158, 178, 220, 272, 272, 281, 285, 286

	O	M	R	W
CJ McDermott	10	3	43	0
MR Whitney	20	5	45	0
AIC Dodemaide	28.3	10	58	6
PR Sleep	26	5	107	3
DM Jones	8	3	23	0

AUSTRALIA 2ND INNINGS

DC Boon	c MD Crowe b Morrison	54
GR Marsh	c Bracewell b Hadlee	23
DM Jones	c MD Crowe b Chatfield	8
AR Border*	lbw b Hadlee	43
MRJ Veletta	c Patel b Bracewell	39
SR Waugh	c Patel b Chatfield	10
PR Sleep	lbw b Hadlee	20
GC Dyer†	c Smith b Hadlee	4
AIC Dodemaide	lbw b Hadlee	3
CJ McDermott	not out	10
MR Whitney	not out	2
Extras	(b 1, lb 9, nb 4)	14
Total	(9 wickets)	230

Fall of wickets 45, 59, 103, 147, 176, 209, 209, 216, 227

	O	M	R	W
RJ Hadlee	31	9	67	5
DK Morrison	16	2	54	1
EJ Chatfield	21	6	41	2
JG Bracewell	24	5	58	1

Toss: Australia   Umpires: AR Crafter and RA French   Match drawn

West Indies v Pakistan

Third Test at Kensington Oval, Bridgetown, Barbados

1987–88

April 22, 23, 24, 26, 27 (1988)

The 1987–88 West Indies versus Pakistan three-match series in the Caribbean was one of the all-time classics. Pakistan won the first Test and could have won the second before the West Indies almost snatched victory, but drawing instead. The scene was set for a thrilling third Test in Barbados, where the West Indies had not lost since 1935.

Asked to bat on a greenish pitch, Pakistan began steadily before losing Mudassar Nazar for 18, while Rameez Raja scored at a healthy rate. He posted a half-century but was soon caught off Winston Benjamin, with the total on 99. Javed Miandad and Salim Malik were also dismissed at crucial moments, with the latter hitting a four and a six before falling for 15. Shoaib Mohammad was in good touch but, like Rameez, was caught by Gordon Greenidge after hitting seven fours in a score of 54. Aamer Malik and Imran Khan also began soundly before both fell to Benjamin, as Pakistan wobbled at 218-7.

The complexion changed as Salim Yousuf and Wasim Akram produced some limited overs-like hitting. Yousuf raced to 32, striking three fours and two sixes before an edged hook shot off Malcolm Marshall broke his nose. Akram meanwhile raced to 38 with four fours and a six, before Abdul Qadir helped Pakistan to 309 all out before stumps. Pakistan's first 10 batsmen reached double figures, but it was telling that none passed 54. The tourists scored at 4.13 runs per over and registered 34 fours and four sixes, but there was some careless batting. Marshall, Benjamin and Curtly Ambrose shared the wickets but copped some stick, while the fourth paceman, Courtney Walsh, was belted for 53 runs in 10 overs.

Pakistan gained the initiative, as Imran had Greenidge lbw before Richie Richardson edged Akram to Aamer, who kept wickets for Pakistan throughout the match. From 21-2, the home side recovered, as Desmond Haynes played stubbornly.

Carl Hooper played some elegant strokes before he was bowled by Akram. Coincidentally, Hooper made the same score and hit the same number of boundaries for his team as Rameez and Shoaib had for Pakistan.

Viv Richards stamped his authority on the match as he creamed a quick 50, and sought more runs while Haynes plodded on. The hosts reached 198-3 after Haynes scored 48 in 287 minutes before the next twist came, Mudassar's medium-pace accounting for Haynes and Gus Logie with successive balls. Jeff Dujon was run out for a duck before Mudassar caught Richards off Akram, and the West Indies crashed to 201-7. Marshall and Ambrose added 24 runs before the wayward Imran had Ambrose lbw, and the score was 226-8 at stumps.

The tail wagged on day three as Marshall and Benjamin struck the ball well. Marshall scored 48 off just 62 balls before he was caught behind. Walsh hit three fours as a last wicket stand of 23 followed the ninth wicket stand of 58, enabling the West Indies to finish just three runs in arrears. Despite the crucial ninth and tenth wicket partnerships, the home side also rued several batsmen not capitalising on good starts.

Pakistan lost Rameez cheaply, before Mudassar and Shoaib pushed the series leaders into a promising position with some admirable batting. But after the batting duo staved off the pacemen, the off-spin of Hooper and Richards proved telling. Hooper ended a 94-run partnership as he dismissed Mudassar, and another 53 runs were added before Shoaib departed for 64 with a return catch to Richards. In a recurring theme, the middle order crumbled. Marshall did the damage. Javed's solid 34 ended with a catch behind, before Aamer was superbly caught by Logie in close. Marshall softened up Salim Malik before Benjamin trapped him lbw, and Pakistan was 177-6 at stumps before a rest day.

Athletic wicketkeeper Jeff Dujon was a permanent fixture in triumphant West Indies teams for many years. His batting was often vital, including in the last Test against Pakistan in 1987–88 as the West Indies drew a fascinating series.

The in-form Marshall trapped Akram lbw early on day four before Yousuf was crucially dropped first ball by Richards. The brave Yousuf scored 28 in a precious 52-run stand with Imran, who subsequently progressed to 43 not out, while Qadir and Jaffer hung around to enable Pakistan to set a target of 266.

Akram dismissed Haynes cheaply, before Richardson struck boundaries frequently and looked ominous. Greenidge also warmed to the task before Jaffer had him caught with the score on 78. Hooper also settled in, but the turning point came when he was run out after the partnership reached 40. Qadir struck gold for Pakistan when he had Richardson stumped after the batsman scored 64 from 72 balls. Logie scratched around for three runs before Qadir bowled him, and the match was delicately poised with a day left. The West Indies needed 112 runs and Pakistan five wickets, with Richards on 26 not out.

Akram dismissed nightwatchman Ambrose for a single, and Richards advanced to 39 before Akram bowled Richards, a monumental breakthrough. The locals were 180-7, but Marshall was not prepared to surrender after taking nine wickets in the match and scoring 48 in the West Indies' first innings. Unfortunately, controversy arose at a crucial time. With the West Indies needing 80 runs, Marshall survived an lbw appeal from a Qadir flipper. Two balls later, Dujon edged a Qadir delivery onto his pad and was caught at short leg, but again the West Indian umpire didn't budge.

Marshall and Dujon chipped away before Akram won an lbw shout against Marshall, and the West Indies required 59 runs with two wickets left. With the pressure on, Pakistan relied heavily on Akram's left-arm pace and Qadir's leg-spin. Qadir, however, became wayward as he may have allowed himself to be affected by the two not-out rulings and a clash with a heckler on the boundary. Dujon meanwhile was very watchful, while Benjamin put his head down and chose the right balls to attack. He struck four fours and two sixes and finished with 40 not out, while Dujon ambled to 29 not out. Benjamin struck a four off Qadir 30 minutes after lunch to seal a thrilling two-wicket win and level the series.

PAKISTAN 1ST INNINGS

Mudassar Nazar	b Ambrose	18
Rameez Raja	c Greenidge b Benjamin	54
Shoaib Mohammad	c Greenidge b Ambrose	54
Javed Miandad	c Richardson b Marshall	14
Salim Malik	b Marshall	15
Aamer Malik	c Hooper b Benjamin	32
Imran Khan*	c Dujon b Benjamin	18
Salim Yousuf†	retired hurt	32
Wasim Akram	c Benjamin b Marshall	38
Abdul Qadir	c Walsh b Marshall	17
Salim Jaffer	not out	1
Extras	(lb 7, nb 9)	16
Total		309

Fall of wickets 46, 99, 128, 155, 186, 215, 218, 297, 309

	O	M	R	W
MD Marshall	18.4	3	79	4
CEL Ambrose	14	0	64	2
WKM Benjamin	14	3	52	3
CA Walsh	10	1	53	0
IVA Richards	6	0	19	0
CL Hooper	12	3	35	0

PAKISTAN 2ND INNINGS

Mudassar Nazar	c Greenidge b Hooper	41
Rameez Raja	c Logie b Marshall	4
Shoaib Mohammad	c & b Richards	64
Javed Miandad	c Dujon b Marshall	34
Salim Malik	lbw b Benjamin	9
Aamer Malik	c Logie b Marshall	2
Imran Khan*	not out	43
Wasim Akram	lbw b Marshall	0
Salim Yousuf†	c Richards b Benjamin	28
Abdul Qadir	c Greenidge b Marshall	2
Salim Jaffer	b Ambrose	4
Extras	(b 3, lb 14, nb 14)	31
Total		262

Fall of wickets 6, 100, 153, 165, 167, 169, 182, 234, 245, 262

	O	M	R	W
MD Marshall	23	3	65	5
CEL Ambrose	26.5	3	74	1
CA Walsh	12	1	22	0
WKM Benjamin	15	1	37	2
CL Hooper	10	1	39	1
IVA Richards	7	3	8	1

WEST INDIES 1ST INNINGS

CG Greenidge	lbw b Imran Khan	10
DL Haynes	c Aamer Malik b Mudassar Nazar	48
RB Richardson	c Aamer Malik b Wasim Akram	3
CL Hooper	b Wasim Akram	54
IVA Richards*	c Mudassar Nazar b Wasim Akram	67
AL Logie	c Javed Miandad b Mudassar Nazar	0
PJL Dujon†	run out	0
MD Marshall	c Aamer Malik b Imran Khan	48
CEL Ambrose	lbw b Imran Khan	7
WKM Benjamin	run out	31
CA Walsh	not out	14
Extras	(b 5, lb 11, nb 8)	24
Total		306

Fall of wickets 18, 21, 100, 198, 198, 199, 201, 225, 283, 306

	O	M	R	W
Imran Khan	25	3	108	3
Wasim Akram	27	1	88	3
Abdul Qadir	15	1	35	0
Salim Jaffer	7	1	35	0
Mudassar Nazar	10	4	24	2

WEST INDIES 2ND INNINGS

CG Greenidge	c Shoaib Mohammad b Salim Jaffer	35
DL Haynes	c Salim Malik b Wasim Akram	4
RB Richardson	st Aamer Malik b Abdul Qadir	64
CL Hooper	run out	13
IVA Richards*	b Wasim Akram	39
AL Logie	b Abdul Qadir	3
CEL Ambrose	c Salim Jaffer b Wasim Akram	1
PJL Dujon†	not out	29
MD Marshall	lbw b Wasim Akram	15
WKM Benjamin	not out	40
Extras	(b 9, lb 6, nb 10)	25
Total	(8 wickets)	268

Did not bat CA Walsh

Fall of wickets 21, 78, 118, 128, 150, 159, 180, 207

	O	M	R	W
Wasim Akram	31	7	73	4
Imran Khan	6	0	34	0
Abdul Qadir	32	5	115	2
Salim Jaffer	5	0	25	1
Shoaib Mohammad	3	1	6	0

Toss: West Indies   Umpires: DM Archer and LH Barker

West Indies won by 2 wickets

Chapter 5:
The Return of South Africa and the Rise of Australia

1990 – 1999

Newlands Cricket Ground, Cape Town, South Africa.

Australia v New Zealand

One-off Test at the WACA, Perth

1989-90

November 24, 25, 26, 27, 28 (1989)

There was no way of knowing what might have happened in the one-off Test between Australia and New Zealand at Perth in 1989–90 had Kiwi right-hand batsman Andrew Jones not been sidelined with a hand injury. But after the match, his absence was all but forgotten after the performance of his replacement, the left-handed Mark Greatbatch, who had scored a century against England in his Test debut nearly two years earlier.

New Zealand also missed off-spinner John Bracewell (finger injury) for the one-off Trans Tasman Test, while Australia missed opening batsman Geoff Marsh (toe injury). Kiwi skipper John Wright won the toss and chose to bowl on a bouncy surface. Mark Taylor scored nine before his departure brought Tom Moody to the crease in his Test debut after replacing his Western Australian team-mate Marsh. Moody looked a little tentative early on, scoring just 12 in more than an hour before lunch, but gradually built confidence and played a commendable innings, while David Boon batted with style and played many forceful shots. Wright dropped Boon at gully off Danny Morrison as Boon was 73, and the second wicket partnership produced 149 runs before Moody edged a leg glance on 61.

Boon posted his century soon after tea and raced from 100 to 150 in just 58 balls before finishing the day on 169, Australia at 296-2. New Zealand suffered another blow as a back injury prevented 19-year-old Test debutant Chris Cairns from bowling after he shared the new ball on day one. Allan Border reached 50 before Morrison beat him for pace, and Boon reached 197 before Wright again missed him at gully, this time off Willie Watson. Boon registered 200 before Wright, off Martin Snedden's bowling, finally held a chance to dismiss him.

Merv Hughes took the most wickets for Australia in the Perth Test of late 1989, but neither he nor his team-mates could remove Mark Greatbatch, who was the cornerstone of New Zealand salvaging a draw

Dean Jones kept the runs flowing after lunch while Steve Waugh, Ian Healy and Merv Hughes made minor but useful contributions. Healy's dismissal produced Dipak Patel's first Test wicket. With the score pushing 500, Hughes and Geoff Lawson fell in quick succession, before Carl Rackemann scored 15 not out in 45 minutes. Jones was on 99 when Morrison trapped him lbw immediately after a drinks break. Australia promptly declared on 521-9, and New Zealand survived 10 overs without loss before stumps.

Local hero Terry Alderman bowled Robert Vance in the first over of day three, and then Greatbatch showed some form, while fellow left-hander Wright was solid until Rackemann bowled him for 36. Martin Crowe showed his style as he and Greatbatch took the Kiwis to 173-2, before Hughes took two quick wickets before tea. Greatbatch was caught behind for 76, then Patel was caught by Boon for zero. The Kiwis kept stuttering, with Martin Crowe lbw to Alderman for 62 before Hughes again made successive breakthroughs, as Ian Smith and Cairns departed. Jeff Crowe scored seven in 90 minutes before Rackemann dismissed him, and the Kiwis were 218-8 when bad light ended play 14 minutes early.

Lawson and Alderman took a wicket each as Australia wrapped up New Zealand's innings early on day four, and the Kiwis were asked to follow on, as they were 290 runs behind. They began poorly, losing Wright to a superb catch by Border at gully after 23 minutes. The score languished on 11 for the next 28 minutes before Vance was caught several balls after he was dropped.

New Zealand's position could have worsened after lunch, but Moody spilled a difficult chance at gully off Alderman to give Greatbatch a reprieve on 12. Determined to capitalise, Greatbatch knuckled down and showed courage, as there was some very tight bowling from the Australian quicks. Greatbatch was rock-solid rather than flashy, and Martin Crowe was steady as he scored 30 in two hours, before part-time bowler Moody claimed his maiden Test scalp with Crowe being caught by Taylor. New Zealand went to tea on 100-3. Then Alderman had Patel lbw, but Greatbatch and Jeff

Crowe steadied and took their side to 168-4 at stumps, with Greatbatch on 69 and his captain 42. Greatbatch, who scored 38 runs in session two and just 25 in session three, took 141 balls to reach 50, after having taken just 78 balls to reach the same score in the first innings.

Jeff Crowe reached 49 in 155 minutes of batting before Hughes had him lbw, then Smith caught first ball as New Zealand slumped to 189-6. Cairns, however, must have learned from watching in terms of resistance, and Greatbatch again scored only 25 in a session. Australia's pacemen tested Greatbatch with short-pitched bowling many times, but he comfortably evaded bouncers and showed good back-foot defence. Greatbatch played the occasional attacking drive when the ball was overpitched, and he rarely played and missed, as his concentration was magnificent. After lunch, Greatbatch reached his century from 341 balls and 462 minutes.

Cairns' 93-minute resistance ended as Hughes had him lbw, raising Australia's hopes as New Zealand trailed by 56 runs with only three wickets remaining. But left-handed duo Greatbatch and Snedden frustrated the hosts and narrowed the deficit to just eight at tea. Rackemann was amazingly economical with 21 maidens in 31 overs, in his first Test for six years.

A defining moment occurred shortly after tea, when Alderman fumbled a slips catch off Lawson to reprieve Greatbatch. The Australians must have fancied dismissing Morrison and Watson cheaply, but neither Greatbatch nor Snedden could be removed. The stonewalling duo added 88 runs in 48.3 overs, with Greatbatch finishing on 146 from 485 balls in a marathon 655 minutes, and Snedden lasted 202 minutes, facing 142 balls for his 33. Greatbatch, Snedden, Boon and Rackemann recorded their highest Test scores in this match, and Boon's sole Test double century was overshadowed by the performance of Greatbatch, who claimed man of the match honours. Cricket author Allan Miller aptly described Greatbatch's innings as "one of the finest backs-to-the-wall innings in the game's history".

AUSTRALIA 1ST INNINGS		
MA Taylor	c Wright b Morrison	9
DC Boon	c Wright b Snedden	200
TM Moody	c Smith b Snedden	61
AR Border*	b Morrison	50
DM Jones	lbw b Morrison	99
SR Waugh	c Greatbatch b Snedden	17
IA Healy†	c JJ Crowe b Patel	28
MG Hughes	c Wright b Snedden	16
GF Lawson	b Morrison	1
CG Rackemann	not out	15
Extras	(b 1, lb 9, w 2, nb 13)	25
Total	(9 wickets dec)	521

Did not bat TM Alderman

Fall of wickets 28, 177, 316, 361, 395, 449, 489, 490, 521

	O	M	R	W
DK Morrison	39.1	8	145	4
CL Cairns	12	2	60	0
MC Snedden	42	10	108	4
W Watson	37	7	118	0
DN Patel	28	5	80	1

NEW ZEALAND 1ST INNINGS		
JG Wright*	b Rackemann	34
RH Vance	b Alderman	4
MJ Greatbatch	c Healy b Hughes	76
MD Crowe	lbw b Alderman	62
DN Patel	c Boon b Hughes	0
JJ Crowe	c Healy b Rackemann	7
IDS Smith†	c Lawson b Hughes	11
CL Cairns	c Healy b Hughes	1
MC Snedden	not out	13
DK Morrison	c Border b Lawson	3
W Watson	lbw b Alderman	4
Extras	(b 1, lb 6, w 4, nb 5)	16
Total		231

Fall of wickets 28, 84, 173, 178, 191, 204, 206, 212, 226, 231

	O	M	R	W
TM Alderman	25.4	7	73	3
GF Lawson	22	5	54	1
CG Rackemann	20	4	39	2
MG Hughes	20	7	51	4
TM Moody	4	1	6	0
AR Border	1	0	1	0

NEW ZEALAND 2ND INNINGS		
JG Wright*	c Border b Lawson	3
RH Vance	c Alderman b Rackemann	8
MJ Greatbatch	not out	146
MD Crowe	c Taylor b Moody	30
DN Patel	lbw b Alderman	7
JJ Crowe	lbw b Hughes	49
IDS Smith†	c Border b Hughes	0
CL Cairns	lbw b Hughes	28
MC Snedden	not out	33
Extras	(lb 14, nb 4)	18
Total	(7 wickets)	322

Did not bat DK Morrison, W Watson

Fall of wickets 11, 11, 79, 107, 189, 189, 234

	O	M	R	W
TM Alderman	32	14	59	1
GF Lawson	38	12	88	1
CG Rackemann	31	21	23	1
MG Hughes	36	8	92	3
TM Moody	17	6	23	1
AR Border	5	2	17	0
DM Jones	3	2	6	0

Toss: New Zealand   Umpires: RJ Evans and PJ McConnell

Match drawn

Australia v Sri Lanka
Second Test at Bellerive Oval, Hobart

1989-90
December 16, 17, 18, 19, 20 (1989)

The last of the two Tests in the 1989–90 Australia-Sri Lanka series was notable, as it was the first Test ever held in the Australian state of Tasmania. A big margin belied the many quality aspects of a great contest.

After Aravinda de Silva scored 167 to help Sri Lanka draw the first Test in Brisbane, the tourists again won the toss and chose to bowl. After being dismissed without scoring in the first innings at Brisbane, David Boon took off for a risky single from the third ball of the second Test, and would have been run out for nought had Sri Lankan skipper Arjuna Ranatunga's throw hit the stumps. There was something in the pitch for bowlers, but Boon and Mark Taylor put on 50 runs before a glance from Taylor down the legside gave wicketkeeper and Test debutant Hashan Tillekeratne his first catch. Rumesh Ratnayake bowled a great spell and went on to dismiss Tom Moody, Boon and Dean Jones, who was out second ball, to leave Australia struggling at 89-4.

The demise of Steve Waugh and Allan Border after steady starts made the score 123-6, before Peter Sleep survived for nearly three hours. Ian Healy, Merv Hughes and Tasmanian Greg Campbell hung around for useful partnerships before Ratnayake dismissed Campbell and Terry Alderman with successive balls to have Australia out for 224. Australia bowled nine overs before stumps, and Sri Lanka crumbled, with two wickets to Alderman and one to Campbell leaving the tourists at 27-3.

Roshan Mahanama and Aravinda de Silva kept Australia wicketless in the first session on day two, and de Silva reached his 50 after hitting seven fours and two sixes. He struck a further two fours and one six before Campbell delighted his home crowd by trapping de Silva lbw for a splendid 75. After progressing to 188-4, Sri Lanka looked set to build a

Australian batsman David Boon, pictured cutting the ball towards fieldsman Asanka Gurusinha during first Test of the 1989–90 series, had the honour of taking strike to the first ball in Test cricket played in his home state of Tasmania.

first innings lead before Sleep's leg-spin caused a collapse. Arjuna Ranatunga fell for 21 before Tillekeratne's first Test innings was a duck, and then Mahanama fell for a resolute 85 when he edged a googly. There was some brief lower order resistance before Hughes claimed three wickets, as Australia gained an eight-run lead on the first innings.

The Sri Lankans hit back as 35 minutes of play remained on day two. An injured Boon had Healy as a runner, but it proved inconsequential, as Boon was caught from the first ball he faced. Moody fell cheaply to Ratnayake again to make the score 10-2, and then Hughes came in as nightwatchman before Australia reached 25-2 at stumps.

Hughes went on to score a vital 30, before Taylor and Border took the total to 121-3 at lunch. They survived until tea as well, with Taylor not offering a chance on his way to 108 while Border was 69 and the total 233-3. After the break, both batsmen perished to sweeps off Aravinda de Silva, with Taylor well caught on the legside while still on 108 before Border was bowled for 85. Jones survived a perilously close lbw appeal before he scored, and subsequently combined with Waugh to push the home side into a very strong position. Waugh raced to 77 at stumps, while Jones was on 51 as Australia led by 395 runs with two days left.

Jones appeared fortunate to survive an appeal for caught behind on the morning of day four. Jones reached 118 and Waugh 134, and then Australia declared at lunch, setting Sri Lanka 522 runs to win. Jones and Waugh added 260 runs as Sri Lanka's six bowlers copped a fair bit of stick. Jones took just 59 balls to go from 50 to 100, while Waugh took 58 balls for his first 50 runs and a further 52 balls to reach his century.

Campbell had Mahanama lbw with just six runs on the board, before Dammika Ranatunga and Asanka Gurusinha proved hard to dislodge. They added 47 runs in 86 minutes, when Gurusinha was caught by Tasmanian all-rounder Rod Tucker, who substituted for Boon and for 12th man Carl Rackemann, who was unwell. From 67-2 at tea, Sri Lanka added 99 runs in the last session for the loss of Dammika Ranatunga, who was solid for more than two hours before needlessly chasing a wide delivery and edging a catch. Aravinda de Silva continued his sparkling form and struck nine boundaries, registering a half-century in just 57 deliveries, before Sri Lanka closed day four on 166-3 after Arjuna Ranatunga provided solid resistance.

The Australians gained the ascendancy before lunch on day five as the overnight not out batsmen were caught, 187-3 becoming 187-5. Tillekeratne was caught with the score on 208, and the tourists were 237-6 at lunch. An Australian victory,

however, was not a foregone conclusion, as Asoka de Silva and Ravi Ratnayeke stonewalled the bowling in the second session after the first 12 minutes were lost to rain. Ratnayeke hit 10 boundaries in a half-century, while Asoka de Silva was much slower.

The total was 304-6 at tea, and Sri Lanka appeared capable of salvaging a draw, until Ratnayeke touched a legside delivery from Campbell and was well caught by the wicketkeeper. Sri Lanka's resistance subsequently ended as Labrooy and de Silva were bowled with the total on 337. Tasmanian Campbell was involved in six wickets in the match, and the (unrelated) de Silvas were among them in both innings. The last-wicket pair lasted 14 minutes before Hughes trapped Ratnayeke lbw with just over 30 minutes remaining. The contest was somewhat tainted as Arjuna Ranatunga accused the Australians of racial abuse, which Allan Miller described in his 1989–90 cricket annual as "a sad end to a brilliant Test match".

Australia captain Allan Border, a tower of strength during the turnaround in the national team's fortunes in the 1980s.

AUSTRALIA 1ST INNINGS

DC Boon	c Mahanama b Ratnayake	41
MA Taylor	c Tillekeratne b Ratnayake	23
TM Moody	c Gurusinha b Ratnayake	6
AR Border*	c EAR de Silva b Ratnayeke	24
DM Jones	c Tillekeratne b Ratnayake	3
SR Waugh	c Tillekeratne b Labrooy	16
PR Sleep	not out	47
IA Healy†	c Tillekeratne b Gurusinha	17
MG Hughes	b EAR de Silva	27
GD Campbell	c Mahanama b Ratnayake	6
TM Alderman	b Ratnayake	0
Extras	(lb 7, w 1, nb 6)	14
Total		224

Fall of wickets 50, 68, 83, 89, 112, 123, 166, 207, 224, 224

	O	M	R	W
JR Ratnayeke	15	2	39	1
GF Labrooy	19	3	61	1
RJ Ratnayake	19.4	2	66	6
CPH Ramanayake	4	0	21	0
AP Gurusinha	6	0	20	1
EAR de Silva	9	6	10	1

AUSTRALIA 2ND INNINGS

MA Taylor	c Gurusinha b PA de Silva	108
DC Boon	c Ratnayake b Labrooy	0
TM Moody	c Tillekeratne b Ratnayake	5
MG Hughes	c Gurusinha b Ratnayake	30
AR Border*	b PA de Silva	85
DM Jones	not out	118
SR Waugh	not out	134
Extras	(b 2, lb 5, w 4, nb 22)	33
Total	(5 wickets dec)	513

Did not bat PR Sleep, IA Healy†, GD Campbell, TM Alderman

Fall of wickets 1, 10, 77, 240, 253

	O	M	R	W
GF Labrooy	22	3	100	1
RJ Ratnayake	35	5	123	2
JR Ratnayeke	19	1	86	0
EAR de Silva	21	2	83	0
PA de Silva	18	1	65	2
CPH Ramanayake	10	0	49	0

SRI LANKA 1ST INNINGS

RS Mahanama	c Healy b Sleep	85
D Ranatunga	c Moody b Alderman	2
AP Gurusinha	c Taylor b Alderman	0
EAR de Silva	c Border b Campbell	2
PA de Silva	lbw b Campbell	75
A Ranatunga*	c Moody b Sleep	21
HP Tillekeratne†	c Taylor b Sleep	0
JR Ratnayeke	c Taylor b Hughes	9
GF Labrooy	b Hughes	11
CPH Ramanayake	not out	4
RJ Ratnayake	c Border b Hughes	0
Extras	(lb 4, nb 3)	7
Total		216

Fall of wickets 11, 15, 18, 146, 188, 192, 193, 201, 216, 216

	O	M	R	W
TM Alderman	23	2	71	2
GD Campbell	23	9	41	2
MG Hughes	21.4	6	68	3
PR Sleep	10	4	26	3
SR Waugh	6	3	6	0

SRI LANKA 2ND INNINGS

RS Mahanama	lbw b Campbell	5
D Ranatunga	c Healy b Hughes	45
AP Gurusinha	c sub b Hughes	20
PA de Silva	c Campbell b Sleep	72
A Ranatunga*	c Jones b Hughes	38
HP Tillekeratne†	c Waugh b Sleep	6
JR Ratnayeke	c Healy b Campbell	75
EAR de Silva	b Campbell	50
GF Labrooy	b Hughes	5
CPH Ramanayake	not out	2
RJ Ratnayake	lbw b Hughes	5
Extras	(b 9, lb 12, nb 4)	25
Total		348

Fall of wickets 6, 53, 94, 187, 187, 208, 332, 337, 337, 348

	O	M	R	W
TM Alderman	30	12	48	0
GD Campbell	33	8	102	3
PR Sleep	36	16	73	2
MG Hughes	31.4	8	88	5
TM Moody	2	0	9	0
DM Jones	4	2	5	0
AR Border	5	4	2	0

Toss: Sri Lanka   Umpires: LJ King and SG Randell

Australia won by 173 runs

Australia v England
Third Test at the Sydney Cricket Ground

1990-91
January 4, 5, 6, 7, 8 (1991)

Ian Healy and Steve Waugh pictured during Australia's run of success in the late 1990s. The situation was much different in January 1991, when Waugh was dropped from the Australian side, but he later became one of the game's modern day champions.

After Australia won the 1989 Ashes series 4-0 and convincingly won the first two Tests of the 1990–91 series on home soil, one could have started to wonder when the next close, hard-fought battle would be. The answer was the third Test at Sydney.

Australia batted first for the first time in the series. Openers Geoff Marsh and Mark Taylor made little impact before Devon Malcolm removed both to make the score 38-2. The other West Indian-born opening bowler, Gladstone Small, was less effective after replacing the injured Angus Fraser. Off-spinner Eddie Hemmings also found the going hard after the 41-year-old was recalled in place of Phil DeFreitas. David Boon and Allan Border took the score to 158-2 at tea, Boon regularly striking the ball superbly. He raced to 97 with his third four in four deliveries, but an attempt to reach a century with his 18th four resulted in a catch behind point from a long-hop. Border hit 10 boundaries before Hemmings bowled him for 78, and Australia was 259-4 at stumps.

Australia lost Steve Waugh for 48 and Dean Jones for 60 in the first session of the second day. Jones was brilliantly stumped down the legside as wicketkeeper Robert 'Jack' Russell was up to the stumps to Small's fast-medium pace. The left-handed Greg Matthews survived a run out chance on 28 and scored a further 100 runs before holing out to Hemmings to produce Phil Tufnell's first Test wicket. Matthews would have been out for 68 had Malcolm not bowled a no-ball, while Ian Healy's 35 was followed by Terry Alderman making his highest Test score of 26 not out. The Ashes looked safely in Australia's keeping as the hosts compiled 518, and England faced just one over before bad light ended play, nearly an hour before stumps was scheduled.

Graham Gooch and Mike Atherton took England to 83-0 at lunch on day three, before Gooch and Wayne Larkins fell in the next session, Gooch caught down the legside and Larkins run out by Border from mid wicket. Bruce Reid claimed the wicket of Robin Smith to make the score 156-3, and then Atherton and David Gower put on 71 runs before stumps.

Atherton reached his century the following morning from the 326th ball he faced, and it was the slowest century in Ashes history in terms of time spent at the crease (424 minutes). Matthews, who bowled 58 overs, was rewarded for his persistence with Atherton's wicket to a catch at short leg, while Gower stole the show in the session, scoring 70 runs with some attractive strokes. Gower reached 123 before falling to a good catch in the gully, and Alec Stewart scored quickly in session two to help England to 426-5 at tea. Alderman had Stewart somewhat dubiously lbw for 91 just

after play resumed. Alderman, England's nemesis in 1989, picked up two wickets with the score on 444 before the Englishmen declared 49 runs behind.

Marsh and Taylor again failed to get going, and both were dismissed after 40 minutes before Australia began the final day's play with an 87-run lead. Some rain fell before the scheduled start. Nightwatchman Healy was on 12 when Gower missed a difficult catch at square leg. Healy consolidated and shared in useful partnerships with Boon and Border, both of whom were caught by Gooch off Tufnell. In just his second Test, left-arm spinner Tufnell took two wickets in successive balls, as Jones popped back a simple return catch just after Border swept a catch to square leg. Waugh prodded the hat-trick ball in Gower's direction at silly point, but Tufnell narrowly missed the three-from-three feat when the fieldsman spilled another tough chance.

Following lunch, Healy reached his highest Test score at the time, 69, before Waugh and the wicketkeeper were dismissed with the total on 166. England was still in with a chance of victory, and the Australian tail comprising Carl Rackemann, Alderman and Reid was hardly imposing, according to their records and reputations with the willow. But the tourists made what turned out to be a fatal mistake in keeping the spinners on. After being bowled by Hemmings cheaply in the first innings, Rackemann defended stoically, and Matthews lasted 72 minutes before Hemmings bowled him for 19. Rackemann meanwhile took 72 minutes to score his first run, an Australian Test record, while Alderman lasted 10 minutes and Reid 28 minutes as time ticked away from England. Rackemann was last out when Malcolm rattled the stumps after belatedly being brought back into the attack. Rackemann's nine runs from 102 balls in 107 minutes was largely responsible for England having been handed a virtually impossible target of 255 runs in 28 overs if they were to have any hope of winning back the Ashes.

Rackemann and Alderman were ineffective with the ball as Gower and Gooch went on the offence. Five fielders were stationed in the deep within just five overs. Eighty-one runs in the first 11 overs however meant the required run rate crept to around 10 per over, and the introduction of spin stymied the run flow. Gower was caught at long off trying to loft a six off Matthews, and then Border had Larkins lbw for a duck. The total reached 100 before Gooch was caught off Matthews, and then Stewart was run out next ball. England's challenge was as good as over, and Smith and Atherton added just 13 runs in half an hour before the tourists finished 142 runs shy of the target after 25 overs were bowled.

AUSTRALIA 1ST INNINGS

GR Marsh	c Larkins b Malcolm	13
MA Taylor	c Russell b Malcolm	11
DC Boon	c Atherton b Gooch	97
AR Border*	b Hemmings	78
DM Jones	st Russell b Small	60
SR Waugh	c Stewart b Malcolm	48
GRJ Matthews	c Hemmings b Tufnell	128
IA Healy†	c Small b Hemmings	35
CG Rackemann	b Hemmings	1
TM Alderman	not out	26
BA Reid	c Smith b Malcolm	0
Extras	(b 5, lb 8, nb 8)	21
Total		518

Fall of wickets 21, 38, 185, 226, 292, 347, 442, 457, 512, 518

	O	M	R	W
DE Malcolm	45	12	128	4
GC Small	31	5	103	1
EE Hemmings	32	7	105	3
PCR Tufnell	30	6	95	1
GA Gooch	14	3	46	1
MA Atherton	5	0	28	0

AUSTRALIA 2ND INNINGS

MA Taylor	lbw b Hemmings	19
GR Marsh	c Stewart b Malcolm	4
IA Healy†	c Smith b Tufnell	69
DC Boon	c Gooch b Tufnell	29
AR Border*	c Gooch b Tufnell	20
DM Jones	c & b Tufnell	0
SR Waugh	c Russell b Hemmings	14
GRJ Matthews	b Hemmings	19
CG Rackemann	b Malcolm	9
TM Alderman	c Gower b Tufnell	1
BA Reid	not out	5
Extras	(lb 16)	16
Total		205

Fall of wickets 21, 29, 81, 129, 129, 166, 166, 189, 192, 205

	O	M	R	W
DE Malcolm	6	1	19	2
GC Small	2	1	6	0
EE Hemmings	41	9	94	3
PCR Tufnell	37	18	61	5
MA Atherton	3	1	9	0

ENGLAND 1ST INNINGS

GA Gooch*	c Healy b Reid	59
MA Atherton	c Boon b Matthews	105
W Larkins	run out (Border)	11
RA Smith	c Healy b Reid	18
DI Gower	c Marsh b Reid	123
AJ Stewart	lbw b Alderman	91
RC Russell†	not out	30
GC Small	lbw b Alderman	10
EE Hemmings	b Alderman	0
PCR Tufnell	not out	5
Extras	(b 1, lb 8, nb 8)	17
Total	(8 wickets dec)	469

Did not bat DE Malcolm

Fall of wickets 95, 116, 156, 295, 394, 426, 444, 444

	O	M	R	W
TM Alderman	20.1	4	62	3
BA Reid	35.1	9	79	3
CG Rackemann	25.5	5	89	0
GRJ Matthews	58	16	145	1
AR Border	19	5	45	0
SR Waugh	14	3	40	0

ENGLAND 2ND INNINGS

GA Gooch*	c Border b Matthews	54
DI Gower	c Taylor b Matthews	36
W Larkins	lbw b Border	0
AJ Stewart	run out (Alderman/Matthews)	7
RA Smith	not out	10
MA Atherton	not out	3
Extras	(lb 1, nb 2)	3
Total	(4 wickets)	113

Did not bat RC Russell†, GC Small, EE Hemmings, PCR Tufnell, DE Malcolm

Fall of wickets 84, 84, 100, 100

	O	M	R	W
TM Alderman	4	0	29	0
CG Rackemann	3	0	20	0
GRJ Matthews	9	2	26	2
AR Border	9	1	37	1

Toss: Australia   Umpires: AR Crafter and PJ McConnell   Match drawn

Pakistan v Sri Lanka
Third Test at Iqbal Stadium, Faisalabad

1991-92
January 2, 3, 4, 6, 7 (1992)

The third and final Test involving Pakistan and Sri Lanka in 1991–92 proved attractive from start to finish, as the match was evenly contested throughout and could have gone either way. An added piece of interest was that Sri Lanka was chasing its first win on foreign soil and first series win over Pakistan, after the first two Tests of the series were drawn.

Imran Khan must have questioned his decision to bowl first after Sri Lankan openers Roshan Mahanama and Chandika Hathurusinghe put on an 81-run stand against an attack that included no spinner. Hathurusinghe hit 10 boundaries and just nine other runs before Waqar Younis bowled him. Wasim Akram made a key breakthrough as he dismissed Asanka Gurusinha cheaply, and Sri Lanka's decent start was somewhat forfeited, as the score was 89-2. Mahanama and Aravinda de Silva were tied down as they took the score to 130-2, before Pakistan quickly gained the upper hand. Salim Jaffer had de Silva caught behind and Arjuna Ranatunga lbw with successive deliveries, after Ranatunga had bagged a pair in the first Test, and rain prevented Sri Lanka batting in the second Test. Mahanama passed 50 before he was out in the same fashion as de Silva, and Sri Lanka sank to 150-5.

Sanath Jayasuriya scored quickly, regularly piercing the field, but Sri Lanka crumbled again after fellow left-hander Hashan Tillekeratne was caught off Waqar for 11. Rumesh Ratnayake hit a four before he was lbw to Waqar, who subsequently had Don Anurasiri caught for a duck. Jayasuriya registered nine fours as he reached 50, before Kapila Wijegunawardene was lbw to Akram, and Sri Lanka finished day one on 205-9. The last wicket partnership was potentially vital, as Pramodya Wickremasinghe scored one run from just five balls in 40 minutes, while Jayasuriya motored to 81 and had hit 14 fours before he was run out.

Pakistan's left-arm quick bowler Wasim Akram made his Test debut in 1985 before playing the last of his 104 Tests in 2002. He was arguably the world's best bowler in the 1990s.

Wijegunawardene was very economical, as Pakistan openers Rameez Raja and Shoaib Mohammad began slowly. It was a game of patience but the Pakistanis seemed to be winning as Rameez worked his way to 63, before Wickremasinghe trapped him lbw with the total on 102. Eight runs later, Shoaib fell similarly, after scoring a painstaking 30 in 208 minutes, and Pakistan finished the day on 117-2 from 54 overs after two stoppages for bad light reduced the day's play.

Pakistan's middle order stuttered just as Sri Lanka's had done. Zahid Fazal and Javed Miandad were unable to score freely, and Miandad was caught off Wickremasinghe before Gurusinha had Salim Malik caught behind, with Pakistan sinking from 141-2 to 146-4. Fazal scored just 13 in 143 minutes before the persevering and accurate Wijegunawardene was rewarded with an lbw. Imran played a dogged captain's innings but his team's innings was unsteady, as Akram and Moin Khan were caught in front of their stumps. Imran hit four fours but scored just six other runs in his 104-minute stay before Wijegunawardene bowled him. Pakistan lost its ninth wicket on the same score that Sri Lanka did, with the sixth lbw of the innings and fourth lbw to Wickremasinghe who claimed his fifth scalp. Tail-enders Jaffer and Aaqib Javed resisted for 51 minutes but were tied down, and Pakistan fell 19 runs short of Sri Lanka's total.

Mahanama lasted 53 minutes but registered only two scoring strokes before Waqar trapped him lbw. Hathurusinghe scored 20 in 80 minutes and Gurusinha 14 in an hour before Sri Lanka finished the day on 68-3. Sri Lanka's situation became more troublesome as only four runs were added on day four, when nightwatchman Wijegunawardene was bowled by Waqar. De Silva scored rapidly but his dismissal for 38 was a real blow as Sri Lanka badly needed him to kick on. Tillekeratne and Ranatunga failed again, although Ranatunga avoided another pair, while Jayasuriya again revived the team's cause without receiving the support he would have liked. He reached 45 before he became Waqar's fifth victim, and then Akram wrapped up the tail as he bowled Anurasiri and Wickremasinghe with successive balls. Due to the low-scoring nature of the game, Pakistan's target of 185 was by no means straightforward.

Fazal opened the innings as Shoaib was unwell, and looked more convincing than Rameez, who was again lbw to Wickremasinghe. Miandad scored just two in 43 minutes before he was caught by Gurusinha off Wijegunawardene, and Malik quickly fell to the same combination. Imran departed just three balls later, with Pakistan in deep trouble at 60-4, and the dismissal of the Pakistan captain was remarkably the 14th

and final lbw of the match. Fazal solidly worked his way to 55 while Akram started confidently and reached 19. This left the deciding Test interestingly balanced with a day remaining, as Pakistan needed 90 runs with six wickets left.

Fazal continued to bat solidly while Akram was equally effective. Fazal scored 23 runs in 80 minutes on day five, and 52 of his runs came in fours, before Gurusinha had him caught. The hosts, however, were soundly placed as just 36 more runs were needed. The game was potentially prone to changing complexion as Akram was caught for 54, leaving Pakistan 156-6. But Moin pushed Pakistan towards the target, and not even the loss of Shoaib with the total on 179 could deny the hosts, extending Sri Lanka's away from home drought. Despite some tidy bowling from Sri Lanka, it was telling that Sri Lanka's bowlers conceded 26 no-balls in Pakistan's first innings and 33 in the match, compared with Pakistan's 18 overall.

Sri Lanka's Sanath Jayasuriya.

SRI LANKA 1ST INNINGS

RS Mahanama	c Moin Khan b Salim Jaffer	58
UC Hathurusinghe	b Waqar Younis	49
AP Gurusinha	c Zahid Fazal b Wasim Akram	3
PA de Silva*	c Moin Khan b Salim Jaffer	12
A Ranatunga	lbw b Salim Jaffer	0
ST Jayasuriya	run out	81
HP Tillekeratne†	c Shoaib Mohammad b Waqar Younis	11
RJ Ratnayake	lbw b Waqar Younis	4
SD Anurasiri	c Shoaib Mohammad b Waqar Younis	0
KIW Wijegunawardene	lbw b Wasim Akram	2
GP Wickremasinghe	not out	1
Extras	(b 3, lb 6, w 2, nb 8)	19
Total		240

Fall of wickets 81, 89, 130, 130, 150, 179, 185, 193, 205, 240

	O	M	R	W
Wasim Akram	22	8	62	2
Salim Jaffer	17	4	36	3
Waqar Younis	21	1	87	4
Aaqib Javed	12.1	3	46	0

SRI LANKA 2ND INNINGS

RS Mahanama	lbw b Waqar Younis	8
UC Hathurusinghe	c Zahid Fazal b Waqar Younis	20
AP Gurusinha	lbw b Aaqib Javed	14
PA de Silva*	lbw b Waqar Younis	38
KIW Wijegunawardene	b Waqar Younis	2
ST Jayasuriya	c Salim Malik b Waqar Younis	45
HP Tillekeratne†	c Moin Khan b Aaqib Javed	14
A Ranatunga	c Javed Miandad b Wasim Akram	6
RJ Ratnayake	not out	5
SD Anurasiri	b Wasim Akram	0
GP Wickremasinghe	b Wasim Akram	0
Extras	(lb 3, nb 10)	13
Total		165

Fall of wickets 28, 43, 67, 72, 105, 136, 146, 160, 165, 165

	O	M	R	W
Wasim Akram	18	2	71	3
Waqar Younis	17	3	65	5
Salim Jaffer	8	2	19	0
Aaqib Javed	8	4	7	2

PAKISTAN 1ST INNINGS

Rameez Raja	lbw b Wickremasinghe	63
Shoaib Mohammad	lbw b Wickremasinghe	30
Zahid Fazal	lbw b Wijegunawardene	13
Javed Miandad	c Gurusinha b Wickremasinghe	14
Salim Malik	c Tillekeratne b Gurusinha	4
Imran Khan*	b Wijegunawardene	22
Wasim Akram	lbw b Gurusinha	13
Moin Khan†	lbw b Wickremasinghe	3
Waqar Younis	lbw b Wickremasinghe	6
Salim Jaffer	not out	8
Aaqib Javed	c sub b Wijegunawardene	10
Extras	(lb 8, w 1, nb 26)	35
Total		221

Fall of wickets 102, 110, 141, 146, 162, 186, 196, 197, 205, 221

	O	M	R	W
RJ Ratnayake	13	2	40	0
KIW Wijegunawardene	31.2	13	47	3
GP Wickremasinghe	32	9	73	5
SD Anurasiri	10	2	28	0
AP Gurusinha	15	9	19	2
A Ranatunga	3	2	2	0
UC Hathurusinghe	2	0	4	0

PAKISTAN 2ND INNINGS

Rameez Raja	lbw b Wickremasinghe	8
Zahid Fazal	c Anurasiri b Gurusinha	78
Javed Miandad	c Gurusinha b Wijegunawardene	2
Salim Malik	c Gurusinha b Wijegunawardene	4
Imran Khan*	lbw b Wijegunawardene	0
Wasim Akram	c de Silva b Wijegunawardene	54
Shoaib Mohammad	b Ratnayake	7
Moin Khan†	not out	22
Waqar Younis	not out	1
Extras	(b 2, lb 3, nb 7)	12
Total	(7 wickets)	188

Did not bat Salim Jaffer, Aaqib Javed

Fall of wickets 31, 52, 60, 60, 149, 156, 179

	O	M	R	W
RJ Ratnayake	9.3	0	43	1
KIW Wijegunawardene	17.2	2	51	4
GP Wickremasinghe	26	6	53	1
AP Gurusinha	12	5	18	1
SD Anurasiri	6	1	18	0

Toss: Pakistan   Umpires: Khalid Aziz and Shakoor Rana   Match referee: DB Carr
Pakistan won by 3 wickets

New Zealand v England

First Test at Lancaster Park, Christchurch

1991–92

January 18, 19, 20, 21, 22 (1992)

A Test match is rarely considered a thriller if it features an innings win, yet the first Test of the New Zealand versus England series in 1991–92 was an exception, despite one team dominating.

New Zealand began well after winning the toss and fielding at the Christchurch venue. Danny Morrison had Graham Gooch caught behind for two, but then things went pear-shaped for the hosts. Despite dampness in the pitch, Morrison and Chris Cairns were very wayward, while England's Alec Stewart was in good form. Graeme Hick was a little uncertain before Cairns had him lbw for 35, but another three hours of play contained 179 runs before the next breakthrough occurred.

Stewart reached 50 before lunch and 100 before tea in a controlled manner. His cuts, drives and pulls were impressive, as was his readiness to hammer loose deliveries. Robin Smith scored quickly, and Kiwi captain Martin Crowe dropped him at slip when 44. Smith struck 16 fours and a six, and was on 96 when he edged Chris Pringle to slip, where Mark Greatbatch made no mistake. Stewart progressed to 148 and had hit 17 fours before a Morrison delivery bounced alarmingly and had Stewart caught by Crowe at slip. It was a crucial breakthrough for the Kiwis just before stumps, but England had the upper hand at 310-4.

New Zealand's bowling remained ineffective on day two, and England's scoring rate was somewhat slower but still effective. A run out accounted for Jack Russell, with the total on 390. Lamb hit 13 fours and a six, but like Robin Smith fell short of a century. Test debutant Dermot Reeve combined with Chris Lewis for the next partnership, which took the total past 500. Reeve made 59, and Lewis hit 13 boundaries, scoring 70 at nearly a run per ball. Phil DeFreitas clubbed the second ball he faced over the long on boundary before Gooch

Zimbabwean-born Graeme Hick had to wait several years before he could play Test cricket for England. A gifted stroke-maker, he finished his Test career with a modest average of 31.32.

declared. The total of 580-9 included 75 fours and three sixes.

Poor weather restricted England's bowlers to only 2.2 overs before stumps, while three runs were scored. No play was possible until early afternoon on day three, when the experienced John Wright and debutant Blair Hartland seemed intent on survival, playing defensively. The score slowly reached 51 without loss before Phil Tufnell's left-arm spin changed the flow.

Tufnell drew Wright into a drive and induced an edge to Lamb at slip. Hartland prodded a catch to Robin Smith in close, and suddenly the Kiwis were 52-2, with two fresh batsmen at the crease. Andrew Jones and Greatbatch hung around for about an hour each, but neither looked convincing. Jones was lbw to Lewis, and Greatbatch caught by Stewart. The spinner struck again when he bowled Shane Thomson, who misread a delivery that drifted into him, and the hosts were in tatters at 91-5.

Dipak Patel hit out against Tufnell. Interestingly, Patel had been largely responsible for Tufnell's figures of 13-3-76-0 in 1986, during Tufnell's first-class debut for Middlesex against Worcestershire, for whom Patel scored 108 in an innings win. But New Zealand's hopes of a recovery were dented when Crowe was caught off Derek Pringle for 20. The Kiwis began day four on 169-6, and lifted as Patel and Cairns went on the attack. The total reached 256 before Patel sought a third run and was run out for 99, having hit 10 fours and two sixes and faced just 134 balls. More unfortunate for Patel was that he never scored a Test century. Reeve's eighth delivery in Test cricket yielded his first wicket, that of Cairns, caught by Hick for 61, when New Zealand was still 102 runs shy of avoiding the follow-on. Ian Smith, Morrison and Pringle showed some resistance, but couldn't prevent England claiming a 268-run lead, and the follow-on was enforced.

Hartland and Wright again established a solid platform. This time Hartland scored 45 in a stand of 81 before he was caught off Tufnell late in the day. Batting bunny Morrison was promoted to nightwatchman and number three, after scoring an unbeaten eight from 53 balls in the first innings. Morrison survived until stumps on day four but was caught behind off Lewis without scoring the next morning. The Kiwis, however, looked like avoiding defeat, as Wright and Jones seemed immovable. They added 101 runs in 213 minutes before Jones was caught behind off Derek Pringle. Crowe also became entrenched at the crease, and Wright was stuck on 99 at tea. New Zealand needed just 57 more runs to make England bat again. Reeve was absent with food poisoning, and DeFreitas limped off. Surely England could not take seven wickets in the last session?

But Wright became another Kiwi to fall for 99, as he advanced a widish Tufnell delivery that bounced into the footmarks, before Russell effected a stumping. The match soon changed dramatically – Tufnell had Greatbatch caught and Thomson lbw in one over. Patel lasted 23 minutes before foolishly skying to mid off, leaving the score 236-7 as 65 minutes remained. Cairns fell to Tufnell for a duck before Ian Smith gloved a Lewis bouncer to Russell. New Zealand had lost 39-6 within 90 minutes.

Crowe and Chris Pringle needed to survive 32 minutes, or score 18 runs in 22 minutes, to salvage a draw. Pringle managed five runs, and New Zealand needed four to guarantee a draw, as Tufnell started an over to Crowe with 11 minutes left. The fielders were in close to pressure Crowe, who saw his chance as he advanced a flighted ball, which dropped. But Crowe's timing was faulty as the ball hit high on the blade and lobbed to extra cover, where Derek Pringle took the catch. The tourists were jubilant, while Crowe lamented choking under pressure. England won the second Test as well, inflicting New Zealand's first home series defeat in 12 years, before the third and final Test was drawn.

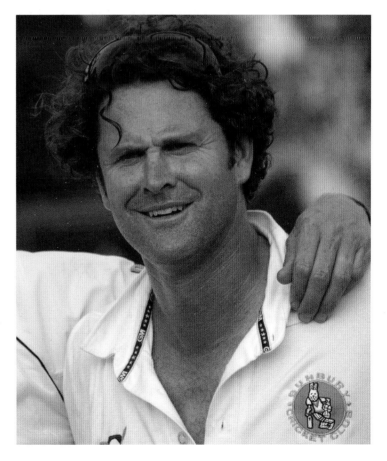

Chris Cairns had injury problems in the first few years of his international cricket career, before becoming one of New Zealand's finest players.

ENGLAND 1ST INNINGS		
GA Gooch*	c Smith b Morrison	2
AJ Stewart	c Crowe b Morrison	148
GA Hick	lbw b Cairns	35
RA Smith	c Greatbatch b Pringle	96
AJ Lamb	b Patel	93
RC Russell†	run out	36
DA Reeve	c Jones b Pringle	59
CC Lewis	b Pringle	70
DR Pringle	c Greatbatch b Patel	10
PAJ DeFreitas	not out	7
Extras	(b 5, lb 10, w 1, nb 8)	24
Total	(9 wickets dec)	580

Did not bat PCR Tufnell

Fall of wickets 6, 95, 274, 310, 390, 466, 544, 571, 580

	O	M	R	W
DK Morrison	33	5	133	2
CL Cairns	30	3	118	1
C Pringle	36	4	127	3
SA Thomson	15	3	47	0
DN Patel	46	5	132	2
AH Jones	3	0	8	0

NEW ZEALAND 1ST INNINGS		
BR Hartland	c Smith b Tufnell	22
JG Wright	c Lamb b Tufnell	28
AH Jones	lbw b Lewis	16
MJ Greatbatch	c Stewart b Tufnell	11
SA Thomson	b Tufnell	5
DN Patel	run out	99
MD Crowe*	c Stewart b Pringle	20
CL Cairns	c Hick b Reeve	61
IDS Smith†	lbw b DeFreitas	20
DK Morrison	not out	8
C Pringle	c Hick b DeFreitas	6
Extras	(b 1, lb 7, nb 8)	16
Total		312

Fall of wickets 51, 52, 73, 87, 91, 139, 256, 279, 306, 312

	O	M	R	W
PAJ DeFreitas	32.4	16	54	2
CC Lewis	30	9	69	1
DR Pringle	15	2	54	1
PCR Tufnell	39	10	100	4
GA Hick	3	0	11	0
DA Reeve	8	4	16	1

NEW ZEALAND 2ND INNINGS		
BR Hartland	c Smith b Tufnell	45
JG Wright	st Russell b Tufnell	99
DK Morrison	c Russell b Lewis	0
AH Jones	c Russell b Pringle	39
MD Crowe*	c Pringle b Tufnell	48
MJ Greatbatch	c Smith b Tufnell	0
SA Thomson	lbw b Tufnell	0
DN Patel	c Pringle b Tufnell	6
CL Cairns	c Smith b Tufnell	0
IDS Smith†	c Russell b Lewis	1
C Pringle	not out	5
Extras	(b 1, lb 7, nb 13)	21
Total		264

Fall of wickets 81, 81, 182, 211, 222, 222, 236, 241, 250, 264

	O	M	R	W
PAJ DeFreitas	23	6	54	0
CC Lewis	22	3	66	2
DR Pringle	21	5	64	1
PCR Tufnell	46.1	25	47	7
GA Hick	14	8	11	0
DA Reeve	2	0	8	0
RA Smith	4	2	6	0

Toss: New Zealand   Umpires: BL Aldridge and RS Dunne
Match referee: PJP Burge   England won by an innings and 4 runs

West Indies v South Africa
One-off Test at Kensington Oval, Bridgetown, Barbados

1991-92
April 18, 19, 20, 22, 23 (1992)

The first time the West Indies and South Africa met in Test cricket came less than two months after they first met in a One Day International. The one-dayer was in the World Cup, when South Africa returned to international cricket after apartheid had caused a 22-year exile. South Africa beat the West Indies by 64 runs before the Africans later fell just one game short of a final berth when rain cruelly ended their run chase against England. There was little doubt that South Africa had captured the attention of much of the cricketing public.

Following the World Cup, South Africa's first Test since 1969–70 was a one-off encounter with the West Indies, still the Test cricket champions. The West Indies, however, were in a transitional period following the retirements of Viv Richards, Gordon Greenidge, Malcolm Marshall and Jeff Dujon. Jimmy Adams, David Williams and Kenny Benjamin made their debut Test appearances, while Carl Hooper and Gus Logie were absent with injury. The match was poorly attended because Barbadians were unhappy with the West Indian selection policy.

South African captain Kepler Wessels was the sole South African with Test experience, and the last of his 24 Tests for Australia took place more than six years earlier. He had played Test cricket against West Indian players Desmond Haynes, Richie Richardson and Courtney Walsh. Wessels sent the hosts in to bat, and the West Indies gained control with a 99-run opening partnership in 93 minutes. The score became 106-2 after Richard Snell accounted for openers Phil Simmons and Haynes, before Tertius Bosch struck after lunch, when Brian Lara was caught behind for 17. Richie Richardson and Keith Arthurton led a revival, with Arthurton driving well and registering regular boundaries. The score reached 219-3 before Snell again struck a key blow, this time as Richardson was caught behind by his namesake Dave Richardson from a loose stroke.

The home side fell apart after tea, going from 240-4 to 262 all out. Arthurton slashed a catch to point off Meyrick Pringle before Allan Donald dismissed Williams and Adams. Snell and Pringle struck again before Patrick Patterson was run out first ball, and South Africa finished day one on 13-0.

Mark Rushmere fell cheaply to Curtly Ambrose the following morning before Andrew Hudson and Wessels turned the game South Africa's way. The West Indian pacemen were less effective than previously, after a rule change meant only one bouncer could be bowled to each batsman per over. On 22, Hudson hooked a short ball from Ambrose, but Walsh dropped a vital catch. Hudson knuckled down and showed impressive concentration and style, while Wessels scored 59 at a steady rate before falling to Ambrose, ending a 125-run partnership. Hudson gained another vital reprieve on 66, as wicketkeeper Williams dropped him off Patterson.

Peter Kirsten and Wessel 'Hansie' Cronje made little impression before being caught by Lara to produce Benjamin's and Adams' maiden Test scalps. Hudson became the first player to score a Test century on debut for South Africa after Wessels scored 162 in his Test debut for Australia in 1982–83. Hudson reached 135 at stumps, as South Africa was just eight runs behind with six wickets remaining.

South Africa led by 17 runs when Adrian Kuiper's very slow 34 ended, as Williams belatedly took a catch. South Africa was unable to build a big lead, as Adams' part-time left-arm spin produced a few wickets. Hudson eclipsed Wessels' debut Test score by one run before he was seventh out, bowled by Benjamin. Donald lasted 23 minutes without scoring before South Africa's lead was confined to 83.

Haynes was very lucky with the second delivery of the home side's second innings, as he played it onto the off-stump without removing a bail. Bosch subsequently dismissed Simmons cheaply, and a recovery was followed by Snell having Haynes caught behind and Richie Richardson lbw, as 66-1 became 68-3. Left-handers Lara and Arthurton steadied the ship, with Lara recording his first Test half-century before treading on his stumps as he played back to a Bosch delivery. The umpires, however, missed the incident and allowed Lara to continue. The hosts nonetheless stumbled again, with Donald sending Arthurton's off-stump cartwheeling before having Lara caught behind. Williams and Ambrose also departed before the West Indies began day four with a 101-run lead.

Adams plugged away and continually showed impressive composure. Following Benjamin's departure, Adams and Walsh added 25 runs before Patterson lasted 86 minutes, despite being beaten many times. Adams pierced the field around cover several times, but Wessels didn't move a fielder to deep cover. Adams produced a potentially match-turning 79 not out, as a decisive last wicket partnership of 62 expanded South Africa's target to 201.

With the pitch now uneven, Ambrose had Hudson caught at slip second ball, before Rushmere was bowled after scratching around for three runs. Wessels and Kirsten, however, survived the remaining 42 overs of the day. Wessels was on 74 and Kirsten 36 as South Africa needed just 79 more runs.

Just one run was added before Wessels edged a drive and was caught off Walsh, who subsequently cut the ball both ways while Ambrose, too, was accurate. Cronje edged Ambrose to Williams before Kuiper inside-edged Walsh, and was well caught as the wicketkeeper dived to his left. Suddenly South Africa was 131-5. Kirsten cut a four to pass 50 before playing a ball onto the stumps, and Walsh followed up with the wicket of Snell, well caught at short leg. Walsh claimed 4-8 in 11 overs as South Africa plummeted to 142-7. The tail crashed quickly, Ambrose yorking Pringle, and Dave Richardson caught behind from a slash after Richardson scored two in 50 minutes. Twenty minutes before lunch, Ambrose bowled Donald first ball to seal an amazing 52-run win for the hosts. The West Indies' 57-year unbeaten record in Barbados remained intact. The 11 West Indian players linked hands, according to Richie Richardson, to demonstrate how united they were.

Top: Fast bowler Patrick Patterson had little success with the ball when the West Indies first contested South Africa in Test cricket, but he was involved in a last wicket partnership that proved vital in the outcome of the match.

Bottom: Kepler Wessels returned to his native South Africa to play international cricket, following his time in Australia several years earlier.

WEST INDIES 1ST INNINGS

DL Haynes	c Wessels b Snell	58
PV Simmons	c Kirsten b Snell	35
BC Lara	c Richardson b Bosch	17
RB Richardson*	c Richardson b Snell	44
KLT Arthurton	c Kuiper b Pringle	59
JC Adams	b Donald	11
D Williams†	c Hudson b Donald	1
CEL Ambrose	not out	6
KCG Benjamin	b Snell	1
CA Walsh	b Pringle	6
BP Patterson	run out	0
Extras	(lb 7, nb 17)	24
Total		262

Fall of wickets 99, 106, 137, 219, 240, 241, 250, 255, 262, 262

	O	M	R	W
AA Donald	20	1	67	2
T Bosch	15	2	43	1
MW Pringle	18.4	2	62	2
RP Snell	18	3	83	4

WEST INDIES 2ND INNINGS

DL Haynes	c Richardson b Snell	23
PV Simmons	c Kirsten b Bosch	3
BC Lara	c Richardson b Donald	64
RB Richardson*	lbw b Snell	2
KLT Arthurton	b Donald	22
JC Adams	not out	79
D Williams†	lbw b Snell	5
CEL Ambrose	c Richardson b Donald	6
KCG Benjamin	lbw b Donald	7
CA Walsh	c Richardson b Snell	13
BP Patterson	b Bosch	11
Extras	(b 17, lb 11, nb 20)	48
Total		283

Fall of wickets 10, 66, 68, 120, 139, 164, 174, 196, 221, 283

	O	M	R	W
AA Donald	25	3	77	4
T Bosch	24.3	7	61	2
MW Pringle	16	0	43	0
RP Snell	16	1	74	4

SOUTH AFRICA 1ST INNINGS

MW Rushmere	c Lara b Ambrose	3
AC Hudson	b Benjamin	163
KC Wessels*	c Adams b Ambrose	59
PN Kirsten	c Lara b Benjamin	11
WJ Cronje	c Lara b Adams	5
AP Kuiper	c Williams b Patterson	34
DJ Richardson†	c Ambrose b Adams	8
RP Snell	run out	6
MW Pringle	c Walsh b Adams	15
AA Donald	st Williams b Adams	0
T Bosch	not out	5
Extras	(b 4, lb 6, w 1, nb 25)	36
Total		345

Fall of wickets 14, 139, 168, 187, 279, 293, 312, 316, 336, 345

	O	M	R	W
CEL Ambrose	36	19	47	2
BP Patterson	23	4	79	1
CA Walsh	27	7	71	0
KCG Benjamin	25	3	87	2
KLT Arthurton	3	0	8	0
JC Adams	21.5	5	43	4

SOUTH AFRICA 2ND INNINGS

AC Hudson	c Lara b Ambrose	0
MW Rushmere	b Ambrose	3
KC Wessels*	c Lara b Walsh	74
PN Kirsten	b Walsh	52
WJ Cronje	c Williams b Ambrose	2
AP Kuiper	c Williams b Walsh	0
DJ Richardson†	c Williams b Ambrose	2
RP Snell	c Adams b Walsh	0
MW Pringle	b Ambrose	4
T Bosch	not out	0
AA Donald	b Ambrose	0
Extras	(b 4, lb 3, nb 4)	11
Total		148

Fall of wickets 0, 27, 123, 130, 131, 142, 142, 147, 148, 148

	O	M	R	W
CEL Ambrose	24.4	7	34	6
BP Patterson	7	1	26	0
CA Walsh	22	10	31	4
KCG Benjamin	9	2	21	0
JC Adams	5	0	16	0
PV Simmons	5	1	13	0

Toss: South Africa   Umpires: DM Archer and SA Bucknor
Match referee: R Subba Row   West Indies won by 52 runs

Sri Lanka v Australia

First Test at Sinhalese Sports Club Ground, Colombo

1992-93

August 17, 18, 19, 21, 22 (1992)

After the first Test of the 1992–93 Sri Lanka versus Australia series, Australian skipper Allan Border said, "This must be the greatest heist since the Great Train Robbery."

This remarkable Test began when Border lost the toss and was asked to bat on a moist pitch that had some life for bowlers. After rain briefly delayed the start, Champaka Ramanayake trapped Tom Moody lbw early on, before Mark Taylor and David Boon steadied things. They took the score to 68-1 before rain forced an early lunch, then seven wickets in the second session gave the home side the upper hand. Boon was caught off part-time medium pacer Chandika Hathurusinghe on 84, before Taylor was lbw to Pramodya Wickremasinghe on 94. Hathurusinghe unexpectedly had Dean Jones lbw, Border bowled and Mark Waugh caught behind in a short space of time, before Greg Matthews became Ramanayake's second lbw victim, and Australia plunged to 124-7.

The hosts inexplicably eased off, as some needlessly defensive field placings and innocuous bowling enabled the tail to wag. Craig McDermott struck three fours and a six in his 22, and Ian Healy batted for just over three hours, scoring an undefeated 66. Shane Warne and Michael Whitney lasted longer than an hour each, as partnerships of 45 and 49 took place for the last two wickets. Australia's 256 was modest, but bigger than what might have been expected, and Sri Lanka started day two on 9-0.

Waugh struck as Hathurusinghe departed for 18, before Roshan Mahanama and Asanka Gurusinha put on an eye-catching partnership. Mahanama was stylish at times, and he hit 13 fours before Healy took a great catch to remove him for 78. Matthews had Aravinda de Silva lbw cheaply, before left-handers Gurusinha and Ranatunga put on 230 runs in 266 minutes, producing the second-biggest partnership for Sri Lanka in Test cricket at the time. Australia's fast, medium and spin bowlers were ineffective as the two left-handers dominated. In his third Test, leg-spinner Warne was treated with disdain as Ranatunga struck three sixes off him in three overs. Sri Lanka led by nine runs at stumps on day two, before Gurusinha and Ranatunga reached their centuries the following morning. Sri Lanka was 367-4 when Ranatunga was caught off Matthews, and then Marvan Atapattu was bowled first ball.

The two quick wickets did not hinder Sri Lanka's progress, as lunch was followed by pocket-sized wicketkeeper and Test debutant Romesh Kaluwitharana launching an astonishing assault on the bowling. He raced to 30 after striking seven fours, mainly with cuts and hooks, and he continued in sparkling form. He was on 77, whereas Gurusinha scored just 18 in the session before falling for 137 just before tea. Sri Lanka topped 500 for the first time in Test cricket, and Ranatunga declared on 547-8, as Kaluwitharana was unbeaten on 132 from a mere 158 balls, having hit 26 fours. Australia began day four after a rest day in a seemingly irreparable position at 26-0, trailing by 265 runs.

Moody again made little impact before succumbing to an accurate Ramanayake delivery, and Taylor again failed to push on after making a solid 40-odd. From 118-2 at lunch, the Australian batsmen plugged away at their uphill battle. Resistance and solid contributions were seen aplenty, although nobody made a big score. Boon's 68 was the highest before he was out to left-arm spinner Don Anurasiri. This ended Boon's 88-run partnership with Jones, who hit nine fours in his 57 in nearly two hours, before a great throw from Gurusinha near square leg ran him out. Anurasiri took another vital wicket as Border was caught at bat-pad with his team still 22 runs behind. Waugh scored 56 before he departed on 319, leaving a gritty Matthews to assume responsibility. Following Healy's demise for 12, McDermott again hit out effectively before Australia finished day four leading by 102 runs with three wickets remaining.

McDermott was 10 runs shy of a maiden Test 50 when Ramanayake had him lbw, before Ramanayake ended Matthews' vital 64 when Australia's lead was 140. Warne and Whitney again hung around for a while, and 40 runs were added for the last wicket. The Sri Lankans could have been better placed considering they conceded 19 no-balls in the first innings and 34 in the second, and allowed a few lower-order partnerships to get away from them. Nonetheless, Sri Lanka needed an attainable 181 runs in 58 overs to record its first Test victory over Australia.

Mahanama and Hathurusinghe provided the platform Sri Lanka sought, with a 76-run opening partnership, before Matthews dismissed Mahanama. Moody ran out Hathurusinghe four minutes later as Sri Lanka slipped to 79-2 with one session remaining, before de Silva struck seven boundaries, racing to 37 at better than a run per ball. With Gurusinha holding his ground, Sri Lanka was 127-2 when de Silva lost his cool for some reason and played a rash slog at McDermott. Border ran about 25 metres to take a superb catch, and there was little sign of what was to follow.

Sri Lanka's batsmen put their team under unnecessary pressure with silly shots when there was no need. Ranatunga and Atapattu were both out second ball, with the former caught off McDermott before the latter was again bowled by Matthews. Kaluwitharana's four was his only scoring stroke before Matthews bowled him as well, and four wickets had fallen for 10 runs. Ramanayake hit a crucial boundary before Matthews had him lbw, and Border showed his faith in Warne by bringing him on after his Test record yielded one wicket for 335 runs. As it turned out, Sri Lanka's last three batsmen presented catches off Warne in the space of 14 runs, as the tourists claimed a scarcely believable 16-run win. Sri Lanka had lost 37-8 in 17.4 overs, with Gurusinha stranded on 31 not out after lasting 135 minutes. After the remaining two Tests were drawn, Australia had a 1-0 series win.

Opening batsman Mark Taylor scored 42 and 43 in Australia's memorable come-from-behind win against Sri Lanka in 1992.

AUSTRALIA 1ST INNINGS

MA Taylor	lbw b Wickremasinghe	42
TM Moody	lbw b Ramanayake	1
DC Boon	c Ramanayake b Hathurusinghe	32
DM Jones	lbw b Hathurusinghe	10
ME Waugh	c Kaluwitharana b Hathurusinghe	5
AR Border*	b Hathurusinghe	3
GRJ Matthews	lbw b Ramanayake	6
IA Healy†	not out	66
CJ McDermott	c Ranatunga b Ramanayake	22
SK Warne	c & b Anurasiri	24
MR Whitney	c & b Wickremasinghe	13
Extras	(lb 10, w 3, nb 19)	32
Total		256

Fall of wickets 8, 84, 94, 96, 109, 118, 124, 162, 207, 256

	O	M	R	W
CPH Ramanayake	20	4	51	3
GP Wickremasinghe	18	4	69	2
UC Hathurusinghe	22	5	66	4
MAWR Madurasinghe	10	1	21	0
AP Gurusinha	2	0	17	0
SD Anurasiri	12	2	22	1

AUSTRALIA 2ND INNINGS

TM Moody	b Ramanayake	13
MA Taylor	c Gurusinha b Anurasiri	43
DC Boon	c Ranatunga b Anurasiri	68
DM Jones	run out (Gurusinha)	57
ME Waugh	c Kaluwitharana b Wickremasinghe	56
AR Border*	c Gurusinha b Anurasiri	15
GRJ Matthews	c Kaluwitharana b Ramanayake	64
IA Healy†	lbw b Hathurusinghe	12
CJ McDermott	lbw b Ramanayake	40
SK Warne	b Anurasiri	35
MR Whitney	not out	10
Extras	(lb 23, w 1, nb 34)	58
Total		471

Fall of wickets 41, 107, 195, 233, 269, 319, 361, 417, 431, 471

	O	M	R	W
CPH Ramanayake	37	10	113	3
GP Wickremasinghe	19	0	79	1
UC Hathurusinghe	27	7	79	1
SD Anurasiri	35	3	127	4
MAWR Madurasinghe	14	1	50	0

SRI LANKA 1ST INNINGS

RS Mahanama	c Healy b Waugh	78
UC Hathurusinghe	c Taylor b Waugh	18
AP Gurusinha	c Jones b Whitney	137
PA de Silva	lbw b Matthews	6
A Ranatunga*	c Warne b Matthews	127
MS Atapattu	b Matthews	0
RS Kaluwitharana†	not out	132
CPH Ramanayake	c Healy b McDermott	0
GP Wickremasinghe	c Matthews b McDermott	21
MAWR Madurasinghe	not out	5
Extras	(b 2, lb 7, w 1, nb 13)	23
Total	(8 wickets dec)	547

Did not bat SD Anurasiri

Fall of wickets 36, 128, 137, 367, 367, 463, 472, 503

	O	M	R	W
CJ McDermott	40	9	125	2
MR Whitney	32	10	84	1
TM Moody	17	3	44	0
ME Waugh	17	3	77	2
SK Warne	22	2	107	0
GRJ Matthews	38	11	93	3
AR Border	4	1	8	0

SRI LANKA 2ND INNINGS

RS Mahanama	c Boon b Matthews	39
UC Hathurusinghe	run out (Moody)	36
AP Gurusinha	not out	31
PA de Silva	c Border b McDermott	37
A Ranatunga*	c Border b McDermott	0
MS Atapattu	b Matthews	1
RS Kaluwitharana†	b Matthews	4
CPH Ramanayake	lbw b Matthews	6
GP Wickremasinghe	c Waugh b Warne	2
SD Anurasiri	c Waugh b Warne	1
MAWR Madurasinghe	c Matthews b Warne	0
Extras	(b 2, lb 3, nb 2)	7
Total		164

Fall of wickets 76, 79, 127, 132, 133, 137, 147, 150, 156, 164

	O	M	R	W
CJ McDermott	14	4	43	2
MR Whitney	5	2	13	0
TM Moody	5	0	10	0
GRJ Matthews	20	2	76	4
ME Waugh	2	0	6	0
SK Warne	5.1	3	11	3

Toss: Sri Lanka   Umpires: KT Francis and TM Samarasinghe
Match referee: FJ Cameron   Australia won by 16 runs

Australia v West Indies
Fourth Test at the Adelaide Oval

1992-93
January 23, 24, 25, 26 (1993)

The first one-run margin in Test cricket took place at the Adelaide Oval on Australia Day in 1993, when Australia contested the West Indies. Australia led the five-match series 1-0 after three Tests and had the chance to win the Frank Worrell Trophy for the first time in 15 years.

West Indies openers Desmond Haynes and Phil Simmons put on an 84-run partnership before Merv Hughes caught Simmons for 46 and then trapped Richie Richardson for two. Brian Lara remained in form following his memorable 277 in the drawn Sydney Test, but the tourists slipped from 129-2 to 134-5, after Tim May's dismissals of Haynes and Keith Arthurton were followed by Hughes dismissing Carl Hooper. In his first Test in four years and in front of his home crowd, May had Haynes stumped from a full-toss down the legside before Arthurton was caught at point. Lara and Junior Murray added 47 runs before rain forced an early tea. Afterwards, Lara fell for 52 when he edged a low catch off a wayward Craig McDermott. Murray continued to bat usefully, and Ian Bishop made 13 before Hughes struck twice in three balls. Kenny Benjamin struck 15 runs, and Murray was unconquered on 49 when Courtney Walsh became Hughes' fifth victim.

Australia scored just two runs for the loss of Mark Taylor in 33 minutes, before bad light ended day one. Taylor edged Bishop before another left-hander, Justin Langer, was quickly struck on the helmet in his Test debut. The following morning, David Boon retired hurt after a vicious Curtly Ambrose delivery thudded into his elbow. Mark Waugh was out second ball before rain delayed play for an hour, and Australia was 41-2 at lunch. Langer remained on 20 when he was caught behind trying to pull a legside delivery. Steve Waugh and Allan Border consolidated before rain cancelled the last session, with Australia 100-3.

Ambrose caused a collapse as Border and Ian Healy were

West Indies pace duo Courtney Walsh and Curtly Ambrose were a formidable force wherever they played, including in Australia, where they helped their team win the 1992–93 Frank Worrell Trophy.

caught by Hooper in one over with the score on 108, before Steve Waugh departed soon after Boon returned. Hughes struck three fours and a six and scored 43 in a 69-run partnership before edging Hooper behind. Shane Warne was lbw three balls later, before May scored six, and McDermott 14 before he backed away and was bowled after the ball struck him. The tourists built on their 39-run lead as McDermott was erratic again. He had Haynes caught behind for 11, before Richardson looked ominous. McDermott hit back when he bowled Simmons, and the visitors slipped further as Lara was caught off Hughes. Arthurton completed a pair as he edged McDermott.

The West Indies reached 124-4 before May bowled superbly to claim five wickets in 32 balls and finish with 5-9 from 6.5 overs. Hooper was caught by Hughes before Murray's defensive shot ballooned to silly mid off. Warne struck when he lured Richardson out of the crease before May dismissed Ambrose, Benjamin and Bishop. The tourists slumped from 145-6 to 146 all out. Australia thus had a tantalising target of 186 for Border to earn his first series win as captain against the West Indies. The pitch seemed fair for both sides as two days of play remained.

The hosts began poorly the next day when an Ambrose delivery in the fifth over cut in and kept low to trap Boon lbw for a duck. Benjamin came on and induced an edge from Taylor, and again Australia was 16-2 before Langer provided a rearguard action. He survived two lbw shouts, and Mark Waugh took 10 runs off one over. But after hitting four fours and scoring 26, Mark Waugh edged Walsh, where Hooper stole Lara's catch in the slips.

The Australians were in trouble first ball after lunch, as Steve Waugh's cut shot resulted in a catch to cover. A subsequent collapse made the score 74-7 to put the West Indies on course for victory. Border fended an Ambrose ripsnorter to short leg, before Healy edged his first ball onto the stumps for his second duck. Ambrose claimed his 10th wicket when he trapped Hughes, before Warne defended admirably while Langer courageously battled some fierce bowling. Langer and Warne slowly added 28 runs before Warne was lbw, and Australia needed 76 runs after tea with two wickets remaining.

On his 31st birthday, May was every bit as tough as Langer, as the duo knuckled down and resisted admirably under enormous pressure. They took every run on offer. Langer reached 50, but the milestone was virtually irrelevant. The partnership produced 42 runs in 46 minutes before Langer was again caught behind, trying to pull, with Australia 42 runs shy of victory. McDermott dug in and runs gradually accumulated. Spectators were anchored to their places.

Australian batsman Craig McDermott watches West Indies wicketkeeper Junior Murray about to take the catch off a Courtney Walsh bouncer that sealed a controversial one-run victory to the West Indies on Australia Day, 26 January 1993.

May drove a three to make the score 180-9, and then it was 181-9 when McDermott spooned a ball towards mid off where Richardson dived in vain. May tucked a subsequent delivery behind square leg but declined a risky second run, meaning Australia still needed one run to avoid defeat. McDermott clipped a ball firmly but Haynes stopped it at short leg to prevent winning runs. Walsh delivered the last ball of an over two minutes before stumps was scheduled, and McDermott tried to evade a short delivery but the ball touched something on the way to the wicketkeeper. Australian umpire Darrell Hair ruled McDermott caught behind as the West Indians celebrated, although replays suggested the ball hit McDermott's helmet grille and missed his bat and gloves. The Australians were distraught, and Border threw his so-called 'worry ball' to the ground in disgust. Subsequently, Ambrose led the West Indies to victory by an innings and 25 runs in the Perth Test.

WEST INDIES 1ST INNINGS

DL Haynes	st Healy b May	45
PV Simmons	c Hughes b SR Waugh	46
RB Richardson*	lbw b Hughes	2
BC Lara	c Healy b McDermott	52
KLT Arthurton	c SR Waugh b May	0
CL Hooper	c Healy b Hughes	2
JR Murray†	not out	49
IR Bishop	c ME Waugh b Hughes	13
CEL Ambrose	c Healy b Hughes	0
KCG Benjamin	b ME Waugh	15
CA Walsh	lbw b Hughes	5
Extras	(lb 11, nb 12)	23
Total		252

Fall of wickets 84, 99, 129, 130, 134, 189, 206, 206, 247, 252

	O	M	R	W
CJ McDermott	16	1	85	1
MG Hughes	21.3	3	64	5
SR Waugh	13	4	37	1
TBA May	14	1	41	2
SK Warne	2	0	11	0
ME Waugh	1	0	3	1

WEST INDIES 2ND INNINGS

DL Haynes	c Healy b McDermott	11
PV Simmons	b McDermott	10
RB Richardson*	c Healy b Warne	72
BC Lara	c SR Waugh b Hughes	7
KLT Arthurton	c Healy b McDermott	0
CL Hooper	c Hughes b May	25
JR Murray†	c ME Waugh b May	0
IR Bishop	c ME Waugh b May	6
CEL Ambrose	st Healy b May	1
KCG Benjamin	c Warne b May	0
CA Walsh	not out	0
Extras	(lb 2, nb 12)	14
Total		146

Fall of wickets 14, 49, 63, 65, 124, 137, 145, 146, 146, 146

	O	M	R	W
CJ McDermott	11	0	66	3
MG Hughes	13	1	43	1
SR Waugh	5	1	8	0
TBA May	6.5	3	9	5
SK Warne	6	2	18	1

AUSTRALIA 1ST INNINGS

MA Taylor	c Hooper b Bishop	1
DC Boon	not out	39
JL Langer	c Murray b Benjamin	20
ME Waugh	c Simmons b Ambrose	0
SR Waugh	c Murray b Ambrose	42
AR Border*	c Hooper b Ambrose	19
IA Healy†	c Hooper b Ambrose	0
MG Hughes	c Murray b Hooper	43
SK Warne	lbw b Hooper	0
TBA May	c Murray b Ambrose	6
CJ McDermott	b Ambrose	14
Extras	(b 7, lb 3, nb 19)	29
Total		213

Fall of wickets 1, 16, 46, 108, 108, 112, 181, 181, 197, 213

	O	M	R	W
CEL Ambrose	28.2	6	74	6
IR Bishop	18	3	48	1
KCG Benjamin	6	0	22	1
CA Walsh	10	3	34	0
CL Hooper	13	4	25	2

AUSTRALIA 2ND INNINGS

DC Boon	lbw b Ambrose	0
MA Taylor	c Murray b Benjamin	7
JL Langer	c Murray b Bishop	54
ME Waugh	c Hooper b Walsh	26
SR Waugh	c Arthurton b Ambrose	4
AR Border*	c Haynes b Ambrose	1
IA Healy†	b Walsh	0
MG Hughes	lbw b Ambrose	1
SK Warne	lbw b Bishop	9
TBA May	not out	42
CJ McDermott	c Murray b Walsh	18
Extras	(b 1, lb 8, nb 13)	22
Total		184

Fall of wickets 5, 16, 54, 64, 72, 73, 74, 102, 144, 184

	O	M	R	W
CEL Ambrose	26	5	46	4
IR Bishop	17	3	41	2
KCG Benjamin	12	2	32	1
CA Walsh	19	4	44	3
CL Hooper	5	1	12	0

Toss: West Indies   Umpires: DB Hair and LJ King
Match referee: DB Carr   West Indies won by 1 run

Sri Lanka v England
One-off Test at Sinhalese Sports Club Ground, Colombo

1992-93
March 13, 14, 15, 17, 18 (1993)

After surrendering a certain maiden Test win over Australia in August 1992, the Sri Lankans found themselves at the same ground seven months later, searching for an equally elusive maiden Test win over England.

England was not in form, having been thrashed 3-0 by India, in India, only a few weeks before the Sri Lanka tour. As if Indian conditions weren't enough, the tourists encountered steamy heat and high humidity in Colombo. With England missing Graham Gooch, Robin Smith opened the batting with Mike Atherton, after wicketkeeper and stand-in captain Alec Stewart won the toss. Sri Lanka's reliance on spin was evident as Champaka Ramanayake was the only paceman chosen. Number three batsman and part-time medium pacer Asanka Gurusinha shared the new ball and delivered five tidy overs before Jayananda Warnaweera's off-spin was introduced. Some conjecture was raised over the legality of the bowling actions of Warnaweera and fellow off-spinner Muttiah Muralidaran, but the touring team had little choice but to focus on the game.

England had 40 runs on the board when Ramanayake had Atherton lbw, before Smith and Mike Gatting survived the rest of the session. Gatting reached 29 after lunch before he was caught off Muralidaran. Smith anchored the innings, while Graeme Hick provided some impetus, and England moved into a solid position. Hick struck seven fours and two sixes, scoring 68 in a partnership of 112 in 140 minutes, before Muralidaran broke through again. Smith and Stewart guided England to 245-3 at stumps, with Smith on 91.

Smith remained the anchorman on day two, while Stewart was more brisk. Smith's century was his first as a Test opener, and he reached 128, with England at a commanding 316-3 before Muralidaran bowled him. Stewart's departure seven runs later was another blow considering Stewart, like Hick,

had found form without converting it into a big score. The left-handed Neil Fairbrother and all-rounder Chris Lewis added 35 runs before Warnaweera bowled Fairbrother to further hinder England's progress. Lewis' demise to a run out eight runs later was something England could ill afford. Then Paul Jarvis was lbw first ball, and Phil Tufnell was similarly dismissed as the tourists lost 9-4, including 1-3. Devon Malcolm thumped two sixes before Warnaweera matched Muralidaran with four scalps, while John Emburey was stranded on one not out in 46 minutes.

Roshan Mahanama gave the home side a flying start with regular boundaries. He raced to 68, with 11 fours in an opening stand of 99 at nearly a run per minute, before off-spinner Emburey showed his knack of snaring a key wicket. Despite some good bowling, England did not strike again on day two, as Sri Lanka reached 140-1 at stumps.

Lewis was rewarded the following morning when Chandika Hathurusinghe was caught behind for 59 at 153-2. A subsequent 50-run partnership unfolded before Tufnell had Gurusinha stumped. The bowlers toiled away in the heat as the England players' shirts became soaked with sweat. Aravinda de Silva and Arjuna Ranatunga put on a handsome partnership as they scored at a steady rate and showed good technique in their strokes. They took their team to 330-3 before catches behind accounted for both, as England struck back to have the locals 339-5. Hashan Tillekeratne took on an anchoring role, but the lower order struggled as Lewis, Emburey and Jarvis struck to have Sri Lanka eight-down and four runs behind. Muralidaran, however, hung around until stumps while Tillekeratne moved to 51 as Sri Lanka led by 28 runs.

Taking the final two wickets after the rest day did not prove a formality as Tillekeratne and Muralidaran kept frustrating the visitors. When Lewis bowled Muralidaran, the batsman had scored 19 in 153 minutes in a partnership of 83. Warnaweera's dismissal left Tillekeratne stranded on 93 not out, as Sri Lanka gained an 89-run lead.

Ramanayake and Gurusinha bowled only briefly, but the latter gave Sri Lanka a bonus with the cheap removal of Atherton. Gatting hit four fours in a quick 18 before a careless shot off Warnaweera cost him. Runs subsequently flowed through Smith and Hick, but faulty shots caused their dismissals when they were well set. Smith perished to Sanath Jayasuriya's left-arm spin for 35, and Hick was caught off Warnaweera after hitting two fours and a six in his 26. England was in tatters at 96-5 when Warnaweera accounted for Stewart. Lewis counterattacked, scoring 45 in an hour, but Fairbrother's dismissal to a run out was another setback before Lewis was caught, making England 153-7.

Emburey provided a rearguard action while Jarvis and Tufnell helped take the score to 188 before Emburey passed 50. He and Malcolm put on 38 precious runs before stumps. Gurusinha's bowling came in handy again when he bowled Emburey after just two runs were scored on day four, while Malcolm staked another claim for batting higher than number 11 as he lasted 64 minutes, albeit for eight not out.

Chasing 140 runs, Sri Lanka faltered early when Lewis had Mahanama caught behind for six. Malcolm bowled only three overs, and fellow pacemen Lewis and Jarvis were economical before spin was utilised. Hathurusinghe was very slow as Gurusinha scored 29 in a 40-run partnership before Emburey bowled him. Sri Lanka lost two wickets on 61, with de Silva falling to Emburey before Hathurusinghe's two-hour innings of 14 ended, as wicketkeeper Stewart claimed his sixth dismissal of the match.

Sri Lankans must have hoped there would be no repeat of their collapse against Australia seven months earlier. One major difference was that Tillekeratne did not play then. He again foiled England as he used his feet well to the spinners, while Ranatunga established himself and batted sensibly. Ranatunga was caught as his team was four runs shy of victory, before the game was over one ball later, as Jayasuriya pulled his first delivery over the boundary. Sri Lanka had now enjoyed Test series wins over India, Pakistan, New Zealand and England.

England opening batsman Mike Atherton battled back injuries for parts of his Test career, which went from 1989 to 2001.

ENGLAND 1ST INNINGS

RA Smith	b Muralidaran	128
MA Atherton	lbw b Ramanayake	13
MW Gatting	c Jayasuriya b Muralidaran	29
GA Hick	c Tillekeratne b Muralidaran	68
AJ Stewart*†	c Tillekeratne b Warnaweera	63
NH Fairbrother	b Warnaweera	18
CC Lewis	run out	22
JE Emburey	not out	1
PW Jarvis	lbw b Warnaweera	0
PCR Tufnell	lbw b Muralidaran	1
DE Malcolm	c Gurusinha b Warnaweera	13
Extras	(b 5, lb 3, w 1, nb 15)	24
Total		380

Fall of wickets 40, 82, 194, 316, 323, 358, 366, 366, 367, 380

	O	M	R	W
CPH Ramanayake	17	2	66	1
AP Gurusinha	5	1	12	0
KPJ Warnaweera	40.1	11	90	4
UC Hathurusinghe	8	2	22	0
M Muralidaran	45	12	118	4
ST Jayasuriya	12	1	53	0
A Ranatunga	3	0	11	0

ENGLAND 2ND INNINGS

RA Smith	b Jayasuriya	35
MA Atherton	c Tillekeratne b Gurusinha	2
MW Gatting	c Tillekeratne b Warnaweera	18
GA Hick	c Ramanayake b Warnaweera	26
AJ Stewart*†	c Mahanama b Warnaweera	3
NH Fairbrother	run out	3
CC Lewis	c Jayasuriya b Muralidaran	45
JE Emburey	b Gurusinha	59
PW Jarvis	st AM de Silva b Jayasuriya	3
PCR Tufnell	c AM de Silva b Warnaweera	1
DE Malcolm	not out	8
Extras	(b 4, lb 2, w 1, nb 18)	25
Total		228

Fall of wickets 16, 38, 83, 91, 96, 130, 153, 173, 188, 228

	O	M	R	W
CPH Ramanayake	3	0	16	0
AP Gurusinha	6	3	7	2
KPJ Warnaweera	25	4	98	4
M Muralidaran	16	3	55	1
ST Jayasuriya	16	3	46	2

SRI LANKA 1ST INNINGS

RS Mahanama	c Smith b Emburey	64
UC Hathurusinghe	c Stewart b Lewis	59
AP Gurusinha	st Stewart b Tufnell	43
PA de Silva	c Stewart b Jarvis	80
A Ranatunga*	c Stewart b Lewis	64
HP Tillekeratne	not out	93
ST Jayasuriya	c Atherton b Lewis	4
AM de Silva†	c Gatting b Emburey	9
CPH Ramanayake	c Lewis b Jarvis	1
M Muralidaran	b Lewis	19
KPJ Warnaweera	b Jarvis	1
Extras	(b 2, lb 13, w 2, nb 15)	32
Total		469

Fall of wickets 99, 153, 203, 330, 339, 349, 371, 376, 459, 469

	O	M	R	W
DE Malcolm	25	7	60	0
PW Jarvis	25.5	1	76	3
CC Lewis	31	5	66	4
PCR Tufnell	33	5	108	1
JE Emburey	34	6	117	2
GA Hick	8	0	27	0

SRI LANKA 2ND INNINGS

RS Mahanama	c Stewart b Lewis	6
UC Hathurusinghe	c Stewart b Tufnell	14
AP Gurusinha	b Emburey	29
PA de Silva	c Jarvis b Emburey	7
A Ranatunga*	c Gatting b Tufnell	35
HP Tillekeratne	not out	36
ST Jayasuriya	not out	6
Extras	(b 1, lb 2, nb 6)	9
Total	(5 wickets)	142

Did not bat AM de Silva†, CPH Ramanayake, M Muralidaran, KPJ Warnaweera

Fall of wickets 8, 48, 61, 61, 136

	O	M	R	W
DE Malcolm	3	1	11	0
PW Jarvis	8	2	14	0
CC Lewis	8	1	21	1
PCR Tufnell	7.4	1	34	2
JE Emburey	14	2	48	2
GA Hick	2	0	11	0

Toss: England   Umpires: KT Francis and TM Samarasinghe   Match referee: CW Smith   Sri Lanka won by 5 wickets

Australia v South Africa
Second Test at the Sydney Cricket Ground

1993-94
January 2, 3, 4, 5, 6 (1994)

Being on the losing side after taking 12 wickets in a Test match would never feel good, and Shane Warne experienced this, as the Australians squandered a Test that was theirs for the taking. The Test provided some resemblance to Australia's losses at Leeds and Birmingham in 1981, only this time the Australians were on home soil while South Africa was the visitor. South Africa had not contested Australia at Test level since 1969–70, and Kepler Wessels now led his homeland against the country he had represented while South Africa was banned from international sport.

The rain-affected first Test in Melbourne was drawn, before Wessels won the toss and chose to bat in the second Test. South Africa began poorly as Andrew Hudson was lbw in the second over, although replays suggested the ball may have missed the stumps. Gary Kirsten and Hansie Cronje batted doggedly and steered the tourists to 91-1 before Cronje was well caught by a diving Mark Waugh behind point, 40 minutes into the second session. Daryll Cullinan struck two fours, and then Warne took five wickets before tea to break the back of the South African innings. Cullinan, Rhodes and Kirsten succumbed to Warne's flipper, and Kirsten's dismissal also featured some quick glovework from Ian Healy. Mark Taylor took a brilliant left-handed catch after Dave Richardson edged a prod, before Wessels drove a low full-toss back to the bowler who dived to take the catch.

Warne dismissed Craig Matthews and Pat Symcox with leg breaks after play resumed, with Symcox out to a wickedly turning delivery from around the wicket. Petrus 'Fanie' de Villiers scored 18 after batting for nearly an hour at number 10, before Craig McDermott dismissed him as the Africans were all out for 169, with Warne taking 7-56. Allan Donald

The new South African flag flies in January 1994 during South Africa's first cricket tour of Australia since 1966–67.

had Taylor caught behind just 20 minutes into the Australian innings, and the locals reached 20-1 after 12 overs when day one concluded.

David Boon and Mark Waugh were dismissed before lunch on day two, while Michael Slater played some attractive strokes on his way to a half-century. After the home side scored 75 runs in the first session, the South Africans were tight, as Slater and Allan Border added just 50 runs between lunch and tea. Australia gained a first innings lead before Border and Slater fell with the total on 179 to dent the team's progress. Border was on 49 when wicketkeeper Richardson jumped to snare an edged cut, before Slater was bowled by Donald for 92. Australia reached 200-5 by stumps, and progressed to 229-5 the next day before Healy was dismissed. The Australian innings neither collapsed nor consolidated, as Damien Martyn was the mainstay in subsequent partnerships of 21, 16 and 15 before he departed for 59. Glenn McGrath exceeded expectations with nine runs, his highest Test score at the time, before Australia finished with a lead of 123.

Hudson failed miserably again, before Kirsten and Cronje provided solidity. McDermott again produced the key breakthrough, this time when Kirsten was bowled for 41, before South Africa finished day three 29 runs behind Australia. Wessels batted bravely after splitting his left hand the previous day when unsuccessfully attempting a catch.

On day four, Cronje again failed to build on a platform before Wessels once more fell to Warne. South Africa was still 13 runs in arrears when Cullinan also fell to Warne for the second time in the match. Rhodes and Richardson put on a 72-run partnership to give the Africans some hope of setting Australia a worthy target, until a collapse of 21-4 seemed to ruin their chances. McGrath and McDermott struck before Warne broke through twice within 20 minutes. Donald, however, survived for 42 minutes while Rhodes hit McDermott for six and played other attacking strokes in a vital 36-run partnership for the last wicket. Australia's target of 117 was still small, and Warne had match figures of 12-128 from 69 overs.

Australia was set back early as de Villiers hit Slater's off stump, before Donald spilled a simple return catch that Boon offered. It seemed crucial as the score reached 51-1 before Boon clipped a catch to short leg. Tim May's entrance as nightwatchman backfired as de Villiers trapped him plumb first ball, and Australia suddenly fell to 56-4 as Taylor edged de Villiers. Border reached seven at stumps, and his team needed 54 runs on day five as the hosts were similarly placed to the Australian teams in the 1981 Leeds and Birmingham Tests.

Border made a fatal error with the second ball of day five when he shouldered arms to a delivery that clipped the top of his off-stump. Donald struck another blow nine runs later when a yorker accounted for Waugh. Healy inside-edged a de Villiers delivery onto the stumps, before Warne was run out to make the score 75-8. As the target was now difficult, Martyn defended persistently under pressure and didn't appear willing to play strokes. McDermott, however, batted confidently and struck four boundaries as the total crept to 110. With Australia back on course for victory, Martyn suddenly aimed a big drive at Donald but succeeded only in hitting a catch straight to Hudson at cover. After scoring 0 and 1, perhaps Hudson had belatedly made a telling contribution.

McGrath scored a single, and crucially retained the strike for the next over, to be bowled by de Villiers. From the third ball, McGrath came forward but pushed the ball in the air and was caught by the bowler. McGrath was distraught as South Africa

Shane Warne took 12 wickets in the Sydney Test of 1994, but was on the losing team after being part of a staggering batting collapse against South Africa.

clinched an incredible five-run win, and de Villiers rather than Warne was the hero, finishing with 10 wickets for the victors. Martyn meanwhile became the scapegoat, and he had to wait six years before he played another Test. Steve Waugh replaced Martyn for the third Test, and excelled with a big century and four wickets, as Australia levelled the three-Test series with a 191-run win.

SOUTH AFRICA 1ST INNINGS

AC Hudson	lbw b McGrath	0
G Kirsten	st Healy b Warne	67
WJ Cronje	c Waugh b McDermott	41
DJ Cullinan	b Warne	9
JN Rhodes	lbw b Warne	4
KC Wessels*	c & b Warne	3
DJ Richardson†	c Taylor b Warne	4
PL Symcox	b Warne	7
CR Matthews	c Taylor b Warne	0
PS de Villiers	c Waugh b McDermott	18
AA Donald	not out	0
Extras	(b 1, lb 4, nb 11)	16
Total		169

Fall of wickets 1, 91, 110, 133, 134, 141, 142, 142, 152, 169

	O	M	R	W
CJ McDermott	18.1	2	42	2
GD McGrath	19	5	32	1
SK Warne	27	8	56	7
TBA May	10	1	34	0

AUSTRALIA 1ST INNINGS

MJ Slater	b Donald	92
MA Taylor	c Richardson b Donald	7
DC Boon	b de Villiers	19
ME Waugh	lbw b Symcox	7
AR Border*	c Richardson b de Villiers	49
DR Martyn	c Richardson b de Villiers	59
IA Healy†	c Richardson b Donald	19
SK Warne	c Rhodes b Symcox	11
CJ McDermott	c Cronje b de Villiers	6
TBA May	not out	8
GD McGrath	b Donald	9
Extras	(b 1, lb 2, nb 3)	6
Total		292

Fall of wickets 10, 58, 75, 179, 179, 229, 250, 266, 281, 292

	O	M	R	W
AA Donald	31.2	8	83	4
PS de Villiers	36	12	80	4
CR Matthews	28	11	44	0
PL Symcox	46	11	82	2

SOUTH AFRICA 2ND INNINGS

AC Hudson	c Healy b McDermott	1
G Kirsten	b McDermott	41
WJ Cronje	b McDermott	38
KC Wessels*	b Warne	18
DJ Cullinan	lbw b Warne	2
JN Rhodes	not out	76
DJ Richardson†	lbw b McGrath	24
PL Symcox	c Healy b McDermott	4
CR Matthews	c Waugh b Warne	4
PS de Villiers	lbw b Warne	2
AA Donald	c Healy b Warne	10
Extras	(b 13, lb 1, nb 5)	19
Total		239

Fall of wickets 2, 75, 101, 107, 110, 182, 188, 197, 203, 239

	O	M	R	W
CJ McDermott	28	9	62	4
GD McGrath	14	3	30	1
TBA May	22	4	53	0
SK Warne	42	17	72	5
AR Border	3	1	8	0

AUSTRALIA 2ND INNINGS

MA Taylor	c Richardson b de Villiers	27
MJ Slater	b de Villiers	1
DC Boon	c Kirsten b de Villiers	24
TBA May	lbw b de Villiers	0
ME Waugh	lbw b Donald	11
AR Border*	b Donald	7
DR Martyn	c Hudson b Donald	6
IA Healy†	b de Villiers	1
SK Warne	run out	1
CJ McDermott	not out	29
GD McGrath	c & b de Villiers	1
Extras	(lb 3)	3
Total		111

Fall of wickets 4, 51, 51, 56, 63, 72, 73, 75, 110, 111

	O	M	R	W
AA Donald	17	5	34	3
PS de Villiers	23.3	8	43	6
CR Matthews	6	5	9	0
PL Symcox	10	3	22	0

Toss: South Africa Umpires: SG Randell and WP Sheahan
TV umpire: IS Thomas   Match referee: JL Hendriks   South Africa won by 5 runs

Pakistan v Australia

First Test at National Stadium, Karachi

1994-95

September 28, 29, 30, October 1, 2 (1994)

Pakistan's Mushtaq Ahmed (right) celebrates after taking a wicket against Australia.

Whenever the last ball of a Test match has the capacity to produce match-winning runs for one team, or a wicket to seal victory for the other team, the Test is bound to be memorable. This was certainly the case at Karachi in 1994, in the first Test of a Pakistan versus Australia series.

Allan Border's retirement paved the way for Mark Taylor to start his reign as Australia's captain. Taylor won the toss and chose to bat on a flat wicket that looked conducive to making runs, but Australia didn't start well. Craig McDermott pulled out with a toe injury and was replaced by Jo Angel. Taylor miscued a legside stroke and was caught-and-bowled by Wasim Akram without scoring. David Boon and Mark Waugh began soundly before falling to Mushtaq Ahmed's leg-spin, then Wasim's dismissal of Michael Slater before lunch left Australia struggling at 95-4.

In his Test debut, the left-handed Michael Bevan batted confidently while Steve Waugh struck regular fours and scored quickly. The duo put on 121 runs in 109 minutes before Waqar Younis bowled Waugh for 73, which included 13 fours. Ian Healy continued the scoring, and Bevan hit 12 fours before falling for 82. Healy posted a half-century and combined with Shane Warne to take the score to 325 before Warne was caught behind at the end of the day's play.

Only 12 runs were added the next morning as Waqar and Wasim cleaned up the tail, before Pakistan's left-handed openers Saeed Anwar and Aamir Sohail put on 90 runs. Bevan took his first Test catch to produce the first wicket, and then a solid-looking Zahid Fazal and free-flowing Anwar took the score to 153, before Tim May crucially had Anwar caught just before tea. Pakistan faltered as May dismissed Fazal soon after the break, before Glenn McGrath dismissed Basit Ali for a duck. Inzamam-ul-Haq and Rashid Latif were caught by Taylor at slip off Warne, and Salim Malik was lbw to Angel as the home side struggled to 209-7 at stumps. Wasim went on to score a crucial 39 while Akram Raza and Waqar made minor contributions before Angel polished off the innings as Australia gained an 81-run lead.

Taylor completed a pair when he edged a Waqar slower ball to the wicketkeeper, and Slater started soundly before again falling lbw just before lunch. Boon and Mark Waugh showed some excellent form in a 122-run partnership, before Waqar wrecked the latter's stumps. Australia's momentum stalled as Wasim fired out Bevan and Steve Waugh for golden ducks, but the tourists were soundly placed with two days left as they led by 262 runs with five wickets remaining.

Boon went from 85 to 114 on day four but he played a lone hand, with Waqar and Wasim going through the tail as Australia lost 19-5. Pakistan required 314 to win with more than a day-and-a-half remaining, and Sohail was the chief scorer in the opening partnership this time, before he was run out with the total on 45. Fazal was caught by Boon for the second time as Pakistan fell to 64-2, before Anwar and Malik led a revival. Australia was rocked when McGrath was unable to bowl more than six overs due to a hamstring injury, while May struggled with a neck injury. Anwar and Malik added 84 runs before Malik succumbed to an Angel bouncer, and Pakistan was 155-3 with one day left.

Warne accounted for nightwatchman Raza early on the final day, before Angel took the prized scalp of Anwar. Australia was poised for victory after Warne dismissed Wasim and Basit to make the score 184-7. Latif batted for just over an hour and scored a crucial 35 before Steve Waugh had him lbw, and then Waqar lasted 37 minutes before skying a catch, giving Warne his eighth wicket of the match. Mushtaq joined Inzamam, as the duo required a last-wicket partnership of 56 for a Pakistani victory, and the 42 minutes that followed will surely not be forgotten by those who saw it.

Despite the absence of McGrath and May, the Australians seemed to have the match in their keeping as Angel and Warne sought the last wicket. Inzamam and Mushtaq whittled away at the target, and a couple of close lbw appeals were turned down. Angel's reaction to Pakistani umpire Khizer Hayat's denial of an appeal against Inzamam led to Angel later being cautioned by match referee John Reid. Mushtaq hit two boundaries and moved to 20, while Inzamam progressed to 58, and Pakistan suddenly needed just three more runs to win.

As fate panned out, a flighted delivery determined the result. Inzamam used his feet and tried to work Warne through mid wicket. He missed, and a stumping beckoned for an Australian win. But Healy also missed the ball, which kept low. It shot between his legs and raced to the boundary for byes (incorrectly ruled leg byes) to seal a Pakistan win.

Taylor reflected in his book *Taylor Made*: "Really, this was the Test match that got away ... We did everything right and lost by a wicket ... I think I've experienced just about every possible emotion – except for the thrill of a victory – that a captain can experience in one Test."

Healy's missed stumping was just one of many decisive incidents throughout the course of the five-day game, and turned out to be one of a number of missed opportunities for Australia in the series. Taylor dropped a vital catch to reprieve Malik in the second Test, before Malik scored 237 and guaranteed a draw. The third Test was also drawn, as Pakistan somewhat fortuitously achieved a 1-0 series win.

AUSTRALIA 1ST INNINGS

MJ Slater	lbw b Wasim Akram	36
MA Taylor*	c & b Wasim Akram	0
DC Boon	b Mushtaq Ahmed	19
ME Waugh	c Zahid Fazal b Mushtaq Ahmed	20
MG Bevan	c Aamir Sohail b Mushtaq Ahmed	82
SR Waugh	b Waqar Younis	73
IA Healy†	c Rashid Latif b Waqar Younis	57
SK Warne	c Rashid Latif b Aamir Sohail	22
J Angel	b Wasim Akram	5
TBA May	not out	1
GD McGrath	b Waqar Younis	0
Extras	(b 2, lb 12, nb 8)	22
Total		337

Fall of wickets 12, 41, 75, 95, 216, 281, 325, 335, 335, 337

	O	M	R	W
Wasim Akram	25	4	75	3
Waqar Younis	19.2	2	75	3
Mushtaq Ahmed	24	2	97	3
Akram Raza	14	1	50	0
Aamir Sohail	5	0	19	1
Salim Malik	1	0	7	0

PAKISTAN 1ST INNINGS

Saeed Anwar	c ME Waugh b May	85
Aamir Sohail	c Bevan b Warne	36
Zahid Fazal	c Boon b May	27
Salim Malik*	lbw b Angel	26
Basit Ali	c Bevan b McGrath	0
Inzamam-ul-Haq	c Taylor b Warne	9
Rashid Latif†	c Taylor b Warne	2
Wasim Akram	c Healy b Angel	39
Akram Raza	b McGrath	13
Waqar Younis	c Healy b Angel	6
Mushtaq Ahmed	not out	2
Extras	(lb 7, nb 4)	11
Total		256

Fall of wickets 90, 153, 154, 157, 175, 181, 200, 234, 253, 256

	O	M	R	W
GD McGrath	25	6	70	2
J Angel	13.1	0	54	3
TBA May	20	5	55	2
SK Warne	27	10	61	3
SR Waugh	2	0	9	0

AUSTRALIA 2ND INNINGS

MA Taylor*	c Rashid Latif b Waqar Younis	0
MJ Slater	lbw b Mushtaq Ahmed	23
DC Boon	not out	114
ME Waugh	b Waqar Younis	61
MG Bevan	b Wasim Akram	0
SR Waugh	lbw b Wasim Akram	0
IA Healy†	c Rashid Latif b Wasim Akram	8
SK Warne	lbw b Waqar Younis	0
J Angel	c Rashid Latif b Wasim Akram	8
TBA May	b Wasim Akram	1
GD McGrath	b Waqar Younis	1
Extras	(b 7, lb 4, nb 5)	16
Total		232

Fall of wickets 1, 49, 171, 174, 174, 213, 218, 227, 229, 232

	O	M	R	W
Wasim Akram	22	3	63	5
Waqar Younis	18	2	69	4
Mushtaq Ahmed	21	3	51	1
Akram Raza	10	1	19	0
Aamir Sohail	7	0	19	0

PAKISTAN 2ND INNINGS

Saeed Anwar	c & b Angel	77
Aamir Sohail	run out	34
Zahid Fazal	c Boon b Warne	3
Salim Malik*	c Taylor b Angel	43
Akram Raza	lbw b Warne	2
Basit Ali	lbw b Warne	12
Wasim Akram	c & b Warne	4
Inzamam-ul-Haq	not out	58
Rashid Latif†	lbw b SR Waugh	35
Waqar Younis	c Healy b Warne	7
Mushtaq Ahmed	not out	20
Extras	(b 4, lb 13, nb 3)	20
Total	(9 wickets)	315

Fall of wickets 45, 64, 148, 157, 174, 179, 184, 236, 258

	O	M	R	W
GD McGrath	6	2	18	0
J Angel	28	10	92	2
SR Waugh	15	3	28	1
SK Warne	36.1	12	89	5
TBA May	18	4	67	0
ME Waugh	3	1	4	0

Toss: Australia   Umpires: HD Bird and Khizer Hayat
TV umpire: Riazuddin   Match referee: JR Reid
Pakistan won by 1 wicket

Australia v England
Third Test at the Sydney Cricket Ground

1994-95
January 1, 2, 3, 4, 5 (1995)

Big wins to Australia in Brisbane and Melbourne drew some resemblance to the corresponding Ashes series four years earlier, and a great third Test again unfolded as England sought to keep the series alive.

England batted first for the first time in the series, and was soon floundering at 20-3. Graham Gooch edged Damien Fleming to Ian Healy in the second over before Craig McDermott flattened Graeme Hick's leg-stump and trapped Graham Thorpe lbw. Mike Atherton survived a close lbw shout, before he and John Crawley rallied with a 174-run partnership, after there had been ample press coverage calling for Atherton to be sacked as captain. The pendulum swung back Australia's way after the new ball was taken, as England fell to 198-7 at stumps. McDermott bowled Atherton through the gate with an off cutter, before Mike Gatting edged behind four balls later without scoring. Crawley edged Fleming to slip, and Steve Rhodes was run out. Australian skipper Mark Taylor deemed it a strange day's cricket, considering Australia took three wickets in the first hour and four in the last 30 minutes, but none in between.

The tourists recovered on day two as Darren Gough swung the bat to good effect and scored 51. Gough hooked a six off McDermott before another hook shot produced a catch to Fleming. Angus Fraser provided solid resistance, and Devon Malcolm made his best Test score: 29. Malcolm clouted two fours and two big sixes off Shane Warne, and slogged McDermott for a four. Lunch was taken as England was all out for 309, and then Australia was 4-0 from 3.3 overs before rain washed out the rest of the day's play.

With the ball moving about on day three, England's pace bowlers were in devastating form as the tourists set about staying in contention for the Ashes. Michael Slater scored 11

Angus Fraser took seven wickets in the Sydney Test of 1995, but it wasn't quite enough for England to achieve the victory it needed to stay in the hunt for the Ashes.

before inside-edging a defensive shot and losing two stumps. David Boon offered no stroke to a ball that flattened his off-stump, and Mark Waugh edged a catch behind to make the score 18-3 with Taylor still on zero. He finally scored from the 36th ball he faced, and Michael Bevan lasted 56 minutes before his dismissal sparked another collapse. Steve Waugh also had a stump dislodged, and then Healy scored 10 before edging to slip on the stroke of lunch as Australia crumbled to 57-6. After Warne and Tim May were caught without scoring, Australia needed 45 more runs to avoid the follow-on.

McDermott batted soundly, and the hosts averted the follow-on thanks to a few mistakes from Malcolm. Malcolm dropped a tough return catch to reprieve Taylor, before being slow in the field when McDermott miscued an airy hit in his direction. A bouncer from Malcolm went over the wicketkeeper's head for four byes to ensure England would have to bat next, but the tourists had a 193-run lead. Taylor was on 49 when he spooned a slow leg break back to Gough, who took his sixth wicket with the next delivery as he destroyed Fleming's stumps.

Gooch and Atherton put on 54 runs in an hour before Gooch was lbw to Fleming, and rain shortened the session. England began day four on 90-1. Atherton progressed to 67 before Fleming dismissed him, while Hick hit 10 fours and a six in a chancy innings. He survived a caught behind appeal on 33, and later played a ball from May onto the stumps without removing a bail. Hick gained another reprieve when he was caught behind off a McDermott no-ball. Hick was just two runs shy of his first Ashes century while Thorpe was three runs shy of a half-century when Atherton sensationally declared the innings closed, leaving Australia with a target of 449.

The eight overs before tea produced an interesting tussle between Malcolm and Taylor, who was hit on the gloves before slashing at a wide delivery and edging a boundary over the slips. Malcolm banged a short ball in next and was promptly hit

for another four. The openers lasted until lunch the next day as a record-winning Test cricket run chase looked a possibility. After Australia began the last day on 139-0, Crawley crucially dropped a straightforward catch to reprieve Slater in the first hour. Slater was on 102 and Taylor 94 at lunch as Australia needed a further 243 to win while England needed 10 wickets. Unfortunately the rain returned and prevented play resuming until 3.30pm. A result looked unlikely, as Australia was intent on survival while time wasn't on England's side.

Slater, however, added just one more run before an airy pull shot was well caught by a running and jumping Phil Tufnell in the deep. Taylor and Boon batted carefully in greasy and tough conditions, and then light rain fell, but play continued. Taylor reached 113 before Malcolm bowled him, and Boon's resistance ended about 30 minutes later when he edged a defensive shot to Hick at slip. Fraser subsequently induced a collapse as Australia lost 10-4, with Bevan and Steve Waugh edging behind before Mark Waugh was plumb lbw. Healy also edged behind, and play was extended beyond 7pm to make up for lost time, with England needing just three more wickets. But with dark clouds hovering, the tourists were forced to use slow bowlers for safety reasons, after the new ball had been used for just 10 overs.

Tufnell, Hick and Gooch couldn't break through as Warne and May survived 77 minutes and put on 52 runs. In what was believed to be the last over, Warne drove wildly at Gooch and was dropped by Malcolm at mid off. Moments later, Warne and May were joyful as the players exited the arena, but another twist unfolded as the umpires realised the final hour's play wasn't completed. May survived four subsequent deliveries from Tufnell, and the Ashes were securely in Australia's grasp for a fourth successive series.

ENGLAND 1ST INNINGS

GA Gooch	c Healy b Fleming	1
MA Atherton*	b McDermott	88
GA Hick	b McDermott	2
GP Thorpe	lbw b McDermott	10
JP Crawley	c ME Waugh b Fleming	72
MW Gatting	c Healy b McDermott	0
ARC Fraser	c Healy b Fleming	27
SJ Rhodes†	run out (SR Waugh/Fleming/Healy)	1
D Gough	c Fleming b McDermott	51
DE Malcolm	b Warne	29
PCR Tufnell	not out	4
Extras	(b 8, lb 7, nb 9)	24
Total		309

Fall of wickets 1, 10, 20, 194, 194, 196, 197, 255, 295, 309

	O	M	R	W
CJ McDermott	30	7	101	5
DW Fleming	26.2	12	52	3
SK Warne	36	10	88	1
TBA May	17	4	35	0
ME Waugh	6	1	10	0
MG Bevan	4	1	8	0

ENGLAND 2ND INNINGS

GA Gooch	lbw b Fleming	29
MA Atherton*	c Taylor b Fleming	67
GA Hick	not out	98
GP Thorpe	not out	47
Extras	(lb 6, w 1, nb 7)	14
Total	(2 wickets dec)	255

Did not bat JP Crawley, MW Gatting, ARC Fraser, SJ Rhodes†, D Gough, DE Malcolm, PCR Tufnell

Fall of wickets 54, 158

	O	M	R	W
CJ McDermott	24	2	76	0
DW Fleming	20	3	66	2
ME Waugh	2	1	4	0
SK Warne	16	2	48	0
TBA May	10	1	55	0

AUSTRALIA 1ST INNINGS

MJ Slater	b Malcolm	11
MA Taylor*	c & b Gough	49
DC Boon	b Gough	3
ME Waugh	c Rhodes b Malcolm	3
MG Bevan	c Thorpe b Fraser	8
SR Waugh	b Gough	1
IA Healy†	c Hick b Gough	10
SK Warne	c Gatting b Fraser	0
TBA May	c Hick b Gough	0
CJ McDermott	not out	21
DW Fleming	b Gough	0
Extras	(b 6, lb 1, nb 3)	10
Total		116

Fall of wickets 12, 15, 18, 38, 39, 57, 62, 65, 116, 116

	O	M	R	W
DE Malcolm	13	4	34	2
D Gough	18.5	4	49	6
ARC Fraser	11	1	26	2

AUSTRALIA 2ND INNINGS

MA Taylor*	b Malcolm	113
MJ Slater	c Tufnell b Fraser	103
DC Boon	c Hick b Gough	17
ME Waugh	lbw b Fraser	25
MG Bevan	c Rhodes b Fraser	7
SR Waugh	c Rhodes b Fraser	0
IA Healy†	c Rhodes b Fraser	5
SK Warne	not out	36
TBA May	not out	10
Extras	(b 12, lb 3, w 1, nb 12)	28
Total	(7 wickets)	344

Did not bat CJ McDermott, DW Fleming

Fall of wickets 208, 239, 265, 282, 286, 289, 292

	O	M	R	W
DE Malcolm	21	4	75	1
D Gough	28	4	72	1
ARC Fraser	25	3	73	5
PCR Tufnell	35.4	9	61	0
GA Hick	5	0	21	0
GA Gooch	7	1	27	0

Toss: England   Umpires: SA Bucknor and DB Hair
TV umpire: WA Cameron   Match referee: JR Reid
Match drawn

Pakistan v Sri Lanka
Second Test at Iqbal Stadium, Faisalabad

1995-96
September 15, 16, 17, 18, 19 (1995)

Sri Lanka's winless trot on Pakistan soil was broken in a memorable Test at Faisalabad in September 1995, although nobody could have seen it coming. Pakistan won the first Test at Peshawar by an innings, and then elected to field first at Faisalabad. Wasim Akram trapped Roshan Mahanama lbw, not offering a shot with the fifth ball of the match, and one might have thought another rout was on the cards. Pakistan however missed Waqar Younis with a stress fracture while Sri Lanka welcomed back Aravinda de Silva.

Indiscreet shots were fatal as Sri Lanka flopped from 32-1 to 33-4. Asanka Gurusinha scored just nine in an hour before pulling an Aaqib Javed delivery from outside off-stump, then Saqlain Mushtaq struck with consecutive deliveries. De Silva offered an easy return catch before Arjuna Ranatunga was caught at short leg from a faulty sweep. Sri Lanka's position could have been worse, but opener Chandika Hathurusinghe was earlier dropped at slip when on one. Hathurusinghe went on to 47 before becoming paceman Mohammad Akram's first Test scalp, as the batsman flicked to mid wicket. Kumar Dharmasena was run out with the total still on 117, and Chamara Dunusinghe hit a six and a four before Wasim trapped him for 12.

Hashan Tillekeratne was Sri Lanka's saviour, batting with composure and determination. He struck three successive fours off Saqlain, and went on to score a century. Fellow left-hander Chaminda Vaas hung around while 64 runs were added, before both batsmen departed with the total on 213. Tillekeratne was caught behind off Saqlain for 115 from just 176 balls, including 20 fours. Muttiah Muralidaran hit a four before Aaqib's third wicket ended Sri Lanka's innings on 223.

Pakistan openers Saeed Anwar and Aamir Sohail put on 42 runs before Muralidaran deceived Sohail and bowled him just before the end of day one. Nightwatchman Saqlain plodded his way through the first session of day two, while Anwar scored 54 before driving a catch to mid wicket. Skipper Rameez Raja pushed things along, while Saqlain became Muralidaran's third scalp after scoring 34 in 224 minutes. A knee injury however kept Muralidaran out of the attack for a while.

Pakistan was just 10 runs shy of Sri Lanka's total when Rameez was caught in close for 75, having struck 12 fours. The hosts led by 25 runs when Shoaib Mohammad was run out, and then Inzamam-ul-Haq registered a half-century as he and Ijaz Ahmed jnr took the total to 288. But Pakistan lost 3-3 after the new ball was taken, with Pramodya Wickremasinghe dismissing Ijaz before Gurusinha claimed Inzamam and Wasim. Inzamam missed the next two days of play after a blow on the helmet from a Wickremasinghe bouncer.

Moin Khan's 30 took Pakistan from 294-8 to 333 all out on day three, and Muralidaran finished with five wickets. The hosts lost more strike power as Wasim had a shoulder injury and couldn't bowl, but Mohammad Akram and Aaqib claimed lbws to dismiss Mahanama and Gurusinha respectively, as Sri Lanka sank to 24-2. Hathurusinghe and de Silva, however, took advantage of Pakistan's depleted attack, and Sri Lanka led by 64 runs at stumps, with Hathurusinghe on 67 and de Silva 78.

Hathurusinghe finished with 83 in six hours when an edged drive was caught at second slip, and the third-wicket partnership of 176 looked like it could go to waste as the tourists collapsed. Tillekeratne was lbw to Aaqib for nought, and Ranatunga caught-and-bowled by Sohail for two. De Silva's resistance ended when he was lbw to Saqlain for 105 scored in 402 minutes, and Sri Lanka led by 130 runs with four wickets remaining.

Dunusinghe scored a useful 27, while Dharmasena showed

The awesome power of Pakistan's Wasim Akram in his prime in 1995, pictured here targeting Australia's Steve Waught at the 'Gabba.

the poise of a recognised batsman. Sri Lanka's chances lifted as Vaas hit seven fours – including three in succession off Sohail – in a brisk 40 before Aaqib bowled him and later claimed his maiden five-wicket haul in Tests. Dharmasena gained two reprieves and lasted nearly three hours before departing for 49, and the last four wickets had added 121 invaluable runs, setting Pakistan a challenging target of 252.

Vaas gave the visitors the ideal start when he had Sohail lbw for a duck in the second over. Anwar and Rameez carefully improved Pakistan's position, although Rameez was dropped at 16. In the last over of the day, however, Muralidaran crucially had Rameez caught in close, and 58-2 was very different from 58-1.

Anwar luckily edged several deliveries safely before Dharmasena bowled him to have Pakistan 99-3. The hosts were in further trouble when Shoaib was lbw to Wickremasinghe for five, while Inzamam was fortunate to be allowed to bat at number four after not fielding in Sri Lanka's second innings. He looked far from settled before presenting Muralidaran a return catch late in the session.

The Pakistanis must have been nervous at lunchtime, with the score at 119-5.

Pakistan's situation worsened to 129-6 when Ijaz miscued a hook to long leg. Moin, however, showed what a fierce competitor he was, while Wasim braved injury to renew Pakistan's chances. The latter scored 26 before Dharmasena bowled him, and 77 runs were still needed with just three wickets left. Moin gained a couple of reprieves, and Saqlain defended again. The total passed 200 as Moin pushed along but, like Anwar, failed to get past 50. A Vaas delivery rose sharply and had Moin well caught by Muralidaran, leaving Pakistan 206-8. Three runs were added when Saqlain was caught, and Mohammad Akram was on strike to Dharmasena for a new over. Mohammad Akram edged his first delivery where Mahanama's slips catch secured a Sri Lankan triumph.

Sri Lanka's first win on Pakistan's turf came just six months after Sri Lanka's first overseas win, in New Zealand. They followed up by beating Pakistan by 144 runs in the third Test at Sialkot, to clinch a memorable series victory.

SRI LANKA 1ST INNINGS

RS Mahanama	lbw b Wasim Akram	0
UC Hathurusinghe	c Saeed Anwar b Mohammad Akram	47
AP Gurusinha	c Wasim Akram b Aaqib Javed	9
PA de Silva	c & b Saqlain Mushtaq	0
A Ranatunga*	c Ijaz Ahmed b Saqlain Mushtaq	0
HP Tillekeratne	c Moin Khan b Saqlain Mushtaq	115
HDPK Dharmasena	run out	0
CI Dunusinghe†	lbw b Wasim Akram	12
WPUJC Vaas	c Ijaz Ahmed b Aaqib Javed	21
GP Wickremasinghe	c Moin Khan b Aaqib Javed	1
M Muralidaran	not out	8
Extras	(b 3, lb 1, nb 6)	10
Total		223

Fall of wickets 0, 32, 33, 33, 117, 117, 149, 213, 213, 223

	O	M	R	W
Wasim Akram	13	6	31	2
Mohammad Akram	14	4	42	1
Aaqib Javed	13	5	34	3
Saqlain Mushtaq	20	3	74	3
Aamir Sohail	7	2	28	0
Shoaib Mohammad	3	2	10	0

SRI LANKA 2ND INNINGS

RS Mahanama	lbw b Mohammad Akram	10
UC Hathurusinghe	c Ijaz Ahmed b Aaqib Javed	83
AP Gurusinha	lbw b Aaqib Javed	12
PA de Silva	lbw b Saqlain Mushtaq	105
HP Tillekeratne	lbw b Aaqib Javed	0
A Ranatunga*	c & b Aamir Sohail	2
HDPK Dharmasena	c Moin Khan b Mohammad Akram	49
CI Dunusinghe†	c Mohammad Akram b Saqlain Mushtaq	27
WPUJC Vaas	b Aaqib Javed	40
M Muralidaran	not out	10
GP Wickremasinghe	b Aaqib Javed	2
Extras	(b 4, lb 10, nb 7)	21
Total		361

Fall of wickets 11, 24, 200, 212, 225, 240, 279, 344, 354, 361

	O	M	R	W
Aaqib Javed	32.3	6	84	5
Mohammad Akram	27	5	78	2
Aamir Sohail	44	12	87	1
Saqlain Mushtaq	36	11	84	2
Ijaz Ahmed jnr	3	0	5	0
Shoaib Mohammad	4	2	9	0

PAKISTAN 1ST INNINGS

Saeed Anwar	c de Silva b Muralidaran	54
Aamir Sohail	b Muralidaran	20
Saqlain Mushtaq	c Mahanama b Muralidaran	34
Rameez Raja*	c sub (DP Samaraweera) b de Silva	75
Inzamam-ul-Haq	b Gurusinha	50
Shoaib Mohammad	run out	12
Ijaz Ahmed jnr	c Dunusinghe b Wickremasinghe	16
Wasim Akram	c Mahanama b Gurusinha	2
Moin Khan†	st Dunusinghe b Muralidaran	30
Aaqib Javed	b Muralidaran	8
Mohammad Akram	not out	0
Extras	(b 4, lb 15, nb 13)	32
Total		333

Fall of wickets 42, 109, 168, 213, 248, 288, 288, 291, 324, 333

	O	M	R	W
GP Wickremasinghe	23	6	53	1
WPUJC Vaas	14	4	35	0
AP Gurusinha	8	1	30	2
HDPK Dharmasena	30	4	79	0
M Muralidaran	23.3	6	68	5
UC Hathurusinghe	6	1	10	0
PA de Silva	13.3	3	39	1

PAKISTAN 2ND INNINGS

Saeed Anwar	b Dharmasena	50
Aamir Sohail	lbw b Vaas	0
Rameez Raja*	c Tillekeratne b Muralidaran	25
Inzamam-ul-Haq	c & b Muralidaran	26
Shoaib Mohammad	lbw b Wickremasinghe	5
Ijaz Ahmed jnr	c Dharmasena b Vaas	8
Moin Khan†	c Muralidaran b Vaas	50
Wasim Akram	b Dharmasena	26
Saqlain Mushtaq	c Ranatunga b Vaas	7
Aaqib Javed	not out	1
Mohammad Akram	c Mahanama b Dharmasena	0
Extras	(nb 11)	11
Total		209

Fall of wickets 6, 58, 99, 108, 119, 129, 175, 206, 209, 209

	O	M	R	W
GP Wickremasinghe	11	1	23	1
WPUJC Vaas	15	2	45	4
M Muralidaran	20	2	83	2
HDPK Dharmasena	22.1	6	43	3
PA de Silva	4	0	15	0

Toss: Pakistan   Umpires: Khizer Hayat and NT Plews   TV umpire:
Ikram Rabbani   Match referee: PL van der Merwe   Sri Lanka won by 42 runs

South Africa v Australia
Second Test at St George's Park, Port Elizabeth

1996-97
March 14, 15, 16, 17 (1997)

Steve Waugh reportedly said, before the second Test in the three-match series in South Africa in 1996–97, that he couldn't see Australia being beaten. His belief was strongly put to the test after Australia won the first Test at Johannesburg by an innings and 196 runs.

Upon winning the toss, Australian captain Mark Taylor chose to field for the first time in a Test, as he felt the pitch was a little under-prepared. Glenn McGrath and Jason Gillespie made the most of the heavily-grassed pitch to reduce South Africa to 22-4. Gary Kirsten and Jacques Kallis were caught off Gillespie without scoring, having faced 19 and 12 balls respectively. Adam Bacher and Hansie Cronje fell to McGrath, before Daryll Cullinan and Herschelle Gibbs took the score to 70 after lunch. Gillespie had Cullinan caught, and 25 runs later dismissed Gibbs and Shaun Pollock with two successive, accurate deliveries to register a five-wicket haul.

South Africa could have been 95-8 but Dave Richardson was ruled not out when he seemingly edged behind. Richardson and Brian McMillan put together a gritty 85-run partnership, and McMillan's 55 helped South Africa pass 200 before finishing on 209 after Shane Warne took the last three wickets. Australia lost Matthew Hayden for a duck when Pollock found the edge, before Taylor and Matthew Elliott focused on survival as Australia scored just 10 runs in the 13 overs before stumps.

After McGrath and Gillespie moved the ball around on day one, South Africa's bowlers swung the ball on day two. Taylor fell early when he chased a Pollock delivery and edged behind, although the home side was handicapped as Pollock strained his hamstring and did not bowl again in the match after taking 2-6 from six overs. Mark Waugh hit three fours in his 20 before Cronje trapped him lbw, and another 16 runs

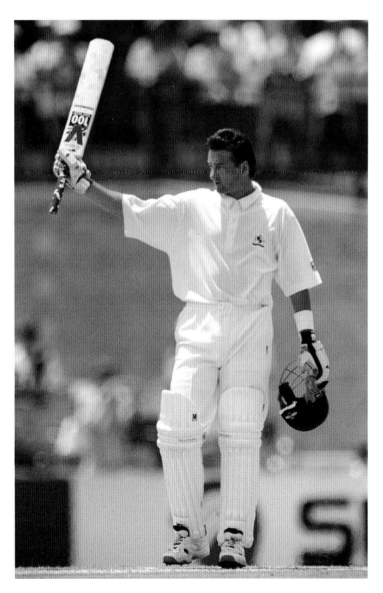

Mark Waugh, pictured here after scoring one of his 20 career centuries, made one of the best and most crucial Test centuries of his career against South Africa in Port Elizabeth in 1997.

South Africa bowler Shaun Pollock was injured for much of the second Test against Australia in Port Elizabeth in 1996–97, as the host team went down by just two wickets.

were added before Australia's batting fell apart after lunch. Most of the batsmen resisted the bowling for a while without looking comfortable, as the total remained low. Elliott was run out before Steve Waugh and Michael Bevan were caught behind off McMillan, and Australia plunged to 70-6. Cronje and the splendidly economical Allan Donald picked up a wicket each, and then Gillespie scored a single in 44 minutes. After tea, the last two wickets fell for five runs as South Africa gained a 101-run lead on the first innings. Taylor thought his players weren't mentally aggressive enough after they batted more than 70 overs for 108 runs. Kirsten and Bacher bettered South Africa's position with an unbroken 83-run partnership in 30 overs before stumps.

Just four runs were added to the overnight score when Gillespie bowled Kirsten. Eleven runs later, Greg Blewett produced a direct hit at the non-striker's end to run out Kallis and precipitate a collapse, which sometimes happens following a run out. South Africa went from 98-1 to 100-4. Bacher was caught for 49, before Cullinan was unlucky to be ruled lbw as replays showed Gillespie should have been called for a front-foot no-ball. Twenty-two runs later, Gibbs was caught off

McGrath to another delivery that replays showed should have been called no-ball. Bevan chipped in with his left-arm wrist-spin when he had McMillan lbw just before lunch, and South Africa led by 238 runs with four wickets remaining.

Bevan struck again when he had Cronje caught behind for 27 after the batsman hit five fours, before Warne trapped Pollock lbw after the injured all-rounder struck four boundaries in his 17. Bevan and Warne picked up another wicket each in quick succession as the home side had crumbled from 87-0 to 168 all out, leaving Australia more than two days to score 270 runs for victory, against an attack that was missing Pollock.

The openers put on 23 runs before McMillan had Taylor lbw. After tea, Hayden and Elliott got in a terrible mess with their running between the wickets, and the former was run out after both batsmen headed for the same end. Australia was in trouble at 30-2, before Elliott and Mark Waugh steadied the ship. The bounce in the pitch became more predictable, and the batsmen defended the accurate deliveries and attacked the loose balls. Eighty-three runs were added before Elliott left his crease and miscued his stroke to present a return catch to left-arm chinaman bowler Paul Adams. The Waugh twins added 32 runs before stumps, and Mark passed 50 after earlier gaining five runs when a ball struck the helmet located behind the wicketkeeper.

The scene was set for a fascinating fourth day, as Australia needed 125 runs and South Africa seven wickets. Twenty-two runs were shaved off the target when Cronje leapt high at cover to brilliantly catch Steve Waugh, just before a drinks break. Blewett looked far from settled before Adams bowled him for seven, and then the score progressed to 204-5 at lunch. Mark Waugh went on to score one of his finest Test centuries, while Bevan hung in as the total crept to 258. Mark Waugh did not look like getting out as he scored 116, included 17 fours and a six, before Kallis bowled him. Bevan subsequently edged Cronje to slip as 258-5 became 258-7, and suddenly the Australians were nervous. Warne clubbed a delivery down the ground, and victory was just five runs away when Kallis trapped Warne lbw with the first ball of an over. "Things were suddenly very tense indeed," Taylor commented in his book, *A Captain's Year*.

Gillespie survived the rest of Kallis' over without scoring, before Cronje bowled to Healy. Cronje strayed onto leg-stump from the third delivery, and Healy instinctively whipped the ball, which flew behind square leg for six as the deep forward square leg and fine leg fielders could do nothing to stop it. Australia clinched a spectacular victory to seal the series, before South Africa bounced back to win the dead rubber Test in Centurion.

SOUTH AFRICA 1ST INNINGS

G Kirsten	c Hayden b Gillespie	0
AM Bacher	c Elliott b McGrath	11
JH Kallis	c Blewett b Gillespie	0
DJ Cullinan	c Warne b Gillespie	34
WJ Cronje*	b McGrath	0
HH Gibbs	b Gillespie	31
BM McMillan	c SR Waugh b Warne	55
SM Pollock	lbw b Gillespie	0
DJ Richardson†	c McGrath b Warne	47
AA Donald	c & b Warne	9
PR Adams	not out	5
Extras	(b 8, lb 8, w 1)	17
Total		209

Fall of wickets 13, 17, 21, 22, 70, 95, 95, 180, 204, 209

	O	M	R	W
GD McGrath	22	7	66	2
JN Gillespie	23	10	54	5
SK Warne	23.4	5	62	3
GS Blewett	4	2	3	0
MG Bevan	2	0	8	0

SOUTH AFRICA 2ND INNINGS

G Kirsten	b Gillespie	43
AM Bacher	c McGrath b Gillespie	49
JH Kallis	run out (Blewett)	2
DJ Cullinan	lbw b Gillespie	2
WJ Cronje*	c Healy b Bevan	27
HH Gibbs	c ME Waugh b McGrath	7
BM McMillan	lbw b Bevan	2
SM Pollock	lbw b Warne	17
DJ Richardson†	not out	3
AA Donald	c Warne b Bevan	7
PR Adams	c Taylor b Warne	1
Extras	(b 1, lb 5, nb 2)	8
Total		168

Fall of wickets 87, 98, 99, 100, 122, 137, 152, 156, 167, 168

	O	M	R	W
GD McGrath	13	3	43	1
JN Gillespie	18	4	49	3
SR Waugh	4.3	0	16	0
GS Blewett	7.3	3	16	0
SK Warne	17.4	7	20	2
MG Bevan	13	3	18	3

AUSTRALIA 1ST INNINGS

ML Hayden	c Cullinan b Pollock	0
MA Taylor*	c Richardson b Pollock	8
MTG Elliott	run out (Bacher)	23
ME Waugh	lbw b Cronje	20
SR Waugh	c Richardson b McMillan	8
GS Blewett	b Donald	13
MG Bevan	c Richardson b McMillan	0
IA Healy†	c Bacher b Cronje	5
SK Warne	lbw b Adams	18
JN Gillespie	not out	1
GD McGrath	c Richardson b Kallis	0
Extras	(b 1, lb 7, w 2, nb 2)	12
Total		108

Fall of wickets 1, 13, 48, 64, 66, 70, 85, 86, 106, 108

	O	M	R	W
AA Donald	23	13	18	1
SM Pollock	6	3	6	2
PR Adams	4	0	5	1
BM McMillan	14	2	32	2
WJ Cronje	14	7	21	2
JH Kallis	9.4	2	18	1

AUSTRALIA 2ND INNINGS

MA Taylor*	lbw b McMillan	13
ML Hayden	run out (Cronje)	14
MTG Elliott	c & b Adams	44
ME Waugh	b Kallis	116
SR Waugh	c Cronje b Kallis	18
GS Blewett	b Adams	7
MG Bevan	c Cullinan b Cronje	24
IA Healy†	not out	10
SK Warne	lbw b Kallis	3
JN Gillespie	not out	0
Extras	(b 11, lb 8, w 3)	22
Total	(8 wickets)	271

Did not bat GD McGrath

Fall of wickets 23, 30, 113, 167, 192, 258, 258, 265

	O	M	R	W
AA Donald	26	6	75	0
BM McMillan	21	5	46	1
WJ Cronje	9.3	1	36	1
JH Kallis	16	7	29	3
PR Adams	21	4	66	2

Toss: Australia   Umpires: RE Koertzen and S Venkataraghavan   TV umpire: DL Orchard
Match referee: R Subba Row   Australia won by 2 wickets

Zimbabwe v New Zealand
Second Test at Queens Sports Club, Bulawayo

1997-98
September 25, 26, 27, 28, 29 (1997)

A two-Test series involving Zimbabwe and New Zealand in September 1997 proved enthralling. New Zealand finished on 304-8 chasing 403 in the first Test at Harare, before the second Test at Bulawayo proved even more fascinating, after Zimbabwe won the toss and made use of a good batting surface.

New Zealand's left-arm opening bowlers David Sewell and Shayne O'Connor were unable to break through in the first session, as Sewell was in his first Test and O'Connor his second. Zimbabwean opener Grant Flower maintained his form from the first Test, in which he scored 104 and 151, while fellow opener Gavin Rennie was solid in his second Test after scoring 23 and 57 in the previous Test. This time Flower batted for three hours, hit 12 fours and was 17 runs shy of another century when he was caught off 18-year-old Daniel Vettori's left-arm spin. Rennie was soon caught off O'Connor, and 148-2 looked a lot better for the visitors than 144-0. However a dropped catch reprieved Guy Whittall on five, and this proved match-turning.

Andy Flower added 70 with Whittall before the former was caught off Vettori, and captain Alistair Campbell made just seven before becoming O'Connor's second victim. Campbell's team, however, reached a solid 263-4 at stumps, with Whittall on 66. Whittall guided the Zimbabwean innings and scored the bulk of the runs as he received solid support, with Dave Houghton and Heath Streak lasting 93 minutes each at number six and eight respectively. After Bryan Strang and Adam Huckle fell without scoring, last batsman Everton Matambanadzo faced 43 balls in 66 minutes, with a lone scoring stroke for four in a 40-run partnership. Whittall finished unconquered on 203, from 359 balls in 453 minutes, with 22 fours and two sixes in Zimbabwe's total of 461. Whittall took 228 balls to reach

New Zealand left-arm spinner Daniel Vettori made his Test debut at the age of 18 in early 1997, and quickly became a fixture in the national team.

100 but only another 127 balls to reach 200.

After New Zealand began day three at 23-0, Blair Pocock went on to score just 27 in 146 minutes before falling lbw to Paul Strang, who similarly dismissed Matthew Horne for five. Craig Spearman's stoic 47 ended with a catch to Huckle off Strang, before vice versa applied to Kiwi captain Stephen Fleming's dismissal. New Zealand crashed to 130-5 just two balls later as Cairns was caught by Rennie, and the tourists were still 100 runs shy of avoiding the follow-on when Adam Parore also fell to Huckle. Huckle and fellow leg-spinner Paul Strang shouldered a lot of responsibility for the hosts, while left-arm medium-pacer Bryan Strang was economical, if not penetrative.

The Kiwis recovered when Nathan Astle struck 13 fours and two sixes in his 218-minute stay before losing his cool and his wicket for 96. But with Chris Harris well set after putting on 97 runs with Astle, the Kiwis avoided the follow-on and were 268-7 at stumps. Harris pushed on while fellow left-hander Vettori, whose highest first-class score was just 29 not out, showed his all-round ability after he took 4-165 from a marathon 58 overs. Vettori's persistence and determination were admirable, and the eighth wicket partnership produced 112 runs before Harris fell for 71. Vettori was only 10 runs shy of 100 when he was last out, and the deficit was just 58. Huckle snared six wickets, but the hosts had failed to ram home the advantage after having the visitors in trouble.

As if to make up for that, Grant Flower raced to 49 runs from 46 balls before he was run out. Astle's part-time bowling accounted for Rennie before Andy Flower fell to Harris as Zimbabwe slipped to 91-3. Whittall was a stumbling block again as Zimbabwe reached 152-3 at stumps, before showing little initiative the following morning. Whittall was run out for 45, and then Campbell played some attacking strokes. His team lost 17-4 before he somewhat surprisingly declared, setting the tourists 286 runs in just over two sessions.

New Zealand began strongly with 41 runs in 38 minutes, and Matambanadzo was taken off after conceding 14 runs in two overs. Huckle broke through when he had Spearman caught by Campbell, and then Horne looked well set before he fell to the same bowler-fielder combination for 29. Campbell again relied on his two leg-spinners, but the Kiwis looked capable of winning. Pocock showed more urgency than in the first innings, this time scoring 62 in 139 minutes before a catch to Paul Strang enabled Huckle to do in New Zealand's second innings what his fellow leg-spinner did in New Zealand's first innings: account for the top three batsmen. Huckle, however, was a little more expensive than he would have liked.

Fleming scored at a decent rate while Astle was restrained, and New Zealand's victory chances looked healthy as the duo put on 69 runs in 71 minutes. But the Kiwis kept losing a wicket just when the team looked like gaining control. Following Astle's demise, Cairns departed for just eight. Fleming reached 75 but the Kiwis could ill afford for him to be run out, as they still needed 46 runs with the rest of the recognised batsmen back in the pavilion. With the required run rate increasing, the climax was akin to those often seen in limited overs matches.

Arriving following Cairns' dismissal, Parore struck a six and scored 23 runs from as many balls before Huckle claimed his 11th wicket of the match. As New Zealand was 260-7, Harris and Vettori had the chance to earn heroic status, if their earlier contributions in the match weren't enough. It was easy to forget that Harris had taken five catches (including one off his bowling), produced two run outs and bowled economically, in addition to his first innings score of 71. But the impending task became stiff, and Vettori was run out to leave the Kiwis needing 11 runs from the last four balls, with two wickets left. Harris opted for safety and no more runs were scored, ensuring a nil-all drawn series in which neither side dominated.

ZIMBABWE 1ST INNINGS

GJ Rennie	c Harris b O'Connor	57
GW Flower	c Fleming b Vettori	83
A Flower†	c Harris b Vettori	39
GJ Whittall	not out	203
ADR Campbell*	c Astle b O'Connor	7
DL Houghton	b Cairns	32
PA Strang	c Harris b Vettori	5
HH Streak	lbw b Cairns	17
BC Strang	c Fleming b Cairns	0
AG Huckle	c Parore b Vettori	0
EZ Matambanadzo	c Fleming b O'Connor	4
Extras	(lb 10, w 2, nb 2)	14
Total		461

Fall of wickets 144, 148, 218, 244, 322, 343, 416, 420, 421, 461

	O	M	R	W
DG Sewell	19	3	81	0
SB O'Connor	27	9	80	3
CL Cairns	36	11	97	3
DL Vettori	58	11	165	4
CZ Harris	14	6	13	0
NJ Astle	7	2	15	0

ZIMBABWE 2ND INNINGS

GJ Rennie	lbw b Astle	24
GW Flower	run out (Spearman)	49
A Flower†	c & b Harris	7
GJ Whittall	run out (Harris)	45
ADR Campbell*	not out	59
DL Houghton	c Harris b Vettori	13
PA Strang	lbw b Vettori	2
HH Streak	run out (Harris)	1
BC Strang	b Cairns	10
AG Huckle	not out	0
Extras	(b 2, lb 7, w 3, nb 5)	17
Total	(8 wickets dec)	227

Did not bat EZ Matambanadzo

Fall of wickets 75, 80, 91, 172, 202, 204, 205, 219

	O	M	R	W
DG Sewell	4	0	9	0
SB O'Connor	5	0	34	0
CL Cairns	11	1	49	1
DL Vettori	18	3	69	2
NJ Astle	9	6	16	1
CZ Harris	17	4	41	1

Toss: Zimbabwe   Umpires: RB Tiffin and S Venkataraghavan
TV umpire: QJ Goosen   Match referee: S Wettimuny
Match drawn

NEW ZEALAND 1ST INNINGS

CM Spearman	c Huckle b PA Strang	47
BA Pocock	lbw b PA Strang	27
MJ Horne	lbw b PA Strang	5
SP Fleming*	c PA Strang b Huckle	27
NJ Astle	c sub (AR Whittall) b Huckle	96
CL Cairns	c Rennie b Huckle	0
AC Parore†	c GW Flower b Huckle	17
CZ Harris	b Huckle	71
DL Vettori	c BC Strang b Huckle	90
SB O'Connor	run out (GW Flower)	7
DG Sewell	not out	1
Extras	(b 1, lb 9, nb 5)	15
Total		403

Fall of wickets 60, 76, 92, 130, 130, 162, 259, 371, 389, 403

	O	M	R	W
HH Streak	15	5	26	0
EZ Matambanadzo	15	4	52	0
PA Strang	47	19	110	3
AG Huckle	40.4	10	109	6
BC Strang	26	12	50	0
GJ Whittall	6	1	14	0
GW Flower	10	2	19	0
ADR Campbell	2	0	13	0

NEW ZEALAND 2ND INNINGS

BA Pocock	c PA Strang b Huckle	62
CM Spearman	c Campbell b Huckle	27
MJ Horne	c Campbell b Huckle	29
SP Fleming*	run out (PA Strang)	75
NJ Astle	c GW Flower b PA Strang	21
CL Cairns	c Houghton b Huckle	8
AC Parore†	c Whittall b Huckle	23
CZ Harris	not out	12
DL Vettori	run out (Houghton)	7
SB O'Connor	not out	0
Extras	(b 5, lb 4, nb 2)	11
Total	(8 wickets)	275

Did not bat DG Sewell

Fall of wickets 41, 89, 138, 207, 221, 240, 260, 275

	O	M	R	W
EZ Matambanadzo	2	0	14	0
BC Strang	8	4	15	0
AG Huckle	32	2	146	5
PA Strang	23	1	81	1
GW Flower	3	1	10	0

India v Pakistan
First Test at MA Chidambaram Stadium, Chennai

1998-99
January 28, 29, 30, 31 (1999)

A spectacular return to India versus Pakistan Test cricket took place in 1999, with this series the first between the countries for nine years, and Pakistan's first tour in India for 12 years. Relations between the two countries remained sensitive, and the first Test involved massive security, after vandalism from Hindu extremists forced the Test to be moved from Delhi to Chennai.

Batting first, Pakistan openers Saeed Anwar and Shahid Afridi hit some cracking off side fours. Three boundaries to Anwar in the eighth over included a missed catch at slip. Afridi departed moments later, before Ijaz Ahmed edged a four off Javagal Srinath, who soon had Anwar lbw without having offered a shot. A Mexican wave swept around the ground, and Inzamam-ul-Haq opened his account with a splendid cover-driven four off Srinath, before leg-spinner Anil Kumble struck with his fifth delivery, inducing a leading edge from Inzamam. Yousuf Youhana also began his scoring with a nice cover drive, before Kumble's dismissal of Ijaz left Pakistan struggling. Srinath comprehensively beat Salim Malik after lunch to make the score 91-5.

Youhana drove Kumble over the boundary before Moin Khan clubbed Sunil Joshi for a massive six over long off. Youhana posted his 50 with an edged four before Sachin Tendulkar's third ball had Youhana lbw. Wasim Akram smacked a couple of Tendulkar full-tosses for four, and Moin went on to score 60 before falling to a great diving slips catch by Sourav Ganguly. Akram thumped Joshi for six before being caught in close off Kumble, who also took the last two wickets to record 6-70, as Pakistan succumbed for 238.

In his Test debut, India's left-handed opener Sadagoppan Ramesh survived Akram's first testing over before cutting Waqar Younis' second ball for four. Ramesh hit two nice boundaries

Indian leg-spinner Anil Kumble, seen here celebrating success.

in three balls off Akram before VVS Laxman hit successive legside fours off Waqar. Ramesh again hit consecutive fours off Akram before India began day two on 48-0.

Laxman drove an early four off Akram before off-spinner Saqlain Mushtaq was introduced, and a missed run-out chance resulted in four overthrows. Akram made a double breakthrough as he trapped the openers lbw, before Tendulkar fell for a duck as he advanced Saqlain and scooped a catch to gully. Another wayward throw cost Pakistan a boundary, and then Rahul Dravid and Mohammad Azharuddin hit some attractive fours before Azharuddin was caught at bat pad to leave India wobbling at 103-4.

Dravid had a couple of near misses before swinging Saqlain for a six. A four off Nadeem Khan took Dravid to a half-century before Saqlain had him lbw, and the off-spinner had five scalps after dismissing Nayan Mongia and Kumble, with India struggling to 188-7. Joshi hit some good boundaries, and Ganguly hit Saqlain for a massive six on his way to a vital 54 before he edged Afridi to slip. Srinath and Joshi hit a four each in one over before Afridi accounted for Srinath and Venkatesh Prasad to restrict India's lead to 16.

Anwar slashed a lucky boundary before Prasad trapped him lbw two balls later, and Pakistan reached 34-1 in the ninth over when bad light ended day two. Afridi quickly hit two fours on day three before Kumble's second delivery accounted for Ijaz. Afridi rode his luck as he edged Srinath just short of first slip before edging a four past second slip. Inzamam also edged Srinath for four, before a cut from Afridi raised Pakistan's 100. Afridi smacked two giant sixes in quick succession, and Inzamam's tenth four raised his 50 before Joshi missed a return catch to reprieve Afridi on 59. Tendulkar again struck in his first over as Inzamam edged a catch, and Youhana hit five fours before being bowled, sweeping at Tendulkar.

Afridi posted a century in only his second Test, and Malik cut some impressive fours before Afridi hit three fours in four balls from Kumble. Pakistan reached 275-4 after tea before crumbling to 286 all out. Joshi removed Malik before Prasad claimed an amazing 5-0. A great delivery had Moin caught behind, before Afridi swung and was bowled. Afridi earned a standing ovation for his chancy 141, which included 21 fours and three sixes. Waqar flicked Srinath for a legside four before Waqar was last out, leaving India a target of 271.

Ramesh flicked a boundary third ball before Waqar struck twice, with Ramesh edging a lazy drive and Laxman trapped lbw. India finished the day on 40-2, and Akram broke through early on day four when a swinging delivery dislodged Dravid's off-bail. Saqlain had Azharuddin lbw not playing a stroke,

before Ganguly was unluckily caught behind as India fell to 82-5. Tendulkar registered an important half-century, and later had a close shave just after tea, before reaching 99 with four fours in a Saqlain over, including two paddles to fine leg. Crucially, Moin missed a stumping chance while Tendulkar was 91 and the score 160-5.

Tendulkar passed 100 before the new ball was taken, but it wasn't long before Saqlain was brought back. The workmanlike Mongia belted Saqlain for six before Akram crucially had Mongia caught for 52, as India needed 53 more runs. Joshi hammered Saqlain for six, and had a couple of narrow escapes before a misfield gifted Tendulkar a boundary. Battling a back injury, Tendulkar slammed successive fours off Saqlain before attempting a third and holing out to mid off.

With Tendulkar gone, the Pakistanis lifted as India needed 17 runs with three wickets left. The Indians faltered as Kumble was lbw to Akram before Joshi tried to push a single but lobbed a return catch to Saqlain. India was 256-9. Two runs were added before a defensive push from Srinath went onto the stumps to seal a thrilling 12-run win to Pakistan. Remarkably, the crowd gave the Pakistanis a standing ovation during their victory lap, an extremely noble moment, in which the appreciation of great cricket overtook any background problems between India and Pakistan.

Waqar Younis is mobbed by team-mates after taking one of his 373 Test wickets for Pakistan.

PAKISTAN 1ST INNINGS

Saeed Anwar	lbw b Srinath	24
Shahid Afridi	c Ganguly b Srinath	11
Ijaz Ahmed	lbw b Kumble	13
Inzamam-ul-Haq	c & b Kumble	10
Yousuf Youhana	lbw b Tendulkar	53
Salim Malik	b Srinath	8
Moin Khan†	c Ganguly b Kumble	60
Wasim Akram*	c Laxman b Kumble	38
Saqlain Mushtaq	lbw b Kumble	2
Nadeem Khan	c Dravid b Kumble	8
Waqar Younis	not out	0
Extras	(lb 5, nb 6)	11
Total		238

Fall of wickets 32, 41, 61, 66, 91, 154, 214, 227, 237, 238

	O	M	R	W
J Srinath	15	3	63	3
BKV Prasad	16	1	54	0
A Kumble	24.5	7	70	6
SB Joshi	21	8	36	0
SR Tendulkar	3	0	10	1

INDIA 1ST INNINGS

S Ramesh	lbw b Wasim Akram	43
VVS Laxman	lbw b Wasim Akram	23
R Dravid	lbw b Saqlain Mushtaq	53
SR Tendulkar	c Salim Malik b Saqlain Mushtaq	0
M Azharuddin*	c Inzamam-ul-Haq b Saqlain Mushtaq	11
SC Ganguly	c Ijaz Ahmed b Shahid Afridi	54
NR Mongia†	st Moin Khan b Saqlain Mushtaq	5
A Kumble	c Yousuf Youhana b Saqlain Mushtaq	4
SB Joshi	not out	25
J Srinath	c Ijaz Ahmed b Shahid Afridi	10
BKV Prasad	st Moin Khan b Shahid Afridi	4
Extras	(b 2, lb 2, nb 18)	22
Total		254

Fall of wickets 67, 71, 72, 103, 156, 166, 188, 229, 246, 254

	O	M	R	W
Wasim Akram	20	4	60	2
Waqar Younis	12	2	48	0
Saqlain Mushtaq	35	8	94	5
Shahid Afridi	7.1	0	31	3
Nadeem Khan	7	0	17	0

PAKISTAN 2ND INNINGS

Saeed Anwar	lbw b Prasad	7
Shahid Afridi	b Prasad	141
Ijaz Ahmed	c & b Kumble	11
Inzamam-ul-Haq	c Laxman b Tendulkar	51
Yousuf Youhana	b Tendulkar	26
Salim Malik	c Dravid b Joshi	32
Moin Khan†	c Mongia b Prasad	3
Wasim Akram*	c Joshi b Prasad	1
Saqlain Mushtaq	lbw b Prasad	0
Nadeem Khan	not out	1
Waqar Younis	c Ramesh b Prasad	5
Extras	(b 1, lb 4, nb 3)	8
Total		286

Fall of wickets 11, 42, 139, 169, 275, 278, 279, 279, 280, 286

	O	M	R	W
J Srinath	16	1	68	0
BKV Prasad	10.2	5	33	6
A Kumble	22	4	93	1
SB Joshi	14	3	42	1
SR Tendulkar	7	1	35	2
VVS Laxman	2	0	10	0

INDIA 2ND INNINGS

S Ramesh	c Inzamam-ul-Haq b Waqar Younis	5
VVS Laxman	lbw b Waqar Younis	0
R Dravid	b Wasim Akram	10
SR Tendulkar	c Wasim Akram b Saqlain Mushtaq	136
M Azharuddin*	lbw b Saqlain Mushtaq	7
SC Ganguly	c Moin Khan b Saqlain Mushtaq	2
NR Mongia†	c Waqar Younis b Wasim Akram	52
SB Joshi	c & b Saqlain Mushtaq	8
A Kumble	lbw b Wasim Akram	1
J Srinath	b Saqlain Mushtaq	1
BKV Prasad	not out	0
Extras	(b 8, lb 10, nb 18)	36
Total		258

Fall of wickets 5, 6, 50, 73, 82, 218, 254, 256, 256, 258

	O	M	R	W
Wasim Akram	22	4	80	3
Waqar Younis	12	6	26	2
Shahid Afridi	16	7	23	0
Saqlain Mushtaq	32.2	8	93	5
Nadeem Khan	13	5	18	0

Toss: Pakistan   Umpires: RS Dunne and VK Ramaswamy
TV umpire: AV Jayaprakash   Match referee: CW Smith   Pakistan won by 12 runs

West Indies v Australia
Third Test at Kensington Oval, Bridgetown, Barbados

1998-99
March 26, 27, 28, 29, 30 (1999)

A classic Test unfolded in Barbados in March 1999 as Australia sought a third consecutive Frank Worrell Trophy series win. Australia and the West Indies had a lopsided win each before the Barbados Test went down to the wire.

With Australia batting first, the hosts sprang a surprise with off-spinner Nehemiah Perry bowling the eighth over. Michael Slater charged Perry's third ball and belted a huge six, before Curtly Ambrose failed to complete the 10th over due to a split in his boot. Soon afterwards, however, the left-handed Matthew Elliott snicked Courtney Walsh to the wicketkeeper after Elliott had edged two fours without looking comfortable. Ambrose soon returned and had Slater edging to first slip, before Mark Waugh inside-edged his second delivery onto the stumps as Australia fell to 36-3.

Australian skipper Steve Waugh survived despite playing and missing many times. He and Justin Langer added 108 runs before Langer was bowled trying to cut Carl Hooper's first ball, immediately after a drinks break. Australia reached 322-4 at stumps with Steve Waugh on 141, while Ricky Ponting progressed to 65 after replacing an injured Greg Blewett.

The chanceless fifth wicket partnership ultimately produced 281 runs in 375 minutes. After being tied down in the 90s, Ponting was caught for 104, before Walsh had Ian Healy lbw, not offering a shot first ball. Steve Waugh, who scored a career-best 200 when Australia reclaimed the Frank Worrell Trophy four years earlier, fell for an agonising 199, this time as Perry won an lbw appeal. After Shane Warne hit a quick 13, Jason Gillespie and Stuart MacGill frustrated the home side. MacGill hit two fours and a six before Australia finished with 490.

The West Indies were 1-1 after just three balls as Ponting ran out Adrian Griffith. A 49-run partnership was followed by McGrath trapping Dave Joseph and Pedro Collins lbw with

Brian Lara's brilliant 153 not out helped the West Indies to a tense one-wicket win over Australia.

successive balls, before Gillespie claimed the prized scalp of Brian Lara to a catch behind, 14 runs later. In the seventh over of day three, Elliott dropped a difficult catch to reprieve Sherwin Campbell before Hooper edged McGrath to slip after an ominous 25 included five fours. McGrath dismissed Jimmy Adams before another run was added and the locals collapsed to 98-6, before Ridley Jacobs helped Campbell steady the ship.

Campbell hit Ponting's first two balls for four before the irregular bowler struck, as Jacobs steered a catch to second slip. 251 for seven. Campbell reached his third Test century before cutting a catch to gully, and then the tail wagged as the last two wickets put on 64 runs to avert the follow-on. Ambrose hit some streaky boundaries in his 28 not out. Walsh crashed a four off Warne before being caught in the deep next ball, and Australia secured a 161-run lead. The tourists subsequently fell to 18-2 in eight overs before stumps, with the out-of-form Elliott caught behind second ball, before Langer was lbw to Ambrose for one.

Slater reached 26 before great fielding from Campbell ran him out. Nightwatchman Gillespie made 14 before Ambrose bowled him, and Mark Waugh failed again. An indiscreet cut shot cost Steve Waugh, and Healy's bad trot continued just after lunch, as Australia sank to 81-7. Warne batted usefully while Ponting hung around without batting freely, as 53 runs were added for the eighth wicket. After Walsh accounted for Warne and MacGill, McGrath hit two fours before the dismissal of a lunging Ponting produced a five-wicket haul for Walsh. The West Indies required 308 runs with a day and a session remaining, and looked promising with an opening stand of 72 before McGrath had Campbell lbw. A googly from MacGill soon had Joseph lbw, and Collins was again lbw to McGrath for nought before the locals ended the day shakily on 85-3.

Gillespie trapped Griffith early on day five before Hooper snicked behind to make the score 105-5. Only Lara stood in the way of an Australian victory. Straight after drinks, Lara clubbed 14 runs in MacGill's first over of a spell, including two successive fours to mid wicket. The score was 161-5 at lunch.

The leg-spin combination of Warne and MacGill was ineffective as a back injury kept Gillespie off the field for a time, and later prevented him sharing the new ball. Lara pulled a huge six off a Warne half-tracker to pass 50 in the 81st over, before racing to a century in the 96th over with a four off Warne. On 77, Lara had a sharp exchange with McGrath after the bowler's bouncer struck Lara's helmet. Adams was beaten by McGrath in the 97th over, ending a vital 133-run stand, before McGrath claimed the fifth and sixth lbws of the innings with successive balls, dismissing Jacobs and Perry. The West Indies needed 54 runs in the last session, with just two wickets left.

Ambrose's batting was useful again, this time in a crucial support role for Lara. After Warne remained ineffective, McGrath and Gillespie bowled in tandem, and a speculative cut for four by Ambrose made the score 295-8 before MacGill returned for one over. On 301-8, Lara edged Gillespie but a diving Healy muffed the catch in front of first slip. Two balls later, Gillespie had Ambrose caught from another edge as the West Indies needed six runs to win. Walsh, who had scored the most Test ducks, survived the rest of the over, which included a no-ball and a yorker.

Lara edged McGrath but two runs resulted, before a wide from a bouncer was soon followed by another bouncer, which Lara hooked for a single to level the scores. Walsh survived one delivery before Gillespie bowled to Lara with an attacking field, which was helpless as Lara creamed a cover drive to the boundary. Lara was mobbed by excited team-mates and spectators as the West Indies snatched the series lead. The Australians, however, hit back with a 176-run win in the final Test, retaining the Frank Worrell Trophy despite another dazzling Lara century.

AUSTRALIA 1ST INNINGS		
MJ Slater	c Lara b Ambrose	23
MTG Elliott	c Jacobs b Walsh	9
JL Langer	b Hooper	51
ME Waugh	b Ambrose	0
SR Waugh*	lbw b Perry	199
RT Ponting	c Hooper b Perry	104
IA Healy†	lbw b Walsh	0
SK Warne	c Lara b Perry	13
JN Gillespie	not out	23
SCG MacGill	run out (Ambrose)	17
GD McGrath	c Joseph b Hooper	3
Extras	(b 4, lb 10, nb 34)	48
Total		490

Fall of wickets 31, 36, 36, 144, 425, 427, 429, 446, 483, 490

	O	M	R	W
CEL Ambrose	31.3	7	93	2
CA Walsh	38	8	121	2
NO Perry	33	5	102	3
PT Collins	35.3	7	110	0
CL Hooper	15.4	4	50	2

AUSTRALIA 2ND INNINGS		
MTG Elliott	c Jacobs b Walsh	0
MJ Slater	run out (Campbell)	26
JL Langer	lbw b Ambrose	1
JN Gillespie	b Ambrose	14
ME Waugh	lbw b Walsh	3
SR Waugh*	b Collins	11
RT Ponting	c Griffith b Walsh	22
IA Healy†	c Jacobs b Collins	3
SK Warne	lbw b Walsh	32
SCG MacGill	c Campbell b Walsh	1
GD McGrath	not out	8
Extras	(lb 5, w 1, nb 19)	25
Total		146

Fall of wickets 0, 12, 35, 46, 48, 73, 81, 134, 137, 146

	O	M	R	W
CA Walsh	17.1	3	39	5
CEL Ambrose	20	2	60	2
PT Collins	9	0	31	2
NO Perry	4	0	11	0

WEST INDIES 1ST INNINGS		
SL Campbell	c SR Waugh b Gillespie	105
AFG Griffith	run out (Ponting)	0
DRE Joseph	lbw b McGrath	26
PT Collins	lbw b McGrath	0
BC Lara*	c Healy b Gillespie	8
CL Hooper	c Warne b McGrath	25
JC Adams	c ME Waugh b McGrath	0
RD Jacobs†	c ME Waugh b Ponting	68
NO Perry	lbw b Gillespie	24
CEL Ambrose	not out	28
CA Walsh	c Slater b Warne	12
Extras	(b 10, lb 3, nb 20)	33
Total		329

Fall of wickets 1, 50, 50, 64, 98, 98, 251, 265, 291, 329

	O	M	R	W
GD McGrath	33	5	128	4
JN Gillespie	28	14	48	3
SK Warne	15.5	2	70	1
SCG MacGill	20	5	47	0
RT Ponting	4	1	12	1
ME Waugh	3	0	11	0

WEST INDIES 2ND INNINGS		
SL Campbell	lbw b McGrath	33
AFG Griffith	lbw b Gillespie	35
DRE Joseph	lbw b MacGill	1
PT Collins	lbw b McGrath	0
BC Lara*	not out	153
CL Hooper	c Healy b Gillespie	6
JC Adams	b McGrath	38
RD Jacobs†	lbw b McGrath	5
NO Perry	lbw b McGrath	0
CEL Ambrose	c Elliott b Gillespie	12
CA Walsh	not out	0
Extras	(b 8, lb 13, w 2, nb 5)	28
Total	(9 wickets)	311

Fall of wickets 72, 77, 78, 91, 105, 238, 248, 248, 302

	O	M	R	W
GD McGrath	44	13	92	5
JN Gillespie	26.1	8	62	3
SK Warne	24	4	69	0
SCG MacGill	21	6	48	1
SR Waugh	5	0	19	0

Toss: Australia   Umpires: EA Nicholls and DL Orchard
TV umpire: HA Moore   Match referee: R Subba Row
West Indies won by 1 wicket

Australia v Pakistan
Second Test at Bellerive Oval, Hobart

1999–2000
November 18, 19, 20, 21, 22 (1999)

Australian fans had reason to be happy with a Test batsman's score of 149 not out in late 1999, unlike in 1981, when Englishman Ian Botham made the score. The occasion in late 1999 was every bit as memorable, with Australia hosting Pakistan.

After Australia won the first Test by 10 wickets, the hosts again chose to bowl first. Glenn McGrath gave Australia a terrific start with the wickets of Saeed Anwar and Ijaz Ahmed in the first 40 minutes. Mohammad Wasim, however, found form, striking four fours in Shane Warne's first two overs. In his second and final Test, paceman Scott Muller was expensive but he bowled Inzamam-ul-Haq, leaving Pakistan struggling at 71-3. After lunch, Pakistan became 120-4 when Yousuf Youhana fell to a splendid slips catch by Mark Waugh off Damien Fleming.

Having played many fine on side strokes, Mohammad scored 91 of Pakistan's first 148 runs before chasing a wide Muller delivery and edging where Adam Gilchrist stole the catch from first slip. Muller struck again when Moin Khan was caught, and Azhar Mahmood was solid before Warne bowled him for 27. After tea, Warne had Saqlain Mushtaq lbw for three and Wasim Akram caught behind for 29. Fleming's second wicket concluded Pakistan's innings on 222, and Australia was 29-0 from 16 overs at stumps, despite Michael Slater and Greg Blewett having some close shaves.

The openers added a further 47 runs before Blewett was superbly caught behind, and Slater was dropped on 36 before Australia reached 134-1 at lunch. A simple catch at point was grassed to reprieve Slater soon after play resumed, and the opener progressed into the 90s as Justin Langer worked towards a half-century. On 97, Slater was reprieved again when a slips catch went down, and three balls later he swished at a full-toss from Saqlain but faulty timing presented an easy catch

to mid wicket. Australia lost Mark Waugh and Langer at 206, with Waugh lbw to Waqar Younis and Langer unluckily ruled caught in close off Saqlain. Ricky Ponting made a duck after thrusting his front pad half-forward and offering no stroke to a brilliant Waqar delivery that swung around his pad to bowl him.

With the total on 236, Saqlain had Gilchrist stumped before Warne was bowled first ball. Saqlain just missed a hat-trick as Fleming narrowly avoided being stumped. Fleming however, was lbw three balls later, before Steve Waugh fell to Akram. Another stumping off Saqlain gave the bowler superb figures of 6-46, as a collapse of 55-9 confined Australia's lead to just 24. Pakistan ended the day on 61-1 after a 50-run opening stand concluded with Mohammad playing a loose stroke off Muller.

Nightwatchman Saqlain hung around the next morning until the 100 was reached, while Anwar played an array of good strokes on both sides of the wicket. Anwar, however, had no answer to a vicious Warne leg break that pitched well outside off-stump before dislodging the leg-stump. Ijaz and Inzamam batted well together and hit semi-regular boundaries in a 136-run partnership, before Ijaz was caught for 82, having played many forceful strokes through the off side. Youhana fell cheaply as Pakistan went to tea on 263-5, before Mahmood was useful again. He was involved in a 57-run partnership, before Inzamam worked his way to 116 at stumps after a good balance of defensive and offensive batting. After Moin fell cheaply, the tourists led by 327 runs at stumps.

Inzamam fell to a sharp right-handed slips catch by Mark Waugh early on day four before a direct hit from Gilchrist ran out Waqar. Warne claimed his fifth scalp after a last wicket stand of 34 boosted Australia's target to a lofty 369. Slater

Adam Gilchrist (left, carrying stumps), celebrates on his way to the dressing rooms after a marathon batting partnership with Justin Langer which took Australia to a record breaking win in the second Test against Pakistan at Bellerive Oval in Hobart, 1999.

survived a perilously close lbw appeal off Akram second ball, and Australia was 26-0 at lunch.

Following the break, Akhtar's sixth over featured 12 runs and a crucial wicket. Slater cut a four before a boundary to mid wicket from a vicious bouncer was followed by an edged catch to gully. Langer opened his account first ball with a boundary to third man. In Akhtar's next over, a 154 km/hr full-toss struck Langer painfully on the gloves. The gutsy Langer and patient Blewett added 42 runs before Blewett edged a low catch to Moin, and then Mark Waugh was plumb lbw first ball from an off cutter. Australia was 81-3.

Steve Waugh and Langer consolidated before and after tea, until an uppish drive from Waugh was well caught by bowler Saqlain. When Akram trapped Ponting, the latter suffered the ignominy of a pair, after a duck in the first Test. Australia was five-down and still 243 runs shy of victory as Langer was joined by Western Australian team-mate and fellow left-hander Gilchrist, who was in his second Test and had hammered 81 in the first.

Gilchrist soon found his stride, and a series of confident strokes took him to 45 before the close of play. Australia required 181 runs and Pakistan five wickets on the last day.

The gritty Langer and free-flowing Gilchrist scored just four runs in the first five overs but subsequently gained momentum. Langer survived two lbw appeals on 211-5 before appearing fortunate to survive a caught behind appeal on 237-5. The batsmen survived a series of bouncers from Akhtar, although one struck Langer on the chin. An off-driven four by Gilchrist off Waqar raised the wicketkeeper-batsman's first Test hundred, and Australia still required 92 runs after lunch. Langer also posted a century, before Gilchrist clouted Saqlain for two successive off side boundaries to make the score 320-5. Gilchrist and Langer took 11 runs from an Akhtar over, Australia zeroing in on victory, before Langer top-edged a slog-sweep to end a match-winning 238-run partnership. Next ball, Gilchrist cut a four to level the scores before slogging the following delivery to cow corner for a famous victory that sealed a series win.

PAKISTAN 1ST INNINGS

Saeed Anwar	c Warne b McGrath	0
Mohammad Wasim	c Gilchrist b Muller	91
Ijaz Ahmed	c Slater b McGrath	6
Inzamam-ul-Haq	b Muller	12
Yousuf Youhana	c ME Waugh b Fleming	17
Azhar Mahmood	b Warne	27
Moin Khan†	c McGrath b Muller	1
Wasim Akram*	c Gilchrist b Warne	29
Saqlain Mushtaq	lbw b Warne	3
Waqar Younis	not out	12
Shoaib Akhtar	c Gilchrist b Fleming	5
Extras	(b 10, lb 6, w 3)	19
Total		222

Fall of wickets 4, 18, 71, 120, 148, 153, 188, 198, 217, 222

	O	M	R	W
GD McGrath	18	8	34	2
DW Fleming	24.5	7	54	2
SA Muller	12	0	68	3
SK Warne	16	6	45	3
GS Blewett	2	1	5	0

AUSTRALIA 1ST INNINGS

MJ Slater	c Ijaz Ahmed b Saqlain Mushtaq	97
GS Blewett	c Moin Khan b Azhar Mahmood	35
JL Langer	c Mohammad Wasim b Saqlain Mushtaq	59
ME Waugh	lbw b Waqar Younis	5
SR Waugh*	c Ijaz Ahmed b Wasim Akram	24
RT Ponting	b Waqar Younis	0
AC Gilchrist†	st Moin Khan b Saqlain Mushtaq	6
SK Warne	b Saqlain Mushtaq	0
DW Fleming	lbw b Saqlain Mushtaq	0
GD McGrath	st Moin Khan b Saqlain Mushtaq	7
SA Muller	not out	0
Extras	(b 2, lb 6, nb 5)	13
Total		246

Fall of wickets 76, 191, 206, 206, 213, 236, 236, 236, 246, 246

	O	M	R	W
Wasim Akram	20	4	51	1
Shoaib Akhtar	17	2	69	0
Waqar Younis	12	1	42	2
Saqlain Mushtaq	24	8	46	6
Azhar Mahmood	7	1	30	1

PAKISTAN 2ND INNINGS

Saeed Anwar	b Warne	78
Mohammad Wasim	c McGrath b Muller	20
Saqlain Mushtaq	lbw b Warne	8
Ijaz Ahmed	c SR Waugh b McGrath	82
Inzamam-ul-Haq	c ME Waugh b Warne	118
Yousuf Youhana	c Ponting b Fleming	2
Azhar Mahmood	lbw b Warne	28
Moin Khan†	c Gilchrist b Fleming	6
Wasim Akram*	c Blewett b Warne	31
Waqar Younis	run out (Gilchrist)	0
Shoaib Akhtar	not out	5
Extras	(lb 6, w 1, nb 7)	14
Total		392

Fall of wickets 50, 100, 122, 258, 263, 320, 345, 357, 358, 392

	O	M	R	W
GD McGrath	27	8	87	1
DW Fleming	29	5	89	2
SK Warne	45.5	11	110	5
SA Muller	17	3	63	1
SR Waugh	4	1	19	0
ME Waugh	2	0	6	0
RT Ponting	2	1	7	0
GS Blewett	2	0	5	0

AUSTRALIA 2ND INNINGS

GS Blewett	c Moin Khan b Azhar Mahmood	29
MJ Slater	c Azhar Mahmood b Shoaib Akhtar	27
JL Langer	c Inzamam-ul-Haq b Saqlain Mushtaq	127
ME Waugh	lbw b Azhar Mahmood	0
SR Waugh*	c & b Saqlain Mushtaq	28
RT Ponting	lbw b Wasim Akram	0
AC Gilchrist†	not out	149
SK Warne	not out	0
Extras	(b 1, lb 4, nb 4)	9
Total	(6 wickets)	369

Did not bat DW Fleming, GD McGrath, SA Muller

Fall of wickets 39, 81, 81, 125, 126, 364

	O	M	R	W
Wasim Akram	18	1	68	1
Waqar Younis	11	2	38	0
Shoaib Akhtar	23	4	85	1
Saqlain Mushtaq	44.5	9	130	2
Azhar Mahmood	17	3	43	2

Toss: Australia Umpires: PD Parker and P Willey TV umpire: SJ Davis Match referee: JR Reid Australia won by 4 wickets

Chapter 6:
The Modern Day Wonders

2000 and beyond

The Ashes are won by England in 2011 at the Sydney Cricket Ground.

India v Australia
Second Test at Eden Gardens, Kolkata

2000-01
March 11, 12, 13, 14, 15 (2001)

VVS Laxman during his monumental 281, which helped India to a remarkable win against Australia after being asked to follow on.

Australia's attempt to achieve 17 successive Test wins turned out to be very unusual, after the Australians achieved a rarity: forcing India to follow on in India. Leading 1-0 after a 10-wicket win in Mumbai, Australia won the toss and batted in the second Test. Matthew Hayden and Michael Slater were cautious but they chose the right balls to attack, and most of their runs came in boundaries. Hayden struck Venkatesh Prasad for successive fours in the 21st over, before Slater whipped off-spinner Harbhajan Singh over the mid-wicket boundary with the last ball before lunch to make the score 88-0.

Another 15 runs were scored when Slater was first out, before Hayden smashed Harbhajan for six over long off, and was soon dropped at slip off Zaheer Khan. Hayden gave Harbhajan some more stick, while Justin Langer also scored most of his runs in boundaries. Just after tea, Hayden perished to a pull shot on 97. Langer departed for 58, and Mark Waugh was elegant before a cut shot produced his downfall. Australia was 252-4 before Harbhajan swung the game India's way. He trapped Ricky Ponting plumb lbw, and then Adam Gilchrist was adjudged lbw next ball, despite the ball clearly pitching outside leg-stump and finding the inside edge. Shane Warne flicked the next ball to short leg where Sadagoppan Ramesh took a right-handed blinder, making the 20-year-old Harbhajan the first Indian to take a Test hat-trick.

Australia was 291-8 at stumps, and another 10 runs were added when Jason Gillespie was fortunate not to be ruled caught behind. Gillespie scored 46 in 190 minutes, including eight fours, while Steve Waugh was gutsy. The partnership produced 133 runs, and then Glenn McGrath scored 21 not out, while his captain registered his first Test century in India. A six over mid wicket took Waugh to 99, before he finished with 110, becoming Harbhajan's seventh victim.

Defending 445, Australia struck with the ninth ball when Ramesh edged Gillespie, before Rahul Dravid drove his first ball for four. A great left-handed catch by Gilchrist accounted for Shiv Das, and India was reeling at 48-3 when Sachin Tendulkar missed a McGrath in-swinger and was lbw. Rahul Dravid cracked Warne for two successive fours before missing a straight ball, and Sourav Ganguly fell to a great catch at gully. Nayan Mongia edged Michael Kasprowicz, and Harbhajan fell to Gillespie as the score plunged to 97-7. McGrath took the next two wickets and had outstanding figures, although number six batsman VVS Laxman punished Warne and Kasprowicz, hitting 12 fours before he was last out on the morning of day three. India's openers put on 45 runs before lunch as the hosts remained 229 behind.

Ramesh made a confident 30 before he was well caught off Warne, and then Laxman came in. He drove Kasprowicz for back-to-back fours, but lost Das, who stepped too far back and was out hit wicket. India was in a hole as Tendulkar again fell for 10 when he edged a drive, before Ganguly found form. He struck eight boundaries before edging McGrath behind for 48. Laxman meanwhile hit multiple boundaries off Warne in the last session, and was in elegant form, his unbeaten 109 narrowing India's deficit to just 20 at stumps.

Kasprowicz, Warne, McGrath, Gillespie and Ponting bowled without success in session one of day four as India progressed to 376-4 at lunch, with Laxman on 171 and Dravid 50. Dravid survived a close lbw appeal just before the break, and then Laxman caressed a lovely cover drive for four immediately after lunch. After McGrath, Ponting, Gillespie, Mark Waugh and Kasprowicz couldn't strike in the second session, Hayden and Slater bowled an over each just before tea, which arrived with India on 491-4. Steve Waugh and Gilchrist were the only Australians not to bowl in the last session, as India, incredibly, had a 315-run lead, 335 runs having been scored for no wickets on the day. Laxman and Dravid were in sublime form, as they didn't offer any catches. Laxman's 275 was the highest Test score by an Indian, while Dravid was on 155.

Laxman departed for 281 when a faulty hit produced a catch behind point. Laxman registered 44 boundaries in his phenomenal 631-minute innings. Mongia didn't last long, and then Dravid ran himself out for 180, which included 20 fours. Khan hit three boundaries off Kasprowicz in a quick 23 not out as India reached 657-7, before a declaration left Australia needing 384 runs from a minimum of 75 overs.

Australia was 24-0 from 12 overs before lunch, and then Slater drove three off side boundaries off Khan in the 13th over. Slater was on 43 when a defensive shot off Harbhajan hit his glove and lobbed to Ganguly. Langer cracked successive fours in Harbhajan's next over before clubbing Venkatapathy Raju for successive sixes. But Langer soon miscued a sweep and was caught at short fine leg, and then Mark Waugh fell lbw to Raju without scoring. Ganguly spilled a vital catch behind square leg to reprieve Steve Waugh, and a draw beckoned as the score was 161-3 at tea. But in the third over of the last session, substitute fielder Hemang Badani dived at short backward square leg to catch Steve Waugh. Amazingly, Australia crashed from 166-3 to 174-8 in just 32 balls.

Ponting paddled a catch to short leg off Harbhajan before Gilchrist and Hayden were lbw as they swept at flighted Tendulkar deliveries. Gilchrist suffered a king pair as he was obviously out this time. Tendulkar also trapped Warne, who tried to cut a ball that nipped in. Gillespie lasted 51 minutes before clipping a catch to short leg, and then McGrath lasted 32 minutes before he thrust his pad at Harbhajan and was lbw in the 69th over. Harbhajan had match figures of 13-196, and a team won after following on for just the third time in Test cricket. Incredibly, Australia was the losing side all three times.

AUSTRALIA 1ST INNINGS

MJ Slater	c Mongia b Khan	42
ML Hayden	c sub (HK Badani) b Harbhajan Singh	97
JL Langer	c Mongia b Khan	58
ME Waugh	c Mongia b Harbhajan Singh	22
SR Waugh*	lbw b Harbhajan Singh	110
RT Ponting	lbw b Harbhajan Singh	6
AC Gilchrist†	lbw b Harbhajan Singh	0
SK Warne	c Ramesh b Harbhajan Singh	0
MS Kasprowicz	lbw b Ganguly	7
JN Gillespie	c Ramesh b Harbhajan Singh	46
GD McGrath	not out	21
Extras	(b 19, lb 10, nb 7)	36
Total		445

Fall of wickets 103, 193, 214, 236, 252, 252, 252, 269, 402, 445

	O	M	R	W
Z Khan	28.4	6	89	2
BKV Prasad	30	5	95	0
SC Ganguly	13.2	3	44	1
SLV Raju	20	2	58	0
Harbhajan Singh	37.5	7	123	7
SR Tendulkar	2	0	7	0

INDIA 1ST INNINGS

SS Das	c Gilchrist b McGrath	20
S Ramesh	c Ponting b Gillespie	0
R Dravid	b Warne	25
SR Tendulkar	lbw b McGrath	10
SC Ganguly*	c SR Waugh b Kasprowicz	23
VVS Laxman	c Hayden b Warne	59
NR Mongia†	c Gilchrist b Kasprowicz	2
Harbhajan Singh	c Ponting b Gillespie	4
Zaheer Khan	b McGrath	3
SLV Raju	lbw b McGrath	4
BKV Prasad	not out	7
Extras	(lb 2, nb 12)	14
Total		171

Fall of wickets 0, 34, 48, 88, 88, 92, 97, 113, 129, 171

	O	M	R	W
GD McGrath	14	8	18	4
JN Gillespie	11	0	47	2
MS Kasprowicz	13	2	39	2
SK Warne	20.1	3	65	2

INDIA 2ND INNINGS

SS Das	hit wicket b Gillespie	39
S Ramesh	c ME Waugh b Warne	30
VVS Laxman	c Ponting b McGrath	281
SR Tendulkar	c Gilchrist b Gillespie	10
SC Ganguly*	c Gilchrist b McGrath	48
R Dravid	run out (SR Waugh/Kasprowicz)	180
NR Mongia†	b McGrath	4
Zaheer Khan	not out	23
Harbhajan Singh	not out	8
Extras	(b 6, lb 12, w 2, nb 14)	34
Total	(7 wickets dec)	657

Did not bat SLV Raju, BKV Prasad

Fall of wickets 52, 97, 115, 232, 608, 624, 629

	O	M	R	W
GD McGrath	39	12	103	3
JN Gillespie	31	6	115	2
SK Warne	34	3	152	1
ME Waugh	18	1	58	0
MS Kasprowicz	35	6	139	0
RT Ponting	12	1	41	0
ML Hayden	6	0	24	0
MJ Slater	2	1	4	0
JL Langer	1	0	3	0

AUSTRALIA 2ND INNINGS

ML Hayden	lbw b Tendulkar	67
MJ Slater	c Ganguly b Harbhajan Singh	43
JL Langer	c Ramesh b Harbhajan Singh	28
ME Waugh	lbw b Raju	0
SR Waugh*	c sub (HK Badani) b Harbhajan Singh	24
RT Ponting	c Das b Harbhajan Singh	0
AC Gilchrist†	lbw b Tendulkar	0
JN Gillespie	c Das b Harbhajan Singh	6
SK Warne	lbw b Tendulkar	0
MS Kasprowicz	not out	13
GD McGrath	lbw b Harbhajan Singh	12
Extras	(b 6, nb 8, pen 5)	19
Total		212

Fall of wickets 74, 106, 116, 166, 166, 167, 173, 174, 191, 212

	O	M	R	W
Zaheer Khan	8	4	30	0
BKV Prasad	3	1	7	0
Harbhajan Singh	30.3	8	73	6
SLV Raju	15	3	58	1
SR Tendulkar	11	3	31	3
SC Ganguly	1	0	2	0

Toss: Australia   Umpires: SK Bansal and P Willey   TV umpire: SN Bandekar   Match referee: CW Smith India won by 171 runs

South Africa v Australia
Second Test at Newlands, Cape Town

2001-02
March 8, 9, 10, 11, 12 (2002)

This Test, Shane Warne's 100th, was memorable in numerous ways, as Australia contested South Africa at Cape Town. A classic Test looked unlikely after Australia dominated the initial stages following its 360-run win in the first Test. The hosts were set back with the loss of paceman Allan Donald, who retired after being injured in the first Test.

After South Africa chose to bat in the second Test, Herschelle Gibbs hit successive boundaries in the fourth over, before edging a wide ball to Mark Waugh. Debutant left-hander Graeme Smith failed when he edged Glenn McGrath to third slip, before experienced left-hander Gary Kirsten edged Brett Lee to second slip. The hosts were 70-4 when a gem of a delivery from Warne pitched outside leg-stump before bowling Neil McKenzie. Good line and length bowling from McGrath accounted for Jacques Kallis and Ashwell Prince after lunch as South Africa fell to 92-6.

Andrew Hall led a recovery on debut and hit some off side fours off Gillespie, while another boundary came from a sweep off Warne. Mark Boucher pulled an impressive four off Lee but departed wastefully two balls later, when he lashed at a wide ball. Paul Adams provided entertainment as he swept Warne for four and struck a six over mid wicket. South Africa passed 200, and Adams scored 35 before edging Gillespie to first slip. Hall's invaluable 70 ended when he too edged Gillespie. South Africa's third debutant, Dewald Pretorius, could boast that he hit the first ball he faced in Test cricket for four off Warne's bowling. Warne dismissed Ntini three balls later and South Africa's innings finished on 239.

Pretorius' second ball yielded an all-run four to Justin Langer, who hit the next ball to the boundary. Matthew Hayden struck two fours in Pretorius' second over and in Ntini's third over, before Langer creamed four fours in Pretorius' third over. Australia was 46-0 from eight overs before stumps, and

Glenn McGrath led Australia's pace attack from 1995 until his retirement in early 2007, and finished with 563 Test wickets at a brilliant average of 21.64.

Langer hammered a four from the first ball he faced on day two. Langer's aggressive innings ended on 37 as he dragged a delivery onto his stumps, before Ricky Ponting struck two of his first three deliveries for four. Boundaries were regular for a while, before Hayden skied a bouncer and was caught at fine leg for 63.

Ponting smacked a six off Hall before edging the unorthodox spin of Adams, who soon deceived Steve Waugh in flight and bowled him off his pads for a duck. Australia faltered to 168-4. A miscued cut from Mark Waugh produced a catch off Ntini, who subsequently had Damien Martyn edging behind as Australia struggled to 185-6. Adam Gilchrist, however, proved a saviour yet again after smashing 204 not out in the first Test. Just before Martyn's dismissal, Gilchrist edged a boundary off Adams before clouting the next ball for a convincing four. After Martyn's demise, Gilchrist hit boundaries in quick succession off Ntini, Adams and Pretorius, before Warne also hit regular boundaries, including a six off Adams. The total reached 317 before Warne's attacking 63 ended when Kallis took a great slips catch, and Gilchrist motored towards his century before Prince took a good low catch at cover to account for Lee. Gillespie and McGrath offered brief resistance, and Gilchrist took 36 runs in two Adams overs before finishing unbeaten on 138 from just 108 balls, Australia having gained a staggering 143-run lead. South Africa was 7-0 when bad light ended the day prematurely.

Gibbs had a couple of close shaves, but he and Kirsten survived the first hour of day three against Warne and McGrath. Gibbs hit three successive fours off Lee, before a prod off Warne was caught at silly point to end the partnership at 84. Smith survived a perilously close lbw appeal off Warne when 12, and soon took 11 runs off a Warne over, while Kirsten looked set for a big score. Smith reached 53 after dispatching two loose Mark Waugh deliveries for four each, before Lee had Kirsten lbw for

87. Kallis struck three fours in a Lee over, and hit sumptuous boundaries off Martyn and Steve Waugh, before an edged four took him to 50. Smith was unlucky to be ruled caught behind for 68, and Warne later had Kallis lbw for 73. South Africa led by 164 runs at stumps, and the lead reached 207 before Warne dismissed Prince.

A gritty McKenzie combined with Boucher to take the hosts to 431-5 before South Africa foolishly lost 9-3. Gillespie had Boucher lbw before Hall was needlessly run out for a duck, and McKenzie run out for 99 after chancing a single and succumbing to a direct hit from Martyn. Adams and Ntini rallied temporarily, and Adams hit two sixes before Warne finished with 6-161 from 70 overs.

With Australia chasing 331, Langer hit two fours in the first over. Pretorius conceded 14 runs in the 10th over, including an inside-edged four to Hayden. Thirteen runs came from Adams' third over, and luck was not on Pretorius' or South Africa's side other than when Langer's free-flowing 58 ended with an inside-edge onto his leg-stump. Australia was 131-1 at stumps, before Hayden and Ponting hit a four each in the first over of day five.

Hayden and Ponting scored freely, and Australia was 201-1 when Hayden reached 96 with a splendid cut for four off Kallis before departing, as he needlessly chased a very wide delivery. Ponting raised his 50 with three successive fours off Pretorius, before 21 runs came in two overs off Ntini and Kallis. Mark Waugh was ruled caught behind for 16, before Steve Waugh hit successive fours off Ntini. The wayward Adams struck twice in quick succession, with accurate deliveries dismissing Steve Waugh and Martyn to make things interesting at 268-5.

Gilchrist continued his form and registered a few fours before a faulty stroke cost him, with the total on 305. Unfazed, Warne hit a quick 15 not out as Australia reached 328-6, before Ponting lofted a six over square leg to raise a century, as well as victory.

SOUTH AFRICA 1ST INNINGS

HH Gibbs	c ME Waugh b Gillespie	12
G Kirsten	c ME Waugh b Lee	7
GC Smith	c Ponting b McGrath	3
JH Kallis	c Gilchrist b McGrath	23
ND McKenzie	b Warne	20
AG Prince	c Gilchrist b McGrath	10
MV Boucher*†	c Gilchrist b Lee	26
AJ Hall	c Gilchrist b Gillespie	70
PR Adams	c Warne b Gillespie	35
M Ntini	c ME Waugh b Warne	14
D Pretorius	not out	5
Extras	(b 4, lb 5, nb 5)	14
Total		239

Fall of wickets 15, 18, 25, 70, 73, 92, 147, 216, 229, 239

	O	M	R	W
GD McGrath	20	4	42	3
JN Gillespie	15	4	52	3
B Lee	16	1	65	2
SK Warne	28	10	70	2
ME Waugh	1	0	1	0

AUSTRALIA 1ST INNINGS

JL Langer	b Ntini	37
ML Hayden	c Hall b Kallis	63
RT Ponting	c Boucher b Adams	47
ME Waugh	c Gibbs b Ntini	25
SR Waugh*	b Adams	0
DR Martyn	c Boucher b Ntini	2
AC Gilchrist†	not out	138
SK Warne	c Kallis b Adams	63
B Lee	c Prince b Kallis	0
JN Gillespie	c Kallis b Adams	0
GD McGrath	lbw b Ntini	2
Extras	(b 2, lb 1, w 2)	5
Total		382

Fall of wickets 67, 130, 162, 168, 176, 185, 317, 338, 343, 382

	O	M	R	W
M Ntini	22.5	5	93	4
D Pretorius	11	1	72	0
JH Kallis	16	1	65	2
AJ Hall	11	1	47	0
PR Adams	20	1	102	4

SOUTH AFRICA 2ND INNINGS

HH Gibbs	c Ponting b Warne	39
G Kirsten	lbw b Lee	87
GC Smith	c Gilchrist b Warne	68
JH Kallis	lbw b Warne	73
ND McKenzie	run out (Martyn)	99
AG Prince	c Ponting b Warne	20
MV Boucher*†	lbw b Gillespie	37
AJ Hall	run out (Lee/Gillespie)	0
PR Adams	not out	23
M Ntini	c Langer b Warne	11
D Pretorius	c ME Waugh b Warne	0
Extras	(b 8, lb 3, w 2, nb 3)	16
Total		473

Fall of wickets 84, 183, 254, 284, 350, 431, 433, 440, 464, 473

	O	M	R	W
GD McGrath	25	7	56	0
JN Gillespie	29	10	81	1
SK Warne	70	15	161	6
B Lee	22	3	99	1
ME Waugh	9	3	34	0
DR Martyn	4	0	15	0
SR Waugh	3	0	16	0

AUSTRALIA 2ND INNINGS

JL Langer	b Pretorius	58
ML Hayden	c Boucher b Kallis	96
RT Ponting	not out	100
ME Waugh	c Boucher b Ntini	16
SR Waugh*	b Adams	14
DR Martyn	lbw b Adams	0
AC Gilchrist†	c McKenzie b Kallis	24
SK Warne	not out	15
Extras	(lb 6, nb 5)	11
Total	(6 wickets)	334

Did not bat B Lee, JN Gillespie, GD McGrath

Fall of wickets 102, 201, 251, 268, 268, 305

	O	M	R	W
M Ntini	24	4	90	1
D Pretorius	14	5	60	1
PR Adams	21.1	0	104	2
AJ Hall	3	0	6	0
JH Kallis	17	2	68	2

Toss: South Africa Umpires: SA Bucknor and RE Koertzen TV umpire: DL Orchard Match referee: CW Smith Australia won by 4 wickets

West Indies v Australia

Fourth Test at Antigua Recreation Ground, St John's, Antigua

2003

May 9, 10, 11, 12, 13 (2003)

Shivnarine Chanderpaul's second innings century helped the West Indies reach the highest successful target in Test cricket.

The final Test of the 2003 series in the Caribbean involving the hosts and Australia had ample controversy, hostility and the highest successful run chase in Test history. A classic occasion seemed unlikely after Australia convincingly won the first three Tests.

Australia batted first and began briskly. Matthew Hayden hit three fours before an indiscreet pull caused his downfall for 14. Justin Langer registered six fours and was reprieved at slip before slashing a catch to gully before lunch. Jermaine Lawson struck a third time when he dismissed another left-hander, Darren Lehmann, two balls after Lehmann hit a four. Australia was 93-3, with Martin Love batting solidly after replacing an unwell Ricky Ponting. Shivnarine Chanderpaul dropped Love and Steve Waugh, before the unfortunate off-spinner Omari Banks bowled Love for 36. Australia was 128-4.

Fifty-three runs later, Waugh edged Merv Dillon behind before Australia became 194-6, when Gilchrist, like Langer and Lehmann, succumbed to the last ball of an over. Like Hayden, Gilchrist miscued a pull. Andy Bichel struck seven fours in a fast 34 before he was caught off a fearsome Lawson, who reduced Australia from 224-6 to 240 all out. Brett Lee, Stuart MacGill and Jason Gillespie were caught behind the wicket: Lee and Gillespie from bumpers, and MacGill just after receiving two bumpers. Lawson took 7-78.

The hosts were 1-1 after one minute when Glenn McGrath dislodged Chris Gayle's middle-stump. Eleven runs came in the third over before Bichel struck with his third ball, with the total on 30 when Daren Ganga gloved a half-tracker to Gilchrist. Nightwatchman Vasbert Drakes survived two close lbw appeals off MacGill before stumps. Devon Smith and Drakes hit some fours the next morning before Lee had Smith caught behind. Brian Lara slashed his first delivery for six, before Drakes was lbw three balls later. The West Indies were 80-4. Lara, who repeatedly exchanged harsh words with his opponents, hit successive fours off Gillespie before Ramnaresh Sarwan did likewise off Lee. The Australians were furious after Lara survived a caught behind appeal off Gillespie.

Lara and Sarwan played some excellent strokes before the pendulum swung, as Bichel took a sharp return catch to dismiss Sarwan, and McGrath then bowled Chanderpaul to make the score 140-6. Lara and Ridley Jacobs scored freely off Gillespie and McGrath, before Jacobs was stupidly run out for 26. Lara pulled three fours in four balls off Bichel, before hitting the fifth ball for a catch to mid off. West Indies 197-8. Banks and Dillon added 27 runs before Lee bowled Dillon, and then Lawson hit three fours in the same over. The hosts levelled Australia's total before Lawson departed. A back strain subsequently restricted

Lawson to six overs, and series referee Mike Procter confirmed two days later that Lawson was reported to the ICC for a suspect action.

With Lawson missing, Langer reached his half-century with a six off Banks while Hayden was just 19, before Hayden increased his scoring rate. Dillon, Banks and Drakes were punished as the left-handed openers played many fine drives and cuts. Lara dropped Hayden at 122-0, before the total reached 171-0 from just 39 overs before stumps. Hayden subsequently posted a century before Langer did likewise. The stand was 242 when Langer departed to a meek push at Gayle. Hayden hit consecutive fours off Dillon, before a new spell for Banks yielded the wickets of Gilchrist and Love in quick succession. Hayden clobbered some boundaries off Banks, including a six that raised Hayden's 150, before the Australians crumbled from 330-3. Lehmann chopped a ball onto his stumps before Hayden was run out for 177. Waugh held firm for two hours but the lower order struggled, while Dillon had some success. McGrath scored a useful 14 in a last wicket stand of 29, and the West Indies required 418 runs.

Only 15 runs came in the first 13 overs before MacGill's second over cost 13 runs, including a huge six by Gayle. Lee bowled fearsomely but fading light caused stumps to be drawn five deliveries early, at 47-0. The hosts slumped to 50-2 the next morning, with Gayle falling to Lee before Smith was caught behind off Gillespie. Lara hit Bichel for two fours in an over before an inswinging yorker from McGrath had Ganga lbw and the West Indies 74-3.

Sarwan again found form and Lara was steady before smashing three sixes off MacGill, including two over long on from successive balls. But the hosts looked gone at 165-4 when Lara sought another six and was bowled by a flighted ball that bounced from the rough. Sarwan, however, kept going, hitting three fours in four balls off MacGill. The 200 was raised before 13 runs were scored in a McGrath over, followed by two fours to Chanderpaul in McGrath's following over.

Following tea, tempers flared when McGrath instigated a disgusting altercation with Sarwan, who subsequently hit MacGill and McGrath for two fours each. Chanderpaul raced to 50 by punishing Gillespie. Sarwan reached his century after the new ball was taken, and then slashed Lee for his 17th four before top-edging a hook next ball for a caught-and-bowled. Jacobs was ruled caught behind next ball after the ball hit his elbow, and the angry crowd hurled bottles onto the field. The score was 288-6. There was a brief rain interruption, and Banks was vitally reprieved on two when Love dropped him. Chanderpaul hooked a six in a Gillespie over that cost 14 runs, before punishing MacGill. Chanderpaul reached an emotional century while a sensible Banks helped the score to a promising 371-6 at stumps.

The target looked tough when Chanderpaul edged Lee behind after adding just a single, but Lee conceded crucial runs before MacGill and Gillespie bowled in tandem. Banks hit two fours in successive overs before whacking MacGill over the cow corner boundary, making the total 402-7. Drakes inside-edged a speculative four, before Banks edged a MacGill full-toss for four more. Moments later, Drakes smacked a four through point to seal the historic run chase.

Top: Matthew Hayden (left) marks his century during Australia's second innings.
Bottom: The Australian slips cordon readies for the catch during the fourth Test against West Indies in Antigua, 2003.

AUSTRALIA 1ST INNINGS

JL Langer	c Banks b Lawson	42
ML Hayden	c Drakes b Lawson	14
ML Love	b Banks	36
DS Lehmann	c Jacobs b Lawson	7
SR Waugh*	c Jacobs b Dillon	41
AC Gilchrist†	c Chanderpaul b Dillon	33
AJ Bichel	c sub (MN Samuels) b Lawson	34
B Lee	c Jacobs b Lawson	9
JN Gillespie	c Jacobs b Lawson	6
SCG MacGill	c Sarwan b Lawson	2
GD McGrath	not out	5
Extras	(b 2, lb 3, w 2, nb 4)	11
Total		240

Fall of wickets 27, 80, 93, 128, 181, 194, 224, 231, 233, 240

	O	M	R	W
M Dillon	18	2	53	2
JJC Lawson	19.1	3	78	7
VC Drakes	15	2	42	0
OAC Banks	20	2	62	1

WEST INDIES 1ST INNINGS

CH Gayle	b McGrath	0
DS Smith	c Gilchrist b Lee	37
D Ganga	c Gilchrist b Bichel	6
VC Drakes	lbw b Lee	21
BC Lara*	c Langer b Bichel	68
RR Sarwan	c & b Bichel	24
S Chanderpaul	b McGrath	1
RD Jacobs†	run out (Lee)	26
OAC Banks	not out	16
M Dillon	b Lee	9
JJC Lawson	c Love b MacGill	14
Extras	(lb 8, w 3, nb 7)	18
Total		240

Fall of wickets 1, 30, 73, 80, 137, 140, 185, 197, 224, 240

	O	M	R	W
GD McGrath	17	6	44	2
JN Gillespie	17	3	56	0
AJ Bichel	14	4	53	3
B Lee	15	2	71	3
SCG MacGill	2.3	0	8	1

AUSTRALIA 2ND INNINGS

JL Langer	c Lara b Gayle	111
ML Hayden	run out (sub [CS Baugh])	177
AC Gilchrist†	c sub (MN Samuels) b Banks	6
ML Love	c sub (MN Samuels) b Banks	2
DS Lehmann	b Dillon	14
SR Waugh*	not out	45
AJ Bichel	c Smith b Dillon	0
B Lee	c sub (SC Joseph) b Dillon	18
JN Gillespie	c Lara b Drakes	5
SCG MacGill	c Lara b Dillon	0
GD McGrath	c Ganga b Drakes	14
Extras	(b 4, lb 9, nb 12)	25
Total		417

Fall of wickets 242, 273, 285, 330, 338, 343, 373, 385, 388, 417

	O	M	R	W
JJC Lawson	6	1	17	0
M Dillon	29	3	112	4
OAC Banks	37	5	153	2
VC Drakes	19	1	92	2
CH Gayle	13	1	30	1

WEST INDIES 2ND INNINGS

CH Gayle	c Waugh b Lee	19
DS Smith	c Gilchrist b Gillespie	23
D Ganga	lbw b McGrath	8
BC Lara*	b MacGill	60
RR Sarwan	c & b Lee	105
S Chanderpaul	c Gilchrist b Lee	104
RD Jacobs†	c Gilchrist b Lee	0
OAC Banks	not out	47
VC Drakes	not out	27
Extras	(b 9, lb 9, w 1, nb 6)	25
Total	(7 wickets)	418

Did not bat M Dillon, JJC Lawson

Fall of wickets 48, 50, 74, 165, 288, 288, 372

	O	M	R	W
GD McGrath	25	10	50	1
JN Gillespie	25	10	64	1
B Lee	23	4	63	4
SCG MacGill	35.5	8	149	1
AJ Bichel	15	3	49	0
SR Waugh	5	0	25	0

Toss: Australia   Umpires: DR Shepherd and S Venkataraghavan
TV umpire: BR Doctrove   Match referee: MJ Procter   West Indies won by 3 wickets

New Zealand v Pakistan

Second Test at Basin Reserve, Wellington

2003–04

December 26, 27, 28, 29, 30 (2003)

New Zealand opener Mark Richardson showed splendid concentration as he scored 82 and 41 against Pakistan in the second Test of 2003–04.

An astonishing recovery best describes the second and deciding Test of the New Zealand versus Pakistan series in 2003–04, after the first Test was drawn.

New Zealand won the toss and elected to bat under dark clouds. Only 2.5 overs were bowled before bad light halted play until after lunch. Back from a hamstring injury, Pakistani quick Shoaib Akhtar fired a delivery through Lou Vincent's defence and into the stumps just before the interruption. With the first ball after the break, Akhtar trapped Stephen Fleming lbw to make the score 1-2. Due to his injury, however, Shoaib wasn't able to bowl lengthy spells.

New Zealand Test debutant Richard Jones scored a gutsy 16 before inside-edging an Abdul Razzaq delivery onto the stumps, then Scott Styris gave a strong exhibition of straight driving. He made a confident 36 before Akhtar produced a rising delivery that had him caught behind. Dogged left-handed opener Mark Richardson played a John Wright-like role, reaching 50 in 262 minutes, while Craig McMillan scored a slow 26. He was unluckily ruled lbw after edging a Shabbir Ahmed delivery onto his pad. Robbie Hart survived a caught behind appeal off Shoaib, who soon struck Hart on the head with a bouncer. But Shoaib felt the pain of his injury, which again restricted him on day two as the Kiwis started at 151-5.

The score was 171-6 when Hart glanced a catch to leg gully, before Jacob Oram found form. He and Richardson added 76 runs before Richardson, who lasted 439 minutes for his 82 runs, lapsed and slashed a wide ball for a catch to point. Oram was joined by another left-hander, Daniel Vettori, and the duo capitalised on Shoaib's lengthy absence. Oram was particularly severe on Danish Kaneria's leg-spin, and the partnership produced 80 runs before Oram fell for 97. Vettori pushed on to 44 before his dismissal. Ian Butler hit a four first ball but was out second ball, and Shoaib had 5-48 as the Kiwis tallied 366.

Oram produced the first wicket in Pakistan's reply as Imran Farhat was caught behind for 20, before a fired-up Butler had Taufeeq Umar and Yasir Hameed in trouble. Butler bowled Yasir for three, and wicketkeeper Hart fumbled a chance to catch Yousuf Youhana. Only eight runs were added on day three when a rising ball from Daryl Tuffey had Taufeeq caught at gully, after the opener scored 16 in 154 minutes. Inzamam-ul-Haq was watchful and looked good until Oram had him lbw for 34, while Youhana was in a stubborn mood. He scored only 29 runs in the session, and went on to score 60 in 246 minutes until he edged Vettori to slip. Soon the score was 171-5 when the new ball was taken, and Butler used it superbly. An indipper bowled Razzaq for 26, and then the score increased to 194-6, before Butler took four quick wickets to claim 6-46 and

have Pakistan out for 196. Mohammad Sami gloved a catch behind, Shoaib was bowled, Moin Khan superbly caught at cover, and Kaneria dubiously lbw from a full-toss. Vincent avoided a pair but again fell early to Shoaib before Fleming scored 24 of the next 35 runs. He advanced Kaneria to drive a boundary before being trapped lbw at the crease next ball. New Zealand led by 245 runs at stumps, with seven wickets remaining after Jones gloved a legside Shoaib delivery to the wicketkeeper. The Kiwis were 95-3 the next morning before Richardson edged a drive to Moin, having scored 41 in a shade over three hours. Shoaib was on a hat-trick after Styris edged a booming drive onto his leg-stump, and McMillan just survived the hat-trick ball, which pitched in the blockhole.

The Kiwis were suddenly in bother at 95-5, which became 96-6 when Tuffey was run out after McMillan called the nightwatchman through for a single and then sent him back. Oram and Vettori were lbw from Shabbir deliveries that nipped in, before inswinging yorkers from Shoaib rattled the woodwork to dismiss Hart and Butler for ducks. Shoaib had 11 wickets for the match, as the hosts lost 8-7, dismissed for 103 and leaving Pakistan a target of 274. The target would be tough, considering the highest successful run chase at Wellington had been 215, which New Zealand achieved against India five years earlier.

Farhat scored 14 in an opening stand of 37 before he gloved a catch to Hart down the leg-side off Oram. Pakistan was 75-2 when Taufeeq was lbw to Vettori for 34, then the tourists were on track when Yasir and Youhana found form. Yasir hit nine fours as he scored a composed 59, before edging the expensive Butler to Hart. Pakistan was 156-3 before Youhana and Inzamam consolidated, punishing any loose balls, and Youhana had a crucial reprieve when Fleming dropped a catch. Youhana and Inzamam reached half-centuries, and Inzamam's took just 66 balls before the Pakistanis were 246-3 at stumps, with Youhana on 73 and Inzamam 57. Interestingly, Inzamam opted not to accept the chance to play an extra 30 minutes on the fourth day, as showers were forecast for day five.

Rain delayed the start of the last day's play by 30 minutes, and then another shower sent the players back to the pavilion before a ball was bowled. Play began just after midday, and Inzamam pulled the opening delivery from Tuffey for four. Inzamam also hit Butler's first ball of the day to the boundary, and Youhana hammered two fours later in the same over, which cost 13 runs. Only 3.5 overs were needed on day five for Pakistan to seal a memorable seven-wicket win, achieved when Youhana whacked a four behind point. Youhana's unbeaten 88 included 14 fours, while Inzamam's 72 yielded nine fours.

NEW ZEALAND 1ST INNINGS		
MH Richardson	c Yousuf Youhana b Shabbir Ahmed	82
L Vincent	b Shoaib Akhtar	0
SP Fleming*	lbw b Shoaib Akhtar	0
RA Jones	b Abdul Razzaq	16
SB Styris	c Moin Khan b Shoaib Akhtar	36
CD McMillan	lbw b Shabbir Ahmed	26
RG Hart†	c Imran Farhat b Shoaib Akhtar	19
JDP Oram	c Moin Khan b Shabbir Ahmed	97
DL Vettori	c Yasir Hameed b Mohammad Sami	44
DR Tuffey	not out	9
IG Butler	c Moin Khan b Shoaib Akhtar	4
Extras	(b 5, lb 14, w 3, nb 11)	33
Total		366

Fall of wickets 1, 1, 41, 94, 145, 171, 247, 327, 361, 366

	O	M	R	W
Shoaib Akhtar	20.3	5	48	5
Mohammad Sami	30	12	64	1
Shabbir Ahmed	37	8	87	3
Danish Kaneria	32	5	86	0
Abdul Razzaq	23	6	62	1

PAKISTAN 1ST INNINGS		
Imran Farhat	c Hart b Oram	20
Taufeeq Umar	c Oram b Tuffey	16
Yasir Hameed	b Butler	3
Yousuf Youhana	c Fleming b Vettori	60
Inzamam-ul-Haq*	lbw b Oram	34
Abdul Razzaq	b Butler	26
Moin Khan†	c Vettori b Butler	19
Mohammad Sami	c Hart b Butler	4
Shoaib Akhtar	b Butler	0
Shabbir Ahmed	not out	0
Danish Kaneria	lbw b Butler	0
Extras	(b 4, lb 3, w 1, nb 6)	14
Total		196

Fall of wickets 27, 30, 60, 112, 168, 171, 194, 195, 196, 196

	O	M	R	W
DR Tuffey	24	9	46	1
IG Butler	20	6	46	6
JDP Oram	22	5	49	2
DL Vettori	22	6	47	1
SB Styris	2	1	1	0

NEW ZEALAND 2ND INNINGS		
MH Richardson	c Moin Khan b Shoaib Akhtar	41
L Vincent	lbw b Shoaib Akhtar	4
SP Fleming*	lbw b Danish Kaneria	24
RA Jones	c Moin Khan b Shoaib Akhtar	7
DR Tuffey	run out (Mohammad Sami/Danish Kaneria)	13
SB Styris	b Shoaib Akhtar	0
CD McMillan	not out	3
JDP Oram	lbw b Shabbir Ahmed	3
DL Vettori	lbw b Shabbir Ahmed	0
RG Hart†	b Shoaib Akhtar	0
IG Butler	b Shoaib Akhtar	0
Extras	(lb 4, w 1, nb 3)	8
Total		103

Fall of wickets 8, 43, 73, 95, 95, 96, 101, 102, 103, 103

	O	M	R	W
Shoaib Akhtar	18	3	30	6
Shabbir Ahmed	17	5	20	2
Mohammad Sami	4	1	12	0
Danish Kaneria	9	2	18	1
Abdul Razzaq	5	1	19	0

PAKISTAN 2ND INNINGS		
Imran Farhat	c Hart b Oram	14
Taufeeq Umar	lbw b Vettori	34
Yasir Hameed	c Hart b Butler	59
Yousuf Youhana	not out	88
Inzamam-ul-Haq*	not out	72
Extras	(b 4, lb 2, nb 4)	10
Total	(3 wickets)	277

Did not bat Abdul Razzaq, Moin Khan†, Mohammad Sami, Shabbir Ahmed, Shoaib Akhtar, Danish Kaneria

Fall of wickets 37, 75, 156

	O	M	R	W
DR Tuffey	14	5	41	0
IG Butler	18.5	1	100	1
JDP Oram	9	1	34	1
SB Styris	6	1	26	0
DL Vettori	23	5	59	1
CD McMillan	4	0	11	0

Toss: New Zealand   Umpires: EAR de Silva and DL Orchard
TV umpire: DB Cowie   Match referee: BC Broad   Pakistan won by 7 wickets

England v Australia
Second Test at Edgbaston, Birmingham

2005
August 4, 5, 6, 7 (2005)

Leading 1-0 in the 2005 Ashes series, Australia was in trouble for the second Test when Glenn McGrath withdrew after rolling his ankle. Ricky Ponting nonetheless elected to bowl first, with Michael Kasprowicz replacing McGrath in a Test that ebbed and flowed dramatically.

Marcus Trescothick cover-drove Brett Lee for three fours in the third over, before Shane Warne crucially dropped Andrew Strauss in the fourth over. Strauss struck successive fours off Warne before Trescothick bludgeoned a huge six over Warne's head, and the left-handed batsmen each hit successive fours off Kasprowicz. The 100 was passed in the 23rd over before a big turning delivery from Warne bowled Strauss. Trescothick hammered 18 runs off Lee in the next over to take England to 132-1 at lunch.

A wild throw from Michael Clarke gifted Michael Vaughan four overthrows before the unfortunate bowler, Kasprowicz, hit back. Trescothick and Ian Bell, who chopped his second delivery for four, edged behind in one over. England was 187-4 when Vaughan skied a catch, but the boundaries kept coming. Andrew Flintoff accumulated six fours and five sixes as he savaged Warne and Lee, before edging a slash off Jason Gillespie just after tea. Geraint Jones fell cheaply before Ashley Giles scored a quick 23. Kevin Pietersen hit three fours in a Lee over, then hoicked a six before being caught. Steve Harmison impressively clubbed Lee for a six and a four in succession, and Simon Jones also cleared the boundary before England was dismissed for 407 in just 79.2 overs, with 54 fours and 10 sixes hit.

After rain forced Australia to start batting on day two, Matthew Hayden was out to his and Matthew Hoggard's first delivery, with a catch clipped to short cover. Ponting registered two fours in Hoggard's next over, then a Harmison delivery

Michael Kasprowicz and Brett Lee put on a last wicket partnership of 59 in the second Ashes Test of 2005, but it wasn't quite enough to take Australia to victory. England bowler Andrew Flintoff talks to umpire Billy Bowden after Kasprowicz was caught out with Australia needing three runs to win the match.

hit Justin Langer in the midriff. Ponting raced to 51 with 10 fours, including three in a row off Simon Jones before Giles had Ponting caught from a mistimed sweep. Damien Martyn hit three fours off Flintoff before he was run out attempting a single, making Australia 118-3 at lunch.

Clarke hit seven fours before he and Simon Katich snicked behind, as the Australians fell to 208-5. Langer and Gilchrist added 54 runs before Australia was dismissed for 308. Flintoff ended the innings with successive inswinging yorkers that trapped Gillespie and Kasprowicz lbw.

Trescothick cover-drove the first ball of England's second innings for four, before Strauss was bowled by a spectacular Warne delivery that landed well outside off-stump. England began day three on 25-1, and quickly crashed to 31-4. Trescothick edged Lee before Vaughan was bowled three balls later, and Hoggard was caught at gully in Lee's next over. Pietersen whacked two sixes in a Warne over before being superbly caught behind for 20. Bell soon fell to Warne and England reached 95-6 at lunch.

A brutish Lee delivery accounted for Geraint Jones, and Warne had Giles and Harmison caught off successive balls as England became 131-9. But things changed as Flintoff fired again, making 73. He smacked two sixes in three balls from Kasprowicz before smashing a six, four and six off successive Lee deliveries. A 51-run, last-wicket partnership stretched Australia's target to 282.

Langer began well before Flintoff again showed his knack for changing the game. He induced an inside edge from Langer onto the stumps and an outside edge from Ponting to the wicketkeeper in one over. Australia was 48-2. Martyn registered some attractive fours, and Hayden struck two boundaries in four balls off Simon Jones, but the latter was instantly followed by an edged catch. A few overs later, Martyn clipped a simple catch to mid wicket.

The pendulum swung again as Katich struck his first and third balls for four, before Clarke drove two fours in three balls from Giles. The left-arm spinner soon struck gold twice, as Katich edged to slip, before Gilchrist advanced his fourth ball and presented a catch to mid on. The promoted Gillespie quickly fell again to a Flintoff yorker, and another 30 minutes of play was allowed before stumps, as Australia was 140-7 and slipping to defeat. Warne counterattacked with successive sixes over square leg off Giles, before a slower ball from Harmison bamboozled Clarke and bowled him. Stumps were drawn with Australia 175-8.

Australia hit back as Warne and Lee took 13 runs off a Harmison over. Harmison's next over featured a streaky four to Warne and a smashing drive by Lee for another four. With Australia needing 62 runs, Warne was bizarrely out hit wicket as he moved back and across, and then a scarcely believable last wicket partnership ensued.

On 227-9, Kasprowicz survived a close lbw appeal before flicking Flintoff for four and then defending a yorker. The next over by Giles yielded three fours including two in succession to Kasprowicz, with the latter off an edge. A wild legside ball from Harmison went for four byes, and then Flintoff returned to bowl as the score was 262-9. Flintoff struck Lee painfully on the fingers, and the tension was immense in the next over, as Lee speculatively inside-edged Harmison for four, survived a yorker and twice played and missed.

On 267-9, Kasprowicz scooped Flintoff, but a diving Simon Jones missed a catch at third man. Flintoff uncharacteristically speared a no-ball past the wicketkeeper for a boundary, before five singles made the score 278-9. Lee then thumped a Harmison full-toss, but only for another single, as he found the fielder in the deep. Harmison soon banged a ball at Kasprowicz's ribcage, and Kasprowicz gloved it down the legside for a catch behind. The hosts clinched a thrilling two-run win, and England subsequently claimed its first Ashes title since 1986–87. In his book *True Colours*, Gilchrist wrote, "If we'd saved the Ashes, it would have been a travesty. England outplayed us."

ENGLAND 1ST INNINGS

ME Trescothick	c Gilchrist b Kasprowicz	90
AJ Strauss	b Warne	48
MP Vaughan*	c Lee b Gillespie	24
IR Bell	c Gilchrist b Kasprowicz	6
KP Pietersen	c Katich b Lee	71
A Flintoff	c Gilchrist b Gillespie	68
GO Jones†	c Gilchrist b Kasprowicz	1
AF Giles	lbw b Warne	23
MJ Hoggard	lbw b Warne	16
SJ Harmison	b Warne	17
SP Jones	not out	19
Extras	(lb 9, w 1, nb 14)	24
Total		407

Fall of wickets 112, 164, 170, 187, 290, 293, 342, 348, 375, 407

	O	M	R	W
B Lee	17	1	111	1
JN Gillespie	22	3	91	2
MS Kasprowicz	15	3	80	3
SK Warne	25.2	4	116	4

AUSTRALIA 1ST INNINGS

JL Langer	lbw b SP Jones	82
ML Hayden	c Strauss b Hoggard	0
RT Ponting*	c Vaughan b Giles	61
DR Martyn	run out (Vaughan)	20
MJ Clarke	c GO Jones b Giles	40
SM Katich	c GO Jones b Flintoff	4
AC Gilchrist†	not out	49
SK Warne	b Giles	8
B Lee	c Flintoff b SP Jones	6
JN Gillespie	lbw b Flintoff	7
MS Kasprowicz	lbw b Flintoff	0
Extras	(b 13, lb 7, w 1, nb 10)	31
Total		308

Fall of wickets 0, 88, 118, 194, 208, 262, 273, 282, 308, 308

	O	M	R	W
SJ Harmison	11	1	48	0
MJ Hoggard	8	0	41	1
SP Jones	16	2	69	2
A Flintoff	15	1	52	3
AF Giles	26	2	78	3

ENGLAND 2ND INNINGS

ME Trescothick	c Gilchrist b Lee	21
AJ Strauss	b Warne	6
MJ Hoggard	c Hayden b Lee	1
MP Vaughan*	b Lee	1
IR Bell	c Gilchrist b Warne	21
KP Pietersen	c Gilchrist b Warne	20
A Flintoff	b Warne	73
GO Jones†	c Ponting b Lee	9
AF Giles	c Hayden b Warne	8
SJ Harmison	c Ponting b Warne	0
SP Jones	not out	12
Extras	(lb 1, nb 9)	10
Total		182

Fall of wickets 25, 27, 29, 31, 72, 75, 101, 131, 131, 182

	O	M	R	W
B Lee	18	1	82	4
JN Gillespie	8	0	24	0
MS Kasprowicz	3	0	29	0
SK Warne	23.1	7	46	6

AUSTRALIA 2ND INNINGS

JL Langer	b Flintoff	28
ML Hayden	c Trescothick b SP Jones	31
RT Ponting*	c GO Jones b Flintoff	0
DR Martyn	c Bell b Hoggard	28
MJ Clarke	b Harmison	30
SM Katich	c Trescothick b Giles	16
AC Gilchrist†	c Flintoff b Giles	1
JN Gillespie	lbw b Flintoff	0
SK Warne	hit wicket b Flintoff	42
B Lee	not out	43
MS Kasprowicz	c GO Jones b Harmison	20
Extras	(b 13, lb 8, w 1, nb 18)	40
Total		279

Fall of wickets 47, 48, 82, 107, 134, 136, 137, 175, 220, 279

	O	M	R	W
SJ Harmison	17.3	3	62	2
MJ Hoggard	5	0	26	1
AF Giles	15	3	68	2
A Flintoff	22	3	79	4
SP Jones	5	1	23	1

Toss: Australia   Umpires: BF Bowden and RE Koertzen

TV umpire: JW Lloyds   Match referee: RS Madugalle   England won by 2 runs

Bangladesh v Australia
First Test at Narayangani Osmani Stadium, Fatullah

2005-06
April 9, 10, 11, 12, 13 (2006)

Australia's Test matches against the so-called 'minnows', such as Bangladesh and Zimbabwe, have often been one-sided, but one encounter that could have gone either way took place at Fatullah in 2006, when Bangladesh remarkably led by 158 runs on the first innings.

Bangladesh's top three batsmen batted superbly in the first session after the toss went their way. Javed Omar struck six fours, but was lbw to Jason Gillespie for 27, before Shahriar Nafees and captain Habibul Bashar kept the run rate high, punishing Brett Lee, Stuart Clark, Gillespie and Shane Warne. The score at lunch was a breathtaking 144-1 from 25 overs, with Nafees' 60 featuring 10 fours and Bashar's 45 eight fours. Wicketkeeper Adam Gilchrist dropped Bashar off Warne in the 24th over, and two boundaries quickly followed in the same over. From the last ball before lunch, Bashar beautifully drove Lee for four, before Nafees cut the sixth ball of the second session for another boundary.

Gillespie and Clark subsequently tightened things up. Nafees reached 99 as he swept Warne for four, before edging the next ball to the fine leg fence to raise his first century. The leg-spin combination of MacGill and Warne conceded four boundaries in six balls at one stage. The score mounted to 238 before Bashar top-edged a catch from a MacGill long-hop, and tea was taken.

Rajin Saleh struck two consecutive fours off Warne before Nafees was bowled by MacGill for a memorable 138. Mohammad Ashraful hit three fours in four balls in MacGill's next over, before Gillespie had Ashraful lbw for 29. Aftab Ahmed also scored 29, and Bangladesh was well placed on 355-5 at stumps. With Warne sidelined due to injury, Bangladesh scored just 58 runs in the first session of day two for the loss of Khaled Mashud to a stumping. The innings fell apart after the

break, MacGill dismissing Mohammad Rafique and Saleh in one over, with the latter pushing to short leg for 67. MacGill finished with eight wickets as Bangladesh totalled 427.

Australia began poorly, with Matthew Hayden lbw to Mashrafe Mortaza in just the third over, before makeshift opener Mike Hussey and number three Ricky Ponting hit two fours each in quick succession. Ponting, however, was lbw to Shahadat Hossain for 21, and Rafique bowled Damien Martyn in his first over as Australia went to tea on 50-3.

Bangladesh held the upper hand as Hussey and Michael Clarke had their stumps hit, with the latter dismissed in Enamul Haque's first over before Haque had Warne edging behind. Australia crashed to 93-6. Gilchrist, however, got his eye in and showed controlled aggression, while a stubborn Lee helped Australia to 145-6 at stumps. Another 11 runs were added before Lee was lbw, and then Gillespie scored 26 in 113 minutes, followed by Clark batting for 39 minutes without scoring. Gilchrist meanwhile blazed away in partnerships of 73 and 39 before he was last out, having hit 15 fours and six sixes in his 144. Australia reached 269 while Rafique picked up five wickets.

Nafees quickly extended Bangladesh's advantage with three fours off Lee in the first three overs, and a few more fours were edged through the slips. Six balls after tea, a yorker from Lee wrecked Nafees' stumps after he made 33 of the first 48 runs. Omar fell 10 runs later, edging a cramped cut shot, before slack running from Bashar and an accurate throw from Clarke caused a run out. Ashraful succumbed to a Clark yorker, and Saleh and Ahmed led a recovery until MacGill had Ahmed lbw, ending a 47-run stand.

Bangladesh was 286 runs in front when the first ball of day four went for four byes. Gillespie, however, struck with his first

ball of the day, as Mashud shouldered arms and had his off-peg struck. Rafique hammered three fours in a Warne over before Warne finally came good and had Rafique lbw and Mortaza bowled with successive balls. Saleh's solid 33 ended as he top-edged a pull off Gillespie, before Warne had Haque lbw with a flipper. The last four wickets fell for just one run. Bangladesh's grip on the match had weakened as Australia's target was 307, and as lunch arrived the openers had 31 runs on the board after 14 overs.

Hayden and Hussey progressed soundly, and Hussey earned a five thanks to four overthrows. Hayden lofted a straight six in the next over, before Hussey edged a sweep onto his stumps. Australia was 64-1 before Hayden and Ponting survived until tea, and Hayden cut a four from the final ball of the session to make the score 114-1. The total reached 173-1 before Hayden risked a single and was run out by a direct hit from Haque. Martyn again failed when a turning ball from Rafique hit his off-stump, making Australia 183-3. Clarke hit two consecutive fours off Haque before Rafique had him caught behind from a cut.

Australia was 212-4 after day four, with Ponting well set on 72. Gilchrist fell for 12 the next morning when he missed a straight ball from Rafique, who had Warne lbw 14 minutes later, and Australia wobbled at 231-6. Lee again provided a solid support role to a senior batsman, and hammered a six over long off. He later drove a four, but edged the next ball to the wicketkeeper, and the game was wide open with Australia 277-7. Six runs later, Ponting top-edged a pull off Hossain towards fine leg, but Mortaza missed a difficult catch that could have swung the game Bangladesh's way. Ponting passed 100 with a cover-driven boundary in the next over, and the tourists needed 17 runs after lunch. It took them five overs, as Ponting waited for loose deliveries and hit three fours before Gillespie scored the match-winning run. Bangladesh was left to rue a number of potentially winning positions, which had all been squandered.

Above: Australian leg-spinner Stuart MacGill took his best innings figures in Test cricket in the first Test against Bangladesh in April 2006.

BANGLADESH 1ST INNINGS

Javed Omar	lbw b Gillespie	27
Shahriar Nafees	b MacGill	138
Habibul Bashar*	c Lee b MacGill	76
Rajin Saleh	c sub (A Symonds) b MacGill	67
Mohammad Ashraful	lbw b Gillespie	29
Aftab Ahmed	c Hayden b MacGill	29
Khaled Mashud†	st Gilchrist b MacGill	17
Mohammad Rafique	b MacGill	6
Mashrafe Mortaza	lbw b MacGill	6
Shahadat Hossain	not out	3
Enamul Haque jnr	c Hayden b MacGill	0
Extras	(lb 16, w 2, nb 11)	29
Total		427

Fall of wickets 51, 238, 265, 295, 351, 398, 416, 417, 424, 427

	O	M	R	W
B Lee	19	5	68	0
SR Clark	25	4	69	0
JN Gillespie	23	7	47	2
SK Warne	20	1	112	0
SCG MacGill	33.3	2	108	8
MJ Clarke	3	0	7	0

BANGLADESH 2ND INNINGS

Javed Omar	c Gilchrist b Gillespie	18
Shahriar Nafees	b Lee	33
Habibul Bashar*	run out (Clarke)	7
Rajin Saleh	c Hayden b Gillespie	33
Mohammad Ashraful	lbw b Clark	4
Aftab Ahmed	lbw b MacGill	17
Khaled Mashud†	b Gillespie	0
Mohammad Rafique	lbw b Warne	14
Mashrafe Mortaza	b Warne	0
Shahadat Hossain	not out	1
Enamul Haque jnr	lbw b Warne	0
Extras	(b 10, lb 7, nb 4)	21
Total		148

Fall of wickets 48, 58, 66, 77, 124, 128, 147, 147, 147, 148

	O	M	R	W
B Lee	8	0	47	1
JN Gillespie	11	4	18	3
SCG MacGill	13	4	30	1
SR Clark	4	2	8	1
SK Warne	13	4	28	3
MJ Clarke	1	1	0	0

AUSTRALIA 1ST INNINGS

ML Hayden	lbw b Mashrafe Mortaza	6
MEK Hussey	b Mohammad Rafique	23
RT Ponting*	lbw b Shahadat Hossain	21
DR Martyn	b Mohammad Rafique	4
MJ Clarke	b Enamul Haque jnr	19
AC Gilchrist†	c Shahadat Hossain b Mohammad Rafique	144
SK Warne	c Khaled Mashud b Enamul Haque jnr	6
B Lee	lbw b Mashrafe Mortaza	15
JN Gillespie	b Mohammad Rafique	26
SR Clark	lbw b Mohammad Rafique	0
SCG MacGill	not out	0
Extras	(lb 4, nb 1)	5
Total		269

Fall of wickets 6, 43, 50, 61, 79, 93, 156, 229, 268, 269

	O	M	R	W
Mashrafe Mortaza	22	3	56	2
Shahadat Hossain	14	2	48	1
Mohammad Rafique	32.2	9	62	5
Enamul Haque jnr	25	4	83	2
Mohammad Ashraful	1	0	11	0
Rajin Saleh	1	0	5	0

AUSTRALIA 2ND INNINGS

ML Hayden	run out (Enamul Haque jnr)	72
MEK Hussey	b Enamul Haque jnr	37
RT Ponting*	not out	118
DR Martyn	b Mohammad Rafique	7
MJ Clarke	c Khaled Mashud b Mohammad Rafique	9
AC Gilchrist†	b Mohammad Rafique	12
SK Warne	lbw b Mohammad Rafique	5
B Lee	c Khaled Mashud b Mashrafe Mortaza	29
JN Gillespie	not out	4
Extras	(b 4, lb 7, w 1, nb 2)	14
Total	(7 wickets)	307

Did not bat SR Clark, SCG MacGill

Fall of wickets 64, 173, 183, 205, 225, 231, 277

	O	M	R	W
Mashrafe Mortaza	22	7	51	1
Shahadat Hossain	20	5	67	0
Mohammad Rafique	38	6	98	4
Enamul Haque jnr	27	5	80	1

Toss: Bangladesh   Umpires: Aleem Dar and Nadeem Ghauri

TV umpire: AFM Akhtaruddin   Match referee: JJ Crowe   Australia won by 3 wickets

Sri Lanka v South Africa
Second Test at P Saravanamuttu Stadium, Colombo

2006
August 4, 5, 6, 7, 8 (2006)

The 2006 Sri Lanka versus South Africa series had some big talking points, with Mahela Jayawardene having scored 374 and Kumar Sangakkara 287 in the first Test. The duo put on a gigantic 624-run partnership in Sri Lanka's innings win, before the second Test proved a thriller.

South Africa began disastrously as Chaminda Vaas trapped Herschelle Gibbs second ball. Andrew Hall edged Lasith Malinga to slip after Hall played and missed at seven of the nine balls he faced. Hashim Amla scored 14 runs in Malinga's third over, with three impressive fours followed by two runs, from an edge that wicketkeeper Prasanna Jayawardene should have caught. Malinga beat Jacques Rudolph for pace in his next over, and Amla hit some nice boundaries before he was ruled lbw to Muttiah Muralidaran.

South Africa recovered from 70-4 as AB de Villiers and captain Ashwell Prince were in superb form and stroked regular boundaries. South Africa went from 113-4 to 231-4 in the second session, before Prince perished to a cut shot two balls after tea for a splendid 86. De Villiers fell for 95 when he was ruled caught behind off Malinga, whose next over yielded three fours to Mark Boucher before Boucher dragged a Muralidaran delivery onto the stumps. Shaun Pollock clobbered a four and a six in a Muralidaran over, and Farveez Maharoof then accounted for Nicky Boje. After Dale Steyn departed, Makhaya Ntini struck two fours off Muralidaran, followed by Pollock hitting a streaky six and a four off successive Malinga deliveries with the new ball. Ntini's dismissal ended South Africa's innings and day one, with 56 fours and two sixes hit in the total of 361.

Ntini struck early when Upul Tharanga miscued a pull, while Sanath Jayasuriya hammered Steyn, who was taken off after conceding 26 runs in three overs. The in-form Sangakkara made 14 when Amla took an overhead catch at short mid wicket from an uppish stroke. Jayasuriya luckily edged a couple of fours, before Mahela Jayawardene slashed at Steyn and was caught behind. Tillakaratne Dilshan hooked his first ball for four, before Ntini returned and reduced Sri Lanka from 85-3 to 86-5 in three deliveries. Dilshan was bowled off the toe of the bat and Jayasuriya was caught at slip.

Chamara Kapugedera and Prasanna Jayawardene led a fightback, both pulling Ntini for six before Jayawardene hit four fours in a Steyn over and Kapugedera smashed Boje for six. Kapugedera fell to Boje for 63 and Jayawardene to a great Steyn delivery for 42. Maharoof and Vaas mixed defence and aggression, and the duo tallied 120 runs, including 21 fours, to take Sri Lanka to 321. South Africa was 6-0 at stumps, after Gibbs avoided a pair with a stylishly-driven boundary.

Malinga delivered Gibbs three successive bouncers early on day three, and Gibbs struck three fours in Malinga's next over. Hall luckily earned a six when Vaas took a catch and stepped on the boundary, before Hall fell to Maharoof for 32. Run outs accounted for Rudolph and Amla, although Rudolph was unlucky, as replays showed the ball touched the rope before Kapugedera produced a direct hit. Gibbs meanwhile looked ominous, and he hoicked Muralidaran for six before departing for 92 when a miscued sweep was superbly caught by a diving Jayasuriya. South Africa's progress slowed until de Villiers hit three successive fours off Malinga to establish a 250-run lead, and Prince and de Villiers departed in the following over. Pollock amazingly pulled a half-tracker for an easy catch, before the visitors' lead passed 300 in the first over of day four. Muralidaran dismissed Boje and Steyn to reduce South Africa to 282-9, before the visitors again enjoyed a last wicket stand. Boucher clubbed a couple of fours and sixes while Ntini registered a four. Muralidaran claimed his 12th wicket of the match when Dilshan held a screamer at short leg to dismiss Boucher. Sri Lanka had never successfully chased a Test target as high as the one confronting them now: 352.

Ntini had Tharanga caught at slip for zero but Steyn was expensive again, his first three overs conceding 30 runs. Jayasuriya struck two fours in Steyn's first over before Sangakkara hit Steyn for a series of boundaries, including an edge over the wicketkeeper. South Africa was severely weakened as a hamstring injury restricted Ntini to just 7.2 overs.

Sangakkara belted the first ball of the second session for four before Jayasuriya hit two fours in three Steyn deliveries and then turned his attention to Pollock, with two fours and a six from successive balls. Sri Lanka was 94-2 when Pollock had Sangakkara caught from a faulty drive, before Amla and Gibbs crucially dropped sitters to reprieve Jayasuriya and Mahela Jayawardene respectively with the score on 115-2. Jayasuriya hit another big six but departed four balls later, Sri Lanka 121-3, ironically as Amla took a great one-handed catch from a ball that kicked and hit Jayasuriya's glove.

A Boje over cost 17 runs before Boje had Dilshan caught by Gibbs. The 200 was raised before Kapugedera was well caught by de Villiers at cover. Mahela Jayawardene however recaptured his brilliant form, and Prasanna Jayawardene helped him take the score to 279-5 the next morning before Hall had the latter lbw. At 282-6, Maharoof gained two vital reprieves with successive deliveries, courtesy of fumbles from Boucher and Amla.

Maharoof was stubborn while Mahela Jayawardene pushed on. The latter reached 123 and took Sri Lanka to the brink of victory at 341-6 despite a slow period of scoring, before Jayawardene advanced Boje and was superbly caught at slip. Sri Lanka painstakingly progressed to 348-7, when Vaas edged a drive and was sensationally caught left-handed by de Villiers at gully. Amidst enormous tension, Muralidaran struck a two before swishing wildly next ball and losing his bails, leaving one wicket standing as Sri Lanka needed two runs. Maharoof managed a single off Boje before Malinga drove into the deep for the winning run.

South African paceman Dale Steyn took a five-wicket haul in Sri Lanka's first innings, but he was also on the receiving end of some brutal batting from Sanath Jayasuriya.

SOUTH AFRICA 1ST INNINGS		
HH Gibbs	lbw b Vaas	0
AJ Hall	c Dilshan b Malinga	0
JA Rudolph	b Malinga	13
HM Amla	lbw b Muralidaran	40
AG Prince*	c HAPW Jayawardene b Muralidaran	86
AB de Villiers	c HAPW Jayawardene b Malinga	95
MV Boucher†	b Muralidaran	32
SM Pollock	not out	57
N Boje	c Sangakkara b Maharoof	11
DW Steyn	c Jayasuriya b Muralidaran	6
M Ntini	c Maharoof b Muralidaran	13
Extras	(nb 8)	8
Total		361

Fall of wickets 0, 4, 31, 70, 231, 256, 273, 307, 327, 361

	O	M	R	W
WPUJC Vaas	18	4	71	1
SL Malinga	18	4	81	3
M Muralidaran	33.5	2	128	5
MF Maharoof	15	2	52	1
ST Jayasuriya	5	0	29	0

SRI LANKA 1ST INNINGS		
WU Tharanga	c Boje b Ntini	2
ST Jayasuriya	c Gibbs b Ntini	47
KC Sangakkara	c Amla b Ntini	14
DPMD Jayawardene*	c Boucher b Steyn	13
TM Dilshan	b Ntini	4
CK Kapugedera	b Boje	63
HAPW Jayawardene†	b Steyn	42
MF Maharoof	b Steyn	56
WPUJC Vaas	c Boucher b Steyn	64
SL Malinga	not out	8
M Muralidaran	c Hall b Steyn	0
Extras	(lb 1, w 2, nb 5)	8
Total		321

Fall of wickets 16, 43, 74, 85, 86, 191, 191, 308, 317, 321

	O	M	R	W
M Ntini	21	3	84	4
DW Steyn	13.1	1	82	5
SM Pollock	16	4	52	0
AJ Hall	15	7	31	0
N Boje	20	6	71	1

SOUTH AFRICA 2ND INNINGS		
HH Gibbs	c Jayasuriya b Muralidaran	92
AJ Hall	c HAPW Jayawardene b Maharoof	32
JA Rudolph	run out (Tharanga)	15
HM Amla	run out (Kapugedera)	8
AG Prince*	c & b Muralidaran	17
AB de Villiers	c Dilshan b Muralidaran	33
MV Boucher†	c Dilshan b Muralidaran	65
SM Pollock	c Tharanga b Muralidaran	14
N Boje	c HAPW Jayawardene b Muralidaran	15
DW Steyn	lbw b Muralidaran	0
M Ntini	not out	5
Extras	(b 9, lb 4, w 1, nb 1)	15
Total		311

Fall of wickets 76, 119, 131, 161, 206, 207, 235, 280, 282, 311

	O	M	R	W
WPUJC Vaas	19	4	53	0
SL Malinga	12	1	55	0
MF Maharoof	21	3	53	1
M Muralidaran	46.5	12	97	7
ST Jayasuriya	9	0	40	0

SRI LANKA 2ND INNINGS		
WU Tharanga	c Gibbs b Ntini	0
ST Jayasuriya	c Amla b Boje	73
KC Sangakkara	c Amla b Pollock	39
DPMD Jayawardene*	c Gibbs b Boje	123
TM Dilshan	c Gibbs b Boje	18
CK Kapugedera	c de Villiers b Boje	13
HAPW Jayawardene†	lbw b Hall	30
MF Maharoof	not out	29
WPUJC Vaas	c de Villiers b Hall	4
M Muralidaran	b Hall	2
SL Malinga	not out	1
Extras	(b 4, lb 8, w 4, nb 4)	20
Total	(9 wickets)	352

Fall of wickets 12, 94, 121, 164, 201, 279, 341, 348, 350

	O	M	R	W
M Ntini	7.2	2	13	1
DW Steyn	22.4	2	81	0
N Boje	39.3	11	111	4
SM Pollock	19	2	60	1
AJ Hall	25	3	75	3

Toss: South Africa   Umpires: Aleem Dar and BF Bowden   TV umpire: TH Wijewardene   Match referee: J Srinath
Reserve umpire: REJ Martinesz   Sri Lanka won by 1 wicket

Australia v England
Second Test at the Adelaide Oval

2006-07
December 1, 2, 3, 4, 5 (2006)

Australia's quest to win back the Ashes began with a victory in the first Test before the second Test at Adelaide proved pivotal in the destiny of the series.

With England batting first after winning the toss, left-handers Andrew Strauss and Alistair Cook put on 32 runs. Strauss departed just after drinks with a flick to short mid wicket. Stuart Clark struck again when Cook edged a flashy drive to the wicketkeeper, and the tourists were an unsteady 58-2 at lunch. Just one run was scored in 28 balls after the break, before Paul Collingwood cut a four. Ian Bell struck 10 runs off a Brett Lee over, although Bell was lucky when an inside edge raced to the fine leg boundary. Collingwood narrowly survived a great Shane Warne delivery, before Collingwood struck the next ball for four, and England reached 144-2 at tea.

Bell punished two successive loose balls from Lee before a miscued hook shot from a bouncer produced a return catch. Lee sent Kevin Pietersen a bouncer second ball, and the batsman pulled a four. An intriguing battle unfolded between Warne and Pietersen, who was cautious at times while ready to punish stray deliveries. Pietersen clouted a six and later hit two fours in succession, and Collingwood also hit two consecutive fours off Warne. Pietersen top-edged the second-last ball of the day but survived, and England finished the day on 266-3.

Collingwood reached his century the following morning before Pietersen had another close shave, as Lee thought he was caught behind. Pietersen hammered three powerful fours in a Glenn McGrath over, and later reached triple figures. Collingwood hit Clark for successive fours and later posted his first 200 in Tests, with a charging four off Michael Clarke. Collingwood fell soon afterwards when he edged behind, and tea was taken with England at 468-4. Pietersen chanced a risky single and was run out for 158, before Warne dismissed Geraint

Michael Clarke plays the cut shot during his first innings 124, which helped Australia towards its total of 513 in reply to England's 551.

Jones cheaply. Ashley Giles began slowly before he and captain Andrew Flintoff took 13 runs off one over, including a six to Flintoff from a top edge. As soon as he whipped a McGrath full-toss for four, Flintoff declared on 551-6.

Justin Langer drove the third ball of Australia's innings for four and fell from the last ball of the second over as a short Flintoff delivery found the shoulder of the bat. Australia was 28-1 from nine overs before stumps, and Matthew Hayden didn't last long on day three before edging a mediocre stroke. Damien Martyn had little impact, and the score was 65-3. It could have been 78-4, but Giles spilled an overhead catch at deep square leg after Ponting pulled airily. Ponting moved to 57 and took Australia to 105-3 at lunch after hitting two successive fours just before the break. Giles' miss was costly as Ponting reached 101 at tea, while Mike Hussey also made runs, including a six off Steve Harmison.

Hussey cover-drove some superb boundaries in the last session, and Ponting reached 142 before edging Matthew Hoggard behind. Clarke immediately hit an elegant boundary, and Hussey reached 91 before he bottom-edged a Hoggard ball onto the off-stump. Clarke just avoided being caught behind and Australia finished the day on 312-5.

Adam Gilchrist looked set for a big score but was caught in the deep for 64. Clarke moved on to a century and shared in a crucial 118-run partnership with Warne as Australia passed 500, before the duo departed in quick succession. Hoggard took his seventh wicket when a swinging delivery bowled Clark, and James Anderson's first wicket ended the innings with Australia 38 runs behind. England reached 31-0, but Clark's sixth delivery had Cook caught at the wicket. The tourists led by 97 runs at stumps.

Day five proved unpredictable. The scoring was slow as Clark and Warne bowled in tandem, and Bell was missed at first slip off Warne. Strauss, however, suffered a poor decision when he was adjudged caught at short leg off his pad. This was compounded two overs later, when Bell was foolishly run out, and then a sweeping Pietersen was bowled by a sharp turning ball from Warne. When Flintoff slashed at Lee and was caught behind, England had crumbled to 77-5.

After lunch, Jones hit a rare boundary but departed softly three balls later when he chased a wide delivery. Giles soon edged another catch to Hayden, and Warne struck again when Hoggard attempted a big drive. Harmison was dismissed lbw, before Anderson lasted 41 minutes, until he too was lbw. Whilst Strauss and Harmison were unfortunate, there were some reckless dismissals, and it was telling that the first, second, third, fifth, seventh, ninth and last dismissals were all from the final ball of an over. The upshot was that Australia needed 168 runs in 36 overs to win.

Ten runs came from the first over, but Langer perished to a cut shot in the third. Hayden swatted Flintoff for four in the sixth over before another cross-batted shot produced a top edge, well caught by Collingwood. Australia was 33-2 before Ponting and Hussey took the score to 68-2 after 13 overs. A few more boundaries kept Australia above the required run rate before Ponting was caught at short extra cover. Martyn hit a four, but steered a catch behind point, and Australia was 121-4 after 22.2 overs. Following five dot balls in the 25th over, Clarke scored a seven thanks to four overthrows, after Pietersen threw wildly with no run out possible, narrowing the equation to just 36 from 11 overs. With Hussey in control, just 10 runs were needed from five overs, and Hussey tied the scores in the 33rd over with a pull for four off Anderson. Hussey drove the next ball through cover for the winning single, and Australia went on to cleansweep the series 5-0, after coming back from the dead in the remarkable second Test.

Australia's 'Mr Cricket' Michael Hussey.

ENGLAND 1ST INNINGS		
AJ Strauss	c Martyn b Clark	14
AN Cook	c Gilchrist b Clark	27
IR Bell	c & b Lee	60
PD Collingwood	c Gilchrist b Clark	206
KP Pietersen	run out (Ponting)	158
A Flintoff*	not out	38
GO Jones†	c Martyn b Warne	1
AF Giles	not out	27
Extras	(lb 10, w 2, nb 8)	20
Total	(6 wickets dec)	551

Did not bat MJ Hoggard, SJ Harmison, JM Anderson
Fall of wickets 32, 45, 158, 468, 489, 491

	O	M	R	W
B Lee	34	1	139	1
GD McGrath	30	5	107	0
SR Clark	34	6	75	3
SK Warne	53	9	167	1
MJ Clarke	17	2	53	0

ENGLAND 2ND INNINGS		
AJ Strauss	c Hussey b Warne	34
AN Cook	c Gilchrist b Clark	9
IR Bell	run out (Clarke/Warne)	26
PD Collingwood	not out	22
KP Pietersen	b Warne	2
A Flintoff*	c Gilchrist b Lee	2
GO Jones†	c Hayden b Lee	10
AF Giles	c Hayden b Warne	0
MJ Hoggard	b Warne	4
SJ Harmison	lbw b McGrath	8
JM Anderson	lbw b McGrath	1
Extras	(b 3, lb 5, w 1, nb 2)	11
Total		129

Fall of wickets 31, 69, 70, 73, 77, 94, 97, 105, 119, 129

	O	M	R	W
B Lee	18	3	35	2
GD McGrath	10	6	15	2
SK Warne	32	12	49	4
SR Clark	13	4	22	1

AUSTRALIA 1ST INNINGS		
JL Langer	c Pietersen b Flintoff	4
ML Hayden	c Jones b Hoggard	12
RT Ponting*	c Jones b Hoggard	142
DR Martyn	c Bell b Hoggard	11
MEK Hussey	b Hoggard	91
MJ Clarke	c Giles b Hoggard	124
AC Gilchrist†	c Bell b Giles	64
SK Warne	lbw b Hoggard	43
B Lee	not out	7
SR Clark	b Hoggard	0
GD McGrath	c Jones b Anderson	1
Extras	(b 4, lb 2, w 1, nb 7)	14
Total		513

Fall of wickets 8, 35, 65, 257, 286, 384, 502, 505, 507, 513

	O	M	R	W
MJ Hoggard	42	6	109	7
A Flintoff	26	5	82	1
SJ Harmison	25	5	96	0
JM Anderson	21.3	3	85	1
AF Giles	42	7	103	1
KP Pietersen	9	0	32	0

AUSTRALIA 2ND INNINGS		
JL Langer	c Bell b Hoggard	7
ML Hayden	c Collingwood b Flintoff	18
RT Ponting*	c Strauss b Giles	49
MEK Hussey	not out	61
DR Martyn	c Strauss b Flintoff	5
MJ Clarke	not out	21
Extras	(b 2, lb 2, w 1, nb 2)	7
Total	(4 wickets)	168

Did not bat AC Gilchrist†, SK Warne, B Lee, SR Clark, GD McGrath
Fall of wickets 14, 33, 116, 121

	O	M	R	W
MJ Hoggard	4	0	29	1
A Flintoff	9	0	44	2
AF Giles	10	0	46	1
SJ Harmison	4	0	15	0
JM Anderson	3.5	0	23	0
KP Pietersen	2	0	7	0

Toss: England   Umpires: SA Bucknor and RE Koertzen   TV umpire: SJ Davis   Match referee: JJ Crowe
Reserve umpire: AD Willoughby   Australia won by 6 wickets

Australia v India
Second Test at the Sydney Cricket Ground

2007-08
January 2, 3, 4, 5, 6 (2008)

Sourav Ganguly scored two half-centuries in Sydney, but was controversially dismissed on the final day as India sank to defeat.

Centuries, some impressive bowling, ample controversy and a thrilling finish ensured there were plenty of memorable aspects in the Sydney Test of 2008, with Australia contesting India.

Australia was 0-1 in the third over as Phil Jaques slashed outside off-stump and edged behind, before left-armer RP Singh struck again when Matthew Hayden edged to slip for 13. Ricky Ponting should have been out for 17, but umpire Mark Benson didn't detect a snick to the wicketkeeper down the leg-side. Ponting sought to capitalise on his reprieve, while

Mike Hussey batted confidently. Hussey survived a stumping chance, and Ponting struck three fours in an RP Singh over to reach 55. Benson subsequently ruled Ponting lbw after he clearly edged a Harbhajan Singh delivery onto his pads. RP Singh struck two balls later when Hussey edged to slip, and then Michael Clarke was plainly lbw after unwisely padding up to a straight Harbhajan delivery. Australia crashed to 134-6 as Adam Gilchrist edged another catch to Sachin Tendulkar at slip.

Left: Andrew Symonds was a huge contributor in Australia's win but it was largely overshadowed by controversy, particularly after alleged racial abuse from Harbhajan Singh towards him.
Right: Sachin Tendulkar looks to the heavens after reaching a splendid century in India's first innings.

Andrew Symonds and Brad Hogg went for their strokes, taking 13 runs off a Harbhajan over before Symonds later hit two successive fours off Anil Kumble. Ishant Sharma should have had Symonds caught behind for 30, but umpire Steve Bucknor thought otherwise. Hogg hammered the first two balls for four after tea, reaching 56, before Symonds survived a very close stumping appeal on 238-6. Boundaries and singles were scored as the Indians seemingly became flat, and Symonds struck a couple of sixes off Harbhajan. Hogg's pugnacious innings produced 79 runs in a 173-run partnership, and Symonds crunched three fours in an over as he and Brett Lee took Australia to 376-7 at stumps. Kumble subsequently took the last three wickets, but not before Lee scored 59 and Mitchell Johnson a quick 28, while Symonds finished unbeaten on 162 as Australia tallied 463.

A near unplayable yorker from Lee wrecked Wasim Jaffer's stumps before VVS Laxman punished some wayward bowling. Three off side drives and a legside stroke brought Laxman four boundaries in a Johnson over. Laxman was in watchful form while Rahul Dravid was solid, and they put on 175 runs before both crucially fell to the last ball of an over. Two balls after driving a boundary to reach 53, Dravid edged Johnson to slip, then Laxman drove a flighted Hogg delivery to short cover. India finished the day on 216-3, leaving the match interestingly poised.

Sourav Ganguly and Tendulkar took the score towards 300, and Tendulkar clubbed Hogg over the long on boundary. Ganguly lifted a catch to mid off three balls later. Lee trapped Yuvraj Singh lbw prior to lunch, before MS Dhoni and Kumble edged behind afterwards, reducing India to 345-7. Tendulkar, however, scored a classy century while Harbhajan played shots effectively, particularly as Johnson's bowling was wayward. Several overs after Harbhajan had an unsavoury exchange with Symonds, Johnson had Harbhajan caught for 63. India led by 11 runs, and RP Singh and Sharma made vital contributions with Tendulkar to secure India a 69-run lead.

After surviving five overs before stumps, Hayden and Jaques gave Australia's second innings a strong start. Hayden hit two successive legside fours off Sharma to raise Australia's 50, and pushed another four later in the over. Jaques scored 42 before sweeping a catch into the deep, then Harbhajan went delirious after inducing a leading edge from Ponting to Laxman in close. Australia was effectively 21-2 at lunch. Hayden went on to carve out an impressive century while Hussey built on a strong start this time, despite some good bowling from India's spinners. Hayden injured his leg and had Ponting run for him, but Hayden played superbly before a reverse sweep off Kumble produced a catch to point. Clarke guided the next ball straight to slip for a catch, and Australia finished day four with a 213-run lead following some weather disruptions.

Hussey and Symonds scored effectively the following morning, with Symonds hitting three fours in an RP Singh over, and Hussey reverse-swept consecutive fours off Kumble. Hussey advanced to 145 not out, while Symonds made 61 before three quick wickets were followed by a declaration, leaving India 333 to win in just over two sessions.

Lee continued Jaffer's misery, with an edge behind from the fifth ball of the innings. Stuart Clark struck in the 10th over after lunch when he trapped Laxman lbw with a low delivery that nipped in. With Hayden off the field, Symonds uncharacteristically dropped an easy slips catch to reprieve Dravid, before Clark struck gold again when Tendulkar inside-edged onto his stumps. Following tea, India needed 254 runs and Australia seven wickets from 46 overs.

Ganguly gave it his best with a series of fours, before Dravid was dubiously adjudged caught behind off Symonds for 38. This was compounded three balls later when Yuvraj clearly edged to Gilchrist. Clarke dropped Ganguly at first slip off Symonds, before Ganguly was controversially caught low down by Clarke at second slip off Lee. Ganguly stood his ground before Australia's appeal was upheld, although replays were unable to prove whether or not the catch was fair.

Dhoni and Kumble resisted well before Symonds produced a turning delivery that had Dhoni lbw without offering a shot. With less than 10 overs left, Australia used Symonds, Hogg, Lee and then Clarke's left-arm spin as three wickets were needed. About 15 minutes remained when the first ball of Clarke's second over bounced off the shoulder of Harbhajan's bat and was caught at slip. Next ball, RP Singh missed his defensive shot and was plumb lbw. With the atmosphere buzzing, there was a slight delay before Sharma survived two deliveries. Sharma prodded forward at the fifth ball of the over and edged to first slip, where Hussey's catch sparked wild scenes of jubilation. Australia had clinched a 2-0 series lead, and went on to win the four-match series 2-1.

Harbhajan Singh and Sachin Tendulkar exchange congratulations during their 129-run partnership in India's first innings.

AUSTRALIA 1ST INNINGS		
PA Jaques	c Dhoni b Singh	0
ML Hayden	c Tendulkar b Singh	13
RT Ponting*	lbw b Harbhajan Singh	55
MEK Hussey	c Tendulkar b Singh	41
MJ Clarke	lbw b Harbhajan Singh	1
A Symonds	not out	162
AC Gilchrist†	c Tendulkar b Singh	7
GB Hogg	c Dravid b Kumble	79
B Lee	lbw b Kumble	59
MG Johnson	c Ganguly b Kumble	28
SR Clark	lbw b Kumble	0
Extras	(b 2, lb 9, w 4, nb 3)	18
Total		463

Fall of wickets 0, 27, 119, 119, 121, 134, 307, 421, 461, 463

	O	M	R	W
RP Singh	26	3	124	4
I Sharma	23	3	87	0
SC Ganguly	6	1	13	0
Harbhajan Singh	27	3	108	2
A Kumble	25.3	0	106	4
SR Tendulkar	5	0	14	0

AUSTRALIA 2ND INNINGS		
PA Jaques	c Yuvraj Singh b Kumble	42
ML Hayden	c Jaffer b Kumble	123
RT Ponting*	c Laxman b Harbhajan Singh	1
MEK Hussey	not out	145
MJ Clarke	c Dravid b Kumble	0
A Symonds	c Dhoni b Singh	61
AC Gilchrist†	c Yuvraj Singh b Kumble	1
GB Hogg	c Dravid b Harbhajan Singh	1
B Lee	not out	4
Extras	(b 3, lb 8, w 3, nb 9)	23
Total	(7 wickets dec)	401

Did not bat MG Johnson, SR Clark

Fall of wickets 85, 90, 250, 250, 378, 393, 395

	O	M	R	W
RP Singh	16	2	74	1
I Sharma	14	2	59	0
Harbhajan Singh	33	6	92	2
A Kumble	40	3	148	4
SR Tendulkar	2	0	6	0
Yuvraj Singh	2	0	11	0

INDIA 1ST INNINGS		
W Jaffer	b Lee	3
R Dravid	c Hayden b Johnson	53
VVS Laxman	c Hussey b Hogg	109
SR Tendulkar	not out	154
SC Ganguly	c Hussey b Hogg	67
Yuvraj Singh	lbw b Lee	12
MS Dhoni†	c Gilchrist b Lee	2
A Kumble*	c Gilchrist b Lee	2
Harbhajan Singh	c Hussey b Johnson	63
RP Singh	c Gilchrist b Clark	13
I Sharma	c & b Lee	23
Extras	(b 4, lb 13, w 6, nb 8)	31
Total		532

Fall of wickets 8, 183, 185, 293, 321, 330, 345, 474, 501, 532

	O	M	R	W
B Lee	32.2	5	119	5
MG Johnson	37	2	148	2
SR Clark	25	3	80	1
A Symonds	7	1	19	0
GB Hogg	30	2	121	2
MJ Clarke	7	1	28	0

INDIA 2ND INNINGS		
R Dravid	c Gilchrist b Symonds	38
W Jaffer	c Clarke b Lee	0
VVS Laxman	lbw b Clark	20
SR Tendulkar	b Clark	12
SC Ganguly	c Clarke b Lee	51
Yuvraj Singh	c Gilchrist b Symonds	0
MS Dhoni†	lbw b Symonds	35
A Kumble*	not out	45
Harbhajan Singh	c Hussey b Clarke	7
RP Singh	lbw b Clarke	0
I Sharma	c Hussey b Clarke	0
Extras	(nb 2)	2
Total		210

Fall of wickets 3, 34, 54, 115, 115, 137, 185, 210, 210, 210

	O	M	R	W
B Lee	13	3	34	2
MG Johnson	11	4	33	0
SR Clark	12	4	32	2
GB Hogg	14	2	55	0
A Symonds	19	5	51	3
MJ Clarke	1.5	0	5	3

Toss: Australia   Umpires: MR Benson and SA Bucknor   TV umpire: BNJ Oxenford
Match referee: MJ Procter   Reserve umpire: RJ Tucker   Australia won by 122 runs

West Indies v Australia

Third Test at Kensington Oval, Bridgetown, Barbados

2008

June 12, 13, 14, 15, 16 (2008)

As in 2003, the best Test in the 2008 West Indies versus Australia series in the Caribbean came after Australia regained the Frank Worrell Trophy. Again, the hosts were set a huge target, although this time they had the chance to level a mere three-match series.

Phil Jaques and Simon Katich started strongly after Australia was invited to bat. Jaques cut a six and pulled a four in the fifth over, and raced to 31 with another four, before perishing next ball to a pull, as wicketkeeper Denesh Ramdin ran towards fine leg. Ricky Ponting hooked successive sixes off Daren Powell, who dropped a hard catch two balls later, and Jerome Taylor trapped Ponting lbw. Australia was 75-2.

Mike Hussey pulled Dwayne Bravo's fourth delivery for six, before Bravo struck twice in his next over. Hussey's hook was well caught by Powell in the deep, and Michael Clarke edged a leg cutter. The return of Fidel Edwards soon after lunch immediately paid dividends, as Katich top-edged a bouncer. Chris Gayle ran from slip for the catch, making Australia 111-5, and Andrew Symonds was crucially reprieved off Bravo's bowling. Xavier Marshall dropped a slips catch, then Symonds gloved a legside catch to Ramdin, but luckily survived.

Symonds hit four fours and a six in left-arm spinner Sulieman Benn's first few overs, and Brad Haddin struck the ball cleanly until Benn had him lbw from a cross-batted shot. Symonds succumbed to an attacking stroke for 52, and Lee was reprieved twice in three balls before rain prematurely ended day one with Australia 226-7. Lee struck a six and a four in quick succession the next morning before the visitors slumped from 244-7 to 251 all out. The total would have been less had there not been four wild wides that went to the boundary.

Gayle clipped a four in his team's first over before Sewnarine Chattergoon was caught behind in the third over. Gayle pulled

Simon Katich was named man of the match in Australia's win over the West Indies in the third Test of 2008.

Lee for four before a powerful drive was superbly caught at mid off by Beau Casson, a left-arm chinaman bowler in his Test debut. West Indies were 26-2. Marshall drove Lee for four, then Ramnaresh Sarwan crunched Lee for six, and Mitchell Johnson's first over contained 12 runs before Sarwan was brilliantly caught by Hussey behind point off Stuart Clark's bowling, bringing the score to 64-3.

Shivnarine Chanderpaul punished Johnson, and Marshall looked impressive before tamely chipping Symonds to mid wicket – 108-4. Bravo clipped a six and a four from successive Casson deliveries, before Johnson had Bravo caught down the legside, at 168-5. Chanderpaul promptly clobbered 18 runs in a Casson over, before the hosts fell from 188-5 to 216 all out. Ramdin was superbly caught by a diving Clarke at gully, and Taylor was caught by Katich off Clarke. Benn and Powell were caught behind, and Chanderpaul was unconquered on 79 when Johnson claimed his fourth scalp, as Edwards edged to second slip. Two dropped catches by Katich off Johnson didn't seem to matter amongst the collapse. Australia was 35-0 at stumps.

Jaques scored a chanceless 108 as he and Katich put on an opening stand of 223. Ponting clipped a first-ball four before gaining a reprieve and hitting Gayle for a straight six. Ponting scored 39, and Hussey was slow before hitting successive fours off Powell, then Katich gave his first chance at 145. Hussey was dismissed before Australia began day four on 330-3. Clarke struck successive boundaries off Benn, until Benn had Katich and Symonds caught for 157 and two respectively. Haddin subsequently punished Benn, before 13 runs came from a Taylor over. Australia's declaration at lunch left the hosts a target of 475, and Chattergoon batted down the order after injuring his ankle while fielding.

Gayle again clipped a four in the first over, then Katich fumbled another easy slips catch to reprieve Marshall on one.

A couple of bouncers cleared Haddin, before Lee was unlucky again, as Casson dropped Gayle at 28-0. A reckless Gayle hit two fours in three balls after Lee went around the wicket, but Clark was unlucky, as a reaching Haddin grassed a snick from Marshall when 22. Lee, however, was safe when Gayle awkwardly pulled a catch to him at mid on, the score at 64-1. Johnson was punished for bowling poorly, as an attacking Marshall and stylish Sarwan were in form, although Marshall was let off again when one of his many boundaries was edged through the slips.

Marshall pulled Clarke's second delivery for six before the bowler struck a few overs later with the score at 159 when Sarwan missed a straight and quicker ball. Casson grabbed his first wicket 22 runs later when Marshall edged a bouncing delivery onto his hip and was caught one-handed by Jaques at short leg. Chanderpaul smashed a couple of long-hops from Casson for four, and Bravo drove the same bowler for six. Bravo struck consecutive fours off Lee not long before stumps, and the score was 239-3 after the first ball of day five, as Chanderpaul edged Clark safely to the boundary.

Bravo struck Casson for successive sixes over cover, before clearing long off in Casson's next over. Bravo, however, fell for 69 when he prodded Casson to silly point, and Clark had Chanderpaul lbw with the new ball as the hosts fell from a threatening 303-3 to a shaky 303-5. But the batting side was not about to surrender. Lee conceded 12 runs in the last over before lunch, and Taylor hit him for successive fours afterwards.

The score fell to 351-7 as Ramdin was lbw and Taylor caught behind. Benn flayed a couple of fours before 375-7 became 375-9, Chattergoon edging a drive to Haddin and Benn skying a slog to Hussey. With one wicket left, there were some near misses, and the tail-enders hit a four each before Powell edged a flashy drive with the target still 88 runs away. The hosts nonetheless had made a fine attempt.

AUSTRALIA 1ST INNINGS

PA Jaques	c Ramdin b Taylor	31
SM Katich	c Gayle b Edwards	36
RT Ponting*	lbw b Taylor	18
MEK Hussey	c Powell b Bravo	12
MJ Clarke	c Ramdin b Bravo	0
A Symonds	c Chattergoon b Bravo	52
BJ Haddin†	lbw b Benn	32
B Casson	lbw b Edwards	10
B Lee	not out	23
MG Johnson	c Benn b Taylor	0
SR Clark	b Edwards	1
Extras	(lb 7, w 21, nb 8)	36
Total		251

Fall of wickets 46, 75, 96, 96, 111, 198, 213, 244, 245, 251

	O	M	R	W
DBL Powell	11	5	43	0
FH Edwards	16.1	3	55	3
JE Taylor	12	2	46	3
CH Gayle	7	2	6	0
DJ Bravo	15	5	61	3
SJ Benn	6	0	33	1

AUSTRALIA 2ND INNINGS

PA Jaques	c Ramdin b Edwards	108
SM Katich	c sub (DJG Sammy) b Benn	157
RT Ponting*	c sub (RS Morton) b Powell	39
MEK Hussey	c Bravo b Benn	18
MJ Clarke	not out	48
A Symonds	c Chanderpaul b Benn	2
BJ Haddin†	not out	45
Extras	(b 5, lb 2, w 5, nb 5, pen 5)	22
Total	(5 wickets dec)	439

Did not bat B Lee, MG Johnson, SR Clark, B Casson

Fall of wickets 223, 299, 330, 358, 360

	O	M	R	W
DBL Powell	16	6	40	1
FH Edwards	14	3	52	1
JE Taylor	22	3	64	0
CH Gayle	16	3	45	0
SJ Benn	47	7	154	3
DJ Bravo	23	4	63	0
XM Marshall	2	2	0	0
RR Sarwan	5	0	9	0

WEST INDIES 1ST INNINGS

CH Gayle*	c Casson b Lee	14
S Chattergoon	c Haddin b Lee	6
RR Sarwan	c Hussey b Clark	20
XM Marshall	c Casson b Symonds	39
S Chanderpaul	not out	79
DJ Bravo	c Haddin b Johnson	29
D Ramdin†	c Clarke b Johnson	1
JE Taylor	c Katich b Clarke	0
SJ Benn	c Haddin b Johnson	3
DBL Powell	c Haddin b Lee	9
FH Edwards	c Ponting b Johnson	1
Extras	(lb 7, nb 8)	15
Total		216

Fall of wickets 11, 26, 64, 108, 168, 188, 189, 195, 204, 216

	O	M	R	W
B Lee	15	2	64	3
SR Clark	15	4	41	1
MG Johnson	11.5	3	41	4
A Symonds	8	4	17	1
B Casson	7	1	43	0
MJ Clarke	2	0	3	1

WEST INDIES 2ND INNINGS

CH Gayle*	c Lee b Clark	26
XM Marshall	c Jaques b Casson	85
RR Sarwan	lbw b Clarke	43
S Chanderpaul	lbw b Clark	50
DJ Bravo	c Jaques b Casson	69
D Ramdin†	lbw b Clark	8
JE Taylor	c Haddin b Johnson	31
S Chattergoon	c Haddin b Lee	13
SJ Benn	c Hussey b Casson	13
DBL Powell	c Haddin b Lee	6
FH Edwards	not out	5
Extras	(b 10, lb 8, w 8, nb 12)	38
Total		387

Fall of wickets 64, 159, 181, 303, 303, 345, 351, 375, 375, 387

	O	M	R	W
B Lee	25.4	3	109	2
SR Clark	24	8	58	3
MG Johnson	12	0	72	1
B Casson	25	3	86	3
MJ Clarke	17	1	38	1
A Symonds	2	0	6	0

Toss West Indies

Umpires: Aleem Dar and MR Benson

TV umpire: GE Greaves

Match referee: RS Mahanama

Reserve umpire: VV Bullen

Australia won by 87 runs

India v England

First Test at MA Chidambaram Stadium, Chepauk, Chennai

2008-09
December 11, 12, 13, 14, 15 (2008)

A superb Test in Chennai in late 2008 was welcome less than three weeks after a terrorist attack on Mumbai. There was strong security at the Chennai Test as mobiles, lunch bags and water bottles were prohibited.

England won the toss and batted on a slow pitch. Only six runs were scored in the first six overs before Harbhajan Singh's off spin was introduced in the ninth. Ten overs later, Andrew Strauss swept two fours in leg-spinner Amit Mishra's first over, and later cut two fours in a Harbhajan over. Alistair Cook batted solidly for 52 before a wild stroke cost him his wicket, with England's total on 118.

Cuts and sweeps were Strauss' forte, although Ian Bell was less convincing, and trapped lbw to Zaheer Khan just two balls after tea. England was 164-2. Strauss reached his century with an edged boundary, before captain Kevin Pietersen perished for a disappointing four when a pull shot went badly wrong. Paul Collingwood edged a four first ball before receiving a rough call on nine, when he was ruled caught at short leg, with replays showing only his pad touched the ball.

Strauss slog-swept a four to reach 123, before chipping the next ball back to Mishra, who took a great diving catch to end a splendid innings. After some lbw appeals were denied, England slipped to 229-6 the next morning, when Andrew Flintoff edged Mishra to short leg. Rahul Dravid spilled a sitter to reprieve James Anderson on six, and Anderson slowly reached 19 before top-edging a catch. Matt Prior scored a dogged 53 not out, including just one boundary, before running out of partners, as England finished with a modest 316.

Virender Sehwag reached nine with a boundary before chopping the next ball onto the stumps. India was 30-1 before off-spinner and debutant Graeme Swann's first over, the last over before tea, was memorable. Gautam Gambhir cut the first

ball for four before surviving an appeal for a catch at short leg. Gambhir was lbw next ball, offering no stroke, before Sachin Tendulkar hit a two and a one. Rahul Dravid pushed at the sixth ball and was struck marginally outside off-stump, but given lbw.

Tendulkar and VVS Laxman led a revival, with Tendulkar clouting Swann for six and later hitting fours off Steve Harmison and left-arm spinner Monty Panesar. Laxman played some wristy strokes before tamely chipping a return catch to Panesar. Flintoff started a new spell moments later, and Tendulkar checked a drive from the first ball and was caught by the bowler. India was 102-5. MS Dhoni drove successive fours off Swann before the reintroduction of Harmison led to Yuvraj Singh edging to Flintoff at slip.

Harbhajan struck three quick boundaries before stumps, and went on to score 40 the next morning before falling to Panesar. Flintoff had Khan lbw, then Dhoni clubbed a catch to Pietersen, making India 219-9. Mishra tonked a four next ball, and was bowled by Flintoff just after lunch with India 75 runs in arrears.

England reached 28-0 following a spate of no-balls from Ishant Sharma before he had Cook caught behind, two balls after Strauss edged a boundary past the slips. Bell quickly registered a four, but departed a few overs later when he edged a Mishra top spinner to short leg. Yuvraj was promptly brought on, and he struck instantly as an arm ball trapped Pietersen. England could have been 43-4 but wicketkeeper Dhoni dropped Strauss, who drove the next ball for four and swung the pendulum.

Strauss and Collingwood played the spinners well, and Collingwood sometimes attacked Mishra. The batting duo ran singles and twos and hit the occasional four, as the pitch was not deteriorating. Strauss and Collingwood posted centuries on day four. Collingwood's milestone was followed by Strauss' departure next ball from a loose drive, ending a 214-run partnership. Sharma varied his length before having Flintoff caught behind, and Collingwood fell for the same score as Strauss – 108 – when a swinging Khan delivery had Collingwood lbw. Khan bowled Swann and Harmison as England's innings stuttered, and it would have been worse had Gambhir not dropped Prior. Prior slapped a four before mishitting to cover next ball, and Pietersen declared to set India 387 runs.

Sehwag gave India an electrifying start after Gambhir hit a four in the first over. Sehwag struck eight fours and two sixes in the next six overs as India raced to 59-0. The total went from 35-0 to 39-0 as Cook missed a sharp catch at gully, before Sehwag uppercut the next ball for six. Changing bowlers made little difference, as Sehwag swept Panesar into the stand in the sixth over. The ninth over was the first not to yield a boundary. Sehwag reached 50 off 32 balls before clouting a four and a six in succession off Panesar, and Swann's second ball was a long-hop which Gambhir dispatched for four. Gambhir was lucky

not to be ruled caught behind at 84-0, before India's 100 was raised after 18 overs with another four from Sehwag. Two balls after whacking Swann over the mid wicket boundary, Sehwag was lbw as he paddled across the line, having scored 83 in a partnership of 117. India was 131-1 at stumps.

India was 141-2 when Dravid edged behind, before Tendulkar survived some aggressive bowling from Flintoff. Gambhir steered a catch to gully, then India's 200 was raised following three fours in seven balls. India was 224-4 when Laxman steered a catch in close, and Yuvraj and Tendulkar gained control as England made numerous bowling changes. Tendulkar was in masterful form while Yuvraj hit the ball hard, and nothing could stop the run flow. The winning runs were registered as Tendulkar's ninth four took his score to 103, while Yuvraj's undefeated 85 included eight fours and a six in the unbroken partnership of 163. Tendulkar dedicated his century to all Indians, before the hosts won the series after the second Test was drawn.

Harbhajan Singh gives Amit Mishra a hug while team-mates join the celebrations following a wicket.

ENGLAND 1ST INNINGS

AJ Strauss	c & b Mishra	123
AN Cook	c Khan b Harbhajan Singh	52
IR Bell	lbw b Khan	17
KP Pietersen*	c & b Khan	4
PD Collingwood	c Gambhir b Harbhajan Singh	9
A Flintoff	c Gambhir b Mishra	18
JM Anderson	c Yuvraj Singh b Mishra	19
MJ Prior†	not out	53
GP Swann	c Dravid b Harbhajan Singh	1
SJ Harmison	c Dhoni b Yuvraj Singh	6
MS Panesar	lbw b Sharma	6
Extras	(lb 7, nb 1)	8
Total		316

Fall of wickets 118, 164, 180, 195, 221, 229, 271, 277, 304, 316

	O	M	R	W
Z Khan	21	9	41	2
I Sharma	19.4	4	32	1
Harbhajan Singh	38	2	96	3
A Mishra	34	6	99	3
Yuvraj Singh	15	2	33	1
V Sehwag	1	0	8	0

ENGLAND 2ND INNINGS

AJ Strauss	c Laxman b Harbhajan Singh	108
AN Cook	c Dhoni b Sharma	9
IR Bell	c Gambhir b Mishra	7
KP Pietersen*	lbw b Yuvraj Singh	1
PD Collingwood	lbw b Khan	108
A Flintoff	c Dhoni b Sharma	4
MJ Prior†	c Sehwag b Sharma	33
GP Swann	b Khan	7
SJ Harmison	b Khan	1
JM Anderson	not out	1
Extras	(b 10, lb 13, w 2, nb 7)	32
Total	(9 wickets dec)	311

Did not bat MS Panesar

Fall of wickets 28, 42, 43, 257, 262, 277, 297, 301, 311

	O	M	R	W
Z Khan	27	7	40	3
I Sharma	22.5	1	57	3
A Mishra	17	1	66	1
Yuvraj Singh	3	1	12	1
Harbhajan Singh	30	3	91	1
V Sehwag	6	0	22	0

INDIA 1ST INNINGS

G Gambhir	lbw b Swann	19
V Sehwag	b Anderson	9
R Dravid	lbw b Swann	3
SR Tendulkar	c & b Flintoff	37
VVS Laxman	c & b Panesar	24
Yuvraj Singh	c Flintoff b Harmison	14
MS Dhoni*†	c Pietersen b Panesar	53
Harbhajan Singh	c Bell b Panesar	40
Z Khan	lbw b Flintoff	1
A Mishra	b Flintoff	12
I Sharma	not out	8
Extras	(b 4, lb 11, nb 6)	21
Total		241

Fall of wickets 16, 34, 37, 98, 102, 137, 212, 217, 219, 241

	O	M	R	W
SJ Harmison	11	1	42	1
JM Anderson	11	3	28	1
A Flintoff	18.4	2	49	3
GP Swann	10	0	42	2
MS Panesar	19	4	65	3

INDIA 2ND INNINGS

G Gambhir	c Collingwood b Anderson	66
V Sehwag	lbw b Swann	83
R Dravid	c Prior b Flintoff	4
SR Tendulkar	not out	103
VVS Laxman	c Bell b Swann	26
Yuvraj Singh	not out	85
Extras	(b 5, lb 11, nb 4)	20
Total	(4 wickets)	387

Did not bat MS Dhoni*†, Harbhajan Singh, Z Khan, A Mishra, I Sharma

Fall of wickets 117, 141, 183, 224

	O	M	R	W
SJ Harmison	10	0	48	0
JM Anderson	11	1	51	1
MS Panesar	27	4	105	0
A Flintoff	22	1	64	1
GP Swann	28.3	2	103	2

Toss: England   Umpires: BF Bowden and DJ Harper   TV umpire: SL Shastri
Match referee: JJ Crowe   Reserve umpire: R Risodkar   India won by 6 wickets

Australia v South Africa
First Test at the WACA, Perth

2008-09
December 17, 18, 19, 20, 21 (2008)

South Africa appeared set back on the eve of its first Test against Australia in the 2008–09 series Down Under, when batsman Ashwell Prince sustained a broken thumb courtesy of team-mate Makhaya Ntini at training. Yet Prince's misfortune led to fellow left-hander Jean-Paul Duminy making a memorable debut, in a Test that was one for the ages.

Matthew Hayden firmly drove two successive boundaries in the first over and another boundary in the third over, before Ntini came around the wicket and had Hayden caught from an unconvincing poke. Ricky Ponting departed first ball as he edged to AB de Villiers at gully, and Mike Hussey also fell for a duck when de Villiers took a great catch off Dale Steyn. The score nearly became 15-4 but Simon Katich just avoided being run out.

Katich hammered three successive fours in Jacques Kallis' first over, and later slashed Ntini over the third man boundary to raise his 50 and Australia's 100. Michael Clarke warmed to the task and punished some loose balls, and the Australians reached 164-3 before losing 2-2 just before tea. Katich missed a Morne Morkel full-toss, and Clarke was caught trying to clobber left-arm spinner Paul Harris.

Andrew Symonds edged two fours in one over, he and Brad Haddin scoring quickly. Eleven runs came in three balls before Symonds was caught from a skier after hitting the previous ball for four. Haddin struck another six before slicing the new ball for a catch, to make the score 298-7. Brett Lee departed five runs later, then Jason Krejza edged a few fours. Mitchell Johnson was lbw from a Morkel yorker with the last ball of day one, before Peter Siddle scored 23 the next morning as Australia reached 375.

South African opener Neil McKenzie fell for two after unwisely pulling from outside off-stump. It took 20 overs for the tourists to register a boundary, after which the next eight

South Africa's AB de Villiers watched the ball closely as he scored 63 and 106 not out to help South Africa to a memorable six-wicket win over Australia.

overs yielded five fours to Hashim Amla and four to Graeme Smith. Off-spinner Krejza broke through as a great delivery bowled Amla through the gate, and then South Africa fell to 110-3 when Smith inside-edged Johnson onto the stumps. De Villiers clubbed a mighty six off Krejza, and Kallis drove two superb fours off Symonds before de Villiers edged successive boundaries off Siddle. Kallis heaved a Krejza half-tracker for six, and the partnership had reached 124 when the game changed dramatically, with Johnson having de Villiers and Kallis edging behind for 63 each.

Johnson had fire in his belly and took 5-2 in an electrifying spell. Duminy appeared unlucky to be ruled caught off his arm. A bouncer to Morkel was followed by a slower ball that had Morkel caught off a leading edge. Harris was caught on the legside late on day two, and Steyn became Johnson's eighth victim. A last wicket partnership of 25 trimmed the deficit to 94, when Mark Boucher was caught off Siddle.

After having a couple of close shaves, Hayden opened his account with a four before being unluckily adjudged caught-and-bowled from a delivery that ballooned off his pad. Katich moved confidently to 37 and edged behind, and Ponting reached 32 before he too was caught by Boucher. Hussey made eight before perishing to a pull. Clarke and Symonds were quiet until Clarke whacked two fours in a Steyn over, and Symonds later pulled Harris for six. Clarke and Symonds succumbed to attacking shots, and Australia was effectively 256-7 when Lee was sensationally caught by a diving de Villiers at slip, after Lee slapped the previous ball for four.

Haddin struck two sixes in a Harris over, and Krejza hit some impressive boundaries off Ntini before falling to another great catch by de Villiers. Johnson hit a quick 21, and Haddin blazed away, while Siddle hung around for 39 minutes. Haddin raced from 78 to 94 in three Harris deliveries before being stumped attempting another six. The target of 414 was just a boundary short of the all-time Test record-winning run chase.

South Africa scored just 13 runs in the first 12 overs, and McKenzie looked in trouble against Lee who had a few appeals turned down. The total was 19 when Johnson had McKenzie caught behind from a push, but Smith found form with some confident boundaries. Smith cut two successive fours off Johnson after tea, before there were two brief rain delays. Smith dominated the scoring while Amla was steady, and Krejza almost had Amla caught behind at 126-1. Smith again cut successive boundaries off Johnson and reached 100, while the total was just 156.

Johnson hit back when a slower ball had Smith lbw for 108. Amla registered 50 when he whipped a half-volley for four, and Lee followed a bouncer with a full ball that Amla edged behind. South Africa 179-3. The next ball soared over Haddin's head for four byes, and the light deteriorated as the scoring accelerated, with Krejza and Siddle ineffective. Kallis struck 13 runs in three balls from Siddle, and Kallis hit the next two balls for four as Krejza delivered a long-hop and a full-toss. A boundary to de Villiers from the last ball of the day took the visitors to 227-3, before their position improved further. Kallis struck Clarke for six, then de Villiers hit two fours in the first over with the new ball.

Johnson struck when Kallis' drive was caught by Hussey, making South Africa 303-4. Johnson unsettled Duminy with some short-pitched balls, but the rookie survived and ensured South Africa's position didn't deteriorate. After lunch, de Villiers clubbed a ball just out of Lee's reach before Duminy swept a four. Duminy struck an exquisite six after advancing Krejza, later belting Clarke to the long-off boundary and steering Johnson between slip and gully. De Villiers pulled a fine four off Johnson to reach 103, before Duminy registered a half-century and the winning runs with a great cover drive.

AUSTRALIA 1ST INNINGS

ML Hayden	c Smith b Ntini	12
SM Katich	lbw b Morkel	83
RT Ponting*	c de Villiers b Ntini	0
MEK Hussey	c de Villiers b Steyn	0
MJ Clarke	c Smith b Harris	62
A Symonds	c McKenzie b Harris	57
BJ Haddin†	c Duminy b Ntini	46
B Lee	c Duminy b Steyn	29
JJ Krejza	not out	30
MG Johnson	lbw b Morkel	18
PM Siddle	c Boucher b Ntini	23
Extras	(lb 7, w 3, nb 5)	15
Total		375

Fall of wickets 14, 14, 15, 164, 166, 259, 298, 303, 341, 375

	O	M	R	W
M Ntini	19.5	1	72	4
DW Steyn	23	4	81	2
JH Kallis	15	2	65	0
M Morkel	20	1	80	2
PL Harris	21	2	70	2

SOUTH AFRICA 1ST INNINGS

ND McKenzie	c Krejza b Johnson	2
GC Smith*	b Johnson	48
HM Amla	b Krejza	47
JH Kallis	c Haddin b Johnson	63
AB de Villiers	c Haddin b Johnson	63
JP Duminy	c Haddin b Johnson	1
MV Boucher†	c Katich b Siddle	26
M Morkel	c Krejza b Johnson	1
PL Harris	c Krejza b Johnson	0
DW Steyn	c Haddin b Johnson	8
M Ntini	not out	5
Extras	(lb 5, w 5, nb 7)	17
Total		281

Fall of wickets 16, 106, 110, 234, 237, 238, 241, 241, 256, 281

	O	M	R	W
B Lee	21	3	59	0
MG Johnson	24	4	61	8
JJ Krejza	25	2	102	1
PM Siddle	16.5	5	44	1
A Symonds	3	1	10	0

AUSTRALIA 2ND INNINGS

ML Hayden	c & b Steyn	4
SM Katich	c Boucher b Kallis	37
RT Ponting*	c Boucher b Harris	32
MEK Hussey	b Ntini	8
MJ Clarke	c Kallis b Steyn	25
A Symonds	c Smith b Harris	37
BJ Haddin†	st Boucher b Harris	94
B Lee	c de Villiers b Kallis	5
JJ Krejza	c de Villiers b Kallis	32
MG Johnson	c Kallis b Morkel	21
PM Siddle	not out	4
Extras	(b 4, lb 7, w 2, nb 7)	20
Total		319

Fall of wickets 25, 59, 88, 88, 148, 157, 162, 241, 278, 319

	O	M	R	W
DW Steyn	19	3	81	2
M Ntini	21	2	76	1
PL Harris	27	3	85	3
JH Kallis	14	4	24	3
M Morkel	16	4	42	1

SOUTH AFRICA 2ND INNINGS

GC Smith*	lbw b Johnson	108
ND McKenzie	c Haddin b Johnson	10
HM Amla	c Haddin b Lee	53
JH Kallis	c Hussey b Johnson	57
AB de Villiers	not out	106
JP Duminy	not out	50
Extras	(b 13, lb 9, w 2, nb 6)	30
Total	(4 wickets)	414

Did not bat MV Boucher†, M Morkel, M Ntini, DW Steyn, PL Harris

Fall of wickets 19, 172, 179, 303

	O	M	R	W
B Lee	27	4	73	1
MG Johnson	34.2	5	98	3
PM Siddle	26	2	84	0
JJ Krejza	24	2	102	0
MJ Clarke	8	0	35	0

Toss: Australia
TV umpire: PR Reiffel
Reserve umpire: MD Martell
Umpires: Aleem Dar and EAR de Silva
Match referee: RS Madugalle
South Africa won by 6 wickets

England v Australia
First Test at Sophia Gardens, Cardiff

2009
July 8, 9, 10, 11, 12 (2009)

The opening showdown of the 2009 Ashes started a fascinating series, as England sought to regain the urn after Australia lost several players to retirement since the 2006–07 series.

Unusually, a Test was played in the capital of Wales. After choosing to bat, England captain Andrew Strauss clipped a splendid boundary from a half-volley in the third over. Alastair Cook fell for 10 when Mike Hussey took a brilliant diving catch to his right at gully, before Ravi Bopara started his scoring with a fluky inside-edged four. Strauss progressed to 30 before Mitchell Johnson struck. A yorker nearly had Strauss lbw, before a bouncer three balls later had Strauss caught off his gloves. Runs flowed briefly, and Bopara played an exquisite cover drive before badly miscuing a Johnson slower ball.

Kevin Pietersen raised England's 100 just after lunch with a great drive, and England went from 97-3 to 194-3 in the session. Paul Collingwood cut two splendid fours in a Nathan Hauritz over, and Ben Hilfenhaus later exchanged words with Pietersen after the batsman pulled away as the bowler ran in. The batsmen had a few close shaves until a diving Brad Haddin snared Collingwood for 64. England was 241-5 when the recall of Hauritz paid dividends, as Pietersen perished to an ungainly sweep.

Andrew Flintoff inside-edged a four and flayed some boundaries, and Matthew Prior also found form. Runs flowed after the new ball was taken, before Peter Siddle rattled the stumps of Flintoff and Prior, who fell to a splendid inswinger for 56. Stuart Broad hit a first-ball four, and accumulated three fours off Siddle the next morning, until Johnson dismissed him. England was 355-8.

Graeme Swann frustrated the tourists as he smacked an unbeaten 47 from 40 balls. Johnson conceded 13 runs in an over, and Swann later struck three consecutive fours off

Rival captains Andrew Strauss and Ricky Ponting at the coin toss.

Hauritz, including one from a reverse sweep. James Anderson scored a useful 26 before he and Monty Panesar fell to Hauritz, England tallying 435.

Phil Hughes gave Australia a flying start, with two fours in succession in Broad's first over, before Flintoff tested Hughes with some short-pitched bowling. With Simon Katich on 10, Flintoff dropped a tough return catch before Hughes edged behind in Flintoff's next over. Ricky Ponting quickly found his stride and registered a half-century in just 70 balls. Katich also posted a half-century, and survived a loud lbw appeal at 152-1. Spinners Swann and Panesar couldn't break through on day two, nor could pacemen Flintoff and Anderson. Katich and Ponting registered centuries late in the day, to make the stumps score 249-1.

Day three began with two maiden overs before some wayward balls were punished, including Swann's opening delivery, a full-toss. Anderson's first over yielded two fours to Ponting, including a textbook cover drive, before Flintoff delivered a wild wide. England finally struck when an Anderson yorker had Katich lbw for 122. A Flintoff bouncer went for four leg byes off Hussey's helmet, then Ponting top-edged a six off the same bowler. Hussey edged behind for just three, before Ponting inside-edged a forceful shot onto his stumps for 150 to leave his side 331-4. The pendulum changed in the ensuing over as Michael Clarke hit 12 runs, and Marcus North opened his account with a four just after lunch.

Clarke hit Panesar for six and the batsmen motored along. A cracking four from Clarke gave Australia the lead, and successive Collingwood deliveries went for four byes. Rain interrupted the last session before play resumed with the lights on, and Clarke fell for 83.

Starting day four on 479-5, Australia raced away, thanks to North and Haddin. Haddin top-edged a hook over Prior for four early on, and North later cover-drove a four despite seven fielders on the off side. After lunch, Haddin hit Anderson for three fours in an over and struck a six each off Swann and Panesar. Haddin passed 100 and soon clubbed a four and a six off successive Collingwood deliveries. Haddin's departure for 121 prompted a declaration. North was undefeated on 125 as Australia led by 239.

England's second innings began disastrously, with Cook and Bopara lbw in successive overs, although Bopara appeared to have been hit too high. Australia's momentum was lost as rain washed out the third session, so England began the last day on 20-2. Pietersen looked foolish in the fourth over, as he offered no stroke and lost his off-stump. Several overs later, Strauss cut Hauritz for four and was out next ball trying to

Paul Collingwood plays a forceful shot during his second innings 74, which helped England draw the first Test

replicate the stroke, making England 46-4. Collingwood was lucky to survive as Hauritz had him in trouble, before Prior tried to cut and was well caught at slip. England was a worrying 102-5 at lunch.

Collingwood and Flintoff were cautious, although Flintoff played the occasional attacking shot. Johnson struck just after drinks when Flintoff edged a feeble prod, and Broad was lucky to survive an lbw appeal first ball. Broad edged Hauritz safely, before off-spinners Hauritz and North bowled 28 successive dot balls. Siddle returned, and Broad twice edged him safely too, before Hauritz had Broad plumb lbw. England looked gone at 159-7.

Siddle gave Swann a torrid time, but Swann played some forceful shots after tea while Collingwood remained dogged. Johnson was wayward with the new ball, although Hilfenhaus trapped Swann as England trailed by 18 runs with 19 overs left. Collingwood had a near miss off Hauritz before edging Siddle to a juggling Hussey, having scored 74 in 344 minutes. Sixty-nine balls remained with one wicket standing and England six runs in arrears. Panesar defended, and Anderson had some narrow escapes before speculatively squirting successive fours off Siddle to put England in front. North came on with four overs left, and Panesar cracked a four. He and Anderson defended against Australia's two off-spinners to secure a sensational draw. The series went on to fluctuate, before England won the final Test to seal the series 2-1.

Australian captain Ricky Ponting leads Michael Clarke, Marcus North, Mitchell Johnson, Ben Hilfenhaus, Mike Hussey and Simon Katich off the field after the draw on day five of the first Ashes Test match in Cardiff, Wales.

ENGLAND 1ST INNINGS

AJ Strauss*	c Clarke b Johnson	30
AN Cook	c Hussey b Hilfenhaus	10
RS Bopara	c Hughes b Johnson	35
KP Pietersen	c Katich b Hauritz	69
PD Collingwood	c Haddin b Hilfenhaus	64
MJ Prior†	b Siddle	56
A Flintoff	b Siddle	37
JM Anderson	c Hussey b Hauritz	26
SCJ Broad	b Johnson	19
GP Swann	not out	47
MS Panesar	c Ponting b Hauritz	4
Extras	(b 13, lb 11, w 2, nb 12)	38
Total		435

Fall of wickets 21, 67, 90, 228, 241, 327, 329, 355, 423, 435

	O	M	R	W
MG Johnson	22	2	87	3
BW Hilfenhaus	27	5	77	2
PM Siddle	27	3	121	2
NM Hauritz	23.5	1	95	3
MJ Clarke	5	0	20	0
SM Katich	2	0	11	0

ENGLAND 2ND INNINGS

AJ Strauss*	c Haddin b Hauritz	17
AN Cook	lbw b Johnson	6
RS Bopara	lbw b Hilfenhaus	1
KP Pietersen	b Hilfenhaus	8
PD Collingwood	c Hussey b Siddle	74
MJ Prior†	c Clarke b Hauritz	14
A Flintoff	c Ponting b Johnson	26
SCJ Broad	lbw b Hauritz	14
GP Swann	lbw b Hilfenhaus	31
JM Anderson	not out	21
MS Panesar	not out	7
Extras	(b 9, lb 9, w 4, nb 11)	33
Total	(9 wickets)	252

Fall of wickets 13, 17, 31, 46, 70, 127, 159, 221, 233

	O	M	R	W
MG Johnson	22	4	44	2
BW Hilfenhaus	15	3	47	3
PM Siddle	18	2	51	1
NM Hauritz	37	12	63	3
MJ Clarke	3	0	8	0
MJ North	7	4	14	0
SM Katich	3	0	7	0

AUSTRALIA 1ST INNINGS

PJ Hughes	c Prior b Flintoff	36
SM Katich	lbw b Anderson	122
RT Ponting*	b Panesar	150
MEK Hussey	c Prior b Anderson	3
MJ Clarke	c Prior b Broad	83
MJ North	not out	125
BJ Haddin†	c Bopara b Collingwood	121
Extras	(b 9, lb 14, w 4, nb 7)	34
Total	(6 wickets dec)	674

Did not bat MG Johnson, NM Hauritz, BW Hilfenhaus, PM Siddle

Fall of wickets 60, 299, 325, 331, 474, 674

	O	M	R	W
JM Anderson	32	6	110	2
SCJ Broad	32	6	129	1
GP Swann	38	8	131	0
A Flintoff	35	3	128	1
MS Panesar	35	4	115	1
PD Collingwood	9	0	38	1

Toss: England
Umpires: Aleem Dar and BR Doctrove
TV umpire: RA Kettleborough   Match referee: JJ Crowe
Reserve umpire: RK Illingworth   Match drawn

India v Australia

First Test at Punjab Cricket Association Stadium, Mohali, Chandigarh

2010-11

October 1, 2, 3, 4, 5 (2010)

The climax to the first Test of the 2010–11 series involving India and Australia was spinetingling, and the course of the match lost little by comparison.

The twists began with the second delivery when India's Virender Sehwag dropped Shane Watson at gully. Boundaries off successive balls were followed by Zaheer Khan trapping Simon Katich next ball, and Ricky Ponting pulling his second delivery for four. Watson hit successive fours off Ishant Sharma, Ponting did likewise to Harbhajan Singh, and wicketkeeper MS Dhoni spilled an edge from Watson at 81-1. Ponting registered several fours soon after lunch, and Watson again struck consecutive fours off the expensive Sharma, who departed with a leg injury. Suresh Raina produced the breakthrough when he ran Ponting out for 71, and Michael Clarke's dismissal left Australia 172-3.

In a very slow period of scoring, Mike Hussey fell for 17 before Watson reached a century. Marcus North hadn't scored when he shouldered arms and lost his off-bail, and the visitors were 224-5 at stumps after Dhoni blundered again, spilling a thin edge from Tim Paine. Paine was very slow for a while, and the first ball of a new spell for Harbhajan had Watson caught at short leg from a prod. Paine and Mitchell Johnson took 11 runs from three Harbhajan deliveries, and the scoring accelerated after lunch as Johnson hit two fours and a six in quick succession, and both batsmen attacked Pragyan Ojha's left-arm spin.

Following the demise of Johnson and Nathan Hauritz, Paine and Ben Hilfenhaus pushed the score past 400. Hilfenhaus struck a six, and then, once the new ball was finally taken after 146.4 overs, he hit two fours in a row. Khan had five wickets when Paine edged to slip for 92, and Doug Bollinger was caught in the deep to conclude Australia's innings at 428.

Indian off-spinner Harbhajan Singh took five wickets in the first Test of the 2010-11 series against Australia.

Sehwag launched an electrifying assault as he cracked some fours off Bollinger, before striking three fours in a Hilfenhaus over and two fours from Hauritz's first deliveries. After Gautam Gambhir fell for 25, India's 100 arrived in the 17th over, and Johnson struck a vital blow before stumps when he had Sehwag caught off a leading edge.

Nightwatchman Sharma had a reprieve the next day until losing his off-stump without offering a stroke. Sachin Tendulkar found form elegantly, almost being run out at 195-3. Rahul Dravid hit 12 fours before edging Bollinger as India became 230-4, before Raina hit regular fours, while Tendulkar went on in sublime form. Johnson missed a catch when Raina was 60, then North surprisingly had Tendulkar lbw for 98. India was 354-5. Dhoni struck 10 runs in three Hauritz deliveries before edging Johnson for a low and somewhat questionable catch, and then Harbhajan was out first ball. Watson dropped a sitter before Khan was bowled in Hauritz's next over, and VVS Laxman belatedly arrived nursing a back injury, with Gambhir as his runner. Raina became Johnson's fifth scalp and Laxman's cheap dismissal left Australia with a 23-run lead.

Watson twice edged Khan for runs before crunching two fours off Sharma as the score raced to 41-0 after five overs, before Harbhajan delivered the sixth over. Harbhajan nearly had Katich lbw before 14 runs came in the next over, bowled by Ojha. Watson scored a quick 56 before pulling Sharma onto his stumps, then Ponting hit a four first ball, and promptly departed. Clarke was caught first ball but reprieved when a no-ball was belatedly called. Clarke, however, fell to a sharp bouncer in Sharma's next over, making Australia 96-3.

Hussey survived a chance to Raina, and Katich had a couple of close shaves before Ojha had him caught behind. Hussey was unluckily ruled lbw after the ball pitched outside leg-stump, and then Paine hit two exquisite fours off successive Ojha deliveries. Australia, however, lost 54-7. North and Paine succumbed to spin before Khan claimed three scalps. A brilliant reverse-swinging delivery dismissed Hauritz, and Hilfenhaus fell to a yorker.

Chasing 216, India was rocked when Gambhir was ruled lbw fourth ball, despite a thick inside edge onto his pad. Hilfenhaus conceded five crucial runs from a wild bouncer before Sehwag slammed the next ball for four. A misfield a few overs later enabled Dravid to register his third four. Bollinger had Dravid nick behind before Tendulkar hit a lovely four first ball. Hilfenhaus subsequently seized the initiative as Sehwag guided a short ball straight to gully, and Raina poked a bouncer to slip. Khan had a couple of narrow escapes as India wobbled to 55-4 at stumps.

India was 76-5 when Hauritz had Khan caught off an edge, and Laxman arrived with Raina as his runner, hitting successive fours in a Hauritz over that cost 14 runs. Bollinger struck paydirt as Tendulkar tried to upper cut and was caught at gully, and Dhoni was disastrously run out. Then Harbhajan was out second ball from a short delivery as India collapsed to 124-8.

Bollinger exited with an abdominal injury, and Laxman found support from Sharma.

The madness began just before lunch as Laxman was nearly run out. Laxman continued bravely, and luck was on Sharma's side as he accumulated a few boundaries and had some near misses off Johnson. Laxman hit a superb four and Watson nearly ran out Sharma at the bowler's end next ball. India needed 11 runs when Sharma was ruled lbw to a Hilfenhaus delivery that would have missed leg-stump. Amidst unbelievable tension, five runs were added before Ojha looked plumb lbw to Johnson, only for umpire Billy Bowden to rule an inside edge. Just as incredibly, substitute fielder Steve Smith shied at the stumps and gave away four overthrows when a direct hit would have run Ojha out! Two balls later, Johnson strayed onto Ojha's pads, resulting in two leg byes to give India a thrilling victory.

India's Sachin Tendulkar, 'The Little Master'.

AUSTRALIA 1ST INNINGS

SR Watson	c Gambhir b Harbhajan Singh	126
SM Katich	lbw b Khan	6
RT Ponting*	run out (Raina)	71
MJ Clarke	c Dravid b Harbhajan Singh	14
MEK Hussey	lbw b Khan	17
MJ North	b Khan	0
TD Paine†	c Laxman b Khan	92
MG Johnson	c Dhoni b Khan	47
NM Hauritz	c Gambhir b Harbhajan Singh	9
BW Hilfenhaus	not out	20
DE Bollinger	c Sharma b Ojha	0
Extras	(b 4, lb 9, nb 13)	26
Total		428

Fall of wickets 13, 154, 172, 218, 222, 275, 357, 373, 427, 428

	O	M	R	W
Z Khan	30	7	94	5
I Sharma	11.4	1	71	0
PP Ojha	51.4	16	113	1
Harbhajan Singh	49	12	114	3
V Sehwag	9.2	1	23	0

INDIA 1ST INNINGS

G Gambhir	lbw b Johnson	25
V Sehwag	c Clarke b Johnson	59
R Dravid	c Paine b Bollinger	77
I Sharma	b Bollinger	18
SR Tendulkar	lbw b North	98
SK Raina	lbw b Johnson	86
MS Dhoni*†	c Watson b Johnson	14
Harbhajan Singh	c Paine b Johnson	0
Z Khan	b Hauritz	6
VVS Laxman	c Clarke b Hauritz	2
PP Ojha	not out	0
Extras	(b 5, lb 13, w 1, nb 1)	20
Total		405

Fall of wickets 81, 106, 151, 230, 354, 382, 382, 399, 401, 405

	O	M	R	W
BW Hilfenhaus	25	2	100	0
DE Bollinger	16	2	49	2
MG Johnson	20	5	64	5
NM Hauritz	29.1	4	116	2
SR Watson	6	0	19	0
MJ North	12	3	39	1

AUSTRALIA 2ND INNINGS

SR Watson	b Sharma	56
SM Katich	c Dhoni b Ojha	37
RT Ponting*	c Raina b Sharma	4
MJ Clarke	c Dhoni b Sharma	4
MEK Hussey	lbw b Harbhajan Singh	28
MJ North	c sub (CA Pujara) b Harbhajan Singh	10
TD Paine†	c sub (CA Pujara) b Ojha	9
MG Johnson	c Dhoni b Khan	3
NM Hauritz	b Khan	9
BW Hilfenhaus	b Khan	6
DE Bollinger	not out	5
Extras	(b 12, lb 4, nb 5)	21
Total		192

Fall of wickets 87, 91, 96, 138, 154, 165, 165, 170, 183, 192

	O	M	R	W
Z Khan	11.5	1	43	3
I Sharma	9	2	34	3
Harbhajan Singh	23	7	40	2
PP Ojha	17	1	59	2

INDIA 2ND INNINGS

G Gambhir	lbw b Hilfenhaus	0
V Sehwag	c Hussey b Hilfenhaus	17
R Dravid	c Paine b Bollinger	13
SR Tendulkar	c Hussey b Bollinger	38
SK Raina	c North b Hilfenhaus	0
Z Khan	c Clarke b Hauritz	10
VVS Laxman	not out	73
MS Dhoni*†	run out (Hilfenhaus)	2
Harbhajan Singh	c Ponting b Bollinger	2
I Sharma	lbw b Hilfenhaus	31
PP Ojha	not out	5
Extras	(b 10, lb 8, w 6, nb 1)	25
Total	(9 wickets)	216

Fall of wickets 0, 31, 48, 48, 76, 119, 122, 124, 205

	O	M	R	W
BW Hilfenhaus	19	3	57	4
DE Bollinger	8	0	32	3
MG Johnson	16.4	2	50	0
NM Hauritz	9	1	45	1
MJ North	4	0	8	0
SR Watson	2	0	6	0

Toss: Australia   Umpires: BF Bowden and IJ Gould
TV umpire: SS Hazare   Match referee: BC Broad   Reserve umpire: S Das   India won by 1 wicket

South Africa v Australia
First Test at Newlands, Cape Town

2011-12
November 9, 10, 11 (2011)

Words such as 'unbelievable', 'incredible' and 'astonishing' could hardly be adequate when describing the first Test of the 2011–12 South Africa versus Australia series. One of many intriguing aspects was the use of the third umpire, as Test teams had the chance to review decisions until two referrals were unsuccessful in each innings. Another intriguing note was 23 wickets falling on day two.

Following a delayed start due to rain, the hosts started strongly after choosing to bowl first. Dale Steyn had Shane Watson edging a magical swinging delivery, before Test debutant Vernon Philander took his maiden wicket. Phil Hughes steered a four but edged the next ball behind, making Australia 13-2. Philander copped a dose of reality when Ricky Ponting hooked him for six, before Morne Morkel beat Shaun Marsh three times in a row. After another delay, Marsh hit Morkel for three fours before a Morkel delivery struck Marsh painfully in the box. Following lunch, Steyn had Ponting lbw with a review, after Ponting survived the original appeal. Australia was 40-3.

Clarke survived a testing over from Steyn, then drove Steyn for four and hit a series of fours off Jacques Kallis and two in a row off Morkel. Marsh survived an lbw appeal off Philander after the hosts reviewed it, before striking successive fours through cover off debutant Imran Tahir. Clarke dispatched three fours in a Philander over, before Steyn had Marsh lbw with the first ball of a new spell.

South Africa regained the upper hand as Mike Hussey and Brad Haddin departed cheaply. Mitchell Johnson supported Clarke, who raised his century and Australia's 200 with his 16th four via a great cover drive. Johnson and Ryan Harris succumbed to faulty strokes before bad light and then rain ended the day with Australia at 214-8. Peter Siddle scored a

handy 20 before he was ninth out, and the innings concluded at 284 as Clarke went for a heave and was bowled for 151, having hit his 21st and 22nd fours earlier in the over.

Johnson bowled two expensive overs and was promptly replaced, before Harris beat Jacques Rudolph's defence and bowled him. South Africa reached 49-1 until Watson struck with the second and sixth deliveries after lunch, with successful referrals to the third umpire after appeals were turned down. Hashim Amla was lbw, then Kallis was caught at slip after edging a ball onto his shoulder.

Graeme Smith and AB de Villiers took 11 runs from the last three balls of a Watson over, before Watson bowled Smith off an inside edge and had Ashwell Prince lbw with successive balls. South Africa crashed further as de Villiers was lbw to Harris after another review from the tourists, and Boucher unsuccessfully used the review system after Watson won an lbw appeal. A boundary produced Philander's first runs before he edged a catch two balls later, and Morkel was run out before Harris wrecked Tahir's stumps. South Africa had avoided the follow-on but looked lost after tallying a miserable 96 in just 24.3 overs and 130 minutes. Little did anyone know what was to follow.

Watson registered a second-ball boundary but Steyn had him lbw next ball, although replays suggested Watson would have had the decision overturned had he reviewed it, because the ball would have cleared the stumps. Hughes was reprieved on three when Smith dropped a sitter, before Hughes flayed a boundary. The pendulum swung, however as Ponting unsuccessfully used the review system after Philander won an lbw appeal.

Hughes was caught low down at slip off Morkel as Australia fell to 13-3 at tea, becoming 13-4 one ball later as Hussey edged a loose drive to gully. The tourists were 15-5 after Clarke unsuccessfully reviewed an upheld lbw appeal from Philander, who struck again when Haddin edged a clumsy shot. Australia fell from 21-6 to 21-9: Harris edged Morkel to slip, Johnson cracked a catch to point off Philander, and Marsh was lbw to Philander after a review from the South Africans following Marsh's relegation in the batting order due to a back injury.

Australia was on course to set a record lowest score in Test cricket, following New Zealand's 26 against England in 1955. Nathan Lyon played at and missed his first delivery, and Siddle edged a four to take the total to 28. Lyon and Siddle played a few confident strokes before Lyon chipped a catch to a diving de Villiers at cover. A stunned Australia was out for 47 in 18 overs and 95 minutes. After being 188 runs in arrears, the hosts had a target of just 236, yet the scoring pattern suggested the chase could be difficult.

Left-handers Smith and Rudolph tallied five fours in the first five overs, when Rudolph edged a half-hearted poke to Haddin. South Africa 27-1. Amla opened his scoring with a driven boundary, and Smith whipped a few full balls for four in quick succession. The total passed 50 when Amla drove a four, before an edged four to Amla was soon followed by an authoritative boundary. The next twist came with the last ball of the day as Hussey dropped a hard-hit chance at gully to reprieve Amla, with the score at 81-1.

The unlucky Harris had Amla dropped again at 88-1, as Watson fumbled at slip. Luck went South Africa's way once more as Smith edged a couple of fours, before Amla drove Johnson for two convincing fours in succession. Eleven runs from a Harris over took the score to 152-1, and Smith hit three fours in a Watson over. Amla motored to 98 with three successive fours off Harris, before cutting Johnson for four to raise his hundred. The cut shot caused Amla's demise, with South Africa just 14 runs shy of victory, before Smith thumped a couple of fours. A single to Smith raised his century and another single ended the contest.

South Africa won this crazy Test by eight wickets, before Australia squared the two-match series with a two-wicket win, chasing 310.

Hashim Amla, whose second innings century helped South Africa to an eight-wicket win.

AUSTRALIA 1ST INNINGS

SR Watson	c Kallis b Steyn	3
PJ Hughes	c Boucher b Philander	9
SE Marsh	lbw b Steyn	44
RT Ponting	lbw b Steyn	8
MJ Clarke*	b Morkel	151
MEK Hussey	c Boucher b Morkel	1
BJ Haddin†	c Prince b Steyn	5
MG Johnson	c Morkel b Philander	20
RJ Harris	c Morkel b Philander	5
PM Siddle	c de Villiers b Morkel	20
NM Lyon	not out	1
Extras	(b 5, lb 7, w 1, nb 4)	17
Total		284

Fall of wickets 9, 13, 40, 143, 158, 163, 202, 214, 273, 284

	O	M	R	W
DW Steyn	20	4	55	4
VD Philander	21	3	63	3
M Morkel	18	2	82	3
Imran Tahir	10	1	35	0
JH Kallis	6	0	37	0

SOUTH AFRICA 1ST INNINGS

JA Rudolph	b Harris	18
GC Smith*	b Watson	37
HM Amla	lbw b Watson	3
JH Kallis	c Ponting b Watson	0
AB de Villiers	lbw b Harris	8
AG Prince	lbw b Watson	0
MV Boucher†	lbw b Watson	4
VD Philander	c Ponting b Harris	4
DW Steyn	not out	9
M Morkel	run out (Siddle)	1
Imran Tahir	b Harris	5
Extras	(lb 4, w 1, nb 2)	7
Total		96

Fall of wickets 24, 49, 49, 73, 73, 77, 77, 81, 83, 96

	O	M	R	W
RJ Harris	10.3	3	33	4
MG Johnson	5	0	26	0
PM Siddle	4	1	16	0
SR Watson	5	2	17	5

AUSTRALIA 2ND INNINGS

SR Watson	lbw b Steyn	4
PJ Hughes	c Rudolph b Morkel	9
RT Ponting	lbw b Philander	0
MJ Clarke*	lbw b Philander	2
MEK Hussey	c Prince b Morkel	0
BJ Haddin†	c Boucher b Philander	0
MG Johnson	c Amla b Philander	3
RJ Harris	c Smith b Morkel	3
PM Siddle	not out	12
SE Marsh	lbw b Philander	0
NM Lyon	c de Villiers b Steyn	14
Extras		0
Total		47

Fall of wickets 4, 11, 13, 13, 15, 18, 21, 21, 21, 47

	O	M	R	W
DW Steyn	5	1	23	2
VD Philander	7	3	15	5
M Morkel	6	1	9	3

SOUTH AFRICA 2ND INNINGS

GC Smith*	not out	101
JA Rudolph	c Haddin b Siddle	14
HM Amla	c Clarke b Johnson	112
JH Kallis	not out	2
Extras	(lb 4, w 1, nb 2)	7
Total	(2 wickets)	236

Did not bat VD Philander, AG Prince, MV Boucher†, Imran Tahir, DW Steyn, M Morkel, AB de Villiers

Fall of wickets 27, 222

	O	M	R	W
RJ Harris	14	2	67	0
PM Siddle	12.2	0	49	1
SR Watson	10	0	44	0
MG Johnson	11	1	61	1
NM Lyon	3	1	11	0

Toss: South Africa
TV umpire: BF Bowden
Reserve umpire: JD Cloete

Umpires: BR Doctrove and IJ Gould
Match referee: RS Mahanama
South Africa won by 8 wickets

Australia v New Zealand

Second Test at Bellerive Oval, Hobart

2011-12

December 9, 10, 11, 12 (2011)

The Kiwis celebrate after Australia's last batsman Nathan Lyon was bowled by Doug Bracewell to win the Second Test at Bellerive Oval in Hobart, Tasmania in 2011.

The second and final Test of the Australia versus New Zealand series in late 2011 was perhaps the most thrilling Test involving the two countries since the 1987 Boxing Day Test. One of many astonishing aspects was the number of boundaries and dismissals from edges.

Australia won the first Test by nine wickets, and started the second Test strongly after captain Michael Clarke chose to bowl. The ball swung early on, and 10 runs were scored off the first seven deliveries, before Martin Guptill edged Peter Siddle behind. New Zealand was 11-2 when James Pattinson had Jesse

Ryder lbw for a duck as the Australians successfully sought a review. When Kiwi skipper Ross Taylor unsuccessfully had an lbw decision reviewed after shouldering arms to Siddle, the score was 25-3.

A few fours were edged before Mitchell Starc had Kane Williamson caught behind from a leg glance. Dean Brownlie cut a four before Pattinson dismissed Brendon McCullum and Reece Young in the next over to make the score 60-6. Brownlie struck some loose balls for four, and a 45-run stand ended when Doug Bracewell edged to slip. The next partnership reaped 41 runs, with Tim Southee hitting three fours before dragging a Starc delivery onto the stumps. Pattinson ended the innings with successive balls, Brownlie chopping onto his wicket and Chris Martin bowled through the gate. The Kiwis managed only 150.

Rain delayed the start of Australia's innings, and then Phil Hughes edged his first ball for four. It was his only scoring shot before pushing a catch to second slip. David Warner drove a boundary, then rain ended the day with Australia 12-1. The ensuing morning, Chris Martin marked his 37th birthday with the wicket of Warner, caught at first slip. Australia was 31-3 when Southee trapped Ricky Ponting plumb lbw, before Clarke survived an lbw appeal after New Zealand reviewed it.

Australia, however, became 35-4 when an out-of-sorts Usman Khawaja poked and was caught behind. Mike Hussey pulled a four off debutant left-arm medium-fast bowler Trent Boult, but the bowler struck next ball, as Hussey nicked behind as he was about to shoulder arms. Haddin drove a catch straight to mid off, and Australia was 75-7 when Clarke's off-stump was hit by a Bracewell delivery, which nipped in.

Pattinson and Siddle rallied before Siddle snicked to second slip, and Williamson soon took a blinder at gully as he dived to his left to snare Pattinson. Australia thus went from 131-7 to 131-9, finishing with 136, as Boult had Starc lbw after the visitors challenged a not out decision.

New Zealand's second innings began with 19 dot balls, and the Kiwis went from 36-0 to 36-2 after the openers were caught off edges. Taylor was dropped at 62-2, before Hussey broke through as Ryder was stumped down the legside. Williamson survived an lbw appeal that Australia reviewed as New Zealand moved from 73-3 to 139-3.

Williamson departed with the third ball of day three as he edged Siddle to Ponting, and then Brownlie opened his account with an elegant boundary. Taylor had a couple of close shaves, registering 50, and his team reached 171-4 before crumbling. The captain edged Pattinson to first slip, and Brownlie drove another boundary before gloving a short Pattinson delivery to Haddin.

Siddle trapped Young lbw and Southee hit off-spinner Nathan Lyon for six and four with successive deliveries, before being caught at long on next ball. Bracewell perished to a slog-sweep two balls later, then Boult struck three precious boundaries off consecutive Siddle deliveries. The last wicket produced 23 runs before Boult holed out, leaving Australia a target of 241.

The hosts overcame a rain-delayed start to be 72-0 at tea, when rain cancelled session three. There were some close shaves: New Zealand didn't seek a review when Hughes was lucky not to be ruled caught behind off his glove before he scored, and Warner inside-edged a four to raise the 50-partnership before the next ball also yielded four runs.

The total was still 72 when Hughes was again caught at slip, before Warner edged another four. Khawaja had one run from 29 balls before driving successive boundaries, and Australia was 122-2 when Khawaja chased a wide ball and was well caught by Taylor at first slip.

The game took a dramatic turn as Australia slid from an impregnable 159-2 to a nervous 159-5. Ponting uncharacteristically punched a Bracewell delivery straight to extra cover, before Clarke snicked a drive to slip in Bracewell's next over. Hussey was lbw first ball after New Zealand won a review, as replays showed the ball would have hit leg-stump. Warner, however, top-edged a pull for four, then clouted the next ball for another boundary, and soon after lunch had raised his maiden century, in only his second Test.

Australia was a promising 192-5 when Haddin luckily edged a boundary, but then Haddin and Siddle were caught off snicks in the next four balls to make Australia a troublesome 194-7. Incredibly, Pattinson inside-edged his first ball for four, and moments later was ruled lbw to Bracewell before having the decision overturned. But two balls later, Pattinson reached and was caught at second slip. Starc had a near-miss first ball before Bracewell produced a corker to splay Starc's stumps, and Australia was 199-9.

Assuming responsibility, Warner clubbed two fours in successive overs before an lbw appeal by Southee against Lyon was upheld, with the total on 216. Replays, however, showed the ball pitched outside leg-stump, so Lyon's review was successful. Four leg byes were followed by a near-miss outside off-stump, and the score was 223-9 when Taylor unsuccessfully challenged a rejected lbw appeal against Lyon.

Lyon impressively drove a four through mid wicket, and another three runs took the score 233-9 before Bracewell settled the issue, finding a gap between bat and pad to wreck Lyon's stumps. It was New Zealand's first Test win over Australia since March 1993.

NEW ZEALAND 1ST INNINGS

BB McCullum	c Haddin b Pattinson	16
MJ Guptill	c Haddin b Siddle	3
JD Ryder	lbw b Pattinson	0
LRPL Taylor*	lbw b Siddle	6
KS Williamson	c Haddin b Starc	19
DG Brownlie	b Pattinson	56
RA Young†	b Pattinson	0
DAJ Bracewell	c Clarke b Siddle	12
TG Southee	b Starc	18
TA Boult	not out	0
CS Martin	b Pattinson	0
Extras	(b 2, lb 12, w 1, nb 5)	20
Total		150

Fall of wickets 10, 11, 25, 56, 60, 60, 105, 146, 150, 150

	O	M	R	W
JL Pattinson	13.5	3	51	5
PM Siddle	13	3	42	3
MA Starc	11	4	30	2
NM Lyon	8	4	13	0

AUSTRALIA 1ST INNINGS

DA Warner	c Taylor b Martin	15
PJ Hughes	c Guptill b Martin	4
UT Khawaja	c Young b Martin	7
RT Ponting	lbw b Southee	5
MJ Clarke*	b Bracewell	22
MEK Hussey	c Young b Boult	8
BJ Haddin†	c McCullum b Bracewell	5
PM Siddle	c Guptill b Bracewell	36
JL Pattinson	c Williamson b Boult	17
MA Starc	lbw b Boult	4
NM Lyon	not out	1
Extras	(b 1, lb 8, nb 3)	12
Total		136

Fall of wickets 7, 24, 31, 35, 58, 69, 75, 131, 131, 136

	O	M	R	W
CS Martin	16	1	46	3
TA Boult	13	4	29	3
TG Southee	12	2	32	1
DAJ Bracewell	10	3	20	3

NEW ZEALAND 2ND INNINGS

MJ Guptill	c Haddin b Siddle	16
BB McCullum	c Hughes b Pattinson	12
JD Ryder	st Haddin b Hussey	16
LRPL Taylor*	c Clarke b Pattinson	56
KS Williamson	c Ponting b Siddle	34
DG Brownlie	c Haddin b Pattinson	21
RA Young†	lbw b Siddle	9
DAJ Bracewell	b Lyon	4
TG Southee	c Hussey b Lyon	13
TA Boult	c Hussey b Lyon	21
CS Martin	not out	2
Extras	(b 4, lb 11, w 5, nb 2)	22
Total		226

Fall of wickets 36, 36, 73, 139, 171, 178, 190, 203, 203, 226

	O	M	R	W
JL Pattinson	21	7	54	3
PM Siddle	25	11	66	3
MA Starc	19	6	47	0
MEK Hussey	5	0	15	1
NM Lyon	7.3	1	25	3
RT Ponting	1	0	4	0

AUSTRALIA 2ND INNINGS

PJ Hughes	c Guptill b Martin	20
DA Warner	not out	123
UT Khawaja	c Taylor b Boult	23
RT Ponting	c Southee b Bracewell	16
MJ Clarke*	c Taylor b Bracewell	0
MEK Hussey	lbw b Bracewell	0
BJ Haddin†	c Taylor b Southee	15
PM Siddle	c Ryder b Southee	2
JL Pattinson	c Guptill b Bracewell	4
MA Starc	b Bracewell	0
NM Lyon	b Bracewell	9
Extras	(b 3, lb 18)	21
Total		233

Fall of wickets 72, 122, 159, 159, 159, 192, 194, 199, 199, 233

	O	M	R	W
CS Martin	16	4	44	1
TA Boult	12	1	51	1
TG Southee	19	3	77	2
DAJ Bracewell	16.4	4	40	6

Toss: Australia
TV umpire: Aleem Dar
Reserve umpire: PR Reiffel

Umpires: Asad Rauf and NJ Llong
Match referee: AJ Pycroft
New Zealand won by 7 runs

Australia v South Africa
Second Test at the Adelaide Oval

2012-13
November 22, 23, 24, 25, 26 (2012)

The number one ranking in Test cricket was at stake as Australia hosted South Africa for three Tests in late 2012. Australia had the better of a rain-affected drawn Test in Brisbane, before the second Test at Adelaide turned out to be one to remember.

With Australia batting first, David Warner struck seven fours in the first 10 overs before fellow left-hander Ed Cowan was bizarrely caught-and-bowled from a Jacques Kallis yorker. Another left-hander, Rob Quiney, edged Morne Morkel to depart for zero, before the next over yielded 11 runs and a wicket as a splendid Kallis delivery wrecked Ricky Ponting's stumps. Australia was 55-3 before the Africans were rocked when Kallis failed to complete his fourth over after injuring his hamstring. This followed the pre-match omission of an injured Vernon Philander, while Dale Steyn also battled injury.

Australia was 102-3 at lunch after Michael Clarke was nearly caught behind, before a remarkable second session started with Warner and Clarke plundering 98 runs in the first 9.3 overs. Morkel and leg-spinners Imran Tahir and Francois 'Faf' du Plessis were belted, and Warner went from 90 to 100 in successive balls. Warner fell for 119 when Morkel induced an edge, before Mike Hussey kept the runs flowing. Clarke reached a century as Australia scored 178 runs in the session.

Incredibly, 202 runs were scored in the next session. Amidst some marvellous strokeplay, Clarke flayed five fours in a Morkel over, on his way to an unbeaten 224 at stumps. Hussey reached 100 with a slog-swept six off Tahir, whose innings figures were 23-0-180-0. Hussey was adjudged caught behind for 64, but he successfully challenged the decision, before Morkel bowled him for 103 with the last ball of the day's play.

South Africa fought back the next morning as Australia lost 10-4 to be 504-9. Clarke added just six runs before Morkel

Rival captains Michael Clarke and Graeme Smith pose with the ICC Test Championship Mace ahead of the Test series involving Australia and South Africa in late 2012.

dislodged his middle-stump, and the bowler finished with five wickets. An aggressive 42 from James Pattinson lifted the total to 550, then Graeme Smith and Alviro Petersen gave South Africa's first innings a great start. Sub-par running cost Petersen his wicket for 54. In Warner's first over, Hashim Amla was stumped for 11, but Smith guided his team to 217-2 at day's end with a fine century. He had survived a stumping chance on 46 before successfully challenging a caught behind ruling on 78.

South Africa faltered the next morning as two wickets fell at 233, before the next three fell at 240, 246 and 250. Jacques Rudolph was caught off Nathan Lyon when well set, before Smith (caught behind) and AB de Villiers (lbw) unsuccessfully challenged upheld appeals off Siddle. Ben Hilfenhaus struck with the new ball when Steyn edged to Ponting, before Rory Kleinveldt's off-stump was sent cartwheeling.

Australia, however, lost an injured Pattinson, who was restricted to only 9.1 overs. Kallis was in discomfort but he warmed to the task soon after lunch and hit three successive fours off Siddle. Kallis later struck three fours in five balls off Siddle, before striking a four and a six in a Clarke over. Clarke soon dismissed Kallis for 58 upon an Australian referral to the third umpire, before Morkel was bowled by Lyon just after the follow-on was averted.

Meanwhile, Test debutant du Plessis showed impressive character after arriving at 233-4. Tahir scored 10 while du Plessis went from 52 to 78 in a last wicket stand of 36, to narrow Australia's lead to 162. The debutant smacked a giant six off Siddle before Hilfenhaus dismissed him, as Clarke took a good catch.

Australia raced to 60-0 after 12 overs following 14 runs from Tahir's first over, before Tahir had Cowan caught off a no-ball in the 16th over. Kleinveldt, however, struck twice in three balls in the 17th over, with Warner caught off a leading edge before Quiney edged to slip to complete a pair. Kleinveldt bowled Cowan through the gate before Ponting inside-edged Steyn onto his wicket. Australia was 111-5 at stumps following the dismissal of nightwatchman Siddle.

Clarke and Hussey looked capable of big scores again, but they were dismissed for 38 and 54 respectively. Matthew Wade scored 18, and then Pattinson and Hilfenhaus put on an unbroken ninth-wicket partnership of 47, before a declaration left the tourists a target of 430.

South Africa was one down after one over, as Smith edged to second slip, before Amla was caught at slip off Lyon in the 12th over. Rudolph survived a close lbw appeal second ball, but later turned a low catch to short leg, before Petersen inside-edged Siddle onto the stumps. The tourists were on the rocks at 45-4, and finished the day at 77-4 from 50 overs.

Having played together in a dominant school team as 17-year-olds, de Villiers and du Plessis were a brick wall in defence on the final day, as Australia sought six wickets. There

South Africa batsman Francois 'Faf' du Plessis scored 78 and 110 not out in his Test debut to save the match against Australia in Adelaide.

were six successive maidens before a 50-run partnership was raised in 45 overs. Clarke subsequently had du Plessis lbw twice, in quick succession, but both decisions were overturned, with the first pitching outside leg-stump and the second hitting the bat.

Siddle penetrated de Villiers' defence after lunch, before Lyon missed a tough chance to catch Kallis. Wade crucially dropped Kallis just before tea, with du Plessis on 94 and the score 212-5. Du Plessis reached a gutsy century after having two close shaves on 98, and then Kallis was caught in close off Lyon after lasting 149 minutes. Steyn lasted 37 minutes before he was caught, while Hilfenhaus and Siddle were badly exhausted in the heat. Siddle suddenly yorked Kleinveldt, and Australia needed two wickets in four overs. Du Plessis, however, staved off Lyon while Morkel staved off Siddle, and du Plessis was a hero with 110 not out in 466 minutes.

Australia's inability to land the knockout blow proved costly. South Africa romped to a 309-run win in the deciding Test, which marked the end of Ponting's Test career. The result belied the nature of the series but showed that moral victories count for little in drawn Tests.

AUSTRALIA 1ST INNINGS

DA Warner	c Smith b Morkel	119
EJM Cowan	c & b Kallis	10
RJ Quiney	c Smith b Morkel	0
RT Ponting	b Kallis	4
MJ Clarke*	b Morkel	230
MEK Hussey	b Steyn	103
MS Wade†	c de Villiers b Morkel	6
PM Siddle	c Smith b Kleinveldt	6
JL Pattinson	c Smith b Steyn	42
BW Hilfenhaus	c Kleinveldt b Morkel	0
NM Lyon	not out	7
Extras	(lb 11, w 1, nb 11)	23
Total		550

Fall of wickets 43, 44, 55, 210, 482, 494, 501, 503, 504, 550

	O	M	R	W
DW Steyn	23.4	4	79	2
M Morkel	30	5	146	5
JH Kallis	3.3	1	19	2
RK Kleinveldt	20.1	4	81	1
Imran Tahir	23	0	180	0
F du Plessis	7	0	34	0

AUSTRALIA 2ND INNINGS

EJM Cowan	b Kleinveldt	29
DA Warner	c du Plessis b Kleinveldt	41
RJ Quiney	c de Villiers b Kleinveldt	0
RT Ponting	b Steyn	16
MJ Clarke*	lbw b Steyn	38
PM Siddle	c de Villiers b Morkel	1
MEK Hussey	c Steyn b Morkel	54
MS Wade†	c de Villiers b Morkel	18
JL Pattinson	not out	29
BW Hilfenhaus	not out	18
Extras	(b 4, lb 10, nb 9)	23
Total	(8 wickets dec)	267

Did not bat NM Lyon

Fall of wickets 77, 77, 91, 98, 103, 173, 206, 220

	O	M	R	W
DW Steyn	17	5	50	2
M Morkel	19	4	50	3
Imran Tahir	14	1	80	0
RK Kleinveldt	19	2	65	3
F du Plessis	1	0	8	0

SOUTH AFRICA 1ST INNINGS

GC Smith*	c Wade b Siddle	122
AN Petersen	run out (Hussey)	54
HM Amla	st Wade b Warner	11
JA Rudolph	c Quiney b Lyon	29
AB de Villiers†	lbw b Siddle	1
F du Plessis	c Clarke b Hilfenhaus	78
DW Steyn	c Ponting b Hilfenhaus	1
RK Kleinveldt	b Hilfenhaus	0
JH Kallis	c Wade b Clarke	58
M Morkel	b Lyon	6
Imran Tahir	not out	10
Extras	(b 7, lb 2, w 3, nb 6)	18
Total		388

Fall of wickets 138, 169, 233, 233, 240, 246, 250, 343, 352, 388

	O	M	R	W
DW Hilfenhaus	19.3	6	49	3
JL Pattinson	9.1	0	41	0
NM Lyon	44	7	91	2
PM Siddle	30.5	6	130	2
MJ Clarke	7	1	22	1
MER Hussey	1	0	7	0
DA Warner	5	0	27	1
RJ Quiney	8	3	12	0

SOUTH AFRICA 2ND INNINGS

AN Petersen	b Siddle	24
GC Smith*	c Ponting b Hilfenhaus	0
HM Amla	c Clarke b Lyon	17
JA Rudolph	c Cowan b Lyon	3
AB de Villiers†	b Siddle	33
F du Plessis	not out	110
JH Kallis	c Cowan b Lyon	46
DW Steyn	c Quiney b Siddle	0
RK Kleinveldt	b Siddle	3
M Morkel	not out	8
Extras	(b 1, lb 1, w 1, nb 1)	4
Total	(8 wickets)	248

Did not bat Imran Tahir

Fall of wickets 3, 36, 45, 45, 134, 233, 234, 240

	O	M	R	W
BW Hilfenhaus	34	16	65	1
PM Siddle	33	15	65	4
MJ Clarke	18	5	34	0
NM Lyon	50	31	49	3
DA Warner	6	0	29	0
RJ Quiney	6	3	4	0
RT Ponting	1	1	0	0

Toss: Australia   Umpires: BF Bowden and RA Kettleborough
TV umpire: Asad Rauf   Reserve umpire: JD Ward
Match referee: RS Madugalle   Match drawn

BIBLIOGRAPHY

BOOKS

Arnold, P 1987, *The Illustrated Encyclopedia of World Cricket*, Golden Press, Sydney.

Ashes Battles and Bellylaughs 1990, Swan Publishing, Byron Bay.

Austin, D et al 1997, *200 Seasons of Australian Cricket*, Pan Macmillan Australia, Sydney.

Baldwin, M 2005, *The Ashes' Strangest Moments*, Robson Books, London.

Booth, L 2012, *Wisden Cricketers' Almanack*, A&C Black, London.

Border, A 1990, *An Autobiography*, Mandarin Australia, Melbourne.

Border, A 1993, *Beyond 10,000*, Swan Publishing, Nedlands.

Chappell, G 1981, *Unders and Overs*, Swan Publishing, Byron Bay.

Crowe, M 1995, *Out on a Limb*, Reed Publishing, Auckland.

Dawson, M 2009, *1000 Memorable Ashes Moments*, HarperCollinsPublishers, Sydney.

Frindall, 1995, *The Wisden Book of Test Cricket*, Vol. II, Headline Books, London.

Frith, D 1993, *Australia versus England: A Pictorial History of Every Test Match Since 1877*, Richard Smart Publishing, Sydney.

Gilchrist, A 2008, *True Colours*, Pan Macmillan Australia, Sydney.

Giller, N 1989, *The World's Greatest Cricket Matches*, Octopus Books, London.

Khan, I 1988, *All Round View*, Chatto and Windus, London.

Miller, A, 1987–88, 1989–90, 1990–91, 1992–93, 1993–94, 1994–95, 1997, 1999, 2000 and 2001, *Allan's Australian Cricket Annual*. Self-published.

Rippon, A 1982, *Classic Moments of the Ashes*, Moorland Publishing, Derbyshire.

Sobers, G 2002, *My Autobiography*, Headline Book Publishing, London.

Taylor, M 1995, *Taylor Made*, Pan Macmillan Australia, Sydney.

Taylor, M 1997, *A Captain's Year*, Pan Macmillan Australia, Sydney.

Ward, A 1994, *Cricket's Strangest Matches*, Robson Books, London.

Yallop, G 1979, *Lambs to the Slaughter*, Outback Press, Collingwood.

ONLINE

Cricinfo: www.espncricinfo.com

Trove: trove.nla.gov.au

UK £19.99

PHOTO CREDITS

Ian Collis Collection: 5(ii), 8–9, 10, 11, 13 (r), 17, 22, 23, 27, 30, 31, 34, 35, 39, 41, 42, 44, 45, 46 (l), 46 (t, b), 49, 51, 52, 53, 54, 58, 60 (b), 62, 65 (t, b), 68 (t, b), 69, 73 (t, b), 75, 77 (t, b), 80, 83, 84 (l, r), 85(t), 87, 88, 89 (t), 91, 92, 93, 95, 97 (b), 101 (l), 103, 104, 105 (r), 107, 108 (t, b), 114, 115 (l), 116, 120, 121(l, r), 122 (t), 124, 125, 126 (b), 132, 134, 136 (t), 140, 141, 143, 144 (l), 145, 148, 149, 151, 152, 153 (t), 159, 160 (r), 161, 162, 164, 167, 168, 169 (r), 172 (t, b), 174, 175, 179, 181 (l, r), 182, 183 (l, r), 185, 186, 191, 192 (t, b), 202, 206, 207, 218, 210, 227 (r), 228 (b), 238, 254, 267.

Ken Piesse Collection: 7 (iii), 14, 21, 28, 59, 60 (t), 69 (t), 76, 79, 81 (t), 85 (b), 89 (b), 97 (l, r, b), 99, 100, 101(l, r), 105 (l), 111 (t, b), 113, 115 (r), 122 (b), 126 (a, c), 128, 129, 131, 135, 136 (b), 138, 139 (l, r), 144 (r), 147, 153 (b), 155, 156, 157 (t, b), 164 (b), 169 (l), 178 (l), 203, 242.

Newspix: 250, 258, 261, 264, 268, 277, 279, 280, 286, 288, 291, 295, 297, 298, 300, 304, 310, 314, 317, 320, 324, 327, 331, 334, 336, 343, 347, 349, 352, 354, 360, 362, 365, 366.

MiD DAY Infomedia Ltd: 7 (i), 165, 212, 213, 215, 245 (t, b), 247, 248, 303, 357.

NHP: 4, 5, 7, 32, 56-57, 63, 64 (r), 67, 71, 72, 73 (m), 81 (b), 160 (l), 177, 178 (r), 188, 189 (t,b), 193, 194, 196-97, 198, 199, 205, 208, 209, 222, 223, 224, 226, 227 (l), 228 (t), 230, 231, 233, 234 (l,r) 235 (l, r, b), 239, 244, 251, 262, 274 (t, b), 283.

Free Domain: 5 (d), 7, 15 (l, r), 18, 19 (l, r), 36 (t, b), 38, 64 (l), 96, 110, 118–19, 194 (b), 236, 256–257, 270, 271, 285, 306, 312–313, 322 (t, b), 339, 340 (l, r), 341, 353, 356.

Cover images: Front cover, top row, from left to right: Jack Hobbs, Don Bradman, Gary Sobers and Kapil Dev. Bottom row: Dennis Lillee, Sachin Tendulkar, Brian Lara and Paul Collingwood. Back cover, clockwise from top left: Victor Trumper, Denis Compton, Bishan Bedi and Clive Lloyd.

The Publishers acknowledge the trademarks of Cricket Australia in these pages and, where used, note that they have been reproduced with the approval of Cricket Australia. The Publishers also acknowledge the work of individuals who share their own photographs and archive material on free domain websites such as wikicommons. If any credit remains unacknowledged, please write to the publisher and this will be corrected in future editions.

ACKNOWLEDGEMENTS

Many thanks to Alan Whiticker from New Holland Publishers for pitching the idea for me to write about 100 classic cricket Tests. Thanks also to Kate Sherington, Diane Ward and the rest of the New Holland Publishers team for helping my project become a reality.